T0074368

Hagenberg Research

Bruno Buchberger · Michael Affenzeller
Alois Ferscha · Michael Haller · Tudor Jebelean
Erich Peter Klement · Peter Paule
Gustav Pomberger · Wolfgang Schreiner
Robert Stubenrauch · Roland Wagner
Gerhard Weiß · Wolfgang Windsteiger
Editors

Hagenberg Research

 Springer

Editors

Bruno Buchberger, Bruno.Buchberger@risc.jku.at
Michael Affenzeller, michael.affenzeller@fh-hagenberg.at
Alois Ferscha, ferscha@soft.uni-linz.ac.at
Michael Haller, haller@fh-hagenberg.at
Tudor Jebelean, Tudor.Jebelean@risc.jku.at
Erich Peter Klement, ep.klement@jku.at
Peter Paule, Peter.Paule@risc.jku.at
Gustav Pomberger, gustav.pomberger@jku.at
Wolfgang Schreiner, Wolfgang.Schreiner@risc.jku.at
Robert Stubenrauch, stubenrauch@softwarepark-hagenberg.com
Roland Wagner, rwagner@faw.jku.at
Gerhard Weiss, gerhard.weiss@scch.at
Wolfgang Windsteiger, Wolfgang.Windsteiger@risc.jku.at

A-4232 Hagenberg
Austria

ISBN 978-3-642-02126-8   e-ISBN 978-3-642-02127-5
DOI 10.1007/978-3-642-02127-5
Springer Dordrecht Heidelberg London New York

Library of Congress Control Number: 2009928635

ACM Computing Classification (1998): D.2, H.3, I.2, C.2, H.5, F.1

© Springer-Verlag Berlin Heidelberg 2009
This work is subject to copyright. All rights are reserved, whether the whole or part of the material is concerned, specifically the rights of translation, reprinting, reuse of illustrations, recitation, broadcasting, reproduction on microfilm or in any other way, and storage in data banks. Duplication of this publication or parts thereof is permitted only under the provisions of the German Copyright Law of September 9, 1965, in its current version, and permission for use must always be obtained from Springer. Violations are liable to prosecution under the German Copyright Law.
The use of general descriptive names, registered names, trademarks, etc. in this publication does not imply, even in the absence of a specific statement, that such names are exempt from the relevant protective laws and regulations and therefore free for general use.

Cover design: KünkelLopka, Heidelberg

Printed on acid-free paper

Springer is part of Springer Science+Business Media (www.springer.com)

Contents

Acknowledgement

This book was sponsored by

- Austrian Ministry of Science and Research (BMWF),
- Austrian Ministry for Transport, Innovation and Technology (BMVIT),
- Upper Austrian Government,
- Johannes Kepler University Linz (JKU),
- Community of Hagenberg,
- Raiffeisenbank Pregarten–Hagenberg.

In the preparation of this manuscript, the support in TeX-programming by Manuel Kauers was very much appreciated.

Hagenberg Research: Introduction

Bruno Buchberger

This book is a synopsis of basic and applied research done at the various research institutions of the Softwarepark Hagenberg in Austria. Starting with 15 coworkers in my Research Institute for Symbolic Computation (RISC), I initiated the Softwarepark Hagenberg in 1987 on request of the Upper Austrian Government with the objective of creating a scientific, technological, and economic impulse for the region and the international community. In the meantime, in a joint effort, the Softwarepark Hagenberg has grown to the current (2009) size of over 1000 R&D employees and 1300 students in six research institutions, 40 companies and 20 academic study programs on the bachelor, master's and PhD level.

The goal of the Softwarepark Hagenberg is innovation of economy in one of the most important current technologies: software. It is the message of this book that this can only be achieved and guaranteed long-term by "watering the root", namely emphasis on research, both basic and applied. In this book, we summarize what has been achieved in terms of research in the various research institutions in the Softwarepark Hagenberg and what research vision we have for the imminent future.

When I founded the Softwarepark Hagenberg, in addition to the "watering the root" principle, I had the vision that such a technology park can only prosper if we realize the "magic triangle", i.e. the close interaction of research, academic education, and business applications at one site, see Figure 1.

This principle proved to be quite successful: research pulls academic education and economic innovation, companies have a motivating and challenging influence on both research and the contents and implementation of curricula, and well trained graduates on all levels guarantee fresh energy for research and competitiveness of companies. In the meantime, this principle has been adopted widely to the extent that, recently (2008), EU President Barroso proclaimed the "Magic Triangle" as the building principle for the new "European Institute for Innovation and Technology" to be founded within the next few months. It is very fulfilling for me to see that this principle now receives such a prominent attention.

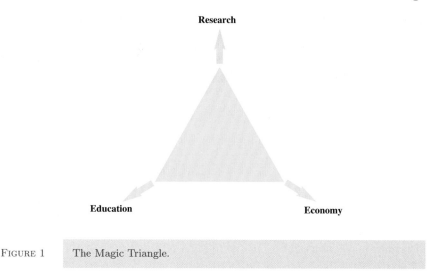

FIGURE 1   The Magic Triangle.

In this book, Hagenberg Research is summarized in various chapters that span the wide range of research topics pursued at the following research institutions in the Softwarepark Hagenberg:

- RISC (Research Institute for Symbolic Computation), the founding institute of the Softwarepark Hagenberg
- FAW (Institute for Application Oriented Knowledge Processing)
- FLLL (Department of Knowledge-Based Mathematical Systems, Fuzzy Logic Laboratorium Linz-Hagenberg)
- RIPE (Research Institute for Pervasive Computing)
- The Software Competence Center Hagenberg
- School of Informatics, Communication and Media, Upper Austria University of Applied Sciences, Research Center Hagenberg

The research strategy we pursue at the Softwarepark Hagenberg emphasizes the flow from formal logic, algorithmic mathematics, to software (and, to a lesser extent) hardware science. In my understanding, logic, mathematics, and software science form a coherent and indistinguishable magma of knowledge and methods (which I like to call the "thinking technology") and this is the strength from which we draw in the Softwarepark Hagenberg.

I am happy and fulfilled to see that this view is providing a solid basis for such a dynamic and future-oriented construct as the Softwarepark Hagenberg. This view also guided me as my personal strategy since the time of writing my PhD thesis in 1965, in which I introduced the theory of Gröbner bases (see [Buc65, Buc70]), which in the meantime became a powerful algorithmic tool for a constantly expanding range of applications in all situations where we have to deal with problems that can be cast in the language of non-linear polynomial systems. The coherent magma of logic, mathematics, and software science can be well demonstrated by the development of the field of Gröbner bases:

- The Gröbner bases method as an algorithmic method is based on a theorem (see [Buc65]) of pure algebra (the Theorem on the characterization of Gröbner bases by the zero-reducibility of the so called S-polynomials, see Section 2 on Gröbner Bases in Chapter I on symbolic computation).
- The proof of the main theorem of Gröbner bases theory, which was quite a challenge at the time of its invention, by recent advances in automated theorem proving in my Theorema Group can now be produced automatically (see [Buc04] and Chapter II on automated reasoning) to the extent that even the key *idea* of the theorem, S-polynomials, can be generated automatically.
- The Gröbner bases method can be applied in a growing number of seemingly quite distinct fields as, for example, coding theory and cryptography, robotics, systems and control theory, invariant theory, symbolics of combinatorial identities etc. (see again Section 2 in Chapter I). Interestingly, it also can be applied to automated theorem proving (notably geometrical theorem proving) and theorem invention and, by recent research in the Theorema Group (see Chapter II), to fundamental questions of software science like the automated generation of loop invariants of algorithms.

In this example, we see how the logic/mathematics/software science "magma" reaches out and bends back to itself in a constant movement of expansion and self-reference conquering higher and higher levels of understanding and methodology. This process, by what we know from Gödel's second theorem, does not have any limitation. Translating this to the "politics" of an institution like the Softwarepark Hagenberg: As long as we base our expansion and growth on research, there is no apparent limit to what we can achieve by our cooperative effort embedded into the international research community.

As the founder of the Research Institute for Symbolic Computation (Johannes Kepler University) and the founder and head of the Softwarepark Hagenberg (1987) I am proud to present the results of our joint research efforts in this book and I look forward to the next steps of our joint growth in intense interaction with the international research community. We will also be particularly happy to welcome our colleagues from all over the world at the research and conference facilities which we are currently expanding by generous grants from the Upper Austrian Government.

I also want to thank my colleagues in the Softwarepark Hagenberg research institutions for years of joint work and for their contributions to this book. My sincere thanks go to the Austrian and Upper Austrian Governmental Institutions and the various Austrian and EU research funding agencies and programs that made it possible to create the Softwarepark Hagenberg and to pursue our research.

Bruno Buchberger
Founder and Head of the Softwarepark Hagenberg

FIGURE 2   The Softwarepark Hagenberg.

References

[Buc65] B. Buchberger. *An Algorithm for Finding the Basis Elements in the Residue Class Ring Modulo a Zero Dimensional Polynomial Ideal.* PhD thesis, University Innsbruck, Mathematical Institute, 1965. German, English translation in: J. of Symbolic Computation, Special Issue on Logic, Mathematics, and Computer Science: Interactions. Volume 41, Number 3–4, Pages 475–511, 2006.

[Buc70] B. Buchberger. An Algorithmical Criterion for the Solvability of Algebraic Systems of Equations. *Aequationes mathematicae,* 4(3):374–383, 1970. German. English translation in: B. Buchberger, F. Winkler (eds.), Groebner Bases and Applications, London Mathematical Society Lecture Note Series, Vol. 251, Cambridge University Press, 1998, pp. 535–545.

[Buc04] B. Buchberger. Towards the Automated Synthesis of a Gröbner Bases Algorithm. *RACSAM (Rev. Acad. Cienc., Spanish Royal Academy of Science),* 98(1):65–75, 2004.

Chapter I
Algorithms in Symbolic Computation

Peter Paule

Bruno Buchberger, Lena Kartashova, Manuel Kauers,

Carsten Schneider, Franz Winkler

The development of computer technology has brought forth a renaissance of algorithmic mathematics which gave rise to the creation of new disciplines like Computational Mathematics. Symbolic Computation, which constitutes one of its major branches, is the main research focus of the Research Institute for Symbolic Computation (RISC).

In Section 1, author P. Paule, one finds an introduction to the theme together with comments on history as well as on the use of the computer for mathematical discovery and proving. The remaining sections of the chapter present more detailed descriptions of hot research topics currently pursued at RISC.

In Section 2 the inventor of Gröbner Bases, B. Buchberger, describes basic notions and results, and underlines the principal relevance of Gröbner bases by surprising recent applications. Section 3, author F. Winkler, gives an introduction to algebraic curves; a summary of results in theory and applications (e.g., computer aided design) is given. Section 4, author M. Kauers, reports on computer generated progress in lattice paths theory finding applications in combinatorics and physics. Section 5, author C. Schneider, provides a description of an interdisciplinary research project with DESY (Deutsches Elektronen-Synchrotron, Berlin/Zeuthen). Section 6, author E. Kartashova, describes the development of Nonlinear Resonance Analysis, a new branch of mathematical physics.

1 The Renaissance of Algorithmic Mathematics

"The mathematics of Egypt, of Babylon, and of the ancient Orient was all of the algorithmic type. Dialectical mathematics—strictly logical, deductive mathematics—originated with the Greeks. But it did not displace the algorithmic. In Euclid, the role of dialectic is to justify a construction—i.e., an algorithm. It is only in modern times that we find mathematics with little or no algorithmic content. [...] Recent years seem to show a shift back to a constructive or algorithmic view point."

To support their impression the authors of [DH81] continue by citing P. Henrici: "We never could have put a man on the moon if we had insisted that the trajectories should be computed with dialectic rigor. [...] Dialectic mathematics generates insight. Algorithmic mathematics generates results."

Below we comment on various aspects of recent developments, including topics like numerical analysis versus symbolic computation, and pure versus applied mathematics. Then we present mathematical snapshots which—from symbolic computation point of view—shed light on two fundamental mathematical activities, *discovery* (computer-assisted guessing) and *proving* (using computer algebra algorithms).

1.1 A Bit of History

We will high-light only some facets of the *recent* history of algorithmic mathematics. However, we first need to clarify what algorithmic mathematics is about.

Algorithmic vs. Dialectic Mathematics

About thirty years ago P.J. Davis and R. Hersh in their marvelous book [DH81] included a short subsection with exactly the same title. We only make use of their example (finding $\sqrt{2}$) to distinguish between algorithmic and dialectic (i.e. non-algorithmic) mathematics. But to the interested reader we recommend the related entries of [DH81] for further reading.

Consider the problem to find a solution, denoted by $\sqrt{2}$, to the equation $x^2 = 2$.

Solution 1

Consider the sequence $(x_n)_{n \geq 1}$ defined for $n \geq 1$ recursively by

$$x_{n+1} = \frac{1}{2}\left(x_n + \frac{2}{x_n}\right),$$

with initial value $x_1 = 1$. Then $(x_n)_{n \geq 1}$ converges to $\sqrt{2}$ with quadratic rapidity. For example, $x_4 = \frac{577}{408} = 1.414215\ldots$ is already correct to 5 decimal places. Note, the algorithm can be carried out with just addition and division, and without complete theory of the real number system.

Solution 2

Consider the function $f(x) = x^2 - 2$ defined on the interval from 0 to 2. Observe that f is a continuous function with $f(0) = -2$ and $f(2) = 2$. Therefore, according to the intermediate value theorem, there exists a real number, let's call it $\sqrt{2}$, such that $f(\sqrt{2}) = 0$. Note, the details of the argument are based on properties of the real number system.

Solution 1 is algorithmic mathematics; solution 2 is the dialectic solution. Note that, in a certain sense, neither solution 1 nor solution 2 is a solution at all. Solution 1 gives us a better and better approximation, but no x_n gives us an exact solution. Solution 2 tells us that an exact solution exists between 0 and 2, but that is all it has to say.

Numerical Analysis vs. Symbolic Computation

Readers interested in the relatively young history of symbolic computation are referred to respective entries in the books [GCL92] and [vzGG99]. Concerning the first research journal in this field, [vzGG99] says, "The highly successful Journal of Symbolic Computation, created in 1985 by Bruno Buchberger, is the undisputed leader for research publication." So in 1981 when the book [DH81] appeared, symbolic computation was still at a very early stage of its development. This is reflected by statements like: "Certainly the algorithmic approach is called for when the problem at hand requires a numerical answer which is of importance for subsequent work either inside or outside mathematics."

Meanwhile this situation has changed quite a bit. Nowadays, symbolic computation and numerical analysis can be viewed as two sides of the same medal, i.e. of algorithmic mathematics. In other words, until today also symbolic computation has developed into a discipline which provides an extremely rich tool-box for problem solving outside or inside mathematics. Concerning the latter aspect, in view of recent applications, including some being described in the sections of this chapter, symbolic computation seems to evolve into a key technology in mathematics.

In fact there are numerous 'problems at hand' which for subsequent (e.g. numerical) work greatly benefit from simplification produced by symbolic computation algorithms. As a simple example, let us consider the problem of adding the first n natural numbers, i.e., to compute the sum

$$x_n := 1 + 2 + \cdots + n = \sum_{k=1}^{n} k.$$

Solution A

Consider the sequence $(x_n)_{n \geq 1}$ defined for $n \geq 1$ recursively by

$$x_{n+1} = x_n + n + 1,$$

with initial value $x_1 = 1$. In other words, this computes the sum x_n by carrying out $n - 1$ additions. For example, $x_4 = x_3 + 4 = (x_2 + 3) + 4 = ((x_1 + 2) + 3) + 4 = 10$.

Solution B

Apply a symbolic summation algorithm (e.g., Gosper's algorithm implemented in most of the computer algebra systems) to *simplify* the sum; i.e., which finds that for $n \geq 1$,

$$x_n = \tfrac{1}{2}n(n+1).$$

Instead of carrying out $n - 1$ additions, this computes the sum x_n by one multiplication and one division by 2. For example, $x_4 = \tfrac{1}{2} \cdot 4 \cdot 5 = 10$. In other words, symbolic computation reduces the numerical task from $n - 1$ operations (additions) to 2!

There are many problems for which better solutions would be obtained by a proper *combination* of numerical analysis with symbolic computation. Such kind of research was the main theme of the Special Research Program SFB F013 *Numerical and Symbolic Scientific Computing* (1998–2008), an excellence program of the Austrian Science Funds FWF, pursued by groups at RISC, from numerical analysis and applied geometry at the Johannes Kepler University (JKU), and at the Johann Radon Institute of Computational and Applied Mathematics (RICAM) of the Austrian Academy of Sciences. Starting in October 2008 this initiative has been continued at the JKU in the form of the Doctoral Program *Computational Mathematics*, another excellence program of the FWF.

Pure vs. Applied Mathematics

Efforts in numerical analysis and symbolic computation to combine mathematics with the powers of the computer are continuing to revolutionize mathematical research. For instance, as mentioned above, a relatively young mathematical field like symbolic computation is growing more and more into the role of a key technology within mathematics. As a by-product the distinction between 'pure' and 'applied' mathematics is taking on a less and less definite form. This stays quite in contrast to a period of 'Hardyism' in the younger history of mathematics.

G. H. Hardy (1877–1947).   FIGURE 1
From http://en.wikipedia.org/wiki/File:Ghhardy@72.jpg

The famous mathematician G.H. Hardy (1877–1947) insisted that all of the mathematics he created during his life time was of no use at all. In the concluding pages of his remarkable *Apology* [Har40] he wrote, "I have never done anything 'useful'. No discovery of mine has made, or is likely to make, directly or indirectly, for good or for ill, the least difference to the amenity of the world. I have helped to train other mathematicians, but mathematicians of the same kind as myself, and their work has been, so far at any rate as I have helped them to it, as useless as my own. Judged by all practical standards, the value of my mathematical life is nil." During that time a pervasive unspoken sentiment began to spread, namely that there is something ugly about applications. To see one of the strongest statements about purity, let us again cite G.H. Hardy [Har40], "It is undeniable that a good deal of elementary mathematics [...] has considerable practical utility. These parts of mathematics are, on the whole, rather dull; they are just the parts which have least aesthetic value. The 'real' mathematics of the 'real' mathematicians, the mathematics of Fermat and Euler and Gauss and Abel and Riemann, is almost wholly 'useless'."

This attitude, sometimes called Hardyism, was "central to the dominant ethos of twentieth-century mathematics" [DH81]. Only towards the end of the seventies this credo began to soften up due to the beginning evolution of computer technology. Bruno Buchberger has been one of the pioneers in this development. Since he became JKU Professor in 1974 he has been pushing and promoting the central role of computer mathematics. With the rapid dissemination of computer technology such ideas were taken up. Attractive positions were created, and the reputation of 'applied' mathematics was increasing. Starting with this process in the U.S.A., the full wave of this development came back to Europe with some delay. Let me cite from a recent article [Due08] of Gunter Dueck, who in 1987 moved to IBM from his position of a mathematics professor at the university of Bielefeld: "Rainer Janssen (mein damaliger Manager bei IBM und heute CIO der Münchner Rück) und ich schrieben im Jahre 1991 einen Artikel mit dem Titel 'Mathematik: Esoterik oder Schlüsseltechnologie?' Dort stand ich noch echt unter meinem Zorn, als Angewandter Mathematiker ein triviales Nichts zu sein, welches inexakte Methoden in der Industrie ganz ohne Beweis benutzt und mit Millioneneinsparungen protzt, obwohl gar nicht bewiesen werden kann, dass die gewählte Methode die allerbeste gewesen ist."

Nowadays the situation is about to change fundamentally. Things have been already moved quite a bit. For example, today 'Hardyists' would say that working in algorithmic mathematics is almost impossible without running into concrete applications! Concrete examples can be found in the sections below, in particular, in Section 5 which describes the use of symbolic summation in particle physics.

To be fair to Hardy one should mention that despite his 'Hardyistic' statements, he was following with interest modern developments, for example, that of computing machines. In particular, he was appreciating the work of Alan Turing. Thanks to Hardy's recommendation, the Royal Society awarded Turing 40 English pounds for the construction of a machine to compute the zeros of the Riemann zeta function [dS04].

Before coming to the mathematical part of this section, another quote of G. Dueck [Due08]: "Damals forderten Rainer Janssen und ich, dass Mathematik sich als Schlüsseltechnologie begreifen sollte. [...] Ja, Mathematik ist eine Schlüsseltechnologie, aber eine unter recht vielen, die alle zusammen multi-kulturell ein Ganzes erschaffen können. Die Mathematik muss sich mit freudigem Herzen diesem Ganzen widmen – dem Leben. Sie muss sich nach außen verpflichtet zeigen, den Menschen und dem Leben etwas Wichtiges zu sein und zu bringen." It is exactly this attitude that one can find at a place like the Softwarepark Hagenberg.

Computer-Assisted Discovery and Proving 1.2

First we comment on *computer-assisted guessing* in the context of mathematical discovery. Then we turn to the activity of proving, more precisely, to *proving methods* where *computer algebra algorithms* are used. Here we restrict to this special type of computed-assisted proving; for *general mathematical proving machines* like the THEOREMA system developed at RISC, see Chapter II.

I.Q. Tests, Rabbits, and the Golden Section

Let us consider the following problem taken from an I.Q. test [Eys66, Aufgabe 13, Denksport I fuer Superintelligente] from the sixties of the last century:

Continue the sequence $1, 1, 2, 3, 5, 8, 13, 21$.

In the 21st century we let the computer do the problem. To this end we load the RISC package `GeneratingFunctions` written by C. Mallinger [Mal96] in the computer algebra system Mathematica:

In[1]:= ≪GeneratingFunctions.m

In the next step we input a little program that can be used to solve such I.Q. tests automatically:

```
In[2]:= GuessNext2Values[Li_] := Module[{rec},
        rec = GuessRE[Li,c[k],{1,2},{0,3}];
        RE2L[rec[[1]],c[k],Length[Li]+1]]
```

Finally the problem is solved automatically with

In[3]:= GuessNext2Values[{1, 1, 2, 3, 5, 8, 13, 21}]

Out[3]= {1,1,2,3,5,8,13,21,34,55}

To produce additional values is no problem:

In[4]:= GuessNext2Values[{1, 1, 2, 3, 5, 8, 13, 21, 34, 55}]

Out[4]= {1,1,2,3,5,8,13,21,34,55,89,144}

Note. The same automatic guessing can be done in the Maple system; there B. Salvy and P. Zimmermann [SZ94] developed the poineering package **gfun** which has served as a model for the development of Mallinger's **GeneratingFunctions**.

What is the mathematical basis for such automatic guessing? The answer originates in a simple observation: Many of the sequences $(x_n)_{n \geq 0}$ arising in practical applications (and in I.Q. tests!) are produced from a very simple pattern; namely, linear recurrences of the form

$$p_d(n)x_{n+d} + p_{d-1}(n)x_{n+d-1} + \cdots + p_0(n)x_n = 0, \qquad n \geq 0,$$

with coefficients $p_i(n)$ being polynomials in n. So packages like Mallinger's **GeneratingFunctions** try to compute-via an ansatz using undetermined coefficients-a recurrence of exactly this type. For the I.Q. example above a recurrence is obtained by

In[5]:= GuessRE[{1, 1, 2, 3, 5, 8, 13, 21}, f[n]]

Out[5]= {{-f[n]-f[1+n]+f[2+n]==0,f[0]==1,f[1]==1}, ogf}

Since only finitely many values are given as input, the output recurrence $f_{n+2} = f_{n+1} + f_n$ $(n \geq 0)$ can be only a *guess* about a possible building principle of an *infinite* sequence. However, such kind of automated guessing is becoming more and more relevant to concrete applications. For instance, an application from mathematical chemistry can be found in [CGP99] where a prediction for the total number of benzenoid hydrocarbons was made. Three years later this predication was confirmed [VGJ02]. Recently, quite sophisticated applications arose in connection with the enumeration of lattice paths, see Section 4, and also with quantum field theory, see Section 5.

In 1202 Leonard Fibonacci introduced the numbers f_n. The fact that $f_0 = f_1 = 1$, and

$$f_{n+2} = f_{n+1} + f_n, \qquad n \geq 0,$$

in Fibonacci's book was given the following interpretation: If baby rabbits become adults after one month, and if each pair of adult rabbits produces one pair of baby rabbits every month, how many pairs of rabbits, starting with one pair, are present after n months?

A non-recursive representation is the celebrated Euler-Binet formula

$$f_n = \frac{1}{\sqrt{5}} \left(\left(\frac{1+\sqrt{5}}{2} \right)^{n+1} - \left(\frac{1-\sqrt{5}}{2} \right)^{n+1} \right), \qquad n \geq 0.$$

The number $(1+\sqrt{5})/2 \approx 1.611803$, the *golden ratio*, is important in many parts of mathematics as well as in the art world. For instance, Phidias is said to have used it consciously in his sculpture.

Mathematicians gradually began to discover more and more interesting things about Fibonacci numbers f_n; see e.g. [GKP94]. For example, a typical sunflower has a large head that contains spirals of tightly packed florets, usually with $f_8 = 34$ winding in one direction and $f_9 = 55$ in another.

Another observation is this: Define g_n as a sum over binomial coefficients of the form

$$g_n := \sum_{k=0}^{n} \binom{n-k}{k}.$$

From the values $g_0 = 1$, $g_1 = 1$, $g_2 = 2$, $g_3 = 3$, $g_4 = 5$, and $g_5 = 8$ it is straight-forward to conjecture that the sequence $(g_n)_{n \geq 0}$ is nothing but the Fibonacci sequence $(f_n)_{n \geq 0}$. In the next subsection we shall see that nowadays such statements can be proved automatically with the computer.

Pi, Inequalities, and Finite Elements

We have seen that linear recurrences can be used as a basis for automated *guessing*. Concerning symbolic computation, this is only the beginning. Namely, following D. Zeilberger's holonomic paradigm [Zei90b], the description of mathematical sequences in terms of linear recurrences, and of mathematical functions in terms of linear differential equations, is also of great importance to the design of computer algebra algorithms for automated *proving*.

For example, consider the sequence $(g_n)_{n \geq 0}$ defined above. To prove the statement

$$f_n = g_n, \qquad n \geq 0,$$

in completely automatic fashion, we use the RISC package Zb [PS95], an implementation of D. Zeilberger's algorithm [Zei90a]:

In[6]:= ≪Zb.m

In[7]:= Zb[Binomial[n-k,k],{k,0,Infinity},n,2]

Out[7]= {SUM[n] + SUM[1 + n] − SUM[2 + n] == 0}

The output tells us that $g_n = \mathrm{SUM}[n]$ indeed satisfies the same recurrence as the Fibonacci numbers. A proof for the correctness of the output recurrence can be obtained automatically, too; just type the command:

In[8]:= Prove[]

For further details concerning the mathematical background of this kind of proofs, see e.g. Zeilberger's articles [Zei90b] and [Zei90a] which were the booster charge for the development of a new subfield of symbolic computation; namely, the design of computer algebra algorithms for special functions and sequences. For respective RISC developments the interested reader is referred to the web page

`http://www.risc.uni-linz.ac.at/research/combinat`

For various applications researchers are using such algorithms in their daily research work-sometimes still in combination with tables. However, there are particular problem classes where symbolic (and numeric) algorithms are going to replace tables almost completely.

Concerning *special sequences* the most relevant table is N. Sloane's handbook [Slo73], [Slo94]. Sloane's home page provides an extended electronic version of it; also symbolic computation algorithms are used to retrieve information about sequences .

Concerning *special functions* one of the most prominent tables is the 'Handbook' [AS64] from 1964. Soon it will be replaced by its strongly revised successor, the NIST Digital Library of Mathematical Functions (DLMF); see `http://dlfm.nist.gov`. The author of this section is serving as an associate editor of this new handbook (and author, together with F. Chyzak, of a new chapter on computer algebra) that will be freely available via the web.

We expect the development of special provers will intensify quite a bit. By special provers we mean methods based on computer algebra algorithms specially tailored for certain families of mathematical objects. *Special function inequalities* provide a classical domain that so far has been considered as being hardly accessible by such methods. To conclude this section we briefly describe that currently this situation is about to change.

Consider the famous Wallis product formula for π:

$$\pi = 2 \cdot \frac{2}{1} \cdot \frac{2}{3} \cdot \frac{4}{3} \cdot \frac{4}{5} \cdot \frac{6}{5} \cdot \frac{6}{7} \cdot \frac{8}{7} \cdot \frac{8}{9} \cdots .$$

This product is an immediate consequence $(n \to \infty)$ of the following inequality (John Wallis, Arithmetica Infinitorum, 1656):

$$\frac{2n}{2n+1} \le \frac{c_n}{\pi} \le 1, \qquad n \ge 0,$$

where

$$c_n := \frac{2^{4n+1}}{2n+1} \binom{2n}{n}^{-2} .$$

In analysis one meets such inequalities quite frequently. Another example, similar to that of Wallis, is

$$\frac{1}{4n} \le a_n \le \frac{1}{3n+1}, \qquad n \ge 0,$$

where

$$a_n := \frac{1}{2^{4n}} \binom{2n}{n}^2 .$$

We shall prove the right hand side, i.e. $a_n \leq 1/(3n+1)$, (the left hand side goes analogously) to exemplify the new Gerhold-Kauers method [GK05] for proving special function/sequence inequalities. As proof strategy they use mathematical induction combined with G. Collins' cylindrical algebraic decomposition (CAD). First observe that

$$a_{n+1} = a_n \frac{(2n+1)^2}{(2n+2)^2} \leq \frac{1}{3n+1} \frac{(2n+1)^2}{(2n+2)^2},$$

where for the inequality the induction hypothesis is used. In order to show that this implies $a_{n+1} \leq 1/(3n+4)$, it is sufficient to establish that

$$\frac{1}{3n+1} \frac{(2n+1)^2}{(2n+2)^2} \leq \frac{1}{3n+4}.$$

But this step can be carried out automatically with any implementation of Collins' CAD; for instance, in Mathematica:

In[9]:= Reduce$[\frac{1}{3n+1} \frac{(2n+1)^2}{(2n+2)^2} \leq \frac{1}{3n+4}, n]$

Out[9]= $-\frac{4}{3} < n < -1 \,||\, -1 < n < -\frac{1}{3} \,||\, n \geq 0$

The Gerhold-Kauers method already found quite a number of non-trivial applications. They range from new refinements of Wallis' inequality [PP08] like

$$\frac{32n^2 + 32n + 7}{4(2n+1)(4n+3)} \leq \frac{c_n}{\pi} \leq \frac{16(n+1)(2n+1)}{32n^2 + 56n + 25}, \qquad n \geq 0,$$

to a proof of the long-standing log-concavity conjecture of V. Moll [KP07]. Further applications and details about the method are given in [Kau08].

We want to conclude by referring to results that emerged from numerical-symbolic SFB collaboration in the context of finite element methods (FEM). In order to set up a new FEM setting, J. Schöberl (RWTH Aachen, formerly JKU) needed to prove the following special function inequality:

$$\sum_{j=0}^{n} (4j+1)(2n-2j+1)P_{2j}(0)P_{2j}(x) \geq 0$$

for $-1 \leq x \leq 1$, $n \geq 0$, and with $P_{2j}(x)$ being the Legendre polynomials. Using the Gerhold-Kauers method together with RISC symbolic summation software, V. Pillwein [Pil07] was able to settle this conjecture. Remarkably, there is still no human proof available!

Last but not least, we mention a recent collaboration of J. Schöberl with C. Koutschan (RISC), which led to a new tool for engineering applications in the context of electromagnetic wave simulation. Formulas derived by Koutschan's symbolic package HolonomicFunctions resulted in a significant speed-up of numerical FEM algorithms e.g. for the construction of antennas or mobile phones. The method is planned to be registered as a patent.

2 Gröbner Bases Theory for Nonlinear Polynomial Systems

2.1 The Relevance of Gröbner Bases Theory

To a great extent, Gröbner bases theory was the starting point of the Research Institute for Symbolic Computation and, hence, the Softwarepark Hagenberg. Gröbner bases theory was initiated in the PhD thesis [Buc65, Buc70] and turned out to be one of the first coherent results in the emerging area of what was later called "computer algebra". Gröbner bases theory allows to handle a big variety of fundamental problems connected to systems of multivariate polynomials, for example the problem of solving such systems (finding all common roots of such systems) or the problem of deciding whether two given multivariate polynomials are "equivalent" with respect to a given system of multivariate polynomials.

Since nonlinear polynomial systems are a mathematical model for a large class of problems in science and engineering, it is no surprise that a general algorithmic method like the Gröbner bases method for handling such systems has an unlimited range of applications. In fact, in many fields of science and engineering, prior to the advent of Gröbner bases theory only linear approximations of the actual problems could be studied. In some cases, if we are satisfied with approximate solutions, linear approximations to the original models may be good enough. However, there are many areas in which only the exact treatment of the exact non-linear problems gives meaningful answers. For example, graph coloring problems can be translated into the problem of solving certain non-linear polynomial systems, see below, where each solution corresponds to a possible coloring. Linear approximations to the systems or approximations to the solutions of the original systems would not make it possible to distinguish between or identify the various colorings.

Over the years, a many applications of Gröbner bases theory, some of them quite surprising, have been found. An overview on these applications, up to 1998, can be found in the proceedings [BW98]. An online-bibliography has been compiled at the occasion of the Special Semester on Gröbner Bases at the Radon Institute for Computational and Applied Mathematics (RICAM) in Linz 2006, which contains over 1000 papers on Gröbner bases, see www.ricam.oeaw.ac.at/specsem/srs/groeb/ (follow link "Bibliography"). A quick way of getting access to the growing literature on Gröbner bases is to use the online citation index "citeseer" (at researchindex.org/). If one enters "Gröbner" or "Buchberger", one will obtain several thousand citations of papers containing contributions to the development, extension and improvement of the Gröbner bases method and its many applications. Also, there are a couple of textbooks available on Gröbner bases, see for example [BW93] and [KR00]. The latter contains a list of most other textbooks on Gröbner bases in its introduction.

Applications of Gröbner bases reach from algebraic geometry or polynomial ideal theory (the original field for which Gröbner bases theory was invented in [Buc65, Buc70]) to invariant theory, coding theory, cryptography and cryptoanalysis, systems theory, control theory, automated geometrical theorem proving, graph theory, invention and proof of combinatorial identities, software engineering, integration of differential equations and many others. Here are some surprising recent applications of Gröbner bases in quite distinct areas:

Origami Construction: The Japanese art of Origami aims at constructing two-dimensional and three-dimensional objects by certain folding operations starting from a square paper sheet. Six classes of folding operations are permitted. The mathematical problem consists in deciding whether a given sequence of operations provenly leads to an object having prescribed properties. For example, ways were proposed to fold a regular heptagon from the initial square using only Origami folding operations. In this case, the question is to *prove* rigorously that a proposed sequence of operations results, indeed, in a heptagon. Gröbner bases can be used for proving or disproving the correctness of arbitrary such sequences of operations for arbitrary properties (that can be described by multivariate polynomials) completely automatically. The method consists, roughly, in translating the sequence of operations into a set of polynomial relations (which is easily possible) and to check whether or not the polynomial that describes the desired property is in the "ideal" generated by the polynomial relations, which is always possible by the Gröbner bases methodology. For details, see for example [ITBR04].

Solution of Linear Boundary Value Problems: Initial value problems for a wide class of differential equations can be solved by symbolic methods. For boundary value problems, there were hardly any symbolic methods available. A generalization of Gröbner bases theory for non-commutative polynomials allows now to obtain symbolic solutions also for boundary value problems. In this new application, the strength of the Gröbner bases method is demonstrated by the fact that the invention of the Green's functions, which was deemed to be an ad hoc creative process for each boundary value problem, is replaced by a completely algorithmic procedure, which is nothing else than just the reduction ("remaindering") operation w.r.t. a (non-commutative) Gröbner basis, which represents the relations between the fundamental operations of functional analysis for boundary problems, see [RBE03].

Optimization of Oil Platforms (the "Algebraic Oil Project"): In this surprising application, the fundamental problem of improved control of the valves on an oil platform, with unknown geometry of the oil caverns under the sea, is attacked. In a "learning phase" the quantity of oil produced in dependence on the position of the valves on the platform is measured. The assumption is made that this dependence can be described by a system of multivariate polynomials (whose coefficients are unknown in the learning phase). With the data collected from sufficiently many measurements, the Gröbner bases method allows then to determine these coefficients (in fact, the system of polynomials generated for modelling the flow will be a Gröbner basis). Now, this multivariate polynomial model of the flow can be used, in the "application phase", to optimize the flow w.r.t. various criteria. This new application of (a numerical variant of) Gröbner bases was proposed in a cooperation between Shell company and the CoCoA Group, see [HKPP06]. The results are practically promising.

Automated Synthesis of Loop Invariants for Programs: The proof that programs meet their specification is one of the fundamental problems in computer science. The method of "loop invariants" for solving this problem requests that, for certain points in the given program, an assertion (formula), called a "loop invariant" is invented for which one can prove that, for every moment the program gets to that point the respective assertion is true for the values of the program variables. The invention of these loop invariants often needs quite some creativity and this is a major obstacle for the practical use of the method of loop invariants. In the *Theorema* Group at RISC, a method was developed by which, for a wide class of programs, these loop invariants can be generated by a combination of symbolic execution of the program, solution of the resulting recursive equations, see Section 1 above, and the use of the Gröbner bases method, see Chapter II on automated reasoning in this book.

Breaking Cryptographic Codes: Gröbner bases are being used both for constructing cryptosystems as well as for trying to break such systems (cryptoanalysis). Breaking an (algebraic) crypto-code basically amounts to solving a system of nonlinear algebraic equations with Boolean coefficients for the values that constitute the bits of the unknown code, i.e. the number of unknowns in the system is the number of unknown bits in the code. Typically, this number is 80 or more. Recently, proposals for algebraic codes that have been deemed to be sufficiently safe have been broken using the Gröbner bases method, see [FJ03]. This was one of the most exciting recent applications of Gröbner bases.

The Determination of Species Relationship in Evolution: In this research area, the probabilities of one species being closer in the evolution with some species than with some other species are determined from an analysis of the genetic codes of species. The result of such an analysis is called the phylogenetic tree of the species. In [CP07] it has recently been shown how this problem of finding the mutual neighborhood probabilities can be cast into the language of multivariate polynomial ideals in Gröbner bases form.

Wavelets: Wavelets are spectra of functions. Each function in a spectrum is determined by a couple of parameters. By combining the functions in a spectrum, i.e. by specifying the values of the individual parameters in a spectrum, (graphical) information can be presented in highly condensed form ("data compression"). The search for suitable spectra of wavelets is an important research topic in wavelet theory. This search leads to systems of algebraic equations that recently have been solved by the Gröbner bases method, see [CPS$^+$01].

Gröbner bases theory is still a very active research area with focus on generalizations of the method (e.g. the non-commutative case), specializations for certain classes of polynomial sets (e.g. toric sets) with higher efficiency, new approaches to compute Gröbner bases for improving the efficiency, numeric variants of the method, and new applications in a big spectrum of different areas.

Gröbner Bases: Basic Notions and Results   2.2

Gröbner bases are sets of multivariate polynomials that enjoy certain uniqueness properties, which make it possible to solve many fundamental problems on such sets algorithmically. The main result of algorithmic Gröbner bases theory is that any finite set of multivariate polynomials can be transformed, by an algorithm, into an equivalent Gröbner basis and that, hence, many fundamental problems on arbitrary sets of multivariate polynomials can be solved algorithmically by, first, transforming the sets into Gröbner bases form and then using the respective algorithms for Gröbner bases. Three examples of such fundamental problems that can be solved algorithmically by transformation into Gröbner bases form are:

- the exact solution of systems of multivariate polynomial equations,
- the problem of deciding whether or not two given multivariate polynomials are equivalent w.r.t. to a given set of multivariate polynomials that define the equivalence,
- the problem of solving "diophantine" equations, i.e. the problem of finding (all) multivariate polynomials that satisfy linear relations whose coefficients are also multivariate polynomials.

We explain here one of the many different, equivalent, ways of defining the notion of Gröbner bases. For this, consider for example the two quadratic bivariate polynomials f_1 and f_2 in the indeterminates x and y:

$$f_1 := -2y + xy \qquad\qquad f_2 := x^2 + y^2.$$

If we fix an ordering on the power products (for example, the lexicographic ordering that ranks y higher than x), each polynomial has a "leading power product", in our case xy and y^2, respectively. Consider now the following linear combination g of f_1 and f_2:

$$g := (y)f_1 + (-x + 2)f_2 = 2x^2 - x^3.$$

Observation: The leading power product x^3 of g is neither a multiple of the leading power product xy of f_1 nor a multiple of the leading power product y^2 of f_2. Now, a set F of multivariate polynomials is called a *Gröbner basis* (w.r.t. the chosen ordering of power products) iff the above phenomenon cannot happen, i.e.

for all $f_1, \ldots, f_m \in F$ and all (*infinitely many* possible) polynomials $h_1, \ldots, h_m$, the leading power product of $h_1 f_1 + \ldots + h_m f_m$ is a multiple of the leading power product of at least one of the polynomials in F.

Example 1. The Set $F := \{f_1, f_2\}$ is not a Gröbner basis. The equivalent Gröbner basis is $\{f_1, f_2, f_3\}$, where $f_3 := 2x^2 - x^3$, which can only be checked by the theorem below.

The following theorem is the crucial result on which the algorithmic usefulness of Gröbner bases hinges.

Theorem 2 (Buchberger). *F is a Gröbner basis iff, for all f_1, f_2, the remainder of the S-polynomial of f_1 and f_2 w.r.t. F is 0.*

The remainder of a multivariate polynomial w.r.t. a set of such polynomials is the rest in a generalized polynomial division, which is an algorithmic process. The S-polynomial of two multivariate polynomials is obtained by multiplying the two polynomials with the lowest possible power products that make the leading power products equal and by subtracting the resulting two polynomials. In the above example, the S-polynomial of f_1 and f_2 is

$$y(-2y + xy) - x(x^2 + y^2) = -x^3 - 2y^2.$$

The proof of this theorem is difficult, see [Buc98] for a concise version. The algorithmic power of the Gröbner bases method is based on this theorem and its proof because the theorem shows, essentially, that the infinite test appearing in the definition of Gröbner bases for checking whether or not a given set F is a Gröbner basis can be replaced by the finite, algorithmic, test on the right-hand side of the theorem! This theorem can now be transformed into an algorithm for *constructing* Gröbner bases, i.e. for the problem to find, for any given multivariate polynomial set F, a set G such that G is a Gröbner basis and F and G generate the same set of linear combinations, see Algorithm 1.

The notion of Gröbner bases, the theorem on the characterization of Gröbner bases by S-polynomials, and the algorithm for the construction of Gröbner bases, together with termination proof, first applications and complexity considerations, were introduced in the PhD thesis [Buc65] and the corresponding journal publication [Buc70]. Buchberger gave the name "Gröbner"

Algorithm 1. Buchberger's Algorithm

Start with $G \leftarrow F$
for all pairs of polynomials $f_1, f_2 \in G$ **do**
    $h \leftarrow$ remainder of the S-polynomial of f_1 and f_2 w.r.t G
    if $h = 0$ **then**
        consider the next pair
    else
        add h to G and iterate
    end if
end for

---

to his theory for honoring his PhD thesis advisor Wolfgang Gröbner (1899–1980).

Example 3. Solving the problem of graph coloring by Gröbner bases. This problem consists in finding all admissible colorings in k colors of a graph with n vertices and edges E. A coloring of the vertices of a graph is admissible if no two adjacent vertices obtain the same color. For example, the left picture in Figure 2 is an admissible coloring in 3 colors of a graph with 4 vertices and edges $\{1,2\}, \{1,3\}, \{2,3\}, \{3,4\}$, whereas the right picture in Figure 2 is not an admissible coloring in 3 colors of the same graph.

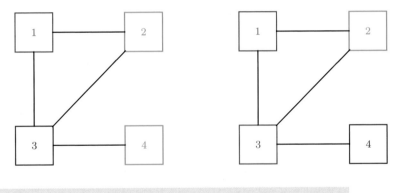

An admissible and a non-admissible coloring of a graph.   FIGURE 2

It is easy to see that the possible colorings of a graph can be obtained by considering all solutions of a certain system of polynomial equations (where the n indeterminates appearing in the polynomials correspond to the colors a the n vertices). We illustrate the construction of the polynomial system in the example:

$\{-1+x_1^3,$ ... the color at vertex 1 is a ternary root of 1, i.e. the three ternary roots of 1 encode the three colors

$-1+x_2^3,$ ... the color at vertex 2 is a ternary root of 1,

$-1+x_3^3,$

$-1+x_4^3,$

$x_1^2+x_1x_2+x_2^2,$ ... the colors at 1 and 2 must be different

$x_1^2+x_1x_3+x_3^2,$

$x_2^2+x_2x_3+x_3^2,$

$x_3^2+x_3x_4+x_4^2\}$

Now, compute a Gröbner basis of this polynomial set (this can be done by using for example Mathematica because, nowadays, Buchberger's algorithm is routinely available in all mathematical software systems) and compute all solutions. The corresponding Gröbner basis is:

$$\{-1+x_1^3, x_1^2+x_1x_2+x_2^2, -x_1-x_2-x_3, -x_1x_2+x_1x_4+x_2x_4-x_4^2\}.$$

One sees that the corresponding Gröbner basis is "decoupled" (this is one of the fundamental properties of Gröbner bases w.r.t. to lexicographic orderings), i.e. it can be completely solved by determining the values of one indeterminate after the other, starting with the first polynomial, which is always a polynomial in the first indeterminate only. In our case, we obtain the following set of solutions:

$$\begin{aligned}
\{ &\{x_1 \to 1, x_2 \to -(-1)^{1/3}, x_3 \to -1+(-1)^{1/3}, x_4 \to 1\}, \\
&\{x_1 \to 1, x_2 \to -(-1)^{1/3}, x_3 \to -1+(-1)^{1/3}, x_4 \to -(-1)^{1/3}\}, \\
&\{x_1 \to 1, x_2 \to (-1)^{2/3}, x_3 \to -1-(-1)^{2/3}, x_4 \to 1\}, \\
&\{x_1 \to 1, x_2 \to (-1)^{2/3}, x_3 \to -1-(-1)^{2/3}, x_4 \to (-1)^{2/3}\}, \\
&\{x_1 \to -(-1)^{1/3}, x_2 \to 1, x_3 \to -1+(-1)^{1/3}, x_4 \to 1\}, \\
&\{x_1 \to -(-1)^{1/3}, x_2 \to 1, x_3 \to -1+(-1)^{1/3}, x_4 \to -(-1)^{1/3}\}, \\
&\{x_1 \to -(-1)^{1/3}, x_2 \to -1+(-1)^{1/3}, x_3 \to 1, x_4 \to -(-1)^{1/3}\}, \\
&\{x_1 \to -(-1)^{1/3}, x_2 \to -1+(-1)^{1/3}, x_3 \to 1, x_4 \to -1+(-1)^{1/3}\}, \\
&\{x_1 \to (-1)^{2/3}, x_2 \to 1, x_3 \to -1-(-1)^{2/3}, x_4 \to 1\}, \\
&\{x_1 \to (-1)^{2/3}, x_2 \to 1, x_3 \to -1-(-1)^{2/3}, x_4 \to (-1)^{2/3}\}, \\
&\{x_1 \to (-1)^{2/3}, x_2 \to -1-(-1)^{2/3}, x_3 \to 1, x_4 \to (-1)^{2/3}\}, \\
&\{x_1 \to (-1)^{2/3}, x_2 \to -1-(-1)^{2/3}, x_3 \to 1, x_4 \to -1-(-1)^{2/3}\} \}
\end{aligned}$$

For example, the solution

$$\{x_1 \to 1, x_2 \to -(-1)^{1/3}, x_3 \to -1+(-1)^{1/3}, x_4 \to -(-1)^{1/3}\} \quad (1)$$

corresponds to the coloring illustrated in Figure 3.

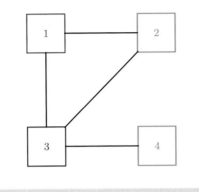

The graph coloring corresponding to the solution (1) of a system of poly-   FIGURE 3
nomial equations.

Oversimplified, the strategy for solving problems with Gröbner bases consists of the following steps:

1. Describe the problem (e.g. "coloring"), if possible, by sets of multivariate polynomials (e.g. polynomials on "roots of unity" instead of "colors").
2. Transform the occurring sets of polynomials into Gröbner basis form.
3. Solve the problem for the corresponding Gröbner bases (which, typically, is simpler than for the original sets). (For instance, find all solutions of the Gröbner basis.)
4. Translate the solutions back to the original sets. (In the case of finding solutions, the solutions of the Gröbner basis are the same as the solutions of the original system.)
5. Interpret the results in the language of the original problem (e.g. translate "roots of unity" into "colors").

3 Rational Algebraic Curves – Theory and Application

3.1 What is a Rational Algebraic Curve?

A plane algebraic curve $\mathcal{C}$ is the zero locus of a bivariate square-free polynomial $f(x, y)$ defined over a field K; i.e.

$$\mathcal{C} = \{\, (a, b) \,|\, f(a, b) = 0 \,\} \,.$$

More specifically, we call such a curve an affine curve, and the ambient plane the affine plane over K, denoted by $\mathbb{A}^2(K)$. By adding points at infinity for every direction in the affine plane, we get the projective plane over K, denoted by $\mathbb{P}^2(K)$. Points in $\mathbb{P}^2(K)$ have (non-unique) projective coordinates $(a : b : c)$ with $(a, b, c) \neq (0, 0, 0)$. In projective space only the ratio of the coordinates is fixed; i.e. if $\lambda \neq 0$ then $(a : b : c)$ and $(\lambda a : \lambda b : \lambda c)$ denote the same point in $\mathbb{P}^2(K)$. A projective plane curve $\hat{\mathcal{C}}$ is the zero locus of a homogeneous bivariate square-free polynomial $F(x, y, z)$ over K; i.e.

$$\hat{\mathcal{C}} = \{\, (a : b : c) \,|\, F(a, b, c) = 0 \,\} \,.$$

An algebraic curve in higher dimensional affine or projective space is the image of a birational map from the plane into this higher dimensional space. In this paper we concentrate on plane algebraic curves. Algebraic curves in higher dimensional space can be treated by considering a suitable birational image in the plane.

For more detailled information on the topics treated in this paper we refer to [SWPD08]. Most of the material for this survey has been developed by the author together with J.Rafael Sendra.

Some plane algebraic curves can be expressed by means of rational parametrizations, i.e. pairs of univariate rational functions. For instance, the tacnode curve (see Figure 4) defined in $\mathbb{A}^2(\mathbb{C})$ by the polynomial equation

$$f(x, y) = 2x^4 - 3x^2 y + y^2 - 2y^3 + y^4 = 0$$

can be represented as

$$\left\{ \left(\frac{t^3 - 6t^2 + 9t - 2}{2t^4 - 16t^3 + 40t^2 - 32t + 9}, \; \frac{t^2 - 4t + 4}{2t^4 - 16t^3 + 40t^2 - 32t + 9} \right) \;\middle|\; t \in \mathbb{C} \right\}.$$

However, not all plane algebraic curves can be rationally parametrized, for instance the elliptic curve defined by $f(x, y) = x^3 + y^3 - 1$ in $\mathbb{A}^2(\mathbb{C})$.

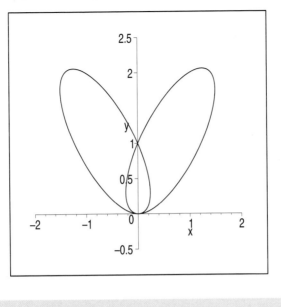

The Tacnode curve.   FIGURE 4

Definition 4. The affine curve $\mathcal{C}$ in $\mathbb{A}^2(K)$ defined by the square–free polynomial $f(x,y)$ is *rational* (or *parametrizable*) if there are rational functions $\chi_1(t), \chi_2(t) \in K(t)$ such that for almost all $t_0 \in K$ (i.e. for all but a finite number of exceptions) the point $(\chi_1(t_0), \chi_2(t_0))$ is on $\mathcal{C}$, and for almost every point $(x_0, y_0) \in \mathcal{C}$ there is a $t_0 \in K$ such that $(x_0, y_0) = (\chi_1(t_0), \chi_2(t_0))$. In this case $(\chi_1(t), \chi_2(t))$ is called an *affine rational parametrization* of $\mathcal{C}$.

Analogously we define projective rational curves.

Some Basic Facts   3.2

Fact 1. *The notion of rational parametrization can be stated by means of rational maps. More precisely, let $\mathcal{C}$ be a rational affine curve and $\mathcal{P}(t) \in K(t)^2$ a rational parametrization of $\mathcal{C}$. The parametrization $\mathcal{P}(t)$ induces the rational map*

$$\mathcal{P} : \mathbb{A}^1(K) \longrightarrow \mathcal{C}$$
$$t \longmapsto \mathcal{P}(t),$$

and $\mathcal{P}(\mathbb{A}^1(K))$ is a dense (in the Zariski topology) subset of $\mathcal{C}$. Sometimes, by abuse of notation, we also call this rational map a rational parametrization of $\mathcal{C}$.

Fact 2. *Every rational parametrization $\mathcal{P}(t)$ defines a monomorphism from the field of rational functions $K(\mathcal{C})$ to $K(t)$ as follows:*

$$\varphi: \quad K(\mathcal{C}) \longrightarrow K(t)$$
$$R(x,y) \longmapsto R(\mathcal{P}(t)).$$

Fact 3. *Every rational curve is irreducible; i.e. defined by an irreducible polynomial.*

Fact 4. *Let $\mathcal{C}$ be an irreducible affine curve and $\mathcal{C}^*$ its corresponding projective curve. Then $\mathcal{C}$ is rational if and only if $\mathcal{C}^*$ is rational. Furthermore, a parametrization of $\mathcal{C}$ can be computed from a parametrization of $\mathcal{C}^*$ and vice versa.*

Fact 5. *Let $\mathcal{C}$ be an affine rational curve over K, $f(x,y)$ its the defining polynomial, and $\mathcal{P}(t) = (\chi_1(t), \chi_2(t))$ a rational parametrization of $\mathcal{C}$. Then, there exists $r \in \mathbb{N}$ such that $\mathrm{res}_t(H_1^{\mathcal{P}}(t,x), H_2^{\mathcal{P}}(t,y)) = (f(x,y))^r$.*

Fact 6. *An irreducible curve $\mathcal{C}$, defined by $f(x,y)$, is rational if and only if there exist rational functions $\chi_1(t), \chi_2(t) \in K(t)$, not both constant, such that $f(\chi_1(t), \chi_2(t)) = 0$. In this case, $(\chi_1(t), \chi_2(t))$ is a rational parametrization of $\mathcal{C}$.*

Fact 7. *An irreducible affine curve $\mathcal{C}$ is rational if and only if the field of rational functions on $\mathcal{C}$, i.e. $K(\mathcal{C})$, is isomorphic to $K(t)$ (t a transcendental element).*

Fact 8. *An affine algebraic curve $\mathcal{C}$ is rational if and only if it is birationally equivalent to K (i.e. the affine line $\mathbb{A}^1(K)$).*

Fact 9. *If an algebraic curve $\mathcal{C}$ is rational then genus$(\mathcal{C}) = 0$.*

3.3 Proper Parametrizations

Definition 5. An affine parametrization $\mathcal{P}(t)$ of a rational curve $\mathcal{C}$ is *proper* if the map

$$\mathcal{P}: \mathbb{A}^1(K) \longrightarrow \mathcal{C}$$
$$t \longmapsto \mathcal{P}(t)$$

is birational, or equivalently, if almost every point on $\mathcal{C}$ is generated by exactly one value of the parameter t. We define the *inversion* of a proper parametrization $\mathcal{P}(t)$ as the inverse rational mapping of $\mathcal{P}$, and we denote it by $\mathcal{P}^{-1}$.

Analogously we define proper projective parametrizations.

Based on Lüroth's Theorem we can see that every rational curve which can be parametrized at all, can be properly parametrized.

Fact 10. *Every rational curve can be properly parametrized.*

Proper parametrizations can be characterized in many ways; we list some of the more practically usefull characterizations.

Fact 11. *Let C be an affine rational curve defined over K with defining polynomial $f(x, y) \in K[x, y]$, and let $\mathcal{P}(t) = (\chi_1(t), \chi_2(t))$ be a parametrization of C. Then, the following statements are equivalent:*

1. *$\mathcal{P}(t)$ is proper.*
2. *The monomorphism $\varphi_{\mathcal{P}}$ induced by $\mathcal{P}$ is an isomorphism.*

$$\varphi_{\mathcal{P}} : \; K(C) \; \longrightarrow \; K(t)$$
$$R(x, y) \longmapsto R(\mathcal{P}(t)).$$

3. *$K(\mathcal{P}(t)) = K(t)$.*
4. *$\deg(\mathcal{P}(t)) = \max\{\deg_x(f), \deg_y(f)\}$.*

Furthermore, if $\mathcal{P}(t)$ is proper and $\chi_1(t)$ is non-zero, then $\deg(\chi_1(t)) = \deg_y(f)$; similarly, if $\chi_2(t)$ is non-zero then $\deg(\chi_2(t)) = \deg_x(f)$.

Example 6. We consider the rational quintic curve C defined by the polynomial $f(x, y) = y^5 + x^2 y^3 - 3\,x^2 y^2 + 3\,x^2 y - x^2$. By the previous theorem, any proper rational parametrization of C must have a first component of degree 5, and a second component of degree 2. It is easy to check that

$$\mathcal{P}(t) = \left(\frac{t^5}{t^2 + 1}, \frac{t^2}{t^2 + 1} \right)$$

properly parametrizes C. Note that $f(\mathcal{P}(t)) = 0$.

A Parametrization Algorithm   3.4

We start with the easy case of curves having a singular point of highest possible multiplicity; i.e. irreducible curves of degree d having a point of multiplicity $d - 1$.

Theorem 7 (curves with point of high multiplicity). *Let C be an irreducible projective curve of degree d defined by the polynomial $F(x, y, z) = f_d(x, y) + f_{d-1}(x, y)z$ (f_i a form of degree i, resp.), i.e. having a $(d-1)$-fold point at $(0 : 0 : 1)$. Then C is rational and a rational parametrization is $\mathcal{P}(t) = (-f_{d-1}(1, t), -t f_{d-1}(1, t), f_d(1, t))$.*

Corollary 8. *Every irreducible curve of degree d with a $(d-1)$-fold point is rational; in particular, every irreducible conic is rational.*

Example 9.

1. Let C be the affine ellipse defined by $f(x,y) = x^2 + 2x + 2y^2 = 0$. So, a parametrization of C is $\mathcal{P}(t) = (-1 + 2t^2, -2t, 1 + 2t^2)$.
2. Let C be the affine quartic curve defined by (see Figure 5)

$$f(x,y) = 1 + x - 15\,x^2 - 29\,y^2 + 30\,y^3 - 25\,xy^2 + x^3 y + 35\,xy + x^4 - 6\,y^4 + 6\,x^2 y = 0 \,.$$

C has an affine triple point at $(1,1)$. By moving this point to the origin,

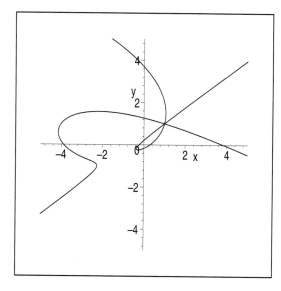

FIGURE 5   Quartic C.

applying the theorem, and inverting the transformation, we get the rational parametrization of C

$$\mathcal{P}(t) = \left(\frac{4 + 6\,t^3 - 25\,t^2 + 8\,t + 6\,t^4}{-1 + 6\,t^4 - t}, \frac{4\,t + 12\,t^4 - 25\,t^3 + 9\,t^2 - 1}{-1 + 6\,t^4 - t} \right) .$$

So curves with a point of highest possible multiplicity can be easily parametrized. But now let C will be an arbitrary irreducible projective curve of degree $d > 2$ and genus 0.

Definition 10. A linear system of curves $\mathcal{H}$ *parametrizes* C iff

1. $\dim(\mathcal{H}) = 1$,

2. the intersection of a generic element in $\mathcal{H}$ and $\mathcal{C}$ contains a non–constant point whose coordinates depend rationally on the free parameter in $\mathcal{H}$,

3. $\mathcal{C}$ is not a component of any curve in $\mathcal{H}$.

In this case we say that $\mathcal{C}$ *is parametrizable by* $\mathcal{H}$.

Theorem 11. *Let $F(x, y, z)$ be the defining polynomial of $\mathcal{C}$, and let $H(t, x, y, z)$ be the defining polynomial of a linear system $\mathcal{H}(t)$ parametrizing $\mathcal{C}$. Then, the proper parametrization $\mathcal{P}(t)$ generated by $\mathcal{H}(t)$ is the solution in $\mathbb{P}^2(K(t))$ of the system of algebraic equations*

$$\left. \begin{array}{l} \mathrm{pp}_t(\mathrm{res}_y(F, H)) = 0 \\ \mathrm{pp}_t(\mathrm{res}_x(F, H)) = 0 \end{array} \right\}.$$

Theorem 12. *Let $\mathcal{C}$ be a projective curve of degree d and genus 0, let $k \in \{d - 1, d - 2\}$, and let $\mathcal{S}_k$ be a set of $kd - (d - 1)(d - 2) - 1$ simple points on $\mathcal{C}$. Then*

$$\mathcal{A}_k(\mathcal{C}) \cap \mathcal{H}(k, \sum_{P \in \mathcal{S}_k} P)$$

(i.e. the system of adjoint curves of degree k passing through $\mathcal{S}_k$) parametrizes the curve $\mathcal{C}$.

Example 13. Let $\mathcal{C}$ be the quartic over $\mathbb{C}$ (see Figure 6) of equation

$$F(x, y, z) = -2xy^2z - 48x^2z^2 + 4xyz^2 - 2x^3z + x^3y - 6y^4 + 48y^2z^2 + 6x^4.$$

The singular locus of $\mathcal{C}$ is

$$\mathrm{Sing}(\mathcal{C}) = \{(0 : 0 : 1), (2 : 2 : 1), (-2 : 2 : 1)\},$$

all three points being double points. Therefore, genus$(\mathcal{C}) = 0$, and hence $\mathcal{C}$ is rational.

We proceed to parametrize the curve. The defining polynomial of $\mathcal{A}_2(\mathcal{C})$ (adjoint curves of degree 2) is

$$H(x, y, z) = (-2\,a_{02} - 2\,a_{20})\,yz + a_{02}y^2 - 2\,a_{11}xz + a_{1,1}xy + a_{20}x^2.$$

We choose a set $\mathcal{S} \subset (\mathcal{C} \setminus \mathrm{Sing}(\mathcal{C}))$ with 1 point, namely $\mathcal{S} = \{(3 : 0 : 1)\}$. We compute the defining polynomial of $\mathcal{H} := \mathcal{A}_2(\mathcal{C}) \cap \mathcal{H}(2, Q)$, where $Q = (3 : 0 : 1)$. This leads to

$$H(x, y, z) = (-2\,a_{02} - 2\,a_{20})\,yz + a_{02}y^2 - 3\,a_{20}xz + \frac{3}{2}\,a_{20}xy + a_{20}x^2.$$

Setting $a_{02} = 1, a_{20} = t$, we get the defining polynomial

$$H(t, x, y, z) = (-2 - 2\,t)\,yz + y^2 - 3\,txz + \frac{3}{2}\,txy + tx^2.$$

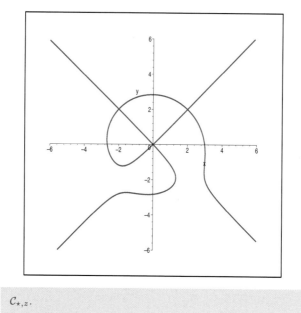

FIGURE 6 $\mathcal{C}_{*,z}$.

of the parametrizing system. Finally, the solution of the system defined by
the resultants provides the following affine parametrization of $\mathcal{C}$

$$\mathcal{P}(t) = \left(12\,\frac{9\,t^4 + t^3 - 51\,t^2 + t + 8}{126\,t^4 - 297\,t^3 + 72\,t^2 + 8\,t - 36},\ -2\,\frac{t(162\,t^3 - 459\,t^2 + 145\,t + 136)}{126\,t^4 - 297\,t^3 + 72\,t^2 + 8\,t - 36} \right).$$

3.5   Applications of Curve Parametrization

Curve parametrizations can be used to solve certain types of Diophantine
equations. For further details on this application we refer to [PV00], [PV02].
    Curve parametrizations can also be used to determine general solutions of
first order ordinary differential equations. This is described in [FG04], [FG06].
    Many problems in computer aided geometric design (CAGD) can be solved
by parametrization. The widely used Bézier curves and surfaces are typical
examples of rational curves and surfaces. Offsetting and blending of such
geometrical objects lead to interesting problems.
    The notion of an offset is directly related to the concept of an envelope.
More precisely, the offset curve, at distance d, to an irreducible plane curve $\mathcal{C}$
is "essentially" the envelope of the system of circles centered at the points of $\mathcal{C}$
with fixed radius d (see Figure 7). Offsets arise in practical applications such

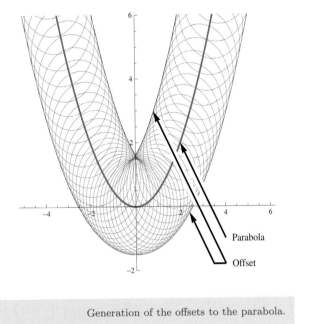

Generation of the offsets to the parabola.   FIGURE 7

as tolerance analysis, geometric control, robot path-planning and numerical-control machining problems.

In general the rationality of the original curve is not preserved in the transition to the offset. For instance, while the parabola, the ellipse, and the hyperbola are rational curves (compare Figure 8), the offset of a parabola is rational but the offset of an ellipse or a hyperbola is not rational.

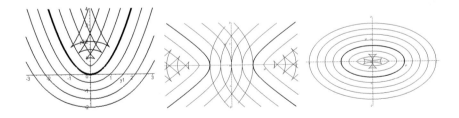

Offsets to the parabola (left), to the hyperbola (center), to the ellipse (right).   FIGURE 8

Let $\mathcal{C}$ be the original rational curve and let

$$\mathcal{P}(t) = (P_1(t), P_2(t))$$

be a proper rational parametrization of $\mathcal{C}$.

We determine the normal vector associated to the parametrization $\mathcal{P}(t)$, namely

$$\mathcal{N}(t) := (-P_2'(t), P_1'(t)).$$

Note that the offset at distance d basically consist of the points of the form

$$\mathcal{P}(t) \pm \frac{d}{\sqrt{P_1'(t)^2 + P_2'(t)^2}} \mathcal{N}(t).$$

Now we check whether this parametrization satisfies the "rational Pythagorean hodograph condition", i.e. whether

$$P_1'(t)^2 + P_2'(t)^2,$$

written in reduced form, is the square of a rational function in t. If the condition holds, then the offset to $\mathcal{C}$ has two components, and both components are rational. In fact, these two components are parametrized as

$$\mathcal{P}(t) + \frac{d}{m(t)} \mathcal{N}(t), \text{ and } \mathcal{P}(t) - \frac{d}{m(t)} \mathcal{N}(t),$$

where $P_1'(t)^2 + P_2'(t)^2 = a(t)^2/b(t)^2$ and $m(t) = a(t)/b(t)$.

If the rational Pythagorean hodograph condition does not hold, then the offset is irreducible and we may determine its rationality.

Example 14. We consider as initial curve the parabola of equation $y = x^2$, and its proper parametrization

$$\mathcal{P}(t) = (t, t^2).$$

The normal vector associated to $\mathcal{P}(t)$ is $\mathcal{N}(t) = (-2t, 1)$. Now, we check the rational Pythagorean hodograph condition

$$P_1'(t)^2 + P_2'(t)^2 = 4t^2 + 1,$$

and we observe that $4t^2 + 1$ is not the square of a rational function. Therefore, the offset to the parabola is irreducible. In fact, the offset to the parabola, at a generic distance d, can be parametrized as

$$\left(\frac{(t^2 + 1 - 4dt)(t^2 - 1)}{4t\,(t^2 + 1)}, \frac{t^6 - t^4 - t^2 + 1 + 32dt^3}{16t^2\,(t^2 + 1)} \right).$$

The implicit equation of the offset to the parabola is

$-y^2 + 32x^2d^2y^2 - 8x^2yd^2 + d^2 + 20x^2d^2 - 32x^2y^2 + 8d^2y^2 + 2yx^2 - 8yd^2 + 48x^4d^2 - 16x^4y^2 - 48x^2d^4 + 40x^4y + 32x^2y^3 - 16d^4y^2 - 32d^4y + 32d^2y^3 - x^4 + 8d^4 + 8y^3 - 16x^6 + 16d^6 - 16y^4 = 0.$

Computer Generated Progress in Lattice 4 Paths Theory

Modern computer algebra is capable of contributing to contemporary research in various scientific areas. In this section, we present some striking success of computer algebra in the context of lattice paths theory, a theory belonging to the area of combinatorics. A lattice is something like the city map of Manhattan, a perfect grid where all streets go either north-south or east-west. A lattice path then corresponds to a possible way a person in Manhattan may take who wants to get from A to B.

Combinatorics deals with the enumeration (counting) of objects, and enumeration questions concerning lattice paths arise naturally: How many ways are there to get from A to B? How many of them avoid a third point C or an entire area of the city? How many go more often north than south? How many avoid visiting the same point twice? How many have an optimal length? Starting disoriented at A and randomly continuing the way at each street crossing, what is the probability of eventually reaching B? What is the expected length of such a random walk?

These and many other questions have been intensively studied already for several centuries. Some are completely answered since long, others are still wide open today. Lattice paths are studied not only for supporting tourists who got lost in the middle of New York, but they are also needed in a great number of physical applications. For example, the laws governing the diffusion of small molecules through a crystal grid depend on results from lattice paths theory.

Paths in the Quarter Plane   4.1

We consider lattice walks confined to a quarter plane. A quarter plane may be imagined as a chess board which at two of its four sides (say, the right and the upper side) is prolonged to infinity. The prolongation removes three of the chess board's corners, only its lower left corner remains. This corner is the starting point of our paths.

Let us imagine that there is a chess piece which is able to move a single step north (N), south (S), west (W), or east (E) at a time. Then, among all the possible paths that this chess piece can perform, we are interested in those where the chess piece ends up again at the board's corner, the starting point of the journey. The number of these paths depends, of course, on the number n of steps we are willing to make. With $n = 2$ steps, there are only

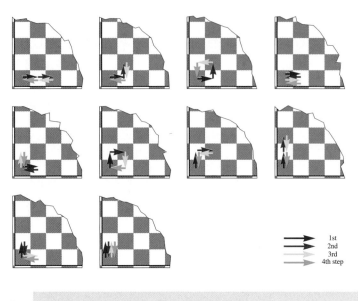

FIGURE 9   All closed Manhattan walks with four steps.

two possible paths: $(0,0) \xrightarrow{\mathrm{E}} (1,0) \xrightarrow{\mathrm{W}} (0,0)$ and $(0,0) \xrightarrow{\mathrm{N}} (0,1) \xrightarrow{\mathrm{S}} (0,0)$. For $n = 3$ steps, there are no such paths, and it is easy to see that there are no such paths whenever n is odd. For $n = 4$ steps, there are ten paths, they are depicted in Figure 9. For $n = 40$ steps, there are exactly as many as $160\,599\,522\,947\,154\,548\,400$ different paths.

That last number can obviously not be obtained by simply writing down all the possible paths. (Not even the fastest computer would be able to finish this task within our lifetime.) The number for $n = 40$ was obtained by means of a formula which produces the number a_n of paths for any given number n of steps. According to this formula, we have

$$a_{2n} = \frac{2}{(n+1)(n+2)} \binom{2n}{n} \binom{2n+1}{n} \qquad (n \geq 0).$$

and $a_n = 0$ if n is odd. This is a classical result and it can in fact be proven by elementary means.

In order to fully understand the combinatorics of our chess piece, it is not sufficient to know the numbers a_n. For a complete knowledge, it is also necessary to know the number of paths that the chess piece can take starting from the corner $(0,0)$ and ending at an arbitrary field (i,j). We can denote this number by $a_{n,i,j}$ and have, for example, $a_{40,6,4} = 2\,482\,646\,858\,370\,896\,735\,656$ paths going in $n = 40$ steps from the corner to the field in the 6th column and the 4th row.

It cannot be expected that there is a simple formula for $a_{n,i,j}$ as there is for $a_n = a_{n,0,0}$. In a sense, the numbers $a_{n,i,j}$ are "too complicated" to admit a formula. But among the sequences which do not have a simple formula, some are still more complicated than others. Combinatorialists have invented a hierarchy of classes for distinguishing different levels of "complicatedness". For a sequence $a_{n,i,j}$, they consider the formal infinite series

$$f(t,x,y) := \sum_{n=0}^{\infty} \sum_{i=0}^{\infty} \sum_{j=0}^{\infty} a_{n,i,j} x^i y^j t^n.$$

This series is called *rational* or *algebraic* or *holonomic*, depending on whether it satisfies certain types of equations whose precise form need not concern us here. The only thing relevant for now is that these notions create a hierarchy

rational series $\subsetneq$ algebraic series $\subsetneq$ holonomic series $\subsetneq$ all series.

A modern research program initiated by Bousquet-Melou and Mishna [BM02, Mis07, BMM08] is the classification of all the series arising from the lattice paths in the quarter plane performed by chess pieces with different step sets than N, S, W, E.

Computer Algebra Support 4.2

Thanks to research undertaken recently by members of RISC (M. Kauers and C. Koutschan) in collaboration with A. Bostan (France) and D. Zeilberger (USA), we are now in the fortunate situation that the combinatorial analysis of lattice paths is completely automatized: there are computer programs which, given any set $\mathcal{S}$ of admissible steps drawn from $\{N, S, E, W, NW, NE, SW, SE\}$, produce a formula for the number of paths that a chess piece can do, if it starts in the corner, is only allowed to make steps from $\mathcal{S}$, and wants to return to the corner after exactly n steps. Also for the more general problem of finding out to which class a series $f(t,x,y)$ describing the full combinatorial nature of the chess piece belongs, there are computer programs available.

Unlike a traditional combinatorialist who would try to *derive* such formulas from known facts about lattice paths, the computer follows a paradigm that could be called *guess'n'prove*. This paradigm, which proves useful in many other combinatorial applications of computer algebra, can be divided into the following three steps:

1. *Gather.* For small values of n, compute the number a_n of paths with n steps by a direct calculation. For instance, for the step set N, S, W, E

taken as example above, a computer is able to find without too much effort that the sequence (a_{2n}) for $n = 0, 1, \ldots$ starts with the terms

$$1, \; 2, \; 10, \; 70, \; 588, \; 5544, \; 56628, \; 613470, \; 6952660.$$

2. *Guess.* Given the initial terms, the computer can next search for formulas matching them. More convenient than a direct search for closed form expressions is a search for recurrence equations matching the data, since this can be done by algorithms reminiscent of polynomial interpolation. Such algorithms are implemented in widely available software packages, for instance in a package by Mallinger implemented at RISC [Mal96]. For the data from our example, this package "guesses" the recurrence equation

$$(n+2)(n+3)a_{2(n+1)} - 4(2n+1)(2n+3)a_{2n} = 0.$$

This equation is constructed such as to fit the first nine terms, but there is a priori no guarantee that it is valid, as we desire, for all n.

3. *Prove.* Experience says that an automatically guessed formula is always correct, but experience is not a formal proof. A formal proof can, however, also be constructed by the computer. We have an algorithm which takes as input a step set and a conjectured recurrence equation, and which outputs either a rigorous formal proof of the recurrence equation, or a counter example. The details of this algorithm are beyond the scope of this text.

There are only two possible reasons for which this *guess'n'prove* procedure may fail. The first is that for the particular step set at hand, the corresponding counting sequence does not satisfy any recurrence. In this case (which may indeed happen) the computer would indefinitely continue to search for a recurrence, because it is at present not possible to detect automatically that no recurrence exists. The second possible case of failure happens when a counting sequence satisfies only extremely huge recurrence equations (say, with millions of terms). In this case, although the computer would *in principle* be able to discover and to prove this recurrence, it may well be that *in practice* it is not, because the necessary computations are too voluminous to be completed by current computer architectures within a reasonable amount of time. The fact that such extremely large objects do actually arise induces a demand for faster algorithms in computer algebra. Such improved algorithms are therefore a natural subject of ongoing research.

4.3 Gessel's Conjecture

Let us now turn to a different imaginary chess piece. This new chess piece is able to move a single step left (E) or right (W), or diagonally a single step down-left (SE) or up-right (NW). We are interested again in the number of paths that take this chess piece from the corner of the (infinitely prolonged) chess board in n steps back to that corner. The counting sequence now starts as

$$1,\ 0,\ 2,\ 0,\ 11,\ 0,\ 85,\ 0,\ 782,\ 0,\ 8004,\ 0,\ 88044,\ 0,\ 1020162,\ 0$$

As an example, the eleven paths consisting of four steps are depicted in Figure 10.

The lattice paths just described were first considered by Gessel and are now known as *Gessel walks*. Gessel observed that there appears to hold the formula

$$a_{2n} = 16^n \frac{(\frac{5}{6})_n (\frac{1}{2})_n}{(\frac{5}{3})_n (2)_n} \qquad (n \geq 0),$$

where the notation $(x)_n$ stands for the product $x(x+1)(x+2)\cdots(x+n-1)$, a variation of the factorial function introduced by Pochhammer. Neither Gessel himself nor any other combinatorialist was, however, able to provide a rigorous proof of this formula. It became known as the Gessel conjecture and circulated as an open problem through the community for several years. Only in 2008, a proof was found at RISC by Kauers, Koutschan, and Zeilberger [KZ08, KKZ08]. Their proof relies on heavy algebraic computations that follow essentially the *guess'n'prove* paradigm described before.

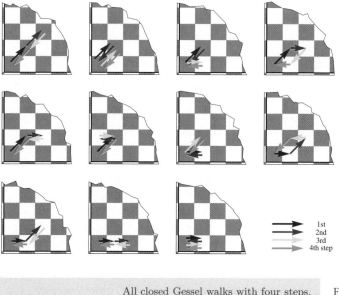

All closed Gessel walks with four steps.   FIGURE 10

The proof of Gessel's conjecture settles the nature of Gessel walks returning to the starting point. The nature of Gessel walks with arbitrary endpoint
(i, j) is more difficult to obtain. This question was addressed by Bostan and
Kauers [BK09a] after the proof of Gessel's original conjecture. By extensive
algebraic calculations, they were able to prove that the series $f(t, x, y)$ encoding the numbers $a_{n,i,j}$ of Gessel walks with n steps ending at (i, j) is *algebraic*.
For at least two different reasons, this is a surprising result. First, it was not
at all expected that $f(t, x, y)$ is algebraic. Combinatorial intuition seemed to
suggest that $f(t, x, y)$ is perhaps holonomic, or not even that. Second, it was
not to be expected that the intensive computations needed for establishing
the algebraicity of $f(t, x, y)$ were feasible for today's computers. As they were,
the combinatorial nature of Gessel walks can now be considered as solved.

It is fair to say that the classification of the Gessel walks is the most
difficult classification problem for lattice paths in the quarter plane. Indeed,
all other kinds of paths can be classified by traditional means relying on
group theory [BMM08]. Gessel's paths are famous partly because they are
the only ones which appear to resist this group theoretic approach. This
is why the clarification of their nature by means of computer algebra, as
previously described, was highly appreciated by the community.

4.4 Lattice Paths in 3D

One of the advantages of a computer algebra approach to lattice paths classification is that computer programs, once written, can be easily adapted to
related problems. Bostan and Kauers [BK08] applied their programs first developed for analyzing the Gessel paths to start a classification of lattice paths
in a three dimensional lattice. In analogy to the problem considered before
in 2D, lattice paths were considered which start in the corner of a space that
extends to infinity in now three different directions, that space may be viewed
as a distinguished octant of the usual Cartesian three dimensional space.

In addition to going north (N), south (S), east (E), or west (W), there are
the additional directions up (U) and down (D). Also combined directions such
as NE or SWU are possible. Basic steps are now more conveniently written
as vectors, e.g., $(1, -1, 0)$ for NE or $(-1, 1, 1)$ for SWU. While in 2D, there
were eight basic steps (N, S, E, W, NE, NW, SE, SW), there are now 26 basic
steps in 3D. For any subset $\mathcal{S}$ of those, we can imagine a chess piece moving
in 3D that is only allowed to take steps from $\mathcal{S}$, and we may ask how many
paths it can take starting from the corner, making n steps, and ending again
in the corner. For these numbers, call them again a_n, there may or may not
be a simple formula. (Usually there is none.) If, more generally, the number
of paths consisting of n steps and ending at a point (i, j, k) is denoted $a_{n,i,j,k}$,
we can consider the infinite series

$$f(t, x, y, z) = \sum_{n=0}^{\infty} \sum_{i=0}^{\infty} \sum_{j=0}^{\infty} \sum_{k=0}^{\infty} a_{n,i,j,k} x^i y^j z^k t^n$$

and may ask whether that series is rational, algebraic, holonomic, or non-holonomic. The answer will depend on the choice S of admissible steps.

In Figure 11, some step sets S are depicted for which the corresponding series is algebraic, holonomic, or non-holonomic. For example, the first step set in the top row is

$$S = \{(-1, 1, 1),\ (0, -1, -1),\ (0, -1, 0),\ (1, 0, 0),\ (1, 0, 1)\}.$$

The distinguished octant to which the paths are restricted is the octant containing $(1, 1, 1)$, which corresponds to the top-right-back corner in the diagrams of Figure 11. The counting sequence for paths returning to the corner with S as above starts

1, 0, 0, 1, 0, 0, 5, 0, 0, 42, 0, 0, 462, 0, 0, 6006, 0, 0, 87516, 0, 0.

For example, the only possible path with three steps is

$$(0, 0, 0) \xrightarrow{(1,0,0)} (1, 0, 0) \xrightarrow{(-1,1,1)} (0, 1, 1) \xrightarrow{(0,-1,-1)} (0, 0, 0).$$

The interested reader may wish to determine the five possible paths with six steps. He or she will find that this is a much more laborious and error prone task than for planar lattice paths.

Most of the possible step sets S in 3D lead to series which are not holonomic, only a fraction of them is holonomic or even algebraic. Out of those, the examples depicted in Figure 11 were chosen such as to illustrate that the position of a step set in the hierarchy is not necessarily related to what might be expected intuitively from the geometric complexity of the step set. For example, the first step set in the third row looks rather regular, yet the corresponding series is not holonomic. On the other hand, the third step set of the first row looks rather irregular, yet the corresponding series is algebraic.

Computer algebra was used in the discovery of these phenomena. The next challenging task is to explain them. As we have seen for Gessel's walks, computer algebra is ready to contribute also in these investigations. It will, in general, be of increasing importance the more the theory advances towards objects that are beyond the capabilities of traditional hand calculations.

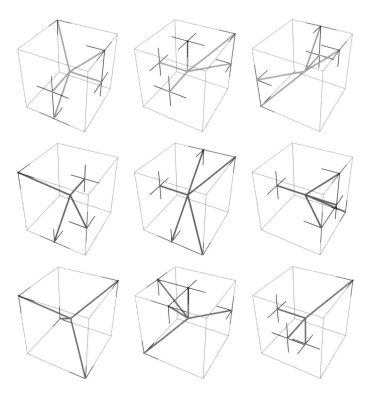

FIGURE 11   Some step sets for lattice walks in 3D whose counting sequences appear
             to be algebraic (first row), holonomic but not algebraic (second row), or
             not holonomic (third row).

5 Symbolic Summation in Particle Physics

Mathematical algorithms in the area of symbolic summation have been intensively developed at RISC in the last 15 years, see e.g., [PS95, Mal96, Weg97,
PR97, PS03, M06]. Meanwhile they are heavily used by scientists in practical
problem solving.

We present in this section a brand new interdisciplinary project in which
we try to deal with challenging problems in the field of particle physics and
perturbative quantum field theory with the help of our summation technology. Generally speaking, the overall goal in particle physics is to study the
basic elements of matter and the forces acting among them. The interaction
of these particles can be described by the so called Feynman diagrams, respectively Feynman integrals. Then the crucial task is the concrete evaluation

of these usually rather difficult integrals. In this way, one tries to obtain additional insight how, e.g., the fundamental laws control the physical universe.

In cooperation with the combinatorics group (Peter Paule) at RISC and the theory group (Johannes Blümlein) at Deutsches Elektronen-Synchrotron (DESY Zeuthen, a research center of the German Helmholtz association), we are in the process of developing flexible and efficient summation and special function algorithms that assist in this task, i.e., simplification, verification and manipulation of Feynman integrals and sums, and of related expressions. As it turns out, the software package Sigma [Sch07] plays one of the key roles: it is able to simplify highly complex summation expressions that typically arise within the evaluation of such Feynman integrals; see [BBKS07, MS07, BBKS08, BKKS09a, BKKS09b].

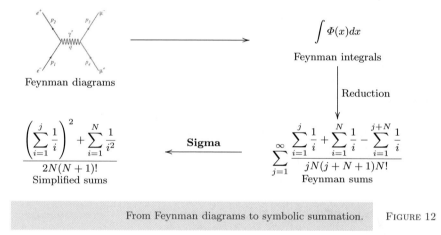

From Feynman diagrams to symbolic summation.   FIGURE 12

After sketching the basic summation tools that are used in such computations, we present two examples popping up at the scientific front of particle physics.

The Underlying Summation Principles   5.1

The summation principles of telescoping, creative telescoping and recurrence solving for hypergeometric terms, see e.g. [PWZ96], can be considered as the breakthrough in symbolic summation. Recently, these principles have been generalized in Sigma from single nested summation to multi-summation by exploiting a summation theory based on difference fields [Kar81, Sch05,

Sch08, Sch09]. As worked out, e.g., in [BBKS07], these methods can help to solve problems from particle physics.

SPECIFICATION (INDEFINITE SUMMATION BY TELESCOPING). *Given an indefinite sum* $S(a) = \sum_{k=0}^{a} f(k)$, *find* $g(j)$ *such that*

$$f(j) = g(j+1) - g(j) \tag{2}$$

holds within the summation range $0 \le j \le a$. *Then by telescoping, one gets*

$$S(a) = g(a+1) - g(0).$$

Example. For the sum expression

$$
\begin{aligned}
f(j) ={}& \frac{(2j+k+N+2)j!k!(j+k+N)!}{(j+k+1)(j+N+1)(j+k+1)!(j+N+1)!(k+N+1)!} \\
&+ \frac{j!k!(j+k+N)!\,(-S_1(j) + S_1(j+k) + S_1(j+N) - S_1(j+k+N))}{(j+k+1)!(j+N+1)!(k+N+1)!}
\end{aligned} \tag{3}
$$

involving the single harmonic sums defined by $S_1(j) := \sum_{i=1}^{j} \frac{1}{i}$ Sigma computes the solution

$$g(j) = \frac{(j+k+1)(j+N+1)j!k!(j+k+N)!\big(S_1(j)-S_1(j+k)-S_1(j+N)+S_1(j+k+N)\big)}{kN(j+k+1)!(j+N+1)!(k+N+1)!} \tag{4}$$

of (2); note that the reader can easily verify the correctness of this result by plugging in (3) and (4) into (2) and carrying out simple polynomial arithmetic in combination with relations such as $S_1(j+1) = S_1(j) + \frac{1}{j+1}$ and $(j+1)! = (j+1)j!$. Therefore summing (2) over j yields (together with a proof)

$$
\begin{aligned}
\sum_{j=0}^{a} f(j) ={}& \frac{S_1(k)+S_1(N)-S_1(k+N)}{kN(k+N+1)N!} + \frac{(2a+k+N+2)a!k!(a+k+N)!}{(a+k+1)(a+N+1)(a+k+1)!(a+N+1)!(k+N+1)!} \\
& \frac{(a+1)!k!(a+k+N+1)!(S_1(a)-S_1(a+k)-S_1(a+N)+S_1(a+k+N))}{kN(a+k+1)!(a+N+1)!(k+N+1)!}.
\end{aligned}
$$

In other words, we obtained the following simplification: the double sum $\sum_{j=0}^{a} f(j)$ with (3) could be simplified to an expression in terms of single harmonic sums. Later we shall reuse this result by performing the limit $a \to \infty$:

$$\sum_{j=0}^{\infty} f(j) = \lim_{a \to \infty} \sum_{j=0}^{a} f(j) = \frac{S_1(k) + S_1(N) - S_1(k+N)}{kN(k+N+1)N!}. \tag{5}$$

In most cases this telescoping trick fails, i.e., such a solution $g(j)$ for (2) does not exist. If the summand $f(j)$ depends on an extra discrete parameter, say N, one can proceed differently with Zeilberger's *creative telescoping paradigm*.

SPECIFICATION (DERIVING RECURRENCES BY CREATIVE TELESCOPING).
Given an integer $d > 0$ and given a sum

$$S(a, N) := \sum_{j=0}^{a} f(N, j) \tag{6}$$

with an extra parameter N, find constants $c_0(N), \ldots, c_d(N)$, free of j, and $g(N, j)$ such that for $0 \le j \le a$ the following summand recurrence holds:

$$c_0(N)f(N, j) + \cdots + c_d(N)f(N + d, j) = g(N, j + 1) - g(N, j). \tag{7}$$

If one succeeds in this task, one gets by telescoping the recurrence relation

$$c_0(N)S(a, N) + \cdots + c_d(N)S(a, N + d) = g(N, a + 1) - g(N, 0).$$

Example. For $d = 1$ and the summand

$$f(N, j) = \frac{S_1(j) + S_1(N) - S_1(j + N)}{jN(j + N + 1)N!}$$

Sigma computes the solution $c_0(N) = -N(N + 1)^2$, $c_1(N)(N + 1)^3(N + 2)$, and

$$g(N, j) = \frac{jS(1, j) + (-N - 1)S(1, N) - jS(1, j + N) - 2}{(j + N + 1)N!}$$

of (7); again the reader can easily verify the correctness of this computation by simple polynomial arithmetic. Hence, summing (7) over $1 \le j \le a$ gives

$$-NS(N, a) + (1 + N)(2 + N)S(N + 1, a) =$$
$$\frac{a(a+1)}{(N+1)^3(a+N+1)(a+N+2)N!} + \frac{(a + 1)\left(S_1(a) + S_1(N) - S_1(a + N)\right)}{(N + 1)^2(a + N + 2)N!} \tag{8}$$

for the sum (6). Later we need the following additional observation: the limit

$$S'(N) := \lim_{a \to \infty} S(N, a) = \sum_{j=0}^{\infty} \frac{S_1(j) + S_1(N) - S_1(j + N)}{jN(j + N + 1)N!} \tag{9}$$

exists; moreover, it is easy to see that the right hand side of (8) tends in the limit $a \to \infty$ to $\frac{(N+1)S_1(N)+1}{(N+1)^3 N!}$. In other words, the infinite series (9) satisfies the recurrence

$$-NS'(N) + (1 + N)(2 + N)S'(N + 1) = \frac{(N + 1)S_1(N) + 1}{(N + 1)^3 N!}. \tag{10}$$

Summarizing, with creative telescoping one can look for a recurrence of the form

$$a_0(N)S(N) + \cdots + a_1(N)S(N + d) = q(N). \tag{11}$$

Finally, Sigma provides the possibility to solve such recurrence relations in terms of indefinite nested sums and products.

Example. We use Sigma's recurrence solver and compute the general solution

$$\frac{1}{N(N+1)N!}c + \frac{S_1(N)^2 + S_2(N)}{2N(N+1)N!}$$

for a constant c of the recurrence (10). Checking the initial value $S'(1) = \frac{1}{2}$ (this evaluation can be done again by using, e.g., the package Sigma) determines $c = 0$, i.e., we arrive at

$$S'(N) = \sum_{j=1}^{\infty} \frac{S_1(j) + S_1(N) - S_1(j+N)}{jN(j+N+1)N!} = \frac{S_1(N)^2 + S_2(N)}{2N(N+1)!}. \quad (12)$$

More generally, we can handle with Sigma the following problem.

SPECIFICATION (RECURRENCE SOLVING). *Given a recurrence of the form (11), find all solutions in terms of indefinite nested sum and product expressions (also called d'Alembertian solution).*

Based on the underlying algorithms, see e.g. [AP94, BKKS09a], the derived d'Alembertian solutions of (11) are highly nested: in worst case the sums will reach the nesting depth $r - 1$. In order to simplify these solutions (e.g., reducing the nesting depth), a refined telescoping paradigm is activated. For an illuminative example see Section 5.3.

One can summarize this interplay of the different summation principles in the "summation spiral" [Sch04] illustrated in Figure 13.

5.2   Example 1: Simplification of Multi-Sums

The first example is part of the calculation of the so called polarized and unpolarized massive operator matrix elements for heavy flavor production [BBK06, BBK07]. Here two-loop Feynman integrals arise which can be reformulated in terms of double infinite series by skillful application of Mellin-Barnes integral representations. One of the challenging sums [BBK06] in this context is

$$S(N) = \sum_{k=0}^{\infty} \sum_{j=0}^{\infty} \overbrace{\frac{\varepsilon^{-\varepsilon\gamma}}{\Gamma(\varepsilon+1)} \Big(\frac{\Gamma(k+1)}{\Gamma(k+2+N)} \frac{\Gamma(\frac{\varepsilon}{2})\Gamma(1-\frac{\varepsilon}{2})\Gamma(j+1-\frac{\varepsilon}{2})\Gamma(j+1+\frac{\varepsilon}{2})\Gamma(k+j+1+N)}{\Gamma(j+1-\frac{\varepsilon}{2})\Gamma(j+2+N)\Gamma(k+j+2)}}^{=:\,f(N,k,j,\varepsilon)}$$

$$+ \frac{\Gamma(k+1)}{\Gamma(k+2+N)} \frac{\Gamma(-\frac{\varepsilon}{2})\Gamma(1+\frac{\varepsilon}{2})\Gamma(j+1+\varepsilon)\Gamma(j+1-\frac{\varepsilon}{2})\Gamma(k+j+1+\frac{\varepsilon}{2}+N)}{\Gamma(j+1)\Gamma(j+2+\frac{\varepsilon}{2}+N)\Gamma(k+j+2+\frac{\varepsilon}{2})} \Big);$$

$$(13)$$

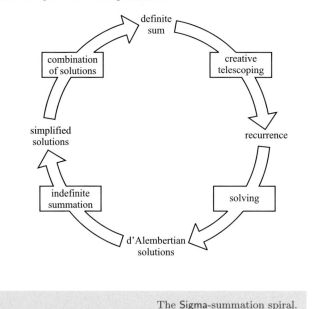

definite
sum

combination
of solutions

creative
telescoping

simplified
solutions

recurrence

indefinite
summation

solving

d'Alembertian
solutions

The Sigma-summation spiral.   FIGURE 13

here N is an integer variable and $\Gamma(x)$ denotes the gamma function, see e.g.
[AAR00], which evaluates to $\Gamma(k) = (k-1)!$ for positive integers k.

Remark. Usually, Feynman integrals (and sums obtained, e.g., by Mellin
Barnes representations) cannot be formalized at the space-time dimension
$D = 4$. One overcomes this problem by an analytic continuation of the space-
time $D = 4 + \varepsilon$ for a small parameter ε. Then one can extract the needed
information by calculating sufficiently many coefficients of the Laurent-series
expansion about $\varepsilon = 0$.

For instance, in our concrete sum (13) one is interested in the first coefficients $F_0(N), F_1(N), F_2(N), \ldots$ in the expansion

$$S(N, \varepsilon) = F_0(N) + F_1(N)\varepsilon + F_2(N)\varepsilon^2 + \ldots \qquad (14)$$

In order to get these components, we proceed as follows. First, we compute,
as much as needed, the coefficients $f_0(N, k, j), f_1(N, k, j), \ldots$ of the series
expansion

$$f(N, k, j, \varepsilon) = f_0(N, k, j) + f_1(N, k, j)\varepsilon + f_2(N, k, j)\varepsilon^2 + \ldots \qquad (15)$$

on the summand level. Then, it follows (by convergence arguments) that for
all $i \geq 0$,

$$F_i(N) = \sum_{k=0}^{\infty} \sum_{j=0}^{\infty} f_i(N, k, j).$$

Remark. The gamma function $\Gamma(x)$ is analytic everywhere except at the points $x = 0, -1, -2, \ldots$, and there exist formulas that relate, e.g., the derivative of the gamma function $\Gamma(x+k)$ w.r.t. x with the sums $S_a(k) = \sum_{i=1}^{k} \frac{1}{i^a}$ for positive integers a.

Due to such formulas, one can compute straightforwardly the first coefficients $f_i(N, k, j)$ in (15) for the explicitly given summand in (13). E.g., $f_0(N, k, j)$ is nothing else than (3). Thus the constant term $F_0(N) = \sum_{k=0}^{\infty} \sum_{j=0}^{\infty} f_0(N, k, j)$ in (14) is given by

$$
\begin{aligned}
F_0(N) = \sum_{k=0}^{\infty} \sum_{j=0}^{\infty} \Big(& \frac{(2j+k+N+2)j!k!(j+k+N)!}{(j+k+1)(j+N+1)(j+k+1)!(j+N+1)!(k+N+1)!} \\
& + \frac{j!k!(j+k+N)!(-S_1(j)+S_1(j+k)+S_1(j+N)-S_1(j+k+N))}{(j+k+1)!(j+N+1)!(k+N+1)!} \Big).
\end{aligned}
\tag{16}
$$

We are faced now with the problem to simplify (16), so that it can be processed further in particle physics. Exactly at that point we are in business with our summation tools from Section 5.1. First observe that the inner sum of (16) is equal to the right hand side of (5). Hence with (12) we find that

$$
\sum_{k=1}^{\infty} \sum_{j=0}^{\infty} f_i(N, k, j) = \frac{S_1(N)^2 + S_2(N)}{2N(N+1)!}.
$$

Finally, we add the missing term $\sum_{j=0}^{\infty} f_i(N, 0, j) = \frac{S_2(N)}{N(N+1)!}$ (derived by the same methods as above). To sum up, we simplified the expression (16) to

$$
F_0(N) = \sum_{k=0}^{\infty} \sum_{j=0}^{\infty} f_0(N, k, j) = \frac{S_1(N)^2 + 3S_2(N)}{2N(N+1)!}.
$$

In [BBK06] the authors derived this constant term and also the linear term

$$
F_1(N) = \frac{-S_1(N)^3 - 3S_2(N)S_1(N) - 8S_3(N)}{6N(N+1)!}
$$

in (14) by skillful application of suitable integral representations.

In contrast, our computations can be carried out purely mechanically with the computer. Essentially, this enables us to compute further coefficients in (14) by just pressing a button (and having some coffee in the meantime):

$$
\begin{aligned}
F_2(N) = \sum_{k=0}^{\infty} \sum_{j=0}^{\infty} f_2(N, k, j) = \frac{1}{96N(N+1)!} \Big(& S_1(N)^4 + (12\zeta_2 + 54S_2(N))S_1(N)^2 \\
& + 104S_3(N)S_1(N) - 48S_{2,1}(N)S_1(N) + 51S_2(N)^2 + 36\zeta_2 S_2(N) + 126S_4(N) \\
& - 48S_{3,1}(N) - 96S_{1,1,2}(N) \Big),
\end{aligned}
$$

$$F_3(N) = \sum_{k=0}^{\infty} \sum_{j=0}^{\infty} f_3(N,k,j) = \frac{1}{960N(N+1)!} \Big(S_1(N)^5 + (20\zeta_2 + 130S_2(N))S_1(N)^3$$

$$+ (40\zeta_3 + 380S_3(N))S_1(N)^2 + \big(135S_2(N)^2 + 60\zeta_2 S_2(N) + 510S_4(N)\big) S_1(N)$$

$$- 240S_{1,1,3}(N) - 240S_{4,1}(N) - 240S_{3,1}(N)S_1(N) - 240S_{1,1,2}(N)S_1(N)$$

$$+ 160\zeta_2 S_3(N) + S_2(N)(120\zeta_3 + 380S_3(N)) + 624S_5(N)$$

$$+ \big(-120S_1(N)^2 - 120S_2(N)\big) S_{2,1}(N) + 240S_{2,2,1}(N)\Big);$$

here $\zeta_r = \sum_{i=1}^{\infty} \frac{1}{i^r}$ denote the zeta-values at r and the harmonic sums [BK99, Ver99] for nonzero integers $r_1, \ldots, r_n$ are defined by

$$S_{r_1,\ldots,r_n}(N) = \sum_{k_1=1}^{N} \frac{\text{sign}(r_1)^{k_1}}{k^{|r_1|}} \sum_{k_2=1}^{k_1} \frac{\text{sign}(r_{m-1})^{k_2}}{k_2^{|r_1|}} \cdots \sum_{k_r=1}^{k_{r-1}} \frac{\text{sign}(r_n)^{k_r}}{k_r^{|r_1|}}. \qquad (17)$$

For instance, we find the linear coefficient $F_1(N)$ in 30 seconds, the quadratic coefficient $F_2(N)$ in 4 minutes and the cubic coefficient $F_3(N)$ in less than one hour.

Example 2: Solving Large Recurrence Relations   5.3

One of the hardest problem that has been considered in the context of Feynman integrals is the calculation of the symbolic Mellin-moments of the unpolarized 3-loop splitting functions and Wilson coefficients for deep–inelastic scattering [MVV04, VMV04, VVM05]: several CPU years were needed for this job. In order to get these results, specialized and extremely efficient software [Ver99] have been developed. Based on deep insight and knowledge of the underlying physical problem fine tuned ansatzes for the computations have been used in addition.

In a recent attempt [BKKS09a, BKKS09b] we explored a different, rather flexible ansatz in order to determine such coefficients. We illustrate this approach for the $C_F N_F^2$-term, say $F(N) = P_{gq,2}(N)$, of the unpolarized 3-loop splitting function; see [BKKS09b, Exp. 1]. Namely, we start with the initial values $F(i)$ for $i = 3, \ldots, 112$ where the first ones are given by

$$\frac{1267}{648}, \frac{54731}{40500}, \frac{20729}{20250}, \frac{2833459}{3472875}, \frac{29853949}{44452800}, \frac{339184373}{600112800}, \frac{207205351}{428652000}, \frac{152267426}{363862125}, \cdots$$

Then given this data, one can establish (within 7 seconds) by Manuel Kauers' very efficient recurrence guesser (see also Section 4.2) the following recurrence:

$$(1 - N)N(N + 1)(N^6 + 15N^5 + 109N^4 + 485N^3 + 1358N^2 + 2216N + 1616)F(N)$$
$$+ N(N+1)(3N^7 + 48N^6 + 366N^5 + 1740N^4 + 5527N^3 + 11576N^2 + 14652N + 8592)F(N+1)$$
$$- (N + 1)(3N^8 + 54N^7 + 457N^6 + 2441N^5 + 9064N^4 + 23613N^3$$
$$+ 41180N^2 + 43172N + 20768)F(N + 2)$$
$$+ (N + 4)^3(N^6 + 9N^5 + 49N^4 + 179N^3 + 422N^2 + 588N + 368)F(N + 3) = 0.$$

We remark that in principle this guess might be wrong, but by rough estimates this unlucky case occurs with probability of about 10^{-65} (if we do not trust in this result, we should not trust any computation: e.g., undetectable hardware errors have a much higher chance to happen).

Given this recurrence, we apply the recurrence solver of Sigma: internally, one succeeds in factorizing the recurrence into linear right hand factors; see [BKKS09b, Exp. 1]. As a consequence, Sigma finds (within 3 seconds) the solution

$$F(N) = -\frac{32}{9}\frac{N^2 + N + 2}{(N - 1)N(N + 1)} + \frac{64}{9}\frac{\left(N^2 + N + 2\right)\sum_{i=1}^{N}\frac{i^4 + 7i^2 + 4i + 4}{(i+1)(i^2 - i + 2)(i^2 + i + 2)}}{(N - 1)N(N + 1)}$$
$$-\frac{8}{3}\frac{\left(N^2 + N + 2\right)\sum_{i=1}^{N}\frac{(i^4 + 7i^2 + 4i + 4)\sum_{j=1}^{i}\frac{(j^2 - j + 2)(j^6 - 3j^5 + 19j^4 - 13j^3 + 44j^2 + 8j + 8)}{(j+1)(j^4 + 7j^2 + 4j + 4)(j^4 - 4j^3 + 13j^2 - 14j + 8)}}{(i+1)(i^2 - i + 2)(i^2 + i + 2)}}{(N-1)N(N+1)}.$$

Next, we activate our sum simplifier (based on refined telescoping [Sch08]) and end up at the closed form

$$F(N) = -\frac{4\left(N^2 + N + 2\right)}{3(N - 1)N(N + 1)}S_1(N)^2 + \frac{8\left(8N^3 + 13N^2 + 27N + 16\right)}{9(N - 1)N(N + 1)^2}S_1(N)$$
$$-\frac{8\left(4N^4 + 4N^3 + 23N^2 + 25N + 8\right)}{9(N - 1)N(N + 1)^3} - \frac{4\left(N^2 + N + 2\right)}{3(N - 1)N(N + 1)}S_2(N)$$

in terms of the harmonic sums given by (17). At this point we make the following remark: we are not aware of the existence of any other software that can produce this solution of the rather simple recurrence given above. Summarizing, we determined the $C_F N_F^2$-term of the unpolarized 3-loop splitting function $F(N) = P_{gq,2}(N)$ by using its first 110 initial values without any additional intrinsic knowledge.

In order to get an impression of the underlying complexity, we summarize the hardest problem. For the most complicated expression (the C_F^3-contribution to the unpolarized 3-loop Wilson coefficient for deeply inelastic scattering, see [BKKS09b, Exp. 6]) M. Kauers could establish a recurrence of order 35 within 20 days and 10Gb of memory by using 5022 such initial values; note that the found recurrence has minimal order and uses 32MB of memory size. Then Sigma used 3Gb of memory and around 8 days in order to derive the closed form of the corresponding Wilson coefficient. The output fills several pages and consists of 30 (algebraically independent) harmonic sums (17), like e.g.,

$$S_{-3,1,1,1}, S_{2,2,1,1}, S_{-2,-2,1,1}, S_{2,-2,1,1}, S_{-2,2,1,1}, S_{-2,1,1,2}, S_{2,1,1,1,1}, S_{-2,1,1,1,1}.$$

In total, we used 4 month of computation time in order to treat all the problems from [MVV04, VMV04, VVM05].

These results from [BKKS09a, BKKS09b] illustrate that one can solve 3-loop integral problems efficiently by recurrence guessing and recurrence solving under the assumptions that sufficiently many initial values (in our case maximally 5022) are known. In order to apply our methods to such problems, methods at far lower expenses have to be developed that can produce this huge amount of initial values. This is not possible in the current state of art.

By concluding, in ongoing research we will try to combine the different ideas presented in Section 5 to find new, flexible and efficient methods that will take us one step further to evaluate automatically non-trivial Feynman integrals.

Nonlinear Resonance Analysis   6

In recent years (2004–2009) a new area of mathematical physics—Nonlinear Resonance Analysis (NRA)—has been developed at RISC. Its theoretical background was outlined in 1998, see [Kar98]. But the way to real-world applications was still long. In particular, appropriate calculation techniques and mathematical model fitting to physical systems had to be worked out. This has been achieved under the projects SBF-013 (FWF), ALISA (OeAD, Grant Nr.10/2006-RU), DIRNOW (FWF, P20164000), and CEN-REC (OeAD, Grant Nr.UA 04/2009). The main points of this work are briefly presented below.

What is Resonance?   6.1

Physical Examples

The phenomena of resonance has been first described and investigated by Galileo Galilei in 1638 who was fascinating by the fact that by "simply blowing" one can confer considerable motion upon even a heavy pendulum. A well-known example with Tacoma Narrows Bridge shows how disastrous resonances can be: on the morning of November 7, 1940, at 10:00 the bridge began to oscillate dangerously up and down, and collapsed in about 40 minutes, see Figure 14. The experiments of Tesla [Che93] with vibrations of an iron column yielded in 1898 sort of a small earthquake in his neighborhood in Manhattan, with smashed windows, swayed buildings, and panic people in the streets.

FIGURE 14   The Tacoma Narrows Bridge. Right picture is taken approximately 40 minutes after the left one.

Nowadays it is well-known fact that resonance is a common thread which runs through almost every branch of physics and technics, without resonance we wouldn't have radio, television, music, etc. Whereas linear resonances are studied quite well, their nonlinear counterpart was till recently Terra Incognita, out of the reach of any general theoretical approach. And this is though nonlinear resonances are ubiquitous in physics. Euler equations, regarded with various boundary conditions and specific values of some parameters, describe an enormous number of nonlinear dispersive wave systems (capillary waves, surface water waves, atmospheric planetary waves, drift waves in plasma, etc.) all possessing nonlinear resonances [ZLF92]. Nonlinear resonances appear in a great amount of typical mechanical systems [KM06]. Nonlinear resonance is the dominant mechanism behind outer ionization and energy absorption in near infrared laser-driven rare-gas or metal clusters [KB05]. Nonlinear resonance jump can cause severe damage to the mechanical, hydraulic and electrical systems [HMK03]. The characteristic resonant frequencies observed in accretion disks allow astronomers to determine whether the object is a black hole, a neutron star, or a quark star [Klu06]. The variations of the helium dielectric permittivity in superconductors are due to nonlinear resonances [KLPG04]. Temporal processing in the central auditory nervous system analyzes sounds using networks of nonlinear neural resonators [AJLT05]. The nonlinear resonant response of biological tissue to the action of an electromagnetic field is used to investigate cases of suspected disease or cancer [VMM05], etc.

Mathematical Formulation

Mathematically, a resonance is an unbounded solution of a differential equation. The very special role of resonant solutions of nonlinear ordinary differential equations (ODEs) has been first investigated by Poincaré [Arn83] who proved that if a nonlinear ODE has *no resonances*, then it *can be linearized* by an invertible change of variables. Otherwise, only resonant terms are important, all other terms have the next order of smallness and can be ignored. In the middle of the 20th century, Poincaré's approach has been generalized to the case of nonlinear partial differential equations (PDEs) yielding what is nowadays known as KAM-theory (KAM for Kolmogorov-Arnold-Moser), [Kuk04]. This theory allows us to transform a nonlinear dispersive PDE into a Hamiltonian equation of motion in Fourier space [ZLF92],

$$i\,\dot{a}_{\mathbf{k}} = \partial \mathcal{H}/\partial a_{\mathbf{k}}^*, \tag{18}$$

where $a_{\mathbf{k}}$ is the amplitude of the Fourier mode corresponding to the wavevector $\mathbf{k}$, $\mathbf{k} = (m,n)$ or $\mathbf{k} = (m,n,l)$ with integer m,n,l. The Hamiltonian $\mathcal{H}$ is represented as an expansion in powers $\mathcal{H}_j$ which are proportional to the product of j amplitudes $a_{\mathbf{k}}$. For the simplicity of presentation, all the methods and results below are outlined for the case of non-zero cubic Hamiltonian $\mathcal{H}_3$ and 2-dimensional wavevector $\mathbf{k} = (m,n)$. A cubic Hamiltonian $\mathcal{H}_3$ has the form

$$\mathcal{H}_3 = \sum_{\mathbf{k_1},\mathbf{k_2},\mathbf{k_3}} V_{23}^1 a_1^* a_2 a_3 \delta_{23}^1 + \text{ complex conj.},$$

where for brevity we introduced the notation $a_j \equiv a_{\mathbf{k}_j}$ and $\delta_{23}^1 \equiv \delta(\mathbf{k_1} - \mathbf{k_2} - \mathbf{k_3})$ is the Kronecker symbol. If $\mathcal{H}_3 \neq 0$, three-wave process is dominant and the main contribution to the nonlinear evolution comes from the waves satisfying the following resonance conditions:

$$\omega(\mathbf{k_1}) + \omega(\mathbf{k_2}) - \omega(\mathbf{k_3}) = 0, \quad \mathbf{k_1} + \mathbf{k_2} - \mathbf{k_3} = 0, \tag{19}$$

where $\omega(\mathbf{k})$ is a dispersion relation for the linear wave frequency. Corresponding dynamical equation yields the three-wave equation:

$$i\,\frac{da_{\mathbf{k}}}{dt} = \sum_{\mathbf{k_1},\mathbf{k_2}} \left[\frac{1}{2} V_{12}^{\mathbf{k}} a_1 a_2 \Delta_{12}^{\mathbf{k}} + V_{\mathbf{k}2}^{1}{}^* a_1 a_2^* \Delta_{\mathbf{k}2}^{1} \right]. \tag{20}$$

The Hamiltonian formulation allows us to study the problems of various nature by the same method: all the difference between the problems of climate variability, cancer diagnostics and broken bridges is hidden in the form of the coefficients of the Hamiltonian, i.e. V_{12}^{k} and V_{k2}^{1*}.

6.2   Kinematics and Dynamics

To compute nonlinear resonances in a PDE with given boundary conditions, one has to find linear eigenmodes and dispersion function $\omega = \omega(m, n)$, and rewrite the PDE in Hamiltonian form by standard methods (e.g. [Arn83], [ZLF92]). Afterwards two seemingly simple steps have to be performed.

Step 1:   Solve the algebraic Sys. (19) in integers and compute the coefficients V_{12}^{k} (they depend on the solutions of the Sys. (19)). This part of the NRA is called *Kinematics*.

Step 2:   Solve the Sys. (20), consisting of nonlinear ODEs; this part of the theory is called *Dynamics*.

In order to show mathematical and computational problems appearing on this way, let us regard one example. Let dispersion function have the form $\omega = 1/\sqrt{m^2 + n^2}$ (oceanic planetary waves) and regard a small domain of wavevectors, say $m, n \leq 50$. The first equation of Sys. (19) reads

$$(m_1^2 + n_1^2)^{-1/2} + (m_2^2 + n_2^2)^{-1/2} = (m_3^2 + n_3^2)^{-1/2}, \qquad (21)$$

the only standard way would be to get rid of radicals and solve numerically the resulting Diophantine equation of degree 8 in 6 variables:

$$(m_3^2 + n_3^2)^2(m_1^2 + n_1^2)(m_2^2 + n_2^2) = \Big[(m_1^2 + n_1^2)(m_2^2 + n_2^2) -$$
$$(m_2^2 + n_2^2)(m_3^2 + n_3^2) - (m_1^2 + n_1^2)(m_3^2 + n_3^2)\Big]^2 \qquad (22)$$

This means that at *Step 1* we will need operate with integers of the order of $(50)^8 \sim 4 \cdot 10^{13}$. This means also that in physically relevant domains, with $m, n \leq 1000$, there is no chance to find solutions this way, using the present computers. At *Step 2* we have $50 \times 50 = 2500$ complex variables $a_j, a_j^*, j = 1, 2, \ldots, 50$; correspondingly Sys. (20) consists of 2500 interconnected nonlinear ODEs. This being a dead-end, a search for novel computational methods is unavoidable.

Kinematics

Two main achievements in this part of our research are

1. the *q-class method* and
2. *topological representation of resonance dynamics,*

which we briefly present below.

The q-class method. Theoretical results of [Kar98] have been the basis for the development of a fast computational algorithm to compute nonlinear resonances outlined in [Kar06]. Various modifications of the q-class method have been implemented numerically ([KK06, KK07]) and symbolically ([KM07, KRF$^+$07]) for a wide class of physically relevant dispersion functions. The efficiency of our method can be demonstrated by following example. Direct computation has been performed in 2005 by the group of Prof. S. Nazarenko (Warwick Mathematical School, UK) with dispersion function $\omega = (m^2 + n^2)^{1/4}$ for the case of 4-term resonance. For spectral domain $m, n \leq 128$, these computations took 3 days with Pentium 4; the same problem in the spectral domain $m, n \leq 1000$, is solved by the q-class method with Pentium 3 in 4.5 minutes.

We illustrate how the q-class method works, taking again Eq. (21) as an example. Two simple observations, based on school mathematics, can be made. First, for arbitrary integers m, n, the presentation

$$\sqrt{m^2 + n^2} = p\sqrt{q}$$

with integer p and square-free q *is unique.* Second, Eq. (21) has integer solutions only if in all three presentations

$$\sqrt{m_1^2 + n_1^2} = p_1\sqrt{q_1}, \quad \sqrt{m_2^2 + n_2^2} = p_2\sqrt{q_2}, \quad \sqrt{m_3^2 + n_3^2} = p_3\sqrt{q_3} \qquad (23)$$

the irrationalities q_1, q_2, q_3 are equal, i.e. $q_1 = q_2 = q_3 = q$. This is only a necessary condition, of course. The number q is called index of a q-class, all pairs of integers (m, n) can be divided into disjoint classes by the index and search for solutions is performed within each class separately. For each class, Eq. (21) takes a very simple form, $p_1^{-1} + p_2^{-1} = p_3^{-1}$, and can be solved in no time even with a simple calculator.

The general idea of the q-class method is, to use linear independence of some functions over the field of rational numbers $\mathbb{Q}$ and can be generalized to much more complicated dispersion functions, e.g. $\omega = m \tanh \sqrt{m_1^2 + n_1^2}$. Though this approach does not work with rational dispersion functions, substantial computational shortcuts have also been found for this case ([KK07]).

Topological representation of resonance dynamics. The classical representation of resonance dynamics by resonance curves [LHG67] is insufficient for two reasons. First, one has to fix a certain wavevector (m, n) and therefore this representation can not be performed generally. Second, no general method exists for finding integer points on a resonance curve. We have introduced a novel representation of resonances *via* a graph with vertices belonging to a subset of a two-dimensional integer grid. We have also proved that there exists a one-to-one correspondence between connected components of this graph and dynamical systems, subsystems of Sys. (20).

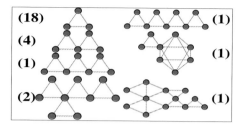

FIGURE 15   Example of topological structure, spectral domain $|k_i| \leq 50$, each blue vertex corresponds to a pair (m, n) and three vertices are connected by arcs, if they constitute a resonant triad. The number in brackets shows how many times the corresponding cluster appears in the given spectral domain.

The topology for the example above is shown in the Figure 15; the dynamical system for the graph component (called *resonance cluster* in physics) consisting of 4 connected resonant triads (Figure 15, bottom left) reads (in real variables)

$$
\begin{cases}
\dot{a}_1 = \alpha_1 a_2 a_9, \quad \dot{a}_2 = \alpha_2 a_1 a_9, \quad \dot{a}_3 = \alpha_4 a_4 a_9, \quad \dot{a}_4 = \alpha_5 a_3 a_9, \\
\dot{a}_5 = \alpha_7 a_8 a_9, \quad \dot{a}_6 = \alpha_{10} a_7 a_8, \quad \dot{a}_7 = \alpha_{11} a_6 a_8, \\
\dot{a}_8 = \alpha_{12} a_6 a_7 + \alpha_8 a_5 a_9, \quad \dot{a}_9 = \alpha_3 a_1 a_2 + \alpha_6 a_3 a_4 + \alpha_9 a_5 a_8.
\end{cases}
\tag{24}
$$

Already this novel representation, both very simple and very informative, has attracted the attention of the peers of the Wolfram Demonstrations Project, and we have been invited to participate in the project[1].

Dynamics

Two main achievements in this part of our research are 1) explicit computation of *dynamical invariants*, [BK09b]; and 2) realization that *dynamical phase* is a parameter of utmost importance in resonance dynamics [BK09c].

Dynamical invariant. In [KL08] it was shown that the dynamics of bigger clusters often can be reduced to the dynamics of smaller clusters, consisting of one or two triads only. Integrability of a triad, with dynamical system

$$
\dot{a}_1 = Z a_2^* a_3, \quad \dot{a}_2 = Z a_1^* a_3, \quad \dot{a}_3 = -Z a_1 a_2,
\tag{25}
$$

is a well known fact ([Whi90, LH04]), and its solution, simplified for the case of zero dynamical phase, reads

---

[1] http://demonstrations.wolfram.com/NonlinearWaveResonances/

$$\begin{cases} C_1(t) = \mathrm{dn}((-t+t_0)\, z\, \sqrt{I_{13}}, \frac{I_{23}}{I_{13}})\, \sqrt{I_{13}} \\ C_2(t) = \mathrm{cn}((-t+t_0)\, z\, \sqrt{I_{13}}, \frac{I_{23}}{I_{13}})\, \sqrt{I_{23}} \\ C_3(t) = \mathrm{sn}((-t+t_0)\, z\, \sqrt{I_{13}}, \frac{I_{23}}{I_{13}})\, \sqrt{I_{23}} \end{cases} \tag{26}$$

Here C_j, $j = 1, 2, 3$ are real amplitudes within the standard representation $a_j = C_j \exp(i\theta_j)$, and t_o, I_{13}, I_{23} are defined by initial conditions. The novelty of our approach lies in that we show ([BK09b]) that this system as a whole can be generally described by *one time-dependent dynamical invariant* of the form:

$$S_0 = Z\,t - \frac{F\left(\arcsin\left(\left(\frac{R_3-v}{R_3-R_2}\right)^{1/2} \right), \left(\frac{R_3-R_2}{R_3-R_1}\right)^{1/2} \right)}{2^{1/2}(R_3-R_1)^{1/2}(I_{13}^2 - I_{13}I_{23} + I_{23}^2)^{1/4}}. \tag{27}$$

Here F is the elliptic integral of the first kind and R_1, R_2, R_3, v are explicit functions of the initial variables B_j, $j = 1, 2, 3$. The same is true for 2-triad clusters. With the reduction procedure [KL08], this means in particular that a resonant cluster consisting of, say, 20 or 100 modes, can theoretically be described by *one dynamical invariant*.

Dynamical phase. Another important fact established in our research is the effect of the dynamical phase $\varphi = \theta_1 + \theta_2 - \theta_3$ on the amplitudes a_j. It was a common belief that for an exact resonance to occur, it is necessary that φ is either zero or constant (e.g. [LHG67, Ped87]). It is evident from the Figure 16 that this is not true.

Applications

Speaking very generally, there exist two ways of using NRA for practical purposes. *Kinematical methods* can be used for computing the form of new technical facilities (laboratory water tank or an airplane wing or whatever else) such that *nonlinear resonances will not appear*. *Dynamical methods* should be used in case reconstruction of the laboratory facilities is too costly a game, for instance while studying stable energy states in Tokamak plasma. It costs hundreds of millions of dollars to construct a new Tokamak. On the other hand, adjustment of dynamical phases can *diminish the amplitudes of resonances* (in this case, these are resonantly interacting drift waves) 10 times and more for the same technical equipment as it is shown in Figure 16.

CENREC

Presently a Web portal for a virtual CEntre for Nonlinear REsonance Computations (CENREC) is being developed at RISC as an international open-source information resource in the most important and vastly developing area of modern nonlinear dynamics – nonlinear resonance analysis. CENREC will contain the following:

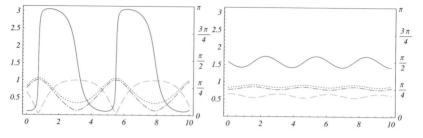

FIGURE 16   Color on-line. Plots of the modes' amplitudes and dynamical phase as
functions of time, for a triad with $Z = 1$. For each frame, the dynamical
phase $\varphi(t)$ is (red) solid, $C_1(t)$ is (purple) dotted, $C_2(t)$ is (blue) dash-
dotted, $C_3(t)$ is (green) dashed. Initial conditions for the amplitudes
are the same for all frames; initial dynamical phase is (from the left
to the right) $\varphi = 0.04$ and 0.4. Here, the horizontal axis denotes non-
dimensional time; vertical left and right axes denote amplitude and phase
correspondingly.

1. A MediaWiki-based hypertext encyclopedia with references to the electronic bibliography and to executable software;
2. An electronically indexed and searchable bibliography, with links to electronic documents (if freely available);
3. A collection of executable symbolic methods accessible via web interfaces
   (http://cenrec.risc.uni-linz.ac.at/portal/).

6.3   Highlights of the Research on the NRA

Natural Phenomena

Intraseasonal oscillations (IOs) in the earth's atmosphere with periods 30-100
days have been discovered in observed atmospheric data in 1960th. They play
an important role for modeling climate variability. All attempts to explain
their origin, including numerical simulations with 120 tunable parameters,
failed [GKLR04]. We developed a model of IOs based on the NRA; this model
explains all known characteristics of IOs and also predicts their appearance,
for suitable initial conditions. The paper on the subject has been published
in the journal Number 1 in general modern physics—*Physical Review Letters*
(*PRL*, [KL07]). The model called a lot of attention of the scientific community: it has been featured in "Nature Physics" (3(6): 368; 2007), listed in *PRL*
Highlights by "The Biological Physicist" (7(2): 5; 2007), etc.

Numerics

The NRA should be regarded as a necessary preliminary step before any numerical simulations with nonlinear evolutionary dispersive PDEs. Instead of using Galerkin-type numerical methods to compute one system of 2500 interconnected nonlinear ODEs for the example regarded in Section 6.2, we have 28 small independent systems and among them 18 are *integrable analytically* in terms of special functions (e.g. in Jacobian or Weierstrass's elliptic functions, see [BK09b]). The largest system to be solved numerically consists of only 12 equations. These theoretical findings are completely general, and do not depend on the form of the dispersion function and the chosen spectral domain, only the form and the number of small subsystems will change (e.g. [KL08, Kar94, KK07]).

Mathematics

Nonlinear resonance analysis is a natural next step after Fourier analysis developed for linear PDEs. The necessary apparatus of a new branch of mathematical physics—definitions, theorems, methods, applications—is already available. The monograph on the subject, authored by E. Kartashova, will be published soon by Cambridge University Press. What is still missing, is an appropriate set of simple basis functions, similar to Fourier harmonics $\exp[i(\mathbf{k}\mathbf{x} + \omega t)]$ for linear PDEs. The form of dynamical invariants gives a hint that the functional basis of the NRA might be constructed, for instance, from three Jacobian elliptic functions $\mathbf{sn}, \mathbf{dn}$ and $\mathbf{cn}$ or their combinations. If this task would be accomplished, the NRA will become a necessary routine part of any university education in natural sciences as is nowadays Fourier analysis.

Acknowledgements

The work described in this chapter was partially supported by the following grants of the Austrian Science Fund (FWF): SFB F1302, SFB F1304, SFB F1305, P19462-N18, P20162-N18, P20164-N18, P20347-N18.

References

[AAR00]   G.E. Andrews, R. Askey, and R. Roy. *Special Functions*. Number 71 in Ency-
           clopedia of Mathematics and its applications. Cambridge UP, 2000.
[AJLT05]   F. Almonte, V.K. Jirsa, E.W. Large, and B. Tuller. Integration and segregation
           in auditory streaming. *Physica D*, 212:137–159, 2005.
[AP94]   S.A. Abramov and M. Petkovšek. D'Alembertian solutions of linear differential
           and difference equations. In J. von zur Gathen, editor, *Proc. ISSAC'94*, pages
           169–174. ACM Press, 1994.
[Arn83]   V.I. Arnold. *Geometrical methods in the theory of ordinary differential equa-
           tions*. A Series of Comprehensive Studies in Mathematics. New York Heidel-
           berg Berlin: Springer-Verlag, 1983.
[AS64]   M. Abramowitz and I. Stegun, editors. *Handbook of Mathematical Functions*.
           United States Government Printing Office, 1964. Reprinted by Dover, 1965.
[BBK06]   I. Bierenbaum, J. Blümlein, and S. Klein. Evaluating two-loop massive op-
           erator matrix elements with Mellin-Barnes integrals. *Nucl. Phys. B (Proc.
           Suppl.)*, 160:85–90, 2006. Proceedings of the 8th DESY Workshop on Elemen-
           tary Particle Theory.
[BBK07]   I. Bierenbaum, J. Blümlein, and S. Klein. Two-loop massive operator ma-
           trix elements and unpolarized heavy flavor production at asymptotic values
           $Q^2 \gg m^2$. *Nucl. Phys. B*, 780:40–75, 2007. [arXiv:hep-ph/0703285].
[BBKS07]   I. Bierenbaum, J. Blümlein, S. Klein, and C. Schneider. Difference equa-
           tions in massive higher order calculations. In *Proc. ACAT 2007*, volume
           PoS(ACAT)082, 2007. [arXiv:hep-ph/0707.4659].
[BBKS08]   I. Bierenbaum, J. Blümlein, S. Klein, and C. Schneider. Two–loop massive
           operator matrix elements for unpolarized heavy flavor production to $o(\epsilon)$.
           Nucl.Phys. B, 803(1-2):1–41, 2008. [arXiv:hep-ph/0803.0273].
[BK99]   J. Blümlein and S. Kurth. Harmonic sums and Mellin transforms up to two-
           loop order. *Phys. Rev.*, D60, 1999.
[BK08]   Alin Bostan and Manuel Kauers. Automatic classification of restricted lattice
           walks. arXiv:0811.2899, 2008.
[BK09a]   Alin Bostan and Manuel Kauers. The full counting function for Gessel walks
           is algebraic, 2009. (in preparation).
[BK09b]   M.D. Bustamante and E. Kartashova. Dynamics of nonlinear resonances in
           Hamiltonian systems. *Europhysics Letters*, 85:14004–6, 2009.
[BK09c]   M.D. Bustamante and E. Kartashova. Effect of the dynamical phases on the
           nonlinear amplitudes' evolution. *Europhysics Letters*, 85:34002–5, 2009.
[BKKS09a] J. Blümlein, M. Kauers, S. Klein, and C. Schneider. Determining the
           closed forms of the $O(a_s^3)$ anomalous dimensions and wilson coefficients from
           Mellin moments by means of computer algebra. Technical Report DESY
           09-002, SFB/CPP-09-22, Deutsches Elektronen Syncrothron, Zeuthen, 2009.
           [arXiv:hep-ph/0902.4091].
[BKKS09b] J. Blümlein, M. Kauers, S. Klein, and C. Schneider. From moments to func-
           tions in quantum chromodynamics. In *To appear in Proc. ACAT 2008*, volume
           PoS(ACAT08)106, 2009. [arXiv:hep-ph/0902.4095].
[BM02]   Mireille Bousquet-Melou. Counting walks in the quarter plane. In *Trends
           Math.*, pages 49–67. Birkhäuser, 2002.
[BMM08]   Mireille Bousquet-Mélou and Marni Mishna. Walks with small steps in the
           quarter plane. ArXiv 0810.4387, 2008.
[Buc65]   B. Buchberger. *An Algorithm for Finding the Basis Elements in the Residue
           Class Ring Modulo a Zero Dimensional Polynomial Ideal*. PhD thesis, Univer-
           sity Innsbruck, Mathematical Institute, 1965. German, English translation in:

J. of Symbolic Computation, Special Issue on Logic, Mathematics, and Computer Science: Interactions. Volume 41, Number 3–4, Pages 475–511, 2006.

[Buc70]   B. Buchberger. An Algorithmical Criterion for the Solvability of Algebraic Systems of Equations. *Aequationes mathematicae*, 4(3):374–383, 1970. German. English translation in: B. Buchberger, F. Winkler (eds.), Groebner Bases and Applications, London Mathematical Society Lecture Note Series, Vol. 251, Cambridge University Press, 1998, pp. 535–545.

[Buc98]   B. Buchberger. Introduction to Groebner Bases. In B. Buchberger and F. Winkler, editors, *Groebner Bases and Applications*, number 251 in London Mathematical Society Lecture Notes Series, pages 3–31. Cambridge University Press, 1998.

[BW93]   T. Becker and V. Weispfenning. *Gröbner Bases: A Computational Approach to Commutative Algebra*. Springer, New York, 1993.

[BW98]   Bruno Buchberger and Franz Winkler, editors. *Gröbner Bases and Applications. Proc. of the International Conference "33 Years of Groebner Bases"*, volume 251 of *London Mathematical Society Lecture Note Series*. Cambridge University Press, 1998. 560 pages.

[CGP99]   F. Chyzak, I. Gutman, and P. Paule. Predicting the Number of Hexagonal Systems with 24 and 25 Hexagons. *MATCH*, 40:139–151, 1999.

[Che93]   M. Cheney. *Tesla Man Out Of Time*. Barnes & Noble, 1993.

[CP07]   J. Chifman and S. Petrovic. Toric Ideals of Phylogenetic Invariants for the General Group-based Model on Claw Trees K1,n. In H. Anai, K. Horimoto, and T. Kutsia, editors, *Algebraic Biology, Proc. of the Second International Conference on Algebraic Biology*, volume 4545 of *Lecture Notes in Computer Science*, pages 307–321, RISC, Hagenberg, Austria, July 2007. Springer.

[CPS⁺01]   F. Chyzak, P. Paule, O. Scherzer, A. Schoisswohl, and B. Zimmermann. The Construction of Orthonormal Wavelets using Symbolic Methods and a Matrix Analytical Approach for Wavelets on the Interval. *Experiment. Math.*, 10:67–86, 2001.

[DH81]   P.J. Davis and R. Hersh. *The Mathematical Experience*. Birkhaeuser, Boston, 1981.

[dS04]   Y. du Sautoy. *The Music of the Primes*. Fourth Estate, London, 2004.

[Due08]   G. Dueck. Mathematik und Weltläufigkeit. *Mitteilungen der DMV*, 16:206–209, 2008.

[Eys66]   Hans J. Eysenck. *Check Your Own I.Q.* Rowohlt, 1966.

[FG04]   R. Feng and X.-S. Gao. Rational General Solutions of Algebraic Ordinary Differential Equations. In J. Gutierrez, editor, *Proc. ISSAC 2004 (Internat. Symp. on Symbolic and Algebraic Computation)*, pages 155–162. ACM Press, New York, 2004.

[FG06]   R. Feng and X.-S Gao. A Polynomial Time Algorithm to Find Rational General Solutions for First Order Autonomous ODEs. *J. Symbolic Computation*, 41:735–762, 2006.

[FJ03]   J.C. Faugere and A. Joux. Algebraic Cryptoanalysis of Hidden Field Equation (HFE) Cryptosystems Using Groebner Bases. In D. Boneh, editor, *CRYPTO 2003*, volume 2729 of *Lecture Notes in Computer Science*, pages 44–60, 2003.

[GCL92]   K.O. Geddes, S.R. Czapor, and G. Labahn. *Algorithms for Computer Algebra*. Kluwer, 1992.

[GK05]   S. Gerhold and M. Kauers. A Procedure for Proving Special Function Inequalities Involving a Discrete Parameter. In *Proceedings of ISSAC'05*, pages 156–162. ACM Press, 2005.

[GKLR04]   M. Ghil, D. Kondrashov, F. Lott, and A.W. Robertson. Intraseasonal oscillations in the mid-latitudes: observations, theory, and GCM results. *Proc. ECMWF/CLIVAR Workshop on Simulations and prediction of Intra-Seasonal Variability with Emphasis on the MJO. November 3-6, 2003.*, pages 35–53, 2004.

[GKP94]   R. L. Graham, D. E. Knuth, and O. Patashnik. *Concrete Mathematics*.
           Addison-Wesley, 2nd edition edition, 1994.
[Har40]   G.H. Hardy. *A Mathematician's Apology*. Cambridge University Press, 1940.
[HKPP06]   D. Heldt, M. Kreuzer, S. Pokutta, and H. Poulisse. Algebraische Modellierung
           mit Methoden der approximativen Computeralgebra und Anwendungen in der
           Ölindustrie. *OR-News*, 28, 2006. issn 1437-2045.
[HMK03]   K. Horvat, M. Miskovic, and O. Kuljaca. Avoidance of nonlinear resonance
           jump in turbine governor positioning system using fuzzy controller. *Industrial
           Technology*, 2:881–886, 2003.
[ITBR04]   T. Ida, D. Tepeneu, B. Buchberger, and J. Robu. Proving and Constraint
           Solving in Computational Origami. In B. Buchberger and John Campbell,
           editors, *Proceedings of AISC 2004 (7 th International Conference on Artifi-
           cial Intelligence and Symbolic Computation)*, volume 3249 of *Springer Lecture
           Notes in Artificial Intelligence*, pages 132–142. Copyright: Springer-Berlin, 22-
           24 September 2004.
[Kar81]   M. Karr. Summation in finite terms. *J. ACM*, 28:305–350, 1981.
[Kar94]   Elena Kartashova. Weakly nonlinear theory in resonators. *Physical Review
           Letters*, 72:2013–2016, 1994.
[Kar98]   Elena Kartashova. Wave resonances in systems with discrete spectra. In V.E.
           Zakharov, editor, *Nonlinear Waves and Weak Turbulence*, volume 182 of *AMS
           Translations 2*, pages 95–130. American Mathematical Society, 1998.
[Kar06]   E. Kartashova. Fast Computation Algorithm for Discrete Resonances among
           Gravity Waves. *JLTP (Journal of Low Temperature Physics)*, 145(1):287–295,
           2006.
[Kau08]   Manuel Kauers. Computer Algebra for Special Function Inequalities. In
           Tewodros Amdeberhan and Victor Moll, editors, *Tapas in Experimental Math-
           ematics*, volume 457 of *Contemporary Mathematics*, pages 215–235. AMS,
           2008.
[KB05]   M. Kundu and D. Bauer. Nonlinear Resonance Absorption in the Laser-Cluster
           Interaction. *Physical Review Letters*, 96:123401, 2005.
[KK06]   E. Kartashova and A. Kartashov. Laminated wave turbulence: generic algo-
           rithms I. *IJMPC (International Journal of Modern Physics C)*, 17(11):1579–
           1596, 2006.
[KK07]   E. Kartashova and A. Kartashov. Laminated wave turbulence: generic algo-
           rithms III. *Physica A: Statistical Mechanics and Its Applications*, 380:66–74,
           2007.
[KKZ08]   Manuel Kauers, Christoph Koutschan, and Doron Zeilberger. Proof of Ira Ges-
           sel's lattice path conjecture. Technical Report 2008-08, SFB F013, Johannes
           Kepler Universität, 2008. (submitted).
[KL07]   E. Kartashova and V. L'vov. A model of intra-seasonal oscillations in the Earth
           atmosphere. *Physical Review Letters*, 98(19):198501, May 2007.
[KL08]   E. Kartashova and V. L'vov. Cluster Dynamics of Planetary Waves. *Europhys.
           Letters*, 83:50012–1–50012–6, 2008.
[KLPG04]   A.L. Karuzskii, A.N. Lykov, A.V. Perestoronin, and A.I. Golovashkin. Mi-
           crowave nonlinear resonance incorporating the helium heating effect in super-
           conducting microstrip resonators. *Physica C: Superconductivity*, 408-410:739–
           740, 2004.
[Klu06]   W. Kluzniak. Quasi periodic oscillations and the possibility of an abserva-
           tional distinction between neutron and quark stars. *Acta Physica Polonica B*,
           37:1361–1366, 2006.
[KM06]   D.A. Kovriguine and G.A. Maugin. Multiwave nonlinear couplings in elastic
           structures. *Mathematical Problems in Engineering*, 2006:76041, 2006.
[KM07]   E. Kartashova and G. Mayrhofer. Cluster formation in mesoscopic systems.
           Physica A: Statistical Mechanics and Its Applications, 385:527–542, 2007.

[KP07]   Manuel Kauers and Peter Paule. A Computer Proof of Moll's Log-Concavity Conjecture. *Proceedings of the AMS*, 135(12):3847–3856, December 2007.

[KR00]   M. Kreuzer and L. Robbiano. *Computational Commutative Algebra I*. Springer New York–Heidelberg, 2000.

[KRF+07]   E. Kartashova, C. Raab, Ch. Feurer, G. Mayrhofer, and W. Schreiner. Symbolic Computations for Nonlinear Wave Resonances. In Ch. Harif and E. Pelinovsky, editors, *"Extreme Ocean Waves"*. Springer, 2007. (submitted).

[Kuk04]   B. Kuksin. Fifteen years of KAM for PDE. In *AMS Translations 2*, volume 212, pages 237–258. American Mathematical Society, 2004.

[KZ08]   Manuel Kauers and Doron Zeilberger. The quasi-holonomic ansatz and restricted lattice walks. *Journal of Difference Equations and Applications*, 14(10):1119–1126, 2008.

[LH04]   P. Lynch and C. Houghton. Pulsation and precession of the resonant swinging spring. *Physica D*, 190:38–62, 2004.

[LHG67]   M.S. Longuet-Higgins and A.E. Gill. Resonant Interactions between Planetary Waves. *Proc. R. Soc. London, Ser. A*, 299:120–140, 1967.

[M06]   Kauers M. Sum Cracker – A Package for Manipulating Symbolic Sums and Related Objects. *J. Symbolic Computat.*, 41(9):1039–1057, 2006.

[Mal96]   Christian Mallinger. Algorithmic Manipulations and Transformations of Univariate Holonomic Functions and Sequences. Master's thesis, RISC-Linz, August 1996.

[Mis07]   Marni Mishna. Classifying lattice walks restricted to the quarter plane. In *Proceedings of FPSAC'07*, 2007.

[MS07]   S. Moch and C. Schneider. Feynman integrals and difference equations. In *Proc. ACAT 2007*, volume PoS(ACAT)083, 2007. [arXiv:hep-ph/0709.1769].

[MVV04]   S. Moch, J. A. M. Vermaseren, and A. Vogt. The three-loop splitting functions in qcd: The non-singlet case. *Nucl. Phys. B*, 688:101–134, 2004. [arXiv:hep-ph/0403192].

[Ped87]   J. Pedlosky. *Geophysical Fluid Dynamics*. New York Heidelberg Berlin: Springer-Verlag, 1987.

[Pil07]   V. Pillwein. Positivity of Certain Sums over Jacobi Kernel Polynomials. *Advances Appl. Math.*, 41:365–377, 2007.

[PP08]   P. Paule and V. Pillwein. Automatic Improvements of Wallis' Inequality. Technical Report 08–18, RISC Report Series, University of Linz, Austria, 2008.

[PR97]   P. Paule and A. Riese. A Mathematica q-analogue of Zeilberger's algorithm based on an algebraically motivated aproach to q-hypergeometric telescoping. In M. Ismail and M. Rahman, editors, *Special Functions, q-Series and Related Topics*, volume 14, pages 179–210. Fields Institute Toronto, AMS, 1997.

[PS95]   P. Paule and M. Schorn. A Mathematica version of Zeilberger's Algorithm for Proving Binomial Coefficient Identities. *J. Symbolic Comput.*, 20(5-6):673–698, 1995.

[PS03]   P. Paule and C. Schneider. Computer proofs of a new family of harmonic number identities. *Adv. in Appl. Math.*, 31(2):359–378, 2003.

[PV00]   D. Poulakis and E. Voskos. On the Practical Solutions of Genus Zero Diopantine Equations. *J. Symbolic Computation*, 30:573–582, 2000.

[PV02]   D. Poulakis and E. Voskos. Solving Genus Zero Diopantine Equations with at Most Two Infinity Valuations. *J. Symbolic Computation*, 33:479–491, 2002.

[PWZ96]   M. Petkovšek, H. S. Wilf, and D. Zeilberger. $A = B$. A. K. Peters, Wellesley, MA, 1996.

[RBE03]   M. Rosenkranz, B. Buchberger, and H. W. Engl. Solving Linear Boundary Value Problems Via Non-commutative Groebner Bases. *Applicable Analysis*, 82(7):655–675, July 2003.

[Sch04]   C. Schneider. The summation package Sigma: Underlying principles and a rhombus tiling application. *Discrete Math. Theor. Comput. Sci.*, 6(2):365–386, 2004.

[Sch05]   C. Schneider. Solving parameterized linear difference equations in terms of indefinite nested sums and products. *J. Differ. Equations Appl.*, 11(9):799–821, 2005.

[Sch07]   C. Schneider. Symbolic summation assists combinatorics. *Sém. Lothar. Combin.*, 56:1–36, 2007. Article B56b.

[Sch08]   C. Schneider. A refined difference field theory for symbolic summation. *J. Symbolic Comput.*, 43(9):611–644, 2008. [arXiv:0808.2543v1].

[Sch09]   C. Schneider. A symbolic summation approach to find optimal nested sum representations. In *Proceedings of the Conference on Motives, Quantum Field Theory, and Pseudodifferential Operators*, To appear in the Mathematics Clay Proceedings, 2009.

[Slo73]   N.J.A. Sloane. *A Handbook of Integer Sequences*. Academic Press, 1973.

[Slo94]   N.J.A. Sloane. *The New Book of Integer Sequences*. Springer, 1994.

[SWPD08]   J.R. Sendra, F. Winkler, and S. Pérez-Díaz. *Rational Algebraic Curves — A Computer Algebra Approach*, volume 22 of *Algorithms and Computation in Mathematics*. Springer-Verlag Heidelberg, 2008.

[SZ94]   B. Salvy and P. Zimmermann. Gfun: A Package for the Manipulation of Generating and Holonomic Functions in One Variable. *ACM Trans. Math. Software*, 20:163–177, 1994.

[Ver99]   J.A.M. Vermaseren. Harmonic sums, Mellin transforms and integrals. *Int. J. Mod. Phys. A*, 14:2037–2076, 1999.

[VGJ02]   Markus Voege, Anthony J. Guttmann, and Iwan Jensen. On the Number of Benzenoid Hydrocarbons. *Journal of Chemical Information and Computer Sciences*, 42(3):456–466, 2002.

[VMM05]   C. Vedruccio, E. Mascia, and V. Martines. Ultra High Frequency and Microwave Non-linear Interaction Device for Cancer Detection and Tissue Characterization, a Military Research approach to prevent Health Diseases. *International Review of the Armed Forces Medical Services (IRAFMS)*, 78:120–132, 2005.

[VMV04]   A. Vogt, S. Moch, and J. A. M. Vermaseren. The three-loop splitting functions in qcd: The singlet case. *Nucl. Phys. B*, 691:129–181, 2004. [arXiv:hep-ph/0404111].

[VVM05]   J. A. M. Vermaseren, A. Vogt, and S. Moch. The third-order qcd corrections to deep-inelastic scattering by photon exchange. *Nucl. Phys. B*, 724:3–182, 2005. [arXiv:hep-ph/0504242].

[vzGG99]   J. von zur Gathen and J. Gerhard. *Modern Computer Algebra*. Cambridge University Press, 1999.

[Weg97]   K. Wegschaider. Computer generated proofs of binomial multi-sum identities. Diploma thesis, RISC Linz, Johannes Kepler University, 1997.

[Whi90]   E.T. Whittaker. *A Course in Modern Analysis*. Cambridge University Press, 1990.

[Zei90a]   D. Zeilberger. A Fast Algorithm for Proving Terminating Hypergeometric Identities. *Discrete Math.*, 80:207–211, 1990.

[Zei90b]   D. Zeilberger. A Holonomic Systems Approach to Special Function Identitites. *J. Comput. Appl. Math.*, 32:321–368, 1990.

[ZLF92]   V.E. Zakharov, V.S. L'vov, and G. Falkovich. *Kolmogorov Spectra of Turbulence*. Springer, 1992.

Chapter II
Automated Reasoning

Tudor Jebelean

Bruno Buchberger, Temur Kutsia, Nikolaj Popov, Wolfgang Schreiner,
Wolfgang Windsteiger

Introduction 1

Observing is the process of obtaining new knowledge, expressed in language, by bringing the senses in contact with reality. Reasoning, in contrast, is the process of obtaining new knowledge from given knowledge, by applying certain general transformation rules that depend only on the *form* of the knowledge and can be done exclusively in the brain without involving the senses. Observation and reasoning, together, form the basis of the scientific method for explaining reality. Automated reasoning is the science of establishing methods that allow to replace human step-wise reasoning by procedures that perform individual reasoning steps mechanically and are able to find, automatically, suitable sequences of reasoning steps for deriving new knowledge from given one.

The importance of automatic reasoning originates in the fact that basically everything relevant to current science and technology can be expressed in the language of logic on which current automated reasoners work, for example the description of systems (specification or implementation of hardware and software), information provided on the internet, or any other kind of facts or data produced by the sciences. As the complexity of the knowledge produced by the observing sciences increases, the methods of automatic reasoning become more and more important, even indispensable, for mastering and developing our working and living environment by science and technology. In the same way as, over the millennia, humans developed tools for enhancing and amplifying their physical power and later developed tools (e.g. devices in physics) for enhancing the observing power, it is now the natural follow-up to develop tools for enhancing and amplifying the human reasoning power.

Mathematical Logic as Basis for Automated Reasoning

As Mathematics can be seen as the science of operating in abstract models of the reality (*thinking*), Mathematical Logic can be seen as the science of operating in abstract models of mathematical thinking (*thinking about thinking*). Since abstract models are expressed using statements, and operating in abstract models is done by transforming and combining these statements, Mathematical Logic studies their *syntax* (how do we construct statements), their *semantics* (what is the meaning of statements) and their *pragmatics* (rules that describe how statements can be transformed in a way that respects semantics). In the era of electronic computing, the importance of automated reasoning increases tremendously, because computers are devices for automatic operation in abstract models (*thinking tools*). Thus, Mathematical Logic becomes also the theoretical basis for studying the design and the behavior of computing devices and programs and, hence, Automated Reasoning is *automated thinking about thinking tools*.

Automated Mathematical Theorem Proving

Since logical formulae have been traditionally used for expressing mathematics, there is a widespread opinion that automated reasoning can be used only for proving mathematical statements, which is sometimes perceived as either redundant (in case of already proven theorems) or hopeless (in case of not yet proven conjectures). First let us emphasize that automated mathematical theorem proving is only a part of automated reasoning—however crucial because it develops techniques which are useful in all other areas of science and technology. Moreover automatic theorem proving is neither redundant (because proving "known" or "trivial" theorems is absolutely necessary in the process of [semi]-automatic verification of complex systems—hardware, software, or combined hardware/software), nor hopeless (because, on the other hand, the proofs of highly nontrivial theorems as the *Four Color Theorem* [AH77] and the *Robbins Conjecture* [McC97] were only possible by the use of automatic theorem proving tools).

Verification and Synthesis

Contemporary technological systems consist of increasingly complex combinations of hardware, software, and human agents, whose tasks are very sophisticated. How do we *express* these sophisticated tasks, how do we *design* and how do we *describe* these technological systems, and how do we *ensure* that the systems always fulfill their tasks? Those who believe that (at least in some organization with a long technological tradition) *these four questions* have been properly answered may take a look at some famous software failures http://en.wikipedia.org/wiki/List_of_notable_software_bugs.

The consequences of design defects in complex technological systems have become a part of our everyday life: computer viruses, unauthorized access to sensitive data (e. g. bank accounts and credit cards), and periodic failures of the programs on our computers and on our mobile phones. The future brings: automotive software for handling the controls and the airbags in our automobiles, generalized internet banking, and the inclusion of computers in most of the objects around us.

Today it is largely accepted that the answer to the above four questions is: both the description of the complex systems (*implementations*), as well as their sophisticated tasks (*specifications*) can be expressed as logical formulae, the design of complex systems can be decomposed in successive and controllable steps of transformation of such logical formulae, and the verification of their correct behavior can be performed by checkable inferences on these formulae.

Semantic Representation of the Information on the Internet

The extraordinary proliferation of the data which is accessible on the internet offers of course an unprecedented richness of information at our fingertips, however the limitations of the current *syntactic* approach are more and more visible. It is often very difficult for the user to select the relevant information among the "noise" of irrelevant one, and it is also impossible to find out pieces of knowledge which require a minimal amount of intelligent processing. These problems can be solved only by a *semantic* approach: the information has to be stored in form of logical statements (probably of very simple structure, but high quantity), and the search engines have to include Automatic Reasoning capabilities.

This chapter summarizes the work performed in the Softwarepark Hagenberg in the field of Automated Reasoning, in particular the work performed at RISC and in the *Theorema* group. Research from other groups in Hagenberg are also tangent with Automated Reasoning, and they are mentioned in the respective chapters.

Theorema: Computer-Supported 2
Mathematical Theory Exploration

At RISC, much of the research on automated reasoning focuses on the *Theorema* Project, which aims at developing algorithmic methods and software tools for supporting the intellectual process of *mathematical theory exploration*. The emphasis of the *Theorema* Project is not so much on the automated proof of yet unknown or difficult theorems but much more on organizing the overall flow of the many small reasoning steps necessary in building up mathematical theories or writing proof-checked mathematical textbooks and lecture notes or developing verified software. The net effect of an exploration, however, may also be that complicated theorems and nontrivial algorithms can be proven correct with only very little user-interaction necessary at some crucial stages in the exploration process, while the individual intermediate reasoning steps are completely automatic. An example of a non-trivial automated algorithm synthesis (the synthesis of a Gröbner bases algorithm) by the *Theorema* methodology is given later in this chapter. The main contribution of the working mathematician who uses *Theorema* will then be the organization of a well structured exploration process that leads from the initial knowledge base to the full-fledged theory.

This design principle of *Theorema* is in contrast to the main stream in automated mathematical theorem proving, which to a great extent has focused on proving individual theorems from given knowledge bases (containing the axioms of the theory, definitions, lemmata etc.). Considering the mathematical theory exploration process (invention of *notions*, invention and proof/refutation of *propositions*, invention of *problems*, invention and verification of *algorithms/methods* for solving problems) and the computer-supported documentation of this process as a coherent process seems to be more natural and useful for the success of automated theorem proving for the every-day practice of working mathematicians than considering the proof of isolated theorems. This point of view has been made explicit, first, in [Buc99] and, later, in [Buc03, Buc06].

The *Theorema* Group has strived to contribute, in various ways, to the computer-support of the mathematical theory exploration process by building

- tools for the automated generation of proofs in various general theories (e.g. elementary analysis, geometry, inductive domains including natural number theory and tuple theory, and set theory),
- and tools for the organization of the theory exploration process and build-up of mathematical knowledge bases (various viewers for proofs including the "focus window" approach, proof presentation including natural language explanation, logico-graphic symbols, user-defined two-dimensional syntax, functors for domain building etc.).

The research goals and the basic design principles of the *Theorema* project were formulated in a couple of early papers, see [Buc96b, Buc96a, Buc96c, Buc97]. Summaries of the achievements in the *Theorema* Project are [BJK+97, BDJ+00, BCJ+06]. A complete list of the publications of the *Theorema* Group can be accessed on-line at www.theorema.org.

The *Theorema* Language and the User Interface   2.1

The typical user interface of *Theorema* is the Mathematica notebook frontend, which allows the combination of mathematical formulae and natural language text (and much more) in a natural way. Figure 1 shows a screenshot of a typical *Theorema* notebook that exhibits the main components of the *Theorema* language. An important design principle of the *Theorema* sys-

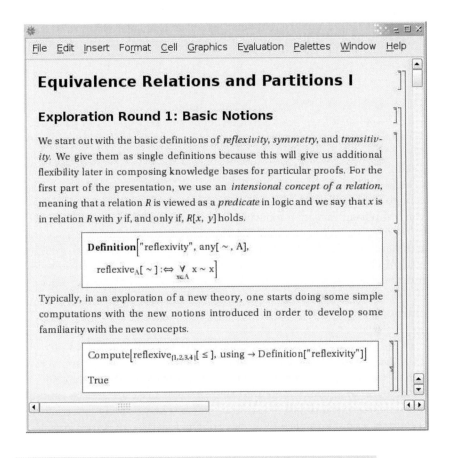

Theorema input in a Mathematica notebook.   FIGURE 1

tem is to come as close to conventional mathematics in the appearance of mathematics in as many aspects as possible, be it in the language in which mathematics is expressed, be it in the way how proofs are presented, and many more.

The *Theorema* language is structured in essentially three layers,

- the *Theorema* formula language,
- the *Theorema* formal text language, and
- the *Theorema* command language.

These three layers correspond to three aspects of mathematical language, namely the logical part of *formulating statements* in a concise and correct way, the organizational part of *structuring knowledge* into definitions, theorems, lemmata, etc., or entire theories, and the description of various *mathematical activities* like proving or computing.

The *Theorema* formula language is a version of higher order predicate logic without extensionality. On this basis, the language offers sets, tuples, and certain types of numbers as basic language components. As an example,

$$\underset{x \in A}{\forall} \; x \sim x \tag{1}$$

is a statement in the *Theorema* formula language. As can be seen in Figure 1, *Theorema* allows standard mathematical notation even in input so that formulae can be written like in conventional mathematical texts. Twodimensional input including also special symbols (like integrals or quantifiers) is standard technology in Mathematica. In order to facilitate *Theorema* input, we provide specialized palettes that paste skeletons for frequently used *Theorema* expressions into a notebook by just one mouse-click.

For composing and manipulating large formal mathematical texts, however, we need to be able to combine the expression language with auxiliary text (labels, key words like "Definition", "Theorem", etc.) and to compose, in a hierarchical way, large mathematical knowledge bases from individual expressions. In the example, in order to define reflexivity by (1) we would use a definition environment.

Definition["reflexivity", any[$A, \sim$],

   reflexive$_A$[$\sim$] : $\Longleftrightarrow$ $\underset{x \in A}{\forall} \; x \sim x$ "$\sim \circlearrowleft$"]

The field "any[*vars*]" declares *vars* as (the free) variables. Each variable v in *vars* can carry a type restriction of the form "$v \in S$" or "type[v]". An optional field "with[*cond*]" tells that the variables must satisfy the condition *cond*. Logically, the variable declaration and the condition are just a shortcut for prefixing every formula in the environment with a universal quantifier. Other examples of formal text are:

Definition["class", any[$x, A, \sim$], with[$x \in A$],

   class$_{A,\sim}$[x] := $\{a \in A \mid a \sim x\}$]

Lemma["non-empty class", any[$x \in A, A, \sim$], with[reflexive$_A$[$\sim$]],

   class$_{A,\sim}$[x] $\neq \emptyset$]

The effect of entering an environment into the system is that its content can be referred to later by *Keyword*[*env_label*]. Knowledge can be grouped using *nested environments*, whose structure is identical except that instead of clauses (formulae with optional labels) there are references to previously defined environments. Typical keywords used for nested environments are "Theory" and "KnowledgeBase", e.g.

Theory["relations",

  Definition["reflexivity"]
  Definition["class"]]

The mathematical activities that are supported in the command language are computing, proving, and solving. Computations are performed based on a semantics of the language expressed in the form of computational rules for the finitary fragment of the formula language, i.e. finite sets, tuples, numbers, and all sorts of quantifiers as long as they involve a finite range for their variable(s). In the example,

Compute[$class_{\{1,2,3,4\},\leq}[3]$, using→Definition["class"],

  built-in→ {Built-in["Sets"], Built-in["Numbers"]}]

would compute the class of 3 in $\{1, 2, 3, 4\}$ w.r.t. $\leq$ using the definition of class (see above) and built-in semantics of (finite) sets and numbers resulting in $\{1, 2, 3\}$ and

Compute[$reflexive_{\{1,2,3,4\}}[\leq]$, using→Definition["reflexivity"],

  built-in→ {Built-in["Quantifiers"], Built-in["Numbers"]}]

would decide by a finite computation, whether the relation $\leq$ is reflexive on $\{1, 2, 3, 4\}$ using the definition of reflexivity and the built-in semantics of quantifiers and numbers resulting in "true". Consider the lemma about non-empty classes stated above, which is a statement about relations on arbitrary not necessarily finite sets. Thus, its validity cannot be verified by computation but must be proven. In order to prove a statement in *Theorema*, we use

Prove[Lemma["non-empty class"], using→Theory["relations"],

  by→SetTheoryPCSProver],

which will try to prove Lemma["non-empty class"] using Theory["relations"] as the knowledge base by SetTheoryPCSProver, a prove method for set theory described in more detail in Section 3.2. In case of success, the complete proof is presented in human readable nicely structured format in a separate window, otherwise the failing proof attempt is displayed. Moreover, *Theorema* features a novel approach for displaying proofs based on focus windows [PB02], a proof simplification tool, and an interactive proof tool [PK05].

2.2 "Lazy Thinking": Invention by Formulae Schemes and Failing Proof Analysis

A main point in the *Theorema* approach to mathematical theory exploration is that mathematical invention should be supported both "bottom-up", by using formulae schemes, and "top-down", by analyzing failing proofs and constructing guesses for necessary intermediate lemmata. This combined approach is called "lazy thinking" and was introduced in [Buc03].

The difficulty of finding proofs for propositions depends, to a large extent, on the available knowledge. Most mathematical inventions, even simple ones like the proof of, say, the lemma that the limit of the sum of two sequences is equal to the sum of the limits, would hardly be possible (even for quite intelligent humans) if mathematical theories were not built up in small steps. In each step, only one new concept is introduced (by an axiom or definition) and all possible simple knowledge is proved first before the proof of any more important theorem is attacked. With sufficiently much intermediate knowledge, it often turns out that the proof of the essential theorems then only needs one single or very few "difficult" ideas that cannot be generated completely automatically.

It is rewarding to scrutinize on what typically happens in a step in which propositions for new notions are conjectured: In fact, in most cases, the type of knowledge conjectured has "rewrite" character: For example, if the notion of multiplication on natural numbers has been introduced, then all possible interactions of this new notion with previous notions like 'zero', 'addition', 'less' etc. that can be formulated as "rewrite properties" should be studied first. For example, distributivity is such a property in rewrite form:

$$(x + y) * z = x * z + y * z.$$

It is an important observation that, when sufficiently many rewrite properties have been proven by using the "fundamental" (sometimes difficult) proof methods in the theory, subsequent proofs of most other possible properties then can be done by simple "rewrite proving" ("symbolic computation proving", "physicists proving", "quantifier free proving", "highschool proving"), i.e. by applying the proven rewrite properties repeatedly just using substitution and replacement. (In the theory of natural numbers, the "fundamental" proving method is induction; in elementary analysis, the "fundamental" proving method is general predicate logic for "alternating" quantifiers '∀ ∃'; etc.). A good theory exploration environment, should support this important observation. In the *Theorema* Project, this observation is a guiding strategy.

How can (rewrite and other) knowledge about notions (introduced by definitions) be "invented", i.e. systematically generated? In the "lazy thinking" approach introduced in [Buc03], two complementary strategies are proposed:

1. The use of "formulae schemes", a bottom-up approach.
2. The use of "analysis of failing proofs", a top-down approach.

A synopsis of the lazy thinking approach to the automation of mathematical theory exploration and some more details can also be found, for example, in [Buc06].

The lazy thinking strategy can be applied both to the invention and verification of theorems and the invention and verification of algorithms ("algorithm synthesis"). Here, we illustrate the method by two examples of algorithm synthesis. There is a rich literature on algorithm synthesis methods, see the survey [BDF+04]. Our method, in the classification given in this survey, is in the class of "scheme-based" methods but is essentially different from previously known such methods by its emphasis on the heuristic usefulness of *failing* correctness proofs.

The algorithm synthesis problem is the following problem: Given a problem specification P (i.e. a binary predicate $P[x, y]$ that specifies the relation between the input values x and the output values y of the problem), find an algorithm A such that

$$\underset{x}{\forall} \ P[x, A[x]].$$

The lazy thinking approach to algorithm synthesis consists of the following steps:

- Consider known fundamental ideas ("*algorithm schemes*") of how to structure algorithms A in terms of sub-algorithms B, C, ... Try one scheme A after the other.
- For the chosen scheme A, try to prove $\underset{x}{\forall} \ P[x, A[x]]$. This proof will probably fail because, at this stage, nothing is known about the sub-algorithms B, C, ... From the *failing proof, construct specifications* Q, R, ... for the sub-algorithms B, C, ... that make the proof work.
- Then A together with any sample of algorithms B, C, ... that satisfy the specifications Q, R, ... will be a correct algorithm for the original problem P.
- If such sub-algorithms B, C, ... are available in the given knowledge base, then we are done, i.e. an algorithm for problem P has been synthesized. If no such algorithms are available, we can apply the lazy thinking method, recursively, for synthesizing algorithms B, C, ... that satisfy Q, R, ... until we arrive at specifications that are met by available algorithms in the knowledge base.

For the (automated) construction of specifications from failing correctness proofs we introduced the following simple (but amazingly powerful) rule: In the failing correctness proof, collect the temporary assumptions

$$T[x_0, \ldots, A[\ldots], \ldots]$$

(where $x_0, \ldots$ are the constants resulting from the "arbitrary but fixed" proof rule) and the temporary goals

$$G[x_0, \ldots, B[\ldots, A[\ldots], \ldots]]$$

and produce the specification for sub-algorithm B:

$$\mathop{\forall}\limits_{X,Y,\ldots} T[X,\ldots,Y,\ldots] \implies G[Y,\ldots,B[\ldots,Y,\ldots]].$$

We illustrate the method in a simple example: We synthesize, completely automatically, an algorithm for the sorting problem, which is the problem to find an algorithm A such that

$$\mathop{\forall}\limits_{X} \text{is-sorted-version}[X, A[X]].$$

We assume that the binary predicate 'is-sorted-version' is defined by a set of formulae in predicate logic. In the first step of the lazy thinking approach, we choose one of the many algorithm schemes in our library of algorithm schemes, for example, the 'Divide-and-Conquer' scheme, which can be defined, within predicate logic, by

$$\mathop{\forall}\limits_{A,S,M,L,R} \text{Divide-and-Conquer}[A, S, M, L, R] \iff$$

$$\mathop{\forall}\limits_{x} A[x] = \begin{cases} S[x] & \Leftarrow \text{is-trivial-tuple}[x] \\ M[A[L[x]], A[R[x]]] & \Leftarrow \text{otherwise} \end{cases}$$

This is a scheme that explains how the unknown algorithm A should be defined in terms of unknown subalgorithms S, M, L, R. With this knowledge we try to prove that

$$\mathop{\forall}\limits_{X} \text{is-sorted-version}[X, A[X]]$$

using one of our automated provers (for induction over tuples). This proof will fail because, at this moment, nothing is known about the subalgorithms S, M, L, R. Analyzing the failing proof for the pending goals and available temporary knowledge at the time of failure we now use the above rule for generating, automatically, specifications for S, M, L, R that will make the proof work. In this example, in approx. 2 minutes on a laptop, the following specifications are generated automatically:

$$\mathop{\forall}\limits_{x} \text{is-trivial-tuple}[x] \implies S[x] = x,$$

$$\mathop{\forall}\limits_{y,z} \begin{matrix} \text{is-sorted}[y] \\ \text{is-sorted}[z] \end{matrix} \implies \begin{matrix} \text{is-sorted}[M[y,z]] \\ M[y,z] \approx (y \times z) \end{matrix},$$

$$\mathop{\forall}\limits_{x} L[x] \times R[x] \approx x.$$

(Here, '$\times$', and '$\approx$' denote "concatenation" and "equivalence" of tuples.) A closer look to the formulae reveals the amazing fact that these specifications on S, M, L, R are not only sufficient for guaranteeing the correctness of A

but are also completely natural and intuitive: They tell us that a suitable algorithm S must essentially be the identity function, suitable algorithms L and R must essentially be "pairing functions" (which split a given tuple X in two parts that, together, preserve the entire information in X) and that M must be a merging algorithm.

Automated Synthesis of Gröbner Bases Theory

Our expectation was that, with lazy thinking, one may be able to synthesize only quite simple algorithms. It came as a surprise, see [Buc04], that, in fact, algorithms for quite non-trivial problems can be synthesized by this method. The most interesting example so far is the problem of Gröbner bases construction with the specification: Find an algorithm Gb, such that

$$\underset{\text{is-finite}[F]}{\forall} \quad \begin{array}{l} \text{is-finite}[\text{Gb}[F]] \\ \text{is-Gröbner-basis}[\text{Gb}[F]] \; . \\ \text{ideal}[F] = \text{ideal}[\text{Gb}[F]] \end{array}$$

(The quantifier ranges over sets F of multivariate polynomials. 'ideal$[F]$' is the set of all linear combinations of polynomials from F.) In Chapter I on symbolic computation it is explained why this problem is non-trivial and why it is important and interesting. In fact, the problem was open for over 60 years before it was solved in [Buc65]. Thus, it may be philosophically and practically interesting that now it can be solved automatically, i.e. the key idea of algorithmic Gröbner bases theory, namely the notion of S-polynomials, and the algorithm based on this key idea can be generated automatically from the specification of the problem by the lazy thinking method.

Namely, we start with the following algorithm scheme, called *"Pair Completion"*, that tells us that the unknown algorithm Gb should be defined in terms of two unknown subalgorithms lc and df in the following way:

$$\underset{\text{Gb,lc,df}}{\forall} \text{Pair-Completion}[\text{Gb}, \text{lc}, \text{df}] \Longleftrightarrow$$

$\underset{F}{\forall} \text{Gb}[F] = \text{Gb}[F, \text{pairs}[F]]$

$\underset{F}{\forall} \text{Gb}[F, \langle\rangle] = F$

$\underset{F,g_1,g_2,\bar{p}}{\forall} \text{Gb}[F, \langle\langle g_1, g_2 \rangle, \bar{p} \rangle] =$

where$[f = \text{lc}[g_1, g_2], h_1 = \text{trd}[\text{rd}[f, g_1], F], h_2 = \text{trd}[\text{rd}[f, g_2], F],$

$$\begin{cases} \text{Gb}\,[F, \langle \bar{p} \rangle] & \Leftarrow h_1 = h_2 \\ \text{Gb}[F \frown \text{df}[h_1, h_2], \langle \bar{p} \rangle \asymp \langle\langle F_k, \text{df}[h_1, h_2] \rangle \underset{k=1,\ldots,|F|}{|} \quad \rangle] & \Leftarrow \text{otherwise} \end{cases}]$$

(Here, our notation for tuples is '$\langle \ldots \rangle$' and '$\frown$' is the append function. The function 'rd' is the one-step reduction function and the function 'trd' is total reduction, i.e. the iteration of 'rd' until an irreducible element is reached.) Now we attempt to prove, automatically, that the above specification holds for the algorithm Gb that is defined in this way from unknown algorithms lc and df. An automatic prover that is powerful enough for this type of proof was implemented in [Cra08]. The proof fails because, at this stage, nothing is known about lc and df. Using the above specification generation rule, one can generate, completely automatically, the following specification for lc.

$$\underset{p,g_1,g_2}{\forall} \begin{array}{c} \mathrm{lp}[g_1]|p \\ \mathrm{lp}[g_2]|p \end{array} \implies \begin{array}{c} \mathrm{lc}[g_1,g_2]|p, \\ \mathrm{lp}[g_1]|\mathrm{lc}[g_1,g_2], \\ \mathrm{lp}[g_2]|\mathrm{lc}[g_1,g_2], \end{array}$$

which shows that a suitable subalgorithm lc is essentially the least common multiple of the leading power products of the polynomials g_1 and g_2. Similarly one automatically obtains that df must essentially be the difference of polynomials. These two ideas are the main ingredients of the notion of S-polynomials, which is in fact the main idea of algorithmic Gröbner bases theory (see Chapter I on symbolic computation). This idea, together with its correctness proof, comes out here completely automatically. This is currently one of the strongest results of the *Theorema* project which creates quite some promises for the future of semi-automated mathematical theory exploration.

3 Natural Style Proving in *Theorema*

The *Theorema* system contains several provers, which differ both in their methods and in the domains which are treated. However, all *Theorema* provers work in *natural style*, that is: the proofs are presented in natural language, and the proof structure and the logical inferences are similar to the ones used by humans. Moreover, in the context of the *Theorema* system one may use provers which have implicit knowledge about the used domain (e.g. number domains), like for instance the PCS prover. This makes certain proofs more compact and readable, in contrast to proving in pure predicate logic with explicit assumptions for such theories.

In this section we summarize shortly the provers of the *Theorema* system, and then we focus on two particular provers: the S-decomposition prover and the set theory prover. All provers are presented in more detail in our survey papers [BJK$^+$97, BDJ$^+$00, BCJ$^+$06] and in the publications available on our home page www.theorema.org.

The provers available in *Theorema* include: a general predicate logic prover, various induction provers containing a simple rewrite prover as a component, a special prover for proving properties of domains generated by functors, the PCS prover for analysis (and similar theories that involve concepts defined by using alternating quantifiers) [Buc01], a set theory prover (using the PCS approach as a subpart), a special prover for geometric theorems using the Gröbner bases method [Rob02], a special prover for combinatorics using the Zeilberger–Paule approach, the cascade mechanism for inventing lemmata on the way to proving theorems by induction, an equational prover based on Knuth-Bendix completion [Kut03], and a basic reasoner [WBR06].

S-Decomposition and the Use of Algebraic Techniques   3.1

Numerous interesting mathematical notions are defined by formulae that contain a sequence of "alternating quantifiers", i.e., the definitions have the structure $p[x,y] \Leftrightarrow \underset{a}{\forall}\, \underset{b}{\exists}\, \underset{c}{\forall}\, \dots q[x,y,a,b,c]$. Many notions introduced, for example, in elementary analysis text books (limit, continuity, function growth order, etc.) fall into this class. Therefore, it is highly desirable that mathematical assistant systems support the exploration of theories about such notions.

The S-decomposition method is particularly suitable both for proving theorems (when the auxiliary knowledge is rich enough) as well as conjecturing propositions (similar to Lazy Thinking) during the exploration of theories about notions with alternating quantifiers. It can be seen as a further refinement of the Prove-Compute-Solve method implemented in the *Theorema* PCS prover [Buc01]. Essentially, the S-decomposition method is a certain strategy for decomposing the proof into simpler subproofs, based on the structure of the main definition involved. The method proceeds recursively on a group of assumptions together with the quantified goal, until the quantifiers are eliminated, and produces some auxiliary lemmata as subgoals.

We present the method using an example from elementary analysis: limit of a sum of sequences; see [Jeb01] for a detailed description of the method. The definition of "f converges to a" is:

$$(\rightarrow) \quad f \rightarrow a \Leftrightarrow \underset{\epsilon}{\forall}\left(\epsilon > 0 \Rightarrow \underset{m}{\exists}\, \underset{n}{\forall}\, (n \geq m \Rightarrow |f[n] - a| < \epsilon)\right).$$

(For brevity, the type information is not included.)

The proof tree is presented in Figure 2 and Figure 3. Boxes represent proof situations (with the goal on top), unboxed formulae represent auxiliary subgoals, and boxes with double sidebars represent substitutions for the metavariables. The nodes of the proof tree are labeled in the order they are produced.

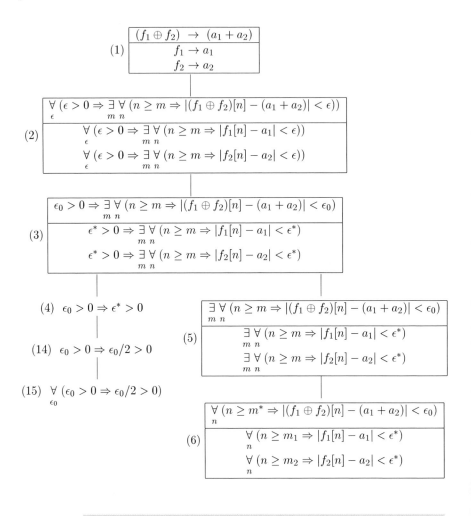

FIGURE 2   S-Decomposition: First part of the proof tree.

The first inference expands the definition of "limit", generating the proof situation (2). *S-decomposition is designed for proof situations in which the goal and the main assumptions have exactly the same structure.* In the example they differ only in the instantiations of f and a. *S-decomposition proceeds by modifying these formulae together, such that the similarity of the structure is preserved, until all the quantifiers and logical connectives are eliminated.* The method is specified as a collection of four transformation rules (infer-

$$(6) \quad \boxed{\begin{array}{c} \forall_{n} \left(n \geq m^* \Rightarrow |(f_1 \oplus f_2)[n] - (a_1 + a_2)| < \epsilon_0\right) \\ \hline \forall_{n} \left(n \geq m_1 \Rightarrow |f_1[n] - a_1| < \epsilon^*\right) \\ \forall_{n} \left(n \geq m_2 \Rightarrow |f_2[n] - a_2| < \epsilon^*\right) \end{array}}$$

$$(7) \quad \boxed{\begin{array}{c} n_0 \geq m^* \Rightarrow |(f_1 \oplus f_2)[n_0] - (a_1 + a_2)| < \epsilon_0 \\ n^* \geq m_1 \Rightarrow |f_1[n^*] - a_1| < \epsilon^* \\ n^* \geq m_2 \Rightarrow |f_2[n^*] - a_2| < \epsilon^* \end{array}}$$

$$(8) \quad n_0 \geq m^* \Rightarrow \\ n^* \geq m_1 \wedge n^* \geq m_2$$

$$(9) \quad \boxed{\begin{array}{c} |(f_1 \oplus f_2)[n_0] - (a_1 + a_2)| < \epsilon_0 \\ |f_1[n^*] - a_1| < \epsilon^* \\ |f_2[n^*] - a_2| < \epsilon^* \end{array}}$$

$$(11) \quad \boxed{\boxed{\begin{array}{c} m^* \leftarrow \max[m_1, m_2] \\ n^* \leftarrow n_0 \end{array}}}$$

$$(10) \quad (|f_1[n^*] - a_1| < \epsilon^* \wedge \\ |f_2[n^*] - a_2| < \epsilon^*) \Rightarrow \\ |(f_1[n_0] + f_2[n_0]) - (a_1 + a_2)| < \epsilon_0$$

$$(12) \quad (|f_1[n_0] - a_1| < \epsilon^* \wedge \\ |f_2[n_0] - a_2| < \epsilon^*) \Rightarrow \\ |((f_1[n_0] + f_2[n_0]) - (a_1 + a_2)| < \epsilon_0$$

$$(13) \quad \boxed{\boxed{\epsilon^* \leftarrow \epsilon_0/2}}$$

S-Decomposition: Second part of the proof tree.   Figure 3

ences) for proof situations and a rule for composing auxiliary lemmata. The transformation rules are described below together with their concrete application to this particular proof.

The inference that transforms (2) to (3) eliminates the universal quantifier and has the general formulation below. (Here, for simplicity, we formulate the inferences for two assumptions only, but extending them to use an arbitrary number of assumptions is straightforward.)

$$\underset{x}{\forall} P_1[x], \underset{x}{\forall} P_2[x] \ \vdash \ \underset{x}{\forall} P_0[x] \ \longmapsto \ P_1[x_1^*], P_2[x_2^*] \vdash P_0[x_0] \qquad (\forall)$$

Like the existential rule, specified later in this section, this rule combines the well-known techniques for introducing Skolem constants and metavariables. However, S-decomposition comes with a *strategy* of applying them in a certain order. The Skolem constant x_0 is introduced before the metavariables (names for yet unknown terms) x_1^*, x_2^*. In the example we use a simplified version of this rule in which the metavariables do not differ. For other examples (e.g. quotient of sequences) this will not work.

The inference from (3) to (4) and (5) eliminates the implication, and has the general formulation:

$$Q_1 \Rightarrow P_1, \ Q_2 \Rightarrow P_2 \ \vdash \ Q_0 \Rightarrow P_0 \ \longmapsto \ \begin{cases} Q_0 \Rightarrow Q_1 \wedge Q_2 \\ P_1, P_2 \vdash P_0 \end{cases} \qquad (\Rightarrow)$$

In contrast to the previous rule, this one is not an equivalence transformation (the proof of the right-hand side might fail even if the left-hand side is provable). This rule is applied in the situations when Q_k's are the "conditions" associated with a universal quantifier (as in the example). The formula $Q_0 \Rightarrow Q_1 \wedge Q_2$ is a candidate for an auxiliary lemma, as is formula (4).

The proof proceeds further with the transformation (5)–(6) (formula (14) will be produced later in the proof) given by the following rule:

$$\underset{x}{\exists} P_1[x], \underset{x}{\exists} P_2[x] \ \vdash \ \underset{x}{\exists} P_0[x] \ \longmapsto \ P_1[x_1], P_2[x_2] \vdash P_0[x^*] \qquad (\exists)$$

where x_1 and x_2 are Skolem constants introduced before the metavariable x^*.

Usually, existential quantifiers are associated with conditions upon the quantified variables. In such a case one would obtain conjunctions (analogous to the situation in formula (3), where one obtains implications). The rule for decomposing conjunctions is:

$$Q_1 \wedge P_1, \ Q_2 \wedge P_2 \ \vdash \ Q_0 \wedge P_0 \ \longmapsto \ \begin{cases} Q_1 \wedge Q_2 \Rightarrow Q_0 \\ P_1, P_2 \vdash P_0 \end{cases} \qquad (\wedge)$$

Similarly to the rule ($\Rightarrow$), this rule produces an auxiliary lemma as a "side effect", using the Q_k's which are, typically, the conditions associated with an existential quantifier. In fact, in the implementation of the method, the rules ($\exists$), ($\wedge$) are applied in one step, as are also the rules ($\forall$), ($\Rightarrow$).

However, in this example there is no condition associated to the existential quantifier, therefore this rule is not used.

The proof proceeds by applying rule ($\forall$) to (6), and then the rule ($\Rightarrow$) to (7). Note that the transformation rules proceed from the assumptions towards the goal for existential formulae, and the other way around for universal formulae. If one would illustrate this process by drawing a line on the formulae in proof situation (2), one obtains an S-shaped curve—thus the name of the method.

Finally, S-decomposition transforms a proof situation having no quantifiers into an implication, thus (9) is transformed into (10), and this finishes the application of S-decomposition to this example. In this moment the original proof situation is decomposed into the formulae (4), (8), and (10). (Obtaining (10) needs an additional inference step, not shown in the figure, which consists in expanding the subterm $(f_1 \oplus f_2)[n_0]$ by the definition of $\oplus$.)

The continuation of the proof is outside the scope of the S-decomposition method. For completing the proof, one needs to find appropriate substitutions for the metavariables, such that the Skolem constants used in each binding are introduced earlier than the corresponding metavariable. For the sake of completeness, we give here a possible follow up (produced automatically by *Theorema*): We assume that the formulae

$$(21) \quad \underset{k,i,j}{\forall} \ (k \geq \max[i,j] \Rightarrow k \geq i \wedge k \geq j),$$

$$(22) \quad \underset{x,y,a,b,\epsilon}{\forall} \ \left(|x - a| < \frac{\epsilon}{2} \wedge |y - b| < \frac{\epsilon}{2} \Rightarrow |(x + y) - (a + b)| < \epsilon \right)$$

are present in the available knowledge as auxiliary assumptions. The prover first tries to "solve" (8), and by matching against (21) obtains the substitution (11). This substitution is applied to (10) producing (12), and by matching the latter against (22), the prover obtains the substitution (13). The substitutions are then applied to the formula (4), which is then generalized (by universal quantification of the Skolem constants) into (15). The latter is presented to the user as suggestions for auxiliary lemmata needed for completing the proof. Of course this subgoal would be also solved if the appropriate assumption was available, however the situation described above demonstrates that the method is also useful for generating conjectures.

The reader may notice that the process of guessing the right order in which the subgoals (4), (8), and (10) should be solved is nondeterministic and may involve some backtracking. This search is implemented in *Theorema* using the principles described in [KJ00].

Moreover, this method can be used in conjunction with algebraic techniques, in particular with Cylindrical Algebraic Decomposition [Col75]. Namely, the substitutions for the metavariables shown at steps (11) and (13) can be also obtained by using CAD–based quantifier elimination. First the proof situations (11) and (12) are transformed into quantified formulae: the metavariables become existential variables, the Skolem constants become universal variables, and the order of the quantifiers is the order in which the respective metavariables and Skolem constants have been introduced during S-decomposition. Then, by successive applications of quantifier elimination, one obtains automatically the witness terms for the existential variables. The method and its application to several examples are described in detail in [VJB08].

3.2 The *Theorema* Set Theory Prover

Many areas of mathematics are typically formulated on the basis of set theory, in the sense that objects or properties are expressed in terms of language constructs from set theory. Most prominently, set formations like

$$\{x \in A \mid P_x\} \quad \text{or} \quad \{T_x \mid x \in A\} \tag{2}$$

occur routinely in virtually all of mathematics. The *Theorema* language described in Section 2.1 supports all commonly used constructs from set theory, such as set formation as shown in (2), membership, union, intersection, power set, and many more. The semantics of the language built into the system immediately allows computations on *finite sets* including also the computation of truth values for statements containing finite sets. Reasoning on *arbitrary sets*, however, amounts to the application of more powerful techniques. This was the starting point for the development of a *set theory prover*, see [Win06] and [Win01], based on the general principles of "PCS" (Proving–Computing–Solving) reasoners introduced in [Buc01] in the frame of the *Theorema* system.

Integration of Proving and Computing

One of the design goals of this prover was the smooth integration of proving, i.e. general reasoning based on inference rules, and computing on numbers, finite sets, tuples and the like. In order to accomplish this task, the set theory prover contains a component that allows to apply computational rules defined in the semantics of the *Theorema* language to formulae occurring in a proof. By this mechanism, the user can even choose, which parts of the language semantics to include in a particular proof.

We demonstrate this in a simple example from a fully mechanized proof of the irrationality of $\sqrt{2}$ taken from a comparison of automated theorem provers carried out by Freek Wiedijk in 2006, see [WBR06]. During the formalization of this proof, one arrives at a formula

$$2m_0^2 = (2m_1)^2, \tag{3}$$

which of course simplifies by simple computation on natural numbers to

$$m_0^2 = 2m_1^2. \tag{4}$$

Compared to other systems, where either

- additional theorems are required to perform the step from (3) to (4)—and consequently separate theorems for all situations similar to this—or
- the simplification from (3) to (4) is carried out by a lengthy sequence of transformation steps based on the axioms for natural numbers,

the step simplifying (3) into (4) is only *one elementary step* based on the semantics of the natural numbers built-into the *Theorema* system. The proofs generated in this way are very elegant and close to how a human would give the proofs—one of the main credos in the design of the *Theorema* system.

The Theoretical Foundations of the Prover

One of the first questions when it comes to set theory is always: "How are the well-known contradictions appearing in naive set theory, e.g. Russell's paradox, avoided?" The *Theorema* set theory prover relies on the Zermelo-Frankel axiomatization of set theory (ZF), meaning that the prover can deal with all sorts of sets whose existence is guaranteed by the Zermelo-Frankel axioms for set theory. This means, in particular, that the *Theorema* language does not forbid "sets" like $\{x \mid x \notin x\} =: R$ nor does it forbid statements like $R \in R$. Rather, the set theory prover refuses to apply any inference step on $R \in R$ on the grounds that R is not formed by any of the set construction principles proven to be consistent in ZF—note that ZF requires $\{x \in S \mid P_x\}$ for some known set S when abstracting a set from a property P_x.

In addition to inference rules based directly on some ZF-axiom, e.g. the inference rule for membership in a set $\{x \in S \mid P_x\}$, the prover also incorporates knowledge *derivable* in ZF. If the prover was intended to be used to prove theorems of set theory based on the ZF axiomatization, it would be cheating if the prover has such knowledge already built in, hence, there is a mechanism to switch off these special rules in case a user wants to use the prover for this purpose. The main field of application for the prover is, however, to prove arbitrary statements whose formalization *uses* language constructs from set theory. An example of such a proof is shown in detail in Figure 4. This is an example of the TPTP library (SET722) of examples for automated theorem provers, and it says that if the composition of functions $g \circ f$ is surjective then also g must be surjective. Note that the knowledge base for this proof only contains the definition of composition, we need not give the definition of surjectivity, because this is built into the prover as a standard concept in set theory. Of course, the proof would also succeed with one's own definition of surjectivity in the knowledge base. The important difference lies in the concise proof produced by this prover because several elementary logical steps are combined into one step when the built-in rule is applied. Note also, that the proof generated by the *Theorema* system comes out exactly as it is displayed in Figure 4 including all intermediate proof explanation text.

(SET722) $\displaystyle\mathop{\forall}_{A,B,C,f,g}$ $f :: A \to B \wedge g \circ f :: A \stackrel{surj.}{\to} C \Rightarrow g :: B \stackrel{surj.}{\to} C$,

under the assumption:

(Definition (Composition)) $\displaystyle\mathop{\forall}_{f,g,x}$ $(g \circ f)[x] := g[f[x]]$.

We assume

(1) $f_0 :: A_0 \to B_0 \wedge g_0 \circ f_0 :: A_0 \stackrel{surj.}{\to} C_0$,

and show

(2) $g_0 :: B_0 \stackrel{surj.}{\to} C_0$.

In order to show surjectivity of g_0 in (2) we assume

(3) $x1_0 \in C_0$,

and show

(4) $\displaystyle\mathop{\exists}_{B1}\ B1 \in B_0 \wedge g_0[B1] = x1_0$.

From (1.1) we can infer

(6) $\displaystyle\mathop{\forall}_{A1}\ A1 \in A_0 \Rightarrow f_0[A1] \in B_0$.

From (1.2) we know by definition of "surjectivity"

(7) $\displaystyle\mathop{\forall}_{A2}\ A2 \in A_0 \Rightarrow (g_0 \circ f_0)[A2] \in C_0$,

(8) $\displaystyle\mathop{\forall}_{x2}\ x2 \in C_0 \Rightarrow \mathop{\exists}_{A2}\ A2 \in A_0 \wedge (g_0 \circ f_0)[A2] = x2$.

By (8), we can take an appropriate Skolem function such that

(9) $\displaystyle\mathop{\forall}_{x2}\ x2 \in C_0 \Rightarrow A2_0[x2] \in A_0 \wedge (g_0 \circ f_0)[A2_0[x2]] = x2$.

Formula (3), by (9), implies:

$A2_0[x1_0] \in A_0 \wedge (g_0 \circ f_0)[A2_0[x1_0]] = x1_0$,

which, by (6), implies:

$f_0[A2_0[x1_0]] \in B_0 \wedge (g_0 \circ f_0)[A2_0[x1_0]] = x1_0$,

which, by (Definition (Composition)), implies:

(10) $f_0[A2_0[x1_0]] \in B_0 \wedge g_0[f_0[A2_0[x1_0]]] = x1_0$.

Formula (4) is proven because, with $B1 := f_0[A2_0[x1_0]]$, (10) is an instance.

FIGURE 4   A proof generated completely automatically by *Theorema*.

Unification 4

Unification is a fundamental symbolic computation process. Its goal is to identify two given symbolic expressions by means of finding suitable instantiations for certain subexpressions (variables). When the term "identify" is interpreted as syntactic identity, one talks about syntactic unification. If "identify" means equality modulo some given equalities, then is it called equational unification. Hence, unification can be seen as solving equations in abstract algebras, which is used almost everywhere in mathematics and computer science.

Research on unification at RISC has been motivated by its applications in automated reasoning, software engineering, and semistructured data processing. The main subject of study was unification in theories with flexible arity functions and sequence variables, called sequence unification. Such theories are a subject of growing interest as they have been recognized to be useful in various areas, such as XML data modeling with unranked ordered trees and hedges, programming, program transformation, automated reasoning, artificial intelligence, knowledge representation, etc. It is not a surprise that these applications, in some form, require solving equations over terms with flexible arity functions and sequence variables. Hence, sequence unification (and its special forms) play a fundamental role there. Intensive research undertaken at RISC on this subject produced important results that shed light on theoretical and algorithmic aspects of sequence unification, including proving its decidability, developing a solving procedure, identifying important special cases and designing efficient algorithms for them, and finding relations with other unification problems. Some of these results are briefly reviewed below.

General Sequence Unification 4.1

Sequence unification deals with solving systems of equations (unification problems) built over flexible arity function symbols and individual and sequence variables. An instance of such an equation is $f(\overline{x}, x, \overline{y}) = f(f(\overline{x}), x, a, b)$, where f, a, b are function symbols, $\overline{x}, \overline{y}$ are sequence variables, and x is an individual variable. It can be solved by a substitution $\{\overline{x} \mapsto (\,), x \mapsto f, \overline{y} \mapsto (f, a, b)\}$ that maps $\overline{x}$ to the empty sequence, x to the term f (that is a shorthand for $f()$), and $\overline{y}$ to the sequence (f, a, b). Solving systems of such equations can be quite a difficult task: It is not straightforward at all to decide whether a given system has a solution or not. Moreover, some equations may have infinitely many solutions, like, e.g. $f(a, \overline{x}) = f(\overline{x}, a)$ whose solutions are the substitutions $\{\overline{x} \mapsto (\,)\}, \{\overline{x} \mapsto a\}, \{\overline{x} \mapsto (a, a)\}, \ldots$.

When solving unification problems, one is usually interested only in most general solutions from which any solution can be generated. Unification procedures try to compute a (preferably minimal) complete set of such most general unifiers. In the sequence unification case, since for some problems this set can be infinite, any complete unification procedure can only give an enumeration of the set. It can not be used as a decision procedure, in general. Hence, to completely solve sequence unification problems, one needs

1. an algorithm to decide whether a given system of equations is solvable and
2. the procedure that enumerates a minimal complete set of unifiers for solvable systems.

In [Kut07], both of these problems have been addressed. Decidability of sequence unification has been proved by reducing the problem to a combination of word equations and Robinson unification, both with linear constant restrictions. Each of these theories is decidable and the Baader-Schulz combination method [BS96] ensures decidability of the combined theory. Since the reduction from sequence unification to this combined theory is solubility-preserving, the reduction together with the combination method and the decision algorithms for the ingredient theories gives a decision algorithm for sequence unification.

Furthermore, a sequence unification procedure is formulated as a set of rules together with a strategy of their application. If a unification problem is solvable, the procedure nondeterministically selects an equation from the problem and transforms it by all the rules that are applicable. The process iterates for each newly obtained unification problem until a solution is computed or a failure is detected. Since each selected equation can be transformed in finitely many ways, the search tree is finitely branching. However, the tree can still be infinite because some unification problems have infinitely many solutions and the procedure goes on to enumerate them. As it is shown in [Kut07], the procedure generates a minimal and complete set of sequence unifiers and terminates if this set is finite.

As the decision algorithm is quite expensive, it is interesting to identify fragments of sequence unification problems for which the unification procedure terminates without applying the decision algorithm. Several such fragments exist: the linear fragment, where each variable occurs at most once; the linear shallow fragment, which is linear only in sequence variables but restricts them to occur only on level 1 in terms; the fragment where there is no restriction in the number of variable occurrences but sequence variables are allowed to be only the last argument in (sub)terms they occur; sequence matching, where one of the sides of equations is ground (variable-free); the quadratic fragment, where each variable can occur at most twice.

These fragments differ on their unification types that is defined by maximal possible cardinality of minimal complete sets of unifiers of unification problems. Unification problems where sequence variables occur only in the last argument position are of type unitary, which means that if such a problem is solvable, it has a single most general unifier. It makes this fragment attractive for automated reasoning and, in fact, the Equational Prover of Theorema [Kut03] can deal with it. The quadratic fragment is infinitary (like the general sequence unification itself), which means that there are some solvable problems with an infinite minimal complete set of unifiers. The equation $f(a, \overline{x}) = f(\overline{x}, a)$ above is an example of such a quadratic problem. However, a nice thing is that, for quadratic problems, one can represent these infinite sets by finite means, in particular, as regular expressions over substitutions. The quadratic fragment has found an application in collaborative schema development in the joint work of T. Kutsia (RISC), M. Florido and J. Coelho (both from Portugal) [CFK07]. All the other mentioned fragments are finitary: For them, solvable unification problems may have at most finitely many most general unifiers.

These fragments have interesting properties and applications. Two of them have already been mentioned above. Among others, the sequence matching capabilities of the Mathematica system [Wol03] should be noted, which makes the programming language of Mathematica very flexible.

It should be noted that all the results on sequence unification in [Kut07], in fact, have been formulated in a more general setting: besides function symbols and individual and sequence variables, the problems may contain so called sequence functions. A sequence function abbreviates a finite sequence of functions all having the same argument lists. Semantically, they can be interpreted as multi-valued functions. Bringing sequence functions into the language allows Skolemization over sequence variables. For instance, $\forall \overline{x} \exists \overline{y} \ p(\overline{x}, \overline{y})$) after Skolemization introduces a sequence function symbol $\overline{g}$: $\forall \overline{x} \ p(\overline{x}, \overline{g}(\overline{x}))$. From the unification point of view, a sequence function can be split between sequence variables. The corresponding rules are part of the unification procedure described in [Kut07].

Flat Matching   4.2

Sequence matching problems, as already mentioned, are those that have a ground side in the equations. An instance of such an equation is $f(x, \overline{y}) = f(a, b, c)$ which has a single solution (matcher) $\{x \mapsto a, \overline{y} \mapsto (b, c)\}$. But what happens if f satisfies the equality $f(\overline{x}, f(\overline{y}), \overline{z}) = f(\overline{x}, \overline{y}, \overline{z})$, i.e. if one can flatten out all nested occurrences of f? It turns out that in such a case the minimal complete set of matchers becomes infinite. The substitutions like $\{x \mapsto f(), \overline{y} \mapsto (f(), a, b, c)\}$, $\{x \mapsto f(), \overline{y} \mapsto (a, f(), b, c)\}$, $\{x \mapsto f(), \overline{y} \mapsto (f(), a, f(), b, c)\}$ and similar others become solutions modulo flatness of f. It is quite unusual for matching problems to have an infinite minimal complete set of solutions. It triggered our interest to matching in flat theories, to study theoretical properties of flat matching, to design a complete procedure to solve flat matching problems, and to investigate terminating restrictions.

But this was only one side of the problem. On the other side, a flat theory is not a theory that is "cooked artificially" to demonstrate that matching problems can be arbitrarily complex. It has a practical application: Flat symbols appear in the programming language of the Mathematica system, by assigning to certain symbols the attribute `Flat`. This property affects both evaluation and pattern matching in Mathematica. Obviously, a practically useful method that solves flat matching equations should be terminating and, therefore, incomplete (unless it provides a finite description of the infinite complete set of flat matchers). Understanding proper semantics of programming constructs is very important to program correctly. Hence, the questions arise: What is the semantics of Mathematica's incomplete flat matching algorithm? What are the rules behind it, how it works? How is the algorithm related to theoretically complete, infinitary flat matching? These questions have not been formally answered before.

[Kut08] addresses both theoretical and practical sides of the problem. From the theoretical side, it gives a procedure to solve a system of flat matching equations and proves its soundness, completeness, and minimality. The minimal complete set of matchers for such a system can be infinite. The procedure enumerates this set and stops if it is finite. Besides, a class of problems on which the procedure stops is described. From the practical point of view, it gives a set of rules to simulate behavior of the flat matching algorithm implemented in the Mathematica system.

Differences between various flat matching procedures can be demonstrated on simple examples. For instance, given a problem $\{f(\overline{x}) = f(a)\}$ where f is flat, the minimal complete flat matching procedure enumerates its infinite minimal complete set of matchers $\{\overline{x} \mapsto a\}, \{\overline{x} \mapsto f(a)\}, \{\overline{x} \mapsto (f(), a)\}, \{\overline{x} \mapsto (a, f())\}, \{\overline{x} \mapsto (f(), f(), a)\}, \ldots$. Restricting the rules in the procedure so that $f()$ is not generated in such cases, one obtains a terminating incomplete algorithm that returns two matchers $\{\overline{x} \mapsto a\}, \{\overline{x} \mapsto f(a)\}$. In order to simulate Mathematica's flat matching, further restrictions should be imposed on the rules to obtain the only matcher $\{\overline{x} \mapsto a\}$. It should be noted that Mathematica's behavior depends whether one has a sequence variable or an individual variable under the flat function symbol. Also, Mathematica treats in a special way function variables (those that can be instantiated with function symbols). [Kut08] analyzes all those cases and gives a formal description of the corresponding rules.

Context Sequence Matching   4.3

Flat matching (and, in general, matching modulo equations with sequence variables) is one generalization of syntactic sequence matching. Another generalization comes from bringing higher-order variables in the terms. T. Kutsia (RISC) in collaboration with M. Marin (Japan) studied extension of sequence matching with function and context variables [KM05, Kut06]. Function variables have already been mentioned above. Context variables are second-order variables that can be instantiated with a context—a term with a single occurrence of a distinguished constant $\bullet$ (called the hole) in it. A context can be applied to a term by replacing the hole with that term. An example of context sequence matching equation is $\overline{X}(f(\overline{x})) = g(f(a, b), h(f(a), f))$, where $\overline{X}$ is a context variable and $\overline{x}$ is a sequence variable. Its minimal complete set of matchers consists of three elements: $\{\overline{X} \mapsto g(\bullet, h(f(a), f)), \; \overline{x} \mapsto (a, b)\}$, $\{\overline{X} \mapsto g(f(a, b), h(\bullet, f)), \; \overline{x} \mapsto a\}$, and $\{\overline{X} \mapsto g(f(a, b), h(f(a), \bullet)), \; \overline{x} \mapsto ()\}$.

Context sequence matching is a flexible mechanism to extract subterms from a given ground term via traversing it both in breadth and in depth. Function variables allow to descend in depth in one step, while with context variables subterms can be searched in arbitrary depth. Dually, individual variables and sequence variables allow moves in breadth: individual variables in one step and sequence variable in arbitrary number of steps. This duality makes context sequence matching an attractive technique for expressing subterm retrieval queries in a compact and transparent way.

Context and sequence variables occurring in matching problems can be constrained by membership atoms. Possible instantiations of context variables are constrained to belong to a regular tree language, whereas the ones for sequence variables should be elements of regular hedge languages. This extension is the main computational mechanism for the experimental rule-based programming package ρLog [MK06].

Relations between Context and Sequence Unification   4.4

Context unification [Com91, SS94] aims at solving equations for terms built over fixed arity function symbols and first-order and context variables. It is one of the most difficult problems in unification theory: Its decidability is an open problem already for more than 15 years. There have been various decidable fragments (obtained by restricting the form of the input equations) and variants (obtained by restricting the form of possible solutions) identified; see, e.g. [Com98, Lev96, SSS02, LNV05] and for more comprehensive overview, [Vil04]. Both sequence unification and context unification generalize the well-known word unification problem [Mak77]. One of them is decidable, while decidability of the other one is an open problem. Hence, a natural question arises: How are these two generalizations of the same problem related with each other?

T. Kutsia (RISC), J. Levy and M. Villaret (both from Spain) gave a complete answer to this problem in [KLV07]. First, they defined a mapping (called curryfication) from sequence unification to a fragment of context unification such that if the original sequence unification problem is solvable, then the curried context unification problem is also solvable. However, this transformation does not preserve solubility in the other direction. To deal with this problem, possible solutions of curried context unification problems have been restricted to have a certain shape, called left-hole context, which can be characterized by the property of having holes in the leftmost leaf in their tree representation, like, for instance, in the context $@(@(\bullet, a), b)$. (In curried problems $@$ is the only binary function symbol and all the other function symbols are constants, but it is not a restriction for solubility, at it was shown in [LV02].) This restriction guarantees solubility preservation between sequence unification and the corresponding fragment of context unification. Next, the left-hole restriction has been extended from the fragment to the whole problem, obtaining a variant, called left-hole context unification (LHCU). To prove solubility of LHCU, another transformation has been defined that transforms LHCU into word equations with regular constraints. The transformation is solubility-preserving and word unification with regular constraints is decidable, which implies decidability of LHCU. Finally, transforming LHCU with inverse curryfication, a decidable extension of sequence unification has been obtained. This transformation also made it possible to transfer some of the known complexity results for context matching to extended sequence matching.

Hence, this work can be summarized as follows: A new decidable variant of context unification has been discovered; A decidable extension of sequence unification has been found and a complete unification procedure has been developed; A new proof of decidability of sequence unification has been given; Complexity results for (some fragments of) extended sequence matching have been formulated.

5 Program Verification

The activities related to program verification in the *Theorema* group refer to various programming styles and to various verification techniques. The *Theorema* system allows to describe algorithms directly in predicate logic, which is sometimes called "pattern based programming". Using some abbreviating constructs (as e. g. `if-then-else`), in *Theorema* one can also use the functional programming style. In both cases the verification benefits from the fact that the properties of the programs are expressed in the same logical language, thus a possibly error prone translation is not necessary. Furthermore, in order to experiment with alternative techniques, *Theorema* provides additionally a simple language for imperative programming.

In this section we focus on the verification of functional programs, however the research on verification of imperative programs is also strongly pursued by our group. For instance, the work on *loop invariants* lead to a complex method which uses algebraic and combinatorial techniques for the automatic generation of polynomial invariants of `while` loops [KPJ05, Kov07]. A very novel and interesting aspect of this method is the nontrivial interplay between logical techniques on one hand, and algebraic techniques on the other hand, which demonstrates the high value of the approach of combining automated reasoning with computer algebra into the field of symbolic computation. Moreover, the recent research on *symbolic execution* [EJ08] introduces a novel approach to the generation of verification conditions exclusively in the theory of the domain of the objects handled by the program—including the termination condition.

Some Principles of Program Verification   5.1

Before a more detailed presentation of our research, we summarize shortly some main principles of program verification. Note that we focus here on the techniques which are based on automated theorem proving, and not, for instance, on model checking techniques.

Program specification (or formal specification of a program) is the definition of what a program is expected to do. Normally, it does not describe, and it should not, how the program is implemented. The specification is usually provided by logical formulae describing a relationship between input and output parameters. We consider specifications which are pairs, containing a precondition (input condition) and a postcondition (output condition).

Formal verification consists in proving mathematically the correctness of a program with respect to a certain formal specification. Software testing, in contrast to verification, cannot prove that a system does not contain any defects or that it has a certain property.

The problem of verifying programs is usually split into two subproblems: *generate* verification conditions which are sufficient for the program to be correct and *prove* the verification conditions, within the theory of the domain for which the program is defined. A survey of the techniques based on this principle, but also of other techniques can be found e. g. in [LS87] and in [Hoa03].

A Verification Condition Generator (VCG) is a device—normally implemented by a program—which takes a program, actually its source code, and the specification, and produces verification conditions. These verification conditions do not contain any part of the program text, and are expressed in a different language, namely they are logical formulae.

Normally, these conditions are given to an automatic or semi-automatic theorem prover. If all of them hold, then the program is correct with respect to its specification. The latter statement we call *Soundness* of the VCG, namely:

Given a program F and a specification I_F (input condition), and O_F (output condition), if the verification conditions generated by the VCG hold, then the program F is correct with respect to the specification $\langle I_F, O_F \rangle$.

Completing the notion of *Soundness* of a VCG, we introduce its dual— *Completeness* [KPJ06]:

Given a program F and a specification I_F (input condition), and O_F (output condition), if the program F is correct with respect to the specification $\langle I_F, O_F \rangle$, then the verification conditions generated by the VCG hold.

The notion of *Completeness* of a VCG is important for the following two reasons: theoretically, it is the dual of *Soundness* and practically, it helps debugging. Any counterexample for the failing verification condition would carry over to a counterexample for the program and the specification, and thus give a hint on "what is wrong". Indeed, most of the literature on program verification presents methods for verifying correct programs. However, in practical situations, it is the failure which occurs more often until the program and the specification are completely debugged.

A distinction is to be made between total correctness, which additionally requires that the program terminates, and partial correctness, which simply requires that if an answer is returned (that is, the program terminates) it will be correct. Termination is in general more difficult. On one hand, it is theoretically proven that termination is not decidable in general (however this does not mean that we cannot prove termination of specific programs). On the other hand, the statement "program P terminates" is difficult or impossible to express in the theory of the domain of the program, but has to be introduced additionally. Adding a suitable theory of computation will increase significantly the formalization and the proving effort. Our approach to this problem is to decompose the total correctness into many simpler formulae (the verification conditions), and to reduce termination of the original program to the termination of a simplified version of it, as shown in the sequel.

5.2   Verification of Functional Programs

In the *Theorema* system we see functional programs as abbreviations of logical formulae (for instance, an `if-then-else` clause is an abbreviation of two implications). Therefore, the programming language is practically identical to the logical language which is used for the verification conditions. This has the advantage that we do not need to translate the predicate symbols and the function symbols occurring in the program: they are already present in the logical language.

Our work consists in developing the theoretical basis and in implementing an experimental prototype environment for defining and verifying recursive functional programs. In contrast to classical books on program verification [Hoa69], [BL81], [LS87] which expose methods for verifying correct programs, we also emphasize the detection of incorrect programs. The user may easily interact with the system in order to correct the program definition or the specification.

We first perform a check whether the program under consideration is *coherent* with respect to the specification of its components, that is, each function is applied to arguments satisfying its input condition. (This principle is also known as *programming by contract.*)

The program correctness is then transformed into a set of first-order predicate logic formulae by a Verification Condition Generator (VCG)—a device, which takes the program (its source code) and the specification (precondition and postcondition) and produces several verification conditions, which themselves, do not refer to any theoretical model for program semantics or program execution, but only to the theory of the domain used in the program.

For coherent programs we are able to define a necessary and sufficient set of verification conditions, thus our condition generator is not only *sound*, but also *complete*. This distinctive feature of our method is very useful in practice for program debugging.

Since coherence is enforced, verification can be performed independently on different programs, thus one avoids the costly process of *interprocedural analysis*, which is sometimes used in model checking. Moreover, the correctness of the whole system is preserved even when the implementation of a function is changed, as long as it still satisfies the specification.

In order to illustrate our approach, we consider powering function P, using the *binary powering* algorithm:

$$P[x, n] = \textbf{If } n = 0 \textbf{ then } 1$$
$$\textbf{elseif } \text{Even}[n] \textbf{ then } P[x * x, n/2]$$
$$\textbf{else } x * P[x * x, (n - 1)/2].$$

This program is in the context of the theory of real numbers, and in the following formulae, all variables are implicitly assumed to be real. Additional type information (e. g. $n \in \mathbb{N}$) may be explicitly included in some formulae.

The specification is:

$$(\forall x, n : n \in \mathbb{N}) \; P[x, n] = x^n. \tag{5}$$

The (automatically generated) conditions for *coherence* are:

$$(\forall x, n : n \in \mathbb{N}) \ (n = 0 \ \Rightarrow \mathbb{T}) \tag{6}$$

$$(\forall x, n : n \in \mathbb{N}) \ (n \neq 0 \wedge \text{Even}[n] \ \Rightarrow \text{Even}[n]) \tag{7}$$

$$(\forall x, n : n \in \mathbb{N}) \ (n \neq 0 \wedge \neg\text{Even}[n] \ \Rightarrow \text{Odd}[n]) \tag{8}$$

$$(\forall x, n, m : n \in \mathbb{N})(n \neq 0 \wedge \text{Even}[n] \wedge m = (x * x)^{n/2} \Rightarrow \mathbb{T}) \tag{9}$$

$$(\forall x, n, m : n \in \mathbb{N})(n \neq 0 \wedge \neg\text{Even}[n] \wedge m = (x * x)^{(n-1)/2} \Rightarrow \mathbb{T}) \tag{10}$$

$$(\forall x, n : n \in \mathbb{N}) \ (n \neq 0 \wedge \text{Even}[n] \ \Rightarrow n/2 \in \mathbb{N}) \tag{11}$$

$$(\forall x, n : n \in \mathbb{N}) \ (n \neq 0 \wedge \neg\text{Even}[n] \ \Rightarrow (n-1)/2 \in \mathbb{N}) \tag{12}$$

One sees that the formulae (6), (9) and (10) are trivially valid, because we have the logical constant $\mathbb{T}$ at the right side of an implication. The origin of these $\mathbb{T}$ come from the preconditions of the 1 *constant-function-one* and the $*$ *multiplication*.

The formulae (7), (8), (11) and (12) are easy consequences of the elementary theory of reals and naturals. For the further check of *correctness* the generated conditions are:

$$(\forall x, n : n \in \mathbb{N}) \ (n = 0 \ \Rightarrow 1 = x^n) \tag{13}$$

$$(\forall x, n, m : n \in \mathbb{N})(n \neq 0 \wedge \text{Even}[n] \wedge m = (x * x)^{n/2} \Rightarrow m = x^n) \tag{14}$$

$$(\forall x, n, m : n \in \mathbb{N})(n \neq 0 \wedge \neg\text{Even}[n] \wedge m = (x*x)^{(n-1)/2} \Rightarrow x*m = x^n) \tag{15}$$

$$(\forall x, n : n \in \mathbb{N}) \ P'[x, n] = \mathbb{T}, \tag{16}$$

where

$$P'[x, n] = \ \textbf{If } n = 0 \textbf{ then } \mathbb{T}$$
$$\textbf{elseif } \text{Even}[n] \textbf{ then } P'[x * x, n/2]$$
$$\textbf{else } P'[x * x, (n-1)/2].$$

The proofs of these verification conditions are straightforward.

Now comes the question: What if the program is not correctly written? Thus, we introduce now a bug. The program P is now almost the same as the previous one, but in the base case (when $n = 0$) the return value is 0.

$$P[x, n] = \ \textbf{If } n = 0 \textbf{ then } 0$$
$$\textbf{elseif } \text{Even}[n] \textbf{ then } P[x * x, n/2]$$
$$\textbf{else } x * P[x * x, (n-1)/2].$$

Now, for this buggy version of P we may see that all the respective verification conditions remain the same except one, namely, (13) is now:

$$(\forall x, n : n \in \mathbb{N}) \ (n = 0 \ \Rightarrow 0 = x^n) \tag{17}$$

which itself reduces to:
$$0 = 1$$

(because we consider a theory where $0^0 = 1$).

Therefore, according to the *completeness* of the method, we conclude that the program P does not satisfy its specification. Moreover, the failed proof gives a hint for "debugging": we need to change the return value in the case $n = 0$ to 1.

Furthermore, in order to demonstrate how a bug might be located, we construct one more "buggy" example where in the "Even" branch of the program we have $P[x, n/2]$ instead of $P[x * x, n/2]$:

$$
\begin{aligned}
P[x, n] = \ & \textbf{If } n = 0 \textbf{ then } 1 \\
& \textbf{elseif } \text{Even}[n] \textbf{ then } P[x, n/2] \\
& \textbf{else } x * P[x * x, (n - 1)/2].
\end{aligned}
$$

Now, we may see again that all the respective verification conditions remain the same as in the original one, except one, namely, (14) is now:

$$(\forall x, n, m : n \in \mathbb{N})(n \neq 0 \land \text{Even}[n] \land m = (x)^{n/2} \ \Rightarrow m = x^n) \tag{18}$$

which itself reduces to:

$$m = x^{n/2} \ \Rightarrow m = x^n$$

From here, we see that the "Even" branch of the program is problematic and one should satisfy the implication. The most natural candidate would be:

$$m = (x^2)^{n/2} \ \Rightarrow m = x^n$$

which finally leads to the correct version of P.

Computer-Assisted Interactive 6
Program Reasoning

As demonstrated in the other sections of this chapter, much progress has been made in automated reasoning and its application to the verification of computer programs and systems. In practice however, for programs of a certain complexity, fully automatic verifications are not feasible; much more success is achieved by the use of *interactive proving assistants* which allow the user to guide the software towards a semi-automatic construction of a proof by iteratively applying predefined proof decomposition strategies in alternation with critical steps that rely on the user's own creativity. The goal is to reach proof situations that can be automatically closed by *SMT (satisfiability modulo theories) solvers* [SMT06] which decide the truth of unquantified formulas over certain combinations of ground theories (uninterpreted function symbols, linear integer arithmetic, and others). In a modern computer science education, it is important to train students in the use of such systems which can help in formal specifying programs and reasoning about their properties.

The RISC ProofNavigator

While a variety of tools for supporting reasoning are around, many of them are difficult to learn and/or inconvenient to use, which makes them less suitable for classroom scenarios [Fei05]. This was also Schreiner's experience when he evaluated from 2004 to 2005 a couple of prominent proving assistants by a number of use cases derived from the area of program verification. While he achieved quite good results with PVS [ORS92], he generally encountered various problems and nuisances, especially with the navigation within proofs, the presentation of proof states, the treatment of arithmetic, and the general interaction of the user with the systems; he frequently found that the elaboration of proofs was more difficult than should be necessary.

Based on these investigations, Schreiner developed the *RISC ProofNavigator* [RIS06, Sch08b], a proving assistant which is intended for educational scenarios but has been also applied to verifications that are already difficult to handle with other assistants. The software currently applies the *Cooperating Validity Checker Lite (CVCL)* [BB04] as the underlying SMT solver. Its user interface (depicted in Figure 5) was designed to meet various goals:

Maximize Survey: The user should easily keep a general view on proofs with many states; she should also easily keep control on proof states with large numbers of potentially large formulas. Every proof state is automatically simplified before it is presented to the user.

Minimize Options: The number of commands is kept as small as possible in order to minimize confusion and simplify the learning process (in total there are about thirty commands, of which only twenty are actually proving commands; typically, less than ten commands need to be used).

Minimize Efforts: The most important commands can be triggered by buttons or by menu entries attached to formula labels. The keyboard only needs to be used in order to enter terms for specific instantiations of universal assumptions or existential goals.

The proof of a verification condition is displayed in the form of a tree structure such as the following proof of a condition arising from the verification of the linear search algorithm [Sch06]:

The RISC ProofNavigator in action.   FIGURE 5

```
[dca]: expand Invariant, Output in zfg
  [tvy]: scatter
    [dcu]: auto
      [t4c]: proved (CVCL)
    [ecu]: split pkg
      [kel]: proved (CVCL)
      [lel]: scatter
        [lvn]: auto
          [lap]: proved (CVCL)
    [fcu]: auto
      [blt]: proved (CVCL)
    [gcu]: proved (CVCL)
```

Here the user expands predicate definitions (command **expand**), performs automatic proof decomposition (command **scatter**), splits a proof situation based on a disjunctive assumption (command **split**), performs automatic instantiation of a quantified formula (command **auto**), and thus reaches proof situations that can be automatically closed by CVCL. Each proof situation is displayed as a list of assumptions from which a particular goal is to be

proved (the formula labels represent active menus from which appropriate
proof commands can be selected):

Formula [C] proof state [dcu] : auto

Constants (with types): anyelem, r, get, length, put, Invariant, content, j_0, anyarray, new, Output,
Input, oldx, i, a, n, olda, any, x.

ed2	$olda = a$
cmz	$oldx = x$
hvv	$n = length(a)$
564	$\forall j \in \mathbb{N} : x = get(a,\ j) \Rightarrow j \geq i$
mys	$i \leq n$
x2w	$r = -1$
cpb	$n \leq i$
k4w	$x = get(a,\ j_0)$
6ha	$j_0 < n$

f5e	$x = get(a,\ -1)$

Parent: [tvy] Children: [t4c]

The software is used since 2007 in regular courses offered to students of
computer science and mathematics at the Johannes Kepler University Linz
and at the Upper Austria University of Applied Sciences Campus Hagenberg;
it is freely available as open source and shipped with a couple of examples:

1. Induction proofs,
2. Quantifier proofs,
3. Proofs based on axiomatization of arrays,
4. Proofs based on constructive definition of arrays,
5. Verification of linear search,
6. Verification of binary search,
7. Verification of a concurrent system of one server and 2 clients,
8. Verification of a concurrent system of one server and N clients.

The last two proofs consist of some hundreds of situations (most of which
are closed automatically, the user has to apply about two dozens commands
only) and were hard/impossible to manage with some other assistants.

The RISC ProgramExplorer

The RISC ProofNavigator is envisioned as a component of a future environment for formal program analysis, the RISC ProgramExplorer, which is
currently under development. Unlike program verification environments (such
as KeY [BHS07]) which primarily aim at the automation of the verification
process, the goal of this environment is to *exhibit* the logical interpretation of
imperative programs and *clarify* the relationship between reasoning tasks one
one side and program specifications/implementations on the other side, and

thus *assist* the user in analyzing a program and establishing its properties. The core features of this environment will be

1. a translation of programs to logical formulas that exhibit the semantic essence of programs as relations on pairs of (input/output) states [Sch08a], e.g. the program

    ```
    { var i; i = x+1; x = 2*i; }
    ```

    becomes the formula

    $$\exists i, i' : i' = x + 1 \land x' = 2 \cdot i'$$

    which can be simplified to $x' = 2x + 2$;
2. the association of verification conditions to specific program positions (respectively execution paths in the program) such that failures in verifications can be more easily related to programming errors.

The environment shall support the following tasks:

- Translating programs to formulas which can be subsequently simplified to exhibit the program's semantic essence;
- Validating specifications by verifying that they satisfy given input/output examples, that they are not trivial, and they are implementable,
- Verifying that the program does not violate the preconditions specified for program functions and atomic operations,
- Verifying that the program ensures the specified postconditions,
- Verifying the correctness of (loop/system) invariants,
- Verifying termination of loops and recursive functions,
- Verifying the correctness of abstract datatype representations.

Particular emphasis is given to a graphical user interface that adequately exhibits the duality between the operational and the logical interpretation of programs and the relationship of verification conditions to properties of particular program parts. A first skeleton prototype of this environment will become available in 2009.

Acknowledgements

The research described in this chapter has been performed in the frame of the following research projects at RISC:

- Austrian Science Foundation (FWF) under Project SFB F1302 (Theorema).
- European Commission Framework 6 Programme for Integrated Infrastructures Initiatives under the project SCIEnce—Symbolic Computation Infrastructure for Europe (Contract No. 026133).

- European Commission Framework 5 Proj Nr. HPRN-CT-2000-00102 (Calculemus).
- INTAS project 05-1000008-8144 "Practical Formal Verification Using Automated Reasoning and Model Checking".
- Upper Austrian Government project "Technologietransferaktivitäten".
- Project "Institute e-Austria Timisoara".

References

[AH77]   K. Appel and W. Haken. Solution of the four color map problem. *Scientific American*, 237:108–121, October 1977.

[BB04]   C. Barrett and S. Berezin. CVC Lite: A New Implementation of the Cooperating Validity Checker. In *Computer Aided Verification: 16th International Conference, CAV 2004, Boston, MA, USA, July 13–17, 2004*, volume 3114 of *LNCS*, pages 515–518. Springer, 2004.

[BCJ⁺06] B. Buchberger, A. Craciun, T. Jebelean, L. Kovacs, T. Kutsia, K. Nakagawa, F. Piroi, N. Popov, J. Robu, M. Rosenkranz, and W. Windsteiger. Theorema: Towards Computer-Aided Mathematical Theory Exploration. *Journal of Applied Logic*, 4(4):470–504, 2006.

[BDF⁺04] D. Basin, Y. Deville, P. Flener, A. Hamfelt, and J. F. Nilsson. Synthesis of Programs in Computational Logic. In M. Bruynooghe and K. K. Lau, editors, *Program Development in Computational Logic*, volume 3049 of *Lecture Notes in Computer Science*, pages 30–65. Springer, 2004.

[BDJ⁺00] B. Buchberger, C. Dupre, T. Jebelean, F. Kriftner, K. Nakagawa, D. Vasaru, and W. Windsteiger. The Theorema Project: A Progress Report. In M. Kerber and M. Kohlhase, editors, *Symbolic Computation and Automated Reasoning (Proceedings of CALCULEMUS 2000, Symposium on the Integration of Symbolic Computation and Mechanized Reasoning)*, pages 98–113. St. Andrews, Scotland, Copyright: A.K. Peters, Natick, Massachusetts, 6-7 August 2000.

[BHS07]   Bernhard Beckert, Reiner Hähnle, and Peter H. Schmitt, editors. *Verification of Object-Oriented Software: The KeY Approach*. Springer, 2007.

[BJK⁺97] B. Buchberger, T. Jebelean, F. Kriftner, M. Marin, E. Tomuta, and D. Vasaru. A Survey of the Theorema Project. In W. Kuechlin, editor, *Proceedings of ISSAC'97 (International Symposium on Symbolic and Algebraic Computation, Maui, Hawaii, July 21-23, 1997)*, pages 384–391. ACM Press, 1997.

[BL81]   B. Buchberger and F. Lichtenberger. *Mathematics for Computer Science I - The Method of Mathematics (in German)*. Springer, 2nd edition, 1981.

[BS96]   F. Baader and K. U. Schulz. Unification in the union of disjoint equational theories: Combining decision procedures. *Journal of Symbolic Computation*, 21(2):211–244, 1996.

[Buc65]   B. Buchberger. *An Algorithm for Finding the Basis Elements in the Residue Class Ring Modulo a Zero Dimensional Polynomial Ideal*. PhD thesis, University Innsbruck, Mathematical Institute, 1965. German, English translation in: J. of Symbolic Computation, Special Issue on Logic, Mathematics, and Computer Science: Interactions. Volume 41, Number 3–4, Pages 475–511, 2006.

[Buc96a] B. Buchberger. Mathematica as a Rewrite Language. In T. Ida, A. Ohori, and M. Takeichi, editors, *Functional and Logic Programming (Proceedings of the 2nd Fuji International Workshop on Functional and Logic Programming,*

November 1-4, 1996, Shonan Village Center), pages 1–13. Copyright: World Scientific, Singapore - New Jersey - London - Hong Kong, 1996.

[Buc96b] B. Buchberger. Symbolic Computation: Computer Algebra and Logic. In F. Bader and K.U. Schulz, editors, *Frontiers of Combining Systems, Proceedings of FROCOS 1996 (1st International Workshop on Frontiers of Combining Systems), March 26-28, 1996, Munich*, volume Vol.3 of *Applied Logic Series*, pages 193–220. Kluwer Academic Publisher, Dordrecht - Boston - London, The Netherlands, 1996.

[Buc96c] B. Buchberger. Using Mathematica for Doing Simple Mathematical Proofs. In *Proceedings of the 4th Mathematica Users' Conference, Tokyo, November 2, 1996.*, pages 80–96. Copyright: Wolfram Media Publishing, 1996.

[Buc97] B. Buchberger. Mathematica: Doing Mathematics by Computer? In A. Miola and M. Temperini, editors, *Advances in the Design of Symbolic Computation Systems*, pages 2–20. Springer Vienna, 1997. RISC Book Series on Symbolic Computation.

[Buc99] Bruno Buchberger. Theory Exploration Versus Theorem Proving. Technical Report 99-46, RISC Report Series, University of Linz, Austria, July 1999. Also available as SFB Report No. 99-38, Johannes Kepler University Linz, Spezialforschungsbereich F013, December 1999.

[Buc01] B. Buchberger. The PCS Prover in Theorema. In R. Moreno-Diaz, B. Buchberger, and J.L. Freire, editors, *Proceedings of EUROCAST 2001 (8th International Conference on Computer Aided Systems Theory – Formal Methods and Tools for Computer Science)*, Lecture Notes in Computer Science 2178, pages 469–478. Las Palmas de Gran Canaria, Copyright: Springer - Verlag Berlin, 19-23 February 2001.

[Buc03] B. Buchberger. Algorithm Invention and Verification by Lazy Thinking. In D. Petcu, V. Negru, D. Zaharie, and T. Jebelean, editors, *Proceedings of SYNASC 2003, 5th International Workshop on Symbolic and Numeric Algorithms for Scientific Computing Timisoara*, pages 2–26, Timisoara, Romania, 1-4 October 2003. Copyright: Mirton Publisher.

[Buc04] B. Buchberger. Towards the Automated Synthesis of a Gröbner Bases Algorithm. *RACSAM (Rev. Acad. Cienc., Spanish Royal Academy of Science)*, 98(1):65–75, 2004.

[Buc06] B. Buchberger. Mathematical Theory Exploration, August 17-20 2006. Invited talk at IJCAR, Seattle, USA.

[CFK07] J. Coelho, M. Florido, and T. Kutsia. Sequence disunification and its application in collaborative schema construction. In M. Weske, M.-S. Hacid, and C. Godart, editors, *Web Information Systems – WISE 2007 Workshops*, volume 4832 of *LNCS*, pages 91–102. Springer, 2007.

[Col75] G. E. Collins. Quantifier elimination for real closed fields by cylindrical algebraic decomposition. In *Second GI Conference on Authomata Theory and Formal Languages*, volume 33 of *LNCS*, pages 134–183. Springer, 1975.

[Com91] H. Comon. Completion of rewrite systems with membership constraints. Rapport de Recherche 699, L.R.I., Université de Paris-Sud, 1991.

[Com98] H. Comon. Completion of rewrite systems with membership constraints. Part II: Constraint solving. *Journal of Symbolic Computation*, 25(4):421–453, 1998.

[Cra08] A. Craciun. *Lazy Thinking Algorithm Synthesis in Gröbner Bases Theory.* PhD thesis, RISC, Johannes Kepler University Linz, Austria, April 2008.

[EJ08] M. Erascu and T. Jebelean. Practical Program Verification by Forward Symbolic Execution: Correctness and Examples. In B. Buchberger, T. Ida, and T. Kutsia, editors, *Austrian-Japan Workshop on Symbolic Computation in Software Science*, pages 47–56, 2008.

[Fei05] Ingo Feinerer. Formal Program Verification: A Comparison of Selected Tools and Their Theoretical Foundations. Master's thesis, Theory and Logic Group,

Institute of Computer Languages, Vienna University of Technology, Vienna, Austria, January 2005.

[Hoa69]   C. A. R. Hoare. An Axiomatic Basis for Computer Programming. *Comm. ACM*, 12, 1969.

[Hoa03]   C. A. R. Hoare. The verifying compiler: A grand challenge for computing research. *Journal of ACM*, 50:63–69, 2003.

[Jeb01]   T. Jebelean. Natural proofs in elementary analysis by S-Decomposition. Technical Report 01-33, RISC, Johannes Kepler University, Linz, Austria, 2001.

[KJ00]   B. Konev and T. Jebelean. Using meta-variables for natural deduction in theorema. In M. Kerber and M. Kohlhase, editors, *Proceedings of the CALCULE-MUS 2000 8th Symposium on the Integration of Symbolic Computation and Mechanized Reasoning*, pages 160–175, St. Andrews, Scotland, August 6-7 2000.

[KLV07]   T. Kutsia, J. Levy, and M. Villaret. Sequence unification through currying. In Franz Baader, editor, *Proc. of the 18th Int. Conference on Rewriting Techniques and Applications, RTA'07*, volume 4533 of *Lecture Notes in Computer Science*, pages 288–302. Springer, 2007.

[KM05]   T. Kutsia and M. Marin. Matching with regular constraints. In G. Sutcliffe and A. Voronkov, editors, *Logic for Programming, Artificial Intelligence, and Reasoning. Proceedings of the 12th International Conference, LPAR'05*, volume 3835 of *LNAI*, pages 215–229. Springer, 2005.

[Kov07]   L. Kovacs. *Automated Invariant Generation by Algebraic Techniques for Imperative Program Verification in Theorema*. PhD thesis, RISC, Johannes Kepler University Linz, Austria, October 2007. RISC Technical Report No. 07-16.

[KPJ05]   L. Kovacs, N. Popov, and T. Jebelean. Verification Environment in Theorema. *Annals of Mathematics, Computing and Teleinformatics (AMCT)*, 1(2):27–34, 2005.

[KPJ06]   L. Kovacs, N. Popov, and T. Jebelean. Combining Logic and Algebraic Techniques for Program Verification in Theorema. In T. Margaria and B. Steffen, editors, *Proceedings ISOLA 2006*, Paphos, Cyprus, November 2006. To appear.

[Kut03]   T. Kutsia. Equational prover of Theorema. In R. Nieuwenhuis, editor, *Proc. of the 14th Int. Conference on Rewriting Techniques and Applications, RTA'03*, volume 2706 of *LNCS*, pages 367–379. Springer, 2003.

[Kut06]   T. Kutsia. Context sequence matching for XML. *Electronic Notes on Theoretical Computer Science*, 157(2):47–65, 2006.

[Kut07]   T. Kutsia. Solving equations with sequence variables and sequence functions. *Journal of Symbolic Computation*, 42(3):352–388, 2007.

[Kut08]   T. Kutsia. Flat matching. *Journal of Symbolic Computation*, 43(12):858–873, 2008.

[Lev96]   J. Levy. Linear second-order unification. In Harald Ganzinger, editor, *Proc. of the 7th Int. Conference Conference on Rewriting Techniques and Applications, RTA'96*, volume 1103 of *LNCS*, pages 332–346. Springer, 1996.

[LNV05]   J. Levy, J. Niehren, and M. Villaret. Well-nested context unification. In R. Nieuwenhuis, editor, *Proc. of the 20th Int. Conference on Automated Deduction, CADE-20*, volume 3632 of *LNAI*, pages 149–163. Springer, 2005.

[LS87]   J. Loeckx and K. Sieber. *The Foundations of Program Verification*. Teubner, second edition, 1987.

[LV02]   J. Levy and M. Villaret. Currying second-order unification problems. In S. Tison, editor, *Proc. of the 13th Int. Conference on Rewriting Techniques and Applications, RTA'02*, volume 2378 of *LNCS*, pages 326–339, Copenhagen, Denmark, 2002. Springer.

[Mak77]   G. S. Makanin. The problem of solvability of equations in a free semigroup. *Math. USSR Sbornik*, 32(2):129–198, 1977.

[McC97]   W. McCune. Solution of the robbins problem. *Journal of Automatic Reasoning*, 19:263–276, 1997.

[MK06]   M. Marin and T. Kutsia. Foundations of the rule-based system RhoLog. *Journal of Applied Non-Classical Logics*, 16(1–2):151–168, 2006.

[ORS92]   S. Owre, J. M. Rushby, and N. Shankar. PVS: A Prototype Verification System. In Deepak Kapur, editor, *11th International Conference on Automated Deduction (CADE)*, volume 607 of *Lecture Notes in Artificial Intelligence*, pages 748–752, Saratoga, NY, June 14–18, 1992. Springer.

[PB02]   F. Piroi and B. Buchberger. Focus Windows: A New Technique for Proof Presentation. In H. Kredel and W. Seiler, editors, *Proceedings of the 8th Rhine Workshop on Computer Algebra, Mannheim, Germany*, pages 297–313, 2002.

[PK05]   Florina Piroi and Temur Kutsia. The Theorema Environment for Interactive Proof Development, December 3 2005. Contributed talk at 12th International Conference on Logic for Programming, Artificial Intelligence, and Reasoning, LPAR'05.

[RIS06]   The RISC ProofNavigator, 2006. Research Institute for Symbolic Computation (RISC), Johannes Kepler University, Linz, Austria, http://www.risc.uni-linz.ac.at/research/formal/software/ProofNavigator.

[Rob02]   Judit Robu. Geometry Theorem Proving in the Frame of the Theorema Project. Technical Report 02-23, RISC Report Series, University of Linz, Austria, September 2002. PhD Thesis.

[Sch06]   W. Schreiner. The RISC ProofNavigator — Tutorial and Manual. Technical report, Research Institute for Symbolic Computation (RISC), Johannes Kepler University, Linz, Austria, July 2006.

[Sch08a] W. Schreiner. A Program Calculus. Technical report, Research Institute for Symbolic Computation (RISC), Johannes Kepler University, Linz, Austria, September 2008.

[Sch08b] W. Schreiner. The RISC ProofNavigator: A Proving Assistant for Program Verification in the Classroom. *Formal Aspects of Computing*, April 2008. DOI 10.1007/s00165-008-0069-4.

[SMT06]   SMT-LIB — The Satisfiability Modulo Theories Library, 2006. University of Iowa, Iowa City, IA, http://combination.cs.uiowa.edu/smtlib.

[SS94]   M. Schmidt-Schauß. Unification of stratified second-order terms. Internal Report 12/24, Johann-Wolfgang-Goethe-Universität, Frankfurt, Germany, 1994.

[SSS02]   M. Schmidt-Schauß and Klaus U. Schulz. Solvability of context equations with two context variables is decidable. *Journal of Symbolic Computation*, 33(1):77–122, 2002.

[Vil04]   M. Villaret. *On Some Variants of Second-Order Unification*. PhD thesis, Universitat Politècnica de Catalunya, Barcelona, 2004.

[VJB08]   R. Vajda, T. Jebelean, and B. Buchberger. Combining Logical and Algebraic Techniques for Natural Style Proving in Elementary Analysis. *Mathematics and Computers in Simulation*, 2008.

[WBR06]   W. Windsteiger, B. Buchberger, and M. Rosenkranz. Theorema. In Freek Wiedijk, editor, *The Seventeen Provers of the World*, volume 3600 of *LNAI*, pages 96–107. Springer Berlin Heidelberg New York, 2006.

[Win01]   W. Windsteiger. *A Set Theory Prover in Theorema: Implementation and Practical Applications*. PhD thesis, RISC Institute, May 2001.

[Win06]   W. Windsteiger. An Automated Prover for Zermelo-Fraenkel Set Theory in Theorema. *JSC*, 41(3-4):435–470, 2006.

[Wol03]   S. Wolfram. *The Mathematica Book*. Wolfram Media, 5th edition, 2003.

Chapter III
Metaheuristic Optimization

Michael Affenzeller

Andreas Beham, Monika Kofler, Gabriel Kronberger, Stefan A. Wagner,

Stephan Winkler

Introduction 1

Motivation and Goal 1.1

Economic success frequently depends on a company's ability to rapidly identify market changes and to adapt to them. Making optimal decisions within
tight time constraints and under consideration of influential factors is one of
the most challenging tasks in industry and applied computer science. Gaining
expertise in solving optimization problems can therefore significantly increase
efficiency and profitability of a company and lead to a competitive advantage.

Unfortunately, many real-world optimization problems are notoriously difficult to solve due to their high complexity. For example, in the context of
combinatorial optimization (where the search space tends to grow exponentially) or in nonlinear system identification (especially if no a-priori knowledge
about the kind of nonlinearity is available) such applications are frequently
found. Exact mathematical methods cannot solve these problems in relevant
dimensions within reasonable time.

Heuristic methods[1] provide a reasonable tradeoff between achieved solution quality and required computing time, as they employ intelligent rules to
scan only a fraction of a highly complex search space.

Typical applications of heuristic methods can be found in production optimization; for example, heuristic algorithms are applied in machine scheduling
and logistics optimization. For efficiently scanning such highly complex and

---

[1] The name "heuristics" is derived from the old Greek word $\varepsilon\nu\rho\iota\sigma\kappa\varepsilon\iota\nu$ which means "to
discover" or "to detect (something)".

exponentially growing search spaces, only heuristic methods can be considered for solving problems in dimensions which are relevant for real-world applications.

The step from heuristics to metaheuristics is an essential one: While heuristics are often designed and tuned for some specific problem, metaheuristics offer generic strategies for solving arbitrary problems. The implementation of concrete solution manipulation operators still depends on the problem representation, but the optimization strategy itself is problem-independent. The success of metaheuristics is based on an interplay between phases of diversification and intensification, but in order to achieve a beneficial equilibrium, fine-tuning is necessary for each problem instance depending on its fitness landscape characteristics.

One of the most prominent representatives of metaheuristics is the class of evolutionary algorithms (EA): New solution candidates (individuals) are generated by combining attributes of existing solution candidates (crossover) and afterwards they are slightly modified with a certain probability (mutation); parent individuals are chosen by means of nature inspired selection techniques. A second well-known example of a rather simple metaheuristic is simulated annealing (SA): This approach is closely related to local search strategies such as hill climbing/descending and generates new solutions iteratively, starting from a usually randomly initialized solution. In contrast to simple hill climbing/descending, moves to worse solutions are permitted with a certain probability which decreases during the heuristic search process; by this means the algorithm first performs exploration (diversification), and later tends to focus on promising regions (intensification).

A multitude of other metaheuristics has been described in the literature, such as for example ant colony optimization (ACO), tabu search (TS), iterated local search (ILS), and scatter search (SS). The evolution of so many diverse metaheuristics results from the fact that no single method outperforms all others for all possible problems. To be a bit more precise, the so-called No-Free-Lunch theorem postulates that a general-purpose universal optimization strategy is impossible and that the only way how one strategy can outperform another is to be more specialized to the structure of the tackled problem. The No-Free-Lunch theorem basically says that, given two arbitrary metaheuristics (including random search), there always exist search spaces for which the first metaheuristic will perform better than the second and vice versa.

This means that even for the most sophisticated metaheuristic a fitness landscape can be constructed for which it performs worse than ordinary random search. Therefore, it always takes qualified algorithm experts to select, parametrize and tune a metaheuristic algorithm for a concrete application.

This situation is illustrated in Figure 1 where the lower layer represents the problem instances with their associated fitness landscape characteristics and the upper layer shows the metaheuristic methods under certain parametrization. There exist some rough rules of thumb derived from empirical testing that indicate which metaheuristics should be chosen for certain problem characteristics.

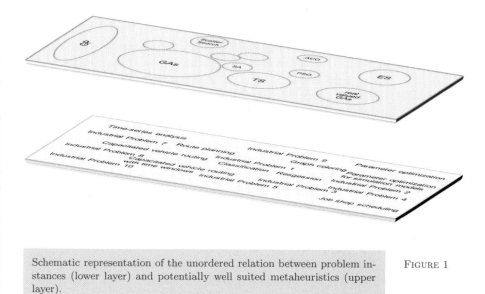

Schematic representation of the unordered relation between problem instances (lower layer) and potentially well suited metaheuristics (upper layer).   FIGURE 1

However, picking an appropriate method for a certain problem instance is a non-trivial task. On the one hand, fitness landscape characteristics may change remarkably for different problem dimensions; on the other hand, the characteristics of a certain metaheuristic may considerably vary for different parameter settings. Therefore, the following aspects are essential for choosing a well suited method and beneficial parameter values for a certain problem instance:

Sensitivity: The importance of good parameter settings for the successful application of metaheuristics cannot be overemphasized. Even a minor change of one parameter value can drastically alter the convergence behavior and the achievable solution quality. Moreover, dependencies between parameters make the analysis and reliable prediction of algorithmic behavior difficult. The detection of robust parameter settings that can be applied in a wide range of applications would be a great benefit for the scientific community. Even more importantly, it would encourage non-experts (for example biologists or economists) to employ metaheuristics more frequently, if good results could be obtained with these parameter settings.

Robustness: Fitness landscape characteristics, such as the distribution of local optima or the landscape ruggedness, play an important role for selecting an appropriate metaheuristic. It is a well-known fact that certain metaheuristics are better suited for some categories of fitness landscapes than others, but a systematic classification or characterization has not been devised yet. There is a clear need for the development of appropriate measures to better characterize fitness landscapes and also for the collection of fitness landscape characteristics for concrete problem instances. Subsequently, the analysis of successful optimization strategies and parameter settings with respect to these fitness landscape characteristics could lead to new insights about problem families and solution spaces.

Scalability: Real-world problems often need to be solved within tight time constraints which limits the choice of adequate metaheuristics. As a result, existing methods must be adjusted to achieve minimal runtime while still yielding the best possible solution quality. For example, this can be achieved by the integration of parallel concepts and the execution on parallel computing systems (see Chapter VII). New algorithmic ideas are also needed to effectively take advantage of the steadily increasing computing power by introducing new self-adaptive parallel metaheuristics.

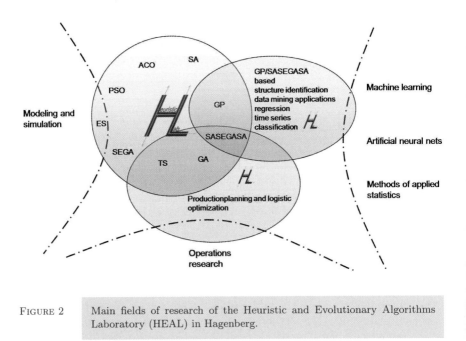

FIGURE 2   Main fields of research of the Heuristic and Evolutionary Algorithms Laboratory (HEAL) in Hagenberg.

In order to face these challenges in the engineering of application oriented metaheuristics, we have developed an environment called HeuristicLab, which serves as a basis for algorithm development and analysis. Since the beginning of its development, HeuristicLab has considered the general aspect of metaheuristics to encapsulate the generic algorithmic components and the problem specific aspects of certain problem classes.

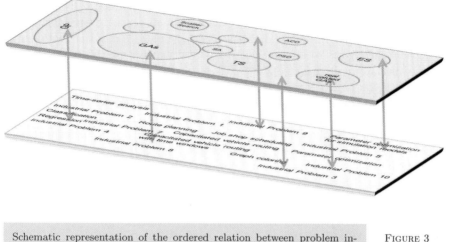

Schematic representation of the ordered relation between problem in-   FIGURE 3
stances (lower layer) and potentially well suited metaheuristics (upper
layer).

Therefore, as illustrated in Figure 2, various different metaheuristic algorithms as well as enhanced hybrid variants denote the core of HeuristicLab by
defining problem independent algorithms as algorithm plugin bundles. This
architecture makes algorithm engineering a lot easier: For attacking a new
problem it is sufficient to implement problem-specific solution manipulation
operators (such as neighborhood operators, crossover and mutation operators) and the whole variety of standard as well as enhanced metaheuristics is
available in HeuristicLab and can be used. This approach has turned out to be
very well suited for algorithm development and analysis. In this environment
many algorithmic enhancements to the general concept of a genetic algorithm
(as for example offspring selection (OS) [AW05] or the relevant alleles preserving GA (RAPGA) [AWW07]) have been developed and applied to many
theoretical benchmarks as well as real-world problems. A good overview of research activities in the field of theoretical and application oriented algorithm
engineering using HeuristicLab can be found in the book [AWWB09] and
the associated homepage[2]. Supplementary information about HeuristicLab
including an up-to-date list of publications can be found on the HeuristicLab
homepage[3].

Furthermore, by using HeuristicLab it becomes very easy to compare various algorithms and also to rapidly obtain an overview about which metaheuristics and which corresponding parameter settings are suited best for a
certain kind of problem. There are concrete plans within the scope of the

---

[2] http://gagp2009.heuristiclab.com/

[3] http://www.heuristiclab.com/

recently started research laboratory *Heureka!*[4] to systematically collect all test runs that will be performed by different metaheuristics in different application domains in a large database. The ultimate goal of this metaheuristic data storage is to systematically analyze which types of metaheuristics are especially suited for concrete fitness landscape characteristics in order to dilute the negative aspects of the No-Free-Lunch theorem. As indicated in Figure 3, this should at least enable us to get some estimate about the usually unknown interrelationships between the problem layer and the layer of theoretically applicable metaheuristics. Still, there are problems for which no suited metaheuristics are known yet and a lot remains to be done also in the field of algorithm engineering in order to fill up these unexplored regions on the map of metaheuristic algorithms with new hybrid metaheuristics.

1.2   Structure and Content

The rest of the chapter is organized as follows: In Section 2 a brief introduction to heuristic optimization is given. Several trajectory-based and population-based metaheuristics are outlined that represent state-of-the-art algorithms of the domain. Section 3 describes generic hybrid enhancements to the general concept of a genetic algorithm that have been developed and applied in various application domains by members of the Heuristic and Evolutionary Algorithms research group in Hagenberg. Two active areas of application treated by the research group are discussed in Section 4 and Section 5. In Section 4 several route planning heuristics are discussed including also some approaches using metaheuristics such as genetic algorithms and tabu search have been performed by members of the Heuristic and Evolutionary Algorithms Laboratory (HEAL). A quite different area of application which we have entered in the last couple of years is described in Section 5: In the context of genetic programming based structure identification, the enhanced algorithmic concepts we have developed are applied to nonlinear structure identification problems using genetic programming. Finally, Section 6 summarizes the chapter and indicates some aspects for future research which are considered important by the authors.

---

[4] Josef Ressel-Centre for Heuristic Optimization, `http://heureka.heuristiclab.com/`.

Bibliographic Remarks 1.3

There are numerous books, journals, and articles available that survey the field of metaheuristic optimization. In this section we summarize some of the most important ones as well as a new book of the authors of this chapter. Representatively, the following books are widely considered very important sources of information about GAs (in chronological order):

- J. H. Holland: *Adaptation in Natural and Artificial Systems* [Hol75a]
- D. E. Goldberg: *Genetic Algorithms in Search, Optimization and Machine Learning* [Gol89]
- Z. Michalewicz: *Genetic Algorithms + Data Structures = Evolution Programs* [Mic92]
- D. Dumitrescu et al.: *Evolutionary Computation* [DLJD00]
- Z. Michalewicz and B. Fogel *How to Solve It: Modern Metaheuristics* [MF00]
- E. Alba *Parallel Metaheuristics: A New Class of Algorithms* [Alb05]
- M. Affenzeller, S. Winkler, S. Wagner, and A. Beham: *Genetic Algorithms and Genetic Programming: Modern concepts and Practical Applications* [AWWB09]

The following journals are dedicated to either theory and applications of genetic algorithms or evolutionary computation in general:

- *IEEE Transactions on Evolutionary Computation* (IEEE)
- *Evolutionary Computation* (MIT Press)
- *Journal of Heuristics* (Springer)

Moreover, several conference and workshop proceedings include papers related to genetic and evolutionary algorithms and heuristic optimization. Some examples are the following ones:

- *Genetic and Evolutionary Computation Conference (GECCO)*, a recombination of the *International Conference on Genetic Algorithms* and the *Genetic Programming Conference*
- *Congress on Evolutionary Computation (CEC)*
- *Parallel Problem Solving from Nature (PPSN)*

Metaheuristic Optimization Techniques 2

Frequently, metaheuristics are categorized by the number of solutions they work on in each iteration. On the one hand, trajectory-based algorithms consider only a single element of the solution space at a time. They jump from one spot in the solution space to another, usually by sampling a new solution from the neighborhood of the current one, and try to reach promising regions in the solution space. The neighborhood of a solution is thereby defined by a neighborhood structure which is a function $\mathcal{N} : \mathcal{S} \rightarrow 2^{\mathcal{S}}$ from the solution space $\mathcal{S}$ to the power set of the solution space that assigns a set of neighbors $\mathcal{N}(s)$ to every solution s [BRA05]. On the other hand, population-based heuristics keep a set of solutions in each iteration. By this means, they can make their decision where to move in the solution space based not only on a single point but on multiple points.

In the following, several representatives of classical trajectory-based and population-based metaheuristics are described (see [BRA05]). More details on metaheuristics and their application to different problems can also be found in [DGG+07]. Furthermore, the topic of hybrid metaheuristics is also briefly touched at the end of this section.

2.1 Simulated Annealing

As stated in [BRA05], simulated annealing (SA) is commonly said to be the oldest among the metaheuristics and one of the first algorithms that contained an explicit strategy to escape from local optima. It was inspired by the annealing process of metal and glass which assume a low energy configuration when cooled down, and is therefore a representative of a nature-inspired optimization algorithm. Its origins go back to the field of statistical mechanics and the Metropolis algorithm published in 1953 [MRR+53]. In 1983 Scott Kirkpatrick, Charles D. Gellart and Mario P. Vecchi generalized this algorithm, introduced the name "simulated annealing" and applied it to problems of computer design and the traveling salesman problem [KGV83].

SA starts with an initial solution s which can be created randomly or using some heuristic construction rule. Similar to iterative first-improvement local search (hill climbing/descending), a solution s' is sampled randomly from the neighborhood $\mathcal{N}$ of the current solution in each iteration. If the sampled solution is better, it is accepted and replaces the current solution. However, if s' is worse, it is not discarded immediately but is also accepted with a probability $P(s'|T_k, s) = e^{-|f(s') - f(s)|/T_k}$ depending on the actual temperature parameter T_k and the quality difference. Algorithm 1 shows a pseudo-code representation of the algorithm.

Due to this stochastic acceptance criterion the temperature parameter T_k can be used to balance diversification and intensification of the search. At the beginning the temperature should be high to enable the algorithm to easily escape from local optima. As the algorithm proceeds, the temperature has to be reduced step by step to focus the search on a promising region of the solution space such that it will converge eventually. The way how the temperature is decreased over time is defined by the cooling scheme. Frequently used cooling schemes include linear, geometric or logarithmic cooling. However, also more complex cooling strategies have been proposed that are not necessarily monotonous and for example suggest reheating phases to diversify the search again from time to time [LM86, Osm93]. The choice of an appropriate initial temperature and cooling scheme is crucial for the performance of the algorithm and therefore has to be adapted for each problem instance to which SA is applied.

Algorithm 1. Simulated annealing

$s \leftarrow$ generate initial solution
$k \leftarrow 0$
$T_k \leftarrow$ initial temperature

while termination criterion not met **do**
    $s' \leftarrow$ choose solution in $\mathcal{N}(s)$ randomly
    if s' is better than s **then**
        $s \leftarrow s'$
    else
        $s \leftarrow s'$ with probability $P(s'|T_k,s) = e^{-\frac{|f(s')-f(s)|}{T_k}}$
    end if
    $T_{k+1} \leftarrow$ adapt temperature T_k
    $k \leftarrow k+1$
end while

return best solution found

Tabu Search 2.2

In 1986 Fred Glover introduced tabu search (TS) in [Glo86]. In contrast to SA, TS is a memory-based method that uses the search history to navigate in the solution space and to prevent stagnation in local optima. Especially in the field of combinatorial optimization TS is considered to be one of the most successful metaheuristics. A detailed description of the algorithm and various applications can be found in [Glo97].

Algorithm 2 outlines a basic TS algorithm. TS can be considered as iterative best-improvement local search with an additional extension to prevent cycles. Without this modification the algorithm would always jump between a local optimum and the best solution in the neighborhood of this local optimum (next best solution). To prevent this behavior and to force the exploration of new areas of the solution space after reaching an optimum, TS uses a short term memory also called tabu list which stores solutions visited in the past in a FIFO list. In each iteration the tabu list is used to generate the allowed set of neighbors $\mathcal{N}_a(s)$ by removing all solutions from the neighborhood of the current solution which have been visited in the last iterations. Then the best solution of the allowed set is chosen as new solution and the tabu list is updated. As storing complete solutions is too inefficient for many applications, the tabu list often contains only the solution components involved in a move. Also multiple tabu lists, one for each solution component, might be used. Finally the algorithm stops, if some termination criterion is met (execution time, number of evaluated solutions, etc.) or all neighboring solutions are tabu and the set of allowed solutions is empty.

Algorithm 2. Tabu search

$s \leftarrow$ generate initial solution
$TL \leftarrow$ empty tabu list

while termination criterion not met **do**
    $\mathcal{N}_a(s) \leftarrow \{s' \in \mathcal{N}(s) | s'$ is not tabu or satisfies an aspiration condition$\}$
    $s' \leftarrow$ best solution $\in \mathcal{N}_a(s)$
    update TL with s and s'
    $s \leftarrow s'$
end while

return best solution found

The size of the tabu list (tabu tenure) represents an important parameter to influence intensification and diversification of the search. A shorter tabu list leads to a more intensive exploitation of a smaller area of the solution space, whereas a longer tabu list forces the algorithm to go to other regions of the solution space more quickly. Selecting an appropriate tabu tenure is a critical step and determines the success of the search. Therefore, several approaches have been discussed to adapt the length of the tabu list automatically during the execution of the algorithm [Glo90, Tai91, BT94]. However, as a longer tabu list might have the effect that a promising region of the solution space is not fully explored, additional aspiration criteria are frequently used which overrule the tabu condition of a solution. For example, if a solution is found in the neighborhood that is tabu but better than the best solution found so far, this solution is also included in the allowed set.

Besides the tabu list as a short term memory, additional memories can also be added in order to control the search process on a higher level. For example, an intermediate term memory can be used to keep track of promising regions of the solution space and to restart the algorithm with a shorter tabu list to perform an intensified search there. Another approach suggests a long term memory to store the frequency of solutions in order to penalize solutions that have been considered already. Additional information on these advanced TS concepts is summarized in [Glo97].

Iterated Local Search 2.3

Iterated local search (ILS) [Stü98, LMS03] is a very general metaheuristic that offers several degrees of freedom. As shown in Algorithm 3, ILS starts with an initial solution on which a local search procedure is applied leading to a (local) optimum $\hat{s}$. In each iteration a new starting point s' is calculated by perturbating the current optimum $\hat{s}$. On that solution local search is applied again which results in another optimum $\hat{s}'$. Finally, the new optimum replaces the old one depending on some acceptance criterion. As in both steps, perturbation and acceptance, the history of the search might be used, ILS is another version of memory-based metaheuristics.

Algorithm 3. Iterated local search

$s \leftarrow$ generate initial solution
$\hat{s} \leftarrow$ perform local search on s

while termination criterion not met **do**
    $s' \leftarrow$ perturbate $\hat{s}$
    $\hat{s}' \leftarrow$ perform local search on s'
    if acceptance criterion is satisfied **then**
        $\hat{s} \leftarrow \hat{s}'$
    end if
end while

return best solution found

Obviously, ILS follows a trajectory of local optima $\hat{s}_1, \ldots, \hat{s}_n$. Thereby the choice of the perturbation scheme is crucial: On the one hand, the new starting point should be located outside the attraction basin of the current local optimum; on the other hand, if perturbation is too strong, ILS behaves like a random multi-start local search. Therefore, the strength of the perturbation has to be selected according to the tackled problem instance. More sophisticated versions of ILS also suggest a variable perturbation procedure that adapts its strength dynamically in order to have a good balance of diversification and intensification of the search.

Due to its very generic formulation, ILS can be seen as a high level definition of trajectory-based metaheuristics. Other algorithms such as variable neighborhood search or simulated annealing can be described as special cases of ILS.

2.4 Evolutionary Algorithms

All metaheuristic algorithms inspired by the Darwinian principle of "survival of the fittest" [Dar98] and the process of evolution are denominated as evolutionary algorithms (EAs). In general, EAs mimic the natural process of species adapting to the environment and simulate this concept to solve combinatorial or continuous optimization problems. The foundations of EAs date back to the 1960s and 1970s. In that time several slightly different algorithms were proposed, but fundamentally all of them followed similar ideas. The most prominent variants of EAs are evolution strategies (ES), developed by Ingo Rechenberg in Germany [Rec73, Rec94], and genetic algorithms (GAs), introduced by John H. Holland and his students in the USA [Hol75b, Gol89]. Although the ES and GA community competed heavily in the early days of EAs, in the recent years effort can be noticed to unite both approaches and to develop a unified and general model for evolutionary computation [DeJ06].

Algorithm 4. Evolutionary algorithm

$P \leftarrow$ generate initial population
evaluate P

while termination criterion not met **do**
    $P_{parents} \leftarrow$ select solutions from P
    $P_{children} \leftarrow$ recombine and/or mutate $P_{parents}$
    evaluate $P_{children}$
    $P \leftarrow$ select from P and $P_{children}$
end while

return best solution found

Algorithm 4 shows the procedure of EAs in a very generalized form. Basically, an EA works on a set of solutions usually called a population. In analogy to genetics, solutions are also often referred to as individuals or chromosomes, the components of a solution are called genes, and the concrete value of a gene is denoted as an allele. In each iteration three different steps are applied:

Selection: First, a selection method is used to pick solutions from the current population that should be modified. If the selection probability of a solution is proportional to the solution quality, which is usually the case for GAs, this steps plays an important role for directing the search process.

Modification: Second, the selected solutions are manipulated. In general, two different modification concepts can be applied either separately or in a combined way. On the one hand, solution components of two or more solutions can be combined to create a new valid and hopefully better solution (crossover). On the other hand, some kind of local modification can be used to change single solutions (mutation).

Replacement: Third, a set of solutions has to be selected from the modified solutions and perhaps also from the current population to build a new generation of parent solutions for the next iteration. Again, if the solution quality is used as a decision criterion whether a solution should become a member of the next generation or not, replacement is also an important factor for navigating the search through the solution space.

The general EA model shown above offers many degrees of freedom to the algorithm designer. How selection, modification, and replacement are implemented depends on the type of EA (GAs, ES, etc.) as well as on the tackled problem. This is probably one of the main success factors of EAs, as they can be easily adapted to particular optimization problems. As a result, many different EA derivatives have been proposed for multiple optimization problems and solution representations. In this context genetic programming (GP) [Koz92b] should also be mentioned as a prominent example which uses GAs to evolve computer programs represented as tree structures. A comprehensive discussion of different EA variants and many application areas can be found in several publications such as [Bäc96, BFM97, DLJD00, HK00, Fog06].

Scatter Search 2.5

Scatter search (SS) and its generalized form called path relinking were developed by Fred Glover in the late 1990s [Glo99, GLM00]. As described in [GLM03b], SS basically consists of five methods:

Diversification Generation Method: The diversification generation method aims to create a set of solutions as different to an existing set of solutions as possible.

Improvement Method: The improvement method tries to improve a solution usually by applying some kind of local search procedure.

Reference Set Update Method: This method is used to build and maintain the reference set containing the "best" solutions found so far. The notion of best is thereby not limited to the solution quality. Other quality criteria such as the diversity of solutions are also taken into account.

Subset Generation Method: The subset generation method operates on the reference set and selects subsets for creating combined solutions. The most common method is to generate all pairs of reference solutions.

Solution Combination Method: Finally, the solution combination method takes the generated subsets of the reference set and combines all solutions of each subset in order to create new solutions. This method is similar to the crossover operator used in EAs.

As outlined in Algorithm 5 these methods are used as follows: First, an initial set of solutions is created using some heuristic method and the initial reference set is selected. Note that the diversification generation method might also be used to get a highly diverse set of initial solutions. Then, in each iteration of the algorithm, an intensification phase and a diversification phase are executed. The intensification phase (inner loop) is repeated as long as the reference set changes (i.e., better solutions are found). The subset generation, combination, and improvement methods are applied to create new solutions; then the reference set is updated if possible. By this means, the regions of the solution space defined by the reference solutions are exploited as much as possible. After the reference set has converged, diversification takes place by applying the diversification generation method on the reference set and choosing a new reference set again.

Algorithm 5. Scatter search

$P \leftarrow$ create initial solutions
$P_{ref} \leftarrow$ choose reference set from P

while termination criterion not met **do**
    repeat
        $P_{sub} \leftarrow$ select subsets from P_{ref}
        $P_{comb} \leftarrow$ apply recombination on P_{sub}
        $P_{comb} \leftarrow$ apply improvement on P_{comb}
        $P_{ref} \leftarrow$ update reference set with P_{comb}
    until P_{ref} converges

    $P \leftarrow$ apply diversification generation on P_{ref}
    $P_{ref} \leftarrow$ choose reference set from P
end while

return best solution found

Originally, SS was designed to optimize solutions encoded as points in the Euclidean space. However, in the recent years it was also shown how SS can be applied to other problems such as linear ordering, route planning, graph coloring, or multi-objective optimization (see for example [GLM03b, GLM03a, NLA+08]).

2.6 Further Metaheuristics

Apart from the typical representatives of trajectory-based and population-based metaheuristics presented above, several other algorithms have been proposed that also belong to either of these two categories. Some of them are listed in the following, even though this list is not complete as the research community focusing on metaheuristic search is very active and new algorithms are frequently published. Additional information about these algorithms can be found in the referenced publications.

- Greedy Randomized Adaptive Search Procedure (GRASP) [FR95]

- Guided Local Search (GLS) [VT99]
- Very Large-Scale Neighborhood Search (VLSN) [AEOP02]
- Variable Neighborhood Search (VNS) [HM01]
- Variable Depth Search (VDS) [LK73]
- Estimation of Distribution Algorithms (EDA) [MP96]
- Evolutionary Programming (EP) [FOW66]
- Ant Colony Optimization (ACO) [DS04]
- Particle Swarm Optimization (PSO) [ESK01]
- Artificial Immune Systems (AIS) [dCT02]

Hybrid Metaheuristics 2.7

In the last years so-called hybrid metaheuristics have become more and more popular that do not strictly stick to one specific metaheuristic approach. In many complex real-world optimization scenarios these algorithms are able to outperform classical metaheuristics by exploiting the advantages of different concepts. However, the development of an effective hybrid approach is in general a difficult task and highly depends on the tackled optimization problem. Various ways of hybridization have been discussed in the literature and a comprehensive overview can be found in [Rai06].

Basically, three different categories of hybrid algorithms can be distinguished: Metaheuristics can be hybridized with each other, metaheuristics can be combined with problem-specific algorithms, or metaheuristics can be used together with other optimization algorithms as for example exact optimization techniques or neural networks.

A typical strategy that belongs to the first category is embedding metaheuristic algorithms in order to improve solutions during the search process of another metaheuristic. For example, memetic algorithms [Mos99, MC03] follow this approach: They combine evolutionary algorithms with trajectory-based metaheuristics to optimize some or all solutions of the population; a local search algorithm is thereby used to intensify the search and to focus the surrounding EA on local optima.

Regarding the second category, metaheuristics can be combined with problem-specific construction heuristics that are used to obtain good starting points for the search (see GRASP) or to transform indirect or incomplete representations into complete and feasible solutions (decoder-based algorithms). The latter strategy is frequently found in algorithms solving combinatorial optimization problems, if a permutation-based solution encoding is used [KPP04]. For example, when solving scheduling problems, an order of jobs can be represented as a permutation; in this case, a schedule builder such as the Giffler-Thompson algorithm [GT60] has to be applied to create concrete schedules which can be evaluated with respect to some objective function [YN97, BWA04].

Last but not least, the combination of metaheuristics with exact optimization techniques is a typical example of an approach that belongs to the last category [DS03, RP08]: On the one hand, exact optimization techniques such as integer linear programming or constraint programming can be used within metaheuristics to reduce the solution space, to efficiently search large neighborhoods, to merge solutions, or to gain additional information to guide the search by solving a relaxation of the tackled problem. On the other hand, many exact optimization techniques rely on good bounds to restrict the area of the solution space that has to be examined; therefore, metaheuristics can be used to quickly obtain good and feasible solutions [Rot07].

3 Algorithmic Advances Based Upon Genetic Algorithms

This section describes some key aspects of our activities in the field of algorithm development. The enhanced algorithmic concepts discussed here aim to hybridize the general concept of genetic algorithms in a generic and bionically inspired way and somehow denoted the beginnings of our research activities in this field. Due to their generality, the enhanced algorithms could be applied successfully to benchmark real world problems in the field of combinatorial optimization, nonlinear structure identification, and simulation-based optimization. Some of these application oriented aspects of these hybrid algorithms are discussed in Section 4 and Section 5.

Before the main ideas of the enhanced GA concepts will be described, we state some considerations about the general functioning of genetic algorithms and their convergence behavior.

3.1 The Unique Selling Points of Genetic Algorithms

Genetic algorithms operate under assumptions that are fundamentally different from those of trajectory-based heuristic optimization techniques such as simulated annealing or tabu search, and also in contrast to population-based heuristics which perform parallel local search as for example the conventional variants of evolution strategies (ES without recombination). When discussing genetic algorithms we also include genetic programming which, from an algorithmic point of view, may be considered as a special case of a genetic algorithm.

A neighborhood-based method usually scans the search space around a current solution in a predefined neighborhood in order to move to more promising directions, and are therefore often confronted with the problem of getting stuck in a local, but not global, optimum of a multimodal solution space.

What makes GAs unique compared to neighborhood-based search techniques is the crossover procedure which is able to assemble properties of solution candidates which may be located in very different regions of the search space. In this sense, the ultimate goal of any GA is to assemble and combine the essential genetic information (i.e. the alleles of a globally optimal or at least high quality solution) step by step. This information is initially scattered over many individuals and must be merged to single solution candidates (chromosomes) by the final stage of the evolutionary search process. This perspective, which is under certain assumptions stated in the variants of the well-known schema theory and the according building block hypothesis [Gol89], should ideally hold for any GA variant. This is exactly the essential property that has the potential to make GAs much more robust against premature stagnation in locally optimal solutions than search algorithms working without crossover.

Schema Theorem and Building Block Hypothesis   3.2

Researchers working in the field of GAs have put a lot of effort into the analysis of the genetic operators (crossover, mutation, selection). In order to achieve better analysis and understanding, Holland has introduced a construct called schema [Hol75a]:

Assuming the use of a canonical GA with binary string representation of individuals, the symbol alphabet $\{0,1,\#\}$ is considered where $\{\#\}$(don't care) is a special wild card symbol that matches both, 0 and 1. A schema is a string with fixed and variable symbols. For example, the schema [0#11#01] is a template that matches the following four strings: [0011001], [0011101], [0111001], and [0111101]. The symbol # is never actually manipulated by the genetic algorithm; it is just a notational device that makes it easier to talk about families of strings.

Essentially, Holland's idea was that every evaluated string actually gives partial information about the fitness of the set of possible schemata of which the string is a member. Holland analyzed the influence of selection, crossover and mutation on the expected number of schemata, when going from one generation to the next. A detailed discussion of related analysis can be found in [Gol89]; in the context of the present work we only outline the main results and their significance.

Assuming fitness proportional replication, the number m of individuals of the population belonging to a particular schema H at time $t + 1$ (i.e., $m(H, t + 1)$) can be calculated and depends on the average fitness value of the string representing schema H and the average fitness value over all strings within the population. Assuming that a particular schema remains above the average by a fixed amount for a certain number of generations, $m(H, t)$ can be calculated directly.

Considering the effect of crossover which breaks apart strings apart (at least in the case of canonical genetic algorithms) we see that short defining length schemata are less likely to be disrupted by a single point crossover operator. The main result is that above average schemata with short defining lengths will still be sampled at an exponential increasing rate; these schemata with above average fitness and short defining length are the so-called building blocks and play an important role in the theory of genetic algorithms.

Using several considerations and proofs given in [Hol75a] one can described effects of mutation, crossover, and reproduction and up with Holland's well known schema theorem:

$$m(H, t + 1) \geq m(H, t)\frac{f_H(t)}{\overline{f}(t)}[1 - p_c\frac{\delta(H)}{l - 1} - o(H)p_m] \tag{1}$$

where $f_H(t)$ is the average fitness value of individuals represented by H, $\overline{f}(t)$ the average fitness of all individuals in the population, $\delta(H)$ the defining length of a schema H (i.e., the distance between the first and the last fixed string position), $o(H)$ the order of H (i.e., the number of non-wildcard positions in H), and p_c and p_m the probabilities of crossover and mutation, respectively.

This result essentially says that the number of short schemata with low order and above average quality grows exponentially in subsequent generations of a genetic algorithm.

The major drawback of the building block theory is given by the fact that the underlying GA (binary encoding, proportional selection, single-point crossover, strong mutation) is applicable only to very few problems as it requires more sophisticated problem representations and corresponding operators to tackle challenging real-world problems.

Keeping in mind that the ultimate goal of any heuristic optimization technique is to approximately and efficiently solve highly complex real-world problems rather than stating a mathematically provable theory that holds only under very restricted conditions, our intention for an extended building block theory is a not so strict formulation that in return can be interpreted for arbitrary GA applications. At the same time, the enhanced variants of genetic algorithms and genetic programming proposed in this section aim to support the algorithms in their intention to operate in the sense of an extended building block interpretation discussed in the following sections.

Stagnation and Premature Convergence   3.3

The fundamental problem which many meta-heuristic optimization methods aim to counteract with various algorithmic tricks is the stagnation in a locally, but not globally, optimal solution. As stated previously, due to their methodology GAs and GP suffer much less from this problem.

Unfortunately, also users of evolutionary algorithms using crossover frequently encounter a problem which, at least in its effect, is quite similar to the problem of stagnating in a local, but not global, optimum. This drawback, in the terminology of GAs called premature convergence, occurs if the population of a GA reaches such a suboptimal state that the genetic solution manipulation operators (crossover and mutation) are no longer able to produce offspring that outperform their parents (as discussed for example in [Fog94], [Aff03]). In general, this happens mainly when the genetic information stored in the individuals of a population does not contain the genetic information which is sufficient to further improve the solution quality.

Several methods have been proposed to combat premature convergence in genetic algorithms (see [LGX97], [Gao03], or [Gol89], e.g.). These include, for example, the restriction of the selection procedure, the operators and the according probabilities as well as the modification of the fitness assignment. However, all these methods are heuristic, and their effects vary with different problems and even problem instances. A critical problem in studying premature convergence therefore is the identification of its occurrence and the characterization of its extent. For example, Srinivas and Patnaik [SP94] use the difference between the average and maximum fitness as a standard to measure genetic diversity, and adaptively vary crossover and mutation probabilities according to this measurement.

Classical Measures for Diversity Maintenance

The term "population diversity" has been used in many papers to study premature convergence (e.g. [SFP93], [YA94]) where the decrease of population diversity (i.e. a homogeneous population) is considered as the primary reason for premature convergence.

The basic approaches for avoiding premature convergence discussed in GA literature aim to maintain genetic diversity. The most common techniques for this purpose are based upon pre-selection [Cav75], crowding [DeJ75], or fitness-sharing [Gol89]. The main idea of these techniques is to maintain genetic diversity by the preferred replacement of similar individuals [Cav75], [DeJ75] or by the fitness-sharing of individuals which are located in densely populated regions [Gol89]. While methods based upon those discussed in

[DeJ75] or [Gol89] require some kind of neighborhood measure depending on the problem representation, the approach given in [Gol89] is additionally quite restricted to proportional selection.

Limitations of Diversity Maintenance

In natural evolution the maintenance of genetic diversity is of major importance as a rich gene pool enables a certain species to adapt to changing environmental conditions. In the case of artificial evolution, the environmental conditions, for which the chromosomes are to be optimized, are represented in the fitness function which usually remains unchanged during the run of an algorithm. Therefore, we do not identify the reasons for premature convergence in the loss of genetic variation in general but more specifically in the loss of what we call essential genetic information, i.e. in the loss of alleles which are part of a global optimal solution. Even more specifically, whereas the alleles of high quality solutions are desired to remain in the gene pool of the evolutionary process, alleles of poor solutions are desired to disappear from the active gene pool in order to strengthen the goal-directedness of evolutionary search.

Therefore, in the following we denote the genetic information of the global optimal solution (which is unknown to the algorithm) as essential genetic information. If parts of this essential genetic information are missing or get lost, premature convergence is already predetermined in a certain way as only mutation (or migration in the case of parallel GAs [Alb05]) is able to regain this genetic information.

A very essential question about the general performance of a GA is whether or not good parents are able to produce children of comparable or even better fitness—after all, the building block hypothesis implicitly relies on this. Unfortunately, this property cannot be guaranteed easily for GA applications in general: The disillusioning fact here is that the user has to take care of an appropriate encoding in order to make this fundamental property hold.

Reconsidering the basic functionality of a GA, the algorithm selects two above average parents for recombination and sometimes (with usually rather low probability) mutates the crossover result. The resulting chromosome is then considered as a member of the next generation and its alleles are therefore part of the gene pool for the ongoing evolutionary process.

Reflecting the basic concepts of GAs, the following questions and associated problems arise:

- Is crossover always able to fulfill the implicit assumption that two above-average parents can produce even better children?
- Which of the available crossover operators is best suited for a certain problem in a certain representation?

- Which of the resulting children are "good" recombinations of their parents chromosomes?
- What makes a child a "good" recombination?
- Which parts of the chromosomes of above-average parents are really worth being preserved?

Conventional GAs are usually not always able to answer these questions in a satisfactory way, which should ideally hold for any GA application and not only for a canonical GA in the sense of the schema theorem and the building block hypothesis. These observations constitute the starting point for generic algorithmic enhancements as stated in the following chapters. The preservation of essential genetic information, widely independent of the actually applied representation and operators plays a main role.

Offspring Selection (OS)   3.4

The ultimate goal of the extended algorithmic concepts described in this chapter is to support crossover-based evolutionary algorithms, i.e. evolutionary algorithms that are ideally designed to function as a building-block assembling machines, in their intention to combine those parts of the chromosomes that define high quality solutions. In this context we concentrate on selection and replacement which are the parts of the algorithm that are independent of the problem representation and the according operators. Thus, the application domain of the new algorithms is very wide; in fact, offspring selection can be applied to any task that can be treated by genetic algorithms (of course also including genetic programming).

The unifying purpose of the enhanced selection and replacement strategies is to introduce selection after reproduction in a way that checks whether or not crossover and mutation were able to produce a new solution candidate that outperforms its own parents. Offspring selection realizes this by claiming that a certain ratio of the next generation (pre-defined by the user) has to consist of children that were able to outperform their own parents (with respect to their fitness values). OS implies a self-adaptive regulation of the actual selection pressure that depends on how easy or difficult it is at present to achieve evolutionary progress. An upper limit for the selection pressure provides a good termination criterion for single population GAs as well as a trigger for migration in parallel GAs.

As already discussed at length, the first selection step chooses the parents for crossover either randomly or in any other well-known way as for example roulette-wheel, linear-rank, or some kind of tournament selection strategy. After having performed crossover and mutation with the selected parents, we introduce a further selection mechanism that considers the success of the apparently applied reproduction. In order to assure that the progression of genetic search occurs mainly with successful offspring, this is done in such a way that the used crossover and mutation operators are able to create a sufficient number of children that surpass their parents' fitness. Therefore, a new parameter called success ratio ($SuccRatio \in [0, 1]$) is introduced. The success ratio is defined as the quotient of the next population members that have to be generated by successful mating in relation to the total population size. Our adaptation of Rechenberg's success rule ([Rec73], [Sch94]) for genetic algorithms says that a child is successful if its fitness is better than the fitness of its parents, whereby the meaning of "better" has to be explained in more detail: Is a child better than its parents, if it surpasses the fitness of the weaker parent, the better parent, or some kind of weighted average of both?

In order to answer this question, we have borrowed an aspect from simulated annealing: The threshold fitness value that has to be outperformed lies between the worse and the better parent and the user is able to adjust a lower starting value and a higher end value which are denoted as comparison factor bounds; a comparison factor ($CompFactor$) of 0.0 means that we consider the fitness of the worse parent, whereas a comparison factor of 1.0 means that we consider the better of the two parents. During the run of the algorithm, the comparison factor is scaled between the lower and the upper bound resulting in a broader search at the beginning and ending up with a more and more directed search at the end; this procedure in fact picks up a basic idea of simulated annealing.

In the original formulation of the offspring selection we have defined that in the beginning of the evolutionary process an offspring only has to surpass the fitness value of the worse parent in order to be considered as "successful"; as evolution proceeds, the fitness of an offspring has to be better than a fitness value continuously increasing between the fitness values of the weaker and the better parent. As in the case of simulated annealing, this strategy gives a broader search at the beginning, whereas at the end of the search process this operator acts in a more and more directed way. Having filled up the claimed ratio ($SuccRatio$) of the next generation with successful individuals using the success criterion defined above, the rest of the next generation $((1 - SuccRatio) \cdot |POP|)^5$ is simply filled up with individuals randomly chosen from the pool of individuals that were also created by crossover, but did not reach the success criterion. The actual selection pressure $ActSelPress$ at the end of generation i is defined by the quotient of individuals that had to be considered until the success ratio was reached and the number of individuals in the population in the following way:

$$ActSelPress = \frac{|POP_{i+1}| + |POOL_i|}{|POP_i|} \tag{2}$$

---

[5] $|POP|$ denotes the number of individuals in a population POP.

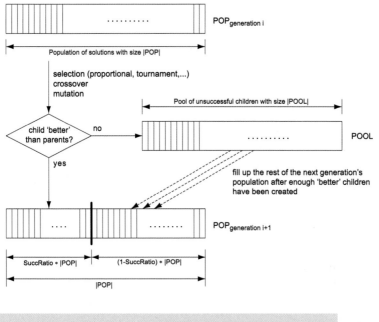

Embedding offspring selection into a genetic algorithm: Flowchart of the   FIGURE 4
embedding of offspring selection into a genetic algorithm.

Figure 4 shows the operating sequence of the concepts described above.

An upper limit of selection pressure (*MaxSelPress*) defines the maximum number of offspring considered for the next generation (as a multiple of the actual population size) that may be produced in order to fulfill the success ratio. With a sufficiently high setting of *MaxSelPress*, this new model also functions as a detector for premature convergence:

If it is no longer possible to find a sufficient number (SuccRatio · |POP|) of offspring outperforming their own parents, even if (MaxSelPress · |POP|) candidates have been generated, premature convergence has occurred.

As a basic principle of this selection model, higher success ratios cause higher selection pressures. Nevertheless, higher settings of success ratio, and therefore also higher selection pressures, do not necessarily cause premature convergence. The reason for this is mainly that the new selection step does not accept clones that emanate from two identical parents per definition. In conventional GAs such clones represent a major reason for premature convergence of the whole population around a suboptimal value, whereas the new offspring selection works against this phenomenon [AWWB09].

With all strategies described above, finally a genetic algorithm with the additional offspring selection step can be devised as stated in Algorithm 6. The algorithm is formulated for a maximization problem; in case of minimization problems the inequalities have to be changed accordingly.

Algorithm 6. Definition of a genetic algorithm with offspring selection

Initialize total number of iterations $nrOfIterations \in \mathbb{N}$
Initialize actual number of iterations $i = 0$
Initialize size of population $|POP|$
Initialize success ratio $SuccRatio \in [0, 1]$
Initialize maximum selection pressure $MaxSelPress \in \,]1, \infty[$
Initialize lower comparison factor bound $LowerBound \in [0, 1]$
Initialize upper comparison factor bound $UpperBound \in [LowerBound, 1]$
Initialize comparison factor $CompFactor = LowerBound$
Initialize actual selection pressure $ActSelPress = 1$
Produce an initial population POP_0 of size $|POP|$

while $(i < nrOfIterations) \wedge (ActSelPress < MaxSelPress)$ **do**
    Initialize next population POP_{i+1}
    Initialize pool for bad children $POOL$

    while $(|POP_{i+1}| < (|POP| \cdot SuccRatio)) \wedge$
        $((|POP_{i+1}| + |POOL|) < (|POP| \cdot MaxSelPress))$ **do**
        Generate a child from the members of POP_i based on their fitness
        values using crossover and mutation

        Compare the fitness of the child c to the fitness of its parents par_1 and par_2
        if $f_c \leq (f_{par_2} + |f_{par_1} - f_{par_2}| \cdot CompFactor)$ **then**
            Insert child into $POOL$
        else
            Insert child into POP_{i+1}
        end if
    end while
    $ActSelPress = \frac{|POP_{i+1}| + |POOL|}{|POP|}$

    Fill up the rest of POP_{i+1} with members from $POOL$
    while $|POP_{i+1}| \leq |POP|$ **do**
        Insert a randomly chosen child from $POOL$ into POP_{i+1}
    end while
    Adapt $CompFactor$ according to the given strategy
    $i = i + 1$
end while

3.5 Consequences Arising out of Offspring Selection

Typically, GAs operate under the implicit assumption that parent individuals of above average fitness are able to produce better solutions as stated in Holland's schema theorem and the related building block hypothesis. This general assumption, which ideally holds under the restrictive assumptions of a canonical GA using binary encoding, is often hard to fulfill for many practical GA applications. Some crucial question about the general functioning of GA-based methods shall be phrased and answered here in the context of offspring selection:

1. *Is crossover always able to fulfill the implicit assumption that two above-average parents can produce even better children?*
   Unfortunately, the implicit assumption of the schema theorem, namely that parents of above average fitness are able to produce even better children, is not accomplished for a lot of operators in many theoretical as well as practical applications. This disillusioning fact has several reasons: First,

a lot of operators tend to produce offspring solution candidates that do not meet the implicit or explicit constraints of certain problem formulations. Commonly applied repair strategies included in the operators themselves or applied afterwards have the consequence that alleles of the resulting offspring are not present in the parents which directly counteracts the building block aspect. In many problem representations it can easily happen that a lot of highly unfit child solution candidates arise even from the same pair of above average parents (think of GP crossover for example, where a lot of useless offspring solutions may be developed, depending on the concrete choice of crossover points). Furthermore, some operators have disruptive characteristics in that sense that the evolvement of longer building block sequences is not supported.

By using offspring selection (OS) the necessity that almost every trial is successful concerning the results of reproduction is no more that strict as only successful offspring become members of the active gene pool for the ongoing evolutionary process.

2. *Which of the available crossover operators is best suited for a certain problem in a certain representation?*

   For many problem representations of certain applications a lot of crossover concepts are available where it is often not clear a priori which of the possible operators is suited best. Furthermore, it is often also not clear how the characteristics of operators change with the remaining parameter settings of the algorithm or how the characteristics of the certain operators change during the run of the algorithm. So it may easily happen that certain (maybe more disruptive) operators perform quite well at the beginning of evolution whereas other crossover strategies succeed rather in the final (convergence) phase of the algorithm.

   In contrast to conventional GAs, for which the choice of usually one certain crossover strategy has to be done in the beginning, the ability to use more crossover and also mutation strategies in parallel is an important characteristic of OS-based GAs as only the successful reproduction results take part in the ongoing evolutionary process. It is also an implicit feature of the extended algorithmic concepts that when using more operators in parallel only the results of those will succeed which are currently able to produce successful offspring which changes over time. Even the usage of operator concepts that are considered evidentially weak for a certain application can be beneficial as long as these operators are able to produce successful offspring from time to time [Aff05].

3. *Which of the resulting children are "good" recombinations of their parents chromosomes?*

   Offspring Selection has been basically designed to answer this question in a problem independent way. In order to retain generality, these algorithms have to base the decision if and to which extent a given reproduction result is able to outperform its own parents by comparing the offspring's fitness with the fitness values of its own parent chromosomes. By doing so, we claim that a resulting child is a good recombination (which is a beneficial building block mixture) worth being part of the active gene pool if the child chromosome has been able to surpass the fitness of its own parents in some way.

4. *What makes a child a "good" recombination?*
   Whereas question 3 motivates the way how the decision may be carried out whether or not a child is a good recombination of its parent chromosomes, question 4 intuitively asks why this makes sense. Generally speaking, OS directs the selection focus after reproduction rather than before reproduction. In our claim this makes sense, as it is the result of reproduction that will be part of the gene pool and that has to keep the ongoing process alive. Even parts of chromosomes with below average fitness may play an important role for the ongoing evolutionary process, if they can be combined beneficially with another parent chromosome which motivates gender specific parents selection [WA05] as is for example applied in our GP experiments shown in the practical part of the book [AWWB09]. With this gender specific selection aspect, which typically selects one parent randomly and the other one corresponding to some established selection strategy (proportional, linear-rank, or tournament strategies) or even both parents randomly, we decrease selection pressure originating from parent selection and balance this by increasing selection pressure after reproduction which is adjusted self-adaptively depending on how easy or difficult it is to achieve advancement.

5. *Which parts of the chromosomes of parents of above-average fitness are really worth being preserved?*
   Ideally speaking, exactly those parts of the chromosomes of above-average parents should be transferred to the next generation that make these individuals above average. What may sound like a tautology at the first view cannot be guaranteed for a lot of problem representations and corresponding operators. In these situations, OS is able to support the algorithm in this goal which is essential for the building block assembling machines GAs and GP.

4 Route Planning

There are many combinatorial optimization problems on which heuristic optimization methods have been applied so far. In this section we will take a closer look at route planning as a representative for combinatorial optimization problems. We will also briefly show how other problem situations can be derived from the classical route planning problems described here.

The traveling salesman problem (TSP) is certainly one of the classical as well as most frequently analyzed representatives of combinatorial optimization problems with a lot of solution methodologies and solution manipulation operators. The problem is that a person has to visit a number of cities starting from and returning to his home city. The goal is to find a tour where every city is visited exactly once and where the travel distances become minimal. While this is the standard definition of the problem, it may not reveal the bigger amount of applications that are behind the TSP. For example the same problem exists in the manufacturing of circuit boards or in laser cutting where the problem is to find on a metal sheet or circuit board a short path between all locations where the machine has to perform some action; usually this is done by moving a tool on the surface. Because of mass production the machine will eventually return to the same position to start with the next unit. Optimizing the distances allows the machine to increase production speed.

A generalization of the TSP is known as the vehicle routing problem (VRP). In addition to the TSP problem of finding the shortest path, this generalization adds the problem of splitting the cities between multiple salesmen. Usually, when talking about the VRP, the terminology changes such that cities are interpreted as customers and each salesman is interpreted as a vehicle. Figure 5 exemplarily shows two solutions to a VRP problem. Generally the VRP describes a whole family of problems which requires the handling of implicit and explicit constraints and which makes it in some ways harder to solve than the TSP. Additionally, there are not many powerful problem-specific methods available, so that the problem is mostly dominated by metaheuristic approaches like tabu search, ant colony optimization and genetic algorithms. These are considered to be among the most powerful problem solving methods for the VRP.

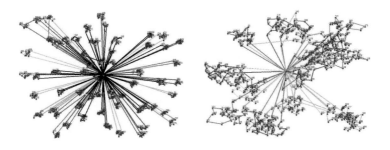

Two possible solutions to 600 customer CVRPtw problems.   FIGURE 5

4.1   The Vehicle Routing Problem

In principle, the vehicle routing problem (VRP) consists of finding an optimal
set of routes such that a number of customers are served in a most efficient
way. VRP stands for a group of problem variants with different requirements,
complexity and difficulty. A survey of the VRP is for example given in [Gol84].

Probably the simplest variant is the so called capacitated vehicle routing
problem (CVRP) where customers are demanding a number of goods delivered to them by a vehicle with limited capacity; typically this demand is
smaller than the capacity of a single vehicle. The sum of all demands on a
route cannot exceed the capacity of the vehicle assigned to this route; the
goal is to find the lowest number of routes servicing the customers in the
shortest possible time. If instead of the capacity the vehicles are limited by
the distance or time they are allowed to travel, the problem becomes known
as the "distance constrained vehicle routing problem" (DVRP), not to con-
fuse with the dynamic VRP which is sometimes also shortened to DVRP.
Distance and capacity restrictions can also be combined to form the "vehicle
routing problem with length constraints" (VRPLC or CVRPLC).

These restrictions form the basic model for a number of additional variants:
If customers have to be visited in a certain time slot, the problem becomes
known as the "vehicle routing problem with time windows" (VRPTW or
CVRPTW). A vehicle now has to visit a customer within a certain time
frame given by a ready time and a due date. It is generally allowed that a
vehicle may arrive before the ready time (in this case it simply waits at the
customer's place), but it is forbidden to arrive after the due date. However,
some models allow early or late servicing but with some form of additional
cost or penalty. These models are denoted "soft" time window models.

If customers are served from several depots, then the CVRP becomes the
"multiple depots vehicle routing problem" (MDVRP); in this variant each
vehicle starts and returns to the same depot. The problem can be solved by
splitting it into several single depot VRP problems if such a split can be done
effectively. Another variant that is often referred to is the pickup and delivery
VRP (PDVRP) where goods have to be picked up at certain locations and
delivered to other locations during the route. The problem can be modeled as
requiring the pickup phase to be finished before the delivery phase or allowing
to interleave these two phases.

Because in the nature of route planning there are also dynamic events that
occur during the execution of a plan, there are also dynamic VRP variants.
Here a new plan has to be computed very quickly for changing problem situations such as changing demands, travel times, customers canceling their
orders or new customers creating new orders. Additionally, so called, "dial-
a-ride" VRP variants received a lot of attention. These treat the problem of
inter-customer pick-up and delivery in a very dynamic order situation. Con-

ceptually, such a model can be thought of as combining urban taxi and bus transportation in that the destinations and routes are completely dynamic, but in part the way and thus the cost is shared among multiple people heading for similar directions. They are thus often referred to as "taxibus"; there are already several cities, e.g. London where such a system has already started operating. It is possible that these systems would be better able to solve the mass transportation requirements of the future.

Because the VRP is a problem with lots of use for real-world companies, many more variants may still exist that are tailored to the needs of a specific problem situation. In this chapter only the most important, and most mentioned ones have been described.

Optimization Goals

Due to the number of different variants and the real life relevance in logistics and industry, several different goals have been identified so far. The most common goals are the minimization of the travel time on the one hand and the minimization of the number of vehicles on the other hand. Other possibilities include to reduce the amount of waiting time at a customer location because of arrival before the customer is ready to be served, or to balance the workload most equally among the different vehicles.

There are several possibilities on how to deal with such a number of different and possibly conflicting goals. The first is to model the solution quality with respect to one goal (f_1) as a fitness value and introduce a feasibility level (a_i) for the other goals $(f_2, \ldots, f_n)$ which has to be satisfied. This can be written as

$$f(x) = f_1(x), \text{ with } f_2(x) < a_1 \wedge f_3(x) < a_2 \wedge \ldots \wedge f_n(x) < a_{n-1}$$

In this way one can search for solutions that minimize the travel time, but for example require a maximum waiting time at a customer location. Another possibility is to weigh the different goals and aggregate them into a single objective value, which can be written as:

$$f(x) = (f_1(x), f_2(x), \ldots, f_n(x)) * (\alpha_1, \alpha_2, \ldots, \alpha_n), \ \alpha_i \in \mathbb{R}$$

In this way it is possible to search for solutions that are optimal with some degree to each of the fitness functions. Note that the multiplication here denotes the scalar product and the resulting fitness is still just single valued. The third possibility is to apply multi-objective optimization techniques. In this case the fitness is actually a vector of values, where each dimension represents the fitness with respect to one goal. Applying multi-object optimization allows to optimize solutions with conflicting goals by using a concept known as Pareto dominance. One solution is said to dominate another solution if it is better with respect to every optimization goal. In the case when all goals have to be minimized, this can be written as

$$x \text{ dominates } y \Leftrightarrow \forall i : f_i(x) < f_i(y).$$

Two solutions are called non-dominated if they are each better than the other in at least one of the goals. Similar to above, for minimization in every objective, this can be written as

$$x \text{ and } y \text{ are non-dominated } \Leftrightarrow \exists i, j : f_i(x) < f_i(y) \wedge f_j(x) > f_j(y).$$

Several different optimization algorithms have been developed that are able to find a set of non-dominated solutions, known as pareto optimal solutions, from which a human expert could choose the best suited one.

The Link between Routing, Assignment and Scheduling

Routing problems such as the TSP and VRP can easily be transformed to an assignment problem or a scheduling problem, allowing one to solve different problem scenarios with relatively little application effort.

If e.g. the TSP is modified such that the locations of the cities, or rather "points", become flexible, it can be transformed into an assignment problem, such as the quadratic assignment problem (QAP). Here the goal is not to find the optimal route, but to minimize the sum of the weighted distances between the points, by assigning the points to a set of given locations. Each point is viewed as having a certain connection strength with other points; the further apart such strongly connected points lie, the worse the solution. Applications of the QAP include facility layout problems in service environments such as hospitals or in a manufacturing scenario, see for example [HK01]. The QAP itself can again be applied to multiple different problem situations, of different domains such as for example microarray layout [dCJR06].

If the term "vehicle" in a VRP is relaxed, numerous scheduling problems can also be modeled as CVRPs or CVRPTWs. An example is the following one: For a single machine we want to schedule a number of jobs for which we know the flow time and the time to go from one running job to the next one. This scheduling problem can be regarded as a VRPTW with a single depot, a single vehicle, and the customers representing the jobs. The cost of changing from one job to another is equal to the distance between the two customers, and the time it takes to perform an action is the service time of the job.

Heuristic algorithms   4.2

The field of inexact algorithms for the CVRP has been very active, far more active than that of exact algorithms; a long series of papers has been published over the recent years. Heuristic algorithms that build a set of routes from scratch are typically called route-building heuristics, while an algorithm that tries to produce an improved solution on the basis of an already available solution is denoted as route-improving.

The Savings Heuristic

At the beginning of the algorithm, each of the n customers (cities) is considered to be delivered with an own vehicle. For every pair of two cities a so-called savings value is calculated; this value specifies the reduction of costs which is achieved when the two routes are combined. Then the routes are merged in descending order of their saving values if all constraints are satisfied. According to [Lap92] the time complexity of the savings heuristic is given as $\mathcal{O}(n^2 \log n)$.

The Sweep Heuristic

The fundamental idea of the sweep heuristic is to perform a radar-like scanning of the customers and assign them to the current route as they would appear on a radar screen. If a constraint would be violated a new route is created. Naturally this heuristic works only well when the problem instance is geographical, meaning that routes are not overlapping each other too much. For the CVRPTW however such an overlap is possible quite easily. The time complexity of sweep heuristics is $\mathcal{O}(n \log n)$, which is equal to the complexity of a sorting algorithm.

The Push Forward Insertion Heuristic

The insertion heuristic, which Solomon described first and termed *I1* performed best in a number of test cases [Sol87]. It extends the savings heuristic insofar as it takes into account the prolongation of the arrival time at the next customer and is thus suitable for the CVRPTW as well. This function evaluates the difference between scheduling a customer directly and servicing it in an existing route between two customers. Mathematically it can be described as

$$I1(i, u, j) = \lambda t_{0u} - (\alpha_1(t_{iu} + t_{uj} - \mu t_{ij}) + \alpha_2(b_{j_u} - b_j)) \tag{3}$$

where t_{ij} denotes the travel time from location i to location j, b_j is the arrival at customer j, b_{j_u} is the arrival time when traveling to customer j over customer u. The parameters are restricted such that $\lambda, \mu, \alpha_1, \alpha_2 \geq 0$ and $\alpha_1 + \alpha_2 = 1$.

Solomon concludes that a hybridization of $I1$ with a sweep heuristic could achieve good solutions with a reasonable amount of computation. Such an approach can be found in [TPS96] where three different properties are taken into account to select the first customer of each route: distance, due date, and the polar angle.

Remark on Sequential Route Building Heuristics

The problem of building one route at a time, as is done in the heuristics described above, is usually that the routes generated in the latter part of the process are of worse quality because the last unrouted customers tend to be scattered over the geographic area. Potvin and Rousseau [PR93] tried to overcome this problem of the insertion heuristic by building several routes simultaneously where the routes are initialized by using Solomon's insertion heuristic. Naturally the difficulty of a parallel route building approach is to define a priori the number of routes to be built. One thus needs to calculate a feasible number of routes that is close to the optimum, or alternatively apply a post processing step where it is tried to merge routes again.

4.3 Metaheuristic Approaches

Genetic Algorithms

Applying genetic algorithms to vehicle routing problems with or without time constraints is a rather young field of research and therefore, even if a lot of work has been performed, no widely accepted standard representations or operators have yet been established. In the following we will in short discuss some of the more popular or promising proposals.

A two phase approach is described in [TOS94]. There a genetic algorithm that performs the clustering of customers into routes is combined with a route construction heuristic to find the shortest path within the clusters. The genetic algorithm of Potvin and Bengio [PB96] has just one phase and operates on chromosomes of feasible solutions only. The selection of parent solutions is stochastic and biased towards the best solutions. Two different crossovers were created specifically for this problem. However, they rarely produce valid solutions and the results therefore have to undergo a repair phase. The reduction of the number of vehicles is performed by two mutation operators, as well as by a local search phase. A cellular genetic algorithm has been proposed in [AD04]. It uses an encoding with unique trip delimiters such that the whole solution representation is syntactically equal to a TSP path encoding. In addition to mutation there is also a local search phase which is conducted after every generation.

The application of offspring selectionon the VRP is described in [AWWB09]. It builds upon the representation of Potvin and Bengio, except that good solutions can also be obtained without using a repair method. Naturally using a repair method eases solving the problem, but offspring selection itself implicitly repairs the genes as only those children are successful that would not require a repair procedure. The GA with offspring selection scaled very well on the CVRP problem instances and achieved average solution qualities within 1% to the best known solution on 75, 100, as well as on 150 customer problem instances. It has also been shown that it is able to exploit the diversity of a population better and thus increases the chance to converge into a very good fitness region.

Ant Colony Optimization

Ant colony optimization (ACO) has been applied successfully to the vehicle routing problem as well. It is a very well-suited metaheuristic to solve the VRP as it basically guides a construction heuristic to create a solution. For the VRP a lot of work has been devoted to build efficient construction heuristics, which however lag behind in solution quality. ACO is able to build on these and improve solution quality further through the use of memory in the form of a pheromone matrix. MACS-VRPTW [GTA99] is a well-known variant of an ant colony system (ACS) for the optimization of the CVRPTW. It uses separate colonies for optimizing the number of vehicles and for optimizing the total travel time. At the time it was introduced it was able to improve the best known solutions for several problem instances.

Tabu Search

Tabu search (TS) is another very successful metaheuristic for solving the VRP. Numerous approaches have been presented to apply TS on the VRP. For single-objective approaches the application of TS is straight-forward, for multi-objective definitions it is necessary to adapt TS to include some kind of archive. Because the way tabu search is designed, namely as metaheuristic with several memories to guide, restart or intensify the search, adding such an archive lies well within the definition of TS. A multi-objective approach is for example described in [Beh07]. Here a number of parallel TS approaches are presented ranging from synchronous to asynchronous methods and including single trajectory searches as well as cooperative approaches. Especially the cooperative approach was able to cover more of the pareto front than those with just a single search trajectory. The asynchronous approach performed fastest, though it did not strictly follow the tabu search idea of best improvement local search. There a master distributes the solutions to be evaluated among several slave nodes and uses an acceptance criterion to decide whether the search should wait for more results of the current neighborhood or proceed by choosing a solution and build the next neighborhood. In each iteration all solutions, even from previous neighborhoods are considered. The algorithm was applied on several benchmark problems on an Origin 3800 and used up to 12 processors. The described TS also uses a restart strategy for diversification of the search when no further improvements can be made for a number of iterations.

5 Genetic Programming Based System Identification

5.1 Genetic Programming

In the previous sections we have summarized and discussed foundations, extensions and applications of genetic algorithms; it has been illustrated how this kind of algorithms is able to produce high quality results for a variety of problem classes. Still, a GA is by itself not able to handle one of the most challenging tasks in computer science, namely getting a computer to solve problems without programming it explicitly. As Arthur Samuel stated in 1959 [Sam59], this central task can be formulated in the following way: *How can computers be made to do what needs to be done, without being told exactly how to do it?*

In this chapter we give a compact description and discussion of an extension of the genetic algorithm called genetic programming (GP) . Similar to GAs, genetic programming works on populations of solution candidates for a given problem and is based on Darwinian principles of survival of the fittest (selection), recombination (crossover), and mutation; it is a domain-independent, biologically inspired method that is able to create computer programs from a high-level problem statement[6].

Research activities in the field of genetic programming started in the 1980s; still, it took some time until GP was widely received by the computer science community. Since the beginning of the 1990s GP has been established as a human-competitive problem solving method. The main factors for its widely accepted success in the academic world as well as in industries can be summarized in the following way [Koz92a]: Virtually all problems in artificial intelligence, machine learning, adaptive systems, and automated learning can be recast as a search for computer programs, and genetic programming provides a way to successfully conduct the search in the space of computer programs.

Similar to the GA, GP is an evolutionary algorithm inspired by biological evolution to find computer programs that perform a user-defined computational task. It is therefore a machine learning technique used to optimize a population of computer programs according to a fitness landscape determined by a program's ability to perform the given task; it is a domain-independent, biologically inspired method that is able to create computer programs from a high-level problem statement (with computer programs being here defined as entities that receive inputs, perform computations, and produce output).

As in the context of any GA-based problem solving process, the representation of problem instances and solution candidates is a key issue also in genetic programming. On the one hand, the representation scheme should enable the algorithm to find suitable solutions for the given problem class, but on the other hand the algorithm should be able to directly manipulate the coded solution representation. The use of fixed-length strings (of bits, characters or integers, e.g.) enables the conventional GA to solve a huge amount of problems and also allows the construction of a solid theoretical foundation, namely the schema theorem. Still, in the context of GP the most natural representation for a solution is a hierarchical computer program of variable size [Koz92a].

So, how can hierarchical computer programs be represented? The representation that is most common in literature and is used by Koza ([Koz92a], [Koz94], [KIAK99], [KKS+03]), Langdon and Poli ([LP02]), and many other authors is the point-labeled structure tree.

As genetic programming is an extension to the genetic algorithm, GP also uses two main operators for producing new solution candidates in the search space, namely crossover and mutation: In the case of genetic programming,

---

[6] Please note that we here in general see computer programs as entities that receive inputs, perform computations, and produce output.

crossover is seen as the exchange of parts of programs resulting in new program structures, and mutation is applied by modifying a randomly chosen node of the respective structure tree: A sub-tree could be deleted or replaced by a randomly re-initialized sub-tree, or a function node could for example change its function type or turn into a terminal node. Of course, numerous other mutation variants are possible, many of them depending on the problem and chromosome representation chosen. Figure 6 shows exemplary operations on structure trees representing formulas in GP.

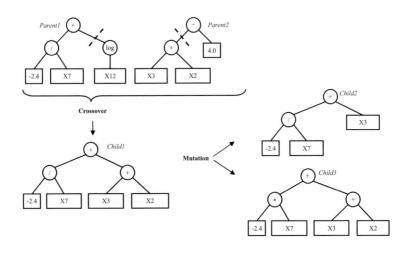

FIGURE 6   Exemplary operations on structure trees representing formulas in GP: The crossover of programs *Parent1* and *Parent2* can for example lead to *Child1*; this model could by mutated be transformed to *Child2* or *Child3*.

Figure 7 illustrates the main components of the GP process as also given for example in [LP02]; please note that this chart shows an enhanced version of the GP cycle also including offspring selection as described in Section 3.4.

We are not going to say much about non tree-based GP systems in this section; still, the reader could be prone to suspect that there might be computer program representations other than the tree-based approach. In fact, there are two other forms of GP that shall be mentioned here whose program encoding differs significantly from the approach described before: *Linear* and *graphical genetic programming*. Explanations and examples can be for example found in [LP02] and [Pol99].

Of course there is a lot of GP-related information available on the Internet including theoretical background and practical applications, course slides and source code. Probably the most comprehensive overview of publications in GP is the GP bibliography maintained by Langdon, Gustafson, and Koza (which is available at http://www.cs.bham.ac.uk/~wbl/biblio/).

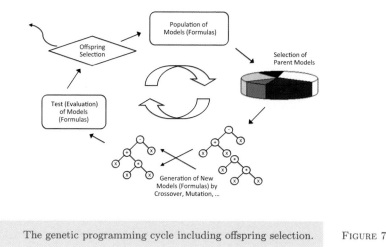

The genetic programming cycle including offspring selection.   FIGURE 7

Data Based Modeling and Structure Identification   5.2

In general, data mining is understood as the practice of automatically searching large stores of data for patterns. Nowadays, incredibly large (and quickly
growing) amounts of data are collected in commercial, administrative, and
scientific databases. Several sciences (e.g., molecular biology, genetics, astro-
physics, and many others) produce extreme amounts of information which
are often collected automatically. This is why it is impossible to analyze
and exploit all these data manually; what we need are intelligent computer
systems that can extract useful information (such as general rules or interesting patterns) from large amounts of observations. In short, "data mining
is the non-trivial process of identifying valid, novel, potentially useful, and
ultimately understandable patterns in data" [FPSS96].

One of the ways how genetic algorithms and, more precisely, genetic programming can be used in data mining is its application in data-based modeling. A given system is to be analyzed and its behavior is to be described
by a mathematical model; the process is therefore (especially in the context
of modeling dynamic physical systems) called system identification. In this
context we use data including a set of variables (features), of which one (or
more) is specified as the target variable(s); target variables are to be described using other variables and a mathematical model. Modeling numerical
data consisting of values of a target variable and of one or more independent
variables (also denoted as explanatory variables) is called regression.

In principle, the main goal of regression is to determine the relationship
of a dependent (target) variable t to a set of specified independent (input)
variables x. Thus, what we want to get is a function f that uses x and a set

of coefficients w such that

$$t = f(x, w) + \epsilon \tag{4}$$

where ϵ represents the error (noise) term.

Applying this procedure we assume that a model can be created with which it will also be able to predict correct outputs for other data examples (test samples); from the training data we want to generalize to situations not known (or allowed to analyze) during the training phase.

When it comes to evaluating a model (i.e., a solution candidate in a GP based modeling algorithm), the formula has to be evaluated on a certain set of evaluation (training) data X yielding the estimated values E. These estimated target values are compared to the original values T, i.e. those which are known from data retrieval (experiments) or calculated applying the original formula to X. This comparison is done by calculating the error between original and calculated target values; there are several ways how to measure this error, one of the simplest and probably most frequently used ones is the mean squared error (mse) function.

Accuracy (on training data) is not the only requirement for the result of the modeling process: Compact and (if possible) minimal models are preferred as they can be used in other applications easier. One of the major problems of in data-based modeling is *overfitting*: It is, of course, not easy to find that models that ignore unimportant details and capture the behavior of the system that is analyzed; due to this challenging character of the task of system identification, modeling has been considered as "an art" [Mor91].

The following two phases in data-based modeling are often distinguished: Structural identification and parameter optimization.

- First, structural identification is hereby seen as the determination of the structure of the model for the system which is to be analyzed; physical knowledge, for example, can influence the decision regarding the mathematical structure of the formula. This of course includes the determination of the functions used, the order of the formula (in the case of polynomial approaches, e.g.) and, in the case of dynamical models, potential time lags for the input variables used.
- Parameter identification is then the second step: Based on training data, the parameters of the formula are determined (optimized) which means that the coefficients and, if used, time lags are fixed.

Using Genetic Programming for data-based modeling has the advantage that we are able to design an identification process that automatically incorporates variables selection, structural identification and parameters optimization in one process.

When applying genetic programming to data-based modeling the function f, which is searched for, is not of any pre-specified form; low-level functions are during the GP process combined to more complex formulas. Given a set of functions $f_1, \ldots, f_u$, the overall function induced by genetic programming can take a variety of forms. Usually, standard arithmetical functions such as addition, subtraction, multiplication, and division are considered, but also trigonometric, logical, and more complex functions can be included.

Thus, the key feature of this technique is that the object of search is a symbolic description of a model, not just a set of coefficients in a pre-specified model. This is in sharp contrast with other methods of regression, including linear regression, polynomial approaches, or also artificial neural networks, where a specific structure is assumed and often only the complexity of this model can be varied.

We have in recent years successfully applied GP-based system identification, especially in the context of identifying models for technical, mechatronical systems as well as in the analysis of medical data sets. In the two following sections we give a compact introduction to these application fields and some examples; an extensive overview of these application fields, a lot of application examples and empirical analysis of algorithmic enhancements of the GP-based system identification process can for example be found in [Win08].

In particular, enhanced gender specific parents selection [AWWB09] (combining random and proportional selection) has been used in GP very successfully, especially in combination with strict offspring selection. This means that both critical parameters of OS, namely success ratio and comparison factor, have been set to 1.0 so that only those children that are better than both parents are selected to become members of the next generation's population.

Application Example: Time Series Analysis   5.3

Whenever (input or output) data of any kind of system are recorded over time and compiled in data collections as sequences of data points, these sequences are called *time series*; typically, these data points are recorded at time intervals which are often, but not always, uniform.

The collection of methods and approaches which are used for trying to understand the underlying mechanisms that are documented in a time series is called *time series analysis*; not only do we want to know what produced the data, but we are also interested in predicting future values, i.e. we want to develop models that can be used as predictors for the system at hand.

There is a lot of literature on theory and different approaches to time series analysis. One of the most famous approaches is the so-called Box-Jenkins approach, which includes separate model identification, parameter estimation and model checking steps.

The main principle can be formulated in the following way: For a given target time series T storing the values $T_{(1)}, \ldots, T_{(n)}$ and a given set of variables $X_1, \ldots, X_N$ we search for a model f that describes T as

$$T_{(t)} = f(X_{1(t)}, X_{1(t-1)}, \ldots, X_{1(t-t_{max})},$$

$$\ldots,$$

$$X_{N(t)}, X_{N(t-1)}, \ldots, X_{N(t-t_{max})}) + \epsilon_t$$

where t_{max} is the maximum number of past values, and ϵ_t is an error term.

Of course, the field of applications of time series analysis is huge and includes for example astronomy, sociology, economics or (as demonstrated below) the analysis of physical systems. Of course it is not at all natural that any physical system, may it be technical or not, can be represented by a simple and easily understandable model.

A lot of research work of members of the Heuristic and Evolutionary Algorithms Laboratory (HEAL) in the area of system identification using GP was done in cooperation with the Institute for Design and Control of Mechatronical Systems (DesCon) at JKU Linz, Austria. The framework and the main infrastructure was given by DesCon who maintain a dynamical motor test bench manufactured by AVL, Graz, Austria; a BMW diesel motor is installed on this test bench, and a lot of parameters of the ECU (engine control unit) as well as engine parameters and emissions are measured. During several years of research on the identification of NO_x and soot emissions, members of DesCon have tried several modeling approaches, some of them being purely data-based as for example those using artificial neural networks (ANNs). Due to rather unsatisfactory results obtained using ANNs, the ability of GP to produce reasonable models was investigated in pilot studies; we are here once again thankful to Prof. del Re for initiating these studies.

In this context, our goal is to use system identification approaches in order to create models that are designed to replace or support physical sensors; we want to have models that can be potentially used instead of these physical sensors (which can be damageable or simply expensive). This is why we are here dealing with the design of so-called *virtual sensors*.

Figure 8 shows a detail of the evaluation of the models produced by GP and ANN on validation data: As we see clearly, both virtual sensors do not capture the behavior completely correctly, but the GP model's fit seems to be better than the one of the ANN model. A more detailed description of the algorithms used and a discussion of the obtained results can be found in [AdRWL05].

A lot of research results in the context of identifying models for diesel engine emissions have been published in cooperation with the Institute of Design and Control of Mechatronical Systems, see for example [WAW04], [dRLF+05], [AdRWL05], [WEA+06] [WAW07b], and [Win08].

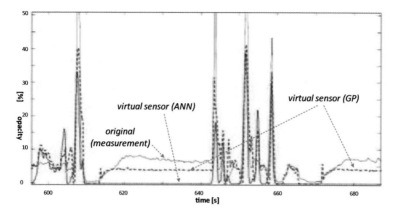

Evaluation of models for particulate matter emissions of a diesel engine   FIGURE 8
(snapshot showing the evaluation of the model on validation/test samples), as given in [AdRWL05].

Application Example: Solving Classification Problems   5.4

Classification is understood as the act of placing an object into a set of categories, based on the object's properties. Objects are classified according to
an (in most cases hierarchical) classification scheme also called taxonomy.
Amongst many other possible applications, examples of taxonomic classification are biological classification (the act of categorizing and grouping living
species of organisms), medical classification and security classification (where
it is often necessary to classify objects or persons for deciding whether a problem might arise from the present situation or not). A statistical classification
algorithm is supposed to take feature representations of objects and map
them to a special, predefined classification label. Such classification algorithms are designed to learn (i.e. to approximate the behavior of) a function
which maps a vector of object features into one of several classes; this is done
by analyzing a set of input-output examples ("training samples") of the function. Since statistical classification algorithms are supposed to "learn" such
functions, we are dealing with a specific area of *machine learning* and, more
generally, *artificial intelligence*.

In a more formal way, the classification problem can be formulated in the
following way: Let the data consist of a set of samples, each containing k
feature values $x_{i1}, \ldots, x_{ik}$ and a class value y_i. We look for a function f that
maps a sample x_i to one of the c classes available:

$$f : X \rightarrow C; \tag{5}$$
$$\forall x_i \in X : f(x_i) = f(x_{i1}, \ldots, x_{ik}) = z_i; z_i \in \{C_1, \ldots, C_c\} \tag{6}$$

where X denotes the feature vector space, z_i the predicted class for a sample i, and C the set of classes; the better a classification function f is, the more the original classifications y_i and the predicted classifications z_i will match when evaluating f on x_i.

There are several approaches which are nowadays used for solving data mining and, more specifically, classification problems. The most common ones are decision tree learning, instance-based learning, inductive logic programming (such as for example Prolog) and reinforcement learning.

In recent years we have successfully applied GP to the analysis of medical data. Concretely, we have used several benchmark data sets from the UCI machine learning repository[7] as well as real world data provided by Prof. Dr. Michael Binder from the Department of Dermatology at the Medical University Vienna, Austria. In all these cases a series of features is given for a set of patients who were potentially suffering from some disease (such as for example a heart disease, skin cancer or hypo- or hyperthyroidism); for all patients the final diagnosis is also given, so that for all patients the classification information (classifying each patient as diseased or healthy) was available. Thus, the main goal here is to identify models that are able to formulate the relationship between measured features of the patients and the eventual medical diagnosis as mathematical equations; such an equation can then be used for example as a diagnosis support model or for explaining the relationship between easily measurable health parameters and diseases.

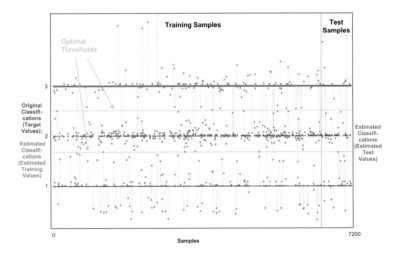

FIGURE 9   Graphical representation of the best result we obtained for the *Thyroid* data set, CV-partition 9: Comparison of original and estimated class values.

---

[7] http://www.ics.uci.edu/~mlearn/

Extensive discussions of empirical test in the context of medical data analysis using GP have been published in [WAW06], [WAW07a], and [Win08], e.g. In these articles we have also compared the results obtained using enhanced GP techniques to those produced by other classification approaches (as for example k-nearest-neighbors, artificial neural networks or support vector machines as described in Section 4.2) as well as standard GP implementations.

Graphical analysis can often help analyzing results achieved to any kind of problem; this is of course also the case in machine learning and in data-based classification. The most common and also simplest way how to illustrate classification results is to plot the target values and the estimated values into one chart; Figure 9 shows a graphical representation of the best result obtained for the *Thyroid* data set (taken from the UCI repository), cross-validation set 9.

Analysis of Population Dynamics in Genetic Programming   5.5

Of course, any modification of the standard GP procedure can have severe effects on internal genetic processes and population dynamics in GP; especially the use of strict offspring selection influences the GP process significantly. This is why we have used several approaches to describe and analyze GP population dynamics as for example the following ones:

- We have analyzed genetic propagation in GP in order to find out which individuals of the population are more or less able to pass on their genetic material to the next generation. On the one hand, better individuals (providing better genetic material) are supposed to pass on their genetic make-up more than other individuals; still, of course for the sake of genetic diversity also solutions that are not that good should also be able to contribute to the genetic process. In [WAW08a] and [Win08] we have summarized empirical studies using several data sets for analyzing the differences in GP population dynamics of different variants of genetic programming.
- When analyzing genetic diversity in GP we systematically compare the structural components of solutions in a GP population and so calculate how similar the individuals are to each other. Of course, on the one hand the GP optimization process is supposed to converge so that eventually all solutions will be more or less similar to each other, but on the other hand the genetic diversity should be maintained as long as possible (or necessary) in order to keep the genetic process active. In [WAW07c], [WAW08b] and [Win08] we have explained methods how to measure structural similarities in models, and we have also analyzed the respective differences discovered in various variants of genetic programming.

5.6   Data Mining and Genetic Programming

Data mining is one necessary step in the process of knowledge discovery. Other equally important steps include the preparation of data for the mining process and interpretation of generated models, see [FPSS96], [HMS01]. The goal of the process is to gain new knowledge about an observed system which can be utilized to improve aspects of the system for instance to gain a competitive advantage.

The power of the hypothesis space of GP and the white-box nature of models generated by GP make GP an interesting algorithm for data mining tasks. In the previous sections we gave a short description of typical data mining tasks where GP can be applied successfully. The conventional approach of data-based modelling with GP, however, has a few drawbacks. Compared to other well known data mining algorithms like CART, C4.5 or SVM, genetic programming is relatively time-consuming. This is not a serious issue if only a few GP runs are necessary, but usually many repetitions are necessary, because multiple genetic programming runs with identical parameter settings generate a diverse set of structurally different models with similar predictive accuracy. One cause for this is the vast and often unrestricted hypothesis space which allows infinitely many equivalent model representations. Also, GP is a heuristic method and has no mechanism to select the simplest or most compact model.

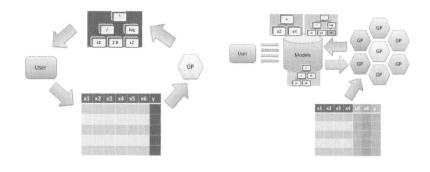

FIGURE 10   The conventional way of data-based modelling with GP (left side) has the drawback of a long feedback loop. The CEDMA approach allows interactive exploration and analysis of models created by GP agents that continuously analyze the data set and store new models in a central model store.

For these reasons it is difficult to extract knowledge out of GP results. The knowledge gained from these experiments is often limited to an insight into which variables play an important role in models for the target variable.

While this insight is often valuable in itself, statistical methods can also provide this insight with less effort. One important feature of GP namely its ability to find a fitting model structure while at the same time optimizing the model parameters cannot be utilized to its full extent.

An extension of the conventional approach that we call cooperative evolutionary data mining agents (CEDMA) can alleviate this problem and make it easier to gain new knowledge about an observed system. In this approach, multiple independent GP processes generate a large number of models for each possible target variable as well as for all input variables. It is useful to search for predictive models for input variables as well, because, if the final model should not include one particular input variable, it can be easily replaced with an appropriate model. The GP runs are parallelized globally to alleviate the problem of time consumption. Figure 10 shows the differences between the conventional approach and the extended CEDMA approach.

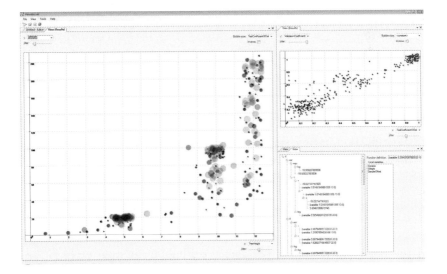

The user can explore the set of identified models and compare and analyze different models for the data set via a graphical user interface that visualizes quality and complexity attributes of specific models in an intuitive way.

FIGURE 11

The CEDMA approach generates a large number of models, however, only a few of them are actually interesting for the user, while most models represent trivial or already known relationships. Therefore, it is necessary to have a user-interface that makes it easy to explore this large set of models. We implemented a graphical user interface that visualizes multiple attributes like the complexity and prognostic quality of all models. Figure 11 shows two screen shots of this model exploration front end. The visualization makes it easy to analyze and compare different models. The user can find interesting models and learn about hidden relationships in an intuitive and interactive manner. The quality of any model can be inspected visually through line charts of the estimated and of the original value of the target variable, and through scatter plots showing the correlations of estimated vs. original values. In this way the user can build up knowledge step by step while drilling down into the details of the identified models. Another benefit of the front end is that the user can start to analyze results while the GP processes are still searching for new models and refining existing models.

In a further step this front end will be extended to make it possible to compose new models via abstraction and combination of other models.

6 Conclusion and Future Perspectives

In this chapter we have discussed basic principles as well as algorithmic improvements and applications of metaheuristics, with a decisive focus on genetic algorithms (GAs) and genetic programming (GP).

New problem independent theoretical concepts have been described and successfully applied to combinatorial optimization problems as well as structure identification in time series analysis and classification. In particular, we have presented enhanced concepts for GAs which enable a self-adaptive interplay of selection and solution manipulation operators. Thereby we delay the disappearance and facilitate the combination of alleles from the gene pool that represent solution properties of highly fit individuals (introduced as *relevant genetic information*).

Moreover, we proposed future research on fitness landscape characteristics and the detection of robust parameter settings for a wide range of problems. The latter is particularly relevant to encourage interdisciplinary use of metaheuristics. The cumbersome search for good parameter settings for each application or problem instance has so far posed a barrier for the broad and successful application of metaheuristics by users who have no solid background in computer science, as for example biologists, chemists, economists, or medical scientists.

Regarding algorithm development, we have observed two extremes: On the one hand, experts in metaheuristics tend to over-engineer and fine-tune metaheuristics for specific benchmark problems that are not representative for real-life applications; on the other hand, users who focus on a specific problem domain frequently lack the necessary programming skills to customize and extend standard algorithms and therefore cannot profit from the multitude of algorithmic improvements which have been introduced since the standard books about genetic algorithms published in the late eighties and early nineties.

In order to close this gap between research and application, we believe that a successive transfer of competence in algorithm development from heuristic optimization experts to users working on real-world applications is necessary. In HeuristicLab, all relevant parts of an algorithm (as for example population initialization, crossover, generational replacement, or offspring selection) can be easily rearranged or replaced via a graphical user interface. Researchers working in other domains will thus no longer have to use metaheuristics as black box techniques (which is frequently the case nowadays), but can use them as algorithms which can be modified and easily tuned to specific problem situations.

These results point the way forward and call for renewed endeavor and scientific curiosity. We will continue to conduct both, fundamental and applied research, in the rapidly growing discipline of metaheuristics, working together with companies in the pursuit of common scientific and economic goals.

Acknowledgements

The research described in this chapter has been performed in the frame of the following research projects of the Heuristic and Evolutionary Algorithms Laboratory (HEAL) in Hagenberg funded by the Austrian Research Promotion Agency (FFG), the Austrian Science Fund (FWF), the Upper Austrian Mechatronics Cluster (MC-cluster) as well as the regional government of Upper Austria (UA):

- GP based techniques for the design of virtual sensors (FWF)
- Cooperative Evolutionary Data Mining (UA)
- Production Planning Optimization (MC-cluster)
- Intelligent Production Steering (MC-cluster)
- Heuristic production fine planning in complex volatile systems (FFG)

Since October 2008 the research activities of the Heuristic and Evolutionary Algorithms Laboratory (HEAL) are consolidated in the Josef Ressel-Centre for Heuristic optimization (Heureka!)[8], which is one of the first three Josef-Ressel centres funded by the Austrian Research Promotion Agency (FFG).

---

[8] http://heureka.heuristiclab.com/

References

[AD04]   E. Alba and B. Dorronsoro. Solving the vehicle routing problem by using cel-
            lular genetic algorithms. In J. Gottlieb and G. R. Raidl, editors, *Evolutionary
            Computation in Combinatorial Optimization*, volume 3004 of *Lecture Notes
            in Computer Science*, pages 11–20, Coimbra, Portugal, 2004. Springer.

[AdRWL05]   D. Alberer, L. del Re, S. Winkler, and P. Langthaler. Virtual sensor design of
            particulate and nitric oxide emissions in a DI diesel engine. In *Proceedings of
            the 7th International Conference on Engines for Automobile ICE 2005*, 2005.
            Document Number: 2005-24-063.

[AEOP02]   Ravindra K. Ahuja, Özlem Ergun, James B. Orlin, and Abraham P. Punnen.
            A survey of very large-scale neighborhood search techniques. *Discrete Applied
            Mathematics*, 123(1-3):75–102, 2002.

[Aff03]   M. Affenzeller. *New Hybrid Variants of Genetic Algorithms: Theoretical and
            Practical Aspects*. Schriften der Johannes Kepler Universität Linz. Univer-
            sitätsverlag Rudolf Trauner, 2003.

[Aff05]   M. Affenzeller. *Population Genetics and Evolutionary Computation: Theo-
            retical and Practical Aspects*. Trauner Verlag, 2005.

[Alb05]   E. Alba. *Parallel Metaheuristics: A New Class of Algorithms*. Wiley Inter-
            science, 2005.

[AW05]   M. Affenzeller and S. Wagner. Offspring selection: A new self-adaptive selec-
            tion scheme for genetic algorithms. In B. Ribeiro, R. F. Albrecht, A. Dobnikar,
            D. W. Pearson, and N. C. Steele, editors, *Adaptive and Natural Computing
            Algorithms*, Springer Computer Science, pages 218–221. Springer, 2005.

[AWW07]   M. Affenzeller, S. Wagner, and S. Winkler. Self-adaptive population size
            adjustment for genetic algorithms. In Alexis Quesada-Arencibia, José Car-
            los Rodríguez, Roberto Moreno-Diaz jr., and Roberto Moreno-Diaz, editors,
            Proceedings of Computer Aided Systems Theory: EuroCAST 2007, Lecture
            Notes in Computer Science, pages 820–828. Springer, 2007.

[AWWB09]   M. Affenzeller, S. Winkler, S. Wagner, and A. Beham. *Genetic Algorithms
            and Genetic Programming Modern Concepts and Practical Applications*. CRC
            Press, 2009.

[Beh07]   Andreas Beham. Parallel tabu search and the multiobjective vehicle routing
            problem with time windows. In *Proceedings of the 21st IEEE International
            Parallel & Distributed Processing Symposium (IPDPS07)*, 2007.

[BFM97]   T. Bäck, D. B. Fogel, and Z. Michalewicz, editors. *Handbook of Evolutionary
            Computation*. Taylor and Francis, 1997.

[BRA05]   Christian Blum, Andrea Roli, and Enrique Alba. An introduction to meta-
            heuristic techniques. In E. Alba, editor, *Parallel Metaheuristics: A New Class
            of Algorithms*, Wiley Series on Parallel and Distributed Computing, chapter 1,
            pages 3–42. Wiley, 2005.

[BT94]   Roberto Battiti and Giampietro Tecchiolli. The Reactive Tabu Search. *ORSA
            Journal on Computing*, 6(2):126–140, 1994.

[BWA04]   Roland Braune, Stefan Wagner, and Michael Affenzeller. Applying genetic
            algorithms to the optimization of production planning in a real-world manu-
            facturing environment. In R. Trappl, editor, *Cybernetics and Systems 2004*,
            volume 1, pages 41–46. Austrian Society for Cybernetic Studies, 2004.

[Bäc96]   Thomas Bäck. *Evolutionary Algorithms in Theory and Practice*. Oxford
            University Press, 1996.

[Cav75]   D. Cavicchio. *Adaptive Search Using Simulated Evolution*. PhD thesis, Uni-
            versity of Michigan, 1975.

[Dar98]   Charles Darwin. *The Origin of Species*. Wordsworth Classics of World Liter-
            ature. Wordsworth Editions, 1998.

[dCJR06]   S.A. de Carvalho Jr. and S. Rahmann. Microarray layout as a quadratic assignment problem. In D. Hudson et al., editor, *Proceedings of the German Conference on Bioinformatics (GCB), volume P-83 of Lecture Notes in Informatics*, pages 11–20. Gesellschaft für Informatik, 2006.

[dCT02]   Leandro N. de Castro and Jonathan Timmis. *Artificial Immune Systems: A New Computational Intelligence Approach*. Springer, 2002.

[DeJ75]   K. A. DeJong. *An Analysis of the Behavior of a Class of Genetic Adaptive Systems*. PhD thesis, University of Michigan, 1975.

[DeJ06]   Kenneth A. DeJong. *Evolutionary Computation: A Unified Approach*. Bradford Books. MIT Press, 2006.

[DGG+07]   Karl F. Doerner, Michel Gendreau, Peter Greistorfer, Walter Gutjahr, Richard F. Hartl, and Marc Reimann, editors. *Metaheuristics: Progress in Complex Systems Optimization*. Operations Research/Computer Science Interfaces Series. Springer, 2007.

[DLJD00]   D. Dumitrescu, B. Lazzerini, L. C. Jain, and A. Dumitrescu. *Evolutionary Computation*. The CRC Press International Series on Computational Intelligence. CRC Press, 2000.

[dRLF+05]   L. del Re, P. Langthaler, C. Furtmüller, S. Winkler, and M. Affenzeller. NO_x virtual sensor based on structure identification and global optimization. In *Proceedings of the SAE World Congress 2005*, 2005. Document Number: 2005-01-0050.

[DS03]   Irina Dumitrescu and Thomas Stützle. Combinations of local search and exact algorithms. In G. Raidl, S. Cagnoni, J. J. R. Cardalda, D. W. Corne, J. Gottlieb, A. Guillot, E. Hart, C. G. Johnson, E. Marchiori, J.-A. Meyer, and M. Middendorf, editors, *Applications of Evolutionary Computing*, volume 2611 of *Lecture Notes in Computer Science*, pages 211–223. Springer, 2003.

[DS04]   Marco Dorigo and Thomas Stützle. *Ant Colony Optimization*. MIT Press, 2004.

[ESK01]   Russel C. Eberhardt, Yuhui Shi, and James Kennedy. *Swarm Intelligence*. The Morgan Kaufmann Series in Artificial Intelligence. Morgan Kaufmann, 1 edition, 2001.

[Fog94]   D. B. Fogel. An introduction to simulated evolutionary optimization. *IEEE Transactions on Neural Networks*, 5(1):3–14, 1994.

[Fog06]   David B. Fogel. *Evolutionary Computation: Toward a New Philosophy of Machine Intelligence*. IEEE Press Series on Computational Intelligence. IEEE Press, 3rd edition, 2006.

[FOW66]   Lawrence J. Fogel, Alvin J. Owens, and Michael J. Walsh. *Artificial Intelligence through Simulated Evolution*. Wiley, 1966.

[FPSS96]   U. M. Fayyad, G. Piatetsky-Shapiro, and P. Smyth. From data mining to knowledge discovery: An overview. *Advances in Knowledge Discovery and Data Mining*, 1996.

[FR95]   Thomas A. Feo and Mauricio G. C. Resende. Greedy randomized adaptive search procedures. *Journal of Global Optimization*, 6:109–133, 1995.

[Gao03]   Y. Gao. Population size and sampling complexity in genetic algorithms. In *Proceedings of the Genetic and Evolutionary Computation Conference (GECCO) 2003*, 2003.

[GLM00]   F. Glover, M. Laguna, and R. Martí. Fundamentals of scatter search and path relinking. *Control and Cybernetics*, 39:653–684, 2000.

[GLM03a]   Fred Glover, Manuel Laguna, and Rafael Martí. Scatter search. In A. Ghosh and S. Tsutsui, editors, *Advances in Evolutionary Computing - Theory and Applications*, Natural Computing Series. Springer, 2003.

[GLM03b]   Fred Glover, Manuel Laguna, and Rafael Martí. Scatter search and path relinking: Advances and applications. In Fred Glover and Gary A. Kochenberger, editors, *Handbook of Metaheuristics*, volume 57 of *International Series in*

Operations Research & Management Science, chapter 1, pages 1–35. Kluwer, 2003.

[Glo86] F. Glover. Future paths for integer programming and links to artificial intelligence. Computers & Operations Research, 13:533–549, 1986.

[Glo90] Fred Glover. Tabu search – part II. ORSA Journal on Computing, 2(1):4–32, 1990.

[Glo97] F. Glover. Tabu Search and Adaptive Memory Programming – Advances, Applications, and Challenges. In R. S. Barr, R. V. Helgason, and J. L. Kennington, editors, Advances in Metaheuristics, Optimization and Stochastic Modeling Technologies, volume 7 of Interfaces in Computer Science and Operations Research, pages 1–75. Springer, Boston, 1997.

[Glo99] Fred Glover. Scatter search and path relinking. In D. Corne, M. Dorigo, F. Glover, D. Dasgupta, P. Moscato, R. Poli, and K. V. Price, editors, New Ideas in Optimization, Advanced Topics in Computer Science, pages 297–316. McGraw-Hill, 1999.

[Gol84] B. L. Golden. Introduction to and recent advances in vehicle routing methods. Transportation Planning Models, pages 383–418, 1984.

[Gol89] D. E. Goldberg. Genetic Algorithms in Search, Optimization and Machine Learning. Addison Wesley Longman, 1989.

[GT60] B. Giffler and G. L. Thompson. Algorithms for solving production-scheduling problems. Operations Research, 8(4):487–503, 1960.

[GTA99] Luca Maria Gambardella, Ric Taillard, and Giovanni Agazzi. Macs-vrptw: A multiple ant colony system for vehicle routing problems with time windows. In New Ideas in Optimization, pages 63–76. McGraw-Hill, 1999.

[HK00] Alain Hertz and Daniel Kobler. A framework for the description of evolutionary algorithms. European Journal of Operational Research, 126:1–12, 2000.

[HK01] Peter M. Hahn and Jakob Krarup. A hospital facility layout problem finally solved. Journal of Intelligent Manufacturing, 12:487–496, 2001.

[HM01] P. Hansen and N. Mladenović. Variable Neighborhood Search: Principles and Applications. European Journal of Operational Research, 130:449–467, 2001.

[HMS01] David J. Hand, Heikki Mannila, and Padhraic Smyth. Principles of Data Mining (Adaptive Computation and Machine Learning). The MIT Press, August 2001.

[Hol75a] J. H. Holland. Adaption in Natural and Artifical Systems. University of Michigan Press, 1975.

[Hol75b] J.H. Holland. Adaptation in Natural and Artificial Systems. University of Michigan Press, Ann Arbor, Michigan, USA, 1975.

[KGV83] S. Kirkpatrick, C. D. Gelatt Jr., and M. P. Vecchi. Optimization by Simulated Annealing. Science, 220(4598):671–680, 1983.

[KIAK99] J. R. Koza, F. H. Bennett III, D. Andre, and M. A. Keane. Genetic Programming III: Darvinian Invention and Problem Solving. Morgan Kaufmann Publishers, 1999.

[KKS+03] J. R. Koza, M. A. Keane, M. J. Streeter, W. Mydlowec, J. Yu, and G. Lanza. Genetic Programming IV: Routine Human-Competitive Machine Learning. Kluwer Academic Publishers, 2003.

[Koz92a] J. R. Koza. Genetic Programming: On the Programming of Computers by Means of Natural Selection. The MIT Press, 1992.

[Koz92b] John R. Koza. The genetic programming paradigm: Genetically breeding populations of computer programs to solve problems. In Branko Soucek and the IRIS Group, editors, Dynamic, Genetic, and Chaotic Programming, pages 203–321. John Wiley, New York, 1992.

[Koz94] J. R. Koza. Genetic Programming II: Automatic Discovery of Reusable Programs. The MIT Press, 1994.

[KPP04] Hans Kellerer, Ulrich Pferschy, and David Pisinger. Knapsack Problems. Springer, 2004.

[Lap92] G. Laporte. The vehicle routing problem: An overview of exact and approximate algorithms. *European Journal of Operational Research*, 59:345–358, 1992.

[LGX97] Y. Leung, Y. Gao, and Z. B. Xu. Degree of population diversity - a perspective on premature convergence in genetic algorithms and its markov chain analysis. *IEEE Transactions on Neural Networks*, 8(5):1165–1176, 1997.

[LK73] S. Lin and B. W. Kernighan. An effective heuristic algorithm for the traveling-salesman problem. *Operations Research*, 21:498–516, 1973.

[LM86] M. Lundy and A. Mees. Convergence of an annealing algorithm. *Mathematical Programming*, 34(1):111–124, 1986.

[LMS03] Helena R. Lourenço, Olivier C. Martin, and Thomas Stützle. Iterated local search. In Fred Glover and Gary A. Kochenberger, editors, *Handbook of Metaheuristics*, volume 57 of *International Series in Operations Research & Management Science*, chapter 11, pages 321–353. Kluwer, 2003.

[LP02] W. B. Langdon and R. Poli. *Foundations of Genetic Programming*. Springer Verlag, Berlin Heidelberg New York, 2002.

[MC03] Pablo Moscato and Carlos Cotta. A gentle introduction to memetic algorithms. In Fred Glover and Gary A. Kochenberger, editors, *Handbook of Metaheuristics*, volume 57 of *International Series in Operations Research & Management Science*, chapter 5, pages 105–144. Kluwer, 2003.

[MF00] Z. Michalewicz and B. Fogel. *How to Solve It: Modern Heuristics*. Springer, 2000.

[Mic92] Z. Michalewicz. *Genetic Algorithms + Data Structures = Evolution Programs*. Springer, 1992.

[Mor91] F. Morrison. *The Art of Modeling Dynamic Systems: Forecasting for Chaos, Randomness, and Determinism*. John Wiley & Sons, Inc, 1991.

[Mos99] Pablo Moscato. Memetic algorithms: A short introduction. In D. Corne, M. Dorigo, and F. Glover, editors, *New Ideas in Optimization*, Advanced Topics in Computer Science, pages 219–234. McGraw-Hill, 1999.

[MP96] Heinz Mühlenbein and Gerhard Paaß. From recombination of genes to the estimation of distributions I. Binary parameters. In H.-M. Voigt, W. Ebeling, I. Rechenberg, and H.-P. Schwefel, editors, *Parallel Problem Solving from Nature - PPSN IV*, volume 1141 of *Lecture Notes in Computer Science*, pages 178–187. Springer, 1996.

[MRR⁺53] N. Metropolis, A. Rosenbluth, M. Rosenbluth, A. Teller, and E. Teller. Equation of state calculations by fast computing machines. *Journal of Chemical Physics*, 21:1087–1092, 1953.

[NLA⁺08] Antonio J. Nebro, Francisco Luna, Enrique Alba, Bernabé Dorronsoro, Juan J. Durillo, and Andreas Beham. AbYSS: Adapting scatter search to multi-objective optimization. *IEEE Transactions on Evolutionary Computation*, 12(4):439–457, 2008.

[Osm93] I.H. Osman. Metastrategy simulated annealing and tabu search algorithms for the vehicle routing problem. *Annals of Operations Research*, 41(1–4):421–451, 1993.

[PB96] J.-Y. Potvin and S. Bengio. The Vehicle Routing Problem with Time Windows - Part II: Genetic Search. *INFORMS Journal on Computing*, 8(2):165–172, 1996.

[Pol99] R. Poli. Parallel distributed genetic programming. In David Corne, Marco Dorigo, and Fred Glover, editors, *New Ideas in Optimization*, Advanced Topics in Computer Science, chapter 27, pages 403–431. McGraw-Hill, Maidenhead, Berkshire, England, 1999.

[PR93] J. Potvin and J. Rousseau. A parallel route building algorithm for the vehicle routing and scheduling problem with time windows. *European Journal of Operations Research*, 66:331–340, 1993.

[Rai06]   Günther R. Raidl. A unified view on hybrid metaheuristics. In Francisco Almeida, Maria J. Blesa Aguilera, Christian Blum, J. Marcos Moreno-Vega, Melquiades Perez Perez, Andrea Roli, and Michael Sampels, editors, *Proceedings of the Hybrid Metaheuristics Workshop*, volume 4030 of *Lecture Notes of Computer Science*, pages 1–12. Springer, 2006.

[Rec73]   I. Rechenberg. *Evolutionsstrategie: Optimierung technischer Systeme nach Prinzipien der biologischen Evolution*. Fromman-Holzboog Verlag, Stuttgart, Germany, 1973.

[Rec94]   Ingo Rechenberg. *Evolutionsstrategie '94*. Frommann-Holzboog, 1994.

[Rot07]   Edward Rothberg. An evolutionary algorithm for polishing mixed integer programming solutions. *INFORMS Journal on Computing*, 19(4):534–541, 2007.

[RP08]   Günther R. Raidl and Jakob Puchinger. Combining (integer) linear programming techniques and metaheuristics for combinatorial optimization. In C. Blum, M. J. Blesa Aguilera, A. Roli, and M. Sampels, editors, *Hybrid Metaheuristics - An Emerging Approach to Optimization*, volume 114 of *Studies in Computational Intelligence*, chapter 2, pages 31–62. Springer, 2008.

[Sam59]   A. L. Samuel. Some studies in machine learning using the game of checkers. In *IBM Journal of Research and Development*, volume 3, pages 211 – 229, 1959.

[Sch94]   H.-P. Schwefel. *Numerische Optimierung von Computer-Modellen mittels der Evolutionsstrategie*. Birkhäuser Verlag, Basel, Switzerland, 1994.

[SFP93]   R. E. Smith, S. Forrest, and A. S. Perelson. Population diversity in an immune systems model: Implications for genetic search. In *Foundations of Genetic Algorithms*, volume 2, pages 153–166. Morgan Kaufmann Publishers, 1993.

[Sol87]   M.M. Solomon. Algorithms for the Vehicle Routing and Scheduling Problem with Time Window Constraints. *Operations Research*, 35(2):254–265, 1987.

[SP94]   M. Srinivas and L. Patnaik. Adaptive probabilities of crossover and mutation in genetic algorithms. In *IEEE Trans. on Systems, Man, and Cybernetics*, volume 24, pages 656–667, 1994.

[Stü98]   Thomas Stützle. *Local Search Algorithms for Combinatorial Problems - Analysis, Algorithms and New Applications*. PhD thesis, TU Darmstadt, 1998.

[Tai91]   E. Taillard. Robust taboo search for the quadratic assignment problem. *Parallel computing*, 17(4-5):443–455, 1991.

[TOS94]   S. Thangiah, I. Osman, and T. Sun. Hybrid genetic algorithm simulated annealing and tabu search methods for vehicle routing problem with time windows. Technical report, Computer Science Department, Slippery Rock University, 1994.

[TPS96]   S. R. Thangiah, J.-Y. Potvin, and T. Sun. Heuristic approaches to vehicle routing with backhauls and time windows. *International Journal on Computers and Operations Research*, 23(11):1043–1057, 1996.

[VT99]   Christos Voudouris and Edward Tsang. Guided local search and its application to the traveling salesman problem. *European Journal of Operational Research*, 113(2):469–499, 1999.

[WA05]   S. Wagner and M. Affenzeller. SexualGA: Gender-specific selection for genetic algorithms. In N. Callaos, W. Lesso, and E. Hansen, editors, *Proceedings of the 9th World Multi-Conference on Systemics, Cybernetics and Informatics (WMSCI) 2005*, volume 4, pages 76–81. International Institute of Informatics and Systemics, 2005.

[WAW04]   S. Winkler, M. Affenzeller, and S. Wagner. New methods for the identification of nonlinear model structures based upon genetic programming techniques. In Z. Bubnicki and A. Grzech, editors, *Proceedings of the 15th International Conference on Systems Science*, volume 1, pages 386–393. Oficyna Wydawnicza Politechniki Wroclawskiej, 2004.

[WAW06]   S. Winkler, M. Affenzeller, and S. Wagner. Using enhanced genetic program-
            ming techniques for evolving classifiers in the context of medical diagnosis -
            an empirical study. In *Proceedings of the GECCO 2006 Workshop on Medi-
            cal Applications of Genetic and Evolutionary Computation (MedGEC 2006)*.
            Association for Computing Machinery (ACM), 2006.

[WAW07a]   S. Winkler, M. Affenzeller, and S. Wagner. Advanced genetic programming
            based machine learning. *Journal of Mathematical Modelling and Algorithms*,
            6(3):455–480, 2007.

[WAW07b]   S. Winkler, M. Affenzeller, and S. Wagner. Selection pressure driven slid-
            ing window genetic programming. In Alexis Quesada-Arencibia, José Car-
            los Rodríguez, Roberto Moreno-Diaz jr., and Roberto Moreno-Diaz, editors,
            Proceedings of Computer Aided Systems Theory: EuroCAST 2007, Lecture
            Notes in Computer Science, pages 272–274. Springer, 2007.

[WAW07c]   Stephan Winkler, Michael Affenzeller, and Stefan Wagner. Variables diversity
            in systems identification based on extended genetic programming. *Proceedings
            of the $16^t h$ International Conference on Systems Science*, 2:470–479, 2007.

[WAW08a]   S. Winkler, M. Affenzeller, and S. Wagner. Offspring selection and its effects
            on genetic propagation in genetic programming based system identification.
            In Robert Trappl, editor, *Cybernetics and Systems 2008*, volume 2, pages
            549–554. Austrian Society for Cybernetic Studies, 2008.

[WAW08b]   Stephan Winkler, Michael Affenzeller, and Stefan Wagner. On the reliability of
            nonlinear modeling using enhanced genetic programming techniques. In *Pro-
            ceedings of the Chaotic Modeling and Simulation Conference (CHAOS2008)*,
            2008.

[WEA+06]   S. Winkler, H. Efendic, M. Affenzeller, L. Del Re, and S. Wagner. On-line
            modeling based on genetic programming. *International Journal on Intelligent
            Systems Technologies and Applications*, 2(2/3):255–270, 2006.

[Win08]   S. Winkler. *Evolutionary System Identification - Modern Concepts and Prac-
            tical Applications*. PhD thesis, Institute for Formal Models and Verification,
            Johannes Kepler University Linz, 2008.

[YA94]   Y. Yoshida and N. Adachi. A diploid genetic algorithm for preserving popu-
            lation diversity - pseudo-meiosis GA. In *Lecture Notes in Computer Science*,
            volume 866, pages 36–45. Springer, 1994.

[YN97]   Takeshi Yamada and Ryohei Nakano. Job shop scheduling. In A. M. Za-
            lzala and P. J. Fleming, editors, *Genetic Algorithms in Engineering Systems*,
            volume 55 of *Control Engineering Series*, chapter 7, pages 134–160. The In-
            stitution of Electrical Engineers, 1997.

Chapter IV
Software Engineering – Processes and Tools

Gerhard Weiss, Gustav Pomberger
Wolfgang Beer, Georg Buchgeher, Bernhard Dorninger, Josef Pichler,
Herbert Prähofer, Rudolf Ramler, Fritz Stallinger, Rainer Weinreich

Introduction 1

Software engineering traditionally plays an important role among the different research directions located in the Software Park Hagenberg, as it provides the fundamental concepts, methods and tools for producing reliable and high quality software. Software engineering as a quite young profession and engineering discipline is not limited to focus on how to create simple software programs, but in fact introduces a complex and most of the time quite costly lifecycle of software and derived products. Some efforts have been made to define software engineering as a profession and to outline the boundaries of this emerging field of research [PP04, Som04]. Several different definitions of the term software engineering appeared since its first mentioning on a NATO Software Engineering Conference[1] in 1968. A good example of an early definition of the term software engineering which is often cited in the literature is the following:

> The practical application of scientific knowledge in the design and construction of computer programs and the associated documentation required to develop, operate, and maintain them. [Boe76]

Another generally accepted definition of software engineering was given by the IEEE Computer Society:

> (1) The application of a systematic, disciplined, quantifiable approach to the development, operation, and maintenance of software; that is, the application of engineering to software. (2) The study of approaches as in (1). [IEE90]

---

[1] Proceedings of the famous 1968 and 1969 NATO Software Engineering Workshops are available at http://homepages.cs.ncl.ac.uk/brian.randell/NATO/index.html

In a first, joint effort of a scientific and industrial initiative a commonly accepted knowledge base had been created with the goal to define the boundaries of the modern software engineering profession. This "Software Engineering Body of Knowledge" (SWEBOK) [ABD$^+$04] introduces the following ten relevant Knowledge-Areas (KAs):

- Software requirements
- Software design
- Software construction
- Software testing
- Software maintenance
- Software configuration management
- Software engineering management
- Software engineering process
- Software engineering tools and methods
- Software quality

In fact, empirical studies show that software products continue to reflect significantly lower quality than other industrial products and that software projects fail significantly more often than other projects. This clearly indicates that software production has not yet advanced from a handicraft to industrial production. As state-of-the art research in the software domain shows, this raises a very broad spectrum of research issues and themes. Software production can not longer be seen as an activity where a single gifted developer implements an unmated algorithm. Instead, to develop software products means to follow a clear process composed of a large number of possibly complex activities which may be spatially and temporally distributed across multiple development teams. Software continues to grow in size and complexity, and software is involved in most everyday activities, such as making a phone call, making payments and driving a car. An IEEE article titled "Why software fails" [Cha05] states that a typical mobile phone contains around two million lines of software code, and according to General Motors the software used in a car will have 100 million lines of code in 2010. This article also highlights the fact that failing software and IT projects tend to seriously hazard the economic activity of companies, as software typically implements and automates essential business activities. Identified reasons for this failure are as follows:

- Unrealistic or unarticulated project goals
- Inaccurate estimates of needed resources
- Badly defined system requirements
- Poor reporting of the project's status
- Unmanaged risks
- Poor communication among customers, developers, and users
- Use of immature technology
- Inability to handle the project's complexity

- Sloppy development practices
- Poor project management
- Stakeholder politics
- Commercial pressures

As several of these reasons indicate, a structured and precise defined set of requirements represents the basis for communication about the development progress, planned quality or changes within the products features over time. One of the major responsibilities of a software project manager is to balance the features and quality of software and the time and costs of development. Software development projects often fail according to an unbalanced focus on a specific aspect at the expense of others (e.g., a focus on the number of demanded software features at the expense of the quality of the software to be developed). Significant progress has been made over the past decades in establishing methods and techniques that help to master demands on software and the software development process. However, as the theory and practice of software engineering shows, a pressing need remains for improving these methods and techniques, inventing new ones, and proving their relevance in an industrial context.

This chapter overviews selected R&D activities conducted in response to this need at Software Competence Center Hagenberg GmbH (SCCH, http://www.scch.at) during the previous years. The chapter's focus is on four related key topics in software science which are of particular practical relevance:

- the software development process (Section 2)
- the quality of software (Section 3)
- architectures for software systems (Section 4)
- domain-specific languages and modeling (Section 5)

The work described in this chapter has been done in close cooperation with the Institute of Business Informatics – Software Engineering (Prof. Pomberger) and the Institute of System Software (Prof. Mössenböck) from Johannes Kepler University (JKU) Linz, which both are long-standing scientific partners of SCCH, with the intention to bridge the gap between latest scientific know-how in the area of software engineering on the one hand and software challenges companies are confronted with in their everyday business on the other hand.

Software Process Engineering 2

Informally spoken, a *software process* is the set of activities, methods, and practices that are used in the production and evolution of software. IEEE de-

fines a *process* as *"a sequence of steps performed for a given purpose"* [IEE90]
and more detailed a *software development process* as *"the process by which
user needs are translated into a software product (...)"*. For our purposes a
software process can be defined as a set of activities, methods, practices, and
transformations that people use to develop and maintain software and the associated work products (see [PCCW93]). It is important to note that we use
the term *software process* intentionally in a broad view referring not only to
an organization's overall software process, but to any process or sub-process
used by a software project or organization and any identifiable activity that
is undertaken to produce or support a software product or software service.
Besides planning, designing, coding, testing this view thus also includes activities like estimating, inspecting, reviewing, measuring, and controlling.

From a business point of view, the processes that software organizations
apply to develop products and services play a critical role in the implementation of strategies and related plans and objectives. Organizations that are
able to control their processes are able to better predict characteristics of their
products and services as well as costs and schedules and can improve the effectiveness, efficiency, and—as a consequence—profitability of their business
[FPC97].

From an engineering and scientific point of view, *software engineering* is
emerging and maturing as an engineering discipline [Sha90, Was96]. Although
it is recognized that due to the great variations among application types
and organizational cultures it is impossible to be prescriptive of the software
process, the concept of *software process* is seen as one of the pillars of a
foundation for a software engineering discipline (see [Was96]). *Software engineering* as an engineering discipline also comprises the scientific treatment
of the software engineering process (see e.g. [BD04]) in order to understand
and systematically improve the software engineering process so that software
systems can be built and evolved with high quality, on time and within budget.

Software process management, on the other side, deals with the activities that are essential for managing the processes associated with developing,
maintaining, and supporting software products in a way, that the produced
products and services adhere to internal and external customer requirements
and that they support the business objectives of the organization producing
them. Key activities identified to be central to *software process management*
are *process definition*, *process measurement*, *process control*, and *process improvement* [FPC97].

The objectives of *software process management* are to ensure that defined
processes are followed and performing as expected, and to make improvements to the processes in order to help meeting business objectives. From
an individual's perspective, the objective of software process management is
to ensure that the processes he/she operates or supervises are predictable,
meet customer needs, and are continually being improved. From the overall

organizational perspective, the objective is to ensure that the above objective is fulfilled for every process within the organization (see [FPC97]).

With software becoming more and more important for our daily life at increasing speed and with faster turnover cycles, in particular the field of *software process improvement* as a means to deliver better quality products and increase efficiency and effectiveness of software development has become an important part of the software engineering discipline. As a consequence, the work with software processes has emerged as a field of its own, similarly to product development, but with the proper *software process* as the product that has to be developed, kept up and maintained. As a consequence, it is no longer appropriate to talk about *software process improvement* or *software process management*, but about *software process engineering*, indicating that the same quality models and process improvement and maintenance efforts applied to software product development should be applied to the proper software process work and its work products (see [Kin01]). Consequently the terms *software process management* and *software process engineering* are often used widely synonymously.

SCCH has carried out a series of application-oriented research projects related to the concepts, models and methods of *software process engineering*, namely:

- Project *HighLight* (ongoing): identification of the specific needs of small and very small enterprises with respect to software process improvement; development of a lightweight process improvement methodology; application of a product line approach to software process modeling.
- Project *Hephaistos* (ongoing): identification of best practices for the integration of business-driven product lifecycle management and engineering-focused product development in multi-product and product family contexts; current focus on the integration of product management, requirements management and architecture management, and change impact analysis.
- Project *GDES-Reuse*: enhancement of a process reference and process assessment meta-model to integrate the concepts of continuous process capability and staged organizational reuse maturity; identification of the relationship of reuse paradigms; development of a process reference model for reuse and of an organizational reuse maturity model for industrial engineering; development of methods for reuse assessment and reuse improvement measure identification and planning.
- Project *SISB*: development of a methodology for the evaluation of engineering strategies as reference framework for process management; identification of "strategy objects" for industrial engineering; mapping and validation of "strategy objects" against best practice process areas.

The remainder of this section shortly provides an overview on relevant concepts related to the field of software process engineering. Based on this, we present details and results of the above listed projects by identifying selected research challenges within the field of software process engineering and demonstrating how the results of the projects contribute to tackling these challenges.

2.1 Concepts Related to Software Process Engineering

This subsection shortly introduces selected key concepts related to software process engineering in order to facilitate the understanding of the subsequent subsection on software process engineering research challenges. These key concepts are: levels of models in software process engineering, benefits and importance of software process engineering, relationship "process quality" – "product quality", best practice software process models and process model classification, software process capability and maturity frameworks, and methods for software process evaluation and improvement.

Levels of Models in Software Process Engineering

Figure 1 depicts the four main levels of models involved in *software process engineering* and identifies the corresponding software process engineering activities associated with model instantiation.

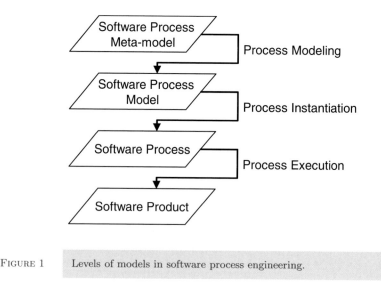

FIGURE 1   Levels of models in software process engineering.

Software process meta-models define the *"conceptual framework for expressing and composing software process models"* [Lon93]. They describe the relevant software process sub-models, their basic concepts, and their relationships and define the notation and language for expressing software process models. *Software process models* are the key result of the *process modeling* activity and serve as abstract representations of software processes. They prescribe a software process in terms of the activities to be carried out, the roles and work product types involved, etc. *Software processes* on the other side are the result of a *process instantiation* for a specific software development endeavor. This step often also includes tailoring or customizing of the software process model to the specific needs and goals of a project. The assignment of tools or other instruments for supporting the carrying out of activities and the assignment of resources to roles is typical for this level. The *execution* of a specific software process within a specific software development endeavor finally leads to the creation of the proper *software product* that in this view itself is seen as an instantiation of the software process.

Generally, software processes are complex entities comprised of a number of steps, resources, artifacts, constraints, etc. Depending on the intended usage, software process models reflect this complexity to a certain degree. Key motivators for meta-model-based process modeling are process model reuse, as sharing and composing process models and process model components require proper interfaces, and the automation of process execution. Examples of process meta-models range from simple models that only explain the basic relationships among activity types and result types (e.g. cascade model [Chr92]) to fully-fledged meta-models for software and systems engineering claiming to be capable of instantiating any software process model and method ([Obj08]). [HSSL02] presents a process meta-model and process model concept for component-based software engineering that incorporate the concept of process capability assessment (see "Software Process Capability and Maturity Frameworks" on page 167) into software process modeling. Pointers to examples for software process models can be found in "Best Practice Software Process Models and Process Model Classification" on page 165.

Benefits and Importance of Software Process Engineering

Software process models play an important role in software engineering. They allow the separation of process aspects from product aspects and provide a basis for the unification of methods and tools. Further general goals pursued with the use of software process models encompass the facilitation of the understanding and communication of the process, the establishment of a basis for the automation of software engineering activities and the establishment of a basis for analyzing and improving an organization's software process (see e.g. [GJ96]). Moreover, the use of software process models provides a series of further, less quantifiable benefits, like better teachability of the process and easier familiarization of new employees with an organization's practices and procedures, increased independence of specific persons and the establishment of a general basis for professionalism and credibility.

Motivated by the overall goal of enhancing performance, improving an organization's software process has become a central topic in software process engineering. Research shows that improving an organization's process quality can lead to substantial gains in productivity, early defect detection, time to market, and quality, that in total add up to significant returns on the investment in software process improvement. Further identifiable benefits refer to improved cost performance, improved estimates and deliveries on schedule, and increased customer as well as employee satisfaction [HCR+94].

Relationship "Process Quality – Product Quality"

Software quality is generally regarded a key to economic success for software developing organizations and has been an issue since the early days of software development. Consequently, a serious of definitions of software quality from many different viewpoints has emerged. According Garvin five such major approaches to the definition of quality can be identified, namely: the transcendent approach of philosophy, the product-based approach of economics, the user-based approach of economics, marketing, and operations management, and the manufacturing-based and the value-based approaches of operations management [Gar84].

Incorporating these different viewpoints for software engineering, ISO/IEC 9126 [ISO01] and ISO/IEC 25000 [ISO05] provide a *quality model for software* that at the top-level decomposes software quality into the aspects of *process quality*, *product quality*, and *quality in use* (see Figure 2). Product quality, in this context, is determined by the degree to which the developed software meets the defined requirements, while quality in use addresses the degree to which a product is fit for purpose when exposed to a particular context of use (see Section 3 on "Software Quality Engineering" for more details).

Process quality within this quality model expresses the degree to which defined processes were followed and completed and assumes that software processes implement best practices of software engineering within an organization. The basic assumption that the quality of a software product is largely influenced by the process used to develop it and that therefore, to improve the quality of a software product, the quality of the software process needs to be improved is the underlying principle of a series of software process capability and maturity frameworks and related methods for software process evaluation and improvement (see subsections below). It is meanwhile explicitly recognized in the international standard on "Software product Quality Requirements and Evaluation" (SQuaRE) together with the assumption

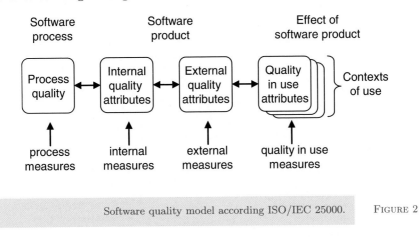

Software quality model according ISO/IEC 25000.   FIGURE 2

that the *quality of a software process* is the extend to which this process is explicitly defined, managed, measured and continuously improved [ISO05]. [SDR⁺02] describes an approach to component based-software engineering, which explicitly adds process capability information to the quality information of software components.

Best Practice Software Process Models and Process Model Classification

The history and evolution of *software process models* dates back to the very beginning of software engineering. While early models suggested a *code and fix cycle*, the first major milestone in software process modeling is the *waterfall development model* [Roy70], that groups activities into major phases based on the ideal assumption of sequential execution, but does not explicitly foresee changes or a prototyping oriented development approach. To overcome these weaknesses the *spiral model* [Boe88] suggests a cyclical, risk-driven development approach, in which - before entering a new cycle - the project risks are analyzed and appropriate measures taken. More recent examples of industry driven software process models are iterative and incremental models like the *Rational Unified Process (RUP)* [Kru03] or its open source subset *Open Unified Process (OpenUP)* [Ope08] that also incorporate principles of agile development.

Further, *standardization* plays a major role in software process modeling. An example of a quasi-standard is the *German V-Model,* which considers the development of a software system from the side of the supplier as well as from the side of the acquirer. It is organized with a focus on work products and provides work product quality standards and state models and also foresees

PRIMARY Life Cycle Processes	ORGANIZATIONAL Life Cycle Processes
Acquisition Process Group (ACQ) ACQ.1 Acquisition preparation ACQ.2 Supplier selection ACQ.3 Contract agreement ACQ.4 Supplier monitoring ACQ.5 Customer acceptance	**Management Process Group (MAN)** MAN.1 Organizational alignment MAN.2 Organizational management MAN.3 Project management MAN.4 Quality management MAN.5 Risk management MAN.6 Measurement
Supply Process Group (SPL) SPL.1 Supplier tendering SPL.2 Product release SPL.3 Product acceptance support	**Process Improvement Process Group (PIM)** PIM.1 Process establishment PIM.2 Process assessment PIM.3 Process improvement
Engineering Process Group (ENG) ENG.1 Requirements elicitation ENG.2 System requirements analysis ENG.3 System architectural design ENG.4 Software requirements analysis ENG.5 Software design ENG.6 Software construction ENG.7 Software integration ENG.8 Software testing ENG.9 System integration ENG.10 System testing ENG.11 Software installation ENG.12 Software and system maintenance	**Resource and Infrastructure Process Group (RIN)** RIN.1 Human resource management RIN.2 Training RIN.3 Knowledge management RIN.4 Infrastructure **Reuse Process Group (REU)** REU.1 Asset management REU.2 Reuse program management REU.3 Domain engineering
Operation Process Group (OPE) OPE.1 Operational use OPE.2 Customer support	

SUPPORTING Life Cycle Processes	
Support Process Group (SUP)	
SUP.1 Quality assurance	SUP.2 Verification
SUP.3 Validation	SUP.4 Joint review
SUP.5 Audit	SUP.6 Product evaluation
SUP.7 Documentation	SUP.8 Configuration management
SUP.9 Problem resolution management	SUP.10 Change request management

FIGURE 3   Software life cycle processes according ISO/IEC 12207.

predefined project execution strategies depending on predefined project types [V-M06]. At an international level the standard ISO/IEC 12207 [ISO95] on *software life cycle processes* provides a best practice software process model (see Figure 3) that also includes organizational and supporting processes. In the form presented in AMD1 and AMD2 to the standard this model also serves as a process reference model for process capability evaluation.

The available software process models vary significantly regarding the level of detail provided and the project or organizational scope covered by the processes defined. Regarding the *level of detail*, [Hum89] distinguishes between *universal level models* providing general guidelines, principles and policies as high-level framework, *worldly level models* providing procedures that implement policies at working level and practices that guide daily work, and *atomic level models* providing detailed refinements like standards, tools, techniques, etc. that are appropriate for process automation.

A further important distinction of software process models at conceptual level in the context of software process evaluation and improvement is the classification into *process implementation models, process assessment models,* and *process reference models.* While *process implementation models* provide the necessary details and guidance to be directly instantiated for process execution (see Figure 1), *process reference models* serve for the evaluation of process capability and benchmarking purposes of the actually implemented processes and—informally spoken—define the requirements for process implementation models from a best practice perspective. *Process assessment models,* finally, break down the requirements of process reference models into measureable indicators of practices and work products and are used within a process evaluation.

Software Process Capability and Maturity Frameworks

A promising means to continuously improve the software development process is to regularly evaluate the software process against some kind of best practice based measurement scale. Also a number of so-called assessment-based methods for software process improvement and corresponding measurement scales have been developed, there are essentially two types of such measurement concepts:

Staged models of process maturity: These models define a maturity scale at *organizational level* and typically relate each of the levels within the maturity scale to recommended practices necessary for achieving this level.

Continuous models of process capability: These models measure the software process at *process level* along two axes—the *process dimension* comprised of a number of processes subject to measurement and typically defined in a *process reference model,* and the generic process *capability dimension* (see Table 1) comprised of process attributes and process capability levels that are applied to characterize each process of the process dimension.

The *Capability Maturity Model (CMM)* [Hum95, PCCW93] is a typical model of the staged type. The approach of continuous process capability was developed within the *SPICE project* [Dor93] and has been standardized within the international standard series ISO/IEC 15504 on *Information Technology – Process Assessment* [ISO03]. According their underlying meta-models, staged models typically provide a predefined road map for organi-

Level 1 PA 1.1	**Performed Process** Process Performance Attribute
Level 2 PA 2.1 PA 2.2	**Managed Process** Performance Management Attribute Work Product Management Attribute
Level 3 PA 3.1 PA 3.2	**Established Process** Process Definition Attribute Process Deployment Attribute
Level 4 PA 4.1 PA 4.2	**Predictable Process** Process Measurement Attribute Process Control Attribute
Level 5 PA 5.1 PA 5.2	**Optimizing Process** Process Innovation Attribute Process Optimization Attribute

TABLE 1   Process capability levels and attributes according ISO/IEC 15504.

zational improvement by identifying improvement priorities generally true for most software organizations. Continuous models, on the other hand, do not prescribe any particular improvement path except the evolution of single processes, but come up with a customizable process dimension.

Models for Software Process Evaluation and Improvement

Beside the process engineering activities built into software best practice process models as own processes or activities, two major types of models for software process evaluation and improvement can be distinguished regarding the issue of scale of the intended improvement activity [Kin01]:

- Software process improvement action life cycle models
- Software process improvement program life cycle models.

Software process improvement action life cycle models are primarily meant for guiding a single improvement action and generally fail to give the necessary guidelines for a full software process improvement program. As they do not address improvement program-level issues, they are typically kept relatively simple. Examples of such models are:

- the Plan-Do-Check-Act (PDCA) model [She31]
- the Process Improvement Paradigm-cycle [Dio93] (see Figure 4).

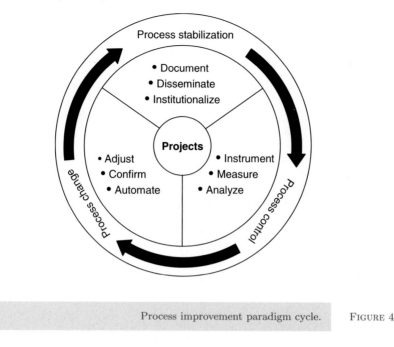

Process improvement paradigm cycle.   FIGURE 4

Models of this type are primarily intended for software process staff, process owners, and non-process professionals having a role in a software process improvement action.

Software process improvement program life cycle models on the other side, put more emphasis on aspects such as initiation, management and coordination of the overall improvement program and in particular on the coordination of individual process improvement actions. Examples of such models are:

- the IDEAL (Initiating-Diagnosing-Establishing-Acting-Learning) cycle [McF96] and
- the ISO 15504-7 cycle [ISO98] (see Figure 5).

These models are mainly intended for people who have been entrusted the management of a large scale process initiative. They are important for staging and managing a successful improvement program and represent a major step towards an institutionalized software process engineering system.

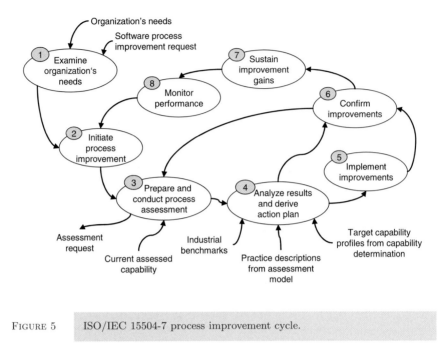

FIGURE 5   ISO/IEC 15504-7 process improvement cycle.

2.2 Software Process Engineering Research Challenges and Application-oriented Research at SCCH

In this section we present selected challenges within the field of *software process engineering* that are tackled by research projects performed at SCCH together with partner companies. The challenges dealt with are:

- Software process improvement for small and very small enterprises
- Integration of product engineering and lifecycle management
- Integrating process capability and organizational reuse maturity
- Alignment of process improvement with strategic goals

Software Process Improvement for Small and Very Small Enterprises

The project *HighLight* is an ongoing research project focusing on the specific needs and requirements of small and medium sized enterprises (SMEs) with respect to software process improvement. Specific attention is devoted to very small enterprises as a relevant subset of SMEs.

SMEs constitute a significant part of the Austrian as well as European industry. In particular software-oriented SMEs, i.e. either SMEs that develop software for customers or SMEs for which software developed in-house represents an essential part of their products or services are confronted with the need to improve the quality of their products in general and of software in particular and to react quickly to changing market and customer needs.

From a software engineering perspective such small development companies have to cope with challenges quite similar to that of large companies, like the need to manage and improve their software processes, to deal with rapid technology advances, to maintain their products, to operate in a global environment, and to sustain their organizations through growth. In the case of small companies however, different approaches to tackle these challenges are required because of specific business models and goals, market niche, size, availability of financial and human resources, process and management capability, and organizational differences [RvW07].

Over the last twenty years the software engineering community has paid special interest to the emerging field of software process improvement as a means to increase software product quality as well as software development productivity. However, the rise of software process improvement was primarily driven through its successful implementation in large companies and there is a widespread opinion stressing the point that the success of software process improvement is only possible for large companies. Nevertheless, within the last five years the software engineering community has shown an increasing interest in tackling the software process improvement challenge for small companies and there is a growing interest of the software engineering community to adapt the models and methods developed for software process improvement in the large to the specific needs of SMEs. [PGP08] presents a systematic review on software process improvement in small and medium software enterprises through analysis of published case studies. The challenge to provide systematic support for software process improvement to small and in particular very small enterprises is meanwhile also subject to international standardization efforts (see [ISO09]).

The overall goal of *HighLight* is therefore to research into, improve and develop innovative concepts, models and methods for the identification and efficient transfer of software engineering best practices to small and medium sized software enterprises. The specific goals and pursued results include:

- the identification of the specific needs, constraints and expectations of SMEs with respect to software process and quality improvement;
- the investigation into the state of the art in software process and quality improvement approaches, methods and standards, particularly with respect to their applicability to SMEs;
- the investigation into the reasons for success or failure of software process and quality improvement initiatives at SMEs and the identification of the critical success factors for such endeavors;

- the compilation of a comprehensive pool of software engineering best practices or pointers to those covering the specific contexts of SMEs;
- the development of a lightweight software process and product improvement methodology specifically targeted for SMEs and particularly tailorable to their strategic and business needs and project and product contexts;
- the validation of the developed concepts, models and methods in selected real-world improvement projects;
- the setup of a forum for discussion and exchange for SMEs interested in software process and quality improvement.

The work within *HighLight* is explicitly based on and driven by the needs and constraints of SMEs with respect to software process and quality improvement. The project builds on existing experience and integrates a process, product and business view on software process and quality management into a lightweight improvement methodology for SMEs. The project focuses on identifying selected development phase, paradigm and—where appropriate— technology-specific software engineering best practices and compiling them into compact, modular and integrated process reference models particularly suited for SMEs. The work will also include the development of concepts and methods for supporting the evolution of an organization's processes through changing paradigms and evolving organizational contexts, in particular company growth and increasing software productization.

As a means to implement such an approach the study of the applicability of concepts from the software product line area [CN02] to software process engineering and the creation of a *"software process line"* for SMEs is envisioned. In such an approach—in analogy to software product features used in software product line approaches to determine the concrete software product within a software product line—the characteristics that describe the organizational, project, product and market context of a software organization are envisioned to determine the software process model out of a *software process model line* that is most appropriate for the respective organization. An initial literature research shows that a similar approach—in a limited scope—has so far only been applied for the definition of project-specific processes for hardware/software co-design in an embedded system domain (see [Was06]).

Furthermore, *HighLight* concentrates on identifying lightweight and efficient methods for transferring the identified best practices into SMEs and will also seek feedback on and try to empirically validate the developed concepts and methodologies. *HighLight* will therefore seek liaison with software development projects at SCCH and within SCCH's partner companies and will establish links with established communities and institutions in the field of software process and quality improvement. Particularly SMEs that generally do not possess any kind of organization development departments will gain a lightweight, efficient and effective method that supports them in adapting to high-quality, state-of-the-art, lean and efficient software engineering processes.

Integration of Product Engineering and Lifecycle Management

The development of software products today is strongly driven by business considerations and market forces throughout the whole lifecycle. Traditional project-focused software development emphasizes distinct project phases and a functionally separated organization with distinct and specialized roles. As a consequence, problems emerge from different stakeholder perspectives on the same underlying product, locally optimized processes, isolated tools, and redundant, inconsistent and often locally stored product data. In real-world contexts these problems are additionally increased, as software organizations often have to manage a number of interrelated and interplaying products and services or as software is only part of the offered product or service. Key challenges in the management of software product development are thus to align the different perspectives to the overall business objectives; to establish consistent and integrated processes, methods and tools that span the different groups; to manage the relationship between the development artifacts produced by the different groups and processes; and to monitor product development progress across the whole lifecycle. The ongoing project *Hephaistos* carried out together with two local project partners tackles these challenges by identifying best practices for the integration of business-driven product lifecycle management and engineering-focused product development.

In this subsection we report about initial, interim results of *Hephaistos* with respect to software process engineering and provide an outlook on further research to be carried out in this context. These interim results are:

- an identification of key problems related to the integration of product engineering and lifecycle management,
- the identification of solution concepts addressing the identified problems, and
- the development of a conceptual model relating the identified solution concepts to core software engineering and management activities.

By analyzing the organizational context of one of the partner companies we identified a number of company-specific problems that were generalized into key problem areas, that also correspond to and are confirmed through issues and obstacles observed in many other industrial projects. These key problem areas related to the integration of product engineering and lifecycle management are [PRZ09]:

- lack of reuse of lifecycle artifacts beyond code, e.g. of requirements, design,
- unclear rationale regarding past informal and undocumented decisions, e.g. regarding requirements or architecture,
- intransparent consequences of changes, in particular during software product maintenance and enhancement,
- imbalance between management oriented lifecycle activities and overemphasized core engineering activities,

- heterogeneous tool-infrastructures lacking integration and interoperability and as a consequence hampering collaboration of roles,
- disruption of workflows and processes as a consequence of limited interoperability of tools that lead to redundant activities and data and increased overhead, error-prone work, and inconsistencies,
- intransparent status of artifacts and work progress due to heterogeneous tool landscapes,
- inability to reconstruct past states, in particular of non-code lifecycle artifacts, and
- missing integration of product management and project management, in particular when software products evolve over years and are maintained and enhanced in a series of ongoing, parallel projects.

Application lifecycle management (ALM) promises to tackle a wide spectrum of the above challenges and over the last years a large number of ALM solutions have been announced. However, the term is quite new, lacks a common understanding and is mostly driven by tool vendors in order to emphasize their move towards integrated tool suites covering the whole application lifecycle.

In order to help analyze and compare these solutions objectively, we identified two main goals of ALM by matching the tool vendors' propositions with the key problem areas listed above. These goals are:

1. Seamless integration of engineering activities at tool and process level across the whole lifecycle of an application;
2. Emphasis on management activities to shift the technical perspective of engineering towards the business perspective of software management.

We then further refined these two main goals into the following solution concepts for the integration of product engineering and lifecycle management [PRZ09]:

Traceability: Traceability is defined as "the degree to which a relationship can be established between two or more products of the development process, especially products having a predecessor-successor or master-subordinate relationship to one another" [IEE90].

Version control: Over the lifecycle of an application multiple versions evolve and require consistent control for managing releases, maintaining defined states and baselines across different artifacts, as well as allowing reverting to these defined states.

Measurement: Retrieving information about products, processes and resources as well as their relationships is the basis for establishing transparency, objective evaluation and planning. The role of measurement is essential for the management of software projects [DeM86] and has to be expanded to the entire application lifecycle.

Workflow support: Workflows bring together a sequence of operations, resources, roles and information flows to achieve a result. Approaches are necessary that provide interoperability of tools and processes to establish workflows across the entire lifecycle of an application.

Collaboration support: As software development is a team endeavor, concepts and tools for collaboration have found their way into software development.

Shared services: In addition to the above solution concepts a number of further basic services were identified like managing users and access rights, etc. which are relevant for every activity and tool applied.

The solution concepts identified above have a strong focus on integration in two directions: firstly, they provide support for the integration of engineering activities over the whole application lifecycle at tool level as well as at process level, addressing the first goal; secondly, the same concepts also enable the integration of engineering activities with management activities by establishing the link between the technical and the business perspective, addressing the second goal. Figure 6 depicts these three dimensions showing the engineering activities and the management activities according to [BD04] on the x-axis and the y-axis respectively. The solution concepts identified above are depicted as third dimension to clearly distinguish them from engineering and management activities and to highlight their role of tying the different engineering and management activities together.

The model depicted in Figure 6 by now has been used to support the definition of a strategy for improving the integration of product engineering and lifecycle management activities and for process improvement in the analyzed company. The strategy is subject to implementation, with a current focus on the integration of product management, requirements management and architecture design. Preliminary results confirm the applicability of the model as guidance for identifying and prioritizing problem areas as well as planning for a tailored ALM solution.

Integrating Process Capability and Organizational Reuse Maturity

The goal of the project $GDES^2$-*Reuse* that we carried out together with *Siemens Corporate Technology* was the development of an assessment-based methodology for evaluating an industrial engineering organization's reuse practices and identifying and exploiting its reuse potential.

While software engineering deals with software only, industrial engineering has to enable the parallel development of different engineering disciplines, like mechanical engineering, electrical engineering, and communications and control system engineering. Industrial engineering projects range from rather

---

[2] Globally Distributed Engineering and Services

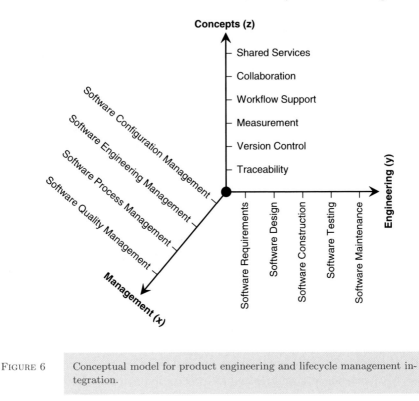

FIGURE 6   Conceptual model for product engineering and lifecycle management integration.

simple and small projects (e.g. semi-automated assembly line) to large and highly complex projects (e.g. nuclear power plants). Like software engineering, industrial engineering today has to cope with increasing demands for more flexible, more reliable, more productive, faster, and cost optimized planning and realization of industrial solutions. Simultaneously, industrial engineering has to deal with more demanding customer requirements, increased complexity of solutions and harder competition in a global market. Increasing reuse has therefore been identified as one key element for increasing quality and productivity in industrial engineering (see [LBB+05]). Reuse is one of the most basic techniques in industrial engineering and pervades all engineering phases and all engineering artifacts. Although recognized as a fundamental and indispensable approach, it is hardly systematized and often only applied in an ad hoc manner. As a consequence the reuse potential in industrial engineering organizations is rarely exploited and in most cases not even known.

On the other side, reuse is well understood in the domain of software engineering (see e.g. [JGJ97, Sam01, MMYA01]) and the distinction between bottom-up reuse concepts like component-oriented reuse and top-down approaches like copy-and-modify, reuse of prefabricates (e.g. application frameworks), the application of platforms, or the system-family or software product line approach [CN02] is well established. In the context of industrial engineering top-down approaches are particularly interesting, as they imply that the reusing organization has a general understanding of the overall structure of an engineering solution.

Our core development work for the overall reuse improvement methodology was preceded by the evaluation of relevant process and product evaluation approaches and standards and respective models and meta-models as well as reuse improvement approaches. This resulted in the selection of a process-centered approach, focusing on the identification of best practices for reuse in industrial engineering based on an adaption of the meta-model of ISO/IEC (TR) 15504 for process reference models and process assessment models as implicitly defined in [ISO03].

The methodology for improvement of reuse in industrial engineering developed within *GDES-Reuse* is intended to be applicable to all kinds of organizations and market segments of industrial engineering and is comprised of three sub-methodologies that are partly also independently applicable:

- a methodology for the *evaluation of the actual situation* of an engineering organization with respect to reuse, that allows to assess to what extent the respective organization fulfills the identified reuse best practices, focused around three distinct, but interplaying and interrelated models: the *process reference model*, the *reuse maturity model*, the *assessment model for reuse in industrial engineering*,
- a methodology for *potentials analysis* that—based on the results of the evaluation and under consideration of external factors and organizational goals—supports the identification of an optimal set of reuse practices for the respective organization, and
- a methodology for *action planning* that—based on the results of the evaluation and the potentials analysis—identifies and prioritizes the necessary measures for introducing or improving reuse.

Table 2 provides an overview of the *process reference model*. The model defines the results necessary for successful reuse and organizes these results according the typical phases of the engineering life cycle which are themselves grouped into categories. The overall objective is to support the representation of evaluation results and to make them comparable across organizational boundaries. Further details on the categories and phases can be found in [SPP+06].

The *reuse maturity model* for industrial engineering defines the results necessary for successful reuse. Based on [PRS00], it organizes these results into distinct organizational reuse maturity stages that build one upon the other in order to provide general guidance for the introduction and improvement of reuse within an engineering organization. The model foresees four maturity stages that are characterized in Table 3.

The *assessment model*, finally, breaks down the reuse results into reuse base practices and input and output artifacts that are used as indicators during evaluation.

Contracting (CON)	Engineering for Reuse (EFR)
CON.1 Acquisition/Initiation CON.2 Customer Requirements Analysis CON.3 Bid Preparation CON.4 Customer Acceptance	EFR.1 Domain Analysis EFR.2 Domain Design EFR.3 Domain Implementation - EFR.3.1 Domain Impl. - Discipline - EFR.3.2 Domain Impl. - Integration
Engineering with Reuse (EWR)	
EWR.1 System Requirements Analysis	**Organizational Support of Reuse (OSR)**
EWR.2 Basic Engineering EWR.3 Detail Engineering: - EWR.3.1 Detail Eng. - Discipline - EWR.3.2 Detail Eng. - Integration EWR.4 Realization and Operational Test EWR.5 Start of Operation EWR.6 Maintenance and Servicing	OSR.1 Reuse Program Management OSR.2 Improvement of Reuse OSR.3 Measurement of Reuse OSR.4 Asset Management OSR.5 Quality Assurance OSR.6 Change Management OSR.7 Problem Resolution

TABLE 2   Structure of the reference model for reuse in industrial engineering.

1 – Chaotic: Reuse is done ad-hoc only and not systematically. If needed, artifacts from previous projects are used as starting point for new ones. Reuse takes place unplanned, uncoordinated, undocumented, informal, occasional, and local and randomly on a small scale. Form and degree heavily depend on persons. Its contribution to achieving business goals is limited.

2 – Systematical: Reuse is pursued systematically. The technical and organizational measures for structured reuse are in place. Solutions are designed modular and the reuse of artifacts is supported by in-house development, purchasing and documentation of artifact usage. Reuse of artifacts is based on conformance with industry specific standards as well as definition and compliance with internal standards or interfaces.

3 – Domain-oriented: The domain specific benefits of reuse are exploited. The business is analyzed and reusable artifacts are defined based on the analysis of recurring requirements. Reusable artifacts are thus customized to the business domain. Reuse is supported by organization and processes. An organization wide infrastructure for reuse is in place and planning, coordination and controlling of a reuse oriented engineering process is established. Domain specific reference architectures are typical at this stage.

4 – Strategic: The whole organization is strategically oriented towards reuse. Reuse is performed systematically and integrated across all phases of the engineering life cycle. This is reflected in the business strategy and in the orientation of all business functions towards reuse, including marketing, sales, acquisition, etc. The portion of reused artifacts is high, as well as the contribution of reuse to achieving business goals.

TABLE 3   Characteristics of reuse maturity stages.

The core objective of the *potentials analysis* methodology is to derive an optimal reuse-oriented target scenario for the engineering processes within the assessed organizational unit based on the organizational unit's business and organizational goals, evaluation results, and exogenous factors like customer or market requirements, available or future technologies, characteristics of competition, etc. The potentials analysis methodology represents the link between the evaluation of the current situation regarding reuse and the method for action planning for improvement of reuse. It serves to identify highly rewarding and not yet implemented reuse practices for subsequent action planning for the implementation of these practices and is rather strategically and tactically oriented. The identification of improvements for reuse in industrial engineering is much more complex compared to "traditional" capability-oriented process improvement. Orthogonal to improving along the process capability dimension it also involves strategic decisions on the overall design of the engineering process, the pursued engineering and reuse paradigms, the desired organizational reuse maturity stages, etc. More details on the potentials analysis method and the related action planning method can be found in [SPPV09].

The methodology deliverables briefly described above are based on the establishment of a conceptual framework through the enhancement of existing meta-models in order to integrate the concept of organizational reuse maturity with the concept of continuous process capability that itself represents a significant achievement of the GDES-Reuse project [SPP⁺06]. All three models, the process reference model (PRM), the reuse maturity model (RMM), and the process assessment model (PAM) for reuse in industrial engineering, capture reuse best practices at different levels of abstraction and organize and represent them from different points of view (see Figure 7):

The PRM as well as the RMM contain the same set of reuse results in the sense of ISO/IEC 15504 process outcomes. While the PRM organizes these reuse results by phases of the engineering life cycle which are themselves grouped into categories of phases, the RMM organizes these reuse results into stages of organizational reuse maturity. The PAM on the other hand picks up the set of reuse results as defined in the PRM and RMM together with the organization of these reuse results by phases from the PRM and breaks down these reuse results into reuse base practices and input and output artifacts as indicators during evaluation. Reuse results represent the core conceptual element of the *GDES-Reuse* methodology providing the bridge between the continuous PRM and the staged RMM and in consequence between the evaluation methodology and the methodology for potentials analysis. From a meta-model point of view the PRM is fully compliant to the requirements of ISO/IEC 15504 [ISO03] for process reference models. It can be interpreted as a partial model of the overall engineering life cycle containing and describing those processes or parts of processes relevant for successful reuse. Consequently the measurement framework for process capability as defined in ISO/IEC 15504 can be directly applied to the reuse results of the PRM

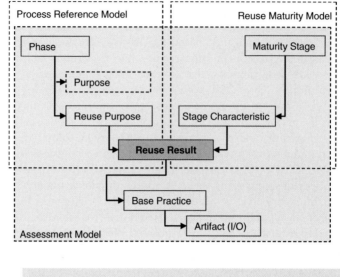

FIGURE 7   Process reference model and reuse maturity model—conceptual framework.

and aggregated towards the phases of the PRM on the one side and towards
the maturity stages of the RMM on the other side.

A major value of the work performed within *GDES-Reuse* lies in the integration and systematization of best practices from a series of reuse approaches
in a single model and in the integration of a "staged" reuse maturity model
with a "continuous" process model. The focus of the work was on providing
a best practice framework for the strategic design of engineering processes in
the sense of which paradigm or development approach or combination of those
to use. The approach chosen to resolve this problem is compliant to established process assessment and improvement approaches like CMMI [CMM06]
or SPICE [ISO03] but much more focused with respect to modelling depth
and thus rather a complement to those models than a substitution of those.

Furthermore, we regard the project's results re-transformable and applicable to the domain of software engineering, as the various reuse paradigms and
approaches developed in the field of software engineering represented a starting point for model development. Moreover, the engineering of control and
communication systems, as one of the core industrial engineering disciplines,
typically includes software engineering as a major sub-discipline.

The methodology for the evaluation of an actual reuse situation has so far
been applied in two real world evaluation projects (see [SPV07]).

Alignment of Processes Improvement with Strategic Goals

Under the umbrella of the project *SISB*[3] together with *Siemens Corporate Technology* we carried out research into methods for the *evaluation and development of engineering strategies* for the industrial solutions business. In this section we highlight results from this research that are relevant for the area of process engineering. These main results are:

- an understanding of the role of engineering strategies in the overall strategy development context of an organization,
- the development of a meta-model for describing engineering strategies,
- the identification of the engineering strategy objects relevant for the industrial solutions business, and
- the development of a methodology to support the evaluation and development of engineering strategies.

In order to understand strategy development at the engineering level we have to relate *engineering strategies* to the overall strategy development efforts in an organization. Typically a distinction is made between the *corporate strategy*, various *division strategies* and various *functional strategies* [VRM03]. While a corporate strategy deals with determining which market segments should be addressed with which resources, etc., a division strategy refines the corporate strategy by addressing the major question how to develop a long term unique selling proposition compared to the market competitors and how to develop a unique product or service. Functional strategies on the other side define the principles for the functional areas of a division in accordance with the division strategy and therefore refine the division strategy in the distinct functional areas, like marketing, finance, human resources, engineering, or software development. Depending on the size and structure of a company there might be no explicit distinction between corporate strategies and division strategies, but nevertheless they are part of the relevant context for the development of functional strategies.

Figure 8 depicts the conceptual framework (meta-model) developed for the description of functional strategies. The core elements of such a strategy are *strategic goals*, *strategy objects* and *strategic statements*. The strategic goals formulated in the engineering strategy are refinements of strategic goals on the corporate respectively divisional level, mapped on the functional area. A strategy object is a topic (e.g. process management) that refines one ore more strategic goals. As the strategy objects—and therefore also the strategic statements—are targeted towards the functional strategic goals it is also assured that the divisional or corporate goals are not violated. Although not necessary on the conceptual level, the grouping of strategy objects facilitates understanding of strategy objects on a more abstract level and also allows focusing of the strategy assessment or development process. The approach for

---

[3] Systematic Improvement of the Solutions Business

grouping strategy objects we finally decided to use, groups strategy objects simultaneously along three dimensions: *strategy key areas* like people, process, products and services, methods and tools; *strategy target groups* denoting the typical responsibility for a strategy object, e.g product management, sales, etc.; and *priority*.

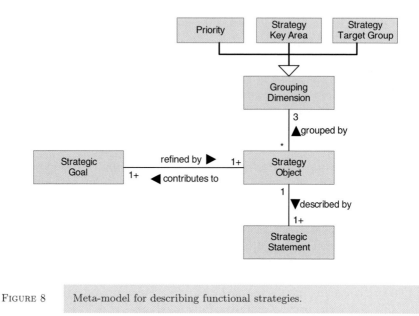

FIGURE 8   Meta-model for describing functional strategies.

Strategy objects in the context of an engineering strategy can be understood as a subject area that needs to be dealt with on a strategic level. In order to identify the strategy objects relevant for the industrial solutions business, strategy objects from the software engineering domain were used as a starting point. These were evaluated and adapted for their use in the industrial solutions business and additional strategy objects were identified. These additional strategy objects were identified by analyzing existing functional strategies from engineering organizations. Examples of strategy objects include architecture management, change management, competence management, domain engineering, tool and data integration, process management, quality management, requirements management, reuse management, and standards management. The full list of identified strategy objects together with their definition, identification of typical topics dealt with, examples of strategic statements and the assignment to the three grouping dimensions is provided in [PSN08]. Additionally, it has to be noted that a major step during the strategy development process is to select—and where necessary add—the appropriate strategy objects according to their importance and urgency.

The general approach of the *methodology* for the systematic assessment of existing engineering strategies is to conduct a strategy development process with an assessment emphasis. The typical strategy development process for functional engineering strategies is shown in Figure 9, structured into the development and prioritization of strategic goals, strategy objects and strategic statements.

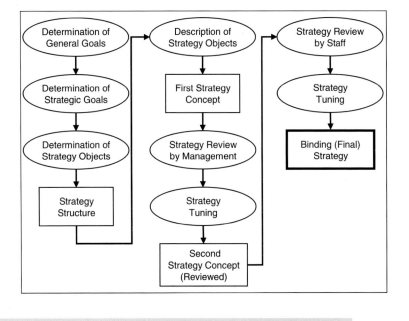

Process of engineering strategy development.   FIGURE 9

As the assessment method simulates parts of a strategy development process the participation of the management responsible for strategy development in a division or company is inevitable. The method itself consists of four main activities:

Engineering strategy assessment – kickoff: Determination of the strategy objects relevant for the company or division and identification of information sources.

Evaluation of strategy objects: Assignment of existing strategic statements to the selected strategy objects and assessment of the maturity of each strategy object and identification of gaps in the engineering strategy.

Consolidation of the evaluation: Adjustment of the assignments of strategic statements as well as of the assessment of the strategy objects together with the responsible management.

Finalization and presentation of results: Finalization of the assessment report and management presentation of the results.

The result of this assessment method is a qualitative report indicating the
general maturity of the engineering strategy regarding form and structuredness, strategy objects that should have been considered in the engineering
strategy, the completeness and maturity of strategic statements for each important strategy object, those strategy objects where existing strategic statements are to weak or few with respect to the relevance of the strategy object,
gaps in the engineering strategy in the sense of strategy objects important
for the company or division without coverage by strategic statements.

In order to validate the identified strategy objects regarding completeness
and coverage of relevant organizational processes, the strategy objects have
been mapped against the key process areas of CMMI [CMM06]. As CMMI
is a widespread process improvement maturity model for the development of
products and services that aims at a wide coverage of engineering disciplines,
it was assumed that the process areas described there cover a wide range of
organizational processes. The detailed mapping of strategy objects against
process areas is described in [PSN08].

As in particular the *strategy key area "Process"* groups all strategy objects
that deal with the management of processes in general, with value chain management, quality management, etc., this grouping allows a customized view
on strategic objects and strategic statements from the point of view of process
engineering. It thus facilitates capturing and understanding the strategic constraints for the process engineering activity as set by the engineering strategy
of an organization.

3 Software Quality Engineering

At about the same rate as software systems have been introduced in our
everyday life, the number of bad news about problems caused by software
failures increased. For example, last year at the opening of Heathrow's Terminal 5, in March 2008, technical problems with the baggage system caused
23.000 pieces of luggage to be misplaced. Thousands of passengers were left
waiting for their bags. A fifth of the flights had to be cancelled and—due to
theses problems—British Airways lost 16 million pounds. An investigation
revealed that a lack of software testing has to be blamed for the Terminal 5
fiasco (ComputerWeekly.com[4], 08 May 2008).

In August 2003 a massive blackout cut off electricity to 50 million people in eight US states and Canada. This was the worst outage in North

---

[4] http://www.computerweekly.com/Articles/2008/05/08/230602/lack-of-software-testing-
to-blame-for-terminal-5-fiasco-ba-executive-tells.htm

American history. USA Today reported: "FirstEnergy, the Ohio energy company . . . cited faulty computer software as a key factor in cascading problems that led up to the massive outage." (USA Today[5], 19 Nov 2003).

These and similar reports are only the tip of the iceberg. A study commissioned by the National Institute of Standards and Technology found that software bugs cost the U.S. economy about \$59.5 billion per year [Tas02]. The same study indicates that more than a third of these costs (about \$22.2 billion) could be eliminated by improving software testing.

The massive economic impact of software quality makes it a foremost concern for any software development endeavor. Software quality is in the focus of any software project, from the developer's perspective as much as from the customer's. At the same time, the development of concepts, methods, and tools for engineering software quality involves new demanding challenges for researchers.

In this chapter we give an overview of research trends and practical implications in software quality engineering illustrated with examples from past and present research results achieved at the SCCH. Since its foundation, SCCH has been active in engineering of high quality software solutions and in developing concepts, methods, and tools for quality engineering. A number of contributions have been made to following areas, which are further elaborated in the subsequent subsections.

• Concepts of quality in software engineering and related disciplines.
• Economic perspectives of software quality.
• Development of tool support for software testing.
• Monitoring and predicting software quality.

Concepts and Perspectives in Engineering of Software Quality   3.1

Definition of Software Quality

Software quality has been an issue since the early days of computer programming [WV02]. Accordingly a large number of definitions of software quality have emerged. Some of them have been standardized [IEE90][6], but most of them are perceived imprecise and overly abstract [Voa08]. To some extent, this perception stems from the different viewpoints of quality inherent in

---

[5] http://www.usatoday.com/tech/news/2003-11-19-blackout-bug_x.htm

[6] The IEEE Standard 610.12-1990 defines software quality as *"(1) The degree to which a system, component, or process meets specified requirements. (2) The degree to which a system, component, or process meets customer or user needs or expectations."*

the diverse definitions. As a consequence, the ISO/IEC Standard 9126:2001 [ISO01] and its successor ISO/IEC Standard 25000:2005 [ISO05] decompose software quality into process quality, product quality, and quality in use. The standard recognizes software as product and reflects Garvin's general observation about different approaches to define product quality [Gar84].

Process quality: Software processes implement best practices of software engineering in an organizational context. Process quality expresses the degree to which defined processes were followed and completed.

Product quality: Software products are the output of software processes. Product quality is determined by the degree to which the developed software meets the defined requirements.

Quality in use: A product that perfectly matches defined requirements does not guarantee to be useful in the hands of a user when the implemented requirements do not reflect the intended use. Quality in use addresses the degree to which a product is fit for purpose when exposed to a particular context of use.

Quality Models

Measurable elements of software quality, i.e. quality characteristics, have to be defined in order to assess the quality of a software product and to set quality objectives. A series of attempts to define attributes of software products by which quality can be systematically described (see [Mil02]) has been combined in the ISO/IEC standards 9126:2001 [ISO01] and 25000:2005 [ISO05] respectively. The standards provides a quality model with six quality characteristics, namely functionality, reliability, usability, efficiency, maintainability and portability, which are further refined in sub-characteristics (see Figure 10).

Bugs, i.e. defects, indicate the deviation of the actual quantity of a quality characteristic from the expected quantity. Defects are often associated with deviations in the behavior of a software system, affecting its functionality. The quality model, however, makes clear that defects concern all quality characteristics of a software system. Hence, a deviation from a defined runtime performance is therefore as much a defect as a deviation from the expected usability or a flawed computation.

Quality models are a valuable vehicle for systematically eliciting quality requirements and for adopting a quality engineering approach covering all relevant qualities of a software product. For example, in the research project *WebTesting*, a guideline for methodical testing of Web-based applications (see [RWW+02] and [SRA06]) has been derived from a domain-specific quality model.

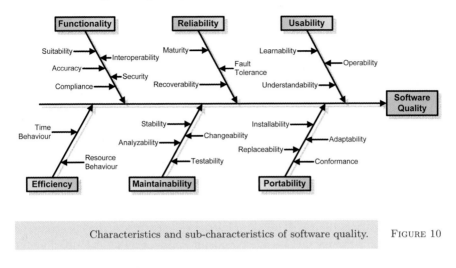

Characteristics and sub-characteristics of software quality.   FIGURE 10

Quality Assurance Measures

Quality must be built into a software product during development and maintenance. Software quality engineering [Tia05] ensures that the process of incorporating quality into the software is done correctly and adequately, and that the resulting software product meets the defined quality requirements.

The measures applied in engineering of software quality are constructive or analytical in their nature. Constructive measures are technical (e.g., application of adequate programming languages and tool support), organizational (e.g., enactment of standardized procedures and workflows), and personnel measures (e.g., selection and training of personnel) to ensure quality a priori. These measures aim to prevent defects through eliminating the source of the error or blocking erroneous human actions. Analytical measures are used to asses the actual quality of a work product by dynamic checks (e.g., testing and simulation) and static checks (e.g., inspection and review). These measures aim to improve quality through fault detection and removal.

Economic Perspective on Software Quality

Applying quality assurance measures involves costs. The costs of achieving quality have to be balanced with the benefits expected from software quality, i.e., reduced failure costs and improved productivity. Engineering of software quality, thus, is driven by economic considerations, entailing what Garvin [Gar84] described as "value-based approach" to define quality.

Value-based software engineering [BAB⁺05] therefore elaborates on the question "How much software quality investment is enough?" [HB06]. In [RBG05] we describe how an analysis of the derived business risks can be used to answer this question when making the investment decision, which can be stated as trade-off. Too little investments in quality assurance measures incur the risk of delivering a defective product that fails to meet the quality expectations of customers and results in lost sales. This risk has to be opposed with the risk of missed market opportunities and, thus, lost sales due to too much quality investments prolonging the time-to-market. Neither too little nor too much quality investments are economically reasonable. From an economic perspective a "good enough" approach to software quality [Bac97] is considered the optimal solution.

Engineering of software quality in practice has to be coherent with economic constraints. Hence, in any application-oriented research, the economic perspective of software quality is a dominant factor. Further examples about economic considerations will be presented in the next subsections as part of the discussion about manual versus automated testing and the prioritization of tests based on the prediction of defect-prone software modules.

3.2   Management and Automation of Software Testing

Software testing is one of the most important and most widely practiced measures of software quality engineering [LRFL07] used to validate that customers have specified the right software solution and to verify that developers have built the solution right. It is a natural approach to understand a software system's behavior by executing representative scenarios within the intended context of use with the aim to gather information about the software system. More specifically, software testing means executing a software system with defined input and observing the produced output, which is compared with the expected output to determine pass or fail of the test. Accordingly, the IEEE Standard 610.12-1990 defines testing as "the process of operating a system or component under specified conditions, observing or recording the results, and making an evaluation of some aspect of the system or component" [IEE90].

Compared to other approaches to engineer software quality, testing provides several advantages, such as the relative ease with which many of the testing activities can be performed, the possibility to execute the program in its expected environment, the direct link of failed tests to the underlying defect, or that testing reduces the risk of failures of the software system. In contrast, however, software testing is a costly measure due to the large number of execution scenarios required to gather a representative sample of the real-world usage of the software system. In fact, the total number of possible execution scenarios for any non-trivial software system is so high that complete testing is considered practically impossible [KFN99]. Test design techniques (e.g., [Bei90, Cop04]) are therefore applied to systematically construct a minimal set of test cases covering a representative fraction of all execution scenarios. Still, testing can consume up to 50 percent and more of the cost of software development [HB06].

As a consequence, automation has been proposed as a response to the costly and labor-intensive manual activities in software testing. Test automation [FG99] has many faces and concerns a broad variety of aspects of software testing: The automated execution of tests, the automated setup of the test environment, the automated recording or generation of tests, the automation of administrative tasks in testing. In all these cases, tool support promises to reduce the costs of testing and to speed up the test process.

In the following, we present results from research projects conducted at SCCH that involved tool-based solutions addressing different aspects of test automation.

- The first example, *TEMPPO*, outlines the tool support for managing large test case portfolios and related artifacts such as test data, test results and execution protocols.
- In the second example, a framework for the automation of unit tests in embedded software development has been used to introduce the paradigm of test-driven development to a large software project in this domain.
- We conclude this subsection with a study about balancing manual and automated software testing subsuming ongoing observations and lessons learned from several research and industrial projects. In addition, we present a tool-based approach (*TestSheets*) for user interface testing as an example for blending automated and manual testing.

Tool Support for Test Management

Testing tools are frequently associated with tools for automating the execution of test cases. Test execution, however, is only one activity in the software testing process, which also involves test planning, test analysis and design, test implementation, evaluating exit criteria and reporting, plus the parallel activity of test management. All of these activities are amenable to automation and benefit from tool support.

In the following we describe a tool-based approach specifically for test management and present some results from the research project TEMPPO (Test Execution Managing Planning and rePorting Organizer) conducted by Siemens Austria and SCCH. The project results are an excellent example for the sustaining benefit that can be achieved by linking science and industry. The project fostered a fruitful knowledge exchange in both directions. Requirements for managing testing in step with actual practice in large software development projects have been elicited by Siemens, and appropriate solution concepts have been developed by researchers at SCCH. The cooperation led to a prototype implementation of a test management environment that addressed a number of research issues significant for tool-based test management in industrial projects.

- A light-weight test process for managing the different stages in the genesis of test cases had to be defined, providing support for the inception of the initial test ideas based on a software requirements specification, the design of test cases and their implementation, the manual test execution as well as the automated execution in subsequent regression testing.
- An efficient structure for organizing and maintaining large hierarchical portfolios of up to several thousand test cases had to be developed. The high volumes of related data included an extendable set of meta-information associated to test cases and a range of artifacts such as associated test scripts, test results and execution protocols accumulated over the whole software development and maintenance lifecycle.
- Changes of the test structure and test cases are inevitable in any large software project once new requirements emerge or test strategies are updated. To accommodate these changes, an integrated versioning and branching mechanism became necessary. It makes sure that results from test executions are linked to the executed version of the test cases even after changes took place.
- Sophisticated query and grouping aids had to be applied for constructing test suites combining a set of test cases for execution. Results from several consecutive test executions had to be merged in a coherent test report for assessing and analyzing the project's quality status.
- Test management as the coordinating function of software testing interacts with a variety of other development and testing activities such as requirements management and change and defect management. For example, the integration of test management and unit testing is described in [RCS03]. These integrations imply interfaces that realize a synchronization between the underlying concepts and workflows of test management and the intersecting activities, which go beyond a mere data exchange between the involved tools.

The prototype developed in the joint research project has been extended with additional features by Siemens and evolved to an industry-strength test management solution. SiTEMPPO[7] (Figure 11) has been successfully applied in projects within the Siemens corporation all over the world, and it is licensed as commercial product for test management on the open market with customers from a broad range of industrial sectors and application domains.

---

[7] http://www.pse.siemens.at/SiTEMPPO

The test management solution SiTEMPPO. FIGURE 11

Automation of Unit Testing in Embedded Software Development

Test-driven development (TDD) [Bec02] has been one of the outstanding innovations over the last years in the field of software testing. In short, the premise behind TDD is that software is developed in small increments following a test-develop-refactor cycle also known as red-green-refactor pattern [Bec02].

In the first step (test), tests are implemented that specify the expected behavior before any code is written. Naturally, as the software to be tested does not yet exist, these tests fail – often visualized by a red progress bar. Thereby, however, the tests constitute a set of precisely measurable objectives for the development of the code in the next step. In the second step (develop), the goal is to write the code necessary to make the tests pass – visualized by a green progress bar. Only as much code as necessary to make the bar turn from red to green should be written and as quickly as possible. Even the intended design of the software system may be violated if necessary. In the third step (refactor), any problematic code constructs, design violations, and duplicate code blocks are refactored. Thereby, the code changes performed in the course of refactoring are safeguarded by the existing tests. As soon as change introduces a defect breaking the achieved behavior, a test will fail and indicate the defect. After the refactoring has been completed, the cycle is repeated until all planned requirements have finally been implemented.

Amplified by the paradigm shift towards agile processes and the inception of extreme programming [BA04], TDD has literally infected the developers with unit testing [BG00]. This breakthrough is also attributed to the framework JUnit[8], the reference implementation of the xUnit family [Ham04] in Java. The framework provides the basic functionality to swiftly implement unit tests in the same programming language as the tested code, to combine related tests to test suites, and to easily run the tests or test suites from the development environment including a visualization of the test results.

TDD has been successfully applied in the development of server and desktop applications, e.g., business software or Web-based systems. The development of embedded software systems would also benefit from TDD [Gre07]. However, it has not been widely used in this domain due to a number of unique challenges making automated unit testing of embedded software systems difficult at least.

- Typical programming languages employed in embedded software development have been designed for runtime and memory efficiency and, thus, show limited support for writing testable code. Examples are limitations in error and exception handling, lack of comprehensive meta-information, rigid binding at compile-time, and little encouragement to clearly separate interfaces and implementation.
- The limiting factor is usually the underlying hardware with its harsh resource and timing constraints that forces the developers to design for runtime and memory efficiency instead for testability. When the code is tuned to produce the smallest possible memory footprint, debugging aids as well as additional interfaces to control and to introspect the state of the software system are intentionally removed.
- Cross-platform development with a separation between host development environments and target execution platforms is a typical approach in building embedded software systems. The development tools run in a host environment, usually including a hardware simulator. Larger increments are cross-compiled and tested on the actual target system once it becomes available.
- In addition, unit testing is concerned with a number of domain-specific issues causing defects that demand domain-specific test methods and tool support. In embedded software development, these specific issues include, for example, real-time requirements, timing problems, and asynchronous execution due to multi-threaded code or decentralized systems.

The goal of the project was to tackle these challenges and to introduce the concept of TDD to the development of embedded software for mobile and handheld devices. Together with the partner company we developed a framework for automated unit testing with the aim to resemble the design of the

---

[8] http://www.junit.org

xUnit family as closely as possible, so unit tests could be written in the restricted C++ language variant used for programming embedded devices. Beyond that, the framework comprises extensions such as to run as application directly on the mobile device or to remotely execute unit tests on the target device via a TCP/IP or a serial connection, while the test results are reported back to the the development environment on the host (Figure 12). Many defects only prevalent on the target hardware can so be detected early in development, before the system integration phase.

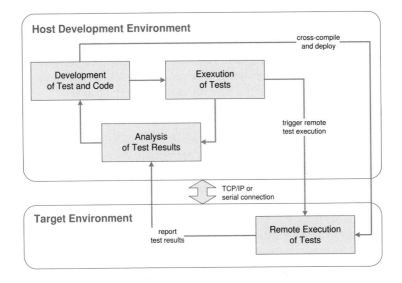

Workflow for unit testing in the host development environment as well as on the target device.   FIGURE 12

Balancing Manual and Automated Software Testing

Questions like "When should a test be automated?" or "Does test automation make sense in a specific situation?" fuel an ongoing debate among researchers and practitioners (e.g. [BWK05]). Economic considerations about automation in software testing led to the conclusion that – due to generally limited budget and resources available for testing – a trade-off between manual and automated testing exists [RW06]. An investment in automating a test reduces the limited budget and, thus, the number of affordable manual tests. The overly simplistic cost models for automated testing frequently found in the literature tend to neglect this trade-off and fail to provide the necessary guidance in selecting an optimally balanced testing strategy taking the value contribution of testing into account [Ram04].

The problem is made worse by the fact that manual and automated testing cannot be simply traded against each other based on pure cost considerations. Manual testing and automated testing have largely different defect detection capabilities in terms of what types of defects they are able to reveal. Automated testing targets regression problems, i.e. defects in modified but previously working functionality, while manual testing is suitable for exploring new ways in how to break (new) functionality. Hence, for effective manual testing detailed knowledge about the tested software system and experience in exploring a software system with the aim to find defects play an important role [BR08]. In [RW06] we propose an economic model for balancing manual and automated software testing and we describe influence factors to facilitate comprehension and discussion necessary to define a value-based testing strategy.

Frequently, technical constraints influence the feasibility of automaton approaches in software testing. In the project *Aragon*, a visual GUI editor as a part of an integrated development environment for mobile and multimedia devices, has been developed [PPRL07]. Testing the highly interactive graphical user interface of the editor, which comprises slightly more than 50 percent of the application's total code, involved a number challenges inherent in testing graphical user interfaces such as specifying exactly what the expected results are, testing of the aesthetic appearance, or coping with frequent changes.

While we found a manual, exploratory approach the preferable way of testing the GUI, we also identified a broad range of different tasks that can effectively be automated. As a consequence we set up the initiative *TestSheets* utilizing Eclipse cheat sheets for implementing partial automated test plans embedded directly in the runtime environment of the tested product [PR08]. This integration enabled active elements in test plans to access the product under test, e.g., for setting up the test environment, and allows to tap into the product's log output. Test plans were managed and deployed together with the product under test.

We found that partial test automation is an effective way to blend manual and automated testing amplifying the benefit of each approach. It is primarily targeted at cumbersome and error-prone tasks like setting up the test environment or collecting test results. Thereby, partial automation enhances the capability of human testers, first, because it reduces the amount of low-level routine work and, second, because it provides room for exploring the product under test from various viewpoints including aspects like usability, attractiveness and responsiveness, which are typically weakly addressed by automated tests.

Monitoring and Predicting Software Quality 3.3

Software quality engineering is an ongoing activity. Beyond measures to achieve software quality, it requires paying close attention to monitor the current quality status of software systems and to anticipate future states as these software systems continue to evolve. In the following we show how a research project integrating software engineering data in a software cockpit can provide the basis for monitoring and predicting software quality of upcoming versions of software products.

Software Cockpits

Continuous monitoring and management of software quality throughout the evolution of a software system [MD08] requires a comprehensive overview of the development status and means to drill-down on suspicious details to analyze and understand the underlying root causes. Software cockpits (also known as dashboards or software project control centers [MH04]) have been proposed as key to achieve this vision by integrating, visualizing and exploring measurement data from different perspectives and at various levels of detail. Typical sources of measurement data are software repositories and corporate databases such as versioning systems, static code and design analysis tools, test management solutions, issue tracking systems, build systems, and project documentation.

Each of these repositories and databases serves a specific purpose and provides a unique view on the project. For a holistic view on software quality, the relevant aspects of these individual views have to be integrated. Thereby, in order to support the analysis of the project situation, it is not enough to simply present the data from different sources side by side. The integration requires modeling and establishing the relationships between the different software repositories and databases at data level [RW08]. The topic of data integration has been successfully addressed by the concept of data warehouses with its associated ETL (extract, transform, load) technologies in database research and practice [KC04].

Data warehouses are the basis for business intelligence solutions, which support managers in making decisions in a dynamic, time-driven environment based on information from diverse data sources across an organization. Test managers and quality engineers operate in a similar environment under pressure to meet high-quality standards and, at the same time, to deliver in a tight schedule and budget. Hence, as partner in the competence network

Softnet Austria[9] we investigated and adopted the idea of business intelligence for software development and quality engineering [LR07].

In a study of existing approaches and solutions offering software cockpits for testing and quality management, we found an overemphasis of the reporting aspect. The main purpose of most of the studied cockpits was to generate static views of aggregated data, usually retrieved from a single data source. In contrast, Eckerson [Eck05] illustrates the nature of cockpits as the intersection between static reporting and interactive analysis. We therefore implemented a software cockpit with the objective to further explore the requirements and solution concepts for interactive data analysis. We based the cockpit on an open source data warehouse as platform for integrating project-specific data sources from development and test tools. The retrieved data was harnessed in customized software metrics and models [Kan02], which were visualized and analyzed via the cockpit. Our first prototype implementation of the software cockpit supported data extraction from open source software engineering tools such as the issue tracking tool Bugzilla or the versioning system CVS.

The three main tiers of the cockpit's architecture are shown in Figure 13 (from bottom to top):

1. *Data adapters* periodically extract relevant data from different repositories and databases, e.g., Bugzilla's issue database or the change log of CVS. The data is transformed to a standard data structure and stored in the central data warehouse.
2. *The data warehouse* organizes the data as cubes amenable for on-line analytical data processing. The data schema supports recording the project history for analyzing the evolution and forecasting of trends.
3. *The user interface* of the cockpit visualizes aggregated information and offers the flexibility to customize views, metrics and models. The Web-based implementation provides easy access to visual representation of the integrated data.

The first prototype of the cockpit has been developed in close cooperation with an industrial software project pursuing an iterative development process. Over a series of rapid prototyping cycles, the Web-based user interface (Figure 14) has evolved including a number of features to visualize and to analyze quality-related measurement data. Building on these results, the software cockpit has been successfully adopted in other projects and organizations, for example, a software product company developing business software involving a development team of more than 100 persons [LRB09].

We identified a number of features that constitute key success factors for the successful implementation and application of software cockpits in practice.

---

[9] http://www.soft-net.at/

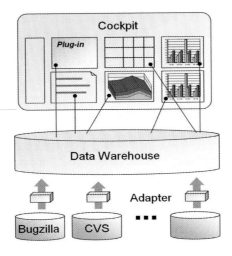

System architecture of the software cockpit.   FIGURE 13

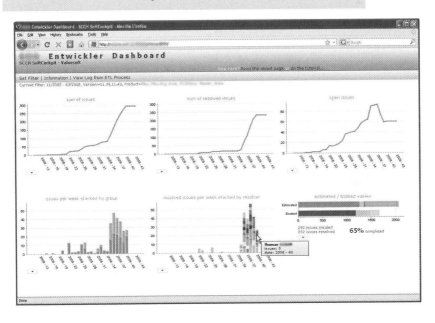

Interface of the software cockpit for developers.   FIGURE 14

- A user-centered design that supports the users' daily activities keeps the administrative overhead at a minimum and is in line with personal needs for feedback and transparency.
- A comprehensive overview of all relevant information is presented as a set of simple graphics on a single screen as the lynchpin of the software cockpit. It can be personalized in terms of user specific views and filters.
- The presented information (i.e. in-process metrics from software development and quality engineering) is easy to interpret and can be traced back to the individual activities in software development. Abstract metrics and high-level indicators have been avoided. This encourages the users to reflect on how their work affects the overall performance of the project and the quality status of the product.
- In addition, the interactive analysis of the measurement data allows drilling down from aggregated measurements to individual data records and in-place exploration is supported by mechanisms such as stacked charting of data along different dimensions, tooltips showing details about the data points, and filters to zoom in on the most recent information.

Predicting Defect-prone Modules of a Software System

Data about the points in time where defects are introduced, reported, and resolved, i.e. the lifecycle of defects [Ram08], is gathered in the data warehouse and can be used to construct the history and current state of defective modules of a software system. The data about the software system's past states can also serve as the basis for predicting future states of a software system, indicating which modules are likely to contain defects in upcoming versions.

The rationale for identifying defect-prone modules prior to analytical quality assurance (QA) measures such as inspection or testing has been summarized by Nagappan et al.: "During software production, software quality assurance consumes a considerable effort. To raise the effectiveness and efficiency of this effort, it is wise to direct it to those which need it most. We therefore need to identify those pieces of software which are the most likely to fail—and therefore require most of our attention." [NBZ06] As the time and effort for applying software quality assurance measures is usually limited due to economic constraints and as complete testing is considered impossible for any non-trivial software system [KFN99], the information about which modules are defect-prone can be a valuable aid for defining a focused test and quality engineering strategy.

The feasibility and practical value of defect prediction has been investigated in an empirical study we conducted as part of the research project *Andromeda*, where we applied defect prediction for a large industrial software system [RWS+09]. The studied software system encompasses about 700

KLOC of C++ code in about 160 modules. Before a new version of the system enters the testing phase, up to almost 60 percent of these modules contain defects. Our objective was to classify the modules of a new version as potentially defective or defect-free in order to prioritize the modules for testing. We repeated defect prediction for six consecutive versions of the software system and compared the prediction results with the actual results obtained from system and integration testing.

The defect prediction models [KL05] we used in the study have been based on the data retrieved from previous versions of the software system. For every module of the software system the data included more than 100 metrics like the size and complexity of the module, the number of dependencies to other modules, or the number of changes applied to the module over the last weeks and months. Data mining techniques such as fuzzy logic-based decision trees, neural networks, and support vector machines were used to construct the prediction models. Then, the models were parametrized with the data from the new versions to predict whether a module is defective or defect-free.

Preliminary results showed that our predictions achieve an accuracy of 78 (highest) to 67 percent (lowest). On average 72 percent of the modules were accurately classified. Hence, in case testing has to be stopped early and some modules have to be left untested, a test strategy prioritizing the modules based on the predicted defectiveness is up to 43 percent more effective than a strategy using a random prioritization. Even in with the lowest prediction accuracy the gain can be up to 29 percent compared to a random testing strategy when only 60 percent of all modules are tested. The gain over time is illustrated in Figure 15. The testing strategy based on average defect prediction results (blue) is compared to the hypothetical best case—a strategy ordering the modules to be tested according to their actual defectiveness (green)—and the worst case—a strategy ordering the modules purely random (red).

The depicted improvements in testing achieved by means of defect prediction are intermediate results from ongoing research. So far, the prediction models have been based on simple metrics derived from selected data sources. Combining the data in more sophisticated ways allows including additional aspects of the software system's history and, thus, promises to further increase the prediction performance [MGF07]. In a specific context of a project, the results can be improved even further by tuning of the applied data mining methods. For the future, we plan to extend this work to a larger set of industrial projects of various sizes and from different domains.

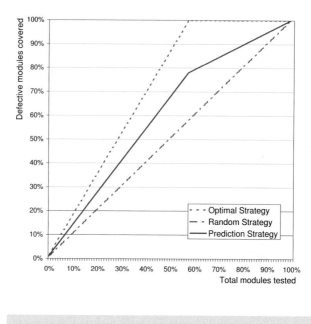

FIGURE 15   Improvement gain achieved by defect prediction.

4 Software Architecture Engineering

A software system's architecture is an abstraction of its implementation, omitting details of implementation, algorithm and data representation, see [BCK03]. The architecture of a software system is often represented by different models, each consisting of abstract elements and relationships. Each of these models can be used to describe a particular abstract view of important structural relationships, facilitating understanding and analysis of important qualities of a software system. The fact that the abstraction defined by an architecture is not made up by one but by different structures and views providing different perspectives on a software system is reflected in a widely accepted definition of software architecture provided by the Bass et al. [BCK03], where software architecture is defined as "the structure or structures of the system, which comprise software elements, the externally visible properties of these elements, and the relationships among them". Architecture is the result of design. This is reflected in a broader definition provided by Medvidovic et al. [MDT07] which state that "a software system's architecture is the set of principal design decisions about a system". This includes design decisions related to structure, behavior, interaction, non-functional properties, the development process, and to a system's business position (see [MDT07]).

The architecture of a software system is one of the most important concepts during software development. It is among the first artifacts produced in the development and contains *early design decisions* [Cle96] that are usually long lasting and expensive to change later in the development. Fundamental system qualities like performance, security, or scalability are determined by a system's architecture. For developers it is a *blueprint* [Gar00] of the system that guides and constrains implementation. For stakeholders it is a means of communication. Formal architecture representations (architecture models) can be used for automatic analysis of important system qualities; informal architecture representations (architecture documentation) are an important means of communication during and system documentation during all phases of a software life-cycle.

Superficially, software architecture research can be classified into two main research areas: general software architecture research and domain-specific software architecture research. General software architecture research encompasses concepts, methods, and tools for creating, describing, and managing software architectures, ideally independent of a particular domain. Domain-specific software architecture research focuses on the application and adaption of general software architecture principles for specific domains and includes the creation of domain-specific architecture languages, tools, reference architectures, and patterns.

In this section we describe both basic and applied research projects in the area of software architectures that are conducted by SCCH with academic and industrial partners. The remainder of this section is structured as follows: Subsection 4.1 provides an overview of the field of software architectures and highlights important research challenges. Subsection 4.2 describes a research cooperation between SCCH and the Software Engineering Group at the Department of Business Informatics, Johannes Kepler University Linz, focusing on languages and tools for comprehensive and integrated software architecture management. Subsection 4.3 describes applied software architecture research for industrial software systems. Finally, Subsection 4.4 describes architecture-related research activities for enterprise information systems.

General Research Areas and Challenges 4.1

In this subsection we provide an overview of research fields and challenges in the area of general software architecture research. Important research fields in this area are architecture design, architecture implementation, architecture analysis and evaluation and architecture documentation [TvdH07, KOS06].

Architecture Design

Architecture design is the activity that creates a system's architecture. While design is performed in all phases of software development fundamental design decisions are usually made before the implementation phase [TMD09]. When creating the initial architecture, a wide range of aspects has to be taken into consideration. Since it is not possible to fulfill the concerns of all stakeholders the architecture of a software system represents a tradeoff between stakeholders concerns [RW05]. Architecture design experience is represented by patterns [MKMG97], styles [MKMG97], and reference architectures [TMD09]. Architecture is also implicitly reused through the use of frameworks [SB03] and middleware [SB03] for a particular domain.

Architecture Implementation

Implementing a defined architecture is in fact the task of mapping the concepts defined during design to implementation artifacts [TMD09]. This process can be performed manually and automatically. If the architecture is implemented manually, a major problem is to ensure that the system implementation conforms to the intended architecture. This problem is known as architectural decay [AGM05], architectural drift [PW92], architectural erosion [PW92] and design erosion [vGB02]. If existing libraries, middleware and frameworks are used, architecture and design is effectively reused and the possible architectural drift is reduced. Since a framework usually defines the architecture for a family of applications in a particular domain, architectural drift is still possible. Approaches for checking architecture conformance like *Lattix* [SJSJ05], *Sotoarc* [Sof07] and *SonarJ* [Hel07] operate at the level of programming-language concepts. They lack high-level architecture support and are not integrated well enough with the development process. Model-driven development [Sch06] can be used for automatically deriving (parts of) an implementation from an architecture. Since architecture is an abstraction of a software system and no specification, only code skeletons can be generated, which have to be implemented manually. The synchronization of the manually modified code with the models used for code generation is a central problem of model-driven software development [HT06].

Architecture Analysis and Evaluation

The purpose of software architecture analysis is to analyze the software architecture to identify potential risks and verify that the quality requirements have been addressed in the design [LH93]. Analysis activities can take place before the system has been build, during it is built and after the system has been built [DN02]. Architecture analysis can be performed manually by using architecture evaluation methods or automatically using architecture analysis tools.

Architecture evaluation methods like the *Software Architecture Analysis Method* (SAAM) [CKK02] or its successor the *Architecture Tradeoff Analysis Method* (ATAM) [CKK02] are scenario-based evaluation methods that have been developed particularly to validate quality attributes, which are usually difficult to analyze. Architecture evaluation methods are time-consuming and resource-intensive processes. They are usually used for evaluating the initial design of a software system with its stakeholders and for assessing the architecture of an already implemented system. They are not intended for continuous architecture analysis.

Architecture Description Languages (ADLs) are formal languages to represent the architecture of a software system [Cle96]. They allow the automatic analysis of system properties before it has been built [Cle95]. An ADL describes a system in terms of components, connectors and their configurations [MT00]. Usually ADLs have a textual as well as a graphical representation [Cle96]. A large number of general purpose and domain-specific ADLs exist [MT00]. Disadvantages of ADLs are lack of tool support [MDT07, MT00], lack of implementation integration [MT00] and lack of standardization. Some ADLs allows code generation in the sense of model-driven software development, which may lead to problems in synchronizing architecture and code as mentioned above. While UML is sometimes discussed as a general purpose ADL, its suitability as an ADL is still subject of study and debate [MDT07]. In most cases UML, is used for architecture documentation as described below.

Architecture Documentation

Since the architecture of a software system is not entirely contained in the implementation it must be documented separately [Hof05]. Documenting software architecture is quite different from architectural descriptions that are created for analysis [IMP05]. While the latter requires a formal description that can be processed by tools, architecture descriptions for documentation purposes are usually described informal using natural language. Researchers have proposed a view-based approach for describing software architectures [RW05, Kru95, CBB$^+$02, HNS99]. An architectural view is a representation of a system from the perspective of an identified set of architecture-related concerns [Int08]. Architecture documentations usually consist of multiple views. The concepts of view-based architecture documentation are defined in the *ISO/IEC 42010 standard: Systems and Software Engineering – Architectural Description* [Int08].

The *Unified Modeling Language* (UML) [Obj07] is the standard modeling language in software development. UML is primary a visual notation [WH05] that consists of over ten different loosely connected individual notations [MDT07]. UML is often used in architecture documentation. UML 2.0 has adapted many features from ADLs [AGM05].

4.2 Software Architecture Management – Languages and Tools

While numerous approaches for individual architecture-related activities exist and have found wide-spread use in practice, architecture is still not supported well enough during software development. Often it is not explicitly and entirely documented; system implementation deviates from the intended architecture; the documented architecture is out-of-date; architecture conformance checking is not performed continuously and can only be performed at a low level of abstraction; and finally the architecture is usually described informal and cannot be used for automatic analysis.

The *Software Architecture Engineering* (SAE) project is a strategic project that addresses these problems. The main idea is to support software architecture related activities like modeling, changing, and validating software architectures as an integral part of other activities in software development. This is achieved by a central integrated and formalized language for describing software architectures (LISA) and an unobtrusive set of integrated architecture tools working on this model (LISA-toolkit).

Integrated Architecture Language

LISA is an architecture description language which can be used for describing and validating architectural structures and properties. It has no explicit textual representation, which is intended for manually creating an architectural description. Instead, LISA-based architecture models are manipulated by the tools provided by the LISA toolkit.

While LISA has been designed as a general purpose ADL, it has been designed with specific aims promising to solve some of problems of architecture engineering described above and with the central aim to raise the abstraction in software development further by extending modeling concepts provided by general purpose programming languages by architectural concepts.

From a technical perspective LISA is an extensible meta-model based on XML-Schema and consists of several integrated and connected sub models. Contrary to other ADLs it puts a special emphasis on linking architecture to implementation and on supporting existing component-models and technologies. The main elements of LISA are shown in Figure 16. The lower layers

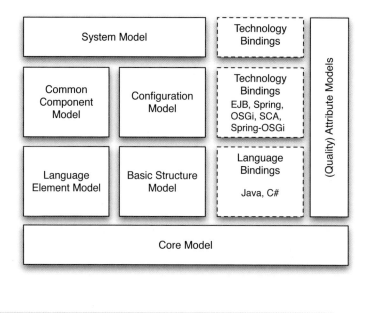

The LISA Model.   FIGURE 16

of the LISA language definition shown in Figure 16 can be used for describing architectural relationships that are defined statically in code. Model elements at these lower layers can be partly extracted from or mapped to source code. Examples are the elements of the *Language Element Model,* which include concepts like classes and interfaces. These elements can be organized by structures in the *Basic Structure Model.* The *Basic Structure Model* can be used for defining elements like functional units, subsystems, deployment units, and layers. Together the elements of the lower layers of the LISA language definition enable functionality provided by architecture management tools. This includes usage and dependency analysis, synchronizing architecture with code, and defining and checking architectural constraints at the level of programming language concepts. Although the lower layers of LISA are aligned with concepts found in concrete programming languages they are still abstract. Bindings to particular programming languages are provided by *Language Binding* definitions as shown in Figure 16.

The upper layers of LISA include the definition of abstract models for describing components, configurations, and whole systems. Again the binding to specific component technologies and models is provided by *Technology Binding Models.* Currently LISA supports bindings for EJB [EJB06], Spring

[Spr08b], OSGi [OSG07], Spring Dynamic Modules for OSGi [Spr08a], and SCA [SCA07]. Examples for elements at the higher layers of LISA are component, contract, port, composite, application, location and tier. These elements can be used for describing and analyzing architectures of component-based and distributed service-oriented software systems. In such systems architectural relationships are not defined in code but through late composition and configuration. Finally, *(Quality) Attribute Models* as shown in Figure 16 can be used for attaching semantic attributes and policies to architectural elements at all levels of abstraction. Such attributes can be used for annotating and validating non-functional attributes of a software system.

Pervasive Architecture Toolkit

LISA is not intended to be used directly by means of a textual representation. Instead creation, manipulation, visualization, and validation of LISA-based architectural models are supported by the LISA-toolkit. To provide unobtrusive and integrated support for architecture related activities during the whole development process, the toolkit is implemented as a set of Eclipse plug-ins and designed to be integrated into software analysis and development tools. An overview of the general structure of the toolkit is shown in Figure 17. A screenshot of the LISA-Toolkit is depicted in Figure 18.

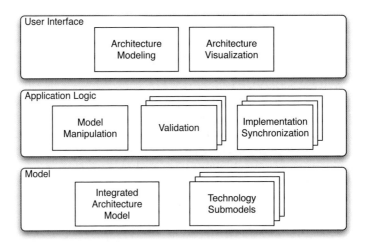

FIGURE 17   The LISA Toolkit.

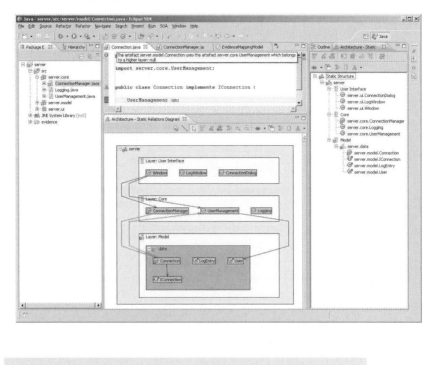

A Screenshot of the LISA Toolkit.   FIGURE 18

As shown in the figure, the toolkit provides an API for editing a LISA-based architecture model as well as functional components for validating architectural constraints and for synchronizing an architecture with a system implementation. In addition, the toolkit provides user interface components for architecture modeling and visualization. All UI components are working on the same architectural model and thus support editing and visualization of different aspects of a system in a consistent way. Violation of architectural constraints defined in the model are immediately shown in all graphical and textual representations of the affected elements.

Examples of available visualizations and modeling tools are shown in Figures 19 and 20. Figure 19 shows usage and dependency relationships of classes and interfaces organized in different layers in an object-oriented software system. The figure shows layer violations (see (1) and (2) in Figure 19) as an example for the violation of architectural constraints.

Figure 20 shows diagrams for representing and editing the architecture of a service-oriented software system using the *Service Component Architecture* (SCA). Instead of classes and interfaces, the main elements at this layer of abstraction are components and contracts. The *Component Decomposition Diagram* provides on overview of the components of the system. In LISA components are independent of a particular implementation technology. The

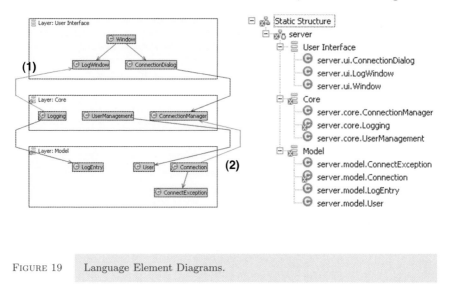

FIGURE 19   Language Element Diagrams.

diagram can be used to explore component structure and decomposition of composite components. Component usage relationships are typically not implemented in source code but rather configured during system assembly or created automatically based on component specifications. The *System Relation Diagram* shows the configuration of a system in terms of components and their relations. Relations and element properties violating architectural constraints are also indicated at this level of abstraction.

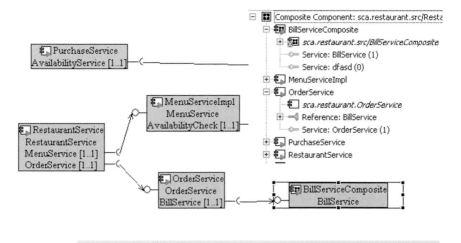

FIGURE 20   Component Diagrams.

Addressed Problem Domains and Research Challenges

The approach supports architecture related activities in different areas of software development and addresses several challenges described above.

Architecture Design: The LISA-toolkit can be used for modeling architectural elements and relationships. A system can be modeled from low level elements at the level of classes and interfaces to higher level components at the level of systems. LISA supports in particular component-based and distributed service-oriented systems.

Architecture Implementation: An architecture model can be used for generating component implementation skeletons and other application parts in the sense of model-driven development. However, the central benefit of the approach in this area is the support for binding architecture to implementation and for continuous synchronization of architecture and implementation. This addresses the problems of outdated architecture description and of architectural drift.

Architecture Analysis and Evaluation: Since the approach is based on a central formalized architecture model, architectural constraints can be defined similar to other architectural description languages. Contrary to other approaches constraints can be defined at the level of the architecture model as well as the level of the implementation and technology binding. Since the same model is used during the whole software life-cycle, architectural constraints can be checked during analysis, implementation and also during maintenance.

Architecture Documentation: Architecture documentation is best supported by a view-based approach as described above. LISA supports architecture documentation by providing diagrams that can be used for describing architectural views.

To summarize, the main elements of the architecture management approach are a central formalized architecture model and set of tools working on this model. Distinct features are the possibility to integrate the architecture tools with other development tools, close integration and synchronization with implementation, the support of component-based systems and the support of existing component models and technologies. First results of the approach have been published in [BW08].

4.3   Software Architectures for Industrial Applications

In the context of this subsection, the term *industrial applications* refers to software, which handles tasks related to manufacturing, process control and -automation. This includes applications for manufacturing operations management (e.g. product tracking, product resource management, product data collection) as well as software for basic control of devices and machines. Of course, industrial applications are not solely restricted to manufacturing industries, the term also applies to software solving similar tasks in areas like aviation, the automotive industry, and building automation.

Challenges and Requirements

Industrial applications tend to have stricter requirements concerning reliability and efficiency (in the sense of ISO-9126) than desktop software. This is particularly the case for software that handles mission- and safety-critical tasks. Reliability means that such industrial applications must provide high availability with minimal downtimes, be robust to failure and be able to fully recover to an operational state in case of faults in underlying or neighbored systems. Efficiency covers the aspects of time and resource behavior. While managing resources like memory efficiently should be important to software applications in general, industrial applications, and especially applications for process control, often must fulfill hard or soft real-time demands. These requirements demand special considerations when designing and implementing industrial applications. Designing real-time systems is particularly challenging [Dou02, Ste00]. Several frameworks aid in designing and developing industrial applications. They range from domain specific control frameworks such as OROCOS [Bru01] to general purpose component frameworks like OSGi [OSG07], which can be used equally for industrial and desktop software.

Case Study ProMoRTE

ProMoRTE [Dor09] is an online (i.e. process controlling) OSGi-based runtime platform for computation algorithms in the steel industry. The following list of requirements was important for designing the architecture of the platform:

- Easy and flexible installation, configuration and operation of computation algorithms at runtime.
- Versioning support for computation algorithms.

- Prescription of unified interfaces for computation algorithms (data access, behavior control).
- Integration with an IDE for developing and maintaining algorithms.
- Support of legacy code to allow the reuse of existing algorithms coded in C/C++.

The pivotal quality requirement addressed the reliability of the platform. Since it had to be deployed in a 24×7 production environment, a maximum of stability and a minimum of downtime was demanded. Manipulations on a certain algorithm (e.g. reconfiguration), failed computations or crashed algorithm executions had not to influence the operation of other algorithms in the platform. In case of a hardware fault or system crash, a full recovery of the platform and all installed algorithms was mandatory. Other important quality demands concerned portability of the system (OpenVMS, Windows, Linux) and performance. Hard real-time capabilities were not deemed necessary, though.

Of course, these requirements affected the architecture of ProMoRTE. To achieve portability we opted to base our implementation on Java. OSGi as the base framework was chosen for its flexible component oriented architecture allowing hot deployment of components (aka bundles) and providing explicit versioning support. Besides, OSGi easily integrates with the popular Eclipse IDE—since Eclipse builds on OSGi, too.

Support of legacy code and the reliability requirement interfered with each other. Incorporating native libraries in Java applications is done via the Java Native Interface. However, direct integration bears the risk of reduced stability and robustness, because defects in native code can not always be handled by the JNI code or the Java application code. Thus, we had to consider a distributed architecture to satisfy the reliability needs, which is shown in Figure 21.

The distribution of process algorithms had in turn an effect on performance, since communication of platform and algorithms had to pass process boundaries. In the end, the negative effects could be coped with. The platform has been operative in the project partner's productive environment for over two years.

Software Architectures for Enterprise Information Systems   4.4

To stay competitive, enterprises need a flexible applications architecture that permits changes and the quick deployment of new functionality with minimal integration effort. Enterprise applications can be integrated at different levels: data, business logic, and presentation. Integration of heterogeneous

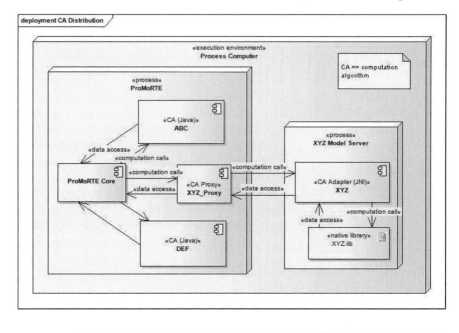

FIGURE 21   Distribution of algorithms with ProMoRTE.

systems both within enterprises (EAI) and between enterprises (B2B) requires standardization. Standardization is a strong trend at all integration
levels. Examples are Web Service standards like SOAP and WSDL as well as
higher-level standards for B2B-integration like ebXML and RosettaNet.

To increase reusability and to flexibly adapt to changing business conditions and processes, enterprise applications are increasingly decomposed into
small reusable and composable elements using standardized interfaces. At
the presentation level such elements are portal components, which can be
composed to web portals and customizable workplaces. At the business logic
layer, the central elements for composition are services. Currently, the term
Service-Oriented Architecture (SOA) is usually used for flexible enterprise
information system architectures based on services using standardized (Web
Service) protocols.

Challenges and Requirements

Central challenges of integrating components at the presentation level are the
integration of the components' user interfaces into a single consistent aggregated application user interface and the support for data exchange between

these components. Data exchange at the presentation level is complicated by two main issues. Presentation level components that are to be integrated may not only be developed by different parties but also managed and operated by different providers. This means that data exchange needs to support remote communication and may cross several different security boundaries. In addition, standardized composition models are needed for integrating components without additional development effort. These issues have been addressed by the Enterprise Portal Project at SCCH, which has been conducted to created customizable workplace solutions in the financial domain.

Central challenges at the business logic level, i.e., for an Service-Oriented Architecture, are the support for service evolution, service reuse, and service management. Similar to the presentation level, services at the business-logic level may be produced and operated by different providers. This means that any changes to the architecture of a SOA-based system may potentially affect not only other departments but even other companies. Equally changes of services operated by a particular company may affect the whole enterprise information architecture. Aspects of service evolution and management in an SOA have been addressed by the *IT4S* project at SCCH.

Enterprise Portal Project (Enipa)

The main result of the *Enipa* project is a component model for enhanced integration of portal components in web portals. The model supports not only the aggregation of components within one web page, but also the composition of component navigation into a central navigation area, the communication between local and remote components, and heterogeneous environments. The approach is based on existing standards like Portlets and WSRP and uses XML for describing component navigation and communication capabilities. It is declarative and may also be used for improving integration capabilities of already existing portal components (see [WZ05] and [WWZ07]).

SOA Evolution and Management (IT4S)

The results of the *IT4S* project are an approach for SOA governance and a versioning approach for service evolution. Notable aspects of the governance approach are an extensible model for describing service metadata of arbitrary service types (not only Web services), support for the process of service specification and service creation, a service browser for service reuse, and the support for service evolution through information about service versioning, service dependencies and service installations [DW06]. The versioning approach consists of a versioning model, of suggestions for release management, evolution scenarios, and a versioning scheme for enterprise services [WZD07]. It also includes compatibility rules for the homogeneous evolution of heterogeneous services [KWZ09].

5 Domain-Specific Languages and Modeling

A domain-specific language (DSL) is a programming language or executable specification language that offers, through appropriate notations and abstractions, expressive power focused on, and usually restricted to, a particular problem domain [vDKV00]. There is a common perception to distinguish between horizontal and vertical domains. Horizontal domains cover different technical software areas as user interface, database, testing, etc. whereas vertical domains are found in business areas like insurance, telephony, or process automation.

Domain-specific languages play an important role in various software engineering methodologies. In generative software development [CEC00], a given system can be automatically generated from a specification written in one or more textual or graphical domain-specific languages [Cza05]. Domain-specific languages have also been applied for end-user programming [MKB06] [PHS+08b]. There has also been a trend in model-driven development towards representing models using appropriate DSLs resulting in the domain-specific modeling discipline [VS06, KT08].

Domain-specific modeling (DSM) proposes to model a software system and to fully generate code from these high-level models. Importantly, both the language used for modeling as well as code generators are specific to a certain domain, in contrast to other model-driven approaches like model-driven architecture [KWB03] that proposes standard modeling languages, e.g. UML.

Domain-specific modeling is about finding concepts from a certain domain and to specify a domain-specific language from these concepts. Tolvanen and Kelly [TK05] identified following driving factors for language construct identification based on an evaluation of 23 case studies:

1. domain expert concepts,
2. developer concepts,
3. generation output,
4. look and feel of the system build, and
5. variability space,

where the combination of the latter two promises most benefits for DSM solutions [TK05, KT08].

The key contribution of domain-specific languages and modeling is to significantly increase both productivity and quality in software development by raising the abstraction level from general-purpose programming languages and modeling notations toward bespoke domains.

For many realistic industrial software systems, a single DSL only solves a limited part of a problem [KT08, LH09]. An entire system, hence, is typically build from a single or multiple DSLs together with system parts developed traditionally by means of general-purpose programming languages.

The Software Competence Center Hagenberg (SCCH) has carried out various application-oriented research projects together with partner companies related to concepts and techniques of domain-specific modeling and languages:

Aragon: development of a graphical-user interface builder for an object-oriented application framework for mobile devices [PPRL07].
Testbed: development of a software testbed for mobile software frameworks [HHK+08].
OdcEditor: development of an end-user programming environment for injection molding machines [PP09].

The remainder of this section focuses on an overview of the field of domain-specific languages and modeling in general and its application to the aforementioned research projects at SCCH.

Overview of the Field 5.1

Domain-specific modeling has two mutual dependent goals [KT08]: First, raise the level of abstraction beyond programming by specifying the solution in a language that directly uses concepts and rules from a specific problem domain. Second, generate final products in a chosen programming language or other form from these high-level specifications.

To achieve these goals, a domain-specific modeling solution consists of following parts (see [KT08]): a domain-specific language, code generators, and a domain framework.

Domain-Specific Language

A domain-specific language (DSL) provides concepts and rules to represent elements in the problem domain on language level. In that, it allows expressing problems of the given domain in a more natural and intuitive way, raises the level of abstraction in the given domain, and brings software specification closer to the domain experts. In distinction to general-purpose programming languages, which are universally applicable to many domains, domain-specific languages are created specifically for problems in the domain and are not intended to problems outside it.

As a formal language, a DSL is defined by its concrete syntax, abstract syntax, and semantics. The concrete syntax (or notation) specifies the concrete appearance of a DSL visible to the user. The notation can be one of various forms—textual, graphical, tabular, etc.—depending on the problem domain at hand. The concrete syntax usually is of increased importance for DSLs, as it—to a great extent—determines acceptance by users.

The goal of the abstract syntax (or meta-model in context of model-driven development) is to describe the structural essence of a language including elements and relationships between elements like containment and references. Concrete and abstract syntax of textual languages are often defined in a single source [KRV07, GBU08] or the concrete syntax defines the abstract syntax implicitly [LJJ07, PP08].

Whereas the formal definition of both abstract and concrete syntax is well elaborated, the language semantics is usually given by the code generators. Formal definition of language semantics is still an open research field, e.g. [Sad08].

In general, DSLs are either standalone, embedded into a host language, or used as domain-specific presentation extensions. A standalone DSL provides full abstraction of the underlying general-purpose programming language used for the solution [KT08]. An embedded DSL is one which extends an existing general-purpose language (e.g. [AMS08]). A domain-specific presentation extension of a general-purpose programming language (e.g. [EK07]) facilitates readability and closes the gap between problem and solution domain. In context of domain-specific modeling, the focus is on standalone DSLs.

Code Generators

A code generator extracts information from a DSL program and generates code in a target language. The target code is either in a general-purpose programming language, which then will be compiled and linked with the domain framework [KT08], or is in some intermediate representation that is interpreted by the domain framework [HHK$^+$08].

Code generation works with transformation rules which specify how the different elements in the DSL program are transformed into target language constructs. For textual output, the transformation techniques model-to-text and text-to-text [LJJ07] are used, depending on the representation of the

DSL program (model or text). For the former one, two main approaches are available [CH03]: visitor-based and template-based.

Domain Framework

A domain framework provides the interface between the generated code and the underlying target platform. Domain-specific frameworks [FJ99] are not specific to the DSM approach but a general approach for software reuse to increase productivity in a specific domain. However, a domain framework can support a DSM approach by providing the immutable part of a solution not visible to users which can be customized and configured by DSL programs. In general, a domain framework is written in a general-purpose programming language by and for software experts, whereas a DSM solution puts a domain-specific language on top of a framework.

Tool Support

The success of a DSM solution largely depends on provided tool support to create and manipulate software models in a given domain-specific language [PP08]. Building a DSM solution should be possible without having to manually program the tool support.

Figure 22 shows the tool chain supporting a DSM approach. A powerful meta-modeling approach is crucial for defining concrete and abstract syntax of a DSL language. The goal is to generate editors, compilers and other language tools from the declarative specification. On the other side, code generation is facilitated by the specification of code generation rules, which specify how the language elements defined in the meta-model should be translated into target code. Today, several powerful DSL frameworks exist which support language engineering for graphical as well as textual DSLs, e.g., EMF and GMF tools for Eclipse [SBPM09], DSL Tools in MS Visual Studio [CJKW07], or the MetaEdit+ environment [KT08]. A comparison of available platforms for textual languages can be found in [PP08].

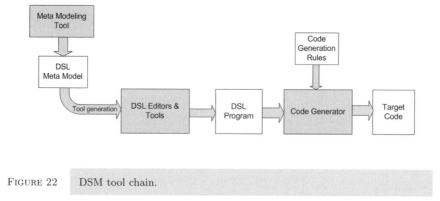

FIGURE 22   DSM tool chain.

5.2 Modeling and Code Generation

In this subsection, we present results from an application-oriented research project carried out by SCCH and its partner company Comneon[10]. The goal of this project was to develop a platform-independent builder tool for man-machine interfaces (MMI) for mobile and embedded devices. Tool support for graphical user interfaces (GUI) or MMIs are recognized as traditional domains where domain-specific modeling can improve both productivity and flexibility by removing the gap between source code and the resulting MMI. In this research project we have developed modeling, meta-modeling, and code generation concepts and have implemented them in the builder tool Aragon [PPRL07]. The tool is used together with the object-oriented C++ framework APOXI developed by Comneon for supporting the multi-stage customization process carried out by domain experts.

As a typical domain framework, APOXI has been designed to meet the special requirements of mobile, embedded devices and provides specific, easy to use and comprehensible APIs for MMI and application development. Application development follows the general idea of application frameworks [Joh99], combined with a strict separation of application behavior and user interface to ease the MMI customization process. Mobile phone manufacturers (MPM) develop customized software solutions based on the framework and customize and adapt their solutions to meet requirements of different mobile phone network operations and market needs resulting in up to 60 different variants of an MMI. MPM developers are typical domain experts that find it difficult to work with plain C++ APIs provided by APOXI. Hence, there is a need for a domain-specific modeling tool to create, adapt, and customize MMIs of embedded devices.

The main challenge for developing a platform-independent MMI builder tool in the domain of mobile and embedded devices were to provide accurate

---

[10] www.comneon.com

feedback of a resulting MMI even in the modeling (design) phase for a large set of different devices and to provide code generators that transforms MMI models into platform-specific code that can be used by the APOXI framework. Figure 23 shows a screen dump of the tool Aragon which has been developed on top of the Eclipse platform.

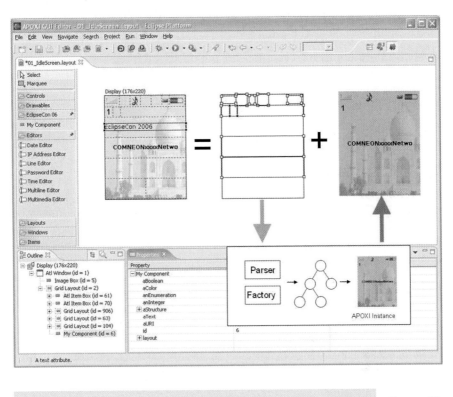

Screen dump of the APOXI GUI Editor.   FIGURE 23

Domain Modeling

Domain modeling in the project started by considering the framework code, i.e., the APOXI framework, the look and feel of resulting MMIs, the requirements of the multi-stage configuration process, and constraints and preferences stemming from the different stakeholders involved. In general, for building MMI solutions of mobile devices a domain expert has to have means to specify the screens with user interface elements, their individual settings, their layout and positioning, containment relations, and how the user interface gestures are connected to application behavior. In distinction to other UI builder tools, Aragon pursues an approach which is target agnostic, i.e., the tool itself is not dependent on the target implementation but fully configured by meta-information which is realized in a target independent and extensible form.

As result, the meta-model, i.e., the abstract syntax of the modeling language, comprises the following concepts:

- Meta-information on UI components provided by a framework (e.g. APOXI) and extensions like windows and menus together with their attributes, and constraints on their configuration, composition, and layout.
- Meta-information on available applications and features provided by applications. This information is required to connect MMI elements with application features implemented in a general-purpose programming language, e.g., the C++ programming language.

Although, this information can be extracted from source code to a large extend, domain experts want to define further constraints concerning composition of UI components that have to be validated and, hence, must be included in the meta-model. Aragon therefore supports a dual approach, i.e., parts of the meta-information is extracted from source code while additional information can be provided by the modeller. However, the meta-model is the sole information Aragon uses for configuring the editor, filling the component palette with elements, guiding the user actions, and validating domain models (e.g. window composition).

In a typical DSM solution, only a few domain experts define the meta-model, whereas users of a DSM solution are not concerned with it. For Aragon, this is not sufficient because of the multi-stage development process including different stakeholders. Besides the framework team that specify meta-model for the APOXI framework and basic applications, also MPM developers define meta-models about new applications and extensions to the APOXI framework. Hence, more powerful tool support to create, maintain, and validate meta-models by users of the DSM solution is required and provided by Aragon resulting in more flexibility compared to other meta-modeling environments [SBPM09, CJKW07, LKT04]. In Aragon therefore, a flexible meta-modeling scheme based on XML is defined which allows adding meta-information by simply adding additional XML files.

For graphical DSLs, the concrete syntax, i.e. the visual representation of the models, is usually defined by specifying the visual representation of the language elements in the meta-model. In Aragon however, the visual representation is not part of the tool, but visual feedback is provided directly by the target framework, e.g. APOXI, as shown in Figure 23. The APOXI instance accepts a MMI model sent by the Aragon tool, e.g. a screen layout, creates the corresponding window object with all child objects and sends back the resulting display image to Aragon. Aragon then merges the resulting image with the invisible domain-model. Besides rendering the corresponding visual representation, some additional information, in particular positioning information of UI elements are extracted from the target platform and sent back to Aragon. This avoids reimplementation of rendering and layout algorithms, which are provided by the domain framework anyway.

The great advantage of this approach for MMI design is, that any divergence between the visual feedback gained in the design stage and the final appearance on the target device is eliminated. Aragon guarantees exact visual feedback according to the target device already in the modeling (or design) phase. Furthermore, the approach used by the Aragon tools is automatically extensible because new user interface elements available in a domain framework, e.g. APOXI, can be displayed in the Aragon editors without further modification of the tools. In addition, by replacing the small interface of Aragon to the target framework, Aragon can easily be adapted to any target platform.

Code Generation

According to the DSM architecture, code generators transform models conforming to a DSL into target code or an intermediate representation which then is interpreted on the target. Aragon supports both forms of code generation, i.e., it allows transforming a window layout alternatively to resource files or to C++ source code. The former one is used for easier customization because resource files may be stored on flash memory of a mobile device and easily replaced. The latter one is more compact and can be loaded fast into memory, which is required for low-end mobile devices due to limited memory and CPU resources.

Because of the textual output of both forms, the Aragon code generators follow the transformation technique model-to-text [LJJ07]. For this technique two main approaches are available [CH03]: visitor-based and template-based. However, both approaches hinder extensibility by DSM users as required for Aragon. The reason is that template languages are often complex and visitors directly operate on the internal representation of a meta-model, which usually shall be hidden to DSM users.

As consequence, we have combined both techniques to a two-phase code generator, which can be extended by DSM users more easily:

1. Domain models given in XML are transformed by means of XSLT into an intermediate model (model-to-model transformation). The XSLT rules can be extended by DSM users.
2. A non-extensible visitor transforms the intermediate model into resulting resource files or C++ source code (model-to-text transformation).

Besides this, Aragon also provides template-based, non-extensible code generators that generate and update C++ source code for applications based on available meta-data of applications. This allows automatic synchronization of meta-model and C++ source code and increases productivity. In this way, common application code concerning registration and feature invocation can be automatically generated from meta-models.

Altogether, the architectural features as described above result in a flexible and extensible tool which, in its core, is independent from the target framework (which is currently APOXI). Actually, being almost APOXI agnostic and only having a tiny interface, Aragon is readily prepared to be used together with other frameworks for MMI design.

5.3 Textual Domain-Specific Languages

In this subsection, we present challenges and results from an application-oriented research project Testbed [HHK+08] aiming the development of a software testbed for unit/integration/system testing of mobile software frameworks.

The field of textual domain-specific languages is well elaborated, mainly from experience over five decades on textual general-purpose programming languages. This includes language definition (concrete and abstract syntax) as well as tool support.

Usually, the concrete syntax (CS) is defined in form of a context-free grammar and the abstract syntax (AS) is either explicitly defined and mapped to concrete syntax, implicitly derived from concrete syntax or concrete and abstract syntax are defined in single source [PP08]. On contrary, other approaches [JBK06, MFF+06] allows the description of a textual concrete syntax for a given abstract syntax in form of a meta-model.

Tool support for textual languages includes text-to-model transformation (parsing), editor support, and code generation. The automatically generation of compiler frontends including scanner and parser for text-to-model transformation is an established area and a lot of such tools (e.g. CoCo/R, LPG, ANTLR) are available. As a consequent further development, actual approaches as enumerated in [PP08] also automatically generate editor support from a context-free grammar definition and provide support for template-based or visitor-based code generation.

For the Testbed project, we followed a DSM approach by providing a textual domain-specific language to specify test cases that can be executed by a test environment. Domain-specific language for testing has been applied by various approaches (e.g. Sinha [SSM03] and Siddhartha [RR99]). In particular, the usage of DSLs for testing of mobile software frameworks has several advantages [HHK+08]:

- Testers usually are not familiar with source code of the system under test (SUT) even are not usually C++ experts.
- Languages like C++ cause many programming errors, most notable errors concerning memory management. Using a high-level testing language prevents many programming errors and facilitates more robust test cases that cannot harm the SUT.
- The use of a separate language (and not the language used to program the SUT) leads to decoupling of the SUT and test cases. Instead of using the API of a SUT directly, high-level language constructs defined by a DSL are more stable with regard of changes of the SUT.
- A DSL also facilitates high-level constructs for testing as well as of the problem domain.

We defined a textual domain-specific language that includes first-class concepts on language level for testing of mobile software frameworks. Besides general-purpose elements for assignment, loops, conditional statements, etc., the language provides following domain-specific elements:

- Statements to verify test results.
- Statements to control test case execution.
- Statements for logging.
- Statements to simulate the protocol stack for both sending and receiving signals of different communication protocols from a test case.

Figure 24 gives an (simplified) example of a test case intended to test a single function of the system under test. The instruction in line 2 simulates a function call to the SUT which in turn sends a signal (MN_ATTACH_REQ) to the protocol stack. This event is consumed and verified from the statement in line 3. To simulate the response back from the protocol stack to the SUT, an SDL signal is created and initialized (lines 4–6) and sent to the SUT in line 7. Triggered by this event, the SUT will call a callback function. This call is consumed and verified by the script in line 8. Test scripts written in the defined language are compiled into an intermediate code that is interpreted by the test environment which can be considered as domain framework in context of a DSM solution.

End-User Programming 5.4

In this subsection, we present results from an application-oriented research project carried out by SCCH and the COMET partner company KEBA AG. The goal of this project was to develop a tool prototype that supports end users (e.g. machine operators) without detail software development expertise to program control programs of injection molding machines. Furthermore,

```
  ExampleTest.tbs  ✕
  1
  2   ExecSync("Driver.Method",{1, 2, 3});
  3   req = WaitForSDLSignal(MN_ATTACH_REQ);
  4   cnf = CreateSDLSignal(MN_ATTACH_CNF);
❸ 5   cnf.Param1.mccs = 1;
  6   // ...              Structure cnf.Param1 has no field mccs
  7   SendSDLSignal(cnf);
  8   cb = WaitForEvent("callback");
  9
```

FIGURE 24   Notation and editing support for testing language.

the modification of control programs must be possible on the touch screen
on the machine directly.

In general, end-user programmers (EUP) are people who write programs,
but not as their primary job function [MKB06]. Instead, they must write
programs in support of achieving their main goal, which is something else.
End-users are often experts of a certain domain, like electrical engineering,
robotics, or plastics. Such domain experts have to transfer their domain
knowledge into a representation that can be understood by the computer.

We have chosen a DSM approach for several reasons. As reported in
[PHS+08a], current modeling notations and languages in the automation
domain do not satisfy the requirements of a programming language, which
can be used by domain experts. On contrary, domain-specific languages
are a proven approach to bring programming closer to application domains
[PHS+08a], and hence, to domain experts. By following a DSM approach,
the challenge is to provide a language or notation that can be used by end-
users on the machine directly. In this context, end-users are domain experts
as machine operators and commissioning specialists.

Language for End-User Programming

A domain-specific language for programming machine cycles of injection
molding machines has to incorporate machine aggregates, aggregate actions,
and blocks of sequential or parallel actions. On the meta-model level, individual aggregate actions of a machine connected together according to sequential
and parallel executions result in the abstract syntax graph for an entire machine cycle.

To visualize a machine cycle to end users, the graph is not displayed directly but by means of a notation (concrete syntax) that arranges individual

nodes and their connections in a two dimensional way, as shown in Figure 25. Nodes representing aggregate actions are placed in horizontal columns resulting in a column for each aggregate. The chosen icons together with the order of columns corresponding to the aggregate position on the actual machine give more specific information for domain experts to identify individual actions of aggregates compared to general-purpose programming languages or software diagrams. Vertically, the actions are placed according to their de-

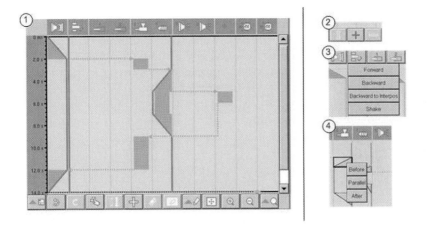

Notation, interaction, and tool support to manipulate machine cycles on touch screens.   FIGURE 25

pendency starting with the very first action of a machine cycle on the top. The vertical dimension of a single action and, hence, of the entire graph, corresponds to the time required to execute an action, or the entire machine cycle respectively. This technique that maps the property duration of an action to a visual dimension facilitates to locate time-consuming actions and to identify actions along the critical path.

The described incorporation of domain aspects (e.g. aggregates and duration) as elements of a visual domain-specific language is a typical example how a DSL can facilitate end-user programming for domain exerts.

Visualization and Interaction

As pointed out earlier, the success of a DSM solution largely depends on provided tool support to create and manipulate software models, e.g. machine cycles, in a given domain-specific language. From our experience, tool support becomes much more important when interaction is done by end-users on touch screens compared to interaction on personal computers with keyboard and mouse pointer devices.

For instance, the modification of a machine cycle by inserting a new action is a non-trivial action on a touch screen that requires special guidelines on individual steps as shown in Figure 25. After pressing the insert button (2), the user has to perform several steps to insert a new action, whereas the editor gives visual feedback about the next step. First, the user selects the corresponding aggregate from the column headers and, afterwards, selects from available actions provided by the selected aggregate (3). Second, the user selects an already existing action and the relative insertion option (4).

For end-user programming, it is also important to achieve a fault tolerance for user interaction so that users can cancel operations at any time. The specification of end-users needs in form of personas [MK08] and usability evaluations provides valuable feedback for the design of both the notation as well as the interaction concepts.

Acknowledgements

Research and development described in this chapter has been carried out by Software Competence Center Hagenberg GmbH (SCCH) in close cooperation with its scientific partners and its partner companies within the frame of the Austrian K*plus* and COMET competence center programs.

References

[ABD+04]   Alain Abran, Pierre Bourque, Robert Dupuis, James W. Moore, and Leonard L. Tripp. *Guide to the Software Engineering Body of Knowledge - SWEBOK*. IEEE Press, Piscataway, NJ, USA, 2004 version edition, 2004.

[AGM05]   Paris Avgeriou, Nicolas Guelfi, and Nenad Medvidovic. Software architecture description and uml. pages 23–32. 2005.

[AMS08]   Lennart Augustsson, Howard Mansell, and Ganesh Sittampalam. Paradise: a two-stage dsl embedded in haskell. In *ICFP '08: Proceeding of the 13th ACM SIGPLAN international conference on Functional programming*, pages 225–228, New York, NY, USA, 2008. ACM.

[BA04]   Kent Beck and Cynthia Andres. *Extreme Programming Explained: Embrace Change (2nd Edition)*. Addison-Wesley Professional, 2 edition, November 2004.

[BAB+05]   Stefan Biffl, Aybüke Aurum, Barry Boehm, Hakan Erdogmus, and Paul Grünbacher. *Value-Based Software Engineering*. Springer Verlag, oct 2005.

[Bac97]   James Bach. Good enough quality: Beyond the buzzword. *Computer*, 30(8):96–98, 1997.

[BCK03]   Len Bass, Paul Clements, and Rick Kazman. *Software Architecture in Practice, Second Edition*. Addison-Wesley Professional, April 2003.

[BD04]   Pierre Bourque and Robert Dupuis, editors. *SWEBOK - Guide to the Software Engineering Body of Knowledge, 2004 Version*. IEEE Computer Society, 2004 version edition, 2004.

[Bec02]   Kent Beck. *Test Driven Development: By Example*. Addison-Wesley Professional, November 2002.

[Bei90]   Boris Beizer. *Software Testing Techniques 2E*. International Thomson Computer Press, 2nd edition, June 1990.

[BG00]   Kent Beck and Erich Gamma. *More Java Gems*, chapter Test-infected: programmers love writing tests, pages 357–376. Cambridge University Press, 2000.

[Boe76]   B. W. Boehm. Software engineering. *Transactions on Computers*, C-25(12):1226–1241, 1976.

[Boe88]   B. W. Boehm. A spiral model of software development and enhancement. *Computer*, 21(5):61–72, May 1988.

[BR08]   Armin Beer and Rudolf Ramler. The role of experience in software testing practice. In *Proceedings of the 34th EUROMICRO Conference on Software Engineering and Advanced Applications*, pages 258–265, Parma, Italy, 2008. IEEE Computer Society.

[Bru01]   H. Bruyninckx. Open robot control software: the OROCOS project. In *Robotics and Automation, 2001. Proceedings 2001 ICRA. IEEE International Conference on*, volume 3, pages 2523–2528 vol.3, 2001.

[BW08]   Georg Buchgeher and Rainer Weinreich. Integrated software architecture management and validation. In *Software Engineering Advances, 2008. ICSEA '08. The Third International Conference on*, pages 427–436, 2008.

[BWK05]   Stefan Berner, Roland Weber, and Rudolf K. Keller. Observations and lessons learned from automated testing. In *Proceedings of the 27th international conference on Software engineering*, pages 571–579, St. Louis, MO, USA, 2005. ACM.

[CBB⁺02]   Paul Clements, Felix Bachmann, Len Bass, David Garlan, James Ivers, Reed Little, Robert Nord, and Judith Stafford. *Documenting Software Architectures: Views and Beyond*. Addison-Wesley Professional, September 2002.

[CEC00]   Krzysztof Czarnecki, Ulrich Eisenecker, and Krzysztof Czarnecki. *Generative Programming: Methods, Tools, and Applications*. Addison-Wesley Professional, June 2000.

[CH03]   Krzysztof Czarnecki and Simon Helsen. Classification of model transformation approaches. In *Proceedings of the 2nd OOPSLA Workshop on Generative Techniques in the Context of MDA*, 2003.

[Cha05]   R. N. Charette. Why software fails. *IEEE Spectrum*, 42(9):42–49, September 2005.

[Chr92]   Gerhard Chroust. *Modelle der SoftwareEntwicklung*. Oldenbourg Verlag München Wien, 1992. in German.

[CJKW07]   Steve Cook, Gareth Jones, Stuart Kent, and Alan C. Wills. *Domain Specific Development with Visual Studio DSL Tools (Microsoft .Net Development)*. Addison-Wesley Longman, Amsterdam, May 2007.

[CKK02]   Paul Clements, Rick Kazman, and Mark Klein. *Evaluating Software Architectures: Methods and Case Studies*. Addison-Wesley Professional, January 2002.

[Cle95]   Paul Clements. Formal methods in describing architectures. In *Monterey Workshop on Formal Methods and Architecture*, September 1995.

[Cle96]   Paul C. Clements. A survey of architecture description languages. In *IWSSD '96: Proceedings of the 8th International Workshop on Software Specification and Design*, Washington, DC, USA, 1996. IEEE Computer Society.

[CMM06]   CMMI for development, version 1.2. Technical report CMU/SEI-2006-TR-008, Carnegie Mellon University, Software Engineering Institute, Pittsburgh, PA 15213-3890, August 2006.

[CN02]   P. Clements and L. N. Northrop. *Software Product Lines: Practices and Patterns.* Addison Wesley Professional Series: The SEI Series in Software Engineering. Addison Wesley, 2002.

[Cop04]   Lee Copeland. *A Practitioner's Guide to Software Test Design.* Artech House Publishers, 2004.

[Cza05]   Krzysztof Czarnecki. Overview of generative software development. pages 326–341. 2005.

[DeM86]   T. DeMarco. *Controlling Software Projects: Management, Measurement, and Estimates.* Prentice Hall PTR, Upper Saddle River, NJ, USA, 1986.

[Dio93]   R. Dion. Process improvement and the corporate balance sheet. *IEEE Software,* pages 28–35, July 1993.

[DN02]   L. Dobrica and E. Niemela. A survey on software architecture analysis methods. *Software Engineering, IEEE Transactions on,* 28(7):638–653, 2002.

[Dor93]   Alec Dorling. Software Process Improvement and Capability Determination. *Software Quality Journal,* 2(4):209–224, December 1993. also in: Information and Software Technology, vol. 35, no. 6/7, June 1993, p. 404.

[Dor09]   Bernhard Dorninger. ProMoRTE: A process model runtime environment based on OSGi. 2009. accepted for publication at 7th IEEE International Conference on Industrial Informatics (INDIN 2009).

[Dou02]   Bruce Powell Douglass. *Real-Time Design Patterns: Robust Scalable Architecture for Real-Time Systems.* Addison-Wesley Longman Publishing Co., Inc., Boston, MA, USA, 2002.

[DW06]   Patricia Derler and Rainer Weinreich. Models and tools for soa governance. In *International Conference on Trends in Enterprise Application Architecture.* Springer Lecture Notes on Computer Science (LNCS), December 2006.

[Eck05]   Wayne W. Eckerson. *Performance Dashboards: Measuring, Monitoring, and Managing Your Business.* Wiley, October 2005.

[EJB06]   Enterprise javabeans 3.0 specification, 2006.

[EK07]   Andrew D. Eisenberg and Gregor Kiczales. Expressive programs through presentation extension. In *AOSD '07: Proceedings of the 6th international conference on Aspect-oriented software development,* pages 73–84, New York, NY, USA, 2007. ACM.

[FG99]   Mark Fewster and Dorothy Graham. *Software Test Automation.* Addison-Wesley Professional, September 1999.

[FJ99]   Mohamed Fayad and Ralph Johnson. *Domain-Specific Application Frameworks: Frameworks Experience by Industry.* John Wiley & Sons, October 1999.

[FPC97]   William A. Florac, Robert E. Park, and Anita D. Carleton. Practical software measurement: Measuring for process management and improvement. Guidebook CMU/SEI-97-HB-003, Software Engineering Institute, Carnegie Mellon University, Pittsburgh, PA 15213, April 1997.

[Gar84]   David A. Garvin. What does product quality really mean? *Sloan Management Review,* 26(1):25–45, Fall 1984.

[Gar00]   David Garlan. Software architecture: a roadmap. In *ICSE '00: Proceedings of the Conference on The Future of Software Engineering,* pages 91–101, New York, NY, USA, 2000. ACM Press.

[GBU08]   Thomas Goldschmidt, Steffen Becker, and Axel Uhl. Classification of concrete textual syntax mapping approaches. pages 169–184. 2008.

[GJ96]   Pankaj K. Garg and Mehdi Jazayeri, editors. *ProcessCentered Software Engineering Environments.* IEEE Computer Society Press, 1996.

[Gre07]   J. Grenning. Applying test driven development to embedded software. *Instrumentation & Measurement Magazine, IEEE,* 10(6):20–25, 2007.

[Ham04]   Paul Hamill. *Unit Test Frameworks*. O'Reilly Media, Inc., October 2004.

[HB06]   LiGuo Huang and Barry Boehm. How much software quality investment is enough: A Value-Based approach. *IEEE Software*, 23(5):88–95, 2006.

[HCR+94] James Herbsleb, Anita Carleton, James Rozum, Jane Siegel, and David Zubrow. Benefits of CMM-based software process improvement: Initial results. Technical Report CMU/SEI-94-TR-013, Software Engineering Institute, Carnegie Mellon University, Pittsburgh, Pennsylvania 15213, August 1994.

[Hel07]   Hello2morro. Sonarj. http://www.hello2morrow.de, 2007.

[HHK+08] Walter Hargassner, Thomas Hofer, Claus Klammer, Josef Pichler, and Gernot Reisinger. A script-based testbed for mobile software frameworks. In *Proceedings of the First International Conference on Software Testing, Verification and Validation*, pages 448–457. IEEE, April 2008.

[HNS99]   Christine Hofmeister, Robert Nord, and Dilip Soni. *Applied Software Architecture*. Addison-Wesley Professional, November 1999.

[Hof05]   Christine Hofmeister. Architecting session report. In *WICSA '05: Proceedings of the 5th Working IEEE/IFIP Conference on Software Architecture (WICSA'05)*, pages 209–210, Washington, DC, USA, 2005. IEEE Computer Society.

[HSSL02] B. Henderson-Sellers, F. Stallinger, and B. Lefever. Bridging the gap from process modelling to process assessment: the OOSPICE process specification for component-based software engineering. In *Proceedings of the 28th Euromicro Conference*, pages 324–331. IEEE Computer Society, 2002.

[HT06]   Brent Hailpern and Peri Tarr. Model-driven development: The good, the bad, and the ugly. *IBM Systems Journal*, 45(3):451–461, July 2006.

[Hum89]   W. Humphrey. *Managing the Software Process*. AddisonWesley Reading Mass., 1989.

[Hum95]   W. Humphrey. *A Discipline for Software Engineering*. SEI Series in Software engineering. AddisonWesley, 1995.

[IEE90]   IEEE Std 610.12-1990: IEEE standard glossary of software engineering terminology, 1990.

[IMP05]   P. Inverardi, H. Muccini, and P. Pelliccione. Dually: Putting in synergy uml 2.0 and adls. In *WICSA '05: Proceedings of the 5th Working IEEE/IFIP Conference on Software Architecture*, pages 251–252, Washington, DC, USA, 2005. IEEE Computer Society.

[Int08]   International Organization for Standardization (ISO). Systems and software engineering - architectural description working draft 3, 2008.

[ISO95]   ISO/IEC 12207:1995, Information technology - Software life cycle processes, 1995. Amd.1:2002; Amd.2:2004.

[ISO98]   ISO/IEC TR 15504-7:1998(e), Information technology - Software process assessment - Part 7: Guide for use in process improvement, 1998.

[ISO01]   ISO/IEC 9126-1:2001, Software engineering - Product quality - Part 1: Quality model, 2001.

[ISO03]   ISO/IEC 15504:2003, Information Technology - Process Assessment, 2003.

[ISO05]   ISO/IEC 25000:2005, Software engineering - Software product Quality Requirements and Evaluation (SQuaRE) - Guide to SQuaRE, 2005.

[ISO09]   ISO/IEC PDTR 29110:2009, Software Engineering - Lifecycle Profiles for Very Small Enterprises (VSE), January 2009.

[JBK06]   Frédéric Jouault, Jean Bézivin, and Ivan Kurtev. Tcs: a dsl for the specification of textual concrete syntaxes in model engineering. In *GPCE '06: Proceedings of the 5th international conference on Generative programming and component engineering*, pages 249–254, New York, NY, USA, 2006. ACM.

[JGJ97]   I. Jacobson, M. Griss, and P. Jonsson. *Software Reuse: Architecture, Process and Organization for Business Success*. Addison-Wesley Professional, 1997.

[Joh99]   Ralph E. Johnson. *Building Application Frameworks: Object-Oriented Foundations of Framework Design*. John Wiley & Sons, 1 edition, September 1999.

[Kan02]   Stephen H. Kan. *Metrics and Models in Software Quality Engineering.*
            Addison-Wesley Longman Publishing, 2002.
[KC04]   Ralph Kimball and Joe Caserta. *The Data Warehouse ETL Toolkit: Practical
            Techniques for Extracting, Cleaning, Conforming, and Delivering Data.* Wiley,
            September 2004.
[KFN99]   Cem Kaner, Jack Falk, and Hung Q. Nguyen. *Testing Computer Software.*
            Wiley, 2 edition, April 1999.
[Kin01]   Atte Kinnula. *Software Process Engineering Systems: Models and Industry
            Cases.* Oulu University Press, 2001. ISBN 951-42-6508-4.
[KL05]   A.G. Koru and H. Liu. Building effective defect-prediction models in practice.
            IEEE Software, 22(6):23–29, 2005.
[KOS06]   P. Kruchten, H. Obbink, and J. Stafford. The past, present, and future for
            software architecture. *Software, IEEE*, 23(2):22–30, 2006.
[Kru95]   Philippe Kruchten. The 4+1 view model of architecture. *IEEE Softw.*,
            12(6):42–50, November 1995.
[Kru03]   Philippe Kruchten. *The Rational Unified Process: An Introduction.* Addison-
            Wesley, 3rd edition, 2003. ISBN 0321197704, 9780321197702.
[KRV07]   Holger Krahn, Bernhard Rumpe, and Steven Völkel. Integrated definition of
            abstract and concrete syntax for textual languages. pages 286–300. 2007.
[KT08]   Steven Kelly and Juha-Pekka Tolvanen. *Domain-Specific Modeling: Enabling
            Full Code Generation.* John Wiley & Sons, March 2008.
[KWB03]   Anneke Kleppe, Jos Warmer, and Wim Bast. *MDA Explained: The Model
            Driven Architecture–Practice and Promise.* Addison-Wesley Professional,
            April 2003.
[KWZ09]   Thomas Kriechbaum, Rainer Weinreich, and Thomas Ziebermayr. Compatibil-
            ity rules for the homogeneous evolution of enterprise services. In *International
            Symposium on Service Science (ISSS)*, pages 189–200. Logos Verlag Berlin,
            March 2009.
[LBB+05]   U. Löwen, R. Bertsch, B. Böhm, S. Prummer, and T. Tetzner. Systema-
            tisierung des Engineerings von Industrieanlagen. *atp - Automatisierungstech-
            nische Praxis, Oldenbourg Industrieverlag*, (4):54–61, 2005. in German.
[LH93]   Wei Li and Sallie Henry. Object-oriented metrics that predict maintainability.
            J. Syst. Softw., 23(2):111–122, November 1993.
[LH09]   Henrik Lochmann and Anders Hessellund. An integrated view on modeling
            with multiple domain-specific languages. In *Proceedings of the IASTED In-
            ternational Conference Software Engineering (SE 2009)*, pages 1–10. ACTA
            Press, February 2009.
[LJJ07]   B. Langlois, C. E. Jitia, and E. Jouenne. Dsl classification. In *Proceedings of
            the 7th OOPSLA Workshop on Domain-Specific Modeling*, 2007.
[LKT04]   Janne Luoma, Steven Kelly, and Juha-Pekka Tolvanen. Defining domain-
            specific modeling languages: Collected experiences. *Proceedings of the 4th
            OOPSLA Workshop on Domain-Specific Modeling*, 2004.
[Lon93]   J. Lonchamp. A structured conceptual and terminological framework for soft-
            ware process engineering. In *Software Process, 1993. Continuous Software
            Process Improvement, Second International Conference on the*, pages 41–53,
            Feb 1993.
[LR07]   Stefan Larndorfer and Rudolf Ramler. TestCockpit: business intelligence for
            test management. In *Work in Progress Session in conjunction with 33rd EU-
            ROMICRO Conf. on Software Engineering and Advanced Applications*, 2007.
[LRB09]   Stefan Larndorfer, Rudolf Ramler, and Clemens Buchwiser. Experiences and
            results from establishing a software cockpit. In *upcoming*, 2009.
[LRFL07]   Stefan Larndorfer, Rudolf Ramler, Christian Federspiel, and Klaus Lehner.
            Testing High-Reliability software for continuous casting steel plants - experi-
            ences and lessons learned from siemens VAI. In *Proceedings of the 33rd EU-
            ROMICRO Conference on Software Engineering and Advanced Applications*,
            pages 255–262, Luebeck, Germany, 2007. IEEE Computer Society.

[McF96]   Bob McFeeley. IDEAL: A user's guide for software process improvement. Handbook CMU/SEI-96-HB-001, Software Engineering Institute, Carnegie Mellon University, Pittsburgh, Pennsylvania 15213, February 1996.

[MD08]   Tom Mens and Serge Demeyer. *Software Evolution.* Springer Verlag, March 2008.

[MDT07]   Nenad Medvidovic, Eric M. Dashofy, and Richard N. Taylor. Moving architectural description from under the technology lamppost. *Information and Software Technology,* 49(1):12–31, January 2007.

[MFF⁺06] Pierre-Alain Muller, Franck Fleurey, Frédéric Fondement, Michel Hassenforder, Rémi Schneckenburger, Sébastien Gérard, and Jean-Marc Jézéquel. *Model-Driven Analysis and Synthesis of Concrete Syntax.* 2006.

[MGF07]   T. Menzies, J. Greenwald, and A. Frank. Data mining static code attributes to learn defect predictors. *IEEE Transactions on Software Engineering,* 33(1):2–13, 2007.

[MH04]   Jürgen Münch and Jens Heidrich. Software project control centers: concepts and approaches. *Journal of Systems and Software,* 70(1-2):3–19, February 2004.

[Mil02]   Dave Miller. *Fundamental Concepts for the Software Quality Engineer,* chapter Choice and Application of a Software Quality Model, pages 17–24. ASQ Quality Press, 2002.

[MK08]   Jennifer Mcginn and Nalini Kotamraju. Data-driven persona development. In *CHI '08: Proceeding of the twenty-sixth annual SIGCHI conference on Human factors in computing systems,* pages 1521–1524, New York, NY, USA, 2008. ACM.

[MKB06]   Brad A. Myers, Andrew J. Ko, and Margaret M. Burnett. Invited research overview: end-user programming. In *CHI '06: CHI '06 extended abstracts on Human factors in computing systems,* pages 75–80, New York, NY, USA, 2006. ACM.

[MKMG97] R. T. Monroe, A. Kompanek, R. Melton, and D. Garlan. Architectural styles, design patterns, and objects. *Software, IEEE,* 14(1):43–52, 1997.

[MMYA01] H. Mili, A. Mili, S. Yacoub, and E. Addy. *Reuse-Based Software Engineering: Techniques, Organizations, and Controls.* Wiley-Interscience, 2001.

[MT00]   Nenad Medvidovic and Richard N. Taylor. A classification and comparison framework for software architecture description languages. *IEEE Trans. Softw. Eng.,* 26(1):70–93, January 2000.

[NBZ06]   Nachiappan Nagappan, Thomas Ball, and Andreas Zeller. Mining metrics to predict component failures. In *Proceedings of the 28th international conference on Software engineering,* pages 452–461, Shanghai, China, 2006. ACM.

[Obj07]   Object Management Group. Uml superstructure specification v2.1.1. OMG Document Number formal/07-02-05 http://www.omg.org/cgi-bin/apps/doc?formal/07-02-05.pdf, 2007.

[Obj08]   Object Management Group. Software & systems process engineering meta-model specification, version 2.0. http://www.omg.org/spec/SPEM/2.0/PDF, April 2008.

[Ope08]   OpenUP - Open Unified Process, 2008. http://epf.eclipse.org/wikis/openup/.

[OSG07]   Osgi service platform release 4, 2007.

[PCCW93] Mark C. Paulk, Bill Curtis, Mary Beth Chrissis, and Charles V. Weber. Capability maturity model for software, version 1.1. Technical Report CMU/SEI-93-TR-02, Software Engineering Institute, Carnegie Mellon University, February 1993.

[PGP08]   F. Pino, F. Garcia, and M. Piattini. Software process improvement in small and medium software enterprises: A systematic review. *Software Quality Journal,* 16(2):1573–1367, June 2008.

[PHS⁺08a] Herbert Prähofer, Dominik Hurnaus, Roland Schatz, Christian Wirth, and Hanspeter Mössenböck. Monaco: A dsl approach for programming automation systems. In *SE 2008 - Software-Engineering-Konferenz 2008*, pages 242–256, Munic, Germay, February 2008.

[PHS⁺08b] Herbert Prähofer, Dominik Hurnaus, Roland Schatz, Christian Wirth, and Hanspeter Mössenböck. Software support for building end-user programming environments in the automation domain. In *WEUSE '08: Proceedings of the 4th international workshop on End-user software engineering*, pages 76–80, New York, NY, USA, 2008. ACM.

[PP04] Gustav Pomberger and Wolfgang Pree. *Software Engineering*. Hanser Fachbuchverlag, October 2004.

[PP08] Michael Pfeiffer and Josef Pichler. A comparison of tool support for textual domain-specific languages. *Proceedings of the 8th OOPSLA Workshop on Domain-Specific Modeling*, pages 1–7, October 2008.

[PP09] Michael Pfeiffer and Josef Pichler. A DSM approach for End-User Programming in the Automation Domain. 2009. accepted for publication at 7th IEEE International Conference on Industrial Informatics (INDIN 2009).

[PPRL07] Josef Pichler, Herbert Praehofer, Gernot Reisinger, and Gerhard Leonhartsberger. Aragon: an industrial strength eclipse tool for MMI design for mobile systems. In *Proceedings of the 25th conference on IASTED International Multi-Conference: Software Engineering*, pages 156–163, Innsbruck, Austria, 2007. ACTA Press.

[PR08] Josef Pichler and Rudolf Ramler. How to test the intangible properties of graphical user interfaces? In *Proceedings of the 2008 International Conference on Software Testing, Verification, and Validation, ICST 08*, pages 494–497. IEEE Computer Society, 2008.

[PRS00] G. Pomberger, M. Rezagholi, and C. Stobbe. *Handbuch für Evaluation und Evaluierungsforschung in der Wirtschaftsinformatik*, chapter Evaluation und Verbesserung wiederverwendungsorientierter Software-Entwicklung. Oldenbourg Verlag, München/Wien, 2000. in German.

[PRZ09] Guenter Pirklbauer, Rudolf Ramler, and Rene Zeilinger. An integration-oriented model for application lifecycle management. 2009. accepted for ICEIS 2009, 11th International Conference on Enterprise Information Systems.

[PSN08] R. Plösch, F. Stallinger, and R. Neumann. SISB - systematic improvement of the solution business: Engineering strategies for the industrial solutions business, version 1.0. Technical report, Software Competence Center Hagengerg, August 2008. (non-public project deliverable).

[PW92] Dewayne E. Perry and Alexander L. Wolf. Foundations for the study of software architecture. *SIGSOFT Softw. Eng. Notes*, 17(4):40–52, October 1992.

[Ram04] Rudolf Ramler. Decision support for test management in iterative and evolutionary development. In *Proceedings of the 19th IEEE international conference on Automated software engineering*, pages 406–409, Linz, Austria, 2004. IEEE Computer Society.

[Ram08] Rudolf Ramler. The impact of product development on the lifecycle of defects. In *Proceedings of the DEFECTS 2008 Workshop on Defects in Large Software Systems*, pages 21–25, Seattle, Washington, 2008. ACM.

[RBG05] Rudolf Ramler, Stefan Biffl, and Paul Grünbacher. *Value-Based Software Engineering*, chapter Value-Based Management of Software Testing, pages 225–244. Springer Verlag, 2005.

[RCS03] Rudolf Ramler, Gerald Czech, and Dietmar Schlosser. Unit testing beyond a bar in green and red. In *Proceedings of the 4th International Conference on Extreme Programming and Agile Processes in Software Engineering, XP 2003*, pages 10–12, Genova, Italy, 2003. LNCS.

[Roy70] W. W. Royce. Managing the development of large software systems:: Concepts and techniques. In *Proc. IEEE WESCON*, pages 1–9. IEEE, August 1970.

[RR99]   Arthur A. Reyes and Debra J. Richardson. Siddhartha: a method for developing domain-specific test driver generators. In *In Proc. 14th Int. Conf. on Automated Software Engineering*, pages 12–15, 1999.

[RvW07]   Ita Richardson and Christiane Gresse von Wangenheim. Why are small software organizations different? *IEEE Software*, 24(1):18–22, January/February 2007.

[RW05]   Nick Rozanski and Eóin Woods. *Software Systems Architecture: Working With Stakeholders Using Viewpoints and Perspectives*. Addison-Wesley Professional, April 2005.

[RW06]   Rudolf Ramler and Klaus Wolfmaier. Economic perspectives in test automation: balancing automated and manual testing with opportunity cost. In *Proceedings of the 2006 international workshop on Automation of software test*, pages 85–91, Shanghai, China, 2006. ACM.

[RW08]   Rudolf Ramler and Klaus Wolfmaier. Issues and effort in integrating data from heterogeneous software repositories and corporate databases. In *Proceedings of the Second ACM-IEEE international symposium on Empirical software engineering and measurement*, pages 330–332, Kaiserslautern, Germany, 2008. ACM.

[RWS⁺09]   Rudolf Ramler, Klaus Wolfmaier, Erwin Stauder, Felix Kossak, and Thomas Natschläger. Key questions in building defect prediction models in practice. In *10th International Conference on Product Focused Software Development and Process Improvement, PROFES 2009*, Oulu, Finnland, 2009.

[RWW⁺02]   Rudolf Ramler, Edgar Weippl, Mario Winterer, Wieland Schwinger, and Josef Altmann. A quality-driven approach to web testing. In *Ibero-american Conference on Web Engineering, ICWE 2002*, pages 81–95, Argentina, 2002.

[Sad08]   Daniel A. Sadilek. Prototyping domain-specific language semantics. In *OOPSLA Companion '08: Companion to the 23rd ACM SIGPLAN conference on Object-oriented programming systems languages and applications*, pages 895–896, New York, NY, USA, 2008. ACM.

[Sam01]   J. Sametinger. *Software Engineering with Reusable Components*. Springer, 2001.

[SB03]   Douglas C. Schmidt and Frank Buschmann. Patterns, frameworks, and middleware: their synergistic relationships. In *ICSE '03: Proceedings of the 25th International Conference on Software Engineering*, pages 694–704, Washington, DC, USA, 2003. IEEE Computer Society.

[SBPM09]   David Steinberg, Frank Budinsky, Marcelo Paternostro, and Ed Merks. *EMF: Eclipse Modeling Framework (2nd Edition) (Eclipse)*. Addison-Wesley Longman, Amsterdam, 2nd revised edition (rev). edition, January 2009.

[SCA07]   Service component architecture specifications, 2007.

[Sch06]   D. C. Schmidt. Guest editor's introduction: Model-driven engineering. *Computer*, 39(2):25–31, 2006.

[SDR⁺02]   F. Stallinger, A. Dorling, T. Rout, B. Henderson-Sellers, and B. Lefever. Software process improvement for component-based software engineering: an introduction to the OOSPICE project. In *Proceedings of the 28th Euromicro Conference*, pages 318–323. IEEE Computer Society, 2002.

[Sha90]   M. Shaw. Prospects for an engineering discipline of software. *Software, IEEE*, 7(6):15–24, Nov 1990.

[She31]   Walter A. Shewhart. *Economic control of quality of manufactured product*. D. Van Nostrand Company, New York, 1931.

[SJSJ05]   Neeraj Sangal, Ev Jordan, Vineet Sinha, and Daniel Jackson. Using dependency models to manage complex software architecture. *SIGPLAN Not.*, 40(10):167–176, October 2005.

[Sof07]   Software Tomography GmbH. Sotoarc. http://www.software-tomography.de/index.html, 2007.

[Som04]   Ian Sommerville. *Software Engineering*. Addison Wesley, seventh edition, May 2004.

[SPP⁺06]   F. Stallinger, R. Plösch, H. Prähofer, S. Prummer, and J. Vollmar. A process reference model for reuse in industrial engineering: Enhancing the ISO/IEC 15504 framework to cope with organizational reuse maturity. In *Proc. SPICE 2006, Luxembourg, May 4-5, 2006*, pages 49–56, May 2006.

[SPPV09]   Fritz Stallinger, Reinhold Plösch, Gustav Pomberger, and Jan Vollmar. Bridging the gap between ISO/IEC 15504 conformant process assessment and organizational reuse enhancement. 2009. (accepted for SPICE Conference 2009, Software Process Improvement and Capability Determination, 2-4 June 2009, Turku, Finland).

[Spr08a]   Spring dynamic modules for osgi(tm) service platforms, 2008.

[Spr08b]   The spring framework - reference documentation, 2008.

[SPV07]   F. Stallinger, R. Plösch, and J. Vollmar. A process assessment based approach for improving organizational reuse maturity in multidisciplinary industrial engineering contexts. In *Proceedings of ESEPG 2007, Amsterdam, 14th June 2007*, June 2007.

[SRA06]   Christoph Steindl, Rudolf Ramler, and Josef Altmann. *Web Engineering: The Discipline of Systematic Development of Web Applications*, chapter Testing Web Applications, pages 133–153. Wiley, 2006.

[SSM03]   A. Sinha, C. S. Smidts, and A. Moran. Enhanced testing of domain specific applications by automatic extraction of axioms from functional specifications. In *Software Reliability Engineering, 2003. ISSRE 2003. 14th International Symposium on*, pages 181–190, 2003.

[Ste00]   David B. Stewart. Designing software components for real-time applications. In *in Proceedings of Embedded System Conference*, page 428, 2000.

[Tas02]   Gregory Tassy. The economic impacts of inadequate infrastructure for software testing, NIST planning report 02-3, May 2002.

[Tia05]   Jeff Tian. *Software Quality Engineering: Testing, Quality Assurance, and Quantifiable Improvement*. Wiley & Sons, 1., auflage edition, February 2005.

[TK05]   Juha-Pekka Tolvanen and Steven Kelly. Defining domain-specific modeling languages to automate product derivation: Collected experiences. pages 198–209. 2005.

[TMD09]   R. N. Taylor, Nenad Medvidovic, and Irvine E. Dashofy. *Software Architecture: Foundations, Theory, and Practice*. John Wiley & Sons, January 2009.

[TvdH07]   Richard N. Taylor and Andre van der Hoek. Software design and architecture the once and future focus of software engineering. In *FOSE '07: 2007 Future of Software Engineering*, pages 226–243, Washington, DC, USA, 2007. IEEE Computer Society.

[V-M06]   V-Modell XT, part1: Fundamentals of the V-Modell XT, version 1.2.1. Technical report, 2006. http://www.v-modell-xt.de/.

[vDKV00]   Arie v. van Deursen, Paul Klint, and Joost Visser. Domain-specific languages: An annotated bibliography. *SIGPLAN Notices*, 35(6):26–36, 2000.

[vGB02]   Jilles van Gurp and Jan Bosch. Design erosion: problems and causes. *Journal of Systems and Software*, 61(2):105–119, March 2002.

[Voa08]   Jeffrey Voas. Software quality unpeeled. *STSC CrossTalk*, (Jun 2008):27–30, 2008.

[VRM03]   M. Venzin, C. Rasner, and V. Mahnke. *Der Strategieprozess - Praxishandbuch zur Umsetzung im Unternehmen*. 2003. in German.

[VS06]   Markus Völter and Thomas Stahl. *Model-Driven Software Development : Technology, Engineering, Management*. John Wiley & Sons, June 2006.

[Was96]   A.I. Wasserman. Toward a discipline of software engineering. *Software, IEEE*, 13(6):23–31, Nov 1996.

[Was06]   Hironori Washizaki. *Product-Focused Software Process Improvement*, volume 4034 of *Lecture Notes in Computer Science*, chapter Building Software Process Line Architectures from Bottom Up, pages 415–421. Springer Berlin / Heidelberg, 2006.

[WH05]   Eoin Woods and Rich Hilliard. Architecture description languages in practice session report. In *WICSA '05: Proceedings of the 5th Working IEEE/IFIP Conference on Software Architecture (WICSA'05)*, pages 243–246, Washington, DC, USA, 2005. IEEE Computer Society.

[WV02]   James A. Whittaker and Jeffrey M. Voas. 50 years of software: Key principles for quality. *IT Professional*, 4(6):28–35, 2002.

[WWZ07]   Rainer Weinreich, Andeas Wiesauer, and Thomas Ziebermayr. A component model for integrating remote applications and services via web portals. *Journal of Object Technology (JOT)*, 6(8), September 2007.

[WZ05]   Rainer Weinreich and Thomas Ziebermayr. Enhancing presentation level integration of remote applications and services in web portals. In *2005 IEEE International Conference on Services Computing (SCC'05)*, volume 2, pages 224–236, Los Alamitos, CA, USA, 2005. IEEE Computer Society.

[WZD07]   Rainer Weinreich, Thomas Ziebermayr, and Dirk Draheim. A versioning model for enterprise services. In *21st International Conference on Advanced Information Networking and Applications Workshops (AINAW'07)*, volume 2, pages 570–575, Los Alamitos, CA, USA, 2007. IEEE Computer Society.

Chapter V
Data-Driven and Knowledge-Based Modeling

Erich Peter Klement

Edwin Lughofer, Johannes Himmelbauer, Bernhard Moser

Introduction 1

This chapter describes some highlights of successful research focusing on knowledge-based and data-driven models for industrial and decision processes. This research has been carried out during the last ten years in a close cooperation of two research institutions in Hagenberg:

- the *Fuzzy Logic Laboratorium Linz-Hagenberg (FLLL)*, a part of the Department of Knowledge-Based Mathematical Systems of the Johannes Kepler University Linz which is located in the Softwarepark Hagenberg since 1993,
- the *Software Competence Center Hagenberg (SCCH)*, initiated by several departments of the Johannes Kepler University Linz as a non-academic research institution under the K*plus* Program of the Austrian Government in 1999 and transformed into a K1 Center within the COMET Program (also of the Austrian Government) in 2008.

Our goal is to derive mathematical models for applications in economy and, in particular, in industry even in situations where comprehensive analytical models (differential or integral equations etc., usually based on physical or chemical laws) are either not available or, if they exist, impossible or too expensive to solve. However, in such complex scenarios quite often expert knowledge (formulated in linguistic terms) or data from past observations of the process to be modeled are available, allowing in many cases suitable knowledge-based and/or data-driven models to be constructed.

The main lines of research described in this chapter reflect some core competencies of the FLLL and the SCCH (especially its area Knowledge-Based Technology): fuzzy systems on the one hand (Section 2), in particular data-driven and evolving systems (Sections 3 and 4) where the FLLL was the leading partner in the cooperation and, on the other hand, the creation of fuzzy regression models and support vector machines (Sections 5 and 6) where the SCCH has particular strength.

Both institutions are very active in these fields in all relevant areas: in the references given at the end many more results of the basic and applied research of FLLL and SCCH can be found, while Section 7 exemplifies some successful cooperations with the industry.

2 Fuzzy Logics and Fuzzy Systems

2.1 Motivation

The development of fuzzy logics and fuzzy set theory started in 1965 with the paper *"Fuzzy sets"* by L. A. Zadeh [Zad65] where this quotation is taken from:

> "More often than not, the classes of objects encountered in the real physical world do not have precisely defined criteria of membership. [...] Yet, the fact remains that such imprecisely defined "classes" play an important role in human thinking, particularly in the domains of pattern recognition, communication of information, and abstraction."

Zadeh's main idea was to generalize the concept of the characteristic function $\mathbf{1}_A \colon X \to \{0, 1\}$ of a subset A of the universe of discourse X to its so-called *membership function* $\mu_A \colon X \to [0, 1]$ which can assume arbitrary values in the unit interval $[0, 1]$: the higher the degree $\mu_A(x)$ for some element $x \in X$ the more x belongs to the set A.

Typically, fuzzy sets (interpreted by their membership functions) are used in connection with linguistic expressions like *small*, *medium* or *large* which, in large parts of human thinking, have fuzzy rather than crisp boundaries and may have a significant overlap rather than forming crisp partitions.

As a consequence, systems using fuzzy sets are particularly well-suited to model human-like reasoning. This is particularly useful if for the problem to be solved no (complete) analytical model (usually derived from physical or chemical laws) is available or if an existing analytical model is too complex to be dealt with in real time. In such situations, fuzzy systems and other methods of soft computing such as neural networks, genetic algorithms or machine learning are able to use additional information existing only in the form of linguistic IF-THEN-rules or in the form of data.

Fuzzy Logics 2.2

Fuzzy logics are many-valued logics where the set $\{0,1\}$ of the two truth values in Boolean logic is replaced by the unit interval $[0,1]$.

The basic logical operation is the generalized conjunction, usually a *triangular norm* (*t-norm* for short). Triangular norms are binary operations on the unit interval $[0,1]$, turning it into an ordered, commutative semigroup with neutral element 1. They originally were studied in the context of *probabilistic metric spaces* [Men42, SS83] (generalized metric spaces where the distance between two objects is measured by a probability distribution rather than by a real number) where they play a crucial role in formulation of an appropriate triangle inequality.

Important examples of t-norms are the minimum, the product and the Łukasiewicz t-norm $T_{\mathbf{L}}$ given by $T_{\mathbf{L}}(x,y) = \max(x+y-1,0)$. By using *additive generators* and *ordinal sums* it is possible to construct and to represent all continuous triangular norms by means of these three prototypical t-norms (for more information on this subject see the books [SS83, KMP00, KM05, AFS06]).

Starting with a (left-)continuous t-norm as an interpretation for the (extended) logical conjunction, implication and negation can be deduced by means of the *residuum*, and a disjunction using a *De Morgan*-type formula. Depending on whether one starts with the minimum, the Łukasiewicz t-norm or the product, one obtains the *Gödel*, the *Łukasiewicz* and the *product fuzzy logic* (see [Háj98, CDM00, Got01]), and their algebraic counterparts are *Heyting*, *MV*-, and *product algebras*, respectively.

Fuzzy Systems 2.3

The best-known fuzzy systems are *fuzzy controllers* which are essentially rule-based systems assigning (with the help of the so-called *compositional rule of inference* and a suitable *defuzzification*) to each input value the corresponding output value, therefore producing an input-output function. The first described laboratory experiment with a fuzzy controller concerned the control of a steam engine [MA75], and the first industrial application reported in the literature concerned the control of a cement kiln [HØ82].

Fuzzy controllers can be understood in the context of fuzzy logics using *T-equivalences* [CCH92, Höh92, Bod03a, Bod03b], i.e., generalized equivalence relations which are reflexive, symmetric and *T*-transitive, the latter property being a transitivity based on some t-norm T. For a deeper analysis of the relationship between fuzzy logics, fuzzy sets and fuzzy controllers see, e.g., [BKLM95, NSTY95, Höh98], an early monograph on fuzzy control is [DHR93]. Here we only mention the two most important and most widely used fuzzy controllers, the *Mamdani* [MA75] and the *Takagi-Sugeno controller* [TS85].

We start with the Mamdani controller which uses fuzzy sets both for input and output and, therefore, needs a defuzzification in order to produce an input-output function as follows:

Let X be an arbitrary input space, let $A_1, \ldots, A_K$ and $B_1, \ldots, B_K$ be normalized fuzzy subsets of X and $\mathbb{R}$ with Borel-measurable membership functions, respectively, let T be a Borel-measurable t-norm, and consider the rulebase $(k = 1, \ldots, K)$

$$\text{IF} \quad x \text{ is } A_k \quad \text{THEN} \quad u \text{ is } B_k.$$

Then the *Mamdani controller* defines the input-output function $F_M \colon X \to \mathbb{R}$ given by

$$F_M(x) = \frac{\displaystyle\int_{\mathbb{R}} \mu_R(x, u) \cdot u \, du}{\displaystyle\int_{\mathbb{R}} \mu_R(x, u) \, du}, \tag{1}$$

provided that $\int_{\mathbb{R}} \mu_R(x, u) \, du > 0$, where the membership function $\mu_R \colon X \times \mathbb{R} \to [0, 1]$ of the fuzzy relation R on $X \times \mathbb{R}$ is given by

$$\mu_R(x, u) = \max\big[T\big(\mu_{A_1}(x), \mu_{B_1}(u)\big), \ldots, T\big(\mu_{A_K}(x), \mu_{B_K}(u)\big)\big].$$

In a strict mathematical sense, the measurability requirements [Hal50] are necessary for (1) being well-defined; in practical situations, these hypotheses, however, are usually (assumed to be) satisfied.

In our definition we have implicitly chosen a special defuzzification method, namely, the so-called *center of gravity* contained in equation (1). We only mention that there are also other methods of defuzzification, e.g., the *center of maximum*.

In most practical examples, the t-norm used for the Mamdani controller is either the minimum or the product; in the first case this particular compositional rule of inference is also referred to as *max-min-inference*, in the latter case as *max-prod-inference* or *max-dot-inference*.

The second important type of fuzzy controllers is the so-called Takagi-Sugeno controller which uses crisp values in the output space. In a way this means that the inference has a built-in defuzzification:

Let X be an input space, let $A_1, \ldots, A_K$ be normalized fuzzy subsets of X with $\sum_{k=1}^{K} \mu_{A_k}(x) > 0$ for all $x \in X$, and $f_1, \ldots, f_K$ be functions from X to $\mathbb{R}$, and consider the rulebase $(k = 1, \ldots, K)$

$$\text{IF} \quad x \text{ is } A_k \quad \text{THEN} \quad u = f_k(x).$$

Then the *Takagi-Sugeno controller* defines the following input-output function $F_S \colon X \to \mathbb{R}$

$$F_S(x) = \frac{\sum_{k=1}^{K} \mu_{A_k}(x) \cdot f_k(x)}{\sum_{k=1}^{K} \mu_{A_k}(x)}. \tag{2}$$

In the special situation, when for $k = 1, \ldots, K$ the functions f_k are constant, i.e., $f_k(x) = u_k$, we speak about a *Sugeno controller* which also can be considered as a special case of the Mamdani controller in the sense that it is a limit of suitable Mamdani controllers (a result which holds for other defuzzification methods too).

These fuzzy controllers have a universal approximation property allowing to approximate any continuous input-output function with arbitrary precision with respect to the sup-norm $||\cdot||_\infty$. This result has been published in several variants (see, e.g., [DGP92, Kos92, NK92, Buc93, Cas95, CD96, Yin98]). The following version was given in [Wan92]:

If X is a compact subset of $\mathbb{R}^n$ and $f \colon X \to \mathbb{R}$ a continuous function then, for each $\varepsilon > 0$, there exist real numbers $u_1, u_2, \ldots, u_K$, fuzzy subsets A_i^k of $\mathbb{R}$ ($i = 1, \ldots, n$; $k = 1, \ldots, K$) having Gaussian membership functions with parameters ξ_i^k and σ_i^k given by

$$\mu_{A_i^k}(x_i) = e^{-\left(\frac{x_i - \xi_i^k}{\sigma_i^k}\right)^2},$$

and a rule base ($k = 1, \ldots, K$)

IF x_1 is A_1^k AND $\ldots$ AND x_n is A_n^k THEN u is u_k

such that the input-output function $F_S \colon X \to \mathbb{R}$ of the corresponding Sugeno controller given by

$$F_S(x_1, \ldots, x_n) = \frac{\sum_{k=1}^{K} \left(\prod_{i=1}^{n} \mu_{A_i^k}(x_i)\right) \cdot u_k}{\sum_{k=1}^{K} \left(\prod_{i=1}^{n} \mu_{A_i^k}(x_i)\right)}$$

satisfies $||F_S - f||_\infty < \varepsilon$.

This approximation theorem is typical for many other universal approximation statements based on the Bolzano-Weierstraß theorem [Rud76] because it is indeed universal concerning the type of input-output functions to be approximated and the precision which can be reached. It is also typical with respect to its purely existential nature and the lack of an upper bound for the number of rules necessary to achieve arbitrary precision. It was shown in [Mos99] that Sugeno controllers using arbitrarily shaped membership functions are nowhere dense (with respect to the sup-norm) in the set of all continuous real functions on a compact domain as soon as the number of rules is bounded from above. For a more detailed discussion of the universal approximation property of fuzzy systems see [KKM99].

3 Data-Driven Fuzzy Systems

3.1 Motivation

Opposed to knowledge-based fuzzy systems, usually built up exclusively based on expert knowledge or human experience (see previous section), data-driven fuzzy systems can be fully automatically generated from numerical or categorical data, which stem from measurements, features extracted from context-based data (images, signals, music) or data bases recording entries of customers etc. This is possible without the necessity of having the underlying physical, chemical etc. laws about the system at hand. Even more, from the view of the data-driven training algorithms the meaning of the system variables plays no role. In some cases, it is even necessary to use data-driven models: for instance when the processes are so complex that a deterministic deduction of analytical models (e.g. differential equations) as well as the collection of expert knowledge is not possible at all.

The big advantage of data-driven fuzzy systems among other data-driven modeling techniques such as neural networks, genetic programming, splines and various machine learning methods, is that

- they are universal approximators (see previous section) and
- at the same time they still allow some insights by providing linguistically [CCHM03] and visually interpretable rules [NK98].

Interpretable models may serve as important components in supervision processes in order to understand models responses better and sometimes to gain some additional insights into the system. For instance, an operator of an industrial system may want to know why a certain decision of a fuzzy classification model was made or he/she is interested in some system dependencies under specific operating conditions in order to intensify his knowledge about the system. Interpretable models may also motivate the operators to an enhanced user interaction, e.g. bringing their own knowledge about several system dependencies into the game. For instance, an operator may change some structural components of the models because he thinks that they are not correctly placed resp. wrongly parametrized. This would lead to a hybrid approach—data on one hand and expert knowledge on the other—and can be essential for maximizing the information flow into the model building process. Interpretability of the generated fuzzy models is guaranteed by their nature to divide a problem into local sub-problems: each rule represents a local model and can be read and understood as an if-then conjunction (see also Section 2). The functions in the consequents of the rules influence the behavior resp. importance of certain variables in the various local regions.

Due to these benefits, data-driven fuzzy systems are nowadays applied in many application fields such as novelty [FT06] and fault detection [LG08], image classification [SNS+08, SDJ99], decision support systems [MLMRJRT00] or identification models in control systems [Abo03] and serve as important components in such applications.

Data-Driven Fuzzy Modeling Approaches 3.2

During the last 20 years a lot of data-driven fuzzy systems approaches were developed and we will describe the most important concepts in these below.

A possibility to obtain the premise structure of a fuzzy system is by exploiting clustering techniques for finding clusters (local groups) in the data which are directly associated with the rules. The fuzzy sets for each variable are obtained by projecting the clusters onto the various (one-dimensional) axes. In this sense, clustering is applied for a reasonable partitioning of the input/output space into various local regions (Figure 1). Approaches which use this concept are the *genfis2* method [YF93] (using subtractive clustering [Chi94] and implemented in MATLAB's fuzzy logic toolbox) and its successor *genfis3* (using fuzzy c-means, a fuzzification of the well-known k-means algorithm [Bez81]), *FMCLUST* [Bab98] (using Gustafsson-Kessel [GK79] clustering) or the approach demonstrated in [ABS02] (applying a Gath-Geva clustering algorithm [HKKR99]). After projection, the (linear) consequent parameters of Takagi-Sugeno-type fuzzy systems are usually obtained by a least squares estimation, either by local learning (estimating parameters for each rule separately) or by global learning (estimating parameters in all rules in one sweep) [Lug08a].

A big family of design methods uses genetic algorithms [CH99] for

- eliciting the optimal number of rules by achieving a reasonable tradeoff between accuracy and model complexity (see e.g. [RS01]) and
- for (fine-)tuning the parameters within an global optimization process.

Also, see Chapter III for more details on genetic algorithms. These are also called genetic fuzzy systems [CHHM01, CGH+04]. A central issue therein is an appropriate coding of the fuzzy systems into strings for ensuring dynamic update of the number of rules, fast convergence and valid individuals in the population when applying genetic operators.

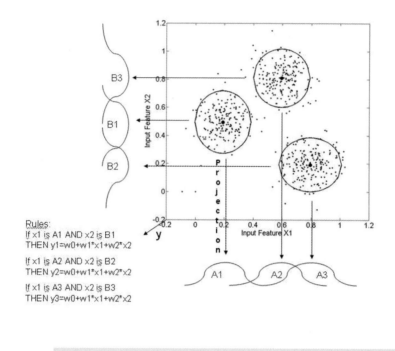

Rules:
If x1 is A1 AND x2 is B1
THEN y1=w0+w1*x1+w2*x2

If x1 is A2 AND x2 is B2
THEN y2=w0+w1*x1+w2*x2

If x1 is A3 AND x2 is B3
THEN y3=w0+w1*x1+w2*x2

FIGURE 1   Horizontal projection of three clusters onto the input axes x_1 and x_2 to form fuzzy sets and three rules.

Another possibility is a numerical optimization procedure for non-linear (antecedent) parameters in the fuzzy systems to minimize the least squares errors (and variants) between estimated and predicted target values. This has the advantage that non-linear parameters are optimized in a deterministic manner (opposed to genetic fuzzy systems) with a clear mathematical formulation of an optimization problem behind (opposed to most of the clustering-based approaches). A well-known method (also integrated in MATLAB's fuzzy logic toolbox) is the *ANFIS* approach [Jan93] exploiting a neuro-fuzzy system architecture and applying an error back-propagation technique for optimizing non-linear antecedent parameters. Another method developed at the FLLL [BLK⁺06] uses the Levenberg-Marquardt algorithm for optimizing non-linear antecedent parameters in triangular and Gaussian fuzzy sets, which uses second order information of the optimization function for fast convergence. *RENO* [BHBE02] exploits a generalized Gauss-Newton like method [SS95] as a second-order approximation method with (regularized) smoothing constraints. A novel development at the FLLL is the so-called *SparseFIS* approach [LK09]. There, rule weights are introduced and optimized in a coherent procedure together with the consequent parameters. Rule selection is achieved by deleting rules with a rule weight lower than ε. A final procedure exploits a semi-smooth Newton method with sparsity constraints on the consequent parameters in order to achieve a sort of local embedded feature selection and to decrease the curse of dimensionality effect in case of high-dimensional data.

Fuzzy classifiers, short for fuzzy classification models, differ from fuzzy regression models in its response to the system: opposed to a predictive numerical value, the response is usually a classification or decision statement represented by a class to which a sample belongs. For the widely classical single model architecture [Kun00], the antecedent parts of the rules are defined in the same way as for Takagi-Sugeno fuzzy systems (2); hence, similar techniques as described above can be applied for learning the antecedent parts. The consequents are singleton class labels instead of fuzzy sets or hyperplanes and are usually estimated by a winner-takes-it-all approach [Kun00]. Confidence values may be assigned by calculating the relative frequencies among the classes per rule [RSA03].

In [ALZ08] a new classifier architecture was introduced based on multi Takagi-Sugeno fuzzy systems. Thereby, one Takagi-Sugeno fuzzy system is trained for each class based on indicator entries in the output (0 when the sample does not belong to the current class and 1 otherwise). This forces the regression surface towards 0 in regions where the corresponding class is not present and towards 1 where it is present. The classification output of a new sample to be classified is produced by a one-versus-rest classification scheme, i.e. by

$$L = class(\mathbf{x}) = \operatorname{argmax}\big(\hat{f}_1(\mathbf{x}), \hat{f}_2(\mathbf{x}), \ldots, \hat{f}_K(\mathbf{x})\big)$$

where $\hat{f}_m(\mathbf{x})$ is the Takagi-Sugeno fuzzy regression model for the m-th class. The confidence $conf$ of the overall output value $L = m \in \{1, ..., K\}$ is elicited by normalizing the maximal output value with the sum of the output values from all K models:

$$conf = \frac{\max\big(\hat{g}_1(\mathbf{x}), \hat{g}_2(\mathbf{x}), \ldots, \hat{g}_K(\mathbf{x})\big)}{\sum\limits_{m=1}^{K} \hat{g}_m(\mathbf{x})}$$

where $\hat{g}_m(\mathbf{x}) = \hat{f}_m(\mathbf{x}) + \big|\min\big(0, \hat{f}_1(\mathbf{x}), \hat{f}_2(\mathbf{x}), \ldots, \hat{f}_K(\mathbf{x})\big)\big|$. This assures that all output values from all Takagi-Sugeno fuzzy systems are forced to be positive, and hence the confidence value well defined.

The idea of a multi model architecture was originally inspired by the regression by indicator matrix technique [HTF01], which, however, suffers from the masking problem due to too low flexibility of linear models. This problem can be solved by the fuzzy regression by indicator matrix approach. For an illustration, Figure 2 (top) shows the masking effect on a multi-class classification problem obtained when using linear regression by indicator matrix (the middle class is completely masked out as nowhere maximal), whereas in

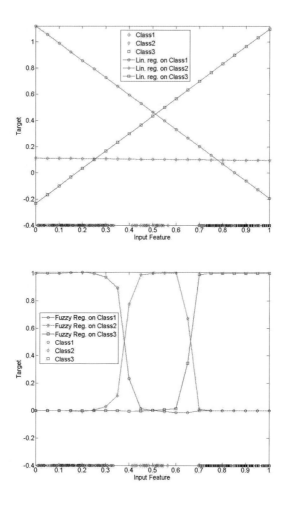

FIGURE 2   Masking problem when applying linear regression of indicator matrix (top), masking problem solved by fuzzy regression of indicator matrix (bottom).

Figure 2 (bottom) the masking effect is solved due to the higher flexibility of the models (going down to zero more rapidly where the corresponding class is not present).

Regularization and Parameter Selection   3.3

An important issue when learning fuzzy systems from data is to ensure a proper run through of the learning algorithm. Often, this is guaranteed when applying conventional approaches as described in the previous section. Sometimes, however, an ill-posed learning problem may arise. For instance, according to significant noise or other specific characteristics in the data, it may happen that a badly conditioned or even singular matrix occurs when estimating the consequent parameters in a (weighted) least squares approach. In this case, a pseudo-inversion process is unstable or even impossible. Hence, it is necessary to include a regularization term in the inversion process. A most common approach for doing so is the so-called Tikhonov regularization [TA77] by adding αI to the inverse matrix. This leads to the weighted least squares approach for the linear consequent parameters $\mathbf{w_i}$ of the i-th rule:

$$\widehat{\mathbf{w_i}} = (R_i^T Q_i R_i)^{-1} R_i^T Q_i \mathbf{y}$$

with R_i the data sample matrix including a columns of ones for the intercept, $Q_i = diag(\Psi_i(k)), k = 1, ..., N$ and y the output vector. A feasible choice of the regularization parameter α is mentioned in [LK08].

Another important issue is an appropriate selection of the parameters in the learning method. Too few rules may lead to an under-fitting of the problem, whereas too many rules may over-fit the training data, approximating more the noise rather than the real tendency of the relationship (see Figure 3). This effect is called the bias-variance tradeoff: the bias error is the error due to too low flexibility of the model and the variance error is due to the sampling variance of the underlying model (usually caused by noise in the data). A possible solution to this is the application of N-fold cross-validation (CV) [Sto74] coupled with a best parameter grid search scenario. The whole data set is divided into N equal folds and each fold is used as test data set and the remaining $N - 1$ folds are used as training data. The errors on the test data folds are averaged to the whole CV error. This procedure is repeated for each parameter setting. In this sense, the CV error estimates the real expected prediction error on new unseen samples quite well, (see also [HTF01]). The parameters leading to the optimal model in terms of the CV error are used for the final training of the fuzzy model.

Regarding the interpretability, usually some additional techniques have to be exploited in order to assure that fuzzy systems generated fully from data assure readable rules and fuzzy sets. A comprehensive study of these techniques is demonstrated in [CCHM03]. Section 5 will present a learning method which is able to extract comprehensible fuzzy regression models.

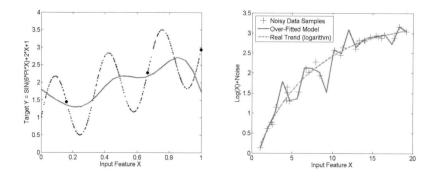

FIGURE 3   Under-fitting of a non-linear relationship caused by too few rules (rule centers marked as big dots)—note the big deviation to the real trend marked by blue dots (left)—and over-fitting caused by noisy data (marked by +) and high model complexity (red curve)—note the big deviation to the real trend (blue dashed line, right).

4 Evolving Fuzzy Systems and On-line Modeling

4.1 Motivation and Solutions

Evolving fuzzy systems are an extension of data-driven fuzzy systems allowing a fast adaptation of the models during on-line mode. This on-line adaptation is necessary, as usually not all possible operating conditions can be covered by off-line simulated or recorded data in advance. Sometimes, a completely new system behavior may demand a feedback from a model in its extrapolation space, which is always quite precarious and risky to follow. A large amount of samples is needed to set up an initial model framework in off-line mode that should achieve high accuracy and guarantee safe production, requiring a high effort for collection, cleaning and (in case of classification) labelling of the data. It is thus a requirement that the models are refined, extended and *evolved* on-line during normal production. Hence, in case of fuzzy systems we speak about *evolving fuzzy systems*. Now, the amount of data and the cycle times for such processes usually do not allow a complete rebuilding of the models from time to time with all the data samples recorded so far. Consequently, this is an on-line processing task which requires an update of some components and parameters of the models in form of incremental learning steps with new data, i.e. the models are evolved sample per sample. Another motivation for the usage of incremental learning algorithms to evolve fuzzy systems is the extraction of fuzzy models from huge data bases which are not able to be loaded at once into the virtual memory (see also [Lug08a]). This requires a sample-wise or at least block-wise loading of the data and building up the models incrementally.

This also means, that incremental learning can be seen as the engine par excellence for modeling and simulating adaptive or evolving processes in real-world. In the supervised case, opposed to reinforcement learning, incremental learning is fully guided by exact class responses or concrete values on the newly loaded samples and hence the learning algorithm exactly knows, in which direction the models need to be updated. In case of small updates, it is sufficient to update some model parameters (non-linear antecedent or linear consequent parameters) in order to move the model appropriately. However, in case of larger updates, such as the inclusion of a new system state, usually additional rules and fuzzy sets have to be evolved. A central question there is when to evolve new rules and when to update the antecedent parameters only in order to find a reasonable tradeoff between stability (convergence to a solution) and plasticity (including new information into the model). This is referred to plasticity-stability dilemma and most of the evolving fuzzy system approaches developed so far tackle this issue.

Pioneering work was done in [Kas01, Kas02] for neuro-fuzzy type systems, developing the so-called *DENFIS* approach. The structure learning is carried out with the help of an evolving clustering method, called *ECM*, i.e., whenever a new cluster is found automatically a new rule is evolved as well. The antecedent fuzzy sets with fixed width for each dimension are then formed around the corresponding center coordinates. *eTS* [AF04] exploits a Takagi-Sugeno fuzzy model and recursively updates the structure of the model based on the potential of the input data, i.e., it implements a kind of incremental version of subtractive clustering, called *eClustering* [AZ06]. A new rule is added when the potential of the data is higher than the potential of the existing rules or a new rule is modified when the potential of the new data is higher than the potential of the existing rules and the new data are close to an old rule. *SAFIS* [RSHS06] as a truly sequential learning algorithm uses the idea of functional equivalence between an RBF neural network and a fuzzy inference system by the application of the GAP-RBF neural network. In on-line *SOFNN* [LMP05] the learning is divided into a parameter and a structure learning, where the former exploits a modified version of recursive least squares [Lju99] and the structure learning includes new adding and pruning techniques. Participatory evolving fuzzy modeling [LHBG09] combines the concept of participatory learning (PL) introduced in [Yag90] with the evolving fuzzy modeling approach *eTS* [AF04]. The PL concept is based on unsupervised clustering and hence is a natural candidate to find rule base structures in adaptive fuzzy modeling procedures.

4.2   The *FLEXFIS Family*

Another approach, developed at FLLL, is the so-called *FLEXFIS* family, which comes with a regression variant [Lug08d], called *FLEXFIS* (short for *FLEXible Fuzzy Inference Systems*) and with a classification variant [LAZ07], called *FLEXFIS-Class* (short for *FLEXible Fuzzy Inference Systems for Classification*). The latter is exploiting both, single-model and the multi-model architecture as described in Section 3.2 (see also Figure 4). Each newly loaded buffer or single sample is processed first through the pre-processing component (e.g. normalization of the data), then through the antecedent learning and rule evolution part and finally through learning and adaptation of consequent parameters after incorporating correction terms for balancing out non-optimal situations. After each cycle, the updated fuzzy model is delivered and can be used for further predictions.

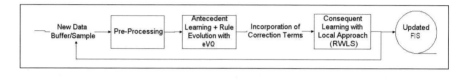

FIGURE 4   Processing chain for incremental learning and evolving Takagi-Sugeno fuzzy models with *FLEXFIS*.

The incremental learning of the antecedent and the rule evolution is done in the clustering space (compare with clustering-based approaches in Section 3.2) based on an evolving version of quantization (called *eVQ* [Lug08c]), extending conventional vector quantization [Gra84] to the on-line mode. This method in its basic form is characterized by three properties:

- Ability to update clusters on a single-pass sample per sample basis without iterating over a data buffer multiple times.
- Ability to evolve clusters in a single-pass incremental manner without the need of pre-parameterizing the number of clusters.
- Calculating the range of influence of clusters in each direction incrementally and synchronously to the cluster centers; these ranges are used as widths for the fuzzy sets projected onto the axes.

The first property is achieved by a specific handling of the learning gain as it steers the degree of shifting the centers and is responsible for a convergence of the rule centers. We do not apply a global learning gain decreasing with the number of iterations, but we define different learning gains for the different clusters according to their significance. The significance of a cluster can be expressed by the number of samples which formed this cluster, i.e. the number of samples for which this cluster was the winning (closest) cluster during the incremental learning process. The second property is achieved by introducing a vigilance parameter steering the tradeoff between plasticity (adaptation of old clusters) and stability (evolution of new clusters) . This also means that already generated clusters are moved in local areas bounded by the vigilance parameter and hence no iteration over the data set a multiple times (as done in the batch off-line variant) is required to force a significant movement of the clusters. Figure 5 shows the application of eVQ on a data set containing 17 (larger and smaller) clusters and compares the obtained partition (ellipsoids) with that one when using conventional batch VQ (bottom image). Also note the movement horizon of a cluster as shown as circle in the left image around the middle cluster at the bottom. Evolution of a new rule goes then hand in hand with evolution of a new cluster as this is projected to the axes (Figure 1).

The adaptation of the consequent parameters is carried out with a recursive fuzzy weighted least squares approach [Lug08a], which is able to update the parameters of each rule separately. This ensures high flexibility when new rules are evolved or older ones are merged, as it does not disturb the convergence of the parameters in the other rules. Furthermore, stability and computational performance are improved as dealing with smaller inverse Hessian matrices to be updated. A specific property of $FLEXFIS$ is that the connection of antecedent and consequent learning is done in a way that a convergence to optimality in the least squares sense is achieved (also coming close to the hypothetical batch solution when feeding all the data at once into the learning algorithm). The bottom image in Figure 6 present the impact of $FLEXFIS$ when adapting an initial fuzzy model (dotted line) to new data samples (marked as pluses) extending the original sample space (marked as dots) by its range significantly. The top image demonstrates the situation when adaptation of linear consequent parameters alone is done. As can be realized from the top image the updated model has not enough flexibility to follow the new trend. Hence, this circumstance was one of the basic motivations to develop evolving fuzzy systems approaches, which also allow an evolution of the rule structure, therefore gaining sufficient flexibility.

The classification variant of $FLEXFIS$, $FLEXFIS$-$Class$ [LAZ07], comes with two types of model architectures, single model architecture with singleton class labels ($FLEXFIS$-$Class$ SM) and multi model architecture ($FLEX$-FIS-$Class$ MM) as defined in Section 3.2. The latter, which exploits $FLEXFIS$ for the evolution of K Takagi-Sugeno fuzzy models for K classes, usually has a higher performance (as will be also shown in Section 7.2) and also has a higher flexibility for including newly upcoming classes on demand (simply a new Takagi-Sugeno fuzzy system is opened up).

A spin-off of $FLEXFIS$-$Class$ was made by building a classifier purely based on the clusters generated by eVQ, hence denoted as eVQ-$Class$ [Lug08b]. There, clusters are updated, evolved and merged in the same manner as in eVQ, and a hit matrix is introduced which tracks the relative frequency counts of each class (column) for each cluster (row). Classifying new samples

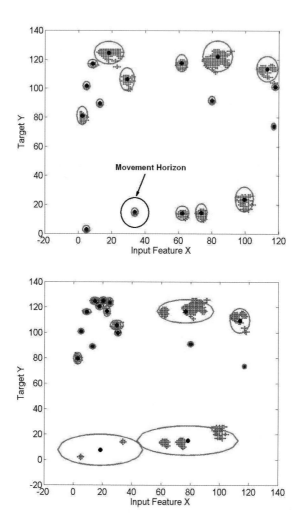

FIGURE 5   Clustering obtained by eVQ (appropriate clustering with 17 clusters, top)
and by conventional VQ when setting the number of clusters to 17 and
the initial centers to a shuffle of the original data samples (bad grouping
effect, bottom).

comes in two variants. Variant A uses the winner-takes-it-all approach by
eliciting the nearest cluster and responding the most frequent class therein.
Variant B performs a weighted classification strategy based on the distance of
the sample to the decision boundary of the two nearest clusters and based on

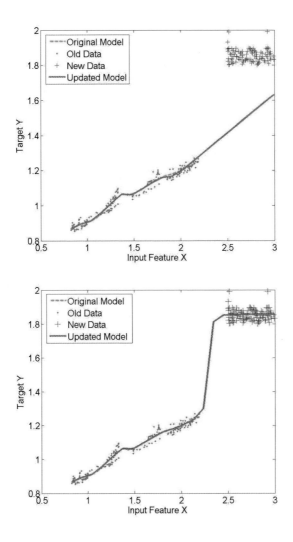

Updated fuzzy model (red curve) based on new samples (marked by +) using adaptation of consequent parameters only (top), updated fuzzy model (red curve) based on new samples (marked by +) applying *FLEX-FIS* (bottom).   FIGURE 6

the relative frequencies of the classes in these two clusters. Mostly, variant B outperforms variant A.

4.3   Handling Drifts and Unlearning Effect in Data Streams

All the evolving fuzzy systems approaches developed so far have a common feature: they are life-long learning approaches, which means that they incorporate all the data samples into the fuzzy models with equal weights in the same order as they are coming in during the on-line process. Hence, older information is treated equally to newer one and fuzzy models reflect a compact information of all the samples seen so far with equal importance. Mostly, this is a beneficial way to evolve the models, especially when a convergence to an optimality criterion or stable state of the model structure is achievable [Lug09]. However, this benefit only applies in case of data streams which are generated from the same underlying data distribution resp. which do not show any *drift* behavior to other parts of the input-output space [Tsy04]. A *drift* refers to a *gradual* evolution of the concept over time. The concept *drift* concerns the way the data distribution slides smoothly through the data/feature space from one region to another. For instance, one may consider a data cluster moving from one position to another. If not outdating the older distribution, a large joint cluster would be the case, under-performing on the new distribution. Hence, it is necessary to gradually out-date previously learned relationships over time. Graduality is important in order to guarantee a smooth out-dating rather than discrete jumps. In [LA09] an extension of the *FLEXFIS* approach is demonstrated, where appropriate mechanisms for automatic detection of drifts and appropriate reaction on drifts are described.

Opposed to an intended gradual forgetting in case of drift occurrences in a data stream, the so-called unlearning effect represents an undesirable forgetting. Unlearning may be caused in steady state situations when using fuzzy sets with infinite support (e.g. Gaussian fuzzy sets as often used in data-driven design of fuzzy systems), where a lot of samples stay at the same region in the data space. The reason for this effect is that the parameters of all linear consequent functions are adapted for each incoming data sample, no matter which firing degree the rules have. In fact, rules with a very low firing degree (i.e. rules which are far away from the constant region) are always adjusted very slightly for each sample, however summing up to a significant contribution with a high amount of data recorded during the steady state. In [Lug09] a strategy was developed for overcoming the unlearning effect by updating only those rules which are firing with a significant degree.

Creating Comprehensible Fuzzy 5
Regression Models

Motivation 5.1

As already mentioned in Section 3, a main reason to introduce fuzzy logic to data-driven modeling is the issue of the interpretability of the generated systems. To achieve easily comprehensible data-driven models with insight into the underlying relations between features, however, usually goes on the expense of accuracy.

It turned out that in many cases the simple application of methods for creating interpretable, computational models from data is not sufficient. There is often the need for higher accuracy, while preserving the interpretability of the systems. Consequently, several approaches were developed recently to optimize existing interpretable fuzzy systems [BHBE02]. This, however, often results again in loss of interpretability. A comprehensive study on various techniques for assuring interpretable data-driven fuzzy systems is demonstrated in [CCHM03]. For the on-line case (applicable to evolving fuzzy systems, see Section 4), FLLL developed a specific approach [LHK05], where complexity reduction mechanisms are carried out on-line after each incremental learning step.

In the following, we want to present a novel approach to data-driven fuzzy modeling (in batch off-line mode) developed at SCCH which aims to create easily comprehensible models while preserving as high accuracy as possible [DH06]. This is achieved by a three-stage approach which separates the definition of the underlying fuzzy sets, the learning of the initial fuzzy rule-based model, and finally a local or global optimization of the resulting model. The benefit of this approach is that it allows to use a language comprising of comprehensible fuzzy predicates and to incorporate expert knowledge by defining problem specific fuzzy predicates. Furthermore, we achieve highly accurate results by applying a regularized optimization technique.

The Underlying Language 5.2

To define the underlying language for our fuzzy models, we have to consider the different types of input attributes that can occur. Fuzzy predicates for categorical attributes, boolean or fuzzy, can be defined easily in a straight forward manner. To be able to handle numeric attributes in rule-based models, it is indispensable to define a discrete set of predicates for these kinds of at-

256   Erich Peter Klement et al.

tributes. The simplest approach is to create fuzzy sets which form a partition
for each dimension and which are evenly distributed over the data range or
have the same cardinality (equi-distance-binning, or equi-frequency-binning).
Although this approach is sufficient for basic calculations, it has strong limitations with respect to accuracy as well as the user's intuition. To overcome
these limitations, several approaches had been proposed which try to fit the
fuzzy sets to the given training data as well as possible [CFM02, KK97]
Alternatively, the fuzzy sets can also be computed ad hoc when creating
the computational models [Jan98, NFI00, ZS96]. Although this leads to very
good numerical results, the drawback of these approaches is again a lack of
linguistic expressions for the resulting fuzzy sets.

   In contrast to the approaches mentioned above, we developed a new algorithm called *CompFS* [Dro04], which creates the fuzzy sets based on the
data set given by considering the semantics of the corresponding linguistic
expressions. To generate k unevenly distributed fuzzy sets according to the
distribution of values in the data set $\mathcal{X}$, first, the centers c_i $(i = 1, \ldots, k)$ of
the fuzzy sets are initialized according to the data distribution. By initializing
the fuzzy set centers with the according quantiles $(q_i = \frac{i-0.5}{k})$, we create an
equi-frequent binning of the data set. To overcome problems which can occur
when using the quantiles, it is necessary to readjust the fuzzy set centers
by using a simple k-means algorithm. Figure 7 shows some examples of how
the fuzzy sets are computed for different data distributions. In all cases, the
resulting fuzzy sets correspond with the user's intuition and can be easily
identified with linguistic expressions ranging from *very small* to *very high*.

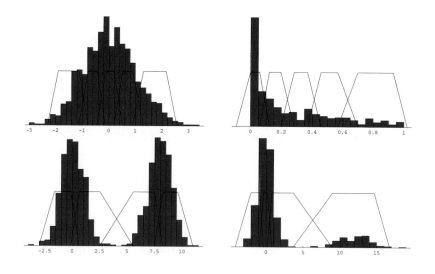

FIGURE 7   Fuzzy sets created using *CompFS*.

Although *CompFS* is capable of computing the fuzzy sets automatically with respect to a given data distribution, it requires the actual number of fuzzy sets as an input. In our experiments it has, however, turned out that the actual choice of this number influences the performance of the resulting model only slightly as long as a sufficiently large number of fuzzy sets is created.

After defining the underlying fuzzy sets, it is necessary to define appropriate predicates using these fuzzy sets. At first linguistic labels are to be defined for each fuzzy set. Depending on the underlying context of the attribute under consideration, these labels can be natural language expressions like *very low*, *medium*, and *large*. Furthermore, we can define the complement and the smallest superset with non-decreasing/non-increasing membership function for these sets. These new fuzzy sets correspond to the linguistic expressions *is not*, *is at least*, and *is at most*, respectively.

Rule Induction 5.3

To create a decision or regression tree for a specific problem, *inductive learning* (i.e. learning from examples) is a widely used approach. Using not only crisp but also fuzzy predicates, decision trees can be used to model vague decisions. Several approaches dealing with such fuzzy decision trees focus on the problem of vague class memberships [PF01, WCQY00]. Viewing decision trees as a compressed representation of a (fuzzy) rule set enables us to use decision trees not only for classification, but also for approximation of continuous output functions. Recent approaches in this direction try to create large trees that solve the resulting optimization problem [Jan98]. These solutions, however, can no longer be interpreted easily—which is usually one of the main advantages of regression trees over numerical optimization methods or artificial neural nets. Using pruning and back-fitting strategies can help to overcome this shortcoming [OW03]. All these approaches, however, tackle the problem of finding accurate yet still comprehensible models from an optimization point of view and do not pay attention to the underlying language used.

In our approach to inductive learning of fuzzy regression trees we pay special attention to comprehensibility. This is achieved by using the general language defined in Section 5.2 and by creating models which are as compact as possible. By introducing a novel transformation on the rule consequences we are able to achieve numerical accuracy without weakening the system's comprehensibility.

A general regression tree consists of a *root node* with a number of *child nodes*. Each of these child nodes can either be a *leaf node* or the root node of a new subtree. If each inner node has exactly two child nodes, the tree is called *binary*. We denote the set of all nodes with $N = \{n^1, \ldots, n^N\}$, the set of all leaf nodes with $L = \{n^{l_1}, \ldots, n^{l_L}\} \subset N$ and the set of inner nodes with $M = \{n^{M_1}, \ldots, n^{M_N}\} \subset N$ where we define the node n^1 to be the root node. To ease notation we will furthermore denote the index set of all leaf nodes with $L = \{l_1, \ldots, l_L\}$.

To each non-leaf node $n^i \in M$, a predicate p^i is associated which is used to decide which of the child nodes to process next. For each inner node $n^i \in M$ the child nodes are denoted as n^i_1 and n^i_2, and without restricting to generality we assume that the left branch (n^i_1) is selected when the corresponding predicate p^i is fulfilled and the right one (n^i_2) otherwise. The uniquely determined path from the root node n^1 to a sub-node $n^j \in N$ is called *complete branch* of the node and will be denoted as b^j. Each leaf node $n^j \in L$ is associated with a constant value $c^j \in \mathbb{R}$ or a local model, i.e., a linear function $c^j \colon X \to \mathbb{R}$.

To ensure comprehensibility of the local linear models, we do not use a simple linear combination of the input dimensions,

$$c^j(\mathbf{x}) = \alpha_0 + \sum_{l=1}^{n} \alpha_l x_l,$$

but of a reformulation with respect to the center of the data under consideration according to

$$c^j(\mathbf{x}) = \alpha_0 + \sum_{l=1}^{n} \alpha_l (x_l - \bar{x}_l). \tag{3}$$

Then $\bar{x}_l$ defines the mean of the samples in the l-th dimension according to b^j_l. This eases interpretation as in contrast to usual Takagi-Sugeno models, the rule output can be interpreted easily. Actually, we can interpret α_0 as the mean output value of all data points the rule applies to. The $\bar{x}_l$'s then characterize this mean with respect to the l-th dimension. The α_l's finally describe the influence of the l-th dimension when x_l is below or above $\bar{x}_l$. For a rough output of the model only α_0 might be displayed. If more detailed information is needed, the k top ranked α_l's can then be displayed.

In the following, we will restrict ourselves to binary regression trees. We overcome the main problem of binary trees—their increasing size for complex problems—by using the flexible underlying language, especially ordering-based predicates as defined in Section 5.2. This enables us to determine the ideal segmentation point automatically and to reduce the overall number of predicates involved.

The basic idea behind *FS-LiRT* (*Fuzzy Set* based *Linear Regression Trees*) is to create a tree where the leaves approximate the desired goal function as well as possible. By associating numerical values (or functions) with the leaf nodes, we finally obtain a Sugeno- or Takagi-Sugeno-type controller. To decide for each node which predicate to take, we use the mean

squared error measure which ensures that the model accuracy increases as
the tree grows.

Post-Optimization of Fuzzy Rule Bases   5.4

In the previous two sections we presented a method for creating easily comprehensible fuzzy models. The trade off for obtaining higher comprehensibility
is a lower accuracy, as smaller models have to involve more general rules/n-
odes. In our approach we overcome this drawback by adding more expressive
output functions to the leaf nodes or by performing post-optimization of the
complete fuzzy system. In [BHBE02], a combination of both is presented,
where—besides the coefficients of the affine linear consequences c^j—the underlying fuzzy sets themselves are fitted by optimizing the positions of the
fuzzy sets' interpolation points. This approach results in a nonlinear optimization problem, as the parameters in the fuzzy sets steering the positions
of these are non-linear parameters. We decided to restrict ourselves to the
optimization of the consequences, which leads to a linear least squares problem which can be solved easier and faster. Moreover, by doing so, we avoid
the danger of ending up in degenerated fuzzy sets which are no longer comprehensible.

The linear least squares problem has a unique solution if and only if the
observation matrix of the system has full rank, what cannot be guaranteed
for our application of optimizing a fuzzy rule base. The rank of the matrix
is dependent on the already given and fixed rule conditions and most of all
on the given data set. Therefore, a regularization of the system is needed to
assure unique and stable solutions. We have chosen to apply the Tikhonov
method. In our case, this amounts to simply adding to the cost function of
the given system the squared sum of the regression coefficients α^j in (3) as
a penalty term (weighted by a *regularization parameter* β). This causes the
absolute values of the coefficient to be kept as low as possible. The higher the
regularization parameter β is chosen, the closer to zero are the coefficients
kept and consequently, the more we will achieve a stable, but also less accurate
solution of our problem.

The presented approach has been applied to various problems in various
kinds of application areas, ranging from metallurgy and paper industry to
energy production. In all these applications, we have received very positive
feedback for the comprehensibility of the models and the achieved accuracy. A
comparison of the proposed method with other approaches showed that with
the same requirements to accuracy we can create smaller, highly interpretable
and more expressive models with *FS-LiRT*. In Figure 8 the visualizations of
a regression tree and an extracted rule base generated by *FS-LiRT* for the
housing data set from the UCI repository [BM98] are shown.

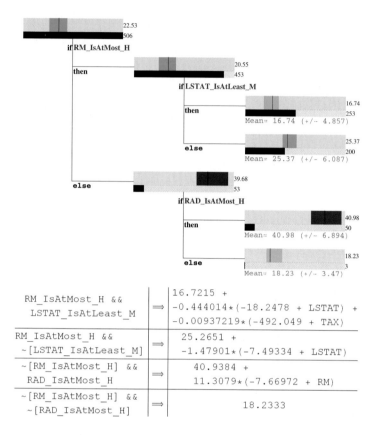

RM_IsAtMost_H && LSTAT_IsAtLeast_M	$\Longrightarrow$	16.7215 + -0.444014*(-18.2478 + LSTAT) + -0.00937219*(-492.049 + TAX)
RM_IsAtMost_H && ~[LSTAT_IsAtLeast_M]	$\Longrightarrow$	25.2651 + -1.47901*(-7.49334 + LSTAT)
~[RM_IsAtMost_H] && RAD_IsAtMost_H	$\Longrightarrow$	40.9384 + 11.3079*(-7.66972 + RM)
~[RM_IsAtMost_H] && ~[RAD_IsAtMost_H]	$\Longrightarrow$	18.2333

FIGURE 8   Regression tree generated by *FS-LiRT* and a rule base extracted from a
tree generated by *FS-LiRT* for the *housing data set*.

6 Support Vector Machines and Kernel-Based Design

6.1 Kernels as Similarities: Motivation and Recent Developments

Kernels are two-placed symmetric functions that can be reproduced as inner
products of points in a Hilbert space. What makes Hilbert spaces special is
that in such spaces one can imagine familiar geometric concepts like hyper-

planes, distances or orthogonality which simplifies the formulation and solution of various optimization problems. Consider for example standard problems of characterizing a cluster of points or the problem of separating the points of different classes which are prevailing problems in machine learning.

The attractivity of kernel methods can be explained by two aspects: firstly, by virtue of the so-called kernel trick (see below) data are mapped implicitly into a higher dimensional feature space in a way that preserves the geometrical notion of the initial optimization procedure based on linear models while extending it to non-linear models; secondly, the representer theorem guarantees that the non-linear optimum can be represented as a superposition of kernel functions which allows to design tractable optimization algorithms [CST01, SS01, Vap95].

As an inner product is a geometric notion, Gram matrices and therefore kernel functions as their generalization on more general index sets (continuum instead of discrete finite set of indices) often emerge in the context of optimization procedures motivated by geometric ideas. These methods find successful applications to classification, regression, density estimation and clustering problems in computer vision, data mining and machine learning.

While the historical roots of kernel methods can be traced back to the mid of the last century, see [Par62], the study of positive-definite functions as kernels of integrals date back to the beginning of the 19th century [Mer09]. It was Mercer who 1909 in [Mer09] characterized kernels in terms of a positive-definiteness condition as a generalization of the classical result from linear algebra.

Recently, learning methods based on kernels like support vector machines, kernel principal component analysis, kernel Gram-Schmidt or Bayes point machines have received considerable advertency, e.g., [HGC01, SS01].

A positive inner product of normed vectors x and y can also be looked at as a similarity quantity S for the vectors under consideration. The smaller the angle between the vectors the higher the degree of similarity. As pointed out in [Mos06b, Mos06a] this geometrically motivated notion of similarity is compatible with the notion of fuzzy similarities in terms of T-equivalences where the so-called T-transitivity plays a crucial role. While for example a min-transitive equivalence relation always turns out to be positive-definite this is not true in general for arbitrary T-equivalences.

The interpretation of kernels as similarity measures is quite helpful when designing kernel-based methods. The question is what is an appropriate similarity measure that fits the problem best. Then, based on such a similarity measure one can turn over to look at the problem from the point of view of a kernel by embedding the problem in an abstract geometric space which allows to reason about the problem in geometric terms.

6.2   Support Vector Machines

Support vector machines (SVM) are based on the concept of separating data of different classes by determining the optimal separating hyper-planes [Vap98]. The idea behind support vector machines is the method of *structural risk minimization*. Instead of optimizing the training error, the attention is turned to the minimization of an *estimate of the test error*. Typically, the SVM is a supervised learning algorithm working on two classes.

Support Vector Machines for Binary Classification

Let us now consider a binary classification problem. We are given empirical data $(x_1, y_1), \ldots, (x_m, y_m) \in \mathcal{X} \times \{-1, 1\}$, where $\mathcal{X}$ is some non-empty set (*domain*) from which *pattern* x_i are taken. The y_i are the so-called *labels*, which determine the affiliation of the pattern to one of the two classes. In the task of learning we want to *generalize* to unseen data points. Given a pattern $x \in \mathcal{X}$ we want to predict the corresponding $y \in \{-1, 1\}$, therefore estimating a function $f \colon \mathcal{X} \to \{-1, 1\}$. One attempt to solve this problem is to introduce a hyperplane that optimally separates the two classes. The SVM approach computes such an optimal separating hyperplane in the form of a decision surface:

$$f(\mathbf{x}) = \operatorname{sgn}\left(\sum_{i=1}^{m} y_i \alpha_i \langle \mathbf{x}_i, \mathbf{x} \rangle + b \right),$$

Only the points closest to maximal margin hyperplane have $\alpha_i > 0$ and these points are called the *support vectors* (SVs). All other points have $\alpha_i = 0$. This means that the evaluation of the decision function depends solely on the points closest to the hyperplane. They are the most informative patterns of the data. The coefficients α_i and b are determined by solving the quadratic programming problem (Wolfe dual of a constrained Lagrangian optimization problem):

$$\text{maximize } W(\alpha) = \sum_{i=1}^{m} \alpha_i - \frac{1}{2} \sum_{i,j=1}^{m} \alpha_i \alpha_j y_i y_j \langle \mathbf{x}_i, \mathbf{x}_j \rangle$$

subject to the constraints

$$\alpha_i \geq 0, \qquad \sum_{i=1}^{m} \alpha_i y_i = 0.$$

This formulation is just capable to deal with linear separation. For general pattern recognition problems the hyperplane needs to be adapted. This is done by mapping the data into another dot product space, where once again a linear separation can be performed. We perform a substitution with symmetric kernels of the shape

$$k(x, x') := \langle \mathbf{x}, \mathbf{x}' \rangle = \langle \Phi(x), \Phi(x') \rangle, \tag{4}$$

$$k \colon \mathcal{X} \times \mathcal{X} \to \quad \mathbb{R}$$
$$(x, x') \mapsto k(x, x').$$

and the map Φ, representing the patterns as vectors in the new dot product space $\mathcal{H}$ (*feature space*), is given by

$$\Phi \colon \mathcal{X} \to \quad \mathcal{H}$$
$$x \mapsto \mathbf{x} := \Phi(x).$$

We will now give some examples of commonly used kernels, as the Gaussian radial basis function(RBF) kernel:

$$k(x, x') = e^{-\frac{||x - x'||^2}{2\sigma^2}},$$

where $\sigma > 0$, the homogeneous polynomial kernel:

$$k(x, x') = \langle x, x' \rangle^d,$$

with $d \in \mathbb{N}$, and the sigmoid kernel:

$$k(x, x') = \tanh(\kappa \langle x, x' \rangle + \delta),$$

with $\kappa > 0$ and $\delta < 0$.

The substitution with (4) is referred to as *kernel trick*—one of the most important steps within SVMs. With such a choice of kernel the data can become linear separable in feature space despite being non-separable in the original input space. The new quadratic programming problem differs only in the replacement of the dot product by the kernel. After the optimal values of α_i and b have been found the final decision function looks as follows:

$$f(\mathbf{x}) = \text{sgn} \left(\sum_{i=1}^{m} y_i \alpha_i k(\mathbf{x}, \mathbf{x}_i) + b \right).$$

To deal with outliers (for example noise in the training data) the so-called *soft margin* approach is introduced. The only difference to the above formulation is that the constraint $\alpha_i \geq 0$ of the quadratic programming problem is replaced by $0 \leq \alpha_i \leq C$, where the parameter C is chosen by the user and can be seen as regularization parameter. A larger C assigns a higher penalty to training errors.

7 Applications

7.1 On-Line Fault Detection at Engine Test Benches

In this application, the task was to supervise the state of engine test benches, basically during the development phase of new engines, in order to prevent severe system failures at an early stage. The likelihood of appearance of a failure increases with the complexity of the system. Failures can affect the system itself, the measuring and monitoring devices, or the control system (which also modifies the system behavior) and can finally even lead to a breakdown of components or the whole system. Since failures affect system performance and system integrity and they become a safety risk for operators, the task was to develop methodologies for automatic detection of such failures at an early stage.

The idea was to set up a generic fault detection framework with a purely data-driven approach, circumventing high efforts in developing analytical fault models, which are usually dedicated for specific engine and have to be re-developed for new engines. The basic task was to automatically identify relationships in form of data-driven approximation models between so-called measurement channels, numerically recorded during the on-line operation mode, and to exploit those relationships for comparing newly recorded data with the confidence bands of the models; this means to examine whether identified models are violated or not and therefore can be used as a trigger for a fault alarm. In order to guarantee the detection of as many as possible faults, each channel is taken as target and from the remaining set of channels the most important ones together with their time delays are selected in order to obtain a high-qualitative approximation model for the target. For this selection, a modified version of forward selection was applied [Mil02]. If for a certain channel no useful approximation exists, which can be seen from a weak model quality or a wide confidence region around the model, the model is skipped as it does not deliver any contribution for fault detection at all. The remaining models (with a high quality) are delivered to the pool of models and are taken further as input to the fault detection logics.

Figure 9 shows the whole fault detection framework including the afore-mentioned components. Initial data-driven models are built up in advance with some pre-collected data, which usually do not cover all operating conditions or system states. Hence, it is necessary to further update the initially

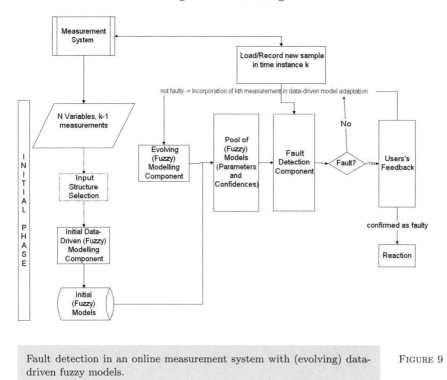

Fault detection in an online measurement system with (evolving) data-driven fuzzy models.   FIGURE 9

built models with new on-line data for refining their parameters and evolving new structural components. For achieving this task, evolving fuzzy systems as described in Section 4 were applied using the *FLEXFIS* approach (see Section 4.2), which in its batch version can be also applied for building initial fuzzy models from an off-line data set. We refer to [AGG+06] for more detailed information on the framework and its off-line components and to [LG08] for the on-line extension with dynamic model updates.

Different data sets from various gasoline and diesel engines were collected, where partially the errors were artificially placed or directly simulated at engine test benches. Finally, detection rates of up to 87% were achieved, mostly fuzzy models could outperform other modeling techniques such as neural networks (based on principal component regression), global and local regression models. Note that the false detection rate could be kept at a very low level (which was one of the major goals). Our methods had these properties:

- Improved fault detection approach (with specific adaptive local error bars) is able to outperform basic fault detection approach (with global error band).
- Analytical fault models (deduced from physical knowledge) perform worse than fuzzy models, especially when the fault level is at least 10%. A reason

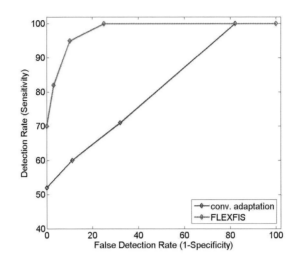

FIGURE 10   ROC curves for *genfis2* with consequent adaptation (blue curve) and
            FLEXFIS (red curve).

for this effect is that they do not cover all measurement channels and
possible relationships in the system.

- For 10% fault levels we still get reasonable results of about 66% detection
  rate, while for tiny 5% deviations we meet the bounds of our approach, as
  at most 26% of these errors can be detected.

The last two properties show the achievable bounds with our data-driven
approach as denoting detection rates for tiny fault levels.

We also inspected the impact of updating the models with evolving fuzzy
systems approach *FLEXFIS*, compared to conventional adaptation of parameters (see Section 4.2) based on real-recorded data from a diesel engine.
Figure 10 represents the ROC ("Receiver Operating Characteristic") curves
of both approaches, whereas the red line indicates the improved ROC curve
when using *FLEXFIS*. The ROC curves show the plot of the false detection
rate (x-axis) against the detection rate (y-axis) when varying the threshold
parameter for triggering a fault alarm or not. The larger the area under this
curve is, the better the method performs. This is because when the method
is able to follow closer the left-hand border and then the top border of the
ROC space (hence spanning a larger area under the curve), it produces a
small false detection rate (x near 0%) while achieving a high detection rate
(y near 100%).

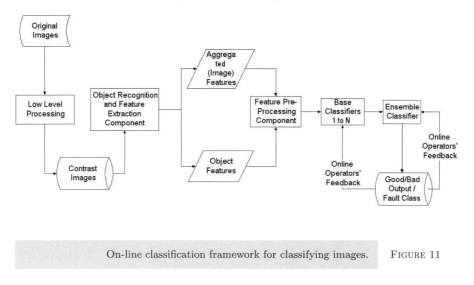

On-line classification framework for classifying images. FIGURE 11

On-Line Image Classification in Surface 7.2
Inspection Systems

In this example, the major task was to set up a classification system which is able to classify images showing surfaces of production items into good and bad ones, hence to provide a quality control statement about the products. Already available classification systems were quite application-dependant: for instance, a manually configured fuzzy system was developed based on expert-knowledge and specifically dedicated to the characteristics of CD imprints. Other classification approaches have strong focus on classical image processing and segmentation techniques and were specifically developed for certain applications. In this sense, it was a big challenge to set up a framework which is applicable to a wider range of surface inspection systems. This was achieved by removing application-dependent elements and applying machine vision and learning approaches based on image descriptors (also called features).

The whole framework consisting of the following components is shown in Figure 11:

- Low-level processing on the images for removing the application dependent elements contrast image: hereby, the assumption is that a fault-free master image is available; for newly recorded images during the production process the deviation to this master images (deviation image) is calculated. The pixels in a deviation image represent potential fault candidates, but need not indicate necessarily a failure in the production item. This depends on the structure, density and shape of the distinct pixel clouds (called regions of interest). An example is presented in Figure 12, where the three different regions of interest are shown in different colors.

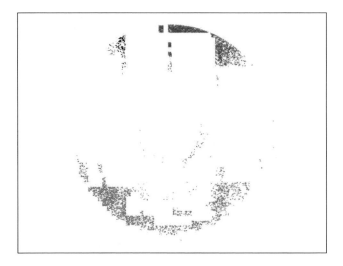

FIGURE 12   Deviation image at a CD imprint inspection system, the different regions of interest (objects) marked with different colors (black, red and green).

- Recognition of regions of interest (objects) in the contrast image: the deviation pixels belonging to the same regions are grouped together; therefore, we exploited various clustering techniques which can deal with arbitrary shape of objects and arbitrary number of objects.
- Extraction of features with a fixed and adaptive feature calculation component: object features characterizing single objects (potential fault candidates) and aggregated features characterizing images as a whole are extracted. Adaptive techniques were developed [EGHL08] for guiding the parameters in the feature calculation component to values such that the between-class spread is maximized for each feature separately, i.e. the single features achieve a higher discriminatory power.
- Building of high-dimensional classifiers based on the extracted features and labels on the images (or even single objects) provided by one or more operators: we exploited several well-known machine learning methods such as k-nearest neighbor algorithm, CART (Classification and Regression Trees) [BFSO93], SVMs [SS01], Baysian classifiers, discriminant analysis [DHS00] or possibilistic neural networks [Was93]. Most of these are recommended as top-10 data mining methods [WKQ$^+$06] and should be in the repertoire of every machine learning scientist. The evaluation was done in a

cross-validation procedure coupled with a best parameter grid search scenario in order to find automatically the optimal parameter setting for each classifier on each data set.

- A feedback loop to the classifiers based on the operator's feedback upon the classifiers decisions for improving the classifiers performance: this requires incremental learning steps during the on-line operation mode as a re-building of the classifiers usually does not terminate in real-time. We used our own developments *FLEXFIS-Class* and *eVQ-Class* (see Section 4.2) for achieving this goal.
- Combining classifiers from different operators for resolving contradictions: this can be solved by so-called ensemble classifiers [Kun04], which combine the responses of several classifiers to an over-all decision. In order to resolve contradictions among operators in on-line mode (following the feedback strategy mentioned above), incremental ensemble classifiers were developed in collaboration with the Katholike Universiteit of Leuven, which are synchronously updated with the base classifiers after each sample.

The on-line classification framework shown in Figure 11 was applied to three real-world surface inspection scenarios:

- Inspection of CD imprints.
- Egg inspection.
- Inspection of metal rotor parts.

On-line image data were recorded for each of these data sets and processed through the framework as shown in Figure 11 for feature extraction and classifier generation; the black images (showing no deviations to the fault-free master and hence can be automatically classified as good) were not used for classifier training and evaluation. This means the remaining data set was always a critical data set on the edge between showing real faults and pseudo-errors. In all three application scenarios, classification rates of over 95% had been achieved, in some case even slightly more than 98% on critical image data sets, for details see [SNS$^+$08]. Taking into account that usually around 96% are non-critical images, which can be easily classified as good, this ends up in a classification rate of over 99.8%, which was a satisfactory number for the end-user companies (a major goal in the project was to achieve a classification rate of at least 99%). A key issue for achieving such a high accuracy was an adaptive feature pre-processing step, which combines object feature and aggregated feature information in an appropriate way [EHL$^+$09].

An interesting topic was the examination of an improvement of on-line incrementally adapted and evolved classifiers over static classifiers, pre-built in off-line mode and letting fixed during the on-line process (as usually done in image classification scenarios). Therefore, we collected on-line image data from CD imprint production, egg inspection and metal rotor parts production processes and stored them in the same order as they were recorded onto hard disc. We implemented an on-line simulation framework which was able to load the features extracted from these images (and stored in feature matrices) sample per sample into the memory and feed them into the incremental classification approaches (*eVQ-Class* and *FLEXFIS-Class*). Hereby, the first third of the data was used for generating initial classifiers in off-line mode, the second third of data for on-line adaptation of the classifiers and the third third for eliciting accuracy on a new on-line test data set (in fact, this were fresh on-line test data as stored at the end of the recording session). The results are shown in Table 1. From these values, it can be clearly seen that an on-line

	CD imprints	*Eggs*	*Rotor*
Static Image Classifiers			
eVQ-Class variant A	75.69	91.55	66.67
eVQ-Class variant B	88.82	90.11	66.67
FLEXFIS-Class SM	78.82	95.20	66.67
FLEXFIS-Class MM	73.53	95.89	54.67
k-NN	79.61	91.51	53.33
CART	78.82	91.78	52.00
Evolved Image Classifiers			
eVQ-Class variant A	89.61	91.12	86.67
eVQ-Class variant B	90.39	93.33	86.67
FLEXFIS-Class SM	78.82	96.21	64.00
FLEXFIS-Class MM	87.65	97.19	78.67
k-NN (re-trained)	90.98	96.06	74.67
CART (re-trained)	90.59	97.02	52.00

TABLE 1   Comparison of the accuracies (in %) between static image classifiers built on the first half of the training data and sample-wise evolved image classifiers with the second half of the training data for the three surface inspection problems.

evolution of the image classifiers is strongly recommended as increasing the accuracies of classifiers significantly, sometimes even about 20%.

Application of SVMs to Texture Analysis   7.3

Though kernel-based methods are appealing because of the well-developed theory of statistical learning, the optimal choice of a kernel for a specific problem is still unsolved.

Recently in [MH08b, Mos09] a novel similarity measure is introduced that takes also structural spatial information of the intensity distribution of the textured image into account, which turns out to be advantageous compared to standard concepts as for example pixel-by-pixel based similarity measures like cross-correlation or measures based on information theoretical concepts that rely on the evaluation of histograms. Examples of such measures include mutual information, Kullback-Leibler distance and the Jensen-Rényi divergence measure. The introduced measure relies on the evaluation of partial sums which goes back to Hermann Weyl's concept of discrepancy [Wey16]. It provides a measure for assessing to which extent a given distribution of pseudo-random numbers deviates from a uniform distribution. It is a crucial property of this discrepancy concept that it is a norm in the geometric sense. Furthermore, for arbitrary integrable (non-periodic) functions it can be proven that the auto-correlation based on this measure shows monotonicity with respect to the amount of spatial translational shift. It is this monotonicity property that makes this discrepancy concept appealing for high-frequent or chaotic structured textures. Moreover, this discrepancy concept can be computed in linear time based on integral images. In [MKH08, MH08a] the discrepancy norm is applied to texture analysis and classification showing that exponential kernels based on this norm lead to higher in-class and a lower inter-class similarities. Due to this effect the resulting number of support vectors can be reduced with the discrepancy norm and, therefore, proves to be more appropriate for texture analysis at least with highly regular patterns than standard concepts like Gaussian or polynomial kernels.

Based on these techniques SCCH developed a patent-pending methodology for texture analysis particularly for quality inspection of woven fabrics which distinguishes by its universal conception and its capability to detect even small defects as demonstrated in Figure 15. Standard approaches usually employ some preprocessing by filter banks, wavelets, or statistical moments which have the disadvantage of using only partial information [TJ93, AKM95]. Various filters and moments are chosen to capture certain characteristics of textures (e.g. contrast, edginess, spatial frequency, directionality, and many others), but it is not granted that the essential information is still available. Classification of different textures usually requires different features. By using support vector machines the feature extraction is performed inherently by choosing a certain kernel. For example, a Gaussian kernel is similar to a radial-basis function network.

Due to the support vector machine approach the system parameters like the window size w of training image patches, the kernel parameters (e.g., σ

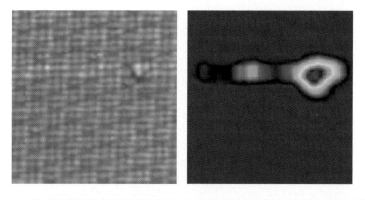

FIGURE 13   Test image of synthetic mesh for paper industry and the resulting defect
analysis for $w = 11$, $\sigma = 0.075$ and $\nu = 0.0025$.

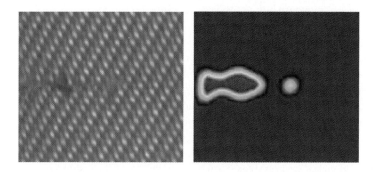

FIGURE 14   Airbag hose image containing defects, and the resulting defect analysis
with $w = 12$, $\sigma = 0.059$ and $\nu = 0.00005$.

FIGURE 15   Airbag hose with very small defect (part of one thread is dirty), and the
result of the SVM with $w = 12$, $\sigma = 0.059$ and $\nu = 0.00005$.

for a Gaussian kernel), as well as the SVM tolerance parameter $\nu = 1/C$ can be determined by performing cross validation. Figures 13–15 present the quality analysis results based on this support vector machine approach.

Acknowledgements

The research of the Fuzzy Logic Laboratorium Linz-Hagenberg (FLLL) described in this chapter was mainly supported by the Upper Austrian Government and by two European projects:

- RTD-Project GRD1-2001-40034 *AMPA—Automatic Measurement Plausibility and Quality Assurance* (in particular the on-line fault detection framework for engine test benches demonstrated in Section 7.1) which was coordinated by AVL List GmbH (Graz), other industrial partners were DaimlerChrysler AG, Guascor Investigación y Desarrollo S.A., and Leuven Measurement Systems International NV.
- STRP-Project STRP016429 *DynaVis—Dynamically Reconfigurable Quality Control for Manufacturing and Production Processes Using Learning Machine Vision* (especially the on-line image classification framework for surface inspection problems presented in Section 7.2) which was coordinated by Profactor GmbH (Steyr), the industrial partners were Sony DADC Austria, Asentics GmbH & Co KG and Atlas Copco.

The research of the Software Competence Center Hagenberg (SCCH) was supported by the Austrian K*plus* and COMET Program.

References

[Abo03]   J. Abonyi. *Fuzzy Model Identification for Control.* Birkhäuser, Boston, 2003.

[ABS02]   J. Abonyi, R. Babuska, and F. Szeifert. Modified Gath-Geva fuzzy clustering for identification of Takagi-Sugeno fuzzy models. *IEEE Trans. Syst. Man Cybern. B*, 32:612–621, 2002.

[AF04]   P. Angelov and D. Filev. An approach to online identification of Takagi-Sugeno fuzzy models. *IEEE Trans. Syst. Man Cybern. B*, 34:484–498, 2004.

[AFS06]   C. Alsina, M. J. Frank, and B. Schweizer. *Associative Functions: Triangular Norms and Copulas.* World Scientific, Singapore, 2006.

[AGG+06]   P. Angelov, V. Giglio, C. Guardiola, E. Lughofer, and J. M. Luján. An approach to model-based fault detection in industrial measurement systems with application to engine test benches. *Measurement Science and Technology*, 17:1809–1818, 2006.

[AKM95]   T. Aach, A. Kaup, and R. Mester. On texture analysis: local energy trans-
            forms versus quadrature filters. *Signal Process.*, 45:173–181, 1995.
[ALZ08]   P. Angelov, E. Lughofer, and X. Zhou. Evolving fuzzy classifiers using
            different model architectures. *Fuzzy Sets and Systems*, 159:3160–3182,
            2008.
[AZ06]   P. Angelov and X. Zhou. Evolving fuzzy systems from data streams in real-
            time. In *Proceedings International Symposium on Evolving Fuzzy Systems
            2006*, pages 29–35, 2006.
[Bab98]   R. Babuska. *Fuzzy Modeling for Control*. Kluwer, Boston, 1998.
[Bez81]   J. C. Bezdek. *Pattern Recognition with Fuzzy Objective Function Algo-
            rithms*. Plenum Press, New York, 1981.
[BFSO93]   L. Breiman, J. Friedman, C. J. Stone, and R. A. Olshen. *Classification
            and Regression Trees*. Chapman and Hall, Boca Raton, 1993.
[BHBE02]   M. Burger, J. Haslinger, U. Bodenhofer, and H. W. Engl. Regularized
            data-driven construction of fuzzy controllers. *J. Inverse Ill-Posed Probl.*,
            10:319–344, 2002.
[BKLM95]   P. Bauer, E. P. Klement, A. Leikermoser, and B. Moser. Modeling of control
            functions by fuzzy controllers. In Nguyen et al. [NSTY95], chapter 5, pages
            91–116.
[BLK+06]   J. Botzheim, E. Lughofer, E. P. Klement, L. T. Kóczy, and T. D. Gedeon.
            Separated antecedent and consequent learning for Takagi-Sugeno fuzzy
            systems. In *Proceedings FUZZ-IEEE 2006*, pages 2263–2269, Vancouver,
            2006.
[BM98]   C. L. Blake and C. J. Merz. UCI repository of machine learning databases.
            Univ. of California, Irvine, Dept. of Information and Computer Sciences,
            1998. http://www.ics.uci.edu/~mlearn/MLRepository.html.
[Bod03a]   U. Bodenhofer. A note on approximate equality versus the Poincaré para-
            dox. *Fuzzy Sets and Systems*, 133:155–160, 2003.
[Bod03b]   U. Bodenhofer. Representations and constructions of similarity-based fuzzy
            orderings. *Fuzzy Sets and Systems*, 137:113–136, 2003.
[Buc93]   J. J. Buckley. Sugeno type controllers are universal controllers. *Fuzzy Sets
            and Systems*, 53:299–303, 1993.
[Cas95]   J. L. Castro. Fuzzy logic controllers are universal approximators. *IEEE
            Trans. Syst. Man Cybernet.*, 25:629–635, 1995.
[CCH92]   J. Coulon, J.-L. Coulon, and U. Höhle. Classification of extremal subob-
            jects over **SM-SET**. In Rodabaugh et al. [RKH92], pages 9–31.
[CCHM03]   J. Casillas, O. Cordon, F. Herrera, and L. Magdalena. *Interpretability
            Issues in Fuzzy Modeling*. Springer, Berlin, 2003.
[CD96]   J. L. Castro and M. Delgado. Fuzzy systems with defuzzification are uni-
            versal approximators. *IEEE Trans. Syst. Man Cybern. B*, 26:149–152,
            1996.
[CDM00]   R. Cignoli, I. M. L. D'Ottaviano, and D. Mundici. *Algebraic Foundations
            of Many-Valued Reasoning*. Kluwer, Dordrecht, 2000.
[CFM02]   G. Castellano, A. M. Fanelli, and C. Mencar. A double-clustering approach
            for interpretable granulation of data. In *Proceedings IEEE Int. Conf. on
            Syst. Man Cybern. 2002*, Hammamet, 2002.
[CGH+04]   O. Cordon, F. Gomide, F. Herrera, F. Hoffmann, and L. Magdalena. Ten
            years of genetic fuzzy systems: current framework and new trends. *Fuzzy
            Sets and Systems*, 141:5–31, 2004.
[CH99]   O. Cordon and F. Herrera. A two-stage evolutionary process for designing
            TSK fuzzy rule-based systems. *IEEE Trans. Syst. Man Cybern. B*, 29:703–
            715, 1999.
[CHHM01]   O. Cordon, F. Herrera, F. Hoffmann, and L. Magdalena. *Genetic Fuzzy
            Systems—Evolutionary Tuning and Learning of Fuzzy Knowledge Bases*.
            World Scientific, Singapore, 2001.

[Chi94]   S. Chiu. Fuzzy model identification based on cluster estimation. *Journal of Intelligent and Fuzzy Systems*, 2:267–278, 1994.

[CST01]   N. Cristianini and J. Shawe-Taylor. *An Introduction to Support Vector Machines and Other Kernel-based Learning Methods*. Cambridge University Press, Cambridge, 2001.

[DGP92]   D. Dubois, M. Grabisch, and H. Prade. Gradual rules and the approximation of functions. In *Proceedings 2nd International Conference on Fuzzy Logic and Neural Networks, Iizuka*, pages 629–632, 1992.

[DH06]   M. Drobics and J. Himmelbauer. Creating comprehensible regression models: Inductive learning and optimization of fuzzy regression trees using comprehensible fuzzy predicates. *Soft Comput.*, 11:421–438, 2006.

[DHR93]   D. Driankov, H. Hellendoorn, and M. Reinfrank. *An Introduction to Fuzzy Control*. Springer, Berlin, 1993.

[DHS00]   R. O. Duda, P. E. Hart, and D. G. Stork. *Pattern Classification*. Wiley, Chichester, 2000.

[Dro04]   M. Drobics. Choosing the best predicates for data-driven fuzzy modeling. In *Proceedings 13th IEEE Int. Conf. on Fuzzy Systems*, pages 245–249, Budapest, 2004.

[EGHL08]   C. Eitzinger, M. Gmainer, W. Heidl, and E. Lughofer. Increasing classification performance with adaptive features. In A. Gasteratos, M. Vincze, and J. K. Tsotsos, editors, *Proceedings ICVS 2008, Santorini Island*, volume 5008 of *LNCS*, pages 445–453. Springer, Berlin, 2008.

[EHL^{+}09]   C. Eitzinger, W. Heidl, E. Lughofer, S. Raiser, J. E. Smith, M. A. Tahir, D. Sannen, and H. van Brussel. Assessment of the influence of adaptive components in trainable surface inspection systems. *Machine Vision and Applications*, 2009. To appear.

[FT06]   D. P. Filev and F. Tseng. Novelty detection based machine health prognostics. In *Proceedings 2006 International Symposium on Evolving Fuzzy Systems*, pages 193–199, Lake District, 2006.

[GK79]   D. Gustafson and W. Kessel. Fuzzy clustering with a fuzzy covariance matrix. In *Proceedings IEEE CDC*, pages 761–766, San Diego, 1979.

[Got01]   S. Gottwald. *A Treatise on Many-Valued Logic*. Studies in Logic and Computation. Research Studies Press, Baldock, 2001.

[Gra84]   R. M. Gray. Vector quantization. *IEEE ASSP Magazine*, 1:4–29, 1984.

[Háj98]   P. Hájek. *Metamathematics of Fuzzy Logic*. Kluwer, Dordrecht, 1998.

[Hal50]   P. R. Halmos. *Measure Theory*. Van Nostrand Reinhold, New York, 1950.

[HGC01]   R. Herbrich, T. Graepel, and C. Campbell. Bayes point machines. *Journal of Machine Learning Research*, 1:245–279, 2001.

[HKKR99]   F. Höppner, F. Klawonn, R. Kruse, and T. A. Runkler. *Fuzzy Cluster Analysis—Methods for Image Recognition, Classification, and Data Analysis*. John Wiley & Sons, Chichester, 1999.

[HØ82]   L. P. Holmblad and J. J. Østergaard. Control of a cement kiln by fuzzy logic. In M. M. Gupta and E. Sanchez, editors, *Fuzzy Information and Decision Processes*, pages 389–399. North-Holland, Amsterdam, 1982.

[Höh92]   U. Höhle. *M*-valued sets and sheaves over integral commutative CL-monoids. In Rodabaugh et al. [RKH92], pages 33–72.

[Höh98]   U. Höhle. Many-valued equalities, singletons and fuzzy partitions. *Soft Computing*, 2:134–140, 1998.

[HTF01]   T. Hastie, R. Tibshirani, and J. Friedman. *The Elements of Statistical Learning: Data Mining, Inference and Prediction*. Springer, New York, 2001.

[Jan93]   J.-S. R. Jang. ANFIS: Adaptive-network-based fuzzy inference systems. *IEEE Trans. Syst. Man Cybern.*, 23:665–685, 1993.

[Jan98]   C. Z. Janikow. Fuzzy decision trees: Issues and methods. *IEEE Trans. Syst. Man Cybern. B*, 28:1–14, 1998.

[Kas01]   N. Kasabov. Evolving fuzzy neural networks for supervised/unsupervised online knowledge-based learning. *IEEE Trans. Syst. Man Cybern. B*, 31:902–918, 2001.

[Kas02]   N. Kasabov. *Evolving Connectionist Systems—Methods and Applications in Bioinformatics, Brain Study and Intelligent Machines*. Springer, London, 2002.

[KK97]   F. Klawonn and R. Kruse. Constructing a fuzzy controller from data. *Fuzzy Sets and Systems*, 85:177–193, 1997.

[KKM99]   E. P. Klement, L. T. Kóczy, and B. Moser. Are fuzzy systems universal approximators? *Internat. J. Gen. Systems*, 28:259–282, 1999.

[KM05]   E. P. Klement and R. Mesiar, editors. *Logical, Algebraic, Analytic, and Probabilistic Aspects of Triangular Norms*. Elsevier, Amsterdam, 2005.

[KMP00]   E. P. Klement, R. Mesiar, and E. Pap. *Triangular Norms*. Kluwer, Dordrecht, 2000.

[Kos92]   B. Kosko. Fuzzy systems as universal approximators. In *Proceedings IEEE International Conference on Fuzzy Systems 1992, San Diego*, pages 1153–1162. IEEE Press, Piscataway, 1992.

[Kun00]   L. Kuncheva. *Fuzzy Classifier Design*. Physica-Verlag, Heidelberg, 2000.

[Kun04]   L. Kuncheva. *Combining Pattern Classifiers: Methods and Algorithms*. Wiley, Chichester, 2004.

[LA09]   E. Lughofer and P. Angelov. Detecting and reacting on drifts and shifts in on-line data streams with evolving fuzzy systems. In *Proceedings IFSA/EUSFLAT 2009 Conference*, Lisbon, 2009. To appear.

[LAZ07]   E. Lughofer, P. Angelov, and X. Zhou. Evolving single- and multi-model fuzzy classifiers with FLEXFIS-Class. In *Proceedings FUZZ-IEEE 2007*, pages 363–368, London, 2007.

[LG08]   E. Lughofer and C. Guardiola. On-line fault detection with data-driven evolving fuzzy models. *Journal of Control and Intelligent Systems*, 36:307–317, 2008.

[LHBG09]   E. Lima, M. Hell, R. Ballini, and F. Gomide. Evolving fuzzy modeling using participatory learning. In P. Angelov, D. Filev, and N. Kasabov, editors, *Evolving Intelligent Systems: Methodology and Applications*. John Wiley & Sons, New York, 2009. To appear.

[LHK05]   E. Lughofer, E. Hüllermeier, and E. P. Klement. Improving the interpretability of data-driven evolving fuzzy systems. In *Proceedings EUSFLAT 2005*, pages 28–33, Barcelona, Spain, 2005.

[Lju99]   L. Ljung. *System Identification: Theory for the User*. Prentice Hall, Upper Saddle River, 1999.

[LK08]   E. Lughofer and S. Kindermann. Improving the robustness of data-driven fuzzy systems with regularization. In *Proceedings IEEE World Congress on Computational Intelligence (WCCI) 2008*, pages 703–709, Hongkong, 2008.

[LK09]   E. Lughofer and S. Kindermann. Rule weight optimization and feature selection in fuzzy systems with sparsity constraints. In *Proceedings IFSA/EUSFLAT 2009 Conference*, Lisbon, Portugal, 2009. To appear.

[LMP05]   G. Leng, T. M McGinnity, and G. Prasad. An approach for on-line extraction of fuzzy rules using a self-organising fuzzy neural network. *Fuzzy Sets and Systems*, 150:211–243, 2005.

[Lug08a]   E. Lughofer. *Evolving Fuzzy Models—Incremental Learning, Interpretability and Stability Issues, Applications*. VDM Verlag Dr. Müller, Saarbrücken, 2008.

[Lug08b]   E. Lughofer. Evolving vector quantization for classification of on-line data streams. In *Proceedings Conference on Computational Intelligence for Modelling, Control and Automation (CIMCA 2008)*, pages 780–786, Vienna, 2008.

[Lug08c]   E. Lughofer. Extensions of vector quantization for incremental clustering. *Pattern Recognition*, 41:995–1011, 2008.

[Lug08d]   E. Lughofer. FLEXFIS: A robust incremental learning approach for evolving TS fuzzy models. *IEEE Trans. Fuzzy Syst.*, 16:1393–1410, 2008.

[Lug09]   E. Lughofer. Towards robust evolving fuzzy systems. In P. Angelov, D. Filev, and N. Kasabov, editors, *Evolving Intelligent Systems: Methodology and Applications*. John Wiley & Sons, New York, 2009. To appear.

[MA75]   E. H. Mamdani and S. Assilian. An experiment in linguistic synthesis with a fuzzy logic controller. *Intern. J. Man-Machine Stud.*, 7:1–13, 1975.

[Men42]   K. Menger. Statistical metrics. *Proc. Nat. Acad. Sci. U.S.A.*, 8:535–537, 1942.

[Mer09]   J. Mercer. Functions of positive and negative type and their connection with the theory of integral equations. *Philos. Trans. Roy. Soc. London*, 209:415–446, 1909.

[MH08a]   B. Moser and P. Haslinger. Texture classification with SVM based on Hermann Weyl's discrepancy norm. In *Proceedings of QCAV09, Wels*, 2008. To appear.

[MH08b]   B. Moser and T. Hoch. Misalignment measure based on Hermann Weyl's discrepancy. In A. Kuijper, B. Heise, and L. Muresan, editors, *Proceedings 32nd Workshop of the Austrian Association for Pattern Recognition (AAPR/OAGM)*, volume 232, pages 187–197. Austrian Computer Society, 2008.

[Mil02]   A. Miller. *Subset Selection in Regression Second Edition*. Chapman and Hall/CRC, Boca Raton, 2002.

[MKH08]   B. Moser, T. Kazmar, and P. Haslinger. On the potential of Hermann Weyl's discrepancy norm for texture analysis. In *Proceedings Intern. Conf. on Computational Intelligence for Modelling, Control and Automation*, 2008. To appear.

[MLMRJRT00] H. Maturino-Lozoya, D. Munoz-Rodriguez, F. Jaimes-Romera, and H. Tawfik. Handoff algorithms based on fuzzy classifiers. *IEEE Transactions on Vehicular Technology*, 49:2286–2294, 2000.

[Mos99]   B. Moser. Sugeno controllers with a bounded number of rules are nowhere dense. *Fuzzy Sets and Systems*, 104:269–277, 1999.

[Mos06a]   B. Moser. On representing and generating kernels by fuzzy equivalence relations. *J. Machine Learning Research*, 7:2603–2620, 2006.

[Mos06b]   B. Moser. On the T-transitivity of kernels. *Fuzzy Sets and Systems*, 157:1787–1796, 2006.

[Mos09]   B. Moser. A similarity measure for images and volumetric data based on Hermann Weyl's discrepancy. *IEEE Trans. on Pattern Analysis and Machine Intelligence*, 2009. To appear.

[NFI00]   O. Nelles, A. Fink, and R. Isermann. Local linear model trees (LOLIMOT) toolbox for nonlinear system identification. In *Proceedings 12th IFAC Symposium on System Identification*, Santa Barbara, 2000.

[NK92]   H. T. Nguyen and V. Kreinovich. On approximations of controls by fuzzy systems. Technical Report 92–93/302, LIFE Chair of Fuzzy Theory, Tokyo Institute of Technology, Nagatsuta, Yokohama, 1992.

[NK98]   D. Nauck and R. Kruse. NEFCLASS-X—a soft computing tool to build readable fuzzy classifiers. *BT Technology Journal*, 16:180–190, 1998.

[NSTY95]   H. T. Nguyen, M. Sugeno, R. Tong, and R. R. Yager, editors. *Theoretical Aspects of Fuzzy Control*. Wiley, New York, 1995.

[OW03]   C. Olaru and L. Wehenkel. A complete fuzzy decision tree technique. *Fuzzy Sets and Systems*, 138:221–254, 2003.

[Par62]   E. Parzen. Extraction and detection problems and reproducing kernel hilbert spaces. *Journal of the Society for Industrial and Applied Mathematics. Series A, On control*, 1:35–62, 1962.

[PF01]   Y. Peng and P. A. Flach. Soft discretization to enhance the continuous
              decision tree induction. In *Proceedings ECML/PKDD01 Workshop In-
              tegrating Aspects of Data Mining, Decision Support and Meta-Learning*,
              pages 109–118, 2001.
[RKH92]   S. E. Rodabaugh, E. P. Klement, and U. Höhle, editors. *Applications of
              Category Theory to Fuzzy Subsets*. Kluwer, Dordrecht, 1992.
[RS01]   H. Roubos and M. Setnes. Compact and transparent fuzzy models and
              classifiers through iterative complexity reduction. *IEEE Trans. on Fuzzy
              Syst.*, 9:516–524, 2001.
[RSA03]   J. A. Roubos, M. Setnes, and J. Abonyi. Learning fuzzy classification rules
              from data. *Inform. Sci.*, 150:77–93, 2003.
[RSHS06]   H.-J. Rong, N. Sundararajan, G.-B. Huang, and P. Saratchandran. Sequen-
              tial adaptive fuzzy inference system (SAFIS) for nonlinear system identi-
              fication and prediction. *Fuzzy Sets and Systems*, 157:1260–1275, 2006.
[Rud76]   W. Rudin. *Principles of Mathematical Analysis*. McGraw-Hill, Düsseldorf,
              1976.
[SDJ99]   R. Santos, E. R. Dougherty, and J. T. Astola Jaakko. Creating fuzzy rules
              for image classification using biased data clustering. In *SPIE Proceedings
              Series*, volume 3646, pages 151–159. Society of Photo-Optical Instrumen-
              tation Engineers, Bellingham, 1999.
[SNS+08]   D. Sannen, M. Nuttin, J. E. Smith, M. A. Tahir, E. Lughofer, and
              C. Eitzinger. An interactive self-adaptive on-line image classification
              framework. In A. Gasteratos, M. Vincze, and J.K. Tsotsos, editors, *Pro-
              ceedings ICVS 2008, Santorini Island*, volume 5008 of *LNCS*, pages 173–
              180. Springer, Berlin, 2008.
[SS83]   B. Schweizer and A. Sklar. *Probabilistic Metric Spaces*. North-Holland,
              New York, 1983.
[SS95]   H. Schwetlick and T. Schuetze. Least squares approximation by splines
              with free knots. *BIT*, 35:361–384, 1995.
[SS01]   B. Schölkopf and A. J. Smola. *Learning with Kernels: Support Vector Ma-
              chines, Regularization, Optimization, and Beyond (Adaptive Computation
              and Machine Learning)*. The MIT Press, 2001.
[Sto74]   M. Stone. Cross-validatory choice and assessment of statistical predictions.
              Journal of the Royal Statistical Society, 36:111–147, 1974.
[TA77]   A. N. Tikhonov and V. Y. Arsenin. *Solutions of Ill-Posed Problems*. Win-
              ston & Sons, Washington, 1977.
[TJ93]   M. Tuceryan and A. K. Jain. Texture analysis. In C. H. Chen, L. F.
              Pau, and P. S. P. Wang, editors, *The Handbook of pattern recognition &
              computer vision*, pages 235–276. World Scientific, River Edge, 1993.
[TS85]   T. Takagi and M. Sugeno. Fuzzy identification of systems and its ap-
              plication to modelling and control. *IEEE Trans. Syst. Man Cybernet.*,
              15:116–132, 1985.
[Tsy04]   A. Tsymbal. The problem of concept drift: definitions and related work.
              Technical Report TCD-CS-2004-15, Department of Computer Science,
              Trinity College Dublin, Ireland, 2004.
[Vap95]   V. Vapnik. *The Nature of Statistical Learning Theory*. Springer, New
              York, 1995.
[Vap98]   V. Vapnik. *Statistical Learning Theory*. Wiley, New York, 1998.
[Wan92]   L. X. Wang. Fuzzy systems are universal approximators. In *Proceedings
              IEEE International Conference on Fuzzy Systems 1992, San Diego*, pages
              1163–1169. IEEE, Piscataway, 1992.
[Was93]   P. D. Wasserman. *Advanced Methods in Neural Computing*. Van Nostrand
              Reinhold, New York, 1993.
[WCQY00]   X. Wang, B. Chen, G. Qian, and F. Ye. On the optimization of fuzzy
              decision trees. *Fuzzy Sets and Systems*, 112:117–125, 2000.

[Wey16]   H. Weyl. Über die Gleichverteilung von Zahlen mod. Eins. *Math. Ann.*, 77:313–352, 1916.

[WKQ⁺06]   X. Wu, V. Kumar, J. R. Quinlan, J. Gosh, Q. Yang, H. Motoda, G. J. MacLachlan, A. Ng, B. Liu, P. S. Yu, Z.-H. Zhou, M. Steinbach, D. J. Hand, and D. Steinberg. Top 10 algorithms in data mining. *Knowledge and Information Systems*, 14:1–37, 2006.

[Yag90]   R. R. Yager. A model of participatory learning. *IEEE Trans. Syst. Man Cybern.*, 20:1229–1234, 1990.

[YF93]   R. R. Yager and D. P. Filev. Learning of fuzzy rules by mountain clustering. In *Proceedings SPIE Conf. on Application of Fuzzy Logic Technology*, volume 2061, pages 246–254. International Society for Optical Engineering, Boston, 1993.

[Yin98]   H. Ying. Sufficient conditions on uniform approximation of multivariate functions by general Takagi-Sugeno fuzzy systems with linear rule consequents. *IEEE Trans. Syst. Man and Cybern. A*, 28:515–520, 1998.

[Zad65]   L. A. Zadeh. Fuzzy sets. *Inform. and Control*, 8:338–353, 1965.

[ZS96]   J. Zeidler and M. Schlosser. Continuous valued attributes in fuzzy decision trees. In *Proceedings 8th Int. Conf. on Information Processing and Management of Uncertainty in Knowledge-Based Systems*, pages 395–400, 1996.

Chapter VI
Information and Semantics in Databases and on the Web

Roland Wagner, Josef Küng, Birgit Pröll
Christina Buttinger, Christina Feilmayr, Bernhard Freudenthaler,
Michael Guttenbrunner, Christian Hawel, Melanie Himsl,
Daniel Jabornig, Werner Leithner, Stefan Parzer, Reinhard Stumptner,
Stefan Wagner, Wolfram Wöß

Introduction 1

The world we are living in is predominated by *information* affecting our business as well as private lives and thus, the time we are living in is commonly referred to as *"information age"* or *"knowledge age"*. Information and *knowledge*, the latter providing the additional potential to infer new knowledge, are contained in *databases*, ranging from traditional ones storing structured data, via, knowledge bases, semantic networks, and ontologies up to the World Wide Web (WWW), which can be regarded as a huge distributed database following the hypertext paradigm of linked information, containing unstructured respectively semi-structured data. *Information systems* enable the retrieval of information and knowledge stored in their database component, e.g., via search engines for the WWW case. Current research approaches enable the management of *semantics*, i.e., the meaning of data, e.g., the Semantic Web aiming at making information on the WWW interpretable for machines.

The Institute of Application Oriented Knowledge Processing (FAW), located in Softwarepark Hagenberg since 1991, is one of the major players in traditional and advanced information systems, data modelling, information retrieval & extraction and WWW-based information systems, including *Web Engineering*. This reputation shows first, in the fact that FAW is heading the annual international conference event *DEXA* (Database and Expert Systems Application), which was co-founded in 1990 by Roland Wagner [DEXA] and established a worldwide recognition of database research as conducted in Softwarepark Hagenberg, second, in the success of numerous industry related projects, e.g., the well known Web-based tourism information system *Tiscover*, which was developed at FAW starting 1995, and, third, in the conduction of multiple basic national & EU research projects in this domain.

In Softwarepark Hagenberg research in part of these areas is also conducted by, among others, *Software Competence Center Hagenberg (SCCH)*, contributing to the topic data warehouses in this chapter, and the *Research Institute of Symbolic Computation (RISC)*.

One primary intention of FAW is to perform *application oriented research*, thus bridging the gap between current research concepts and research-oriented industry requirements, as shown in the work presented in this chapter. We present current research topics dealt with at FAW and SCCH by particular research groups, which adhere to different requirements and cope with different application areas. The presented topics have in common that their focus of interest is the *management of information and knowledge*, i.e., on the one hand their proper *storage*, by means of ontologies or semantic networks, on the other hand their *"intelligent" retrieval* based on semantic aspects, by means of similarity queries respectively case based reasoning as well as Web information extraction for the case of unstructured data on Web pages and their *analysis and interpretation* based on a proper storage in data warehouses. Thus, the subchapters comprise:

- *Ontologies* (authored by Feilmayr, Pröll, Wöß): Current advanced information and knowledge applications often use ontologies as their knowledge repository, mainly due to their potential to manage semantics. We present an approach for ontology development and discuss their application for information extraction purposes.
- *Semantic Networks* (authored by Freudenthaler, Küng, Stumptner): One of the first approaches to handle semantics was to build up networks in which the edges were enriched by additional information that represents the meaning (semantics). A well known and standardized solution is called topic maps. In this chapter we introduce these concepts and show an application example.
- *Adaptive Modeling* (authored by Himsl, Jabornig, Küng, Leithner): Developing information systems contains at least one modelling task in the early stage of the project. During the last few years the idea of adaptive modelling (adapting the corresponding meta model during the modelling process) came up and a sophisticated tool supporting in particular visual meta- and instance-modelling has been developed.
- *Web Information Extraction* (authored by Buttinger, Feilmayr, Guttenbrunner, Parzer, Pröll): Web information extraction (IE) is commonly defined as extracting structured data out of unstructured data as it appears on Web pages. Besides an introduction into the fundamentals of (Web) information extraction we present three information extraction systems tackling different application domains and outline selected concepts resulting from their development.

- *Similarity Queries* and *Case Based Reasoning* (authored by Freudenthaler, Küng, Stumptner): A recurring challenge in information systems is dealing with similarity. Often data are not accurate enough that equality is given or, users want to find the most similar object(s) to a given query. At FAW a vague query system (VQS) has been developed that enriches traditional data base systems by similarity queries. The second part in this chapter is on Case Based Reasoning (CBR) where similarity plays a crucial role, too.
- *Data warehouses* (authored by Hawel, Wagner S.): Today the huge amount of data often is stored in so called data warehouses, particular database systems that are optimized for managing and analyzing this data mass. In this book we address two selected sub-topics: Regression tests and active data warehousing.

Ontologies 2

An ontology defines a shared vocabulary, which can be thereupon used to model a domain. In the following subchapter we first, provide a definition and introduce some basic concepts of ontologies, second, we propose an ontology development methodology, and third, we discuss recent approaches of applying ontologies for the information extraction purpose. Ontologies and their usage in the GRID domain are dealt in Chapter VII.

Basics 2.1

The term Ontology derives from philosophy (from the Greek ωυ, genitive συτος: of being <part. of ειναι: to be> and -λογια: study, theory)[1] and in general it is the study of what kind of things exists, as well as of the basic categories of being and their relations. In computer science ontologies are primarily used in applications related to knowledge management, natural language processing, e-commerce, information retrieval, information integration and they are the core element in all of the Semantic Web applications. The Semantic Web and Semantic Web technologies offer a new approach of managing information and processes, the fundamental principle of which is the creation and use of semantic metadata.

[Gru93] coined the commonly agreed definition: *"An ontology is an explicit and formal specification of a conceptualization"*. The conceptualization

---

[1] Cambridge Encyclopedia Vol. 55

is formal and hence permits reasoning by computer; and that a practical ontology is designed for some particular domain of interest. Guarino [Gua98] classified ontologies in different types according to their level of generality. Upper-level ontologies describe very general concepts such as space or time and are domain-independent. A domain ontology is a conceptualization that is specific to a domain.

A more formal definition is to define an ontology as a structure of a 4-tuple

$$O := (C, R, I, A).$$

Ontologies consist of concepts C (sometimes called classes), properties R of each concept (also called relations), describing features and attributes of the concept, and restrictions on properties. An ontology together with a set of individual instances I of classes constitutes a knowledge base. A is a set of axioms. According to Gruber, formal axioms are used to verify the consistency of the ontology itself and further an automated reasoner can infer new conclusions from the given knowledge, thus making implicit knowledge explicit.

The Web Ontology Language OWL^2 , which builds on Resource Description Framework RDF^3, provides a mechanism for modelling components of an ontology.

The example of an ontology statement (also known as triple) in Figure 1 comprises a concept Person, holding a property hasName, which links a person to a string—the person's name.

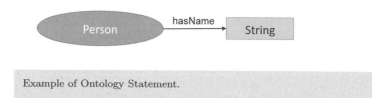

FIGURE 1   Example of Ontology Statement.

An ontology, a formal model, can be used to provide formal semantics to any sort of information: databases, catalogs, text documents, Web pages, etc. The association of information with formal models makes the information more amenable to machine processing and interpretation. Semantic annotation of unstructured content based on ontologies is getting a relevant topic.

Research challenges include algorithms for automatic ontology learning and -population from text, their evaluation and applications, setting up proprietary evaluation frameworks for assessment. Content, development methodology, automated reasoning aspects, and tool support are all-

---

[2] http://www.w3.org/2004/OWL

[3] http://www.w3.org/RDF

important for turning the development and use of ontologies into a true scientific and engineering discipline.

DynamOnt – Dynamic Ontology   2.2

The DynamOnt project aims at developing a methodology and toolset, which enables domain experts to do rapid prototyping of ontologies while adhering to best-practice principles of ontology engineering through the use of consistency checks and guided questions. The main objective was to develop a methodology that allows domain experts who are neither IT-specialists nor formal ontologists, to create ad-hoc categorizations or segmentations of arbitrary "knowledge spaces", without having to compromise on the quality of the evolving conceptual model. In order to design interactive guidance for domain experts to create sensible lower ontologies DynamOnt aims at supporting the process of evolving existing glossaries or taxonomies into group-specific ontologies. A main contribution was to converge different traditions within *ontology engineering* (foundational approaches, linguistic approaches, computer science, IEEE/W3C standards) as well as approaches from terminology management and computational linguistics. The methodology also aims at supporting conceptualizations at different levels of formality [GWG06].

Figure 2 shows an overview of the DynamOnt components. The central idea is the dynamic generation and maintenance of the knowledge model supporting different levels of model rigour ranging from simple project glossaries to formal domain ontologies [GBPW05a].

A typical scenario is a group of people working collaboratively on a project. As part of their work they create knowledge-based output, primarily in the form of documents. Since the team may consist of experts from different domains, countries and cultures they do not share a common vocabulary, yet. Therefore, the users will create a glossary, either starting from existing collections of terminology or by creating new ones. Over time, the glossary increases in size and complexity and additional structural elements will become necessary to manage the evolving term repository. In DynamOnt, the maintenance of the knowledge model is based on such a refinement process. DynamOnt allows users both, to organize the entries of the glossary and to create a taxonomy. Subsequently, additional relations and attributes can be added. Guided questions lead the users to a more structured knowledge model. Using upper level ontologies like $DOLCE^4$ or $SUMO^5$, DynamOnt guides the user by asking questions (e.g. "Is this attribute constant over time?") and automatically detects possible inconsistencies or errors in the ontology.

---

[4] http://www.loa-cnr.it/DOLCE.html

[5] http://www.ontologyportal.org/

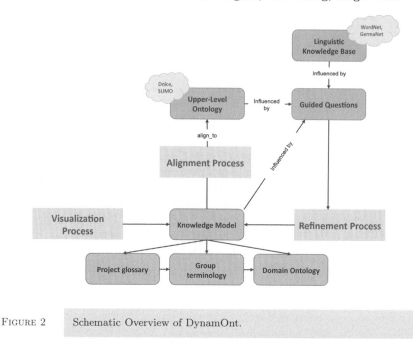

FIGURE 2   Schematic Overview of DynamOnt.

Furthermore, the refinement process is influenced by linguistic knowledge bases. Therefore, the newly created ontology is related to existing projects such as *WordNet* or *GermaNet* by automatically adding links whenever possible and selectively prompting users where required. An adequate visualization will help the user to better understand the given knowledge model. As a result, the DynamOnt system will lead to tightly coupled document-, content-, terminology-, and ontology repositories that will offer large improvements in productivity to heterogeneous, distributed groups of knowledge workers. Moreover, it enables individuals to manage their personal knowledge and content resources.

The DynamOnt project is funded by FIT-IT Semantic Systems program under FFG 809256/5512 and was a cooperation of Salzburg Research, FAW, Institute of Software Technologies and Interactive Systems (Technical University Vienna) and factline Webservices GmbH.

Ontologies in Information Extraction 2.3

In the following we will discuss the application of ontologies for the purpose of information extraction. Refer to Section 5 for an introduction to information extraction (IE), its challenges in the Web domain, as well as the use of ontologies in IE applications.

There are various IE techniques available for analyzing text and extracting relevant information, which allow for recognition of named entities and even relations, events and scenarios (see Section 5).

Semantic annotation (aka. semantic tagging) is a lightweight form of IE, in that it tags semantic models of, e.g., an ontology, to natural language items, as they appear in a text. Thus, it may also be characterized as the dynamic creation of interrelationships between ontologies and documents in a bi-directional manner covering creation, evolution and population of ontological models [RS06]. Semantic annotation realizes named entity recognition and can be used as a preliminary phase within a more complex IE process. IE in addition recognizes properties of named entities and interrelations between named entities, and thus, enables the extraction of events and even scenarios.

Ontologies may support semantic annotations as well as information extraction. The later is referred to as *ontology-based information extraction (OBIE)* and comprises two tasks, in that ontologies and IE benefit from each other [VNCN05]:

An Ontology constitutes the knowledge base of an IE application: The ontology is then primarily used for semantic annotation, but can also be the basis for, e.g., information verification purposes within the later stages of the IE process.

Information Extraction is used for ontology population and enhancement:
   In this context texts are used as knowledge sources in order to build and further enrich ontologies.

In our IE related application-oriented research work we base on the advantages of OBIE in the following areas:

1. Usage of *prototypical ontology excerpts as knowledge base for proof-of-concept IE prototypes*, e.g., JobOlize (refer to Section 5.2).
2. Development of *real-world domain ontologies* for IE purposes, e.g., MAR-LIES ontology, (refer to Section 5.4), and tourism ontology cDOTT, see below.
3. Usage of *ontologies for verification of IE results*, as applied in MARLIES (refer to Section 5.2).
4. Development and application of *extraction domain ontologies*, as described below.
5. *Ontology Population*, as described below.

cDOTT – a Core Domain Ontology for Tourism and Travel

Based on our longtime experience in the development of information systems and mobile applications in the tourism domain [GWP+08, PR00], we are currently developing an *ontology for the tourism and travel domain*, which can be used for, e.g., IE systems, recommender systems and mobile event handling systems. The domain of tourism is commonly known as a knowledge-intensive domain, where online information plays a crucial role for the whole life-cycle of a journey, comprising pre-trip, on-trip and post-trip phases. In this light, there is an urgent need for an ontology with a strict teleological orientation. For the tourism domain, this means to have a core domain ontology comprising the most important concepts (such as accommodation, gastronomy, event, attraction, transportation), while enabling its extension enhancement with other related ontologies for the purpose of concept expansion and reasoning. This approach leads to a loose-coupling of ontologies. The benefit of our solution is the possibility to reuse existing concepts of different application contexts, e.g., a time ontology [FGP+09] (see also Sections 5.4 and 5.3).

Development and Application of Ontology-driven Extraction (ODIE) and Ontology Population

Previous and current research work demonstrate that ontologies are considered as key technology for IE, where they can assist in a variety of ways. For the future, ontologies will even get a higher significance with respect to the IE field. Ontology-driven extraction (ODIE) constitutes a new approach of OBIE and introduces among others *extraction domain ontologies* storing IE rules besides the domain content and thus, allowing for a rapid start of an extraction process. Even when using only a simple domain ontology, which only covers part of target data, satisfactory results can be achieved, and meaningful feedback for ontology enhancement or redesign can be generated [SN07]. We are on the way to develop an ODIE system, where ontologies enhanced knowledge is automatically processed in order to build the required IE rules according to a specified IE task. Thus, the domain experts get enabled to develop and maintain a (Web) IE system without or only marginal involvement of software engineers. A corrective feedback component, which is based on the results of an IE assessment component, facilitates a semi automatic ontology population so as to further alleviate the system's maintenance.

Semantic Networks 3

Every network (consisting of vertices and edges) in which the edges represent the semantic relation between the vertices (concepts, objects) is called a *semantic network*. These networks were one of the first approaches for knowledge representation in the 1950s and early 1960s. Today several standardized representation forms for semantic networks are in usage, among others RDF (resource description format), RDF-schema, OWL (Web Ontology Language) and, Topic Maps.

Semantic Networks and Decision Support 3.1

In the 1960s the wish for a system was raising which could support experts of various fields in decision taking. A Decision Support System (DSS) can be defined as:

"A computer program that provides information in a given domain of application by means of analytical decision models and access to databases, in order to support a decision maker in marketing decisions effectively in complex and ill-structured (non-programmable) tasks." [KM95]

Whenever there is a fixed goal but no algorithmic solution or when there are numerous and user-dependant solutions, it is useful to provide support to an expert by a Decision Support System. The goal of DSS is to improve decisions by better understanding and preparation of the tasks which lead towards evaluation and choosing. Usually it is not possible to fully automatize information processing to reach the conclusion. Only if an information processing task can be started as an algorithm then the decision making process is structured, it can be implemented in a computer program and the solution to the problem is automated.

Structured problems are routine because they are unambiguous, this means that there is a single solution method. If a certain problem is less structured then there exist more alternative solution methods and solutions may not be equivalent. Mainly in management there are many situations where decisions have to be taken in non-programmable problems.

Classification of DSS

Due to a great user-need for nearly each domain there were implementations of Decision Support Systems. To make this abundance of systems manageable more easily, it is useful to classify them. Taking the categorization below in consideration it should become clear that most systems are hybrid and not driven by a single DSS component. Decision Support Systems can be categorized the following way:

1. Data-Driven Decision Support Systems: This type of Decision Support Systems provides the possibility of access and manipulation of well-structured data. Business Intelligence Systems are good examples for data-driven DSS.
2. Model-Driven Decision Support Systems: Model-driven DSS offer access and manipulation functionality for models like financial models, representation models or optimization models. These systems use data (parameters) which usually are provided by a user to analyze a certain situation. These systems mainly are not data-intensive.
3. Knowledge-Driven Decision Support Systems: Knowledge-driven DSS normally are considered to support users in management positions. Problem-solving and analysis functionality are important components of such systems.
4. Document-Driven Decision Support Systems: A relatively new category of DSS are document-driven Decision Support Systems, frequently called "Knowledge Management Systems". The aim of these systems generally is provide support for the management of un-structured documents or web pages. A well designed and well adapted (full-text) search engine is a powerful tool in connection with document-driven Decision Support Systems.

Topic Maps

"Topic Maps have their roots in the first years of the 1990s. The so called 'Davenport Group' was discussing the problem of interchanging computer documentation. The basic concepts Topic, Association and Occurrence (TAO), discussed in this manner, became the Topic Map standard some years later. A Topic describes or rather represents any subject from real world, e.g., concepts and entities . . . . These Topics need to be categorized made possible by Topic Types. For instance a Topic 'Austria' would be of type 'Country'. To define relations between topics there is the association-concept. An Association has a type, e.g., 'written by' and two or more members. An example for an association between a document and a person could be 'p23234.pdf written by Reinhard Stumptner'. The type of the Association is 'written by'. Furthermore it has two members: the document 'p23234.pdf' and the person 'Reinhard Stumptner'. The third main concept is the Occurrence. Occurrences are used for linking a topic to information sources of any type. Such information sources in general are outside of the topic map." [FSFK07]

Generally speaking, Topic Maps provide techniques to make connections between pieces of information.

VCDECIS

As described in [FSFK07], the term Decision Support System (DSS), Knowledge Management System (KMS) and Knowledgebase (KB) designate an approach to improving organizational outcomes and organizational learning by introducing a range of specific processes and practices for identifying and capturing knowledge, know-how, expertise and other intellectual capital and for making such knowledge assets available for transfer and reuse across the organization. While knowledge transfer (an aspect of Knowledge Management) has always existed in a certain form, for example through on-the-job discussions with peers, formally through apprenticeship, professional training and mentoring programs—since the late twentieth century—technologically through knowledge bases, expert systems and other knowledge repositories, knowledge management programs seek to consciously evaluate and manage the process of accumulation and application of intellectual capital. A key distinction made by Knowledge Management practitioners is between tacit and explicit knowledge. The former is often subconscious and internalized, and individuals may or may not be aware of what they know and how they accomplish particular results. At the opposite end of the spectrum is explicit knowledge—this refers to knowledge that individuals hold explicitly and consciously in mental focus, and may communicate to others, and especially to such knowledge when codified into written or another permanent form. These two opposite characteristics of knowledge require different approaches in Knowledge Management:

Tacit knowledge requires systems which can access knowledge resources to learn best practice, enables the communication between people and indicates context between knowledge and its sources; And explicit knowledge which can be codified in documents requires a person-to-document-approach such as Document Management Systems and Databases combined with search tools.

Ikujiro Nonaka and Hirotaka Takeuchi ("The Knowledge Creating Company") argued that on the one hand, a successful knowledge management program needs to convert internalized tacit knowledge into explicit codified knowledge in order to share it, but on the other hand, individuals and groups must also internalize and make personally meaningful explicit knowledge once they retrieve it from its codified form. The amount of data and documents in intranets of enterprises or web appearances of the enterprises increases, at present ever more strongly. However, the content in these documents for enterprises is essential for commercial success. In this great quantity of information important knowledge can be lost easily.

The idea of VCDECIS is a content- and knowledge management system, which is able to provide important information generally stored in the form of documents. It is designed to serve as a knowledge-based system and meets all requirements specified in the sense of knowledge management. The Concept of VCDECIS is tied to organizational objectives, as improved performance and quality, competitive advantage and a higher level of innovation.

The development is based on the following Taxonomy of Decision Support Systems (DSS):

Communication-driven DSS: supports more than one person or institution working on shared tasks.

Document-driven DSS: manages, retrieves and manipulates unstructured information in a variety of electronic formats.

Data-driven DSS: emphasizes on access and interpretation of data (time-series, statistics, databases, ...).

Knowledge-driven DSS: provides specialized problem solving expertise stored as facts, rules, procedures, or in similar structures.

In VCDECIS each aspect can be found, communication-, document-, data- and knowledge driven DSS. Therefore the system has an integrated design of independent elements and well defined interfaces. The support of collaborative work as enabled by a so-called communication-driven DSS was decisive for the implementation of VCDECIS as web application. The whole content is stored on a web server and satisfies all necessity of Knowledge Sharing. The system's goal is a proper management of literature in the meaning of document-driven DSS is actualized with tools such as a semantic network for the machine-readable content context, search engines and a navigator for content browsing and publishing. On the highest level a knowledge-based system acts as knowledge-driven DSS.

Topic Map

"VCDECIS is a specialized knowledge-based system for the field of Structural Health Monitoring. It can be termed a knowledge-based Content Management System (CMS) whose main components are a Topic Map for knowledge representation, an easy to use web portal and an integrated search engine for full-text search within the content. To improve runtime-performance of the Topic Map it is stored not in its original XML structure but in a rational database. Attributes (facets) of topics are kept separately in a database of the same kind. Full-text search functionality is provided by the open-source software package Lucene. The search engine and the Topic Map navigation are integrated into VCDECIS web portal whereby search results can be "opened" for navigation in the Topic Map. The core of the VCDECIS content management uses a topic map as a form of semantic network for the knowledge representation. It allows the integration of heterogeneous information such as any kind of addressable data (documents, links, ...) and concepts from projects, institutions, scientific issues ...to datasets from databases.

In many fields of Computer Science there exists a need to represent knowledge and meaning in order to make communication between humans and computers possible or rather make it more efficient.

Thus a separation into two layers, Topics and their Occurrences, is reached. As already mentioned a topic map can represent information using topics (to represent any concept), associations (to represent the relationships between topics) and occurrences (which represent relationships between topics and information resources relevant to them). The topic map of VCDECIS distinguishes between two types of topics—topics and content topics. While topics are created to hold information of concepts and define context among them, content topics represent metadata of occurrences. Content topics are characterized by the possibility of having associations to topics only, not to other content topics. Due to the fact that VCDECIS' content is in the center of attention, the ability to aggregate content/occurrences using content topics turned out to be advantageous." [FSFK07]

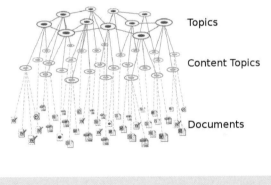

Topics

Content Topics

Documents

Topics and content topics.   FIGURE 3

Application and Utilization

As explained in [FSFK07], VCDECIS' document upload platform is an easy to use web-based user interface to manage any kind of documents or files in the and link them with topics of a Topic Map. In a first step of an upload process, information like name, keywords and so on are specified and in a second step it is associated with topics like person, institution et cetera. Furthermore, administrators of the system have the possibility to create new topics. Topic and association types generally are static and cannot be expanded by the user.

Add content: The user is assisted by an upload tool running on a web browser while uploading documents on the web server. The upload tool offers a simple graphical user interface and is extensively self-explanatory for convenient filing. The procedure of adding content is done within three steps, namely upload files, create topics and "content topics" (aggregation of occurrences) and finally the definition of associations. Within this procedure content is stored to the web server, indexed by the full-text search engine and linked to relevant topics of the semantic network. The document is placed within this knowledge network with the advantage that the user does not need to remember complicated hierarchies or other form of organization of a file system.

Content search: The retrieval of documents and topics within VCDECIS is supported by sophisticated search tools. The content search can be applied either in the scope of all entries of the topic map or in the documents by means of a full text search.

Content browsing: Based on associations and semantic links the user can navigate to "neighboring" documents (same project, same author, identical scientific issue ...). The so-called Navigator is besides the search engine an essential tool for the retrieval of knowledge and information.

Content publishing: As VCDECIS is a web application and access by "external" users such as project partners, the publication scope are intended to be defined by clients, which is an elementary property of all topics and content topics. The system offers three level of authority—internal, private and public. While public topics do not need any user-login for access via internet, a topic defined as private or internal only grants access to a certain group of users or company members.

4 Adaptive Modeling

In successful business and IT projects of today's enterprises there are modeling activities in business reengineering, logistics, supply chain management, industrial manufacturing and so on. Models foster the communication between stakeholders, because they enforce a certain standardization of the respective domain language. Therefore, they speed up requirement elicitation and then serve as a long-time documentation of system analysis efforts. Modeling is here to stay even if models are not intended as blueprints in Software development projects they add value. For example, there are huge business process redocumentation projects in major enterprises. Research in model-driven engineering is important. In these efforts there exists a different focus on modeling than model-driven engineering. We have a look at the working domain expert. Often, it is necessary to adapt the modeling method and, in particular, to adapt the used modeling language to the current needs of the domain. It may become necessary to introduce new modeling elements, to deprecate an existing model element, to add properties to an existing modeling element, to detail the semantics or to change the appearance of a model element.

Over the last three years we have been anxious to get an overview of the current research in the domains of metamodeling, domain specific modeling and model transformation, including the most recent developments like Eclipse GMF [GMF09] and Microsoft DSL [CJKW07], in order to survey the suitability of concepts for the business modeling domain. As a result it came up that the concepts could not be directly applied. To provide metamodeling features for the business domain and directly to end-users the first order principles are intuitivity and usability. Rather complex methods like MOF [omg06] or most proprietary methods implemented by, e.g., (Meta)-CASE tools [Met01, KP02, REN01, Kel97, LMB$^+$01], are hardly accepted by users in this domain. Nevertheless, metamodeling features would add substantial value when applied to the business domain in a user-friendly intuitive style.

The result was a visualization-oriented metamodeling concept that has been implemented in a Modeling-Platform called AMMI. The concept as well as the platform allows the intuitive visualization-oriented creation of metamodels and to use them as a schema for (instance-)modeling. Further a central feature of the concept is the support for an "Iterative Modeling Process". Presumption to this was that our experiences showed that it is not applicable to create the perfect fitting metamodels in advance. Well, for some basic tasks snapshot modeling will be sufficient but often the domain evolution has to result in an evolution of the modeling language. Initially basic metamodels will be created and used to model the domain. Over several building cycles the metamodel can be changed and the already existing instances will be adapted automatically to create a more fitting domain representation. However, the building cycles are not limited in respect to dynamic changes in the domain.

Iterative Modeling Process   4.1

As mentioned, unlike most of the research that has been done in Domain Specific Modeling, Metamodeling and Model Transformation we can place the origin of this work in the area of corporate modeling. In numerous projects from business process reengineering to enterprise-wide IT-Architectures, modeling is an essential prerequisite for success. Moreover, it is hardly possible to achieve sustainable improvements without an appropriate abstraction of the real corporate structures and processes. This is where modeling has to take place. But on the other hand modeling must not become an end in itself. It has to be strongly focused on that what needs to be analyzed.

Otherwise it will be nearly impossible to maintain the results, considering that corporate structures and processes are frequently subject of changes. As consequence of organizational changes the model repository and even modeling methods may have to be adapted to keep them valid. This adaptation process is more than a tool function; it is moreover an organizational process that has to be implemented.

This is one major area where we see a huge deficit in the current research. Tool vendors highlight their features to support metamodeling and praise their solution as flexible and adaptive. The organizational aspects that come up with adaptiveness are not considered sufficiently. Metamodeling and in particular an iterative modeling process can lead to unintended situations when they are implemented in an inappropriate way within an organizational structure. As a metamodel defines a common language that is used, e.g., company-wide, any changes on metamodel have to be planed carefully. Standardized and predefined change- and authorization processes must be implemented. Modeling is used across different companies, company departments and over different areas of application. Providing the service of modeling and modeling tools to users is nowadays the task of the service-oriented IT-Management. A de-facto standard for service-oriented IT-Management is the IT-Infrastructure-Library (ITIL). The idea is to use this de-facto standard, especially the area of "Service Support" (SSP) as basis for a "Modeling Support Process" (MSP). Moreover the MSP is an instance of the SSP and describes how a "Modeling Service" can be supported and continuously improved in organizations. See [HJL+07] for an in-depth discussion of this organizational integration.

4.2 Visual Reification

As highlighted earlier we see intuitivity as a key feature to apply metamodeling successfully to the business domain. As a tribute to this we discuss our tool against the background of a design rationale that we have coined "visual reification". Visual reification is the principle that the visual representation of the metamodel is at the same time also a visual representation of a model that adheres to the meta model. Or to say it differently, in painting a metamodel the user also paints a correct and in particular a visually correct model. With visual reification metamodeling is no longer an abstract visualization independent task, it is now intuitive WYSIWYG modeling.

This design rationale is at the core of end-user oriented meta modeling that is targeted by our efforts. The basic argument is that metamodeling becomes more intuitive and less complex if the model specification mechanism, i.e., the meta modeling capability, is oriented towards the appearance of the model. In our tool we make the visual reification principle a first class citizen. We are not biased in favor of the visual reification principle. We rather want to understand under which circumstances and for which features it adds value. Therefore we make it available in our tool and in order to make it available to sophisticated investigation and empirical evaluation in particular. We think that the visual reification principle is a contribution in its own right, because it helps to start a systematic discussion of the pragmatics of metamodeling features and their alternatives.

Furthermore, we will see that the principle is an ideal that we are sometimes tempted to violate in order to have the appropriate expressive metamodeling power and pragmatics at hand. A couple of available metamodeling tools use the principle in some way as a design rationale, however, they use it only implicitly. With our tool the design rationale becomes explicit.

AMMI – The adaptive Meta- and Instance Modeling Platform   4.3

All this concepts are implemented in a modeling platform called AMMI. The platform's core components are open source technologies, in particular the Eclipse Rich Client Platform and the Hibernate Persistence Framework. The metamodel definition language defined here [DHJ$^+$08, Jab06] was integrated to allow either conceptual or visual-true graphical definition of metamodels and to support the iterative modeling process. The tool integrates a model adaptation engine for the adaptation of instances after metamodel changes and to enable model evolution. A meta-layer is implemented for textual or graphical definition of metamodels and to enable the creation of metamodel instances an instance-layer has been developed on top of the meta-layer. For metamodel-based analysis on the repository of meta- and instance models an analysis and reporting module is available on a vertical analysis-layer. All layers are integrated as modules within the platform and can be optionally removed to create either only a metamodeling- or instance modeling or analysis tool. Beside this the access to each module is role dependent and can be restricted by an administration module that manages roles, users and user groups. The role specific access to modules and the central metamodel repository prevent from the decentralized definition or adaptation of metamodels by unauthorized users. Right from the start it was always an issue to support a simple integration into a company's IT-infrastructure. This was the main reason to develop platform independent and to use JAVA technologies. Moreover relational databases are still de-facto standard in today's enterprises. To take this into account the persistence layer was designed generic to support different data stores. At the current state of development the implementation for relational databases using the object relational framework

Hibernate is integrated. Nevertheless, other implementations like XMI flat-files are possible. At this time the tool is used in several Austrian companies including Voestalpine Europlatinen1 to completely support their modeling requirements with a predefined metamodel repository called ITSAM (IT Service and Architecture Management). ITSAM includes metamodels to visualize and analyze business processes as well as business architectures compliant to ITIL [iti06] and CobiT [cob07].

Figure 4 shows a screenshot of the tool's meta layer where metamodels can be created. As example, an organizational metamodel (organigram) is defined. The first (left) editor shows the metamodel in the conceptual style. The second editor visualizes the same metamodel but here the visual reification principle is applied. It is obvious that both metamodeling styles are structurally equal. In the first editor the MetaConnection "has Skill" is selected. You can see that there are two visual representations, created as reference copies. Instances of "has Skill" can now be drawn between instances of "Actor" and "Skill" as well as between instances of "Role" and "Skill". Multiplicities are defined for both reference copies and will be interpreted for each separately.

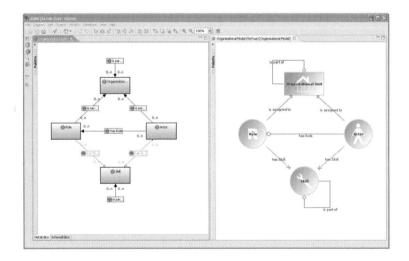

FIGURE 4   Conceptual style vs. visual reification.

Figure 5 demonstrates the use of MetaObjects to specify visual compartments (or container, compositions). The MetaObject acts as a container for child MetaObjects. For example we assume that an "Actor" can now be visually a child of an "Organizational Unit". Moreover we introduce the new MetaObject "Facility" and define that an "Actor" can be a child of a "Facility". The left editor once again shows the conceptual notation. You can see that it is possible to define that a MetaObject can be a child of several parent MetaObjects by the use of reference copies. The visual reification principle is applied in the second editor. Both visualizations are structurally equal. For the container layout the xy-layout is used, which allows to place child figures free inside its parent figure's bounds. Nevertheless, also stack layout, border layout and toolbar layout algorithms are available. The latter one can be used, e.g., to define UML compartments like "Classes", "Attributes" and "Methods".

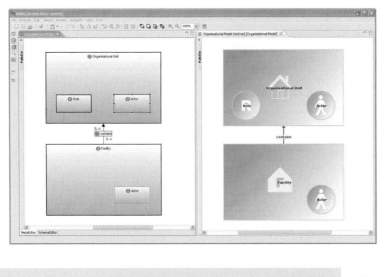

Visual reification with compartments.   FIGURE 5

In Figure 6 you can see a screenshot of the tool's instance layer where instance models based on metamodels are created. The editor visualizes a minimal process for an incoming order. For every selected element available attributes are shown in a property view. You can find the property view for the selected element "Calculate Capacity" in the lower part of the screen. Values and references to other model elements can be defined here. In this example references to incoming/outgoing information objects and documents have been created.

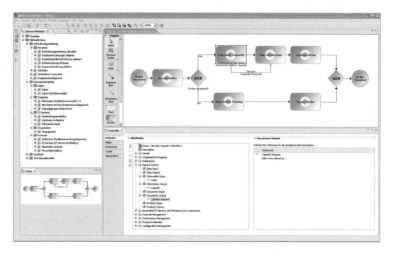

FIGURE 6   Instance of a process model.

5   Web Information Extraction

Information extraction (IE) is commonly defined as *extracting structured data out of unstructured data*, as it is provided, e.g., in textual documents. During the last decade IE heavily gained in importance not least to the massive and permanently growing amount of unstructured data, which is available online [Bro07]. There is a wide range of techniques to cope with this challenging task, which is partly based on information retrieval methods and techniques and, due to its addiction to the natural language, subject to linguistic research.

Web information extraction (Web IE) takes as input Web pages instead of local textual documents and addresses the given peculiarities of this domain, e.g., *semi-structured data*, distributed text sources, and design issues. Techniques range from screen scrapping tools, relying on structural and layout tags of Web pages, to *Natural Language Processing (NLP)* based and machine learning approaches. Even if some general approaches exist, e.g., text engineering frameworks, the majority of application systems are domain dependent, relying on a domain specific vocabulary and grammar.

This subchapter provides a short introduction into the fundamentals of IE respectively Web IE, presents available tools and identifies current challenges in the field. Thereafter, three IE systems tackling different application domains are presented and selected concepts resulting from their development are outlined.

Information Extraction in a Nutshell   5.1

IE is a technology, which analyzes natural language text in order to extract information of interest. The process takes text as input and produces fixed-formated data according to a given specification [Cun06]. IE results can thereupon be used for semantic tagging of text, semantically enriched search engines, recommender systems etc.

Information Extraction Process

The traditional IE process comprises four major steps [AI99]:

1. the system identifies individual *tokens*, i.e. words, from the text of a document.
2. these tokens are *annotated on basis of a vocabulary*.
3. the tokens are then assembled and set into *relation* in order to produce new facts according to a set of rules.
4. the facts are translated into the required *output* format.

The facts to be extracted are also called *information extraction templates*, where each template commonly consists of several slots in the form of attribute-value-pairs. For example, a template contact might consist of slots name, street, street number, zip-code, country, and email address.

Information Extraction as Compared to Information Retrieval

IE is often compared to *information retrieval (IR)*, as they share some basic concepts for text processing. However, they clearly differ in their intention and task processing. IR is initiated by a user posing his or her current information need in form of a query, e.g., a number of terms, to the system. The system thereon searches for text documents respectively Web pages that might be relevant for the user and presents surrogates, e.g., URLs, of the original sources to the user (see search engines like Google).

Whereas IE analyzes a text according to a specified template and presents the information extracted from several sources itself to the user. E.g., a user might want to get a list of contact data of high category hotels in Vienna providing a swimming pool facility to be extracted from the Web. However, IE takes over numerous concepts of IR, among them:

Tokenization: splitting a text into tokens (words).

Stemming: reducing the tokens to their stemmed form, to allow a proper matching of word derivations, e.g., the plural form "hotels" is stemmed to "hotel".

Application of a thesaurus: replacing tokens by their synonym, to allow the semantically identity of words, e.g., "automobile" gets replaced by "car".

Part-of-speech (POS)-tagging: identifying essential parts of the text according to the language's grammar as prominent NLP concept.

Similarity concepts: dealing with string similarities for the purpose of, e.g., error correction by applying diverse algorithms, e.g., Damerau Levenshtein metric and phonetic algorithms.

Term weighting: assigning of terms the importance of a token within the text by, e.g., applying $tf * idf$ weighting.

Performance evaluation: reapplying recall and precision as performance measures.

MUC Conferences

IE grew out of work performed in the realm of the *Message Understanding Conferences (MUC)* in the late 1980s and 1990s. The Conference was initiated and financed by DARPA to encourage the development of IE methods in form of a competition. The task was to fill specified templates in a predetermined domain, comprising among others military, terror attacks, joint-ventures, microelectronics, and astronomy. The results achieved by the competing IE systems were measured against human-annotated data in a controlled test environment.

The MUC program arrived at a definition of IE split into five tasks [Cun06].

Named Entity recognition (NE):   finds and classifies information items of interest in text, e.g., names, places, etc.

Co-reference resolution (CO):   identifies identity relations between NEs.

Template Element construction (TE):   adds descriptive information to NE results (using CO).

Template Relation construction (TR):   finds relations between TE entities.

Scenario Template production (ST):   fits TE and TR results into specified event scenarios.

Most current IE applications focus on NE and TE. Complexity of TR and ST is much higher, thus, hardening proper extraction quality.

Information Extraction Assessment

Extraction quality is evaluated by taking as basis the traditional IR performance measures *precision*, i.e., the number of slots it filled correctly, divided by the number of fills it attempted, and *recall*, i.e. the number of slots it filled correctly divided by the number of possibly correct fills, as taken from the manual extraction. Beyond, *F-measure* or balanced *F-score* is a popular measure that combines precision and recall as their weighted harmonic mean.

[MKSW99] proposes a more specific view on the involved parameters in that the type of incorrectness, i.e. substitution (incorrect slot), deletion (missing slot), and insertion (spurious slot) is considered. Precision and recall are then defined by:

$$P = \frac{C}{M} = \frac{C}{C + S + I}$$
$$R = \frac{C}{N} = \frac{C}{C + S + D}$$

N: total number of slots in the reference.

M: total number of slots in the hypothesis.

C: number of correct slots—those slots in the hypothesis that align with slots in the reference and are scored as correct.

S: number of substitutions (incorrect slots)—slots in the hypothesis that align with slots in the reference and are scored as incorrect.

D: number of deletions (missing slots or false rejections)—slots in the reference that do not align with any slots in the hypothesis.

I: number of insertions (spurious slots or false acceptances)—slots in the hypothesis that do not align with any slots in the reference.

In addition a *slot error rate (SER)* calculating the ratio of the total number of different types of slot errors divided by the total number of slots in the reference, which is fixed for a given test is proposed.

$$SER = \frac{S + D + I}{N} = \frac{S + D + I}{C + S + D} = \frac{\text{Total number of slot errors}}{\text{Total number of slots in reference}}.$$

Web Peculiarities

Web IE takes as input *Web pages* instead of local textual documents and addresses the given peculiarities of this domain, some of them representing the core characteristics of Web applications in contrast to software applications [KPRR06]:

Composition and navigation aspects: Web sites are hypertexts, i.e. a composition of a varying number of Web pages, which are linked to each other. For most applications IE must deal with the entire set of Web pages, thus, a Web crawler has to be incorporated into the IE system's architecture, which collects the Web pages and stores them in a document corpus building the source for the further extraction process.

Structuredness of information on a Web page: Web pages typically contain a mixture of structured, semi-structured, and unstructured data. *Structured* means, that the content is produced out of a database and presented in a way, that the schema behind can easily be inferred. *Semi-structured* is attributed to the description language HTML, which is used for the greater part of Web pages. HTML proposes layout tags and a small set of semantically tags, thus, enabling meta-tagging of tokens or parts of the text. *Unstructured* means the presence of natural language phrases, that require the application of NLP techniques as traditional text documents do.

Heterogeneity aspects: A mayor characteristics of Web applications is the importance of their look and feel. Competitors want to differ from each other and therefore, design their Web sites in a very heterogeneous way, concerning the content, e.g., with respect to its granularity as well as the structure and the look and feel.

Web site evolution: Web sites tend to be permanently changed, due to evolving Web technologies and mostly forced by competitive reasons. These changes do not only address the content, but also the design and overall structure of the Web site. The architecture of Web sites evolved from linked static HTML pages to highly interactive Web applications based on client-side scripting and AJAX technology at the present time. The later still being a tough nut to crack.

Improper use of technology: Web standards with regard to HTML validity or Web accessibility exist. However, the greater part of Web designers and Web application developers do not adhere to them. Invalid HTML pages, e.g., the use of tables just for the look & feel purpose, harden IE in real world environments.

Information Extraction Tools

Techniques and tools to cope with the Web peculiarities identified above have been developed. They range from screen scrapping tools, via rule based approaches to machine learning approaches.

- *Screen Scrapping tools* (also referred to as *wrappers*) rely on structural and layout tags of Web pages. Wrappers are procedures in order to extract a defined information item by specifying its occurrence on a Web page, e.g., with respect to its location in the Web page's *domain object model (DOM)* or with respect to a certain layout tag. Thus, screen scrapping is adequate for extracting data from homogeneously structured Web pages, but bears deficiencies for the case of heterogeneously designed Web pages, as there is a proprietary wrapper needed for each Web page, and for the case of evolution of the Web site. Exemplary tools are:

- *Solvent* [Sol] is part of the *SIMILE* project operated by MIT. It generates wrappers, in the form of XPath statements, for information items identified on an exemplary Web page by a user, which are further on used by the Piggy Bank Application [Pig].
- *Lixto* [BEG+05], realizes a visual approach for wrapper generation and is robust against minor structural changes in the code of the source page.

• *Rule-based IE approaches* rely on a (domain dependent) knowledge base consisting of lists and rules. A current approach is to enrich the knowledge base by incorporating a (domain) ontology, which is capable to store data and their relations (see Section 2) and thus, allow for an improved analysis of semantic aspects in documents respectively on Web pages. Most rule-based IE systems are proprietary developments, however, some text engineering frameworks exist, e.g., GATE (Generalized Architecture for Text Engineering, see below) and UIMA (Unstructured Information Management Application) a former IBM development, now operated by Apache.

• *Machine learning approaches*, which relieve from manual rule development in that rules representing extraction patterns are derived from a learning set of Web pages and can thereupon be applied to new Web pages.

GATE is applied for the IE scenarios discussed in the next section. This is why we take a somewhat more detailed view on this framework at this point.

GATE (Generalized Architecture for Text Engineering)

GATE [CMBT02] provides a GNU-licensed open source framework comprising a pipeline architecture and a graphical development environment. GATE proposes a grammar, called *JAPE*[6] (a version of CPSL – Common Pattern Specification Language), which enables finite state transduction over annotations based on regular expressions. The GATE pipeline allows for the definition of cascading components (processing resources) and passes a document or Web page from one resource to the next. Available components comprise: Tokenizer, Gazetteers, which match lists of domain dependent terms against the document, Sentence Splitter, which performs, e.g., POS-tagging, and Transducers, which execute implemented JAPE rules.

---

[6] a Java Annotation Patterns Engine

IE Scenarios and Applied Concepts

In the following we present information extraction systems as applied in three different domains. We will discuss their architecture and some innovative concepts that have been developed in order to cope with the given domain requirements: JobOlize, performing information extraction from job offers as presented on the Web, affords improved extraction quality through the incorporation of structural Web page segmentation aspects; TourIE, extracting essential tourism data out of heterogeneously designed accommodation Web sites, includes an SVM supported crawler for the collection and classification of Web pages and implements nested rules for the purpose of template relation (TR) extraction, and MARLIES, aiming at the recognition of entities and their relations in the manufacturing domain.

5.2 JobOlize – Headhunting by Information Extraction in the era of Web 2.0

E-recruitment is one of the most successful e-business applications supporting both, headhunters and job seekers. In the EU in 2007, 70% of all job offers were published online, and more than 56% of employments were results of online offers [WKE+07]. The explosive growth of online job offers makes the usage of information extraction techniques to build up job portals and allow matchmaking between offers and job profiles of job seekers at least in a semi-automatic way a necessity. Existing approaches like Monster or Stepstone, however, hardly cope with the heterogeneous and semi-structured nature of job offers as they appear on the Web.

The information extraction system *"JobOlize"* [BPP+08] is targeted on *arbitrarily structured IT job offers* on the Web with one job offer being presented on a single Web page (see right hand side of Figure 8). The information to be extracted comprises IT skills, language skills, operation areas and graduations. Even more demanding, the templates IT skill and language skill require information on an appropriate skill level of the applicant, e.g., mother tongue for language skill. The prototype developed by FAW has been partly funded by the Austrian Research Promotion Agency FFG under grant 813202 and has been used for further development of the Austrian online job portal *www.joinvision.com*.

In the following we will focus on two significant issues arising from the requirements for JobOlize. First, we will discuss the extraction approach, combining existing NLP-techniques with a new form of context-driven extraction incorporating Web page segmentation aspects and thus, improving extraction quality. Second, we will describe functionality and implementation aspects of the annotation manipulation user interface. This component allows users a proper adaptation of the extraction results while preserving the look and feel of the original Web page in that it is realized as a rich client interface on basis of Web 2.0 techniques.

Context-Driven Information Extraction Incorporating Web Page Segmentation

The architecture of JobOlize, depicted in Figure 7, is divided into two core components, a knowledge base providing a domain ontology as well as an extraction rule base and a pipeline consisting of different extraction components. Parts of the system are realized on basis of the text engineering framework *GATE* (see Section 5.1).

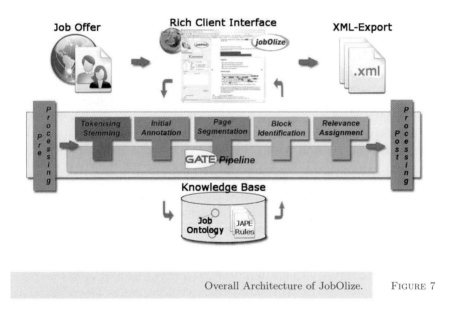

Overall Architecture of JobOlize.   FIGURE 7

e-Recruitment Domain Ontology. For representing the annotation vocabulary used by JobOlize, a light-weight domain ontology has been developed containing 15 core concepts of job offers which should be extracted. A design goal in this respect was to build on reasonable concepts of existing ontologies in the area of e-recruitment and human resource (HR) management, backed up by our experience in developing ontologies [GBPW05b]. Our ontology also considers specialization hierarchies of IT skills (e.g., "Oracle" and "MySQL" are specializations of "DBS") and equivalence relationships (e.g., "DB" is semantically equivalent to "DBS"), which are of particular interest for the extraction process. Finally, to consider also job offers in different languages, each concept contains a language property.

Extraction Rule Base. The second part of our knowledge base contains about 50 extraction rules ranging from very simple ones, responsible, e.g., for matching input tokens with ontology concepts to rather complex ones for, e.g., job title detection, using the rule language JAPE (see Section 5.1).

Pipeline of Extraction Components. On basis of the second core part of our architecture, the pipeline, annotations of web pages are incrementally built up by streaming input pages through the different components of the pipeline, each of them being responsible for a certain annotation task, thereby adding new or modifying already existing annotations. Thus, JobOlize reuses existing NLP-based components for tokenizing and stemming as provided by the GATE framework and furthermore realizes customized components on basis of Java for pre-processing the input Web pages (e.g., eliminating JavaScript code), for post-processing (e.g., exporting annotated Web pages as XML documents) and for the core task of identifying those tokens of the input Web page, which are relevant for our purposes, e.g., IT-skill with an associated skill-level like "basic knowledge in Java programming". The identification of relevant tokens is performed on basis of four different customized components, as described in the following, which are making use of the above mentioned knowledge base.

Initial Annotation. The first component is responsible for an initial annotation of the tokens of the input Web page with appropriate concepts defined by our domain ontology. For most of the tokens, this task is straightforward, but considering the domain concepts IT-skill and language skill, context-driven processing is required in order to determine their corresponding levels. In particular, not only the position of the skill level with respect to the skill type itself is taken into account by means of appropriate JAPE rules, but also, e.g., if it is located within the same sentence or not.

Page Segmentation. The remaining three components promote the basic idea of context-driven extraction even further, with the ultimate goal to improve the quality of the extraction results. For this, the Web page is first segmented into three parts, a top part, a content part and a bottom part, simply taking the content itself into account. This is done by identifying common text fragments between two job offers of the same Web site on basis of the well-known Longest-Common-Subsequence algorithm (LCS). These common text fragments represent the top and bottom parts of a page and contain tokens which are most probably irrelevant for further processing. For example, the occurrence of "powered by Typo3" within the bottom page would lead to an IT-skill annotation of "Typo3" during the initial annotation phase, being refined by page segmentation, i.e., classified as irrelevant.

Block Identification. The content part of the Web page identified before, is further divided into so-called blocks, representing a couple of tokens which "visually" belong together and are normally grouped under a header title. For the identification of such blocks, first, context in terms of layout information (e.g., a <b>-tag) and structural information (e.g., a <li>-tag) is considered by appropriate JAPE rules. In a second step, context in form of content information is used to categorize the identified blocks. In particular, on basis of their header title and the corresponding domain concepts defined by our ontology, blocks are categorized and annotated as requirements, responsibilities, offer characteristics and contact details, i.e., those chunks of information most commonly found in job offers.

Relevance Assignment. The final component of our extraction process assigns pre-defined relevance values, ranging from 0 to 1, to the initial annotations, depending on the block category, the annotated token is contained in. E.g., in case that a token annotated as IT-skill is part of the requirements block it gets a relevance of 1, whereas if it is part of the bottom part, it gets a relevance of 0.25, only. During post-processing, annotated IT-skills with a relevance lower than a certain threshold, are eliminated from the result.

Evaluation results. An evaluation of the prototype showed that the context-driven extraction process incorporating Web page segmentation outperforms a conventional extraction, as expected. E.g., for IT-skills precision and f-measure increased by 30% and 20%, respectively. For more details on the evaluation see [BPP$^+$08]

Annotation Manipulation via a Rich Client Interface

For ensuring an acceptable quality of the extraction results, information extraction out of arbitrarily structured and heterogeneous job offers is reasonable in a semi-automatic way only. Thus, the annotation results generated automatically by the extraction system have to be assessed by a user and potentially corrected accordingly. For this task, we provide a rich client interface which allows the user to visualize the results of the extraction process in terms of the annotated Web pages and the possibility to manipulate existing annotations or to add additional ones directly in a Web browser. The screenshot in Figure 8 depicts on the left hand side a menu sidebar and on the right hand side the original Web page.

Annotation Highlighting. Within the sidebar, the user can choose from an annotation list (see Figure 8 (1)), representing the concepts of our domain ontology, which of the automatically generated annotations should be indicated within the Web page on the right hand side. To preserve the look and feel of the original Web page, annotations are indicated by marking the concerned parts of the Web page with corresponding colours and highlighting those, being currently focused on, by means of a flash effect.

Annotation Details. The details of annotations (e.g., the relevance values assigned) are shown for each annotation, both, within the sidebar (see Figure 8 (2)) and directly within the Web page, activated by a mouse over effect.

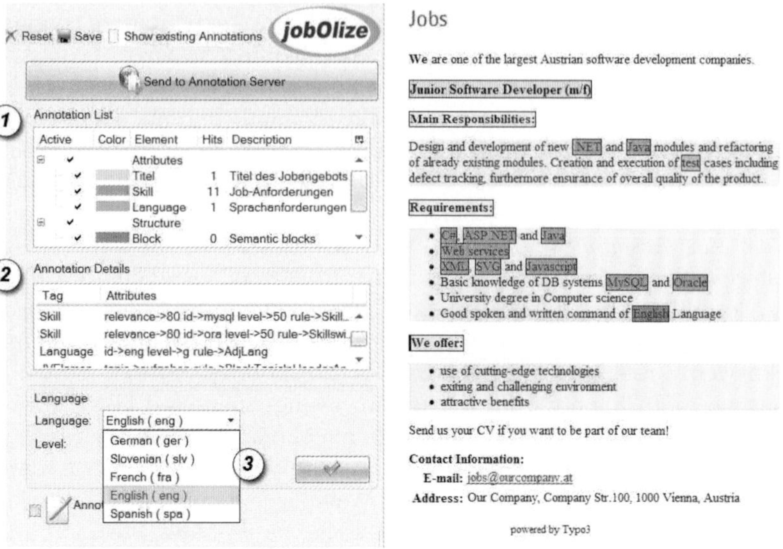

FIGURE 8   Rich Client Interface of JobOlize.

This functionality also serves as a simple form of explanation component, which allows tracing back the genesis of a certain annotation.

Annotation Manipulation. Finally, the details of each of the automatically generated annotations can be manipulated in accordance with the underlying job ontology, the annotation can be completely deleted or new ones can be added. Thus, e.g., a language skill can be modified from German to English (see Figure 8 (3)). Manipulations are immediately propagated to the Web page at the right hand side.

Implementation Aspects. Concerning implementation aspects, the rich client interface is realized as a Firefox extension using *XUL* (XML User Interface Language [XUL], allowing for portability of the application, JavaScript and *CSS*. The primary reason to favor the Firefox extension mechanisms instead of alternatives like Apache's MyFaces [MyF], was the rather easy realization of a rich client interface experience as in native desktop applications, considerably reducing programming effort. Annotation highlighting as well as manipulation is based on DOM. As a pre-requisite for asynchronously initiating the extraction process (executed on the server) directly from within the rich client interface, the underlying extraction system had to be ported to the used Tomcat Web server.

TourIE – Ontology-based Information Extraction from Tourism Web Sites   5.3

Since the beginning of the World Wide Web, tourism industry, i.e., airlines, car rental companies, and accommodation owners, takes advantage of this medium to bring its products to the living room of the prospective tourist. During the last decade the required data storage was commonly done in local databases and, for the majority of tourism Web sites, maintained manually. Currently, the enlarging amount of semi-structured and unstructured data on heterogeneously designed tourism Web sites demands for information extraction (IE) mechanisms for semi-automatic acquisition of structured data in order to build up, e.g., tourism Web portals or tourism recommender systems.

The *TourIE* prototype, which has been developed by FAW [Fei07, Par08] in cooperation with the tourism portal provider Tiscover AG[7], focuses on accommodation Web sites aiming at the extraction of some of the most prominent information specified in a search for accommodations by a tourist [DO01]: accommodation's name, available facilities, room price, location, swimming, accommodation category, images, etc. [FGP+09]. This particular sub-domain of the travel and tourism industry bears a number of challenges for the purpose of information extraction primarily caused by the immateriality of the accommodation's products at the time of the booking decision. Rooms, holiday packages, etc. demand for comprehensive information featuring varying complexity and structure [WK99], which is reflected in open variants for their presentation on Web pages. Even if a large number of accommodation owners decide to subscribe to a Web portal and thus, present their products in a more structured and better comparable way, resulting in a homogeneous presentation of the accommodations, a considerable number of accommodation Web sites are maintained individually and, thus, feature a number of heterogeneity aspects.

Heterogeneity of Tourism Web Sites

Figure 9 shows Web pages of three individually maintained accommodation Web sites together with the exemplary TourIE extraction templates accommodation's name, facilities, and price and demonstrates some of the heterogeneities discussed in the following.

Heterogeneity of content model. The content model contains the extent of information provided, ranging from basic data only, e.g., accommodation's name, short textual description, and contact data, to all-encompassing infor-

---

[7] www.tiscover.com

| FIGURE 9 | Heterogeneously designed accommodation Web sites. |

mation including sensitive price information per person or room/apartment on a seasonal basis together with diverse price reductions, thus, establishing the basis for an electronic booking process.

Heterogeneity of structure model. The representation of tourism information ranges from structured to unstructured data. E.g., facilities can be either presented in form of a list or separated by commas within a textual paragraph. Also multimedia data, e.g., a pool facility represented as icon or as image, is subject to the information extraction purpose.

Heterogeneity of composition and navigation model. Different to other applications, e.g., job offer extraction, in the majority of cases accommodation Web sites comprise several Web pages (see Section 5.1), requiring an additional crawler component.

Heterogeneity of presentation model demands for the inspection of layout tags, which provoke that, e.g., a textual item is presented in bold or underlined and, thus, e.g., raising the relevance of a text item for being the accommodation's name.

These heterogeneities imply that simple screen scrapping methods (see Section 5.1) are unfeasible for TourIE, and demand for a rule based approach employing a domain specific ontology and domain specific rules incorporating structural and NLP related aspects.

Employment of a Rule/Ontology Based Approach

Overview of TourIE Architecture

Figure 10 shows the overall architecture of TourIE. The extraction process comprises three intertwined processing phases, first, a pre-processing phase, which integrates a Web crawler as predominant component, second, an information extraction phase, which incorporates a GATE pipeline (see Section 5.1) basing upon the tourism specific knowledge base, and third, a post-processing phase, assigning relevance judgments to potential template candidates, which are thereafter used for their ranking within a specified XML document.

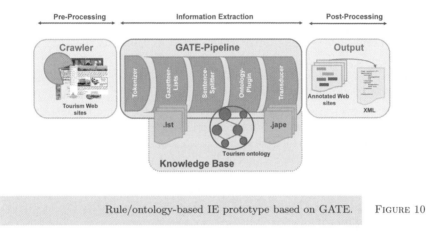

Rule/ontology-based IE prototype based on GATE.   FIGURE 10

The GATE pipeline employed for TourIE (see Figure 10) cascades for the most part available processing resources adapted to the tourism domain, i.e.

1. a tokenizer,
2. gazetteer lists, responsible for the token matching in order to identify NLP-related co-reference aspects,
3. a sentence splitter,
4. the ontology plugin, which constitutes a self-developed component enabling the access to the tourism domain ontology, and
5. a transducer, interpreting tourism specific Jape rules and thus, resolving more complex template relations like contact data or room price.

Annotation via Tourism Domain Ontology and Ontology-Plugin

At this stage, the TourIE domain ontology represents a simplified excerpt of the tourism domain comprising concepts and relations focusing on the specified templates of the TourIE prototype. However, the development of a comprehensive tourism domain ontology is on its way (see Section 2). The ontology plugin constitutes the Java-developed interface to the tourism prototype ontology. Thus, the tokens on an accommodation Web page can be matched with labels of concepts and individuals of the ontology and can thereupon be annotated with appropriate label names and property values. E.g., a token "double" gets annotated with a corresponding room type level. Furthermore, the ontology is used in the post-processing phase to verify some parts of the extracted templates, e.g., correspondence of zip code and city name. In order to cope with typing or translation errors referring to the tokens on the Web page, similarity matching is implemented, in that a token can be matched with differing ontology-labels. According to that, amongst others, a Porter stemmer is used in order to reduce tokens to their base form and Damerau-Levenshtein-Metric is employed as similarity measure.

Extraction of Template Relations via Jape Rules

The complexity of templates in TourIE ranges from simple extraction of named entities to rather complex extraction of template relations. Price extraction is an example for the latter one and is often encompassing a table data extraction task (see Section 5.4). Even if price extraction is also addressed by researchers dealing with different application domains, tourism prices hold a major challenge due to their complex data structure. The exemplary Web pages in Figure 9 include price information, which is dependent on room category (superior, standard) and room type (single, double). The code excerpt below shows a simplification of the rule "price", which in case of determined consecutive annotations "RoomCategory", "RoomType", and "Money" on a Web page, sets them into relation in order to fill the template "room price".

```
Rule: price                          (
(                                      ({Split})*
({RoomCategoryLabel})?                 {MoneyAnnotation})
{RoomTypeLabel}                        )+
({Split})?                           ):price
({RoomCategoryAnnotation})?          -->
({Split})?                           :price.Price={}
```

Crawling and SVM Supported Classification of Web Pages

The inclusion of a Web crawler is a necessity for accommodation Web sites, which are composed of a more than a single Web page and thus, have their entire information about the accommodation split over several linked Web pages. *WebSPHINX* [MB98], an easy extendable crawler, was chosen and extended in a way to limit search to a given depth and a maximal number of Web pages in order to reduce crawling time. The TourIE crawler is responsible for first, the collection of the entire set of Web pages belonging to the accommodation Web site and second, the classification of Web pages according to specified types, e.g., price related Web pages, providing information for further improving extraction quality in the post-processing phase.

Web page classification is realized by applying a support vector machine (SVM), which is based on supervised learning methods and learns its model from a set of manually classified examples. By hand of the learned model it is possible to classify unknown examples. Basically an SVM is able to categorize linear separable data of a binary class problem; a kernel extension enables its application for non-linear separable data. Moreover, the implementations of SVM provide multi class classification, realized by reducing the multi class problem to a binary problem. There are two different strategies to implement this reduction: one-versus-one or one-versus-all. Training samples are given in the form $\{(x_1, y_1), \ldots, (x_m, y_m)\}, x_i \in X, y_i \in \{-1, 1\}$ where every sample x_i is labeled with -1 or 1. With this examples an hyperplane consisting of a normal vector w a bias b and a training example x_i is calculated $y_i = sgn(\langle w, x_i \rangle + b)$. In the scope of text classification SVMs provide some advantages like the use of different kernels or the ability to handle large, spare feature vectors svm1.

The SVM supported classification realized in TourIE uses a bag-of-words as features. Together with adapted concepts for stemming, term frequency normalization and stop word elimination classification quality resulted in recall and precision values of approximately 0.84 for both on the test data. Evaluation of the overall TourIE prototype showed satisfying results with recall up to 0.76, precision up to 0.62, and a corresponding F-measure value of 0.73 for template relations.

MARLIES – Supply of Demands in Manufacturing 5.4

Sourcing and procurement are mayor tasks of *supply chain management*, which increasingly benefit from Web technologies in that producers respectively service suppliers make information on their services retrievable online for the prospective consumers. Thus, especially for small and medium enterprises, the Web acts as an intermediary to attract new consumers from all

over the world. The wide range of branches, the degree of specialization, as
well as the size and resources of service supplying companies provoke, that
their Web sites promoting their services highly vary in extent, detail and
trendiness. In spite of the improved accessibility of information these heterogeneities and the mere number of existing Web sites entail that a search for
manufacturers, offering exactly the service the consumer is in demand for,
turns out to be a very tricky and time consuming task. Information extraction
technologies constitute the prerequisite to enable the semi-automatic support
for finding the best fitting service supplier.

  MARLIES is an information extraction system targeted at extracting contact data and detailed data on services offered by companies in the manufacturing industry via their Web sites. The system constitutes one component of
the intermediary system www.tech2select.com, which is operated by the Austrian company Tech2select GmbH. Its development by FAW is partly funded
by the Austrian Research Promotion Agency FFG under grant FFG 817789.
Services as treated by MARLIES are machines or manufacturing processes
promoted by a supplier. In order to build the base for a business assignment the services must be specified in sufficient detail, including information
on the processable material and dimension, which are further described by
measurements, units and values.

  On account of the given requirements an ontology and rule based approach
was implemented. The major challenges of MARLIES are on the one hand
the proper ontological modelling of highly structured and complexly related
technical data, which constitutes the basis for the realized approach of an
ontology aware annotation, on the other hand, the extraction of relations
between the data units while tackling structural provocations, as related data
on a service might be spread over several Web pages and is often concealed
in nested tables.

MARLIES Architecture

Figure 11 illustrates the components of MARLIES. A crawler collects Web
pages of a service supplier's Web site and classifies them into Web pages containing contact data and data on proposed services by use of an SVM (see
SVM Supported Classification of Web Pages of TourIE). Due to the mentioned complexity of the domain the MARLIES pipeline, which is again based
on GATE, comprises a number of specialized processing resources, which are
partly intended for structural analysis, e.g., a transducer responsible for the
analysis of fonts. The interface to the MARLIES ontology, which contains
among others machines (production units), processes, materials, dimensions,
and relations in between, is based on the OntoRoot Gazetteer, a plug-in provided by GATE, thus, allowing ontology aware annotation of Web pages. The
post-processing component prepares the extraction results for delivery to the

customer database, in that the best fitting result is determined according to some relevance assessment, which incorporates classification and verification results. The customer database establishes the base of the intermediary Web application, which further on matches service supplies and service demands.

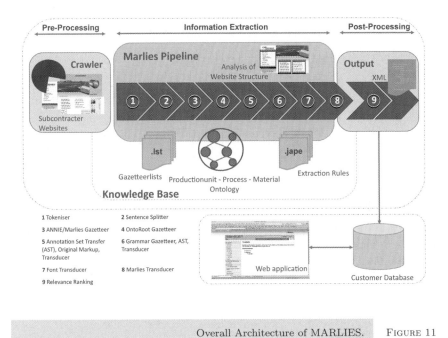

Overall Architecture of MARLIES.   FIGURE 11

Enabling Ontology Aware Annotations

One major challenge in MARLIES is to identify the relations between production units, their dimensions and the materials they are able to process. Thus, beyond a syntactical extraction, a more semantic interpretation of relations between tokens is needed. Hence, rules matching annotations against ontology properties had to be employed, which are capable of producing ontology-aware annotations, meaning that the annotations are assigned to and enriched by the concepts of the MARLIES ontology at processing time. As a prerequisite, the ontology resources, i.e., classes and instances, have to be pre-processed using an adapted tokenizer and a sentence splitter. Figure 12 shows an example, which demonstrates, that the token "vertical" is assigned to "turnings centers" instead of "furnances" by interpreting the corresponding ontology properties at processing time.

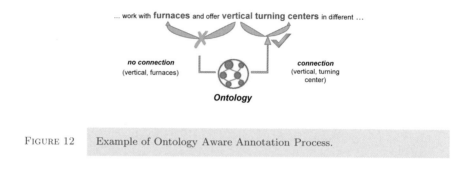

FIGURE 12   Example of Ontology Aware Annotation Process.

Employing Table Data Extraction Concepts

A large part of production unit related data is presented in tables. These tables are heterogeneously designed as the service supplier respectively the Web page designer sees its best fit. Moreover, HTML tables are often not used in their intended way and, thus, adhering to the HTML validity demands, but they are misused for design purposes. As shown in Figure 13 diameter denoting a measure and mm denoting a unit appear in the column heading. The machines and their corresponding attributes are listed in one or several table rows. The appropriate data items have to be set into relation and the dimension value has to be split into its minimum and maximum value. One extraction result in the example is a hobbing machine of type Pfauter P 400, with a min. diameter of 15 mm and a max. diameter of 400 mm.

machine type	description	ø (mm)	to module	weight max.	toothing quality
toothing machines:					
Pfauter P 400	hobbing machine	15 - 400	6		8 - 9
Pfauter P 900	hobbing machine	30 - 900	10		8 - 9
Pfauter P 900	hobbing machine	30 - 900	10		8 - 9
Pfauter PE 1200	hobbing machine	30 - 1200	20		6 - 7
Pfauter P 1250	hobbing machine	50 - 1250	16		8 - 9
Lorenz SN 8	shaping machine	30 - 750	10		8 - 9

Result

Hobbing machine – Pfauter P 400	Diamater (min): 15 mm
	Diamater (max): 400 mm

☐ ... measure
☐ ... unit
☐ ... machine

FIGURE 13   Example of Table Data Extraction.

The table data extraction process employed in MARLIES cascades several components, among them the preparatory grammar and font components.

The grammar component analyzes the underlying text and identifies, whether it is a continuous text or some table content. It comprises a gazetteer, an annotation set transfer and a transducer (see Figure 11). The font component identifies different formatting styles, e.g., font and font size, and thereby helps finding headers and relevant tokens. It comprises an annotation set transfer and a font transducer, which is responsible for the execution of JAPE-rules.

The development of MARLIES is still in progress at the publishing time of this book, why evaluation results cannot be provided at this stage.

Similarity Queries and Case Based Reasoning 6

Identity, Equality and Similarity have been studied at least since the age of the Greek philosophers. In general, Similarity between two objects is given when one object has partially the same attribute values as the other, or one object can be easily transformed into the other. Unfortunately, similarity is not an objective concept. For different persons—even for the same person in different circumstances—the same two objects can be various similar.

Exploring concepts of similarity has been a research issue in Hagenberg, in particular at FAW, since its foundation in 1990. First we concentrated on similarity of objects in Databases. Later on, investigating similarity questions geometric models [AKW06, AKWP06] and in Case Based Reasoning became an additional topic of interest.

Similarity Queries in Databases 6.1

Database management systems (DBMS) represent the de facto standard for managing data in real world applications. The applied technology is optimized for the efficient retrieval of records that are meeting the specified query conditions exactly. If there is no record fitting the specified query conditions, the system returns an empty result set. In many cases this is useful and even desirable. If the query "The data of employee Scott" fails, obviously no data is available for this person and it makes sense, if the database system returns an empty result set. But, in many other cases the user would be helped a lot when the system provides him the most the objects most similar to the query condition.

VQS – Vague Query System

The main goal was to develop an application domain independent system which is able to enhance already existing data bases with the functionality of similarity searching. This means that even if a database is quite old and at the time of its creation nobody thought about similarity searching VQS can be taken and customized and vague queries are working. Figure 14 shows the architecture of the system.

For carrying out vague queries a system requires additional knowledge behind the attribute values. Something like similarity functions or other concepts for measuring similarity are needed. Beside simple similarity functions for numeric and date values VQS attribute values can be mapped to points in a multidimensional space. Hence, similarity is defined through distances in this space. This solution seems to be very problem adequate. In many cases numeric co-ordinates for nonnumeric attribute values are given. For instance: Geographic co-ordinates for villages, RGB-values for colours, and so on. [KP97]

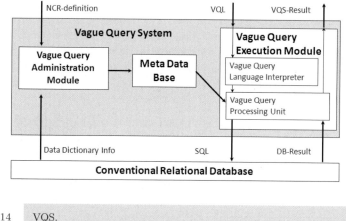

FIGURE 14   VQS.

An extra query language (VQL-Vague Query Language) is defined as an extension of SQL. Its most important concept is the operator 'IS' ('is similar to') which forces the vague query system to take objects which are 'near' to this query condition into the result set in the case that no object matches exactly to the query condition. Also an interpreter (Vague Query Language Interpreter) and the corresponding processing unit is introduced which transfers these more user friendly VQL-statements into SQL-statements considering the semantic background information held in additional metadata.

In VQL tables and views of a relational database can be used as data sources. Views can base on other views and so on. VQS is able to look for assigned semantic background information along this view definitions, down until to basing table attributes are reached. The implementation of this feature is very sophisticated. It considers renaming of attributes and joins in the view definition. On the other hand, with this solution we can support different similarity measures for the same objects within one system.

The similarity operator of the basic vague query system could not be used in the join-condition. Therefore the first extension of VQS was a vague join capability [KP98, KP99]. Then a corresponding multidimensional index structure has been developed [DKW01] and fuzzy 'greater than' and 'less than' operators have been introduced [BK04].

Case-based Reasoning   6.2

This chapter introduces the methodology "Case-based Reasoning" (CBR). As described in [FGSK08], [FGSK09] and [FSFK08], Case-based Reasoning is a cyclic problem solving process whereby already known knowledge is stored in form of cases. A case consists of a problem and an appropriate solution. These cases are stored in a so-called case base. CBR is "a recent approach to problem solving and learning (...) [AP94]".

The objectives of Case-based Reasoning are: no development of new solutions for new problems, reutilization of solutions from similar problems, no new problem solving process and rapid and cost-efficient solutions.

One of the most important fundamentals of Case-based Reasoning is the CBR-Cycle according to [AP94]. This cycle consists of four main phases which a new problem has to pass: Retrieve, Reuse, Revise and Retain.

The following description of the four main phases of CBR relies on [FGSK08], [FGSK09] and [FSFK08]. If a new problem appears, a new case is formulated and no new problem solving process should be started. In the phase "Retrieve" this new case is compared to cases in the case base where already known cases and general knowledge are stored. Matching cases relying on similarity calculation are selected.

In the phase "Reuse" the most similar case from the case base is combined with the new problem/case. The CBR-System can now suggest a solution by reusing the solution of an already known case and adapt it to the new problem.

In the phase "Revise" the retrieved solution is checked whether it can be applied to the current problem without changes. If the retrieved solution is faulty in the scope of the new case, it has to be adapted to the new problem.

Finally, in the phase "Retain" the new problem/case with a retrieved and perhaps adapted solution creates a new case which is stored in the case base again. The case base has learned and consequently can solve future problems more probably. If the current problem could not be solved with the CBR-

System (e.g. no similar case could be found in the case base), a human expert can deal with it and find the appropriate solution. If this expert can solve the problem, the human solution should be combined with the current problem and form a new case for integration into the case base. So, similar future problems can also be solved with the CBR-System.

6.3 Similarity Measures

As described in [FGSK09], similarity measures play a great role for CBR. These measures are essential to be able to compare new problems/cases with the cases in the case base. It is fundamental to choose the right similarity measure for given data. A very short selection of a few possible similarity measures could be:

- Similarity measure by Hamming: for bivalent attributes (true-false, yes-no, man-woman, 0-1, ...)
- Assessed similarity measure by Hamming:

  - Some attributes can be more important than others
  - One has to give priority to attributes through different assessments

- Generalized similarity measure: Not only binary attributes but also attributes with any values can be compared.
- Other similarity measures:

  - Tversky-contrast-model
  - Similarity measure by Rosch
  - Similarity measures for graph representation
  - Etc.

The following example shows how the similarity between cases can be calculated [FGSK09]. Therefore, the Generalized Similarity Measure by Hamming is used defined by the following formula:

$$sim(x, y) = \frac{\sum_{i=1}^{n} w_i sim_i(x_i, y_i)}{\sum_{i=1}^{n} w_i}$$

Figure 15 shows a very small case base with only five cases (only for illustration). The attributes are "Global Frequency", "Piping Element", "Sensor", "Pipe Temperature" and "Capacity Utilization". Each case $x_1, \ldots, x_5$ has its individual parameter values.

Case	Attributes				
	Global Frequency (in Hz)	Piping Element	Sensor	Pipe Temperature (in °C)	Capacity Utilization (in %)
x_1	80,4	Plug Flow Reactor	Accelerometer 15a	58,6	80
x_2	87,7	Plug Flow Reactor	Accelerometer 24c	75,5	65
x_3	72,3	Plug Flow Reactor	Accelerometer 18b	78,4	53
x_4	92,7	Branch Connection	Accelerometer 21a	71,9	90
x_5	78,4	Branch Connection	Accelerometer 24c	85,1	50

Similarity Measures – Case Base.   FIGURE 15

If a new case y appears, one want to know, which case in the case base is the most similar one to the new case y, see Figure 16 [FGSK09].

Case	Attributes				
	Global Frequency (in Hz)	Piping Element	Sensor	Pipe Temperature (in °C)	Capacity Utilization (in %)
y	80,1	Plug Flow Reactor	Accelerometer 18b	63,9	50

Similarity Measures – New Case y.   FIGURE 16

To be able to use the Generalized Similarity Measure by Hamming, for each attribute functions have to be defined, e.g. how similar is 58.6 °C to 63.9 °C or how similar is an Accelerometer 15a to an Accelerometer 18b. An example to define functions is shown in the following listing:

- "Global Frequency = $sim_{GF}(x_{GF}, y_{GF})$ = For each hertz (Hz), which differs from case x_i to case y, the similarity value is reduced by 0,01
- Piping Element = $sim_{PE}(x_{PE}, y_{PE})$ =

  - Plug Flow Reactor: Similarity value of 1
  - Branch Connection: Similarity value of 0

- Sensor = $sim_S(x_S, y_S)$ =

  - Accelerometer 18b: Similarity value of 1
  - Accelerometer 15a: Similarity value of 0.75
  - Accelerometer 21a: Similarity value of 0.85
  - Accelerometer 24c: Similarity value of 0.5

- Pipe Temperature = $sim_{PT}(x_{PT}, y_{PT})$ = For each degree Celsius (°C), which differs from case x_i to case y, the similarity value is reduced by 0.01

- Capacity Utilization $= sim_{CU}(x_{CU}, y_{CU}) =$ For each percentage point (%), which differs from case x_i to case y, the similarity value is reduced by 0.01. [FGSK09]"

Now, a new table with the similarities between the cases of the case base and the new case y can be generated. Attributes can be more important than others, so one can define so-called weighting coefficients (w_i) for calculating the similarity (see the last line in Figure 17 [FGSK09]).

Case	Attributes				
	Global Frequency (in Hz)	Piping Element	Sensor	Pipe Temperature (in °C)	Capacity Utilization (in %)
x_1	1	1	0,75	0,95	0,7
x_2	0,92	1	0,5	0,88	0,85
x_3	0.92	1	1	0,86	0,97
x_4	0,87	0	0,85	0,92	0,6
x_5	0,98	0	0,5	0,79	1
w_i	1	0,8	0,2	0,75	0,5

FIGURE 17   Similarity Measures – Similarities and Weighting Coefficients.

An example to calculate the similarity between a case in the case base and the new case y is shown in the following calculation:

$$sim(x, y) = \frac{(1 * 1 + 0,8 * 1 + 0,2 * 0,75 + 0,75 * 0,95 + 0,5 * 0,7)}{3,25} \approx 0,93$$

Using this formula for the other cases $x_2 \ldots x_5$, the following similarities can be calculated: x_1: 0,93, x_2: 0,89, **x_3: 0,94**, x_4: 0,62 and x_5: 0,67.

As one can see, the case x_3 is the most similar case to the new case y. If there would be a new problem, the case x_3 would be used to retrieve a similar solution [FGSK09].

Applications of Case-based Reasoning for Structural 6.4
Health Monitoring

Simple Structures

"Due to aging and corrosion, structures, which are part of the traffic infrastructure, have to be inspected regularly. In the case of lamp posts Austrian Codes require an inspection interval of 6 years. The onsite inspection consists of measurements and visual inspection whereupon the latter is partly subjective. As the conservative way of assessment involves experts who combine measurement analysis and visual inspection to conduct a classification of thousands of lamp posts a year it is obvious that a certain amount of subjectivity influences the result. Moreover, time between contract award and delivering results is short. Increased objectivity hand in hand with less time will also increase result-quality. In order to reach higher result-objectivity paired with less time-effort, automated processes become a must. (. . .) Consequently, beside cost reduction and time saving, comparably simple knowledge gathering processes are main benefits of the system. (. . .) Therewith, the similarity between the cases' attributes can be expressed and for a new case the most similar cases can be provided. The system currently is in the state of a "research prototype" whereby the results of first experiments were quite promising. The results of lamp post assessment done by an expert and done by the Case-based Reasoning system were equal with a 90% probability. The error rate of 10% generally results from the experts' subjectivity, from shortcomings (from CBR's point of view) in the inspection process and of course from matters of fine tuning of the system. In addition to gaining objectivity CBR helps to save time. Normally it takes an expert around 15–20 days to classify around thousand lamp posts. With CBR this is possible within a few minutes plus around one day of experts' review. (. . .) The application of systems for automated classification of measurements of simple structures, e.g. of lamp posts promises good results and even offers the possibility of a fully automated process. [FFSK09]"

Piping Systems

This chapter shows possible opportunities of CBR in the field of Structural Health Monitoring for the EU-project SafePipes.

Three possible approaches are introduced in the following paragraphs:

The first approach is the interpretation of measuring data for periodic measurements. Hereby, one can rely on measuring data of similar structures whereby the geometric data of a new structure is uploaded. With this given data the system can provide similar structures and distance information. The system could classify states of a structure, provide characteristics like "risk level" for example and suggest essential actions.

Another approach is the provision of information to support structure design. Weak points of buildings should be pointed out and improve structure design.

Finally Case-based Reasoning could be used for an integrated alert system for permanent monitoring. For the domain of SafePipes this aspect might be the most interesting one. Relying on historic measuring data of a structure the system could point out changes of its dynamics to detect impacts or damages. The alert system for permanently monitored structures should detect damages at a very early point of time to allow counteractive measures.

7 Data Warehouses

A Data warehouse (DWH) is a systems that is able to manage a huge amount of data and supports efficient complex analysis tasks to support decisions. In this chapter we want to give a small insight into DWH research in Hagenberg. Among others FAW is working on the ETL (Extract Transfer Load) process and SCCH on active data warehousing. Besides, FLLL is successfully researching in gaining knowledge from data warehouses, see Section 5 in Chapter V.

7.1 Automated Regression Tests of ETL Modules

Goal of this work was—as software regression test in general do—to ensure correctness of new versions of ETL module. The implemented test system acts as an extension of common ETL software. It bases on the following Idea (like several other black box test frameworks do but, until now not for a DWH ETL process): There is a predefined input data set and the corresponding output given. Whenever a (new) ETL version is to be tested the system takes the test set and checks the correctness of the result.

Since the structure of input data changes quiet often during the life of a DWH this guarantee of correctness is a vitally important in particular when bugs in a new version do not cause a program abort (They just produce wrong data in the DWH.) and crucial decisions are derived from this DWH.

Adaptive Data Warehousing using Workflow Engines   7.2

A major goal of active data warehouses (ADW) is to automatically perform complex analysis tasks. However, this goal is only insufficiently implemented in current active data warehousing architectures, which generally focuses on more frequent updates to the DWH. Traditionally, data warehouses are used to support non-routine decision making tasks within the strategic decision making. Routine decision tasks, on the other hand, are more likely to be found at the tactical and operational level of an organization. Although these routine decision tasks are well structured, they can be complex and may require detailed domain knowledge. A characteristic of routine decision tasks is that the same analyzes are repeated rather frequently. In conjunction with the clear scope that routine decision tasks encompass, these tasks are ideal candidates for automated analysis.

Once automated analyses are established, the results can be used to automatically trigger actions in the operational systems. This implements the closed loop that brings business intelligence to the operational systems. A complex analysis can be perceived as a directed graph where each vertex represents a partial analysis and each edge a condition which connects subsequent analyses. Such a graph exhibits all properties that can be found in a workflow. Thus, we propose an ADW architecture for automated analysis based on workflow technology.

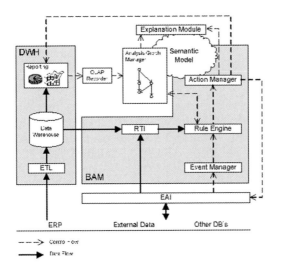

Prototype architecture.   FIGURE 18

Architecture

The proposed active data warehouse architecture extends the general ADW architecture with analysis rules [ZLH06] as shown in Figure 18.

The Analysis Graph Manager (AGM) is the glue that brings together DWH and business activity monitoring (BAM). It manages analysis graphs, which are recorded interactively by analysts using ad-hoc reporting tools or directly modelled with the Analysis Graph Manager.

For each vertex in the analysis graph, the Rule Engine performs its corresponding analysis. Based on the results, the Rule Engine determines the next vertex in the analysis graph or triggers a predefined action.

Advantages

Besides releasing the analyst routine decision tasks, workflows make the analysts domain knowledge explicit and well documented. The workflow steps of an analysis graph can be augmented with additional explanations for non-domain experts and analysis graphs can be specified in the same way manual decision making takes place; the business problem does not have to be transformed into a declarative statement.

Considering the tremendous amount of data that will be generated in the future, we believe automated analysis will become a key technology to integrate data warehousing into the operational business.

Acknowledgements

The projects described in this chapter have been partially funded by the European Union FP6-NMP 13898, Fit-IT FFG 809256/5512, FFG 813202, FFG 817789, Austrian Kplus and COMET competence center programs, the Upper Austrian Government (OÖ2010), Tiscover AG, Tech2select GmbH, JoinVision E-Services GmbH and VCE (Vienna Consulting Engineers).

References

[AI99]   Douglas E. Appelt and David J. Israel. Introduction to information extraction technology. A tutorial prepared for IJCAI-99, Stockholm, Schweden, 1999.

[AKW06]   Saiful Akbar, Josef Küng, and Roland Wagner. Multi-feature integration on 3d model similarity retrieval. In *ICDIM*, pages 151–156. IEEE, 2006.

[AKWP06]   Saiful Akbar, Josef Küng, Roland Wagner, and Ary Setijadi Prihatmanto. Multi-feature integration with relevance feedback on 3d model similarity retrieval. In Gabriele Kotsis, David Taniar, Eric Pardede, and Ismail Khalil Ibrahim, editors, *iiWAS*, volume 214 of *books@ocg.at*, pages 77–86. Austrian Computer Society, 2006.

[AP94]   Agnar Aamodt and Enric Plaza. Case-based reasoning: foundational issues, methodological variations, and system approaches. In *AI Commun.*, pages 39–59. IOS Press, March 1994.

[BEG⁺05]   Robert Baumgartner, Thomas Eiter, Georg Gottlob, Marcus Herzog, and Christoph Koch. Information extraction for the semantic web. In *Reasoning Web*, pages 275–289, 2005.

[BK04]   Ulrich Bodenhofer and Josef Küng. Fuzzy orderings in flexible query answering systems. *Soft Comput.*, 8(7):512–522, 2004.

[BPP⁺08]   Christina Buttinger, Birgit Pröll, Jürgen Palkoska, Werner Retschitzegger, Manfred Schauer, and Reinhold Immler. Jobolize - headhunting by information extraction in the era of web 2.0. In *Proceedings of the 7th International Workshop on Web-Oriented Software Technologies (IWWOST 2008)*, Yorktown Heights, New York, July 2008.

[Bro07]   Michael L. Brodie. Computer science 2.0: A new world of data management. In Christoph Koch, Johannes Gehrke, Minos N. Garofalakis, Divesh Srivastava, Karl Aberer, Anand Deshpande, Daniela Florescu, Chee Yong Chan, Venkatesh Ganti, Carl-Christian Kanne, Wolfgang Klas, and Erich J. Neuhold, editors, *VLDB*, page 1161. ACM, 2007.

[CJKW07]   Steve Cook, Gareth Jones, Stuart Kent, and Alan Wills. *Domain-specific development with visual studio dsl tools*. Addison-Wesley Professional, 2007.

[CMBT02]   H. Cunningham, D. Maynard, K. Bontcheva, and V. Tablan. Gate: A framework and graphical development environment for robust nlp tools and applications. In *Proceedings of the 40th Annual Meeting of the ACL*, 2002.

[cob07]   COBIT, Control Objectives for Information and related Technology, Version 4.1, 2007. http://www.itgi.org.

[Cun06]   Hamish Cunningham. Information Extraction, Automatic. Preprint, 18th November 2004, at http://gate.ac.uk/sale/ell2/ie/main.pdf. *Encyclopedia of Language and Linguistics, 2nd Edition, Elsevier*, 5:665–677, November 2006.

[DHJ⁺08]   Dirk Draheim, Melanie Himsl, Daniel Jabornig, Josef Küng, Werner Leithner, Peter Regner, and Thomas Wiesinger. Concept and pragmatics of an intuitive visualization-oriented metamodeling tool (accepted with minor revisions). In *Journal of Visual Languages and Computing (JVLC)*. Elsevier, 2008.

[DKW01]   Tran Khanh Dang, Josef Küng, and Roland Wagner. The sh-tree: A super hybrid index structure for multidimensional data. In Heinrich C. Mayr, Jirí Lazanský, Gerald Quirchmayr, and Pavel Vogel, editors, *DEXA*, volume 2113 of *Lecture Notes in Computer Science*, pages 340–349. Springer, 2001.

[DO01]   S. Dolcinar and R. Otter. *Marktforschung für die österreichische Hotelklassifizierung*. Austrian Chamber of Commerce, Vienna, 2001.

[Fei07]   Christina Feilmayr. Ontologiebasierte informationsextraktion in webbasierten tourismusinformationssystemen. Master's thesis, Johannes Kepler University, Linz, December 2007.

[FFSK09]   Bernhard Freudenthaler, Martin Fritz, Reinhard Stumptner, and Josef Küng. Case-based Reasoning for the Automated Assessment of Simple Structures in Terms of Structural Health Monitoring (Submitted for publication). In *7th International Workshop on Structural Health Monitoring 2009*, 2009.

[FGP+09]   Christina Feilmayr, Christoph Grün, Birgit Pröll, Hannes Werthner, and Robert Barta. Covering the semantic space of tourism - an approach based on modularized ontologies. In *Workshop on Context, Information And Ontologies*. ESWC2009, March 2009. Accepted for publication.

[FGSK08]   Bernhard Freudenthaler, Georg Gutenbrunner, Reinhard Stumptner, and Josef Küng. Case-based Decision Support for Bridge Monitoring. In *Third International Multi-Conference on Computing in the Global Information Technology 2008*, 2008.

[FGSK09]   Bernhard Freudenthaler, Georg Gutenbrunner, Reinhard Stumptner, and Josef Küng. Case-Based Decision Support for Bridge Monitoring (Submitted for publication). In *International Journal On Advances in Intelligent Systems*, 2009.

[FSFK07]   Ernst Forstner, Reinhard Stumptner, Bernhard Freudenthaler, and Josef Küng. VCDECIS–knowledge online advanced content management using a semantic network. In *DEXA Workshops*, pages 312–316. IEEE Computer Society, 2007.

[FSFK08]   Bernhard Freudenthaler, Reinhard Stumptner, Ernst Forstner, and Josef Küng. Case-based Reasoning for Structural Health Monitoring. In *Fourth European Workshop on Structural Health Monitoring 2008*, 2008.

[GBPW05a]   Eva Gahleitner, Wernher Behrendt, Jürgen Palkoska, and Edgar Weippl. On cooperatively creating dynamic ontologies. In *HYPERTEXT '05: Proceedings of the sixteenth ACM conference on Hypertext and hypermedia*, pages 208–210, New York, NY, USA, 2005. ACM Press.

[GBPW05b]   Eva Gahleitner, Wernher Behrendt, Jürgen Palkoska, and Edgar Weippl. On cooperatively creating dynamic ontologies. In *HYPERTEXT '05: Proceedings of the sixteenth ACM conference on Hypertext and hypermedia*, pages 208–210, New York, NY, USA, 2005. ACM Press.

[GMF09]   Eclipse   graphical   modeling   framework   (gmf),   2009. http://www.eclipse.org/gmf/.

[Gru93]   Thomas R. Gruber. A translation approach to portable ontology specifications. *Knowl. Acquis.*, 5(2):199–220, June 1993.

[Gua98]   Nicola Guarino. Formal ontology and information systems, 1998.

[GWG06]   Andreas Gruber, Rupert Westenthaler, and Eva Gahleitner. Supporting domain experts in creating formal knowledge models (ontologies), 2006.

[GWP+08]   Christoph Grün, Hannes Werthner, Birgit Pröll, Werner Retschitzegger, and Wieland Schwinger. Assisting tourists on the move- an evaluation of mobile tourist guides. In *ICMB '08: Proceedings of the 2008 7th International Conference on Mobile Business*, pages 171–180, Washington, DC, USA, 2008. IEEE Computer Society.

[HJL+07]   Melanie Himsl, Daniel Jabornig, Werner Leithner, Peter Regner, Thomas Wiesinger, Josef Küng, and Dirk Draheim. An iterative process for adaptive meta- and instance modeling. In Roland Wagner, Norman Revell, and Günther Pernul, editors, *DEXA*, volume 4653 of *Lecture Notes in Computer Science*, pages 519–528. Springer, 2007.

[iti06]   ITIL, IT Infrastructure Library, Version 3, 2006. http://www.ogc.gov.uk.

[Jab06]   Daniel Jabornig. An adaptive tool for meta and instance modeling. Master's thesis, Johannes Kepler University, Linz, 2006.

[Kel97]   S. Kelly. *GOPRR Description (Appendix 1)*. PhD thesis, 1997.

[KM95]   Michael Klein and Leif Methlie. Knowledge based decision support systems, 1995.

[KP97]   Josef Küng and Jürgen Palkoska. Vqs - a vague query system prototype. In
            DEXA Workshop, pages 614–618, 1997.
[KP98]   Josef Küng and Jürgen Palkoska. Vague joins - an extention of the vague
            query system vqs. In *DEXA Workshop*, pages 997–1001, 1998.
[KP99]   Josef Küng and Jürgen Palkoska. An incremental hypercube approach for
            finding best matches for vague queries. In Trevor J. M. Bench-Capon, Gio-
            vanni Soda, and A. Min Tjoa, editors, *DEXA*, volume 1677 of *Lecture Notes
            in Computer Science*, pages 238–249. Springer, 1999.
[KP02]   S Kent and O Patrasciu. *Kent Modelling Framework Version - Tutorial
            (Draft)*. Computing Laboratory, Canterbury, UK, December 2002.
[KPRR06]   G. Kappel, B. Pröll, S. Reich, and W. Retschitzegger. *Web Engineering -
            Systematic Development of Web Appplications*. Wiley, 2006.
[LMB⁺01]   A. Ledeczi, M. Maroti, A. Bakay, G. Karsai, J. Garrett, C. Thomason,
            G. Nordstrom, J. Sprinkle, and P. Volgyesi. The Generic Modeling Envi-
            ronment. In *Workshop on Intelligent Signal Processing, Budapest, Hungary*,
            volume 17, May 2001.
[MB98]   Robert C. Miller and Krishna Bharat. Sphinx: a framework for creating per-
            sonal, site-specific web crawlers. *Comput. Netw. ISDN Syst.*, 30(1-7):119–130,
            1998.
[Met01]   *MetaCase. Domain-Specific Modelling: 10 Times Faster Than UML (White
            Paper)*. MetaCase Consulting, Finland, 2001.
[MKSW99]   John Makhoul, Francis Kubala, Richard Schwartz, and Ralph Weischedel.
            Performance measures for information extraction. In *In Proceedings of
            DARPA Broadcast News Workshop*, pages 249–252, 1999.
[MyF]   Myfaces (accessed may 2008). http://www.myfaces.org.
[omg06]   omg. *Meta Object Facility (MOF) Core Specification Version 2.0*, 2006.
[Par08]   Stefan Parzer. Klassifizierung und informationsextraktion aus touristischen
            webseiten unter anwendung einer support vector machine und regelbasierter
            methoden. Master's thesis, Johannes Kepler University, Linz, Januar 2008.
[Pig]   Piggy bank (accessed februar 2009). http://simile.mit.edu/wiki/Piggy_Bank.
[PR00]   Birgit Pröll and Werner Retschitzegger. Discovering next generation tourism
            information systems: A tour on tiscover. *Journal of Travel Research*, 39:182–
            191, 2000.
[REN01]   J. Janneck R. Essar and M. Naedele. *The Moses Tool Suite - A Tutorial.
            Version 1.2*. Computer, Engineering and Networks Laboratory, ETH Zurich,
            2001.
[RS06]   P. Warren R. Studer, J. Davies. *Semantic Web Technologies -Trends and
            Research in Ontology-Based Systems*. John Wiley and Sons, 2006.
[SN07]   Vojtech Svatek and Marek Nekvasil. The ex project: Web information extrac-
            tion using extraction ontologies, 2007.
[Sol]   Solvent (accessed februar 2009). http://simile.mit.edu/wiki/Solvent.
[VNCN05]   Paola Velardi, Roberto Navigl, Alessandro Cucchiarelli, and Francesca Neri.
            Ontology Learning from Text: Methods, Evaluation and Applications, volume
            123, chapter Evaluation of OntoLearn, a Methodology for Automatic Learning
            ofDomain Ontologies. Frontiers in Artificial Intelligence and Applications, ios
            press edition, July 2005.
[WK99]   Hannes Werthner and Stefan Klein. *Information Technology and Tourism -
            A Challenging Relationship*. Spinger, Vienna, 1999.
[WKE⁺07]   Tim Weizel, Wolfgang König, Andreas Eckhardt, Sven Laumer, and Jens Lip-
            pert. *Recruting Trends 2007 - European Union - An empirical survey with
            the top 1.000-enterp. in the EU*. Number 2007-798. 2007.
[XUL]   Xul (accessed may 2008). http://developer.mozilla.org/.
[ZLH06]   Michael Zwick, Christian Lettner, and Christian Hawel. Implementing au-
            tomated analyses in an active data warehouse environment using workflow
            technology. In Dirk Draheim and Gerald Weber, editors, *TEAA*, volume 4473
            of *Lecture Notes in Computer Science*, pages 341–354. Springer, 2006.

Chapter VII
Parallel, Distributed, and Grid Computing

Wolfgang Schreiner
Károly Bósa, Andreas Langegger, Thomas Leitner, Bernhard Moser,
Szilárd Páll, Volkmar Wieser, Wolfram Wöß

Introduction 1

The core goal of parallel computing is to speedup computations by executing independent computational tasks concurrently ("in parallel") on multiple units in a processor, on multiple processors in a computer, or on multiple networked computers which may be even spread across large geographical scales (distributed and grid computing); it is the dominant principle behind "supercomputing" respectively "high performance computing".

For several decades, the density of transistors on a computer chip has doubled every 18–24 months ("Moore's Law"); until recently, this rate could be directly transformed into a corresponding increase of a processor's clock frequency and thus into an automatic performance gain for sequential programs. However, since also a processor's power consumption increases with its clock frequency, this strategy of "frequency scaling" became ultimately unsustainable: since 2004 clock frequencies have remained essentially stable and additional transistors have been primarily used to build multiple processors on a single chip (multi-core processors). Today therefore every kind of software (not only "scientific" one) must be written in a parallel style to profit from newer computer hardware.

Hagenberg Research

In Hagenberg, research on parallel, distributed, and grid computing is primarily pursued by the Research Institute for Symbolic Computation (RISC), the Institute for Application Oriented Knowledge Processing (FAW), the Software Competence Center Hagenberg (SCCH), and the Heuristic and Evolutionary Algorithms Laboratory (HEAL) of the Upper Austria University of

Applied Sciences in the Campus Hagenberg. In fact, RISC has been one of the first institutes to recognize the importance of parallel computation and has worked in this area since the early 1980s (see Section 2). RISC has also initiated the Austrian Center for Parallel Computation (ACPC) [ACP] and the Austrian Grid initiative [Aus] in which among other institutes RISC and FAW are collaborating (see Section 3). Also the industrial relevance of the area is not neglected: the SCCH pursues application-oriented research with economic partners (see Section 4) and the RISC Software Company operates the Austrian Grid Development Center (AGEZ) which fosters cooperations between the Austrian Grid and industry.

A common theme of the parallel/grid computing activities in Hagenberg is that they are not pursued for their own sake but are driven by the concrete needs of particular application areas that are in our center of expertise:

Symbolic Computation: RISC has developed parallel hardware, software, and algorithms for symbolic computation (see Section 2).

Medical Informatics: RISC has in collaboration with the Upper Austrian Research (UAR) department for MI and the FAW developed a grid variant for the medical simulation software SEE++ (see Section 3.1).

Data Systems: FAW has worked on providing uniform access to heterogeneous data sources distributed over large-scale networks (see Section 3.3).

Computational Intelligence: SCCH has implemented on Graphics Processing Units data-parallel algorithms for machine learning (see Section 4).

Metaheuristic Optimization: HEAL has worked on parallel implementations of heuristic optimization strategies (see Chapter III).

This combination of expertise, as well in parallel and grid computing as in several application areas, and the strong contact among the research groups and other (academic and industrial) partners in Hagenberg represents a unique strength that characterizes our activities in this research area. Via the Austrian Grid initiative and the Austrian Grid Development Center located in Hagenberg, these links also extend to other Austrian groups working in this area. The research competence also translates in corresponding educational activities (as well the Johannes Kepler University Linz as the School of Informatics, Communications and Media of the Upper Austria University of Applied Sciences offer courses in parallel and grid computing) from which qualified staff in corresponding research activities can be drawn.

Outline

In the remainder of the introduction, we give a survey on parallel computing theory, hardware architectures, programming languages, software, algorithms, and formal models; state of the art reports on the field are provided e.g. by the European conference series Euro-Par [Eur] or the American SC (former "Supercomputing") series [Sup]. The rest of the chapter is mainly dedicated to our own activities in this area.

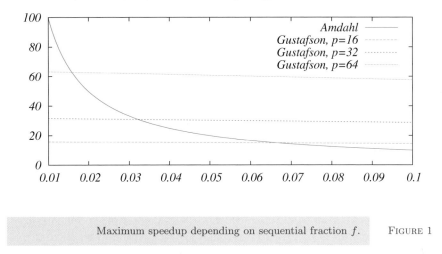

Maximum speedup depending on sequential fraction f.   FIGURE 1

Performance   1.1

The central performance measure in parallel computing [HP06] is the *(absolute) speedup* $S_p = T/T_p$ where T is the time for the solution of a problem by the best sequential program and T_p is the time for the solution by a parallel program executed with p processors. We expect $0 < S_p \le p$; with $S_p \simeq p$ we have the best case of a program with "linear" speedup. Nevertheless anomalies yielding a "super-linear" speedup $S_p > p$ may arise, typically because multiple processors have more (fast) cache memory available.

While the speedup only accounts for the gain of parallel computing, the *(absolute) efficiency* $E_p = S_p/p$ is a measure for the "return of investment": we expect $0 < E_p \le 1$; if E_p is significantly smaller than 1, we have paid a disproportionally high price for the speedup gained. In practice, therefore the goal is to achieve high speedup with a reasonable level of efficiency.

If a fraction f of a problem can be only solved by sequential computation, *Amdahl's Law* $(S_p \le 1/f)$ states that the speedup S_p of a parallel solution to the problem is (independently of p) limited by the inverse of f, i.e. a problem with only 1% inherently sequential computation content cannot achieve a speedup higher than 100! This negative result puts therefore an absolute bound on the gain of parallel computation for a problem of fixed size.

However, for many problems an increase in the problem size s lets the size of its "parallel part" grow in proportion with s while the size of the "sequential part" remains unchanged. If we increase in such problems the parallel part in proportion with p, *Gustafson's Law* $(S_p \le f + p \cdot (1 - f))$ states that also the speedup grows correspondingly; the program is then called "scalable". This positive result therefore establishes that parallel computation can be effectively applied to solving problems of ever growing size (see Figure 1).

Due to these results, the focus of the analysis of parallel programs has turned from a mere speedup analysis to *scalability analysis*: here we investigate how much the problem size s must grow with an increasing processor number p such that the speedup S_p of a parallel program grows in proportion with p or, in other words, its efficiency E_p remains constant (*isoefficiency*).

1.2 Architectures

Flynn's taxonomy classifies parallel hardware architectures in two categories:

Single instruction, multiple data (SIMD):   units are tightly synchronized: at any time, all units execute the same instruction (on different data);
Multiple instructions, multiple data (MIMD):   units are loosely synchronized: at any time, different units may execute different instructions.

Due to its greater flexibility, today most architectures are of the MIMD type; nevertheless they may exhibit SIMD features for special purposes (e.g. numerical computations or graphics processing).

Instruction Level Parallelism

Since long, parallelism is exploited inside processors to speed-up program execution [HP06]. Instructions are split into sequences of small steps that are fed into *instruction pipelines* such that the execution of multiple instructions may overlap. *Superscalar processors* provide redundant functional units to which multiple instructions are simultaneously dispatched. To simplify the scheduling of multiple units, Intel's IA-64 (Itanium) architecture has introduced *explicitly parallel instruction computing (EPIC)* where a parallelizing compiler has to generate a program with parallel machine instructions.

Multi-Core Computing

Today a single processor (CPU) encompasses multiple cores; dual-core and quad-core processors are typical, but processors with 128 cores and more have already been announced. The technology is widely used, not only for general purpose CPUs, but also for embedded processors and graphics processors (GPUs). In essence, each core represents a full processor; multiple cores typically share a (level 2) cache and bus interface. From the usage point of view, multi-core processors can be essentially considered as SMP systems.

Symmetric Multiprocessing (SMP)

In SMP systems (also called *shared memory multiprocessors*), multiple processors are connected to a single shared main memory, usually via a bus through which all memory requests are serialized; each processor can access each memory location in the same way and at the same speed (*uniform memory access*, short *UMA*). SMP personal computers, workstations, and servers are commercially available with 2, 4, or 8 (multi-core) processors. SMP systems are controlled by a single operating system (OS) instance that schedules processes to processors and thus automatically balances the workload of multiple applications, multiple users, and/or multiple tasks.

Massively Parallel Processing (MPP)

MPP systems (also called *distributed memory multiprocessors*) scale to a large number of processors (in June 2008 the world's fastest computer [Top] was the IBM Roadrunner MPP with 6480 Opteron dual-core processors and 12240 PowerXCell processors with 9 cores each). Therefore an MPP system is composed in a modular way from nodes that comprise processors and local memory and that are connected via a scalable network. A processor has only direct access to the local memory; for interaction among processors on different nodes, messages are exchanged over the network. Typically each node runs a local OS instance; processes are placed on nodes by the programmer.

A special class of MPPs are *virtual (or distributed) shared memory* systems where, by a combination of hardware and software mechanisms, a shared memory is implemented on top of MPP hardware. To users and programs these systems look like SMPs (with an operating system that automatically maps processes to processors); however, access to memory on remote nodes is significantly more costly (*non-uniform memory access*, short *NUMA*).

Cluster Computing

Computer clusters [Buy99] (also called *Beowulf systems* after a project that pioneered this approach) are essentially MPPs whose computing nodes are plain computers (e.g. multi-core PCs) which are connected either by common networks (e.g. Ethernet) or by special high performance links (e.g. Myrinet). Clusters have become very popular because, for suitable applications, they may provide good performance at comparatively low costs. Consequently the June 2008 "Top 500" supercomputer list [Top] counts 400 clusters but only 98 specially designed MPPs (these however lead the list w.r.t. performance).

Grid Computing

A *(computational) grid* [FK98] is a networked infrastructure consisting of computing nodes, storage elements, and special devices that are geographically widely distributed but accessible from any node connected to the grid (the term "grid" was introduced as a metaphor for making computational resources as easily accessible as electricity in the power grid). In contrast to a computer cluster that is owned and administrated by a single institution, a grid is composed of resources that belong to multiple institutions (administrative domains) without central control and global knowledge. A main challenge in grid computing is thus to provide services for the lookup of resources and for their secure and efficient use by remote users. One of the largest grid activities is the European project *Enabling Grids for E-SciencE (EGEE)* [EGE] which provides the computational infrastructure for the Large Hadron Collider (LHC) experiment at the CERN laboratory.

1.3 Programming

Writing programs for parallel computers is a difficult and error-prone task; in the ideal case therefore a *parallelizing compiler* automatically generates a parallel program from a program written in a conventional sequential language. However, it has turned out to be very difficult to automatically extract efficiently exploitable parallelism from a sequential program (apart from limited instruction-level parallelism). Therefore most approaches to parallel programming rely on explicit parallel programming constructs, parallelization annotations, and/or parallel programming libraries.

Parallel Language Extensions

Various dialects of conventional programing languages with explicit parallel programming constructs have been proposed. For example, *High-Performance Fortran (HPF)* [HPF] pioneered a data-parallel programming model with a parallel *FORALL* construct which was taken over into the Fortran 95 standard. *Unified Parallel C (UPC)* [UPC] provides a uniform programming model for both shared and distributed memory hardware: shared variables are physically associated to particular processors but can be read and written by all processors; synchronization constructs coordinate the parallel execution.

Parallel Declarative Languages

Declarative languages are based on abstract concepts like mathematical functions (*functional languages*) or logic relations (*logic languages*) whose operational interpretation gives rise to parallel execution. Nevertheless, parallel constructs or annotations are used for exhibiting the efficiently exploitable parallelism. *Glasgow Parallel Haskell (GPH)* [GPH] and *Eden* [Ede] are extensions of the functional programming language Haskell by annotations for parallel execution. Also the concurrent language *Erlang* [Erl] developed by Ericsson for programming telecommunication systems has a functional core.

Multithreaded and Socket Programming

Modern operating systems support the concept of *threads*, i.e. light-weight processes that operate in a shared memory and that can be efficiently scheduled among multiple cores or multiple processors of an SMP system. *POSIX threads (PThreads)* [But97] is a widely supported standard for multi-threaded programming in C/C++: by library calls threads can be created, synchronized, and terminated. The language *Java* developed by Sun and Microsoft's *C#* language embed threads into an object-oriented language framework.

Furthermore, most operating systems support *Internet sockets* [SFR03] for network communication; corresponding programming libraries are available in C/C++, Java, C#, and other languages. The combination of threads and sockets is a low-level but nevertheless powerful workhorse for parallel computing: it allows to write parallel/distributed programs that utilize multi-core processors, SMPs, and computer clusters.

OpenMP

OpenMP [Ope] is a standard for *shared* memory parallel programming in C/C++, Fortran, and other languages. The core of OpenMP is a set of "pragmas", i.e. program annotations by which the programmer directs the compiler to generate parallel threads (for the parallel execution of loops or for the parallel execution of program sections) and to appropriately synchronize them. OpenMP operates on a considerably higher level than a plain multi-threading API: it leaves the sequential program structure essentially unchanged and takes care of low level issues of data organization; nevertheless, by library routines also explicit multi-threaded programming is possible. OpenMP is widely supported and OpenMP programs are portable among most multi-core/SMP architectures (but not MPP systems or computer clusters).

Message Passing Interface (MPI)

MPI [MPIa] is a standard for *distributed* memory parallel programming in C/C++, Fortran, and other languages. The core of MPI is an application programming interface for writing parallel programs in which processes interact only by exchanging messages; each process may be therefore placed on a separate computing node of an MPP or on a separate computer in a cluster (nevertheless MPI programs may use multi-threading libraries for exploiting shared memory parallelism within a node). Besides operations for point-to-point communication, MPI supports a large set of *collective operations*, e.g.

for broadcasting a message to a group of processes, or for collecting their results; a specific implementation of MPI may execute these operations in a more efficient way than by point-to-point messages, if it exploits the specific features of the underlying communication infrastructure. MPI is supported by practically every vendor and for all parallel computing architectures, i.e. SMP systems, MPP systems, and computer clusters; MPI can be therefore considered as the most portable standard for parallel programming today.

Grid Middleware

On top of grid hardware, the layer of *grid middleware* implements services and tools for deploying and executing grid applications. The *Open Grid Software Architecture (OGSA)* [OGS] provides a reference model for service-oriented grid computing; OGSA can be seen as an adaptation of the concept of web services to support the requirements of the grid. Today one of the most popular grid middleware products is the *Globus Toolkit* [Glo] which implements OGSA-compliant services supporting security, information infrastructure, resource management, data management, communication, fault detection, and portability. While Globus is powerful but complex, the *gLite* [gLi] middleware developed and used by the European grid project EGEE implements a somewhat more light-weight approach to service-oriented grid computing. All these middleware products do not provide a parallel programming model but rather support the concepts of "batch jobs" as the units of grid execution.

1.4 Algorithms

A fundamental classification of parallel algorithms and applications is based on the core target of parallelization:

- *Data parallel* algorithms focus on the distribution of data among multiple processors each of which processes some part of the data;
- *Task parallel* algorithms focus on the distribution of activities among multiple processors each of which performs some of these activities.

In one case, the distribution of data determines how activities are mapped to processors while in the other one the distribution of activities determines which data have to be transferred to each processor; in practice, real programs exhibit features of both principles.

Another important classification is based on the ratio between the communication/synchronization and the computation required for executing a parallel program. In *fine-grained* parallel algorithms, the ratio is high, i.e. processes have to communicate a lot to perform their tasks; algorithms of this kind can be implemented efficiently only on multi-core/SMP architectures with shared memory communication. In *coarse-grained* parallel algorithms, the ratio is low, i.e. only little communication is necessary, which makes this type of algorithms suitable also for MPP systems and computer clusters with network communication. In *embarrassingly parallel* algorithms, the ratio is essentially zero i.e. the processors can operate in an independent way; such applications can be easily executed also on grids (examples of this kind are "parameter studies" where the same computation must be performed for a range of different input parameters).

A parallel program can be systematically developed from an algorithmic idea in four phases [Fos95]: *partitioning* the problem solution into independent tasks, determining the *communication* required between tasks, *agglomerating* tasks to bigger processes to reduce the communication requirements, and *mapping* processes to processors. In practice, however, not every parallel program has to be designed from scratch: various widely applicable parallel program "patterns", "skeletons", or "frameworks" [Pat] have emerged.

One of these patterns is the *manager/worker model* with one manager process and a set of worker processes (see Figure 2). The manager maintains a pool of tasks to be performed and records the status of each task ("open", "active", "closed"). Initially, the manager sends one open task to each worker (marking it as "active") and then waits for results. Whenever a worker has completed its task, it sends the result back to the manager who sets the status of the task to "closed" and assigns, if there are still open tasks left, a new one to the worker. When all tasks are closed, the program terminates.

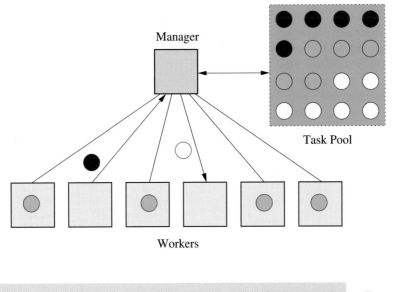

The manager/worker model.   FIGURE 2

The main advantage of this model is that it automatically balances the workload among processors: even if some tasks turn out to be "bigger" than others, all workers remain fully occupied as long as there remain open tasks to be performed. The scheme can also be generalized in that workers may generate new (sub-)tasks that are sent to the manager. Manager/worker algorithms can be efficiently executed on MPP systems and clusters with a moderate number of processors. However, if the number of workers is too high, the central manager becomes a bottleneck. In this case, the scheme can be generalized to multiple layers of (sub-)managers.

1.5 Modeling and Reasoning

A core problem of parallel programs is that their behavior is in general *non-deterministic*: unlike sequential programs, two subsequent runs of a parallel program with the same inputs may exhibit different behaviors and produce different outputs. This is a consequence of the MIMD principle where different processors execute without a central control; consequently, in different executions events at different processing units may happen in different orders. Traditional strategies for ensuring program correctness by systematic testing have therefore only limited value; more and more they are complemented by formal methods to verify correctness properties of parallel programs.

For this purpose, a formal model of a parallel system is constructed, e.g. as a finite state machine which can be analyzed by a *model checker* [CGP99]. A desired correctness property is formally specified (typically in some variant of temporal logic [Lam02]) and then automatically verified with respect to *all* possible behaviors of the model. If there exists any behavior that violates the property, it is detected and returned as a counterexample. Model checkers such as *Spin* [Spi] have been successfully applied to the verification of hardware systems and communication protocols; they also play an increasingly important role in the verification of (sequential and concurrent) software. To verify infinite state models, systems for *computer-assisted proving* such as PVS [PVS] or RISC's Theorema (see Chapter II) may be applied.

2 Parallel Symbolic Computation

For three decades the Research Institute for Symbolic Computation (RISC) has pursued research on parallel and distributed computing, in particular on parallel languages, software, and algorithms for symbolic computation (computer algebra and theorem proving, see Chapters I and II); a survey of the field is provided by the PASCO conference series [PAS]. RISC is also member of the European SCIEnce project (Symbolic Computation Infrastructure for Europe) that develops a grid infrastructure for symbolic computation [SCI09]. Our research has for example produced the following results:

- the *L-machine*, the first parallel computer built in Austria [Buc78, Buc85],
- systolic algorithms for *multiprecision arithmetic* [BJ91, RJ07],
- work on *parallel logic programming* and the development of ‖*Maple*‖ (parallel Maple) for the implementation of parallel variants of the Gröbner bases algorithm invented by Bruno Buchberger [Sie93, Sie94],
- work on *dataflow computing* [Sch91, Loi92] and *parallel functional programming* for computer algebra [Sch95, Sch96],
- the development of *PACLIB*, a parallel (shared memory multiprocessor) variant of the computer algebra library SACLIB [HNS95, Sch94],
- the development of the *MathBroker* framework for executing, describing, and querying mathematical web services [CS02, BCS05, BS06],
- the development of *Distributed Maple*, a system for distributed programming in the computer algebra system Maple [Dis, SMB03, BS05].

The remainder of this section focuses on the last item, the development of Distributed Maple and its application to parallel computer algebra.

Distributed Maple   2.1

Commercial computer algebra systems such as Maple or Mathematica provide large software libraries that already implement a lot of mathematical functionality; consequently most computer algebra researchers prefer to implement their code in the scripting languages of these systems rather than writing it from scratch in some compiled programming language. The goal of "Distributed Maple" [Dis, SMB03] is to write *parallel* computer algebra code in the Maple language and have it executed on multiple processors respectively on multiple computers of a network.

User Interface

The user interacts with Distributed Maple via a conventional Maple frontend by executing Maple commands that establish the distributed session in which tasks are created for execution on any connected machine:

```
> dist[initialize]([[compute,linux], [speedy,solaris]]);
connecting compute...
connecting speedy...
                                  okay
> t1 := dist[start](int, x^n, x):
```

```
> t2 := dist[start](int, x^n, n);
> dist[wait](t1) + dist[wait](t2);
```

$$\frac{x^{(n + 1)}}{n + 1} + \frac{x^n}{\ln(x)}$$

```
> dist[terminate]();
```

```
okay
```

First we load a file `dist.maple` which represents the interface to the distributed backend by a Maple package `dist`. By `dist[initialize]`, we ask the system to start the backend and create two new Maple kernels on machine `compute` of type `linux` and on machine `speedy` of type `solaris`, respectively. The machine types are used to lookup the specific startup information which is located in a configuration file `dist.systems`.

After the session has been successfully established, two calls of the command `dist[start]` start two tasks that evaluate the Maple expressions `int(x^n, x)` and `int(x^n, n)`, respectively. The corresponding calls of `dist[wait]` block the current execution until the tasks have terminated and return the corresponding task results. Finally, the session is stopped and resources are freed by calling `dist[terminate]`.

Architecture

Since the Maple kernel is closed source, we have developed a Java-based parallel execution framework which is independent of Maple, i.e. it can embed *any* kind of computational kernel. The overall structure of a distributed program session is depicted in Figure 3; each computational node connected to the session is composed of two components:

Scheduler: The program `dist.Scheduler` implements the distributed scheduler which coordinates the node interaction. The initial scheduler process (created by the Maple kernel attached to the user interface) reads all system information from file `dist.systems`; it then starts instances of the scheduler on other machines.

Maple Interface: The program `dist.maple` executed by every Maple kernel implements the interface between kernel and scheduler. Unix pipes are used to exchange messages (which embed Maple objects in a linear format).

When the session is established, every instance of the scheduler accepts tasks from the attached computation kernel and distributes these tasks among all kernels connected to the session. During the execution, dynamic connections between remote scheduler instances are created on demand.

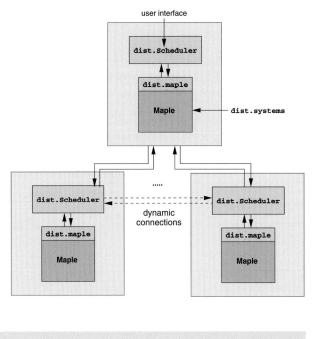

Distributed Maple software architecture.   FIGURE 3

Programming Model

In contrast to many other software systems based on the message passing model of parallelism, the parallel programming model of Distributed Maple is based on the *functional model* of parallelism: a program creates concurrent tasks that eventually deliver a result; tasks are first order objects that can be handled as any other Maple values. The core of the programming interface consists of two functions:

dist[start](*f*, *a*, ...): This call creates a task that evaluates the expression *f(a, ...)*; the call immediately returns a reference *t* to this task.

dist[wait](*t*): This call blocks the execution of the current task until the task represented by *t* has terminated; the call then returns the result of *t*. Multiple tasks may independently wait for the result of the same task.

On which computational kernel a task is scheduled for execution is entirely in the responsibility of the runtime system. Tasks may create other tasks; arbitrary kinds of Maple objects (including task references) may be passed as task arguments and returned as task results.

Sometimes the performance of a parallel program is improved by processing the results of a set of tasks not in a fixed order but in that order in which the results happen to arrive. This can be achieved by using the following non-deterministic form of task synchronization.

dist[select](*tlist*):   This call blocks the current task until *any* task in the list of task handles *tlist* has terminated. The call then returns a list r where $r[1]$ is the result of this task and $r[2]$ is its index in *tlist*.

Furthermore, if a parallel program processes large data in multiple phases separated by task interactions, it may be more efficient to let tasks preserve their states across the phases rather than creating for every phase new tasks to which the data have to be passed. For this purpose, Distributed Maple supports the concept of "shared objects" that may implements various forms of inter-task communication such as communication channels.

Fault Tolerance

Since the software is intended for execution in distributed environments with potentially faulty behavior, it incorporates extensive support for fault-tolerance which is novel in this application area [BS05]. This allows to write programs that take many days without risking to lose computations by the failure of a computing node or of a communication link.

The mechanisms that ensure fault tolerance are essentially as follows:

- task descriptions and task results are permanently logged on stable storage such that they can be recovered whenever necessary;
- connectivity between every pair of nodes is constantly monitored; if a node becomes unreachable, appropriate measures are taken.

Fault recovery is "on the fly" (i.e. the user does not notice any disruptions of the software): computations do not fail if some node fails, if a connection to a node fails, or if the software running on a node crashes. Furthermore, if nodes or connections fail only temporarily, they are automatically reconnected to the session when they become operational again. The processes on a node terminate their execution properly, if the node becomes disconnected from the session such that no "hang-over" processes are left. Only if many nodes fail or become unreachable in a short time period, the session fails but can be restarted (with all previously computed results still available from the stable storage). By the functional model of parallelism, the overhead of the fault tolerance framework is very small (compared to message passing software that ensures fault tolerance by checkpointing complete system states).

2.2 Parallel Computer Algebra Algorithms

A major motivation for the development of Distributed Maple was the parallelization of parts of CASA, a Maple library developed by various researchers at RISC for solving problems in algebraic geometry [CAS, MW96]. The basic

objects of CASA are algebraic sets represented e.g. as systems of polynomial equations. Algebraic sets represented by bivariate polynomials model
plane curves. Algebraic sets represented by trivariate polynomials model surfaces in space; intersections of such surfaces define space curves. With the
help of Distributed Maple, we have developed parallel variants of various
CASA algorithms, e.g. for the reliable plotting of algebraic plane or space
curves [MSW00, SMW00c, SMW00a, SMW00b].

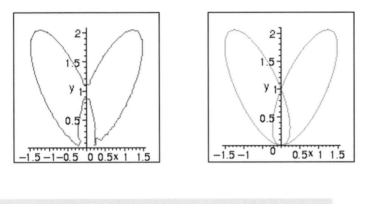

Maple's `implicitplot` versus CASA's `pacPlot`.   FIGURE 4

Conventional methods for plotting algebraic curves often yield qualita-
tively wrong solutions, i.e., plots where some "critical points" (e.g. singularities) are missing. For instance, the left diagram in Figure 4 shows a plot of
the plane curve $2x^4 - 3x^2y + y^4 - 2y^3 + y^2$ generated by Maple's command
`implicitplot`. The numerical approximation fails to capture two singularities; even if we improve the quality of the diagram by refining the underlying grid, only one of the missing singularities emerges. On the other hand,
CASA's algorithm `pacPlot` produces the correct diagram shown to the right.
This is achieved by a hybrid combination of exact symbolic algorithms for
the computation of all critical points and of fast numerical methods for computing the interconnections between the points. Since the algorithm spends
virtually all of its time in the computation of the critical points, this step is
the target of parallelization. In more detail, the problem solved by this step is
to find for an algebraic curve $a(x, y)$ every real solution ("root") $\langle x, y \rangle$ of the
system $\{a = 0, \frac{\partial a}{\partial x} = 0\}$. Since exact real arithmetic is not possible, each root
is actually "isolated" by a pair of intervals $\langle [x', x''], [y', y''] \rangle$ whose bounds
x', x'', y', y'' are rational numbers with $x' \leq x \leq x''$ and $y' \leq y \leq y''$.

The algorithm computing the set of all intervals that isolate the critical
points is sketched in Algorithm 1. We have parallelized this algorithm on
various levels (underlined in Algorithm 1): parallel resultant computation,

Algorithm 1. Computation of critical points

---

function CRITICALPOINTSET($a(x,y)$)
   $P \leftarrow \emptyset$
   $S \leftarrow \{\langle p(y), q(x,y)\rangle \mid \exists p'(y):$
         $\langle p'(y), q(x,y)\rangle \in \mathrm{triangulize}(a(x,y), \frac{\partial a(x,y)}{\partial x}), p(y) \in \mathrm{factorize}(p'(y))\}$
   for $\langle p(y), q(x,y)\rangle \in S$ **do**
     $r(x) \leftarrow \mathrm{resultant}_x(p(y),\ q(x,y))$
     $X \leftarrow \mathrm{realroot}(r(x))$
     $Y \leftarrow \mathrm{realroot}(p(y))$
     for $x \in X$ **do**
       $q'(y) \leftarrow \mathrm{squarefree}(q(x,y),\ x.0,\ p(y))$
       $q''(y) \leftarrow \mathrm{squarefree}(q(x,y),\ x.1,\ p(y))$
       for $y \in Y$ **do**
         if $\mathrm{test}(q'(y),\ q''(y),\ y,\ p(y))$ **then**
           $P \leftarrow P \cup \{\langle x, y\rangle\}$
         end if
       end for
     end for
   end for
   for $p \in P$ **do**
     $\mathrm{refine}(p)$
   end for
   return P
end function

---

parallel real root isolation, parallel solution test, and parallel interval refinement.

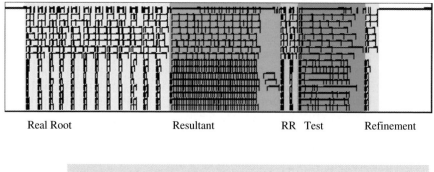

   Real Root   **Resultant**   **RR Test**   **Refinement**

FIGURE 5   Plotting of algebraic plane curves.

Figure 5 illustrates the trace of an execution of the parallel version of `pacPlot` in a cluster with 16 processors listed on the vertical axis; each horizontal line denotes a task executed on a particular machine. We can clearly distinguish the real root isolation phase followed by the phases for resultant computation, the second real root isolation, the solution tests and the solution refinements. With this parallelization, we achieved a speedup of 14 in a heterogeneous local cluster of 16 workstations and a speedup of 13 in a combination of local workstations and a remote multiprocessor.

Grid Computing 3

In Hagenberg, research on grid computing is mainly pursued in the context of the Austrian Grid [Aus], a national initiative that is funded by the Austrian Ministry for Science and Research and whose main goal is to support and to coordinate grid research in Austria. Another important purpose is to stimulate cooperations among the relevant scientific areas and the various grid research groups in Austria. Numerous universities in Austria participate in the Austrian Grid (among others, the Johannes Kepler University Linz, the University of Innsbruck, and the University of Vienna).

First Phase 2004–2006:   The project started in 2004 with 24 participating partner institutions and with 137 people involved. In the first phase, 34 research projects were funded (24 dedicated to middleware research and 10 to application development). Until the end of 2006, around 2,7 Million Euro were invested into the project.

Second Phase 2007–2009:   By the end of 2007, 22 partners take part and 95 people are employed. Furthermore, 28 research projects are funded (14 related to basic grid research, 9 to application development, 3 to infrastructure research, 1 to public relations, and 1 to project coordination).

To achieve the goals of the initiative, an appropriate hardware and software infrastructure is established and maintained (see Figure 6). In the first phase of the project, the backbone of the grid was an Altix 350 machine with 96 Intel Itanium2 1.4 GHz CPUs organized into three grid nodes (64 CPUs in Linz, 16 CPUs in Innsbruck, and 16 CPUs in Salzburg). This machine has a performance of 550 Gigaflop/s and provides more than 1 TB storage space. In 2008, the backbone was expanded by an SGI 4700 comprising 128 Intel Itanium2 1.6 GHz CPUs and 7 TB storage space; the overall performance of this machine is 1.6 Teraflop/s. There is no network dedicated exclusively to the Austrian Grid; rather the grid nodes are connected to each other via the *Austrian Academic Computer Network (ACOnet)* that provides 10 Gigabit Ethernet connections among the major academic institutions; the partners in Hagenberg (RISC and FAW) are connected to this infrastructure via the Johannes Kepler University Linz by a 1 Gigabit Ethernet connection.

In the second phase of the initiative the *Austrian Grid Development Center (AGEZ)* was established. The main goal of this unit is to transfer the results of the Austrian Grid research to the Austrian industry and to raise the public awareness about the potential and possibilities of grid computing. The AGEZ realizes projects together with Austrian companies and is in charge of dissemination, consulting, and training activities. It is directed by Prof. Buchberger and operated by the RISC Software Company in Hagenberg; the overall goal is to establish it as a persistent entity which serves as the main contact for the Austrian industry regarding grid computing.

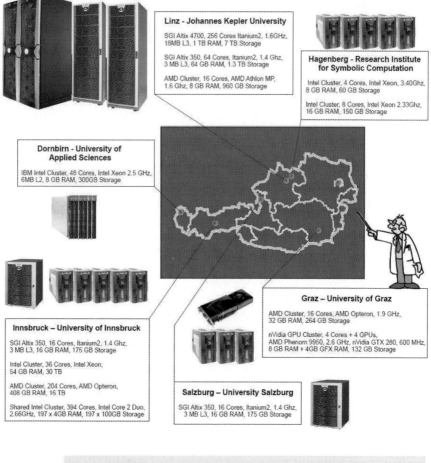

Linz - Johannes Kepler University

SGI Altix 4700, 256 Cores Itanium2, 1.6GHz,
18MB L3, 1 TB RAM, 7 TB Storage

SGI Altix 350, 64 Cores, Itanium2, 1.4 Ghz,
3 MB L3, 64 GB RAM, 1.3 TB Storage

AMD Cluster, 16 Cores, AMD Athlon MP,
1.6 Ghz, 8 GB RAM, 960 GB Storage

**Hagenberg - Research Institute
for Symbolic Computation**

Intel Cluster, 4 Cores, Intel Xeon, 3.40Ghz,
8 GB RAM, 60 GB Storage

Intel Cluster, 8 Cores, Intel Xeon 2.33Ghz,
16 GB RAM, 150 GB Storage

**Dornbirn - University of
Applied Sciences**

IBM Intel Cluster, 48 Cores, Intel Xeon 2.5 GHz,
6MB L2, 8 GB RAM, 300GB Storage

Graz – University of Graz

AMD Cluster, 16 Cores, AMD Opteron, 1.9 GHz,
32 GB RAM, 264 GB Storage

nVidia GPU Cluster, 4 Cores + 4 GPUs,
AMD Phenom 9950, 2.6 GHz, nVidia GTX 280, 600 MHz,
8 GB RAM + 4GB GFX RAM, 132 GB Storage

Innsbruck – University of Innsbruck

SGI Altix 350, 16 Cores, Itanium2, 1.4 Ghz,
3 MB L3, 16 GB RAM, 175 GB Storage

Intel Cluster, 36 Cores, Intel Xeon,
54 GB RAM, 30 TB

AMD Cluster, 204 Cores, AMD Opteron,
408 GB RAM, 16 TB

Shared Intel Cluster, 394 Cores, Intel Core 2 Duo,
2.66GHz, 197 x 4GB RAM, 197 x 100GB Storage

Salzburg – University Salzburg

SGI Altix 350, 16 Cores, Itanium2, 1.4 Ghz,
3 MB L3, 16 GB RAM, 175 GB Storage

FIGURE 6   Hardware resources of the austrian grid by the end of 2008.

3.1   Grid-Enabled SEE++

This section presents research carried out by RISC in the frame of both
the Austrian Grid Phase 1 [Aus] and the *"Enabling Grids for E-sciencE 2"*
(EGEE2) [EGE] project. The goal of this activity was the development of
a grid-enabled variant of the medical software system SEE++ [Buc04, SEE]
which was originally developed by the former Upper Austria Research (UAR)
department for medical informatics (MI) in Hagenberg (now a unit of the
RISC Software Company) for the biomechanical 3D simulation of the human

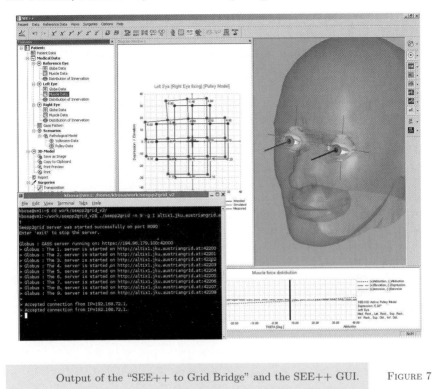

Output of the "SEE++ to Grid Bridge" and the SEE++ GUI.   FIGURE 7

eye and its muscles (see Figure 7); the work was performed by a collaboration of RISC and UAR MI with support by FAW.

SEE++ supports the diagnosis and treatment of *strabismus*, a usually persistent or regularly occurring misalignment of the eyes where eyes point in different directions such that a person may see double images. SEE++ simulates a typical medical examination called *Hess-Lancaster test*, from which the reason for the pathological situation of the patient can be estimated. The outcome of such an examination consists of two *gaze patterns* of blue points and of red points respectively (see the diagram in the middle of Figure 7).

The blue points represent the image seen by one eye and the red points the image seen by the simulated other eye; in a pathological situation there is a deviation between the blue and the red points. The default gaze pattern that is calculated from the patient's eye data by SEE++ contains 9 points. Bigger gaze patterns with 21 and 45 are possible and provide more precise results for the decision support in case of some pathologies, but their calculations are more time consuming. It is also possible to give the measured gaze pattern of a patient as input. In this case, SEE++ takes some default or estimated eye data and modifies a subset of them until the calculated gaze pattern of the simulated eye (red points) matches the measured gaze pattern (green points). This procedure is called *pathology fitting*.

Strabismus can be rarely corrected sufficiently after the first surgical treatment. One of the main goals of the SEE++ software system is to give support to make the treatment of strabismus easier and more efficient. Still the doctors have to spend lots of time with changing the eye parameters by a manual trial and error method and waiting for the results. The current pathology fitting algorithm is time consuming (it runs several minutes) and gives only a more or less precise estimation for the pathology of the patient. Doctors want to see quickly the results from such a decision support system, but for reaching adequate response times it is not sufficient to use only local computational power. For this, a large scale distributed resource would be appropriate that provides the ability to perform higher throughput by taking advantage of many networked computers.

The goal of "Grid-Enabled SEE++" is to adapt and to extend SEE++ in several steps and to develop an efficient grid-based tool for "Evidence Based Medicine", which supports the surgeons in choosing optimal surgery techniques for the treatments of different syndromes of strabismus. For this purpose, we have developed a *parallel version of the Hess-Lancaster test* [BSBK05, BSBK07] executed in the grid and have prototyped (in collaboration with FAW) a *grid-enabled medical database* [BSBK05]. Since we met with some limitation of the Globus Toolkit 4 [BSBK07], we also implemented another *SEE++ version for the gLite grid middleware* [BS08b]. In the following, we describe these activities in more detail.

Parallel Hess-Lancaster Test

To develop "Grid-Enabled SEE++", we combined the SEE++ software with the Globus Toolkit [Glo] (applying both the older *pre-Web Service* and the newer *Web Service* framework of this grid middleware) to develop a parallel version of the simulation of the Hess-Lancaster test.

The core component of our development is a "SEE++ to Grid Bridge" [BSBK05], via which the unchanged SEE++ client can get access to the infrastructure of the Austrian Grid. The bridge acts as a SEE++ server to the SEE++ clients and as a Globus client to the Grid. The usage of grid resources is completely transparent to the clients. Before the bridge accepts the computational requests from the SEE++ clients, it starts grid-enabled SEE++ servers in the grid. These processes behave as some kind of "executer" programs for the computation tasks such that the remarkable latencies of the job submissions for the computational requests can be avoided.

This "SEE++ to Grid Bridge" splits gaze pattern calculation requests of clients into subtasks (which contain only some points of the pattern) and distributes them among the servers (data parallelism, see Section 1.4). Since the calculations of each gaze points is completely independent from each other, there is no communication among the server processes. By this, we speeded up this simulation by a factor of 12–14 with 30–45 processors which demonstrates how a the computational power of the Austrian Grid can be effectively exploited for a real-world application.

A Grid-Enabled Medical Database

Next, we developed (in collaboration with FAW) the prototype of a grid variant of a medical database component for SEE++ [Mit05], which stores medical data and eye model parameters. These pathological cases can be utilized as initial estimations of a grid-based pathology fitting algorithm [BSBK05].

Since this database is designed for storing patient records, security is a very important aspect. The security implementation ensures that every database access is secured appropriately by checking the caller's identity. Furthermore, the access layer employs many techniques to maximize security (such as supporting username/password based authentication and applying strong encryption of stored user passwords with a SHA-512 salted hash code).

The overall goal is to develop a distributed grid-enabled database system that allows "Grid-Enabled SEE++" to give efficient support to "Evidence Based Medicine". To establish such a grid-based database without a major modification in the existing data access layer, an abstraction layer has to be introduced as provided by the *Grid Semantic Data Access Middleware* (G-SDAM) developed by FAW (see Section 3.3).

Design of Grid-Based Pathology Fitting

Pathology Fitting is a non-linear optimization problem in a multidimensional parameter space where some of the patient's eye model parameters are modified until the calculated gaze pattern matches the measured one. In this way, the pathological reason of strabismus can be determined automatically.

Unfortunately, a gaze pattern does not uniquely determine the values of eye model parameters. Furthermore, the gaze patterns can in practice not be measured with perfect precision, hence the simulated gaze patterns cannot be completely the same as the measured one. At the moment, SEE++ uses a heuristic that is able to exclude most of the pathologically irrelevant solutions (solutions which are possible in the mathematical model, but cannot occur in a real human eye) and give an approximation of the correct solution.

As a first step on speeding up pathology fitting, we extended the pathology fitting component of SEE++ by parallel gaze pattern calculation, since a single pathology fitting process often requires the calculation of 60–100 gaze patterns. However, the speedup achieved by this implementation was limited to a factor of two, because the gaze pattern calculations are triggered by consecutive optimization steps.

Another attempt at speeding up the fitting process may be based on the fact that a gaze pattern does not uniquely determine a simulation model and the current algorithm may not find always the best solution (despite of the introduced heuristics, the quality of outcome still depends on the initial estimation for the current pathological case), we can exploit the grid infrastructure to attempt to find better solutions:

1. by searching in the database concurrently for similar cases as the one presented to the pathology fitter and
2. by starting concurrent pathology fitting processes with these cases as the starting points of the optimizations (parameter study).

Initial work on improving the optimization process is reported in [Wat08].

Comparison of Globus and gLite

In the frame of the EGEE-2 project [EGE], we have developed an alternative to the original Globus-based version of "Grid-Enabled SEE++" by applying the grid middleware gLite [gLi]. In some benchmarks, we have compared the effectiveness of both solutions in different situations where 1, 3, 9, 25, 30 or 45 processors were used on the grid. The basis for this experimental comparison was the parallel grid-enabled simulation of Hess-Lancaster test.

The test cases based on Globus 4 were executed on the Austrian Grid site altix1.jku.austriangrid.at, which contains 64 Intel Itanium processors (1.4GHz) and resides at the Johannes Kepler University (JKU) in Linz. The "SEE++ to Grid Bridge" and SEE++ clients were always executed at the RISC institute located in Hagenberg which has a one Gigabit/sec connection to the JKU. In case of 25 or more processors, we used some processes on the grid site altix1.uibk.ac.at in Innsbruck that comprises 16 CPUs of the same type. The test cases based on gLite were performed on some clusters of the architecture of the *Int.EU.Grid* Project [Int]. The server jobs were randomly disseminated among some clusters in Germany (122 CPUs), Poland (32 CPUs), Slovakia (32 CPUs) and Spain (20 CPUs).

In these tests, we speeded up the simulation by a factor of 12–14 in Globus and by a factor 9–13 in gLite (see Figure 8). Apparently the results achieved with Globus look better, but the measured values do not reflect the whole picture: in the tests based on Globus we employed homogeneous hardware and there were fast connections between the bridge and the servers with relatively consistent quality. In the gLite tests, the environment was heterogeneous and communication latencies were higher with large variations. These facts may imply that the differences between the values concerning to Globus and gLite on Figure 8 are caused more by the disparity of the hardware architectures of the two testbeds than by the applied middleware.

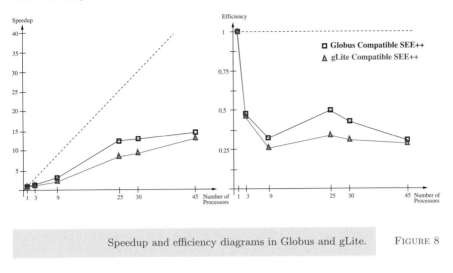

Speedup and efficiency diagrams in Globus and gLite.   FIGURE 8

Parallel Supercomputing in the Grid   3.2

In this section, we outline an ongoing research activity of RISC in the frame of the Austrian Grid Phase 2 with the goal of developing a distributed programming software framework and a corresponding programming interface (API) for grid computing. This work shall assist applications whose algorithmic structures do not lend themselves to a decomposition into big sequential components whose only interactions occur at the begin and the end of the execution of a component (such that they can be scheduled by a meta-level grid workflow language that implements communication between components by file-based mechanisms). Our solution shall empower applications to perform scheduling decisions on their own by utilizing the information provided by an API about the grid environment at hand in order to adapt the algorithmic structure to the particular runtime situation.

In the grid no application can execute efficiently, if it is not aware of the fact that it does not run in a homogeneous cluster environment (with low latency and high bandwidth between all nodes) but in an environment with heterogeneous nodes and connections that dramatically vary between three different levels: the processors within a grid node, the grid nodes within the same network, and grid nodes in different networks linked by wide-area connections. Thus the API shall not hide this fact from the application but rather reflect the information provided by the grid management and execution environment to the programming language level so that the application can utilize this information and adapt its behavior to it, e.g., by mapping closely interacting activities to nodes within a network and minimizing communication between activities executing on nodes in different networks.

The API shall however hide low-level execution details from the application by providing an abstract execution model that in particular allows to initiate activities and communicate between them independently of their physical location. The execution engine has to map these abstract model features to the appropriate underlying mechanisms: to initiate an activity on a local machine or on a machine within the same administrative authority, simply a process may be started; to initiate an activity on a remote node means to contact a corresponding service on that machine, provide the appropriate credentials, and ask the service to start the activity.

Software Framework

In our approach [BS08a], we adapt the algorithmic structure of a parallel program to particular grid resources by assigning to a parallel program an appropriate schema that describes a generalized communication structure and that is especially designed for heterogeneous network environments (the schema classifies connections among the processes as often used respectively rarely used links). The schema can be specialized by some parameters according to some characteristics of the program. The outcome of this procedure is a *specification* of the preferred communication structure of the program in heterogeneous networks. We map this specification to a predicted performance model of an available physical network architecture in order to decrease the communication overhead during the execution as much as possible.

Figure 9 depicts the overall framework which consists of three major components (components denoted by ellipses represent third party software products which we may substitute in a later phase):

Scheduling Mechanism: This mechanism employs the performance prediction tool *Network Weather Service (NWS)* [WSH99] which is used by many middleware products to gather qualitative information about the current state of the execution infrastructure (network and CPUs) and to predict its short-term performance. Before each execution of a parallel program on the grid, the scheduling mechanism maps the specified communication structure of the program to the topological hierarchy of the physical grid architecture such that it minimizes the assessed execution time. The output is a mapping description called *execution plan.*

Deployment Mechanism: This mechanism is based on the startup mechanism of MPICH-G2 [MPIc, KTF03], a grid-enabled implementation of the MPI standard based on the library MPICH [MPIb]. The Deployment Mechanism takes the generated execution plan and starts the processes of the program on the corresponding grid nodes according to the plan.

Topology-Aware API: It is not enough to discover the characteristic of an available physical grid architecture, but a *topology-aware* programming environment must exploit this information. The main purpose of this API

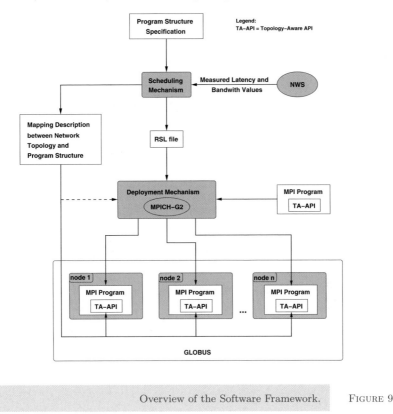

Overview of the Software Framework.   FIGURE 9

is to inform a parallel program how its processes are assigned to some physical grid resources and which roles are assigned to these processes.

Application

The framework can be e.g. used to efficiently execute in the grid a program based on a hierarchical variant of the manager/worker model (see Section 1.4) with a tree of processes organized in three levels: the root process acts as the global manager, the processes on the second level represent local managers, and the leaf processes are the workers that perform the actual computations.

With the help of NWS, the scheduling mechanism determines an adequate distribution of the processes to grid nodes such that the workers on the third level are organized as big local groups (preferring clusters and LANs) and the point-to-point communications between the processes on the second level and the corresponding workers are as efficient as possible. Based on this execution plan, the deployment mechanism allocates the chosen group of grid nodes and starts the processes on them. Finally, the topology-aware API informs the processes at runtime how they are distributed on the allocated pool of grid nodes and maps them to the predefined roles in the specified hierarchical schema (global manager, local manager and worker) such that the program is executed with minimal communication overhead.

Advantages of the Approach

The major advantages of our approach (against other topology-aware software frameworks, like MPICH-G2) are the following:

- It takes the point-to-point structure of a parallel program into consideration and tries to fit it to a heterogeneous grid network architecture.
- It leverages existing topology-aware software frameworks: in particular, the efficient collective operations of MPICH-G2 can be still used.
- It eliminates the algorithmic challenges of topology-aware programming, i.e. a programmer deals only with the computational problem at hand.
- The users need not be aware of the grid or manually provide the information about the physical topology structure of the network/grid.
- The distribution of the processes is always conformed to the actual loading of the network resources.

A prototype of the framework will become operational by the middle of 2009.

3.3 Data Grids

In a changing world with a steadily increasing amount of electronic data, systems which are able to easily manage and access these data become more and more important. As the grid is an immense infrastructure enabling access to autonomous systems spread at different places, it is best suited for the maintenance of distributed data sources. If the requirement of managing large amounts of data is joined with the possibility of connecting numerous computer systems as the grid does, a system emerges that has the capability to organize remote data in a way such that users can easily access it and data-intensive applications can use it efficiently. Such an architecture is called *Data Grid* [FKT01].

Because there are many ways to implement such a system (as will be shown in the section *Application Areas* below), there are different approaches on how to define it. Chervenak et al. [CFK+01] proposed that data grids mainly support two two basic functionalities. Firstly, they have to enable high-speed and reliable data transfer; secondly, scalable replica discovery and management mechanisms have to be provided. Additionally, services are needed that provide the management of replica. There are many other requirements that a data grid has to fulfill for specific application areas. For instance, the goal of the G-SDAM project (described later in Section *Semantic Data Integration*) is to semantically integrate distributed and heterogeneous information into a single virtual information space. This will enable scientists to share data more easily and with less manual pre-processing.

In order to provide these mechanisms, *metadata* (i.e. data about the data themselves) are required, e.g. attributes such as time of creation, time of last modification, size on disk, as well as data semantics. With these metadata it is possible to create unique and persistent identifiers with the aim of distinguishing between different objects such as users and entities. To classify and organize these identifiers, so called logical namespaces are created. With these it becomes possible to control access, enable discovery, and manage wide area latencies. Another crucial characteristic of data grids is the functionality to restrict access. Since information is an important good, users might want to restrict the distribution of their data. So authentication and authorization mechanisms are realized to control coarse- to fine-grained access.

Application Areas

This section gives an overview of some applications in heterogeneous research fields to demonstrate the universal need and application areas of data grids. Most of the applications use data grids to integrate distributed data sets which provide and store large amounts of data.

BIRN (Biomedical Informatics Research Network): This research network[1] in the application field of biomedical informatics is a geographically distributed knowledge base with the goal to advance the diagnosis and treatment of diseases. The main contributors are clinical and biomedical scientists who use this grid by enhancing and processing the data. One of the main features which is very important for this purpose is the data integration aspect. The model of *federation* (see below) is used for federating data sources. The difficulty this community has to deal with is not only that a large amount of data is generated but also that existing data sets and storage systems are highly heterogeneous (ranging from relational databases over ontologies to spatial atlases).

GriPhyN (Grid Physics Network): This petabyte-scale data grid[2] is mainly used and administrated by experimental physicists and information technology researchers; it will provide an information and data management system for the data intensive science of the 21st century. Mainly three science projects profit from this grid. The first one is in the field of astronomy, the *The Sloan Digital Sky Survey*. This project is about measuring the universe by recording the sky and determining distances between celestial objects and galaxies. Another project is LIGO, which is about *Detecting Einstein's Gravitational Waves*. Because of the accuracy of the

---

[1] http://www.nbirn.net

[2] http://www.griphyn.org

measurements and the demand of very close examination, large amounts of peripheral data are generated and have to be stored. The third project is called *High-Energy Particle Physics* and is about the Large Hadron Collider (LHC) which is generating an astronomical amount of data. Even if the prime data of the CERN CMS detector is divided by a factor of ten, still more than a petabyte of data per year is generated. This huge amount of data is federated to different locations across Europe; it needs the functionalities of a data grid in order to be managed and processed in an automated way.

NEES (Network for Earthquake Engineering Simulation): The NEES network[3] is operating from 2004 to 2014; it consists of 15 large-scale, experimental sites that provide special functions like shake tables and earthquake effect simulations. To provide the needed computational power and data management/storage, NEESgrid was developed. As the researchers are located throughout the USA, it is important to distribute data to them as well as to provide and manage the necessary metadata. To gain access to the repository and to the environment, users can access the grid via a web-based user interface. The management of rights is also a very important feature of this data grid application.

NVO (National Virtual Observatory): The research area of this application[4] is similar to that of the Sloan digital sky survey of the GriPhyN network. This is an area where huge amounts of data are generated which have to be stored, managed, and processed. Therefore, also in this project, a data grid is in use which is called *TeraGrid*[5]. The main objectives are the exposure of massive data to massive computing and to run applications to visualize and explore these data. In the future, additional projects will be able to use the TeraGrid and the protocols and infrastructure of NVO.

Model Classification of Data Grids

This section outlines the various characteristics of data grids. Depending on the application scenario, they more or less differ in their architectures. While some implementations have a single source, others integrate existing data sources that interact with each other. Figure 10 shows the most common models found in data grids.

The first model is called *monadic*. All the information gathered is stored in a central repository which answers the queries submitted by users and systems and provides the data. It is obvious that this central system is the single point of failure. Therefore, a backup system is often provided to support the central system but this does not improve the locality of data. This model does not integrate replica management and hence minimizes the architectural

---

[3] http://www.nsf.gov/news/special_reports/nees/about.jsp

[4] http://www.us-vo.org/

[5] http://www.teragrid.org/

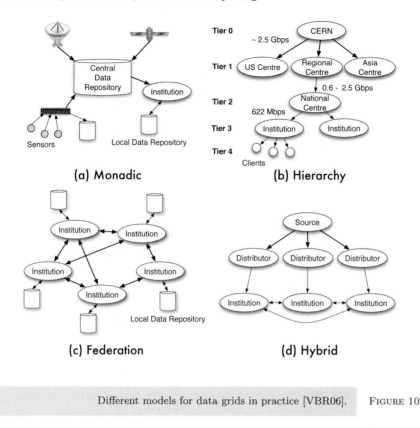

Different models for data grids in practice [VBR06]. FIGURE 10

overhead. One disadvantage, however, is that all the traffic has to be delivered to the central node. The performance of the system heavily depends on the network bandwidth. The NEES project, which has already been mentioned, uses such a model for its data grid.

The second model shown is the *hierarchical* model. It is organized like a tree, so there is a single source that distributes data to other systems. An example therefore is the CERN grid as shown in Figure 10 (b). CERN produces data that are delivered to regional centers such as the *US Centre* or the *Asian Centre*. The *Regional Centre* itself provides these data to the national centers which deliver them to the institutions that are connected with the users. It can be seen that the information flow is top-down only; each connection has a particular bandwidth associated.

The characteristics of the third model called *federation* is that existing systems can be easily integrated into the data grid. The figure shows that every institution provides its data stored in its database to the other institutions. Therefore it is important that an appropriate authentication mechanism guarantees optimized security features. This model is for example implemented in the BIRN project discussed above. When using the federation model, it is possible to use data replication in order to fetch the data needed, such that a copy is stored on the own system. Thus a replica discovery and management mechanism is needed in order to keep the whole system consistent.

The last model is the *hybrid* one. Hybrid models are actually not different models, but rather combinations of one or more other models. In practice, it is sometimes necessary that information has to be provided mainly by a single source (like in the hierarchical model), but in the bottom-most tier the institutions also have to be connected and have to provide data for each other similar to the federation models. Hence, it is not always possible to use a single model, because the possibilities and benefits of more are desirable [VBR06].

Semantic Data Integration for E-Science Grids

The research focus of the Institute for Application Oriented Knowledge Processing (FAW) in the Austrian Grid project is semantic data integration. A data integration middleware is implemented which enables transparent access to distributed and heterogeneous information systems based on ontologies. The *Resource Description Framework* (RDF) and the *Web Ontology Language* (OWL) are used as global data model and the declarative query language SPARQL *(*SPARQL*)* (an recursive acronym for SPARQL Protocol and RDF Query Language) is used as declarative query language. The grid middleware is called *Grid-enabled Semantic Data Access Middleware* (G-SDAM)[6]; its core component is developed as an independent sub-project called *Semantic Web Integrator and Query Engine* (SemWIQ)[7]. While until 2008 the development was focused around SemWIQ, the grid integration and release of G-SDAM is scheduled for the last project year at the end of 2009.

As explained earlier, data integration is one of the base requirements in many scientific applications. Many grid computations require large amounts of input data to be analyzed. If data from different independent sources are used, a dedicated data integration middleware may provide a transparent view without the demand to map and align the existing data to a common structure whenever data has to be retrieved.

The G-SDAM/SemWIQ approach is based on the following assumptions:

- data sources are already existing or have been created independently and are therefore fully autonomous,
- data sources are geographically distributed,
- data are stored in various information systems (e.g. relational database systems, file systems, accessible via Webservices only),
- data structures and semantics are heterogeneous because they are developed and maintained autonomously,
- the semantics of data is usually difficult to interpret without human communication and interaction (this also applies to metadata).

---

[6] http://gsdam.sourceforge.net

[7] http://semwiq.faw.uni-linz.ac.at

Within the middleware developed for the Austrian Grid, the heterogeneous data models and structures are aligned to common domain ontologies when data sources are registered at so-called mediators. Each *Global Repository Node* (GRN) within G-SDAM is providing a SemWIQ mediator instance. The required transformation of data representations is done on-the-fly during data retrieval. This enables large-scale data mining across geographically distributed and heterogeneous data sources because all data are represented in the same common data model.

Within G-SDAM, data can be retrieved by executing SPARQL queries against a SemWIQ mediator running on a GRN. Any data source to be integrated has to provide a SPARQL end-point and can then be registered by one or more GRNs[8]. Because usually a data source does not provide a SPARQL endpoint by default (only native RDF stores do), a wrapper is placed on top of the data source. This mediator-wrapper architecture is depicted in Figure 11.

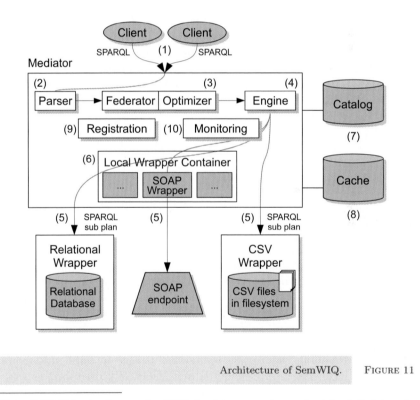

Architecture of SemWIQ.   FIGURE 11

---

[8] Note: G-SDAM actually uses SemWIQ for data processing and retrieval. It integrates the Grid Security Infrastructure and OGSA-compliant Web services. An OGSA-DAI *Data-Source* implementation will also be provided.

Clients establish a connection to the mediator and request data by submitting SPARQL queries (1). Patterns in such *global* queries adhere to a virtual data graph which refers to classes and properties from arbitrary RDFS or OWL vocabularies. The parser (2) calculates a canonical query plan which is modified by the federator/optimizer component (3). The federator decomposes the global query, scans the registry and statistics for relevant registered data sources and produces a federated query plan. The optimizer uses several rules based on heuristics as well as statistics collected periodically from the registered data sources to generate an optimized global query execution plan. The query execution engine (4) processes this global plan which includes remote sub-plans executed at remote endpoints (5). The SPARQL protocol is used between mediator and wrapper endpoints and sub-plans are therefore serialized back into lexical queries. In [LWB08] the query processing pipeline is presented in detail.

The registry catalog (7) stores descriptions and statistics about each registered data source [BLW06] and a local RDF cache (8) will be used in future to cache triples for global join operations and frequently recurring queries. The registration component (9) is responsible for the (de-)registration of data sources via Web services. Finally, the monitoring component (10) is periodically fetching statistics from registered data sources. In October 2008 the new sub-project RDFStats[9] was integrated into the data source monitor. Now it also includes histograms for the data distributions which significantly aids the optimization of global queries.

Global Domain Ontologies and Vocabularies

Aligning data from heterogeneous data models (the relational model, XML, CSV, etc.) and schemes (e.g. different database schemes for the same domain) is a difficult task. The semantic information required to interpret existing data is usually available as metadata and documentation intended for human readers. However, this information is often not sufficient; it requires human communication and manual alignment when transforming various data sets into a common format before data can be analyzed systematically.

If it is possible to define formal mappings from several source data models to a single common data model, the transformation can be done automatically during data retrieval. However, this requires a very expressive common data model, since it has to cover various individual semantics of each source model. The Resource Description Framework is able to fulfill this requirements. The RDF-based data model is mathematically described as sets of triples forming an RDF graph; most important, the semantics of RDF data can be extended on the basis of RDF itself. Further important features are globally unique data identifiers (specified as URIs) and the open world assumption which allows to merge globally distributed RDF graphs to extend

---

[9] http://semwiq.faw.uni-linz.ac.at/rdfstats

locally incomplete information. RDF data may be described by RDF Schema or OWL, which additionally allows to use description logic constraints in order to automatically classify instances based on deductive reasoning.

Based on the W3C standards, several vocabularies (terminological ontologies, i.e. without instances also known as the *A-box*) may be used to describe data (see Figure 12). During the past years of Semantic Web research, many vocabularies have already been published and may be reused. Together with the Kanzelhöhe Solar Observatory (partner of the Austrian Grid project), further vocabularies have been developed to describe observations in general and solar observations in particular.

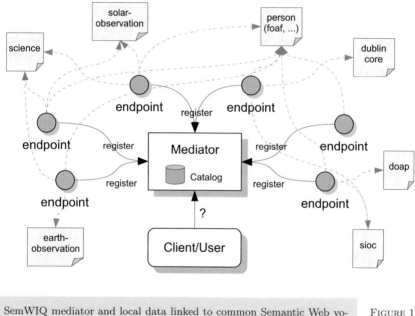

SemWIQ mediator and local data linked to common Semantic Web vocabularies (RDF Schema/OWL) published on the Web—each G-SDAM Global Repository Node (GRN) is equipped with a SemWIQ Mediator instance. A SemWIQ endpoint may be part of the grid or not.   Figure 12

Often the argument is raised that finding integrated data models or domain ontologies is a difficult task which requires expert support. This is absolutely true: the effort is even required within G-SDAM/SemWIQ. However, this task can be done by a core community who may develop and maintain the vocabularies with collaboration tools developed exactly for that purpose (e.g. OntoWiki[10]). The mapping of a data source has to be done only once upon data source registration. During the mapping process it is possible to add semantic links to other data sources on the Web.

---

[10] http://ontowiki.net/

Future Research Directions

Currently, the Semantic Web Integrator and Query Engine used for G-SDAM supports the semantic aspect fulfilling the requirements for virtually sharing scientific data from heterogeneous data repositories. However, it does not yet include typical data grid aspects like replica management or fine-grained authorization. After the full integration of SemWIQ into the Grid (G-SDAM release), which mainly includes GSI (Grid Security Infrastructure) integration and publishing OGSA-compliant (*Open Grid Services Architecture*) Web services, future research will investigate the integration of G-SDAM into the existing data grid middleware. To integrate G-SDAM into OGSA-DAI (*OGSA Data Access and Integration*), a special G-SDAM *DataSource type* will be implemented. The OGSA-DQP middleware, which is a sub-project of OGSA-DAI enables parallel, distributed query processing by utilizing computational Grid resources. In future work, the applicability of OGSA-DQP for query federation and optimization in SemWIQ will be investigated.

4 GPU Computing for Computational Intelligence

Since 1999 the Software Competence Center Hagenberg (SCCH) pursues application-oriented research in the field of computational intelligence in cooperation with international scientific and economic partners. Computational intelligence is an active field of research comprising machine learning like supervised and unsupervised learning, fuzzy logics, and automated reasoning. Beside the methodological aspects regarding recognition capabilities for e.g. computer vision problems, it is a major goal to design and implement the methods in way that makes them adequate for real-time in-line process control as they are e.g. encountered in industrial quality inspection problems.

Many of these methods are characterized by the *high dimensionality of data* on which they operate and the *high arithmetic intensity* caused by computationally intensive mathematical models. These are often limiting factors for the applicability in time-critical applications. Parallelization represents the only viable solution for breaking the usability boundaries of the existing algorithms of which many exhibit inherent data-parallelism (see Section 1.4). This suggests that GPU (graphics processing unit) computing, an emerging technology which uses the massive data-parallel and floating point arithmetical capabilities of graphics hardware is a good candidate to deal with application speed problems.

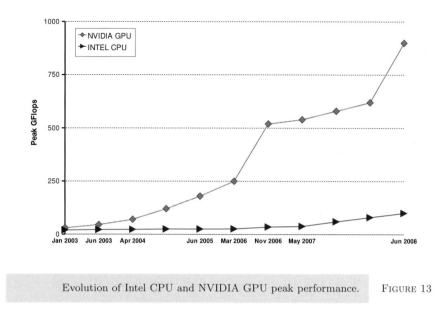

Evolution of Intel CPU and NVIDIA GPU peak performance.   FIGURE 13

General Purpose Computing on GPUs   4.1

The landscape of parallel computing has substantially changed in the last
years. It has not only become clear that "the future is parallel" [FR96], but
current trends also show that computing power through parallelism will be
provided by many-core (massively parallel multi-core) architectures [ABC$^+$06].
The success of on-chip parallelism is best reflected in the evolution of the
graphics processing units. During the last six years, GPUs went through a
set of substantial changes, which turned these initially explicitly graphics oriented devices into *massively parallel, general purpose* computing tools. Driven
by the needs and pressure of the multi-billion dollar computer gaming market, the race of graphics hardware manufacturers resulted in the increase of
floating point arithmetic performance with remarkable leaps. This has led to
a quickly growing, substantial gap between the raw performance of CPUs and
GPUs. The significant floating point performance superiority of the graphics
hardware (see Figure 13) lies in the fundamental architectural differences.

The introduction of fully programmable commodity GPUs that provide
high computational speed for graphics applications was also an important
event in the scientific computing world. Current GPU-based solutions provide affordable and compact supercomputing power with performance in the

teraflop range[11] [NVI08c]. Researchers in the field of scientific and high performance computing, motivated by the potential, affordability, and increasing
programmability of graphics hardware became interested in harnessing GPUs
for general purpose computing. This collective initiative has became known
as General Purpose computation on GPUs (GPGPU) [GPG].

GPU Architecture

GPUs were originally designed for computer graphics and visualization. However, from a fixed function processing unit GPUs have evolved into massively
parallel many-core processors, exceeding by far the capabilities of current
CPUs. Optimized for sequential code execution, a great amount of CPU
transistors is devoted to control and instruction level parallelism. In contrast, GPUs are designed for highly parallel execution with less transistors
reserved for control and more devoted to computation. Beside using the transistors in a more efficient way, the GPU architecture has a less complex design
which facilitates to increase the number of transistors. Also, the importance
of throughput rather than latency allows higher arithmetic intensity for the
same number of transistors [OLG+07]. Knowing that latency will lag bandwidth in the near future [Pat04], the GPU architecture (centered around the
importance of throughput) has a start-line advantage compared to CPUs.

Based on the stream architectural concept [KRD+03, Owe05], the processing units of GPUs contain several *streaming multiprocessors*, each being
a multi-core *stream processor*. Modern GPUs have an extensive set of special
features, e.g. hardware support for multi-threading, floating point units capable of executing per clock cycle a multiply-add, multiply, and "superfunc"
operation (i.e. rsqrt, sin or cos), special function instructions (e.g. exponential function, reciprocal instructions, trigonometric functions). Tailored for
floating point arithmetic for 3D graphics, the GPU hardware is not intended
for general use (i.e. can not replace the CPU). As a conclusion, GPUs are
considered *floating point coprocessors* or *arithmetic accelerators* (like FPGAs
or ClearSpeed FPU boards) and require control by the CPU (i.e. host).

GPUs are centered around the *graphics pipeline*: different tasks executed
concurrently on a large set of data. The pipeline is divided in space rather
than time (as is the case for CPUs), different stages execute different tasks in
parallel and feed their results to the consequent stage. Initially, to each stage
a different hardware element corresponded, i.e. a special purpose compute
unit tailored to the specific operations of the respective stage. The vertex
and pixel shader units are traditionally the programmable parts.

The initial fixed-function nature of GPUs ensured the simplicity of the
design which resulted in highly efficient task-parallel execution. However, the

---

[11] The NVIDIA Tesla deskside supercomputer consists of a standard desktop PC equipped
with 3-4 Tesla C1060 boards with up to 960 processing cores and 933 GFlops peak arithmetic performance per board.

varying arithmetical intensity of the executed operations on different units causes load balancing issues in such a pipeline architecture, as the speed of execution depends on the slowest stage of the pipeline. On the other hand, the necessity for more flexible programmability of the vertex and pixel-fragment stages resulted in their feature-wise convergence. These two factors led to the design concept of the modern GPUs, the *unified shader architecture*. As these stages are the most computation-intensive and highly parallel stages of the pipeline, by unifying (physically and function-wise as well) the programmable parts of the GPU, the computational power gets concentrated in a single unit. This facilitates load balancing and opened up the possibility of the previously limited general purpose use. From a parallel computing point of view, the unification is a step toward a more general stream architecture. Both leading graphics hardware manufacturers, NVIDIA and AMD[12] have been using unified architecture in their GPUs on the G80 (GeForce 8 family) platform since 2006 [LNOM08, NBGS08] respectively R500/Xenos platform since 2005 [AB06]. NVIDIA provides the Tesla, AMD the FireStream [AMD] specialized GPGPU platforms for high performance and scientific computing.

GPU Computing

The architecture of the graphics hardware (designed to support both task- and data-parallelism) requires a special programming approach. Therefore traditional graphics programming is inherently data- and task-parallel. With the unified architecture, the data-parallel nature of the many-core GPUs gets accentuated, creating a favorable platform for general purpose programming. The programmable unit of GPUs are SIMD, therefore a general purpose code must exhibit data-parallelism in order to exploit the massive hardware concurrency capabilities. GPUs are characterized by fine-grain parallel execution, *thousands of lightweight threads* need to be executed concurrently in order to keep the GPU busy. The efficiency of an algorithm is strongly influenced by the degree of concurrency which is dependent on the dimensionality of the input data. A fine partitioning of the computational domain is necessary in order to provide sufficient concurrency for efficient execution. Concurrent thread execution is able to hide the latency of the main memory by switching from threads groups blocked by ongoing memory operations to other threads.

General purpose programming of GPUs is carried out in a SPMD (single program multiple data) fashion: multiple data elements are concurrently processed by the same program. The data elements are typically 32bit floating point or integer values, but the latest architectures[13] already support 64bit, double precision floating point arithmetic (although at lower speed). While the general SPMD model allows simultaneous execution of the program on

---

[12] The former graphics hardware manufacturer ATI was acquired by AMD in 2006.

[13] The AMD platform with the ATI RV670/RV770 and the NVIDIA platform with the GT200 introduced double precision support.

different instruction points by different cores, for efficiency reasons GPUs necessitate restrictions. Allowing different execution paths over all threads would require substantial amount of control hardware. Instead, a block of threads is executed in SIMD manner on a single multiprocessor. Threads from different blocks can take different execution paths, but if divergent branching occurs in threads running on the same core, all branches need to be evaluated, leading to inefficiency. From a programming point of view, this limits the use of branching (i.e. usage of conditional statements). However, coherent thread grouping (i.e. threads from the same group executing the same branch) can be achieved by carefully structuring the data-parallel execution.

The *stream programming* model [Owe05] represents the basis of the modern GPGPU languages and programming environments. This approach concentrates on expressing parallelism, modelling communication patterns and memory use in the application. It formulates the computation as arithmetic *kernels* that operate on data, structured into *data streams* [OHL+08]. A key difference compared to a general stream programming approach which executes an *arbitrary Turing machine* is that on GPUs *a single function* processes the data stream [Ven03]. The Sh [Sh] shading language offering stream programming abstractions and BrookGPU [Bro], a compiler and runtime environment implementation of the Brook stream programming language were the first to be successfully abstracting the GPU as a stream processor. A commercial platform for GPU computing is NVIDIA's CUDA [CUD] which consists of GPGPU language extensions for C, the CUDA compiler, and runtime library. NVIDIA also offers implementation of the BLAS and FFT numerical libraries with CUBLAS [NVI08a] and CUFFT [NVI08b].

Graphics oriented GPUs have been becoming more and more capable of solving general computing problems. Specifically those problem classes that are suitable to be expressed using the data-parallel paradigm are good candidates. The problem size as well as the arithmetic intensity of the respective algorithm is crucial to keep the GPU busy. Typically, applications which operate on large data sets are eligible to be implemented on GPUs. The stream memory architecture is very powerful. Even *memory bound* GPGPU algorithms, having preponderant memory access operations, and therefore low arithmetic intensity, can outpace the CPU version which suffers from the memory bottleneck of the traditional Von Neumann style architectures [Ven03]. Arithmetically intensive operations often take significantly less cycles on GPUs, as an extensive set of special function instructions is supported (e.g. trigonometric and logarithmic functions in CUDA). As a result of all these advantages, GPU-based solutions are gaining recognition with the numerous real-life applications ranging from fluid dynamics to N-body problems, computer vision and many more (see [AMD, OHL+08, CUD, GPG]). Typical speedups range from 10 to 100, but speedups as high as 270 (sum products) and 470 (k nearest neighbor search) exist [AMD, CUD].

Nonetheless, the graphics oriented hardware design still carries its limitations. Beside the inherently non GPU-parallelizable algorithms (e.g. not data-parallel or exhibiting communication patterns not suitable for GPUs) there are several limitations of current GPGPU tools and platforms:

- There exists no fully IEEE 754 compliant floating point arithmetic (e.g. deviations in rounding, no NaN support).
- Double precision arithmetic is less efficient; it achieves below half of the advertised single precision speed.
- Full 32bit arithmetic is inefficient.
- There is no support for recursion.
- Global synchronization is inefficient.
- PCI-X bandwidth and latency represent a bottleneck; moving data between host and global memory can represent a serious bottleneck.
- There is no single tool which supports the efficient, flexible and easy programming of both of the two major graphics hardware platforms.

A GPU-based SVM Classifier 4.2

As an introductory step for GPU computing at SCCH, we developed a GPU-based parallelization of the support vector machines classifier algorithm [P08].

Support vector machines (SVMs) are currently considered one of the most powerful learning methods and provide state-of-the art solution for various application areas, e.g. text categorization, texture analysis, gene classification and many more. The SVM concept is heavily used in several industrial applications at SCCH. Consult [SS01] for a detailed explanation on SVMs.

The SVM algorithms exhibit data-parallelism suggested by the dominance of vector-oriented operations. In several time-critical industrial applications (e.g. classification of textures), a limiting factor is represented by the high data dimensionality which on the other hand is a source of concurrency in a data-parallel implementation. At the same time, kernel functions with high arithmetic intensity (e.g. Gaussian RBF) are also a source of speed concerns in traditional implementations. This suggests that a GPGPU implementation can provide means to increase the usability of SVM-based algorithms which are limited by sequential execution.

Our work aimed to provide a parallel SVM classifier algorithm for GPU, to implement the algorithm using the NVIDIA CUDA platform and to compare its performance and behavior with the library LIBSVM [CBM$^+$08], an established CPU-based implementation. The binary SVM classification problem corresponds to the evaluation of the decision function

$$f(\mathbf{x}) = \text{sgn}\left(\sum_{i=1}^{m} \alpha_i y_i \mathrm{K}(\mathbf{x}, \mathbf{x}_i) + b\right)$$

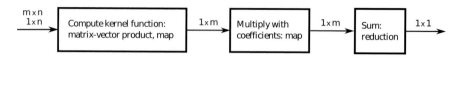

FIGURE 14   SVM decision function evaluation with stream programming.

where α_i, y_i are weight coefficients, $K(\mathbf{x}, \mathbf{x}_i)$ is a kernel function, $\mathbf{x}_i$ are the support vectors, b the bias, and $\mathbf{x}$ is the data instance to be classified (for a detailed explanation see [SS01]).

Identifying the parallelizable parts of the decision function represents the first step. These are then mapped to the data-parallel computational primitives map and reduce (i.e. parallel computing idioms, see [OLG+07, OHL+08]), respectively the data-parallel matrix-vector product. This mapping ensures that the algorithm fits smoothly in the stream programming model. The evaluation of the decision function is represented by the consequent application of data-parallel operations (kernels) on the data stream in their order of application in the decision function. The initial data-stream consisting of the support vectors and the data instance vector is reduced to a single value, the decision value. The scheme is illustrated in Figure 14.

An initialization step setting up the GPU environment precedes the actual classification phase. This step consists of CUDA library initialization and copying trained classifier data (support vectors, coefficients and parameters) to the GPU—these remain constant through the classification phase. This step represents an overhead compared to a CPU implementation. Based on the presented data-parallel scheme, the classifier implementation consists of CUDA kernels for each step of the evaluation of the decision function. As most of the computation is offloaded to the GPU, expensive communication with the host is limited to the transfer of input/output. The dot-product based kernel function makes use of the CUBLAS library provided with CUDA.

The benchmark results support the initial expectations: significant speedup is achievable while the classifier performance is not affected by the single precision arithmetic. We measured speedups up to 26.8 compared to the CPU implementation. Considering the application areas this can be quite significant, e.g. in object tracking it could substantially increase the frequency of frame processing which yields smoother and more precise tracking. The average deviation of decision values[14] computed on GPU from the CPU results are in the range of 10^{-4}–10^{-7}. This can be considered very low, did in our tests not cause misclassification, and does probably not influence typical

---

[14] While this is not a strict measure of the misclassification risk caused by the loss of computational accuracy, we use these empirical observations to characterize the general behavior of the GPU classifier.

SVM classifiers. The benchmarking was conducted on a GeForce 8800 Ultra GPU and a single core of an Intel Xeon 5060 3.2Ghz CPU.

We were able to draw some important conclusions from benchmarking and profiling results. In the following we summarize these and point out the strengths and weaknesses of our GPU-based SVM classifier implementation:

- Arithmetically more complex kernel functions yield increased speedup. This opens up the possibility for using specialized kernels without the risk of application slowdown.
- Low data dimensionality (i.e. a small number of support vectors or a low dimension vector space) strongly affects the algorithm, as this limits the level of thread concurrency. We propose two possible workarounds: either a hybrid implementation by moving the inefficient steps back to the CPU, or, if the application allows, grouped execution on several data instances.
- "Padding" the data vectors to dimensions which are multiples of 32 (the block size of the shared memory) yields significant speedup.
- The GPU overhead does not represent a significant drawback in situations where the initialization time is negligible, e.g. in real-time classifiers where many data instances are consequently fed to the classifier. However, when only a small number of data instances are classified at once (i.e. the initialization time is proportionately high), it becomes a limiting factor.

Note that our approach intends to deal with a large range of problems defined by widely varying data dimensions. Such an approach might not be able to produce the highest possible performance in every situation (various hardware capabilities, various problems sizes). As data-parallelism is crucial, ideally, a CUDA algorithm should be able to adapt its execution scheme to keep the GPU occupancy as high as possible. This "self tuning" capability is hard to realize. However, in specific applications, where the problem size is previously known, tuning of the execution parameters for the actual problem size requires less effort and it is less error-prone.

Acknowledgements

The research described in this chapter has been performed in the frame of the Austrian Grid project funded by the Austrian BMBWK (Federal Ministry for Education, Science and Culture) under the contracts GZ 4003/2-VI/4c/2004 and GZ BMWF-10.220/0002-II/10/2007, in the frame of the Enabling Grids for E-sciencE (EGEE-2) project sponsored by the European Commission, and in the frame of the Special Research Program (SFB) "Numerical and Symbolic Scientific Computing" project SFB F013/F1304 "Symbolic Differential Computation" funded by the Austrian Science Fund (FWF).

References

[AB06]   Jeff Andrews and Nick Baker. Xbox 360 System Architecture. *IEEE Micro*, 26(2):25–37, March–April 2006.

[ABC+06] Krste Asanovic, Ras Bodik, Bryan Christopher Catanzaro, et al. The Landscape of Parallel Computing Research: A View from Berkeley. Technical Report UCB/EECS-2006-183, EECS Department, University of California, Berkeley, December 2006.

[ACP]   ACPC – Austrian Center for Parallel Computation. http://www.gup.jku.at/ information/acpc/acpc.php.

[AMD]   AMD.   ATI Stream Technology.   http : / / ati . amd . com / technology / streamcomputing/index.html.

[Aus]   Austrian Grid Project. http://www.austriangrid.at.

[BCS05]   Rebhi Baraka, Olga Caprotti, and Wolfgang Schreiner. A Web Registry for Publishing and Discovering Mathematical Services. In *IEEE International Conference on e-Technology, e-Commerce, and e-Service (EEE-05)*, pages 190–193, Hong Kong, April 29–March 1, 2005. IEEE Computer Society Press.

[BJ91]   B. Buchberger and T. Jebelean. Systolic Algorithms in Computer Algebra. In *NATO ASI on Parallel Processing on Distributed Memory Multiprocessors*, Ankara, Turkey, 1991.

[BLW06]   Martin Blöchl, Andreas Langegger, and Wolfram Wöß. Registration of Heterogeneous Data Sources in the Case of the Grid Semantic Data Access Middleware (G-SDAM). In *Proceedings of the Austrian Grid Symposium (AGS'06)*. OCG, 2006.

[Bro]   BrookGPU. http://graphics.stanford.edu/projects/brookgpu/.

[BS05]   Karoly Bosa and Wolfgang Schreiner. Tolerating Stop Failures in Distributed Maple. *Scalable Computing: Practice and Experience*, 6(2):59–70, July 2005.

[BS06]   Rebhi Baraka and Wolfgang Schreiner. Semantic Querying of Mathematical Web Service Descriptions. In Mario Bravetti et al, editor, *Third International Workshop on Web Services and Formal Methods (WS-FM 2006)*, volume 4184 of *Lecture Notes in Computer Science*, pages 73–87, Vienna, Austria, September 8–9, 2006. Springer.

[BS08a]   Karoly Bosa and Wolfgang Schreiner. Initial Design of a Distributed Supercomputing API for the Grid. Technical report, Research Institute for Symbolic Computation (RISC), Johannes Kepler University Linz, Austria., 2008.

[BS08b]   Karoly Bosa and Wolfgang Schreiner. The Porting of a Medical Grid Application from Globus 4 to the gLite Middleware. In Peter Kacsuk at al., editor, *Proceedings of DAPSYS 2008*, pages 51–61. Springer, September 2008.

[BSBK05] Karoly Bosa, Wolfgang Schreiner, Michael Buchberger, and Thomas Kaltofen. SEE-GRID, A Grid-Based Medical Decision Support System for Eye Muscle Surgery. In Jens Volkert et al., editor, *Proceedings of 1st Austrian Grid Symposium 2005*, pages 61–74, Hagenberg, Austria, December 01 - 02 2005. Austrian Computer Society (OCG).

[BSBK07] Karoly Bosa, Wolfgang Schreiner, Michael Buchberger, and Thomas Kaltofen. A Grid Software for Virtual Eye Surgery Based on Globus 4 and gLite. In *Proceedings of ISPDC 2007*, pages 151–158. IEEE Computer Society, 2007.

[Buc78]   Bruno Buchberger. Computer-Trees and Their Programming. In *4th Colloquium "Les arbres en algebre et en programmation"*, pages 1–18, University of Lille, France, February 16–18, 1978.

[Buc85]   Bruno Buchberger. The L-Machine: An Attempt at Parallel Hardware for Symbolic Computation. In *Symposium on Applied algebra, Algebraic algorithms, and Error Correcting Codes (AAECC)*, volume 229 of *Lecture Notes in Computer Science*, pages 333–347. Springer, 1985.

[Buc04]   Michael Buchberger. *Biomechanical Modelling of the Human Eye.* PhD thesis, Johannes Kepler University, Linz, Austria, March 2004.

[But97]   David R. Butenhof. *Programming with POSIX Threads.* Addison-Wesley, 1997.

[Buy99]   Rajkumar Buyya. *High Performance Cluster Computing.* Prentice Hall, 1999.

[CAS]   CASA — Computer Algebra System for Algebraic Geometry. http://www.risc. uni-linz.ac.at/software/casa.

[CBM⁺08]   Shuai Che, Michael Boyer, Jiayuan Meng, et al. A Performance Study of General-Purpose Applications on Graphics Processors Using CUDA. *Journal of Parallel and Distributed Computing,* 68:1370–1380, 2008.

[CFK⁺01]   A. Chervenak, I. Foster, C. Kesselman, C. Salisbury, and S. Tuecke. The Data Grid: Towards an Architecture for the Distributed Management and Analysis of Large Scientific Datasets. *Journal of Network and Computer Applications,* 23(3):187–200, 2001.

[CGP99]   Edmund M. Clarke, Orna Grumberg, and Doron A. Peled. *Model Checking.* MIT Press, 1999.

[CS02]   Olga Caprotti and Wolfgang Schreiner. Towards a Mathematical Service Description Language. In *International Congress on Mathematical Software (ICMS),* Bejing, China, August 20–28, 2002. World Scientific Publishers.

[CUD]   CUDA Zone. http://www.nvidia.com/object/cuda_home.html.

[Dis]   Distributed Maple. http://www.risc.uni-linz.ac.at/software/distmaple.

[Ede]   Eden: Parallel Functional Programming. http://www.mathematik.uni-marburg. de/~eden.

[EGE]   Enabling Grids for E-sciencE (EGEE). http://www.eu-egee.org.

[Erl]   Erlang. http://www.erlang.org.

[Eur]   Euro-Par Conference Series — European Conference on Parallel and Distributed Computing. http://www.europar.org.

[FK98]   Ian Foster and Carl Kesselmann. *The Grid 2: Blueprint for a New Computing Infrastructure.* Morgan Kaufmann, 2nd edition, 1998.

[FKT01]   I. Foster, C. Kesselman, and S. Tuecke. The Anatomy of the Grid: Enabling Scalable Virtual Organizations. *Lecture Notes in Computer Science,* 2150, 2001.

[Fos95]   Ian Foster. *Designing and Building Parallel Programs: Concepts and Tools for Parallel Software Engineering.* Addison-Wesley, 1995.

[FR96]   M. J. Flynn and K. W. Rudd. Parallel Architectures. *ACM Computing Surveys,* 28(1):67–70, 1996.

[gLi]   gLite — Lightweight Middleware for Grid Computing. http://glite.web.cern.ch.

[Glo]   The Globus Toolkit. http://www.globus.org/toolkit.

[GPG]   General-Purpose Computation Using Graphics Hardware. http://www.gpgpu. org.

[GPH]   Glasgow Parallel Haskell (GPH). http://www.macs.hw.ac.uk/~dsg/gph.

[HNS95]   Hoon Hong, Andreas Neubacher, and Wolfgang Schreiner. The Design of the SACLIB/PACLIB Kernels. *Journal of Symbolic Computation,* 19:111–132, 1995.

[HP06]   John L. Hennessy and David A. Patterson. *Computer Architecture: A Quantitative Approach.* Academic Press, 4th edition, 2006.

[HPF]   High Performance Fortran (HPF). http://hpff.rice.edu.

[Int]   Int.EU.Grid Project. http://www.interactive-grid.eu/.

[KRD⁺03]   Ujval J. Kapasi, Scott Rixner, William J. Dally, et al. Programmable Stream Processors. *IEEE Computer,* 36(8):54–62, August 2003.

[KTF03]   N. Karonis, B. Toonen, and I. Foster. MPICH-G2: A Grid-Enabled Implementation of the Message Passing Interface. *Journal of Parallel and Distributed Computing (JPDC),* 63(5):551–563, May 2003.

[Lam02]   Leslie Lamport. *Specifying Systems: The TLA+ Language and Tools for Hardware and Software Engineers.* Addison Wesley, 2002.

[LNOM08]   Erik Lindholm, John Nickolls, Stuart Oberman, and John Montrym. NVIDIA Tesla: A Unified Graphics and Computing Architecture. *IEEE Micro,* 28(2):39–55, March–April 2008.

[Loi92]   Hans-Wolfgang Loidl. A Parallelizing Compiler for the Functional Programming
           Language EVE. In *Austrian-Hungarian Workshop on Transputer Applications*,
           pages 1–10, Sopron, Hungary, October 8–10, 1992. Hungarian Academy of Sci-
           encesTechnical Report KFKI-1992-34/M,N.

[LWB08]   A. Langegger, W. Wöß, and M. Blöchl. A Semantic Web Middleware for Virtual
           Data Integration on the Web. In *Proceedings of the European Semantic Web
           Conference 2008, Tenerife*, pages 493–507. Springer, 2008.

[Mit05]   Daniel Mitterdorfer. Grid-Capable Persistance Based on a Metamodel for Med-
           ical Decision Support. Master's thesis, Upper Austria University of Applied
           Sciences, Hagenberg, Austria, July 2005.

[MPIa]   MPI (Message Passing Interface) Forum. http://www.mpi-forum.org.

[MPIb]   MPICH Project. http://www-unix.mcs.anl.gov/mpi/mpich1/.

[MPIc]   MPICH-G2 Project. http://www.hpclab.niu.edu/mpi/.

[MSW00]   Christian Mittermaier, Wolfgang Schreiner, and Franz Winkler. A Parallel
           Symbolic-Numerical Approach to Algebraic Curve Plotting. In Vladimir Gerdt
           and Ernst W. Mayr, editors, *CASC-2000, Third International Workshop on
           Computer Algebra in Scientific Computing*, pages 301–314, Samarkand, Uzbek-
           istan, October 5–9, 2000. Springer, Berlin.

[MW96]   Michael Mnuk and Franz Winkler. CASA - A System for Computer Aided Con-
           structive Algebraic Geometry. In J. Calmet and C. Limongelli, editors, *Interna-
           tional Symposium on the Design and Implementation of Symbolic Computation
           Systems (DISCO'96)*, volume 1128 of *Lecture Notes in Computer Science*, pages
           297–307, Karsruhe, Germany, 1996. Springer.

[NBGS08]   John Nickolls, Ian Buck, Michael Garland, and Kevin Skadron. Scalable Parallel
           Programming with CUDA. *Queue*, 6(2):40–53, March–April 2008.

[NVI08a]   NVIDIA. CUDA CUBLAS Library Documentation, March 2008. http://
           developer.download.nvidia.com/compute/cuda/2_0/docs/CUBLAS_Library_2.0.
           pdf.

[NVI08b]   NVIDIA. CUDA CUFFT Library Documentation, March 2008. http://
           developer.download.nvidia.com/compute/cuda/2_0/docs/CUFFT_Library_2.
           0.pdf.

[NVI08c]   NVIDIA. NVIDIA Tesla Personal Supercomputer, 2008. http://www.nvidia.
           com/object/personal_supercomputing.html.

[OGS]   Open Grid Services Architecture WG (OGSA-WG). http://forge.gridforum.
           org/sf/projects/ogsa-wg.

[OHL+08]   John D. Owens, Mike Houston, David Luebke, Simon Green, John E. Stone,
           and James C. Phillips. GPU Computing. *Proceedings of the IEEE*, 96(5):879–
           899, May 2008.

[OLG+07]   John D. Owens, David Luebke, Naga Govindaraju, Mark Harris, Jens Krüger,
           Aaron E. Lefohn, and Timothy J. Purcell. A Survey of General–Purpose Compu-
           tation on Graphics Hardware. *Computer Graphics Forum*, 26(1):80–113, March
           2007.

[Ope]   The OpenMP API Specification for Parallel Programming. http://openmp.org.

[Owe05]   John Owens. Streaming Architectures and Technology Trends. In Matt Pharr,
           editor, *GPU Gems 2*, chapter 29, pages 457–470. Addison Wesley, 2005.

[P08]   Szilárd Páll. GPU Computing Approach for Parallelizing Support Vector Ma-
           chine Classification. Master's thesis, Johannes Kepler University Linz, July 2008.

[PAS]   Parallel Symbolic Computation (PASCO) '07. http://www.orcca.on.ca/
           conferences/pasco2007/site/index.html.

[Pat]   Parallel Programming Patterns. http://www.cs.uiuc.edu/homes/snir/PPP.

[Pat04]   David A. Patterson. Latency Lags Bandwith. *Communications of the ACM*,
           47(10):71–75, October 2004.

[PVS]   PVS Specification and Verification System. http://pvs.csl.sri.com.

[RJ07]   L. Ruff and T. Jebelean. Functional Based Synthesis of a Systolic Array for GCD Computation. In V. Zsok Z. Horvath, editor, *Implementation and Application of Functional Languages*, volume 4449 of *LNCS*, pages 37–54. Springer, 2007.

[Sch91]   Wolfgang Schreiner. ADAM – An Abstract Dataflow Machine and its Transputer Implementation. In Arndt Bode, editor, *Second European Conference on Distributed Memory Computing (EDMCC2)*, volume 487 of *Lecture Notes in Computer Science*, pages 392–401, Munich, Germany, April 22–24, 1991. Springer.

[Sch94]   Wolfgang Schreiner. Virtual Tasks for the PACLIB Kernel. In *Parallel Processing: CONPAR 94 - VAPP VI Third Joint International Conference on Vector and Parallel Processing*, volume 854 of *Lecture Notes in Computer Science*, pages 533–544, Linz, Austria, September 6–8, 1994. Springer.

[Sch95]   Wolfgang Schreiner. Application of a Para-Functional Language to Problems in Computer Algebra. In A. P. Wim Böhm and John T. Feo, editors, *High Performance Functional Computing*, pages 10–24, Denver, Colorado, April 9–11, 1995. Lawrence Livermore National Laboratory Report CONF-9504126.

[Sch96]   Wolfgang Schreiner. A Para-Functional Programming Interface for a Parallel Computer Algebra Package. *Journal of Symbolic Computation*, 21:593–614, 1996.

[SCI09]   The SCIEnce Project (Symbolic Computation Infrastructure for Europe), 2009. http://www.medicis.polytechnique.fr/science.

[SEE]   SEE-KID. http://www.see-kid.at.

[SFR03]   W. Richard Stevens, Bill Fenner, and Andrew M. Rudoff. Unix Network Programming: The Sockets Networking API, 2003.

[Sh]   Sh High Level Metaprogramming Language. http://libsh.org.

[Sie93]   Kurt Siegl. Parallelizing Algorithms for Symbolic Computation Using ‖MAPLE‖. In *ACM SIGPLAN Symposium on Principles and Practice of Parallel Programming*, pages 179–186, San Diego, CA, May 19–22, 1993. ACM Press.

[Sie94]   Kurt Siegl. A Parallel Factorization Tree Gröbner Basis Algorithm. In Hoon Hong, editor, *International Symposium on Parallel Symbolic Computation (PASCO)*, volume 5 of *Lecture Notes Series in Computing*, pages 356–362, Hagenberg, Austria, September 26–28, 1994. World Scientific.

[SMB03]   Wolfgang Schreiner, Christian Mittermaier, and Karoly Bosa. Distributed Maple: Parallel Computer Algebra in Networked Environments. *Journal of Symbolic Computation*, 35:305–347, 2003.

[SMW00a] Wolfgang Schreiner, Christian Mittermaier, and Franz Winkler. Analyzing Algebraic Curves by Cluster Computing. In Peter Kacsuk and Gabriele Kotsis, editors, *Distributed and Parallel Systems – From Instruction Parallelism to Cluster Computing, DAPSYS'2000, 3rd Austrian-Hungarian Workshop on Distributed and Parallel Systems*, pages 175–184, Balatonfüred, Hungary, September 10–13, 2000. Kluwer, Boston.

[SMW00b] Wolfgang Schreiner, Christian Mittermaier, and Franz Winkler. On Solving a Problem in Algebraic Geometry by Cluster Computing. In Arndt Bode, Thomas Ludwig, Wolfgang Karl, and Roland Wismüller, editors, *6th International Conference on Parallel Computing (Euro-Par 2000)*, volume 1900 of *Lecture Notes in Computer Science*, pages 1196–1200, Munich, Germany, August 29 – September 1, 2000. Springer.

[SMW00c] Wolfgang Schreiner, Christian Mittermaier, and Franz Winkler. Plotting Algebraic Space Curves by Cluster Computing. In X.-S. Gao and D. Wang, editors, *4th Asian Symposium on Computer Mathematics*, pages 49–58, Chiang Mai, Thailand, December 17-21, 2000. World Scientific Publishers, Singapore.

[Spi]   On-the-Fly, LTL Model Checking with Spin. http://spinroot.com.

[SS01]   Bernhard Schölkopf and Alexander J. Smola. *Learning with Kernels: Support Vector Machines, Regularization, Optimization, and Beyond (Adaptive Computation and Machine Learning)*. The MIT Press, 2001.

[Sup]   SC*XY* Conference Series — The International Conference for High Performance Computing, Networking, Storage, and Analysis. http://supercomputing.org.

[Top]   Top 500 Supercomputing Sites. http://www.top500.org.

[UPC]   Berkeley UPC — Unified Parallel C. http://upc.lbl.gov.

[VBR06]   Srikumar Venugopal, Rajkumar Buyya, and Kotagiri Ramamohanarao. A Taxonomy of Data Grids for Distributed Data Sharing, Management, and Processing. *ACM Comput. Surv.*, 38(1):3, 2006.

[Ven03]   Suresh Venkatasubramanian. The Graphics Card as a Streaming Computer. *CoRR*, cs.GR/0310002, 2003.

[Wat08]   Johannes Watzl. Investigations on Improving the SEE-GRID Optimization Algorithm. Diploma thesis, Research Institute for Symbolic Computation (RISC), Johannes Kepler University, Linz, Austria, June 2008.

[WSH99]   Rich Wolski, Neil T. Spring, and Jim Hayes. The Network Weather Service: a Distributed Resource Performance Forecasting Service for Metacomputing. *Future Generation Computer Systems*, 15(5–6):757–768, 1999.

Chapter VIII
Pervasive Computing

Alois Ferscha

Pervasive Computing has developed a vision where the "computer" is no longer associated with the concept of a single device or a network of devices, but rather the entirety of situative services originating in a digital world, which are perceived through the physical world. It is expected that services with explicit user input and output will be replaced by a computing landscape sensing the physical world via a huge variety of sensors, and controlling it via a plethora of actuators. The nature and appearance of computing devices will change to be hidden in the fabric of everyday life, invisibly networked, and omnipresent. Applications and services will have to be greatly based on the notions of context and knowledge, and will have to cope with highly dynamic environments and changing resources. "Context" refers to any information describing the situation of an entity, like a person, a thing or a place. Interaction with such computing landscapes will presumably be more implicit, at the periphery of human attention, rather than explicit, i.e. at the focus of attention.

In this chapter we will address some of the Pervasive Computing research challenges and emerging issues of interaction in Pervasive Computing environments. After computing devices pervade into objects of everyday life, computers will be "invisible", but physical interfaces will be "omnipresent"—hidden in literally "every thing". It will contrast implicit and explicit interaction approaches at the frontiers of pervasive, integrated and thus "hidden" technology. In the outlook, we will give a more systematic prospect of emerging lines of research.

1   What is Pervasive Computing?

Computer science nowadays appears to be challenged (and driven) by techno-logical progress and quantitative growth. Among the technological progress challenges are advances in sub-micron and system-on-a-chip designs, novel communication technologies, microelectromechanical systems, nano and ma-terials sciences. The vast pervasion of global networks over the past years, the growing availability of wireless communication technologies in the wide, local and personal area, and the evolving ubiquitous use of mobile and em-bedded information and communication technologies are examples of chal-lenges posed by quantitative growth. A shift is currently perceived from the "one person with one computer" paradigm, which is based on explicit human computer interaction, towards a ubiquitous and pervasive computing land-scape, in which implicit interaction and cooperation is the primary mode of computer supported activity. This change—popularly referred to as "Perva-sive Computing"—poses serious challenges to the conceptual architectures of computing, and the related engineering disciplines in computer science.

Historically, Pervasive Computing has its roots in ideas first coined by the term Ubiquitous Computing. *"The most profound technologies are those that disappear. They weave themselves into the fabric of everyday life until they are indistinguishable from it"* was Mark Weiser's central statement in his seminal paper in Scientific American in 1991 (Weiser 1991). The conjec-ture that *"we are trying to conceive a new way of thinking about computers in the world, one that takes into account the natural human environment and allows the computers themselves to vanish into the background"* has fer-tilized the embedding of ubiquitous computing technology into a physical environment which responds to people's needs and actions. Most of the ser-vices delivered through such a "technology-rich" environment are adapted to the context, particularly to the person, the time and the place of their use. Along Weiser's vision, it is expected that context-aware services will evolve, enabled by wirelessly ad-hoc networked, mobile, autonomous special purpose computing devices (i.e. *"information appliances"*), providing largely invisi-ble support for tasks performed by users. It is expected that services with explicit user input will be replaced by a computing landscape sensing the physical world via a huge variety of sensors, and controlling it via a manifold of actuators in such a way that it becomes merged with the virtual world. This interaction principle is referred to as *implicit interaction*, since input to such a system does not necessarily need to be given explicitly or attentively. Applications and services will have to be greatly based on the notion of con-text and knowledge, will have to cope with highly dynamic environments and changing resources, and will thus need to evolve towards a more implicit and proactive interaction with users.

A second historical vision impacting the evolution of pervasive computing claimed for an intuitive, unobtrusive and distraction free interaction with technology-rich environments. In an attempt of bringing interaction *"back to the real world"* after an era of keyboard and screen interaction, computers started to be understood as secondary artifacts, embedded and operating in the background, whereas the set of all physical objects present in the environment started to be understood as the primary artifacts, i.e., the *"interface"*. Instead of interacting with digital data via keyboard and screen, physical interaction with digital data, i.e., interaction by manipulating physical artifacts via *"graspable"* or *"tangible"* interfaces, was proposed. Inspired by the early approaches of coupling abstract data entities with everyday physical objects and surfaces like Bishop's Marble Answering Machine, Jeremijenko's Live Wire and Wellner's Digital Desk, tangible interface research has evolved, where physical artifacts are considered as both representations and controls for digital information. A physical object thus represents information, while at the same time acting as a control for directly manipulating that information or underlying associations. With this seamless integration of representation and control into a physical artifact also input and output device fall together. In this view, artifacts can exploit physical affordances suggesting and guiding user actions, while not compromising existing artifact use and habits of the user. Recent examples for *"embodied interaction"*, where input and output are fused into physical object manipulation, include architecture and landscape design and analysis, object shape modeling interfaces using brick like blocks or triangular tiles. Although the first attempts towards realizing the ubiquitous and pervasive computing vision in the early nineties fell short due to the lack of enabling hard- and software technologies, now, about ten years later, new approaches are viable due to technological progress and quantitative growth.

While the first attempts of the pervasive computing vision in the mid nineties fell short due to the non-availability of enabling hard- and software technologies, are now, about fifteen years later, viable. Pervasive computing initiatives and projects have emerged at major universities worldwide, and national and international research funding authorities (IST Future and Emerging Technologies programme of the EU, DARPA, NSF, many national Science Foundations in Asia, etc.) have accelerated the efforts of a rapidly growing, vibrant research community. Preliminarily suffering from a plethora of unspecific terms like "Calm Computing", "Hidden or Invisible Computing", "Ambient Intelligence", "Sentient Computing", "Post-PC Computing", "Universal Computing", "Autonomous Computing", "Everyday Computing", etc., the research field is has now consolidated from its origins in distributed systems and embedded systems, and has started to codify its scientific concerns in technical journals, conferences, workshops and textbooks (e.g. the Journals on Personal and Ubiquitous Computing (Springer Verlag), Pervasive and Mobile Computing (Elsevier), IEEE Pervasive, IEEE Internet Computing, Int. Journal of Pervasive Computing and Communications (Emerald), or the annual conferences PERVASIVE (International Conference on Pervasive Computing), UBICOMP (International Conference on Ubiquitous Computing), MobiHoc (ACM International Symposium on Mobile Ad Hoc Networking and Computing), PerComp (IEEE Conference on Pervasive Computing and Communications), ISWC (International Symposium on Wearable Computing), IWSAC (International Workshop on Smart Appliances and Wearable Computing), MOBIQUITOUS (Conference on Mobile and Ubiquitous Systems), WMCSA (IEEE Workshop on Mobile Computing Systems and Applications), AmI (European Conference on Ambient Intelligence)—and an explosive growth in the number of related conferences in Asia.

This process of "consolidation" is by far not settled today, so that even the term "Pervasive Computing" must be regarded verdant. A clear research focus, however, that has crystallized over the past 12 to 24 months is addressing the very fundamental issue of cooperation in networked embedded systems. While the Institute for Pervasive Computing at the Johannes Kepler University of Linz and RIPE (Research Institute of Pervasive Computing at the Softwarepark Hagenberg) has been working over the past eight years along the paradigm shift of distributed and mobile systems towards (wirelessly) networked embedded systems (under the umbrella "Pervasive Computing"), this epoch of paradigms, architectures, methods, algorithms, protocols and hardware-software systems for "communicating devices" appears to be declining. A new generation of research challenges going way beyond the aspect of mere communication or connectivity (among devices) has evolved, now addressing the principles of "spontaneous, yet meaningful interaction in context"—among not only "devices', but more generally among "digital artifacts". For this reason, and for this report we therefore select just two aspects of this next generation of pervasive computing challenges (and give a more consolidated perspective in the outlook of this chapter):

1. ensembles of (context) Aware Digital Artifacts, and
2. embodied Interaction (i.e., interfaces embedded into artifacts, subject to physical interaction).

2 Ensembles of Digital Artifacts

As we observe an increasing number of real-world objects with embedded computing capabilities like vehicles, tools and appliances, computers, mobile phones and portable music players (we refer to such technology-enriched physical objects as Digital Artifacts, or just artifacts), the issue of their interaction becomes a dominant issue of HCI research. Technology integrated into everyday objects like tools and appliances, and environments like offices, homes and cars, etc. turns these artifacts into entities subject to human-artifact interaction whenever humans use those appliances or become active in those environments. Moreover, built with networked embedded systems technology, they become increasingly interconnected, diverse and heterogeneous entities subject to artifact-artifact interaction, raising the challenge of an operative, and semantically meaningful interplay among each other (see Figure 1).

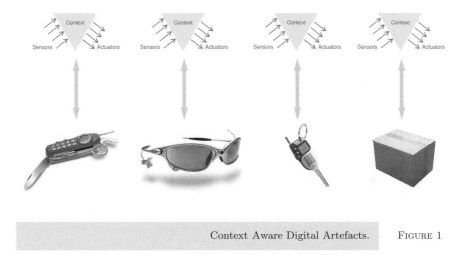

Context Aware Digital Artefacts.   FIGURE 1

One approach to address this challenge is to design and implement systems able to manage themselves in a more or less autonomous way. While self-management stands for the ability of a single artifact to describe itself, to select and use adequate sensors to capture information describing its context, self-organizing stands for the ability of a group of possibly heterogeneous peers to establish a spontaneous network based on interest, purpose or goal, and to negotiating and fulfilling a group goal. A way of implementing artifacts is based on miniaturized stick-on embedded computing systems, integrating sensor, actuator and wireless communication facilities. Such stick-on solutions can then be attached or built into everyday objects, and executing software stacks that implement selforganization in a totally distributed style. Interaction at the application level is invoked based on the analysis of self-describing profile data exchanged among nearby artifacts. Self-management builds up the basis for the self-organization of artifact ensembles, which stands for their ability to establish a spontaneous network based on individual interest, purpose or goal, and to negotiate and fulfill a group goal through cooperation. Research on self-managing and -organizing systems has attracted much interest in the computer science community [HKH+04, IU97, MS01, Zig].

2.1   Context Awareness

Context awareness refers to the ability of the system to recognize and localize objects as well as people and their intentions. The context of an application is understood as "any information that can be used to characterize the situation of an entity", an entity being "a person, place or object that is considered relevant to the interaction between a user and an application, including the user and applications themselves". A key architecture design principle for context-aware applications is to decouple mechanism for collecting or sensing context information and its interpretation, from the provision and exploitation of this information to build and run context-aware applications. To support building context-aware applications, software developers should not be concerned with how, when and where context information is sensed. Sensing context must happen in an application independent way, and context representation must be generic for all possible applications.

The ability to describe itself is an important aspect of an autonomous digital artifact, which allows for expressing all kinds of context information. The use of a self-description is twofold: it provides local applications with an awareness of the artifact's context on the one hand, and it serves as a basis for achieving awareness about other artifacts by exchanging the self-descriptions on the other hand. We agree with the definition of awareness given in [FHR+06a], where it is defined as "an understanding of the activities of others, which provides a context for your own activities". We consider the concept of self-describing artifacts as a promising approach of implementing implicit interaction among autonomous systems, particularly with regard to an open-world assumption (i.e. interacting artifacts do not know each other in advance) where an ad-hoc exchange of self-descriptions upon encountering other artifacts in required in order to get an awareness of their context. We therefore follow the approach of autonomous digital artifacts able to exchange the self-description upon becoming aware of the existence of another artifact in a direct "peer-to-peer" manner. Further interaction can then be parametrized and contextualized considering the provided context information of the interaction counterpart. In [FR07], we have presented a context-aware profile for self-description and its exchange for arbitrary artifacts, and surveyed work regarding self-description and profiles. Examples of the integration and miniaturization of sensor and wireless communication hardware is given in Figure 2.

A second examples of one of our successful digital artifact designs is the SPECTACLES system Figure 3. It represents a modular, autonomous, lightweight, wirelessly communicating wearable display device, that can be integrated into the physical structure of an eyeglasses frame. As an autonomous, wearable display system it is enabled to communicate with its environment wirelessly (technologies like BT and WiFi are integrated), sense different environmental parameters, and display different kinds of media (video, audio, image, text). Besides the output facilities, the computational platform of

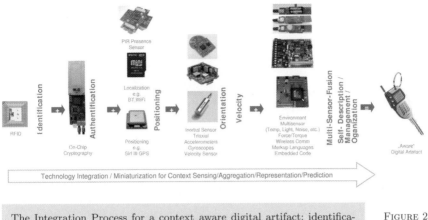

The Integration Process for a context aware digital artifact: identifica-   FIGURE 2
tion, authentication, positioning and tracking technologies are combined
with multi-sensor systems, wireless communication, storage and computational resources, to be invisibly embedded into an everyday object like
a car key, giving an "aware" digital artifact.

SPECTACLES is designed to be flexible enough to support the integration
of input devices like cameras, accelerometers and other sensor units that can
act as a means for natural human-computer-interaction and as a source for
recognizing the context.

Spatial Abstraction 2.2

Clearly, the traditional approach of instructive systems [Wan04] with their
passive, deterministic, context-free and pre-programmed nature appears less
appropriate as an architecture for service ensembles as conglomerates of individual devices. A more *autonomous* system architecture [Hor01] is demanded,
coordinating the activities within service ensembles in a self-organized or goal-
oriented style. Towards such an *autonomous* system quality we identify two
aspects of system properties, the first relating to the individual devices, the
second to spontaneous configurations (or ensembles) of such devices:

1. *self-management*, which stands for the ability of a single device to acquire
   information that can help to understand its situation or *context* [Dey01],
   and to adapt to changing contexts at runtime, and
2. *self-organization*, i.e. the ability of devices to spontaneously (upon service
   requests) join into ad-hoc service ensembles to e.g. negotiate and achieve
   ensemble goals through coordinated actions.

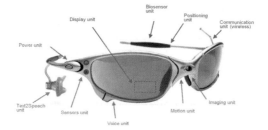

FIGURE 3   SPECTACLES: A wearable computer system comprising a PXA270 XS-
cale CPU on a gumstix verdex motherboard (400MHz 16 MB FLASH,
64 MB RAM), an optics subsystem with display adapter board and micro camera unit (Kopin K230LV AMLCD – 320×240 PixelSymbol), accelerometer and digital compass (ADXL 330 and HMC6352), a global positioning system (USGlobalSat EM-408 SiRF III GPS receiver), wireless
communication units (LAN9117 Ethernet controller, Marvell 88W8385
Modul – 802.11(b) and 802.11(g), BT 2.0) and an autonomous power
management system.

Our focus here is on devices which are equipped with sensors, actuators, as
well as with computing and wireless communication technology to support
ad-hoc networking. Since these devices can have various different kinds of
appearance (like shape, size, mobility, etc.) and digital technology embedding
(e.g. mobile phones, smart appliances, smart rooms, etc.), we refer to them as
"digital artifacts". Common to our notion of a smart artifact is its ability to
collect information from sensor data to understand their context, to represent
and reason about its perception of the environment, to share this perception
with and to collaboratively adjust with other digital artifacts within certain
zones influence, and to autonomously act in order to achieve ensemble goals.
    Both self-management and self-organization have received much research
attention in computer science over the past years [HMG05, JBL+06, KC03,
MMTZ06, SFH+03a]. Particularly have self-organization principles as inspired by nature attracted the attention of computer scientists [HG03, KE01,
MMTZ06, SFH+03a, ZGMT04]. In the respective literature, self-organization
is defined as a process in which *"patterns at the global level of a system
emerge solely from interactions among lower-level components"* [CFS+01],

where pattern refers to structure and organization in both space and time. Self-organization hence is way beyond centralized coordination, and complex collective behavior results from contextual local interactions between components [SFH+03a]. Local interactions in turn are based on individual goals and the perception of the respective environment. The essence of self-organization is that system structure, and thus collective behavior, often appears without explicit trigger or pressure from outside the system, but is inertial to the system and results from interactions within the system. System structure can evolve in time and in space, may maintain stable form or exhibit transient phenomena, or may grow or shrink in size, number or feature.

As digital artifacts are situated in physical space, it is ultimately important to consider their spatial properties and in particular spatial relationships between them. We therefore address spatial abstractions as essential for the self-organization of digital artifact ensembles. Actually, most of the known phenomena of self-organization and -adaptation in nature are phenomena of self-organization in space [MZ05], and [ZM04] identifies the concept of space and the awareness of distributed components of their surrounding to play an important role for mechanisms of self-organization. However, as self-organization is based on (direct or indirect) contextual local interactions between the components of a system, both the inference of high-level contextual information from spatial relationships, as well as standardized means for exchanging spatial information between the components through so-called self-descriptions are issues of research (see [HE03, SFH+03b]). With regard to spatial information about an artifact's environment, challenges we observe are the *maintenance of a spatial model* of the environment as well as the provision of a *spatial programming model* for defining spatially-aware behavior.

Components of a Digital Artifact   2.3

To technology-enriched physical objects we refer to as *digital artifacts*. One way of implementing such artefacts is based on miniaturized computer systems to be attached to or embedded in everyday objects, which integrate *sensors* (for acquiring context information from the environment), *actuators* (for reacting to the environment), *communication facilities* (for communicating with other artifacts and IT-systems), a *runtime system* (for storing and processing sensed data or data received from other artifacts), and provide *external services* to their surroundings (see Figure 4). It is typically a mobile device with a small form factor, constrained processing capabilities and limited energy resources due to battery operation, it is *context-aware* due to its sensors and operates autonomously (i.e. without any centralized control), and it acts according to certain defined goals (which may be achieved cooperatively by interacting with other artifacts).

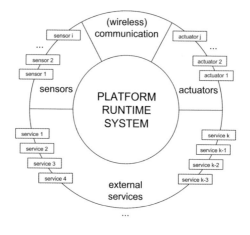

FIGURE 4   Components of a digital artifact.

We are convinced that in an environment with numerous autonomous entities, interaction has to be achieved in a distributed, non-centralized way, and we thus think that *peer-to-peer concepts* are more suitable for the cooperation among artifacts than client-server architectures. In order to support interaction, we suggest using some kind of *self-description* that is exchanged among entities upon coming within communication range. It contains context information that is relevant for the interaction (e.g. physical properties like an artifact's size, weight or color, its spatial contexts like position and direction, or its capabilities in terms of provided services), and is extensible with regard to supporting a variety of application scenarios. However, an artifact need not comprise the full functionality shown in Figure 4, and thus may not be able to interact with other artifacts on its own, but only on behalf of another artifact serving as a "proxy" [FHdSR+07]. The focus of this work is on two particular properties of an artifact, namely *autonomy* and *context-awareness*. As artifacts are by nature distributed throughout physical space, we consider their inherent spatial properties, in particular their position, direction and shape, as well as spatial relationships between them, as valuable context information for a variety of applications, and propose a *model for building spatially-aware applications.*

Self-Description 2.4

The ability to *describe itself* is an important aspect of an autonomous digital artifact, which allows for expressing all kinds of context information. The use of a self-description is twofold: it provides local applications with an awareness of the artifact's context on the one hand, and it serves as a basis for achieving awareness about other artifacts by exchanging the self-descriptions on the other hand. We agree with the definition of *awareness* given in [DB92], where it is defined as "an understanding of the activities of others, which provides a context for your own activities". We consider the concept of self-describing artifacts valuable for *interacting autonomous systems*, particularly with regard to an *open-world assumption* (i.e. interacting artifacts do not know each other in advance) where an ad-hoc exchange of self-descriptions upon encountering other artifacts is required in order to get an awareness of their context. In [FHdSR+07, FHR+08] we propose a *Digital Artifact Service* which is responsible for exchanging the self-description upon becoming aware of the existence of another artifact. Further interaction can then be parametrized and contextualized considering the provided context information of the interaction counterpart.

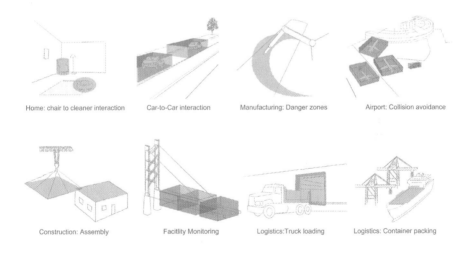

Home: chair to cleaner interaction   Car-to-Car interaction   Manufacturing: Danger zones   Airport: Collision avoidance

Construction: Assembly   Facitlity Monitoring   Logistics:Truck loading   Logistics: Container packing

Zones of Influence of Digital Artifacts and Potential Areas of Application (upper row). Multiple and Dynamic Zones of Influence in Car2Car Scenarios (lower row).   FIGURE 5

2.5 Spatial Awareness

With *spatial awareness* we refer to the knowledge an artifact has about its own and other artifacts' spatial properties (e.g. position), as well as about spatial relations to or between other artifacts (e.g. distance). To spatial properties and relations we refer to as spatial context. Several categories for representing spatial context information can be distinguished:

- *quantitative* (i.e. using numerical values) vs. *qualitative* (i.e. using abstract symbols),
- *absolute* (i.e. with respect to an extrinsic frame of reference) vs. *relative* (i.e. with respect to the spatial context of another artifact),
- *static* (i.e. at a certain point in time) vs. *dynamic* (i.e. the degree of change at a point in time), and
- *point in time* (i.e. a snapshot at a certain time) vs. *time series* (i.e. a trajectory of context values over a sequence of points in time).

Our approach for representing *spatial properties* is the use of so-called *Zones-of-Influence (ZoI)*, which typically contain absolute quantitative static values given at a point in time. They are a means for explicitly defining geographical areas (referred to as *shapes* in the following) of an artifact that are relevant for applications, as well as their positions and directions in space. Moreover, by relating ZoIs of artifacts with respect to certain spatial properties, *spatial relations* among them such as "intersects" and "on the left hand side" can be defined, as well as dynamic relations such as "moving away" or "growing". Besides the representations of spatial properties and relations at certain points in time, time series of spatial contexts can be considered too.

3 Quantitative Space: Zones-of-Influence

In order to deal with space computationally, it has to be represented in a standardized way such that it can be processed by a computer. In this regard, we distinguish two types of space: quantitative space and qualitative space. *Quantitative space* deals with numerical values of spatial characteristics, which are represented with Zones-of-Influence as discussed in this section. The second type is *qualitative space*, which is based on symbolic abstractions (i.e. symbols are used for representation rather than numeric values) of quantitative spatial information (as provided by sensors for example).

The implementation of *space awareness* based on the exploitation of spatial properties (e.g. position) and relations (e.g. distance) among physical objects in the real world, we associate XML-based *self-descriptions* with each and every artifact (or object) subject to a space awareness service. As an example, in our software framework for an autonomous computing platform (Peer-It)

[FHR$^+$08], a descriptive model for the space surrounding an object has been developed. Basically, the ZoI of an object refers to the spatial outreach to which an object can perceive the presence of another object, or be perceived by others. ZoIs, as geometrical descriptions of the vicinity of an object, hence, describe the extent of the subspace within which an object can interact with another object (it is possible to define arbitrary three-dimensional shaped ZoI's). The ZoI concept builds on technological sensors for distance (like microwave, ultrasound or radio based sensors), and orientation (like compasses, accelerometers or gyroscopes) embedded into a digital artifact, to be able to scan its vicinity for other objects. Interaction with another object can be initiated by

- overlapping or intersecting ZoI-geometries or
- by relating position, orientation, size, or any other item of information in the self-description of an object to the self-description of another object.

Digital artifacts hence can become "spatially aware" about each other. They can build up knowledge about where other artifacts are, how far or close they are, and reason about their orientation.

A single artifact can be associated with multiple simultaneous ZoIs, see e.g. multiple ZoIs for a car, e.g. to support

- a car theft application (red),
- a pedestrian safety application (yellow),
- a drive-by-wire application (green), or
- a obstacle avoidance application (purple) in Figure 5.

The spatial properties of an object encoded into its ZoI can either be static (i.e. not changing over time) or dynamic (i.e. dependent on a respective context—see e.g. the Car2Car speed dependent interactions in a drive-by-wire situation in Figure 5, bottom).

The position of a ZoI is referred to as *anchor point*, and its shape and size are specified relative to the anchor point. Applications now that implement space awareness usually make use of the ZoI geometry of an artifact, and its respective anchor point. Basically, when an object artifact the ZoI of another artifact, their self-descriptions are exchanged via wireless communication, and related to each other wrt. orientation and distance of their anchor points. The so generated "spatial information" can then be used to control the behavior of an artifact.

Spatial properties such as *position* and *direction* are usually acquired from corresponding sensors. Every sensor provides readings which are given for two- or three-dimensional space, and with respect to its specific reference system. In the following, common representations for position and direction are presented, and the representation of Zones-of-Influence is explained in detail.

For the property *position*, an indoor location sensor (see [HSK04, HB01, Leo98]) may provide three-dimensional *Cartesian coordinates* relative to a certain point in the building, and a GPS receiver provides *spherical polar coordinates* in a reference frame for the whole earth. A comprehensive overview of coordinate systems can be found in [Dan]. As mentioned already, the focus of this work is on *multiple interacting artifacts* which may use different spatial sensor. In order to recognize relations by comparing their sensor readings, a common coordinate system is required. The most common coordinate system, which is used by GPS, is the World Geodic System WGS84 [IoD]. In this system, points are typically represented as spherical polar coordinates in *longitude, latitude* and *altitude*. However, it is possible to convert these polar into *Cartesian coordinates* using the *earth centered* (i.e. its origin is the center of the earth) and *earth fixed* (i.e. coordinates of a point on the earth's surface do not change). In such a Cartesian *ECEF* system, positional relations between two points on the *surface of the earth* require special treatment; for example, the shortest Euclidean distance between them differs from the actual distance on the surface.

There are also different reference systems for the property *direction* (in literature often referred to as orientation). A common direction system is the *North-East-Down (NED)* system defined by the x-axis pointing to the north, the y-axis pointing to the east and the z-axis heading towards the center of the earth. For the representation of directions, different systems are used, for example *Euler angles* or orientation *Quaternions*. The former is usually used for navigation applications, where a sequence of rotations around the axes is given by the following values: *yaw* (i.e. a rotation around the z-axis in a NED system), *pitch* (i.e. a rotation around the y-axis in a NED system) and *roll* (i.e. a rotation around the x-axis in a NED system). It should be noted that, if *multiple different reference systems* are to be used together, there must be means for either transforming values among them or in a common system.

A precondition for using spatial properties with digital artifacts is to embed them into the artifacts' self descriptions. There are many ways for representing spatial properties like position, direction and shape. A virtually unmanageable huge number of markup languages, partially developed for specific application domains, exists by now. Prominent examples are the Keyhole Markup Language (KML)[1] which is used for describing three-dimensional geospatial data in Google Earth, and the Geography Markup Language (GML)[2] which serves as a modeling language and interchange format for geographic systems. Due to the complexity of these standards, we decided to develop *markup elements* tailored to the description of spatial properties and qualitative relations. However, as the architecture allows to exchange the components which are responsible for parsing the spatial context contained in self-descriptions (see Section 5), it is easily possible to use other means for their representation.

---

[1] http://code.google.com/apis/kml/

[2] http://www.opengeospatial.org/standards/gml

In order to cope with the characteristics of *space-aware digital artifacts* we define a Zones-of-Influence definition to be contained in the top-level structuring element `DADescriptionElement` of an artifact's self-description. The XML description of the respective ZoI element consists of the following items:

Name: Serves as an identification of the zone as well as a semantic identifier for applications. The name must be unique per artifact.

Position: Defines the position of the so-called anchor point of the zone (e.g. using WGS84 ECEF coordinates), defining a reference point for recognizing relations like distance and orientation to other zones. It is typically the value sensed by some position sensor; however, it can also be determined by other static or dynamic contexts. It should be noted that this point need not be the physical position of the artifact nor the center of the zone's shape. In order to be able to compare sensor values from different sensors using different reference systems, the used reference system has to be specified using the XML attribute `refSystem`.

Direction: Defines the direction of the anchor point in space, which determines how the overall zone is oriented in space (e.g. using Euler angles). As for position, the direction can be static or dynamic and the reference system has to be specified using the attribute `refSystem`.

Shapes: Each ZoI consists of one or more shapes defining the spatial extension of the zone. A shape can be a predefined basic shape like a sphere or a cube, or an arbitrary freeform shape. Each shape requires specific parameters describing its characteristics (e.g. width, height and depth for cuboids). The position and direction of a single shape are given relative (and according to the respective reference system) to the anchor point's position and direction of the overall zone (with the elements `Position` and `Direction`) using the XML elements `RelativePosition` and `RelativeDirection`, respectively.

An important aspect of a zone is that its spatial properties (i.e. position, direction and shape) can be dynamic, since the properties of moving artifacts are subjects to change. A ZoI is called dynamic if at least one spatial property depends on a dynamic context as for example determined by a physical sensor. In order to allow for modelling dynamic zones, references to sensor data sources are introduced. It specifies both where the data can be acquired from, and how the values are to be interpreted for their use in an artifact's self-description. A `SensorData` element can provide either a primitive or a complex type (as known from programming languages). The accessor component defined by the attribute accessor is responsible for fetching the corresponding value whenever it is referenced. We have defined an `OSGiSensorDataService` that provides sensor data using an interface with a single method which returns a String containing a potentially complex datatype, which is parsed using the semicolon as delimiter. An example for the usage of this service is depicted in the XML fragment below:

```
<DADescriptionElement type="SensorData" name="Position"
accessor="OSGiSensorDataService">
    <SvcName> at.jku.pervasive.fact.IsenseTracker </SvcName>
    <Param> COM1 </Param>
    <UpdateInterval> 10 </UpdateInterval> <!-- in [Hz] -->
    <Values>  <!-- service provides CSV value -->
        <x type="token" token=";" nrToken="0"/>
        <y type="token" token=";" nrToken="1"/>
        <z type="token" token=";" nrToken="2"/>
    </Values>
</DADescriptionElement>
```

A *dynamic Zone-of-Influence* references such a `SensorData` element, whereas primitive elements are referenced by their name and a prefix @ (e.g. @Position), and complex types are referenced using a "dot notation" (e.g. @Position.x) as the following example shows. Mathematical calculations can be specified using the @Eval definition containing mathematical expressions as parameters.

```
<DADescriptionElement type="ZoI">
    <Name> CurrentRadioRange </Name>
    <Position refSystem="WGS84ECEF">
        <X> @Position.x </X>
        <Y> @Position.y </Y>
        <Z> @Position.z </Z>
    </Position>
    <Shape type="sphere">
        <Radius> @Eval(@SNR/10) </Radius>
    </Shape>
</DADescriptionElement>
```

Aside the quantitative abstractions of space expressed with ZoIs above, there is, however, also need and potential to express and exploit more quantitative expressions of space to control the behavior of digital arefacts. We look into more details of these possibilities in the sequel.

4 Qualitative Space: Spatiotemporal Relations

Qualitative abstractions of space represent spatial information with *abstract symbols* such as "inside", "left", "far away" or "towards" instead of *numeric values* such as "3.52m away". Qualitative space abstractions do have several advantages. First, qualitative models allow for dealing with *coarse and imprecise spatial information*, which is an important property whenever exact sensor information is not available or precise answers are not required [CFH97, HN02, MDF05]. Second, processing quantitative knowledge is more complex and thus computationally more expensive [Fre92], which is of particular relevance for *embedded systems* with constrained resources such as processing power, storage capacity or limited communication bandwidth. Third, and of great importance with regard to *human computer interaction*, is the similarity of qualitative representations to their expression in natural languages [RM04]. Not all inferences need the precision of quantitative methods [For97, FR93]. Often qualitative predicates are sufficient.

A considerable amount of research is dedicated to *qualitative spatial representation and reasoning*, which is concerned with *abstracting* continuous spatial properties and relations of the physical world, and *inferring* knowledge from the respective qualitative representations. Research in this field is driven by the observation that spatial reasoning in our everyday life is mostly driven by qualitative abstractions than a-priori quantitative knowledge, and it has led to an increasing interest in the investigation of spatial concepts from a *cognitive viewpoint* [CH01]. Today, though, qualitative spatial reasoning has mainly been studied in the context of artificial intelligence (e.g. for robot navigation of high-level computer vision) and geographic information systems (GIS). Comprehensive *overviews* of this topic are given in [CH01, Her94, HN02], among others. Detailed discussions on *linguistic and cognitive aspects* can be found in [BF04, CFH97, Her94, Ten05]. The main challenge was to allow machines to represent and reason about space and spatial relations without using quantitative techniques.

In the following subsections, we will describe how different types of relations can be *recognized* by comparing zone descriptions and *represented* in a qualitative way (see Section 4.1), and which high-level contexts can be *inferred* by means of closure and composition operations on the one hand, and logical or temporal combinations of relationships on the other hand (see Section 4.2). Finally, a rule-based approach for inferring relations as well as for *maintaining* and *querying* a repository of relationships is discussed in Section 4.3.

Relationship Recognition and Representation   4.1

The recognition of spatial relationships is based on a *pairwise comparison of zone descriptions*, namely their quantitative spatial data (as provided e.g. by sensors). However, qualitative relations may also be recognized by dedicated sensors such as the ultrasonic peer-to-peer sensor presented in [HKG+05], or using a location tracking system (e.g. [Eka]) which allows to assign symbols to location areas and thus provides some qualitative topological relations. This means that, as soon as an artifact receives the self-description of another one, it compares the absolute quantitative information of zones contained therein (e.g. the shape which is a-priori known, or the position provided by a GPS module) with its own zones and calculates *binary relations* from it. The latter artifact is often referred to as primary object in literature [CH01], the former one—i.e. the artifact which recognized the spatial relation—is referred to as reference object. As we relate zones, we refer to them as *primary zone p* and *reference zone r*, respectively. Note that an artifact can have multiple zones, and zones of a single artifact can also be related with respect to each other.

A *binary relation* in general is defined as an association between two sets. We just consider spatial relations over a single set of zones Z, in which each zone $x \in Z$ is associated with another zone $y \in Z$ to which a spatial relation R exists; in this case, it holds that $(x, y) \in R$. Such a relation is often denoted as $R(x, y)$, and it is read as "x is in relation R to y". Taking for example the distance relation, and assuming that two artifacts a and b are aware of their two-dimensional location from e.g. an indoor tracking system, they could exchange their position information and compute the Euclidean distance among each other—which is a quantitative distance relation between their *physical zones*.

Qualitative spatial reasoning is commonly realized in form of calculi over sets of *jointly exhaustive and pairwise disjoint* spatial relations (i.e. non-overlapping relations covering the whole space, also referred to as *base relations*), which are in turn defined over sets of spatial entities. Thus, in order to represent spatial relations in a qualitative way, it is necessary to decide on a certain kind of *spatial entity* first among which the binary relations are defined. With regard to positional and directional relations, mainly points [Fre92, Mor04] and line segments [AEG94, MRW00] have been used for representing physical objects in space; the representation of extended objects is discussed in [CBGG97, Ege89, RCC92], among others. We decided to use *points* for positional and directional relations between disjoint zones (i.e. each zone is represented by its *anchor point*), and their *extension* for topological relations (i.e. the zones' shapes are related). However, it should be noted that points may no longer be a suitable abstraction for positional and direction relations in the case that two zones are nearby or even overlap; instead, it will be necessary to incorporate the artifacts' extensions in order to recognize meaningful relations (see [Her94]).

Qualitative spatial relations can be classified in two categories, namely static and dynamic ones. First, *qualitative static spatial relations* represent spatial relations between zones at a certain point in time. We distinguish four types which are shown in Figure 6, whereas two zones p (the primary zone) and r (the reference zone) are placed in two-dimensional Euclidean space; however, the relations are defined correspondingly in three dimensions. For *topological* relations, five relations between regions are defined according to the *RCC-5 calculus*; a more detailed qualitative representation distinguishing eight relations is provided by the *RCC-8 calculus* [CBGG97, Ege89]. For *orientation* and *direction* relations, a cone-based qualitative representation which partitions the space in a 360° range in four equally sized sectors is used. In this regard, orientation relations describe where the primary zone is placed relative to the reference zone [CH01, Her94], wherefore the space around the reference zone is partitioned and the relation is denoted by the region in which the primary zone is located. Similarly, directional relations relate the direction of the primary zone (as given by its intrinsic direction axis) with that of the reference zone, wherefore the space around the primary zone is partitioned according to the direction axis of the reference zone and the region in which the direction axis of the primary zone points denotes the directional relation. *Distance* relations partition the space around the reference zone r in circular ranges, where the range of an outer distance relation is bigger than that of an inner one [CFH97, IHM03].

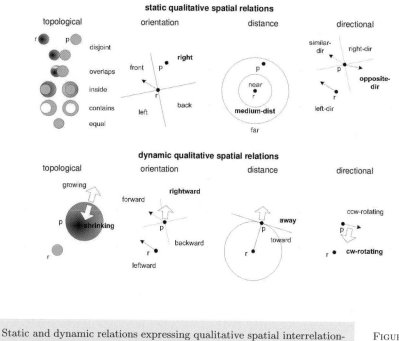

Static and dynamic relations expressing qualitative spatial interrelationship (among digital artifacts in 2-D).   FIGURE 6

Correspondingly, four types of *qualitative dynamic spatial relations* represent how a zone's spatial relation is changing in terms of metric values at a certain point in time. However, such changes need not result in changes of the corresponding static spatial relations; for example, two zones may be "moving away" from each other at a certain point in time, but the static spatial relation "near" may still exist. Dynamic *topological* relations represent a change in the scale of the primary with respect to the reference zone, as for example that it is growing. For dynamic *orientation* relations, the space is partitioned in the same way as for static ones, but around the primary zone; the region in which the thick arrow points denotes the dynamic relation. Dynamic spatial relations can be recognized either by comparing the corresponding spatial relations at least two successive points in time, or by using spatial sensors already providing quantitative relations (see [KKG05]).

There are some important things to consider. First, the presented spatial relations—both their existence and meanings—depend on the *application domain* in which they are used. Our approach to cope with this challenge is that the developed middleware (see Section 5) supports different spatial relations with varying meanings for one or more application domains. This specifically concerns the meaning of the spatial abstractions, namely how the space is partitioned for a certain relation. A related issue is the *granularity* of positional and directional relations, which can be changed by partitioning the space in a bigger number of intervals. Third, for dynamic relations, there must be means for representing the *absence of relative motion*, wherefore four additional relations—"stable-size" (for topology), "stable-orient" (for orientation), "stable-dist" (for distance) and "stable-dir" (for direction)—are introduced.

These relations build up a powerful basis for qualitative spatial reasoning, but can be extended with further relations in order to increase their granularity, cover other types of spatial context or be conform to certain application needs. Once a relation has been recognized at a certain point in time, it is inserted in the *relations repository*.

Another important thing to consider are *frames of reference*, as they influence the *semantics of spatial relations*; common classifications of reference frames can be found in [Fra98, MTBF03, MSER99, Ten05]. A further classification distinguishing three types of reference frames can be found in [AEG94, CFH97, HCF95], where the focus of this work is on the first two of them:

Intrinsic: relations are given by inherent properties of the reference zone (e.g. it fixes the front side of the reference zone r according to its direction axis for orientation relations, or the zone's size interests distance relations)

Extrinsic: relations are determined by external factors (e.g. the North Pole serves as a reference direction for orientation relations, and the earth reference frame's scale defines distances)

Deictic: relations are represented from an external viewpoint

As mention, a self-description may not only contain quantitative descriptions of Zones-of-Influence, but also *qualitative relations between them*. This allows artifacts to exchange relations they are aware of among each other, which is a precondition for inferring relations to artifacts out of communication range. We define the XML element `DADescriptionElement` with the attribute `type = "QualitativeRelation"` for their representation in self-descriptions, as shown in the following example. Both the reference and primary zone are addressed using the schema `<artifact identification>` : `<name of the zone>`, whereas `@local` is used for the artifact which contains this relation in its self-description.

```
<DADescriptioneElement type="QualitativeRelation">
    <Name> front </Name> <!-- unique relation name -->
    <ReferenceZoI> @local:PhyicalBoundaryZoI </ReferenceZoI>
    <PrimaryZoI> 00-00-00-70-05-75-67-1B:PhysicalBoundaryZoI </PrimaryZoI>
</DADescriptionElement>
```

Relationship Inference   4.2

The previous sections described how spatial relations are recognized by comparing zone descriptions, and represented in a qualitative way. In this section, we deal with the issue of how conclusions can be drawn from such qualitative representations of relations. This is subject of the field of qualitative spatial reasoning. A huge number of calculi have been developed so far, which focus on different spatial properties such as orientation and direction, and use different kinds of spatial entities; a state-of-the-art overview of *qualitative spatial and temporal calculi* can be found in [DFWW06, WFDW07].

Our approach is to infer relations from one or more other relations by means of *logical rules* as discussed in Section 4.3, making knowledge explicit which is implicitly available in the relationship repository. The qualitative relations stored in the repository are not only relations recognized by a comparison of ZoIs, but also such which are included in other artifacts' self-descriptions. An inferred relation need not be of the same type like the ones from which it is inferred, as it is the case for operations provided by qualitative spatial calculi; instead, new relations at a higher semantic level can be inferred from relationship combinations.

A precondition for inferring relations is that they are stored in a relationship repository, each one with the following information:

- *name* of the relation (e.g. "left"),
- *type* of the relation (e.g. "orientation"),
- *identification* of the reference and primary zone between the relation exists, and
- *time* interval in which the relation exists.

We distinguish between two types of relationship inference. The first type is based on a *composition of relations* between zones. Compositional reasoning has received much attention in the research community [CH01, Fre92, Her94, Hol07a]. It deals with the following question: "given the relation between two entities x and y, as well as y and z, what is the relation between x and z?" Formally, a composition operation is modeled as follows:

$$R \circ S = \{(x, z) | \exists y \in Z : (x, y) \in R \land (y, z) \in S\},$$

where R and S are qualitative relations and Z is the set of known Zones-of-Influence. The result of a composition operation depends on the meaning of the relation [MDF05], and it is often a compound relation (i.e. a set of alternatively possible base relations). A related technique for inferring qualitative relations from existing ones is the utilization of the relation property *transitivity* [HF07], which correspond to a composition of relations where all three relations—the two composed ones as well as the resulting relation—are the same. Although this approach is universal in the sense that it can be applied to arbitrary relations without the need for considering their meaning, it is quite limited as many relations like distance and intrinsic orientation are not transitive.

The second type is the inference of new high-level relations by a *logical and temporal combination* of existing ones. For the temporal combination, a representation of the dimension time is required. A *discrete time* model with constant time difference Δt between two successive points in time is used therefore, which is motivated by the fact that relations which occur at "nearly" the same point in time—which again depends on the application domain and thus must be adjustable by the application—should have the same discrete point in time. The temporal entities among which relationships can be defined are *time intervals* in the discrete time T. An interval $[s, e]$ is defined by an ordered pair of a start-point s and an end-point e, and it equals a set of successive points in time: $[s, e] = \{t \in T | s \leq t \leq e\}$. We follow the argumentations in [All83] and [For97], that the use of intervals corresponds to our intuitive notion of time. Moreover, as with qualitative spatial relations, this discretization of time allows for *qualitative abstractions of temporal relations* such as "*a* occurred before *b*", which is helpful whenever exact temporal relationships are not of relevance or unavailable. With this definition of intervals, it is also possible to represent points in time as time intervals, where the start- and end-point are equal.

According to [All83], *13 qualitative temporal relations* between intervals can be distinguished at a time, like for example "before", "equals" and "during". As we have proposed in [Hol07b], *time intervals in which certain relations exist* can be temporally related therewith, like for example that $near(y, x)_{[t,t+5\Delta t]}$ *overlaps* with the relation $left(z, x)_{[t+2\Delta t,t+11\Delta t]}$, where x, y and z denote Zones-of-Influence and the subscript intervals represent the discrete time intervals in which the respective relations exist.

4.3   Rule-Based Qualitative Reasoning

We use a declarative, *rule-based approach* for combining relations and *inferring* new ones, as well as for *querying* and *maintaining* the repository of existing relationships. The *JBoss Drools rule-engine* [JBo] is used therefore, which serves as a layer of abstraction between the application programming layer and the low-level relationship recognition which provides information about qualitative spatial relations at certain points in time. Rules can be constructed by a human expert in a natural manner, be it with mappings of rules to natural language sentences (as supported by [JBo]) or by using a graphical user interface that facilitates the process of selecting and combining relations to rules. Rules are constructed by a *human domain expert* and stored in a rule base, and an *inference engine* matches them against facts in the *relations repository*. Rules fire upon changes in the repository, whereas a rule is executed for each combination of facts for which it is fulfilled. A so-called agenda is responsible for resolving conflicts and executing the rules in an appropriate order, as their execution may have an impact on the repository and thus may cause some rules to be removed from the agenda for example. Both rules and facts can be added and removed at runtime.

Rules are defined using *first-order-logic*, and they consist of a *conditional part* as well as a *consequence part* which specifies one or more actions which are executed in the case of fulfilled conditions (see below). The former specifies patterns on relations in the working memory, while the main purpose of the latter is to insert new facts and remove or modify existing ones. An important feature is that inserted facts can be used in the conditions of other rules.

We distinguish three types of rules:

maintenance rules: perform maintenance operations on the repository,
inference rules: infer relationships from existing ones, and
query rules: query the history of relationships.

A relation that is recognized at time t is inserted with the interval $[t, t]$ in the repository. Every time a new relation is inserted, or the time-interval of an existing one changes, all rules are executed by the rule engine. Amongst others, there are two *maintenance rules* for managing the relationships stored in the repository. The first one limits the length of the history, which may cause relations to be removed from the repository or their intervals' starting points to be adapted. The second one *merges relations belonging together*; it therefore checks the repository for pairs of relations with the same name and zone identification, whose intervals are not in an "after" or "before" relation to each other as shown in Figure 6. For each such pair, it replaces the interval of one relation with the union of the two intervals, and removes the other relation from the repository. Merging relations is also necessary for logical *or* and *not* combinations, in contrast to logical *and* combinations where an intersection of the respective intervals is processed.

The second type are the actual *inference rules*, which are used for inferring new relations from existing ones. They can—logically and temporally—combine relations like in the "leaving" example of Section 4.2, and insert a new relation with the respective interval in the repository upon recognition. The following JBoss Drools code fragment shows the rule for the relation "leaving", which is a temporal combination of the spatial relations "near", "medium-dist" and "far". Another rule may then combine the relation "leaving", which is generated by the first rule, with the spatial relation "right" using a logical *and*.

```
rule "leaving"
    when
        Relation(name=="near", $rZ1:rZone, $pZ1:pZone, $i1:interval)
        Relation(name=="medium-dist", rZone==$rZ1, pZone==$pZ1, $i2:interval)
        Relation(name=="far", rZone==$rZ1, pZone==$pZ1, $i3:interval)
        eval($i1.meets($i2) && $i2.meets($i3)) <!-- temporal relations -->
    then
        Relation $r1 = new Relation("leaving", $rZ1, $pZ1,
            $i1.merge($i2.merge($i3))); <!-- outer bounds of intervals -->
        insertLogical($r1, true);
```

The third type of rules are *query rules*. During the application execution, newly recognized relationships are inserted in the repository, and others are removed or their intervals changed. At any time, it is possible to query the repository for certain relationships or combinations of them, where conditions on their names, zone identifications and intervals can be defined. The rule engine we use supports queries with dedicated rules having a conditional part only, and their results can be iterated at application level by referring to the name of the query. However, other ways for spatiotemporal queries are can be found in literature [HKBT05, VL07], whereas SQL-like queries also seem to be a suitable alternative.

5 Middleware for Space Awareness

We propose a *service-oriented architecture* for the implementation of the runtime system of spatially aware digital artifacts. Such a service-oriented design provides exchangeability of components by defined interfaces, and facilitates the reuse of already existing blocks of functionality. Our implementation builds upon the *Equinox OSGi framework*[3]. The basis component of the middleware is the *Digital Artifact Service*, whose central responsibility is the exchange of self-descriptions among artifacts. On top of it, there are services for the maintenance and visualization of received ZoI-descriptions as well as for recognizing and inferring spatial relations among them. An *overview of the architecture*, which consists of six services described in Sections 5.2 and 5.1, can be seen in Figure 7.

---

[3] http://www.eclipse.org/equinox

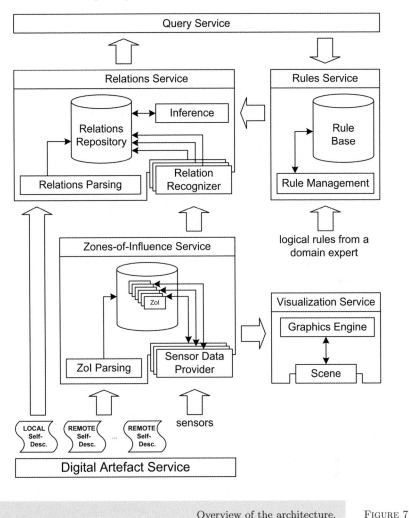

Overview of the architecture.   FIGURE 7

The Digital Artifact Service   5.1

The Digital Artifact Service provides means for *discovering* other artifacts and *exchanging* self-descriptions among them. It builds up an interface for interacting with artifacts that are *within communication range*, and has to provide the following functionality:

- *Notification* about available and no-longer available artifacts as well as about changed self-descriptions.

- *Retrieval* of the self-descriptions of artifacts which have been notified to be available.
- *Management* of self-description elements of the local artifact at runtime (e.g. adding and removing ZoIs).

Due to the use of OSGi, the implementation of a *Digital Artifact Service* that wraps and utilizes existing services can be achieved without modifying existing code. For instance, a Digital Artifact Service can be composed of existing services for the discovery, communication and exchange of self-descriptions as shown in Figure 8. In addition to discovering artifacts and exchanging self-descriptions, it is also possible to utilize *simulation-input* of e.g. the Java-based *J-Sim*[4] simulation environment, which allows for programming artifacts as individual Java components that communicate with others via ports, whereas the composition is done in the Tcl script language.

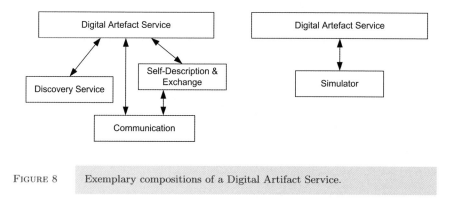

FIGURE 8   Exemplary compositions of a Digital Artifact Service.

For a prototypical implementation of the Digital Artifact Service, we have utilized *UPnP* since it already provides means for discovery of as well as for communication between devices.

5.2 Services for Spatial Relationship Awareness

On top of this Digital Artifact Service, several services for *achieving spatial relationship awareness* have been implemented as shown in Figure 7. A short overview of their functionality and responsibilities is given in the following:

Zones-of-Influence (ZoI) Service: The major responsibility of the *ZoI Service* is to provide an *up-to-date model* of the current spatial situations (i.e. the spatial contexts) of artifacts by maintaining a ZoI object for every zone

---

[4] http://www.j-sim.org

included in the self-descriptions of artifacts that are known to be available. Particularly for *dynamic zones*, namely those for which the spatial properties (e.g. the position, orientation and shape) are determined by sensor values, the *ZoI Service* has to fetch them using the corresponding *Sensor Data Provider*. To maintain such an up-to-date model, the *ZoI Service* registers itself as a listener at the *Digital Artifact Service* and creates new ZoI objects, removes no-longer available ZoIs and adjusts the properties of existing ones according to the availability of ZoI descriptions of reachable artifacts and corresponding changes of them.

Visualization Service: The *Visualization Service* can be used for visualizing ZoI objects currently maintained by the *ZoI Service*. It allows to *plug in different scenes*, in order to parametrize which ZoIs are visualized (e.g. by their position or shape type) and how they are visualized. This service is mainly intended to be used for the visualization of application scenarios and for evaluation purposes.

Relations Service: The *Relations Service* accesses the *ZoI Service* in order to retrieve Java objects of currently maintained zones, and it provides a repository of spatial relations between them. For the recognition of relations, it utilizes *pluggable relation recognizers* which operate on ZoI objects and/or the results of other recognizers. Therefore, a recognizer typically registers itself as a listener of the *ZoI Service* to get notified about changes of zones as well as their spatial properties. With this mechanism, it is possible to use *domain-specific relations* by simply plugging in corresponding recognizers as required. We basically distinguish between *quantitative and qualitative relation recognizers*, whereas qualitative ones typically utilize (the results of) quantitative ones. Recognized relations are inserted in the repository, in order to be used by applications or other recognizers as well as for the inference of further relations with rules provided by the Rules Service (see Section 4.3). The insertion takes place at *discrete points in time* as discussed in Section 4.2, whereas the *time interval*—with that point in time as start- and end-time—is added to the relation object.

Rules Service: The *Rules Service* is an interface to the rules repository containing maintenance-, inference- and query-rules by providing means for removing, modifying and adding them at runtime. Rules are typically stored in rule files, either in XML or in a form specific to the rule engine. While the first one is useful when the generation of rules has to be done programmatically or visually supported using a graphical user interface for example, the latter is the first choice whenever humans have to edit the rules manually. For the chosen rules engine [JBo], a conversion between XML and the engine-specific format is always possible.

Query Service: Finally, the *Query Service* is the actual main interface to the application layer. However, due to the OSGi-based architecture, applications can also access the services underneath. The *Query Service* accesses both the *Rules Service* and the *Relations Service* in order to deploy query rules and get the respective results.

The development process of a spatially aware application is now exemplified for the case of a vibro-tactile notification and directional guidance device, LifeBelt. With LifeBelt we have developed a device intended to act as a notification and guidance system based on sense of vibration. The system addresses the challenge of overseeing and overhearing in situations when there is abundance of visual and auditory stimulations, like in situations of danger or panic. In such scenarios it is important to notify the user with information about a potential threat in an un-obstructive yet demanding manner, so that his attention is not diverted. Intended as a wayfinding guide in emergency evacuation scenarios, LifeBelt generates notifications about distance and orientation to the nearest exit, as shown in Figure 9. The notification is generated via eight embedded tactor elements, lined up in the fabric of a wrist belt and are connected to the belt micro-controller. Selectively vibrating tactors indicate direction, the intensity of vibration represents the respective distance.

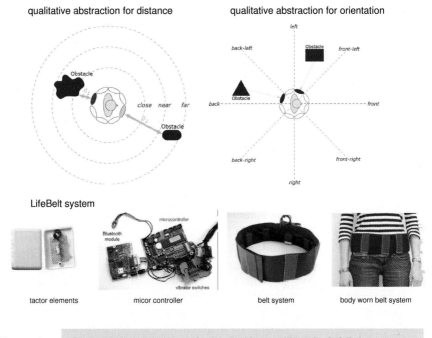

FIGURE 9   Qualitative abstractions of space implemented in the LifeBelt.

The development process involves *(i)* the identification of spatial relations between objects which are relevant for the application, along with their type (e.g. static orientation), the possible values (e.g. front, right, back and left), their semantics (i.e. how the space is partitioned), dimensionality, etc. In a LifeBelt scenario we would identify individuals, obstacles in the scene and the location of exits as artifacts, and relate them to each other spatially. *(ii)*, sec-

ond, the ZoIs needed for recognizing the relations identified in the first step
are modelled for each artifact. As for the individuals, radial zones of influence
could be assumed, whereas the shape of obstacles could be expressed by ZoIs
with congruent geometry. In step *(iii)*, the respective sensors for determining
the spatial properties position, direction and spatial extension are identified
and integrated. Here, positioning and distance sensors (ultrasonic, microwave
scanners, SNR based wireless communication systems etc.) appear appropriate. Sensors and their interfaces are encoded into the self-description of the
respective artifacts. *(iv)*, relation recognizers are implemented according to
the identified relations and ZoIs, so that finally *(v)*, a rule-based modeling
of the application behavior can be coded by mapping spatial relations or
combinations to the triggering of actions. The inferencing of new high-level
relations and the triggering of application-level actions are well supported by
the framework.

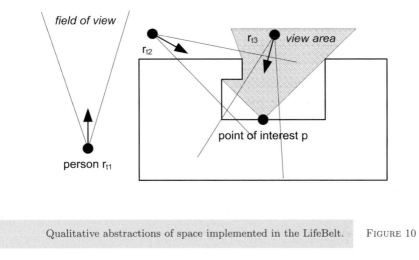

Qualitative abstractions of space implemented in the LifeBelt.   FIGURE 10

Particularly for the explanation of the latter consider a person with a
certain field of view moving towards a point of interest (exit) in Figure 10.
The person is represented by a moving point-shaped ZoI w, and a masonry
with a certain point of interest (emergency exit) which is represented by a
static freeform ZoI p representing the region from which the exit can be seen.
The individual and masonry are equipped with digital artifacts which *autonomously* exchange their self-descriptions upon coming within reach. Two
types of relations are of interest, namely if the masonry's ZoI p (i.e. its anchor point) is in front of the individual's ZoI w, and if p also contains w.
The former is a static orientation (with a $35°$ angle for the relation front in
our example) and the latter a static topological relation. If and only if both
spatial conditions are fulfilled (as it is the case for w at time $t3$ in Figure 10),
the person has presumably looked at the exit. Position and direction of w

are acquired from the location tracking system, whereas ZoI p is fixed (i.e. no sensors are required therefore) as the assumed masonry cannot move.

The following XML fragment shows the representation of ZoI p in the masonry's self-description. In order to be able to compare sensor values from different sensors using *different reference systems*, the used reference system is specified using the XML attribute `refSystem`. Direction and position are acquired from respective Sensor Data Providers, and the shape of the ZoI is represented using a polygon.

```
<DADescriptionElement type="ZoI">
  <Name> Masonry </Name>
  <Position refSystem="WGS84ECEF2D">
    <X> @Position.x </X>
    <Y> @Position.y </Y>
  </Position>
  <Direction refSystem="NEDEuler2D">
    <Yaw> @Direction.yaw </Yaw>
  </Direction>
  <Shape type="Freeform2D">
    <Point x="0.0" y="0.0"/>
    <Point x="-36.0" y="-52.0"/>
    <Point x="-9.0" y="-52.0"/>
    <Point x="-9.0" y="-84.0"/>
    <Point x="-22.0" y="-118.0"/>
    <Point x="108.0" y="-118.0"/>
  </Shape>
</DADescriptionElement>
```

The *rule* is pretty simple. It checks for the concurrent existence of the two relations `front` and `contains` within the *same time interval* (which is checked with the function `isCurrent()`), and inserts a new relation `$r` in the repository whose interval is the intersection of those two relations. The existence of this interval can be queried from the application; in addition, a certain action such as a vibro impulse can be executed in the consequence part of the rule as a feedback for the person.

```
rule "TowardsExit"
  when
    Relation(name=="Orientation",value=="front",
      $p:pZoI,$r:rZoI,$i1:interval)
    Relation(name=="Topology",value=="contains",
      pZoI==$p,rZoI==$r,$i2:interval)
    eval($i1.isCurrent() && $i2.isCurrent())
  then
    /* trigger action at application level, e.g. vibration on LifeBelt */
end
```

6 Embodied Interaction

Extending the notion of a digital artifact, a physical object can represent information while at the same time acts as a control for directly manipulating that information or underlying associations. With this seamless integration of representation and control into a physical artifact also input and output device fall together. Placed meaningfully, such artifacts can exploit physical affordances suggesting and guiding user actions, while not compromising existing artifact use and habits of the user. More recent examples for "embedded interaction", where input and output are fused into physical object manipulation, include architecture and landscape design and analysis, object shape modeling interfaces using brick like blocks or triangular tiles.

Brygg Ullmer and Hiroshi Ishii introduced "Tangible User Interfaces" (TUIs) [IU97] and related them to "Graspable Interfaces" [Fit96], as both involving physical artifacts as *(i)* representations and *(ii)* controls for digital information. A central characteristic of tangible interfaces is the seamless integration of representation and control within physical objects. Manipulating physical controls hence stands for directly manipulating their underlying associations (digital information). Input and Output devices fall together.

According to their definition, TUIs are interfaces that "give physical form to digital information, employing physical artifacts both as representations and controls for computational media". Four characteristics concerning representation and control can be formulated:

- Physical representations are computationally coupled to underlying digital information.
- Physical representations embody mechanisms for interactive control.
- Physical representations are perceptually coupled to actively mediated digital representations. (visual augmentation via projection, sound ...)
- Physical state of tangibles embodies key aspects of the digital state of a system. (TUIs are persistent: turn off the electrical power and there is still something meaningful here that can be interpreted)

In addition to their definition, tangible interfaces rely on a balance between physical and digital representations, and digital representations are needed to mediate dynamic information. There have been many research efforts devoted to tangible user interfaces, but it has proven difficult to create a definition or taxonomy that allows to compare and contrast disparate research efforts, integrate TUIs with conventional interfaces, or suggest design principles for future efforts. Kenneth Fishkin addressed this problem, presenting a taxonomy [Fis04] which uses *(i)* metaphor and *(ii)* embodiment as its two axes of the TUI design space.

Fishkin's taxonomy [Fis04] uses the concepts of embodiment and metaphor to classify TUI's. The rationale behind this is that TUI research has evolved so broadly, that a simple binary definition to decide whether an interface is tangible or not is just not sufficient. The proposed solution is to create a two dimensional taxonomy that allows for a scale of tangibility, weighted along the two axes of embodiment and metaphor. The definition of embodiment is effectively a measure of how close the digital output is to the input, and also to what extent the user thinks that the states of the system are inside the device. The scale is defined as ranging from "Distant" (the output is removed from the input) through "Environmental" (output is around the user) to "Nearby" (the output is near to the input), ending up with "Full" embodiment (the output device is the input device).

Key characteristics of TUIs can hence be summarized as follows:

- By coupling digital information to everyday physical objects and environments, physical representations link to digital information both computationally and perceptually.
- The interfaces are a physical objects rather than abstract entities.
- The physical representation incorporates the control process.
- A tangible interface is persistent and carries the physical state.
- TUIs exploit physical affordances and suggest (and guide) action.
- TUIs distributed interaction across a range of objects.
- Interaction is thus spread throughout a space.
- Interaction beyond enforced sequentiality (avoids WIMP *"click-after-click"* interaction).

As TUIs are devices that give physical form to digital information, employing physical artifacts as representations and controls of the computational data, the physical/digital mapping raises an important design challenge. To be successful, the spatial mapping relationship of the TUI's objects and their use must be *(i)* spatially congruent (e.g. computer-mouse, mapped to cursor movement), or at least well learned (e.g. QWERTY-keyboard mapped to alphabet), *(ii)* must unify the input space and the output space (as opposed to the decoupling of action space and perception space when working with WIMP metaphor interfaces), and *(iii)* should enable trial-and-error activity, since in a natural world, human activity is goal-related and exploratory (the costs of speculative exploration of the task space should be low). Good TUIs offer a one-to-one coupling of physical and digital objects, and each digital object has a representation in the real world.

TUIs [UI00] or *"embodied interaction"* [Dou01] [FMH98] aim at interacting with applications executing in the background by providing natural and intuitive means of interaction, claiming to be more efficient and powerful compared with traditional interaction methods in specific cases. TUIs couple physical representations (e.g. spatially manipulable physical artifacts) with digital representation (e.g. graphics and sounds), making bits directly manipulable and perceptible by people [Fit96] [HKSSR97]. In general, tangible interfaces are related to the use of physical artifacts as representations and controls for digital information [UI00]. An important class of applications is defined by the use of TUIs a remote control. Typically, home electronic devices are equipped and controlled with button based remote controls. Attempting to complement the traditional remote control (RC) by a TUI raises a variety of design issues (see the previous section of this report), but also carries potential to improve on the usability of remote controlled device. Since the process of designing TUIs in many cases starts with a problem analysis of an existing interface paradigm or technology (to be improved or replaced), we take the analysis of an RC as an example of reference. Take as TUI development challenge a universal RC, able to control not only one, but a whole set of devices or appliances. With such an RC, in order to control a certain device, the user needs to perform the following general sequence of operations:

1. Device discovery. Device discovery is necessary when the user is situated in a non-familiar space, as the user must know whether the desired device is available or not.
2. Device selection. The user must select, out of a whole ensemble of devices, which one to control. Alternatively, a certain device can be implicitly selected based on the user's context (i.e. information about his situation), preferences, and history.
3. Connection. The RC must be able to connect to the selected device. Thus, a communication channel must be established between the control artifact and the device such that control commands from the artifact can be relayed to the device.
4. Device control. A device offers a set of services, and the user manipulates the control artifact to set up input values for the services. To do so, the following steps are performed:

   • Service discovery. If the user is not already familiar with the device, then it needs to know the services provided by the device. In many cases, the user already knows which service it needs to control. For example, it is common knowledge that air conditioning devices have at least two services: temperature and fan power.
   • Service selection. The user chooses one of the services to control. For example, in the air conditioner case, it chooses temperature.
   • Control parameter steering. The user sets up values for the controllable parameters of the service.

Considerable research and development efforts have been devoted to step 1 ([Upn], [Wal99], [Blu], [VZT05]), step 2 ([VKP+03], [Nfc], [KLH02]), step 3 ([Blu], [Wif], [Zig]), and step 4a ([VKP+03], [Blu]). As for steps 4b and 4c, a combined approach for controlling the environment with physical artifacts, which allows to browse and select both devices and their services as well as to steer the input values of a selected service with simple gestures, is described in [HRLF06]. The study explains how only two types of gestural manipulations with a cube-shaped TUI that can be intuitively associated to service selection and to steering, respectively: Flip and Turn. In general, the geometry of objects suggests manipulation affordances in a TUI. The geometry of a physical object defines a number of stable mechanical equilibria of the object placed on a planar horizontal surface. A flip-gesture now moves the object from one stable equilibrium to another, by changing the object's orientation wrt. the surface. Thus, a flip-manipulation triggers a change of the selected service. A box can hence be used to select from up to six services. A turn-gesture is a rotation of an object along a defined axis. This can be used to steer the parameter value of the selected service. Both gestures are geometric rotations of objects, which can be traced by integrated accelerometers and gyroscopes. Flipping and turning hence reveals to be a universal approach to implement a RC TUI.

As for the more general case of RC TUIs, considerable research efforts have targeted the realization of a "universal interaction device". One approach are mobile computing platforms (usually PDAs or smartphones) that can be used for interacting with multiple services. Examples are the "Universal Information Appliance" [ELM+99], the "Universal Interactor" [HKSSR97], or the "Personal Universal Controller" in [KS03]. The main issues are discovery of devices and services [VKP+03] and composition of user interfaces [PLF+01], [KS03]. Discovery is supported by service oriented frameworks, communication protocols and standards such as UPnP [Upn], Jini [Wal99], Bluetooth [Blu] and URC [VZT05]. Proposed approaches for device selection include browsing, pointing and touching [VKP+03], [Nfc], or automatic selection based on context clues and user history [KLH02]. Connection is supported by wireless technologies such as Bluetooth, Zigbee [Zig], and WiFi [Wif]. In general, the universality of the control device means the ability to control multiple services, with as little a priori information as possible about the services. Such a handheld control device suffers from some of the shortcomings of today's remote controls: the device is complicated and therefore hard to use, it offers non-intuitive control means, it requires to be available at all times. Furthermore, more than a single TUI could be used to control the same service. The redundancy of physical objects in the user's environment together with a dynamic mapping of objects and movements to services and parameters can ensure that a control object is always handy for any device that the user decides to control. Tangible User Interface (TUI) research has studied the capabilities of physical objects as rich input devices. Specific movements of objects were considered for control. Tilting user interfaces [Rek96] use the tilt of a portable device as input for the device. In [FRHR05], various artifacts and associated gestures are used for device control. Some publications present TUIs where multiple faces are associated to different functions and flipping is used to select a function. In [Fit96], flipbricks are described as part of graspable user interfaces. Different commands, such as "cut", "copy", "paste", are associated to each face of a flipbrick, and one of them can be activated by flipping the brick. The ToolStone device described in [RS00] uses also the rotation of the device, in addition to flipping, to further increase the selectable functionalities. With respect to the involved gestures, flipping and turning have turned out to be manipulations TUIs that can be generically mapped to abstract control actions. An approach for using physical objects for home device control is reported in [KS03], where everyday objects and an augmented table are employed for configuring and using interfaces to applications. More recently, Bennet and O'Modhrian proposed the term "Enactive Interfaces" as a classification of interfaces that allow the expression and transmission of "enactive knowledge". I refers to enactive knowledge (as opposed to symbolic or iconic knowledge) as a form of knowledge that is stored in bodily sensori-motor responses. Similar ideas have been articulated in phenomenology (Daseins-Theorie), claiming that we "know" things well only if we engage with them. Enactive knowledge can hence be built up by direct engagement with the things in our environment. Assuming those things representing the input interfaces to computer systems, then an enactive interface can be understood as a particularly direct means of communication between humans and computers. It is argued that *"Enactive interfaces are desirable because they allow the user to utilize their pre-conceived knowledge of interacting with the world when using the interface."*

Enactive interfaces (EIs) build on the theory for Enactive Instruments, which has developed criteria for embodied interaction, i.e. the embodiment of services in physical artifacts. These are:

- Embodied activity is situated. The agent is situated in an environment.
- Embodied activity is timely. Real-world activity requires real-time constraints.
- Embodied activity is multimodal. Concurrent use of multiple sensory modalities with the possibility of cross coupling between the modalities.
- Embodied activity is engaging. The agent is required by the system and is actively engaged with it.
- The sense of embodiment is an emergent phenomenon. It may and will change over time.

TUI's differ from EI's in two main aspects: timeliness and engagement. Bennet and O'Modhrian consider them as not simple binary states, but continua both *(i)* from nonengaging through to fully engaging and *(ii)* from non-timely through to very timely. They build a two dimensional design space along the two axis 'engagement' and 'timeliness', within which it is possible to place any TUI, with the result that it will be possible to plot how "enactive" a TUI is: *"The utility of this graph is that designers of TUI's can gauge the enactive potential of the system they are designing, and modify their design so as to achieve the desired position within the tangible-enactive space."*

Grasping Digital Information 6.1

The idea of understanding the touching and grasping of things as an act of computer input goes back to George Fitzmaurice, who in his PhD thesis on "Graspable UIs" attempted for a first definition: *A Graspable UI design provides users concurrent access to multiple, specialized input devices which can serve as dedicated physical interface widgets, affording physical manipulation and spatial arrangements. Hence input control can be "space-multiplexed". That is, different devices can be attached to different functions, each independently (but possibly simultaneously) accessible. This, then affords the capability to take advantage of the shape, size and position of the physical controller to increase functionality and decrease complexity. It also means that the potential persistence of attachment of a device to a function can be increased. By using physical objects, we not only allow users to employ a larger expressive range of gestures and grasping behaviors but also to leverage off of a user's innate spatial reasoning skills and everyday knowledge of object manipulations. These physical artifacts are essentially "graspable functions"—input devices which can be tightly coupled or 'attached' to virtual objects for manipulation, or for expressing actions. These artifacts need to have spatially-aware computational devices."*

Human gesticulation as a modality of human-machine interaction has been widely studied in the field of Human-Computer Interaction. With the upcoming Pervasive and Ubiquitous Computing research field, the explicit interaction with computers with mouse, keyboard and screen in the WIMP metaphor has given way to a more implicit interaction involving all human senses. As an important part of this tendency, gestures and movements of the human body represent a natural and intuitive way to interact with physical objects in the environment. Thus, manipulation of objects can be regarded as a means of intuitive interaction with the digital world. This paradigm underlies the research on Tangible User Interfaces (TUIs) or *"Embodied Interaction"*. It aims at facilitating "remote control" applications by providing natural and intuitive means of interaction, which are often more efficient and powerful compared with traditional interaction methods. TUIs couple physical representations (e.g. spatially manipulable physical artifacts) with digital representation (e.g. graphics and sounds), making bits directly manipulable and perceptible by people. In general, tangible interfaces are related to the use of physical artifacts as representations and controls for digital information. We witness the advent of applications, appliances and machinery that are richer and richer in information technology, providing large palettes of services to end users. This richness brings up many challenges to the user interface designer, which must face the task of offering the user simple, natural, and intuitive interfaces to systems and services.

Interaction with digital information based on physical *"things"* that we touch or grasp, shake or toss, flip or turn, can be understood as "remote controls" in an abstract sense. Input commands can be expressed via the delivery of a certain gesture, exposed to a certain artifact. To develop an example of a graspable or tangible interface, we consider the challenge of designing concepts of remote media controls, like a TV remote control.

The number and usability of remote controls for home entertainment systems like TV sets, set-top boxes, satellite receivers and home entertainment centers has reached overstraining complexity: about eight to ten remote controls with about sixty to eighty push-buttons each are typical for a home

entertainment system setting today. To be able to harness the ever growing remote control interaction complexity, we propose physical shortcuts to
express the most frequently used control commands.

Contemporary remote controls for home entertainment systems, such as
television sets, sound systems and set-top boxes, are designed according to
a one button per function paradigm. Function overload of modern entertainment systems hence makes button based remote controls a rather confusing
user interface. While some of the buttons are not used at all and some are
used occasionally, there are usually a few functions that are used frequently:
hopping channels/stations (TV or radio), controlling the volume and switching on/off. Recent television platforms like IPTV set-top boxes, additionally
provide a graphical user interface in order to navigate through a hierarchical
menu structure, demanding even more buttons or yet another remote control.

Power Grip

Precision Grip

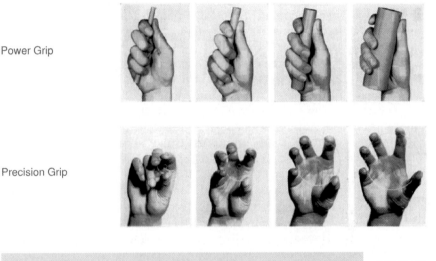

The kinematics and capabilities of the human hand when grasping and   FIGURE 11
holding physical objects: power grip (above) and precision grip (below).
From: J. R. Napier: "The Prehensile Movement of the Human Hand",
The Journal of Bone and Joint Surgery, 38-B (4), pp 902–913, London,
1956.

Inspired by the observed inadequacy of the button-based remote control
designs with respect to frequently invoked control commands, alternative
control designs are recommended. As one such alternative, in some of our
work we have proposed physical shortcuts, allowing to issue control commands with gestures natural to the human hand. These physical shortcuts
are implemented as gestures for tangible artifacts, requiring a convincing affordance and a simple but sufficiently versatile gesture set. Operating tradi-

tional remote controls follows a certain pattern, illustrated with the example of watching TV:

- grabbing the remote control to switch on the TV,
- pushing some buttons while watching TV,
- putting away the remote control when done.

Analyzing this informal interaction protocol reveals that the human hand already undertakes a lot of actions prior to the intended launching of a command, like grasping, holding or turning it to a faceup position. These hand gestures, are already expressing intent for a command launch, which could already be used to invoke the command itself. This observation and the design motivation of making command invocation easier and quicker, encourages the use of tangible artifacts that can be manipulated using one's hands and that support a "grab-to-switch-on" functionality. An important essential in the design process for a tangible remote control is the functioning of the human hand when it comes to grip and control: a human hand can fundamentally execute two different kinds of grip: a power grip and a precision grip (see Figure 11).

TUIs to serve as media remote controls have some coverage in the HCI literature. While tangible objects such as augmented toys incorporate both form and function and therefore clarify the interaction style [HL07], it is apparently harder to design tangible artifacts for abstract tasks such as controlling a media center. In [ClDJG02], for instance, so called "navigational blocks" (wooden cubes containing a micro-processor and labeled with a unique ID) are proposed to be flipped to one of their six sides in order to query information about certain elements in a virtual gallery. In [SG07] a commercial mobile phone is enhanced with near field communication capabilities and an accelerometer in order to control a personal computer using simple gestures. A cylindrical tangible user interface with embedded displays and sensors, TUISTER, is presented in [BGK04]: upper and lower half of the cylinder can be twisted against each other, enabling interaction with respect to the absolute space orientation in order to infer which one of the two halfs was twisted (to differentiate between fine grained and coarse browsing in hierarchical structures). [FHR06b] gives an example on how to control a PC's media player using a tangible artifact incorporating accelerometers, magnetometers and gyroscopes, with respect to a pairing mechanism (the artifact allowed to sequentially control more than one actuator using RFID tags). A tangible media control system is also presented in [PAW07], allowing to control objects (such as a cube that can be flipped to each of its sides) augmented with RFID tags and a tracking system to control e.g. a software midi synthesizer. [BSKH05] shows the results towards remote control in a living room through tangible user interfaces. One of the projects, Flip'n'Twist, uses a cube and a dial for media control by flipping the cube to its different sides and turning the dial. Each side of the cube sets the media control system in a distinct state (such as play, seek and volume control) and lets the user utilize the dial for fine grained operations. [SG07] classifies 13 different computational toys that can be considered tangible user interfaces. The five cube shaped artifacts allow various interaction styles, such as stacking, shaking, turning, flipping and touching, regarding adjacency, sequence and network topology of multiple devices if applicable. Cube shaped TUIs have been proposed, comprising accelerometers and a proximity sensor is presented that can determine which side is facing up, whether one of three predefined gestures was performed and if the side facing up has changed (transition). The cube presented in this report can distinguish more then these states and transitions as it incorporates an additional gyroscope in order to track rotations around the vertical axis. To keep power consumption low, the gyroscope is powered only when it is needed. Accelerometer technology can at the same time be used to distinguish which side of a cube shaped tangible user interface was facing up. Cubes that comprise a display on each side and a speaker have been proposed, addressing applications such as quizzes, a math/vocabulary trainer and a letter matching game. Observations of our previous prototypes for media control using a cube (amongst others, see Figure 12) as the tangible artifact [FR07], we have realized that a system relying on a cube that can be flipped to its sides to distinguish among different modes of operation requires the user

- to be very skilled in the usage of the cube
- or to have a look at the cube each time interaction occurs in order to find out where to flip it, if the cube has corresponding annotations.

It is easy to get confused and to lose track of the current state, and hence to act appropriate in the respective state. Additionally, it is hard to find a certain side of the cube if it is currently facing down or away from the user. By turning or flipping the cube to find the corresponding side, unintentional interaction could occur, leading to disaffection and desperation. Thus it appears useful to use other gestures for cube interaction than flipping. That way, the cube has a base orientation with the button facing up and the label being readable by the user. The possible gestures include tilting the cube to the front/back/left/right, pressing the button and turning the cube around the z-axis (the one heading upwards "through" the button). Each gesture leads back to the base orientation thus providing the user a known situation to start from. In [BGK04] an accelerometer based gesture control for a design environment is presented that allows users to map arbitrary gestures to certain functions (personalization). Besides controlling a VCR by supporting commands such as on, off, play, stop, forward and many more the gesture control system is also suited to navigate in a 3D design software. A respective user study shows that different users use different gestures for a certain command—for instance at least 20 gestures were mapped to the VCR record task by the test persons. While personalization is an important issue, a fixed set of gestures is a wise choice for simplicity's sake: users can execute the

tasks they want to accomplish (controlling a TV set) instead of personalizing
their tangible user interface.

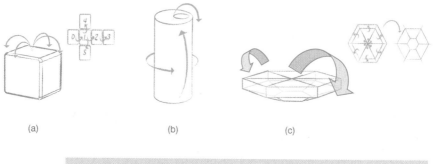

(a)   (b)   (c)

FIGURE 12   The possible alphabets based on gestures expressed with TUIs are related
to their geometrical shape: (a) cube, (b) can, (c) hexagon.

As now for the design of a TUI based media remote control, simplicity
should be the guiding element of the process. Aside the analysis of the kinematics of the human hand (Figure 11), also the observation of well trained
human hand gestures can deliver important information on how to design the
artifact. Taking for example the hand gestures people are expressing with artifacts of their daily life, e.g. a soft drink can or a cigarette box, it is easy
to see, how form determines handling (Figure 13). It is well known, that,
for example in a coffeehouse situation, people tend to grasp available objects
and play with them in predictable styles: while the can is being turned and
rolled, the box is rather flipped, turned, rotated, tossed, or swapped along
its main axes. We can assume, that this playful handling of objects comes
naturally, and hence has high potential for tangible remote controls, since
movements and hand gestures do not have to be trained, but are already well
conditioned.

Above the "experienced" handling of objects, suggesting to design TUIs
by mapping well learned hand gestures to command alphabets, also the shape
and form of the artifact can lead to intuitive acceptance, or uninspired mis-
designs. Efficient mapping of gestures to commands, i.e. the design of gesture
alphabets is already rooted in the basic form of the TUI. Figure 12 (a) shows
an equilateral cube with rounded edges and corners. The cube can be flipped
to every face as discrete motion and turned about every axis as continuous
motion. Figure 12 (b) depicts a cylindric shape like a can which can be continuously rotated about the x- and z-axis. It is also possible to flip it over
the horizontal edge as a discrete movement. The hexagon, as illustrated in
Figure 12 (c), has an arched bottom with six faces. The user topples the
interface by tipping it on the top as discrete move limited to six states. A
rotation about the z-axis is possible, but the edgy form forces a gradual ro-

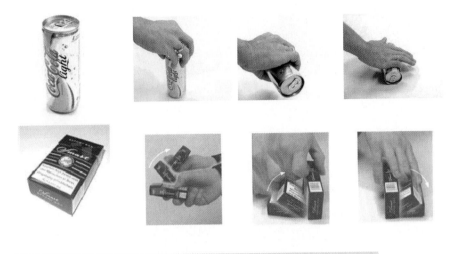

FIGURE 13

Hand gestures that "come naturally": everyday objects based on their shape, size, geometry and weight "invite" for playful handling.

tation and not a continuous one. Empirical user testing with the cube, the can and the hexagon reveals that the cube is the best shape if a combination of discrete (flip) and continuous (turn) gestural expressions are desired.

Besides form, also the overall appearance of a TUI has critical impact onto its "intuitive" use. The "affordance" [Nor99] of an object, i.e. its ability to express just those action possibilities an actor can perform with that object (or in other words: the ability of an object or product to use it in the right way) can significantly contribute to an easy use design. Figure 14 shows different designs of TUIs with obviously different affordances. Experiments for example involving adults and children with the objects in Figure 14 demonstrated which shapes are suggestive for which gestures: The cube has a pleasant size for a hand and encourages the user to grab, flip and rotate it. Moreover, people tend to press their fingertips into the holes at the cube's edges. The two red knobs animate the user to turn it and drag it over flat surface, like a table or board. The two knobs distinguish only in the way they were touched: knob (b) is preferably touched and moved with forefinger and thumb, while knob (d) is picked with the whole hand. The green cuboid "invites" to touch or finger press the cavity on its top side, to rotate it around vertical edges or flip it alongside faces.

Having in mind a tangible remote control that is supplementary to a vendor provided remote control control, with the aim to quickly invoke the most frequently demanded commands, an analysis of a minimum meaningful set of commands suggests to focus on changing volume, switching the channel or navigating the menu, switching ON and OFF and bring the system to

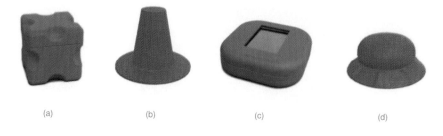

(a)   (b)   (c)   (d)

FIGURE 14   TUI designs with different "affordance", i.e. the ability to express by its
form how it should be properly used.

its origin state. These functions can be mapped to gestures which can be
expressed by the cube TUI (Figure 15 (a)): Flipping up and down, turning
left and right, shaking and resting (Figure 15). As additional function and
orientation support the cube is equipped with a button to switch between
the set-up mode and the operation mode of the set-top box. Operating mode
functions are volume and channel change which are activated by pressing the
mode button. To change the volume the user has to rotate the cube hori-
zontally. A clockwise rotation increases the volume, an anticlockwise reduces
it. Switching the channel is caused by flipping the cube up and down. These
gestures are also used in the set-up mode without pressing the button to
navigate through the menu. To set the TV set in standby mode, the cube
must be placed into the cradle. A fast shaking of the cube from left to right
sight and back navigates back to into the home state.

The cube platform itself is based on an AT-Mega168 micro-controller, with
additional electronics involving 3 axis acceleration sensors and a gyroscope,
together with IEEE 802.15.4 wireless communication components. A finite
state machine based software architecture is deployed for artifact based hand
gesture recognition, which are converted into standardized IR remote control
commands (Figure 16).

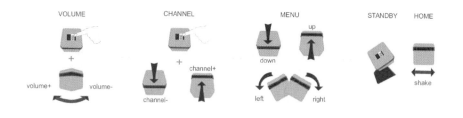

FIGURE 15   Mapping of command alphabets to TUI hand gestures.

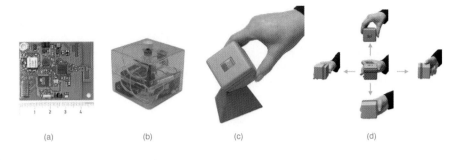

(a)   (b)   (c)   (d)

The cube TUI prototype: Built upon the Atmel AT-Mega168 CPU and   FIGURE 16
equipped with accelerometer, gyroscope, push-button and IEEE 802.15.4
wirelss communication electronics (a), the hardware board together with
power supply is embedded into the cube cabinet (b). The cube cradle (c)
serves as a "switch off/switch on" interface (c), while gestures expressed
with the cube in hand are interpreted and converted into standardized
remote control commands.

Outlook 7

At the Johannes Kepler University of Linz (JKU), since the year 2000 the
Institut für Pervasive Computing (IPC) has developed its own "Pervasive
Computing Research Agenda", based on its core competencies in architecture
and software for networked embedded systems (see Figure 17).

Settling around middleware solutions and service architectures, the research lines of focus strive "awareness", as the means for semantic interactions, "intelligence", as the technological backing for systems able to perceive,
learn, plan and act, "natural interfaces", as a search for a confluence among
man and machines and their mutual interplay, and "appliances", as the physical appearance of an "ambient intelligence". Translating the findings in the
focused research lines into industrial applications, ultimately implement a
pipeline of innovations from research to industry in a compelling way.

IPC and RIPE has its stranding in the international scientific community. It is frequently asked for consultancies for the EU, and hosts international conferences and events in the field, like PERVASIVE 2004, the worlds
most renowned scientific conference in Pervasive Computing, or ISWC'09,
the leading conference in Wearable Computing. IPC/RIPE are engaged in
a number of (international) research projects with industrial partners and
in competitive funding programs like EU FP6, FP7 and national programs
like FIT-IT. In the recent FP7 project PANORAMA, for example, it is re-

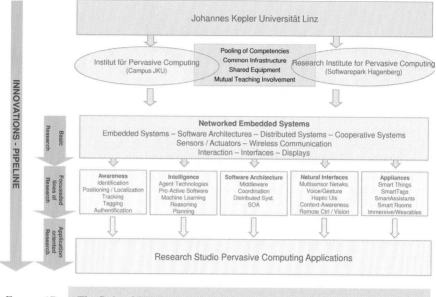

FIGURE 17   The Role of RIPE in the Pervasive Computing Research Agenda at the
University of Linz.

sponsible for the WP Research Agenda. Some of the recent involvements
in projects are InterLink (funded by IST FET), BEYOND THE HORIZON
(funded by IST FET), CRUISE NoE – Creating Ubiquitos Intelligent Sensing
Environments (IST FP6), BISANTE, EU/IST, Broadband Integrated Satellite Network Traffic Evaluation, or SPECTACLES (Autonomous Wearable
Display Systems) in cooperation with Silhouette International. Application
oriented research, for which IPC/RIPE seeks the Research Studio platform,
is manifested in successful cooperation projects like INSTAR (Information
and Navigation Systems Through Augmented Reality) (Siemens AG, Munich, CT-SE-1), Peer-to-Peer Coordination (Siemens AG, Munich, CT-SE-
2), Context Framework for Mobile User Applications (Siemens AG, Munich,
CT-SE-2), WebWall, Communication via Public Community Displays, Connect Austria, or VRIO, Virtual Reality I/O, with GUP JKU, IBM Upper
Austria, to name a few.

IPC/RIPE is already successfully engaged in the Research Studio "Pervasive Computing Applications" (PCA) inside the Research Studios division of
the Austrian Research Centers GmbH – ARC from 2005 to 2008, now part of
the Research Studios Austria Forschungsgesellschaft mbH. PCA actively com-
mits to and shapes the change of information and communication technologies
(ICT) by a focused research agenda. The availability and fast experimental
turn-around time of cutting edge research infrastructure makes the studio a
very attractive partner for near-industrial research. PCA supports three re-

search areas: Context and Sensors (e.g. a Wireless Motion Tracking board), Smart Appliances and Environments (e.g. Virtual Machines for Embedded Environments) and Intuitive Interfaces (e.g. Tangible Remote Controls). In 2007, the Telekom Austria presented the Telekom Austria Cube, a design study for the navigation within IPTV portals of the near future—a prominent example for the capabilities of the studio concerning custom electronic design (integration of multiple sensor data and processing with wireless communication technology) and miniaturization. PCA is currently involved in the FIT-IT research program SPECTACLES, developing space constrained electronics for a wearable display, or DISPLAYS, developing architectures for interactive display landscapes, amongst others.

In the consulting work for the European Commission (DG Information Society and Media) IPC/RIPE when preparing for the Research Programme of FET in FP7, and while heading the TC "Pervasive Computing and Communications" (2005–2007), we created the term "Networked Societies of Artifacts", to refer to the research agenda raised by the evolution of technology-rich artifacts (devices, services, objects of everyday use, appliances, etc.) cooperatively attempting goals with society-like behavior. Such self-managed "digital artifacts", going beyond their capability to localize and recognize other artifacts, are attempting to spontaneously form "goal tribes", i.e. configure ensembles of possibly complementing competencies, to act in a sensitive, proactive, and responsive, but most of all cooperative and coordinated way. Understanding such networked societies of artifacts implemented as pervasive computing systems (embedded, miniaturized, sensor-rich, actuator-enabled, wirelessly communicating, context-aware and adaptive to context, self-configuring, self-managing and self-organizing, remembering and learning, etc.), but enhanced with societal principles of behavior (cooperation, coordination), leads to Pervasive Cooperative Systems.

Evidently, such systems raise the need for radically new (formal) models, architectures, operational principles, methods and algorithms, software and hardware systems for social, cooperative system behavior, cooperative management and cooperative organization (on top of "self-management" and "self-organization"), cooperative goal-orientedness, cooperative sensing, cooperative learning, cooperative memorizing, cooperative reasoning and retrieval, cooperative service delivery, to name a few. It appears worthwhile to look into those research challenges with "cooperation" being the (induced!) principle of system design, rather than a concept or feature, implemented in hard-/software. In our contribution in very recent EU FP7 research proposals we have already expressed aspects of related research issues. In the EASE (Eternally Adaptive Service Ecosystems) project proposal the principle of cooperation is manifested in a system framework for the decentralized deployment and execution of long-lived, highly-adaptive and context-aware services—taking inspiration on cooperation from natural ecosystems. The project will investigate and experiment with the modelling and deployment of services as "cooperative" individuals in an ecosystems of other services. In the SOCIONICAL project (FP7 FET)—which has just started—, by looking at three types of interactions and cooperation among individual entities "in the small",

1. among humans,
2. among humans and digital artifacts, and
3. among digital artifacts themselves,

we will ask for (and make attempts to predict) the effects and consequences of massive, seemingly unpredictable occurrences and mutual causal inter-relationships among such local interactions and cooperation on the global properties of the system as a whole ("in the large"). In the (FP7 FET)—also just launched—project OPPORTUNITY (Activity and Context Recognition with Opportunistic Sensor Configurations) we have raised the issue of coop-erative sensing, i.e. the spontaneous, goal-oriented, cooperative configuration of sensor ensembles to opportunistically collect data about the user and his environment in a scalable way. Even at the level of applications, in the DIS-PLAYS project, the principle of cooperation will be addressed with a software architecture that configures fragmented, dispersed or tiled display hardware (like e.g. screens), to "cooperatively" deliver complex multimedia content to the user in a situated, context controlled way.

Based on our previous contributions in the field of Pervasive Computing, ranging from cooperative embedded sensor-actuator systems (e.g. P2P Co-ordination Framework, DigitalAura), autonomous systems (e.g. Cooperative Digital Artifacts, Peer-It), identity management (e.g. 2D Barcode, RFID, ZigBee, BT or WiFi based solutions), software architectures for context and activity recognition and prediction (e.g. Context Framework), and "uncon-ventional user interfaces", like tangible interaction (TA Cube, SpaceSwitch, VibraBelt, SmartCase, etc.), implicit interaction (PowerSaver, Smart Living, SensorChair, Driver Identification, etc.) or display systems (e.g. SPECAT-CLES, WebWall, SmartShopwindow, SmartMovieposter, Ambient Facades, AR Car Navigation, Digital Graffiti, etc.), we will consider to address *(i)* Co-operative Computing Frameworks and Architectures, *(ii)* Principles of Co-operative Management and Cooperative Organization of Networked Embed-ded Systems as well as *(iii)* Strategic Application Domains (like e.g. Energy Efficiency, Green-IT, Smart Material, Wearable Computing or Cooperative Displays Systems).

Acknowledgements

This survey of Pervasive Computing research activities reflects the work of many ambitious and gifted people, currently or formerly engaged in the IPC and RIPE research institutes. The work on spatially aware digital arti-facts was mostly done by Clemens Holzmann (qualitative spatial relations) and Manfred Hechinger (middleware), and was well supported by the whole FACT project team. The work on embodied interaction was mostly done by Stefan Resmerita (Gestural Interaction) and Simon Vogl (TA Cube). I gratefully acknowledge the work, contribution and support by my partners, co-investigators and co-workers—they all deserve the credits for the foundational findings behind this write-up: P. Aumayr, P. Baumgartner, W. Beer, V. Christian, B. Emsenhuber, H. Dobler, J. Doppler, M. dos Santos Rocha, M. Franz, St. Gusenbauer, M. Hechinger, D. Hochreiter, G. Holl, C. Holzmann, E. Kashofer, M. Keller, C. Klein, M. Lenger, M. Leitner, P. Lukowicz, M. Matscheko, R. Mayrhofer, L. Mehrmann, J. Mitic, W. Narzt, R. Oberhauser, T. Obermüller, St. Oppl, G. Pomberger, St. Resmerita, A. Riener, H. Schmitzberger, M. Steinbauer, P. Thon, S. Vogl, B. Wally, D. Zachhuber, A. Zeidler and K. Zia.

References

[AEG94]   Alia I. Abdelmoty and B.A. El-Geresy. An intersection-based formalism for representing orientation relations in a geographic database. In 2nd ACM Workshop on Advances In Geographic Information Systems, Workshop at CIKM 1995, Gaitherburg, MD, USA, December 1-2, 1994, pages 44–51. ACM Press, December 1994.

[All83]   James F. Allen. Maintaining knowledge about temporal intervals. Communications of the ACM, 26(11):832–843, 1983.

[BF04]   John A. Bateman and Scott Farrar. Towards a generic foundation for spatial ontology. In 3rd International Conference on Formal Ontology in Information Systems, FOIS 2004, Torino, Italy, November 4-6, 2004, pages 237–248, Amsterdam, 2004. IOS Press.

[BGK04]   A Butz, M Groß, and A Krüger. Tuister: a tangible ui for hierarchical structures. In in Proceedings of PI03: Workshop on Real World User Interfaces, held at Mobile HCI 2003, pages 223–225. ACM Press, 2004.

[Blu]   The bluetooth specification. http://www.bluetooth.org.

[BSKH05]   Andreas Butz, Michael Schmitz, Antonio Krüger, and Harald Hullmann. Tangible uis for media control: probes into the design space. In CHI '05: CHI '05 extended abstracts on Human factors in computing systems, pages 957–971, New York, NY, USA, 2005. ACM.

[CBGG97]   Anthony G. Cohn, Brandon Bennett, John Gooday, and Nicholas M. Gotts. Representing and reasoning with qualitative spatial relations about regions. In Spatial and Temporal Reasoning, pages 97–134. Kluwer Academic Publishers, 1997.

[CFH97]   Eliseo Clementini, Paolino Di Felice, and Daniel Hernández. Qualitative representation of positional information. Artificial Intelligence, 95(2):317–356, 1997.

[CFS+01]   Scott Camazine, Nigel R. Franks, James Sneyd, Eric Bonabeau, Jean-Louis Deneubourg, and Guy Theraula. Self-Organization in Biological Systems. Princeton University Press, Princeton, NJ, USA, 2001.

[CH01]   Anthony G. Cohn and Shyamanta M. Hazarika. Qualitative spatial representation and reasoning: An overview. Fundamenta Informaticae, 46(1-2):1–29, 2001.

[ClDJG02]   Ken Camarata, Ehen Yi luen Do, Brian R Johnson, and Mark D Gross. Navigational blocks: navigating information space with tangible media. In *In Proceedings of the 7th international conference on Intelligent user interfaces*, pages 31–38. ACM Press, 2002.

[Dan]   Peter H. Dana. Coordinate systems overview. http://www.colorado.edu/ geography/gcraft/notes/coordsys/coordsys.html, last visited on December 12th, 2007.

[DB92]   Paul Dourish and Victoria Bellotti. Awareness and coordination in shared workspaces. In *Proceedings of the ACM Conference on Computer-Supported Cooperative Work, CSCW'92, Toronto, USA, November 1-4, 1992*, The Power of Simple Shared Workspaces, pages 107–114, 1992.

[Dey01]   Anind Dey. Understanding and using context. *Personal and Ubiquitous Computing*, 5(1):4–7, 2001.

[DFWW06]   Frank Dylla, Lutz Frommberger, Jan O. Wallgrün, and Diedrich Wolter. SparQ: A toolbox for qualitative spatial representation and reasoning. In *Qualitative Constraint Calculi: Application and Integration, Workshop at KI 2006, Bremen, Germany, June 14, 2006*, pages 79–90, 2006.

[Dou01]   Dourish, Paul. *Where the Action Is: The Foundations of Embodied Interaction*. MIT Press, 2001.

[Ege89]   Max J. Egenhofer. A formal definition of binary topological relationships. In *FODO*, volume 367 of *LNCS*, pages 457–472. Springer, 1989.

[Eka]   Ekahau Inc. Positioning engine. http://www.ekahau.com, last visited on December 12th, 2007.

[ELM+99]   K. F. Eustice, T. J. Lehman, A. Morales, M. C. Munson, S. Edlund, and M. Guillen. A universal information appliance. *IBM Systems Journal*, 38(4):575–601, 1999.

[FHdSR+07]   Alois Ferscha, Manfred Hechinger, Marcos dos Santos Rocha, Rene Mayrhofer, Andreas Zeidler, Andreas Riener, and Marquart Franz. Building flexible manufacturing systems based on peer-its. *EURASIP Journal on Embedded Systems*, October 2007.

[FHR+06a]   Alois Ferscha, Manfred Hechinger, Andreas Riener, Heinrich Schmitzberger, Marquart Franz, Marcos dos Santos Rocha, and Andreas Zeidler. Context-aware profiles. In *Proceedings of the 2nd International Conference on Autonomic and Autonomous Systems (ICAS 2006)*, page 48, Los Alamitos, CA, USA, April 2006. IEEE CS Press.

[FHR06b]   Alois Ferscha, Clemens Holzmann, and Stefan Resmerita. The key knob. In *Proceedings of the 26th IEEE International Conference on Distributed Computing Systems Workshops (ICDCSW'06)*, page 62, Los Alamitos, CA, USA, July 2006. IEEE CS Press.

[FHR+08]   Alois Ferscha, Manfred Hechinger, Andreas Riener, Marcos dos Santos Rocha, Andreas Zeidler, Marquart Franz, and Rene Mayrhofer. Peer-it: Stick-on solutions for networks of things. *Pervasive and Mobile Computing Journal*, 4(3):448–479, June 2008.

[Fis04]   Kenneth P. Fishkin. A taxonomy for and analysis of tangible interfaces. *Personal and Ubiquitous Computing*, 8(5):347–358, 2004.

[Fit96]   George W. Fitzmaurice. *Graspable User Interfaces*. PhD thesis, Computer Science Dept., Univ. of Toronto, 1996.

[FMH98]   Kenneth P. Fishkin, Thomas P. Moran, and Beverly L. Harrison. Embodied user interfaces: Towards invisible user interfaces. In Stéphane Chatty and Prasun Dewan, editors, *EHCI*, volume 150 of *IFIP Conference Proceedings*, pages 1–18. Kluwer, 1998.

[For97]   Kenneth D. Forbus. Qualitative reasoning. In *The Computer Science and Engineering Handbook*, pages 715–733. 1997.

[FR93]   C. Freksa and R. Röhrig. Dimensions of qualitative spatial reasoning. In N. Piera Carreté and M. G. Singh, editors, 3rd *IMACS Workshop on Qualitative Reasoning and Decision Technologies, QUARDET 1993, Catalunya, Spain, June 16-18, 1993*, pages 483–492, 1993.

[FR07]   A. Ferscha and S. Resmerita. Gestural interaction in the pervasive computing landscape. 2007.

[Fra98]   Andrew U. Frank. Formal models for cognition - taxonomy of spatial location description and frames of reference. In *Spatial Cognition, An Interdisciplinary Approach to Representing and Processing Spatial Knowledge*, volume 1404 of *LNCS*, pages 293–312. Springer, 1998.

[Fre92]   Christian Freksa. Using orientation information for qualitative spatial reasoning. In *International Conference GIS - From Space to Territory: Theories and Methods of Spatio-Temporal Reasoning, Pisa, Italy, September 21-23, 1992*, volume 639 of *LNCS*, pages 162–178. Springer, 1992.

[FRHR05] Alois Ferscha, Stefan Resmerita, Clemens Holzmann, and Martin Reichör. Orientation sensing for gesture-based interaction with smart artifacts. *Journal of Computer Communications*, 28(13):1552–1563, August 2005.

[HB01]   J. Hightower and G. Borriello. A survey and taxonomy of location systems for ubiquitous computing. Technical report, Seattle, WA, USA, August 2001. Extended paper from Computer, 34(8) p57-66, August 2001.

[HCF95]   Daniel Hernández, Eliseo Clementini, and Paolino Di Felice. Qualitative distances. In *Spatial Information Theory: A Theoretical Basis for GIS, International Conference COSIT 1995, Semmering, Austria, September 21-23, 1995*, volume 988 of *LNCS*, pages 45–57. Springer, 1995.

[HE03]   David Hales and Bruce Edmonds. Evolving social rationality for MAS using "tags". In 2nd *International Joint Conference on Autonomous Agents and Multiagent Systems, AAMAS 2003, Melbourne, Australia, July 14-18, 2003*, pages 497–503, New York, NY, USA, 2003. ACM Press.

[Her94]   Daniel Hernández. *Qualitative Representation of Spatial Knowledge*, volume 804 of *LNCS*. Springer, 1994.

[HF07]   Clemens Holzmann and Alois Ferscha. Towards collective spatial awareness using binary relations. In 3rd *International Conference on Autonomic and Autonomous Systems, ICAS 2007, Athens, Greece, June 19-25, 2007*, page 36. IEEE CS Press, 2007.

[HG03]   Francis Heylighen and Carlos Gershenson. The meaning of self-organization in computing. *IEEE Intelligent Systems*, 18(4):72–75, 2003.

[HKBT05] Marios Hadjieleftheriou, George Kollios, Petko Bakalov, and Vassilis J. Tsotras. Complex spatio-temporal pattern queries. In 31st *International Conference on Very Large Data Bases, VLDB, Trondheim, Norway, August 30 - September 2, 2005*, pages 877–888. ACM, 2005.

[HKG+05] Mike Hazas, Christian Kray, Hans-Werner Gellersen, Henoc Agbota, Gerd Kortuem, and Albert Krohn. A relative positioning system for co-located mobile devices. In 3rd *International Conference on Mobile Systems, Applications, and Services, MobiSys 2005, Seattle, Washington, USA, June 6-8, 2005*, pages 177–190. ACM, 2005.

[HKH+04] David Holstius, John Kembel, Amy Hurst, Wan, Peng-Hui, and Jodi Forlizzi. Infotropism: living and robotic plants as interactive displays. In *Proceedings of DIS'04: Designing Interactive Systems: Processes, Practices, Methods, & Techniques*, Museums and public displays, pages 215–221, 2004.

[HKSSR97] Todd D. Hodes, Randy H. Katz, Edouard Servan-Schreiber, and Lawrence A. Rowe. Composable ad-hoc mobile services for universal interaction. In *MOBICOM*, pages 1–12, 1997.

[HL07]   Steve Hinske and Matthias Lampe. Semantic mapping of augmented toys between the physical and virtual world. In *Workshop on Tangible User Interfaces in Context and Theory at CHI 2007*, 2007.

[HMG05]   Klaus Herrmann, Gero Muhl, and Kurt Geihs. Self-management: The solution
           to complexity or just another problem? *IEEE Distributed Systems Online*,
           6(1), 2005.

[HN02]   Jerry R. Hobbs and Srini Narayanan. Spatial representation and reasoning.
           In *Encyclopedia of Cognitive Science*. MacMillan, London, UK, 2002.

[Hol07a]   Clemens Holzmann. Inferring and distributing spatial context. In 2nd Eu-
           *ropean Conference on Smart Sensing and Context, EuroSSC 2007, Kendal,
           England, October 23-25, 2007*, volume 4793 of *LNCS*, pages 77–92. Springer,
           2007.

[Hol07b]   Clemens Holzmann. Rule-based reasoning about qualitative spatiotemporal
           relations. In 5th *International Workshop on Middleware for Pervasive and
           Ad-Hoc Computing, MPAC 2007, Newport Beach, CA, USA, November 26-
           30, 2007*, pages 49–54. ACM Press, 2007.

[Hor01]   Paul Horn. Autonomic computing: Ibm's perspective on the state of informa-
           tion technology. Technical report, International Business Machines Corpora-
           tion (IBM), New Orchard Road, Armonk, NY 10504, USA, October 2001.

[HRLF06]   Clemens Holzmann, Stefan Resmerita, Michael H. Leitner, and Alois Ferscha.
           A paradigm for orientation-based universal remote control. In *Proceedings
           of the 3rd International Workshop on the Tangible Space Initiative (TSI
           2006), in conjunction with Pervasive 2006*, pages 425–432, Dublin, Ireland,
           May 2006.

[HSK04]   Mike Hazas, James Scott, and John Krumm. Location-aware computing
           comes of age. *IEEE Computer*, 37(3):95–97, 2004.

[IHM03]   Amar Isli, Volker Haarslev, and Ralf Möller. Combining cardinal direction
           relations and relative orientation relations in qualitative spatial reasoning.
           CoRR, cs.AI/0307048, 2003.

[IoD]   National Imagery and Mapping Agency: Department of Defense. World
           geodetic system 1984, its definition and relationships with local geodetic
           systems, third edition, national geospatial-intelligence agency. http://earth-
           info.nga.mil/GandG/publications/tr8350.2/ wgs84fin.pdf, last visited on De-
           cember 12th, 2007.

[IU97]   Hiroshi Ishii and Brygg Ullmer. Tangible bits: Towards seamless interfaces
           between people, bits and atoms. In *Proceedings of ACM CHI 97 Conference
           on Human Factors in Computing Systems*, volume 1 of *PAPERS: Beyond
           the Desktop*, pages 234–241, 1997.

[JBL+06]   Márk Jelasity, Özalp Babaoglu, Robert Laddaga, Radhika Nagpal, Franco
           Zambonelli, Emin Gün Sirer, Hakima Chaouchi, and Mikhail I. Smirnov.
           Interdisciplinary research: Roles for self-organization. *IEEE Intelligent Sys-
           tems*, 21(2):50–58, 2006.

[JBo]   JBoss.org. Drools 4.0 rules engine. http://labs.jboss.com, 2007.

[KC03]   Jeffrey O. Kephart and David M. Chess. The vision of autonomic computing.
           IEEE Computer, 36(1):41–50, 2003.

[KE01]   James Kennedy and Russell C. Eberhart. *Swarm Intelligence*. The Mor-
           gan Kaufmann Series in Evolutionary Computation. Morgan Kaufmann, San
           Francisco, CA, USA, March 2001.

[KKG05]   Gerd Kortuem, Christian Kray, and Hans Gellersen. Sensing and visualizing
           spatial relations of mobile devices. In 18th *annual ACM Symposium on User
           Interface Software and Technology, UIST 2005, Seattle, WA, USA*, pages
           93–102, New York, NY, USA, 2005. ACM Press.

[KLH02]   Khomkrit Kaowthumrong, John Lebsack, and Richard Han. Automated se-
           lection of the active device in interactive multi-device smart spaces. In *In
           Workshop at UbiComp'02: Supporting Spontaneous Interaction in Ubiquitous
           Computing Settings*, 2002.

[KS03]   Christian Kray and Martin Strohbach. Gesture-based interface reconfigura-
            tion. In *Workshop "AI in mobile systems" (AIMS 2003) at Ubicomp'03*,
            2003.

[Leo98]   Ulf Leonhardt. *Supporting Location-Awareness in Open Distributed Systems*.
            PhD thesis, Department of Computing, Imperial College, London, UK, may
            1998.

[MDF05]   Reinhard Moratz, Frank Dylla, and Lutz Frommberger. A relative orientation
            algebra with adjustable granularity. In *Workshop on Agents in Real-Time
            and Dynamic Environments at IJCAI 2005, Edinburgh, Scotland*, 2005.

[MMTZ06]   Marco Mamei, Ronaldo Menezes, Robert Tolksdorf, and Franco Zambonelli.
            Case studies for self-organization in computer science. *Journal of Systems
            Architecture*, 2006. in press.

[Mor04]   Reinhard Moratz. Qualitative spatial reasoning about oriented points. Tech-
            nical Report SFB/TR 8 Report No. 003-10/2004, University of Bremen, Bre-
            men, Germany, October 2004.

[MRW00]   Reinhard Moratz, Jochen Renz, and Diedrich Wolter. Qualitative spatial rea-
            soning about line segments. In Werner Horn, editor, 14th *European Confer-
            ence on Artificial Intelligence, ECAI 2000, Berlin, Germany, August 20-25,
            2000*, pages 234–238. IOS Press, 2000.

[MS01]   Todd Miller and John Stasko. The infocanvas: information conveyance
            through personalized, expressive art. In *Proceedings of ACM CHI 2001
            Conference on Human Factors in Computing Systems*, volume 2 of *Short
            talks: expressing emotion through art, music, and technology (expressing
            emotions)*, pages 305–306, 2001.

[MSER99]   Alexandra Musto, Klaus Stein, Andreas Eisenkolb, and Thomas Röfer. Quali-
            tative and quantitative representations of locomotion and their application in
            robot navigation. In Thomas Dean, editor, *IJCAI*, pages 1067–1073. Morgan
            Kaufmann, 1999.

[MTBF03]   Reinhard Moratz, Thora Tenbrink, John A. Bateman, and Kerstin Fischer.
            Spatial knowledge representation for human-robot interaction. In *Spatial
            Cognition III, Routes and Navigation, Human Memory and Learning, Spatial
            Representation and Spatial Learning*, volume 2685 of *LNCS*, pages 263–286.
            Springer, 2003.

[MZ05]   Marco Mamei and Franco Zambonelli. Spatial computing: the TOTA ap-
            proach. In Özalp Babaoglu, Márk Jelasity, Alberto Montresor, Christof Fet-
            zer, Stefano Leonardi, Aad P. A. van Moorsel, and Maarten van Steen, editors,
            Self-star Properties in Complex Information Systems, volume 3460 of *LNCS*,
            pages 307–324. Springer, 2005.

[Nfc]   The near field communication forum. http://www.nfc-forum.org.

[Nor99]   Donald A. Norman. Affordance, conventions, and design. *Interactions*,
            6(3):38–43, 1999.

[PAW07]   Trevor Pering, Yaw Anokwa, and Roy Want. Gesture connect: facilitating
            tangible interaction with a flick of the wrist. In Brygg Ullmer and Albrecht
            Schmidt, editors, *Proceedings of the 1st International Conference on Tangible
            and Embedded Interaction 2007, Baton Rouge, Louisiana, USA*, pages 259–
            262. ACM, 2007.

[PLF+01]   Shankar Ponnekanti, Brian Lee, Armando Fox, Pat Hanrahan, and Terry
            Winograd. ICrafter: A service framework for ubiquitous computing environ-
            ments. In Gregory D. Abowd, Barry Brumitt, and Steven A. Shafer, editors,
            Ubicomp, volume 2201 of *Lecture Notes in Computer Science*, pages 56–75.
            Springer, 2001.

[RCC92]   David A. Randell, Zhan Cui, and Anthony G. Cohn. A spatial logic based
            on regions and connection. In Bernhard Nebel, Charles Rich, and William
            Swartout, editors, 3rd *International Conference on Principles of Knowledge*

Representation and Reasoning, KR 1992, Cambridge, Massachusetts, USA, October 25-29, 1992, pages 165–176. Morgan Kaufmann, 1992.

[Rek96]   Jun Rekimoto. Tilting operations for small screen interfaces. In *Proceedings of the ACM Symposium on User Interface Software and Technology*, Papers: Interaction Techniques (TechNote), pages 167–168, 1996.

[RM04]   Jochen Renz and Debasis Mitra. Qualitative direction calculi with arbitrary granularity. In 8th *Pacific Rim International Conference on Artificial Intelligence, PRICAI 2004, Auckland, New Zealand, August 9-13, 2004*, volume 3157 of *LNCS*, pages 65–74. Springer, 2004.

[RS00]   Jun Rekimoto and Eduardo Sciammarella. Toolstone: Effective use of the physical manipulation vocabularies of input devices. In *Proceedings of the ACM Symposium on User Interface Software and Technology*, Sensing User Activity, pages 109–117, 2000.

[SFH+03a]   Giovanna Di Marzo Serugendo, Noria Foukia, Salima Hassas, Anthony Karageorgos, Soraya Kouadri Mostéfaoui, Omer F. Rana, Mihaela Ulieru, Paul Valckenaers, and Chris van Aart. Self-organisation: Paradigms and applications. In *Engineering Self-Organising Systems*, volume 2977 of *LNCS*, pages 1–19. Springer, 2003.

[SFH+03b]   Giovanna Di Marzo Serugendo, Noria Foukia, Salima Hassas, Anthony Karageorgos, Soraya Kouadri Mostéfaoui, Omer F. Rana, Mihaela Ulieru, Paul Valckenaers, and Chris van Aart. Self-organisation: Paradigms and applications. In 1st *International Workshop on Engineering Self-Organising Applications, ESOA 2003, Workshop at AAMAS 2003, Melbourne, Australia, July 15, 2003*, volume 2977 of *LNCS*, pages 1–19. Springer, 2003.

[SG07]   Eric Schweikardt and Mark D. Gross. A brief survey of distributed computational toys. In Tak-Wai Chan, Ana Paiva, David Williamson Shaffer, Kinshuk, and Jie-Chi Yang, editors, *DIGITEL*, pages 57–64. IEEE Computer Society, 2007.

[Ten05]   Thora Tenbrink. Semantics and application of spatial dimensional terms in english and german. Technical Report SFB/TR 8 Report No. 004-03/2005, University of Bremen, Bremen, Germany, March 2005.

[UI00]   Brygg Ullmer and Hiroshi Ishii. Emerging frameworks for tangible user interfaces. *IBM Systems Journal*, 39(3&4):915, 2000.

[Upn]   Universal plug and play. http://www.upnp.org.

[VKP+03]   Pasi Välkkynen, Ilkka Korhonen, Johan Plomp, Timo Tuomisto, Luc Cluimans, Heikki Ailisto, and Heikki Seppä. A user interaction paradigm for physical browsing and near-object control based on tags. In *Proceedings of Physical Interaction Workshop on Real World User Interfaces, in the Mobile HCI Conference 2003, Udine, IT*, pages 31–34, 2003.

[VL07]   Jose Ramon Rios Viqueira and Nikos A. Lorentzos. SQL extension for spatio-temporal data. *International Journal on Very Large Data Bases (VLDB)*, 16(2):179–200, 2007.

[VZT05]   Gregg Vanderheiden, Gottfried Zimmermann, and Shari Trewin. Interface sockets, remote consoles, and natural language agents: A v2 urc standards whitepaper. White paper, URC Consortium, February 2005.

[Wal99]   J. Waldo. The jini architecture for network-centric computing. *Communications of the ACM*, 42(7):76–82, July 1999.

[Wan04]   Yingxu Wang. On autonomous computing and cognitive processes. In 3rd *International Conference on Cognitive Informatics, ICCI'04, August 16-17, 2004*, pages 3–4. Theoretical and Empirical Software Engineering Research Center, Dept. of Electrical & Computer Engineering, University of Calgary, 2500 University Drive NW, Calgary, Alberta, Canada T2N 1N4, IEEE CS Press, 2004.

[WFDW07] Jan Oliver Wallgrün, Lutz Frommberger, Frank Dylla, and Diedrich Wolter. SparQ user manual v0.7. Technical report, University of Bremen, Bremen, Germany, July 2007.

[Wif] The wireless fidelity alliance. http://www.wi-fi.org.

[ZGMT04] Franco Zambonelli, Marie Pierre Gleizes, Marco Mamei, and Robert Tolksdorf. Spray computers: Frontiers of self-organization for pervasive computing. In 13th IEEE International Workshops on Enabling Technologies, WETICE 2004, Modena, Italy, June 14-16, 2004, pages 403–408. IEEE CS Press, 2004.

[Zig] The zigbee alliance. http://www.zigbee.org.

[ZM04] Franco Zambonelli and Marco Mamei. Spatial computing: An emerging paradigm for autonomic computing and communication. In 1st International IFIP Workshop on Autonomic Communication, WAC 2004, Berlin, Germany, October 18-19, 2004, volume 3457 of LNCS, pages 44–57. Springer, 2004.

Chapter IX
Interactive Displays and Next-Generation Interfaces

Michael Haller

Peter Brandl, Christoph Richter, Jakob Leitner, Thomas Seifried,

Adam Gokcezade, Daniel Leithinger

Until recently, the limitations of display and interface technologies have restricted the potential for human interaction and collaboration with computers. For example, desktop computer style interfaces have not translated well to mobile devices and static display technologies tend to leave the user one step removed from interacting with content. However, the emergence of interactive whiteboards has pointed to new possibilities for using display technology for interaction and collaboration. A range of emerging technologies and applications could enable more natural and human centred interfaces so that interacting with computers and content becomes more intuitive. This will be important as computing moves from the desktop to be embedded in objects, devices and locations around us and as our desktop and data are no longer device dependent but follow us across multiple platforms and locations.

In face-to-face meetings, people share a wide range of verbal and non-verbal cues in an attempt to communicate clearly. In a business meeting, for example, people often collaborate around a table. The space between them is typically used for sharing communication cues such as gaze, gesture and non-verbal behaviors, and sometimes for interacting with real objects on the table, such as papers and models. There is free and easy interchange of ideas and natural communication. As displays become available in our everyday surroundings, co-located collaborators will more easily be able to access their digital information and media during their social and work exchanges. Furthermore, as our local and remote devices become increasingly able to communicate amongst each other, collaborators can more readily share personal data, or include remote colleagues in their discussions.

A key activity that often occurs during these collaborative exchanges, and one that is not well supported with current computing environments, is brainstorming. Technology is often abandoned for traditional media (e.g. notepads, whiteboards, flipcharts, and napkins) during collaborative brainstorming ses-

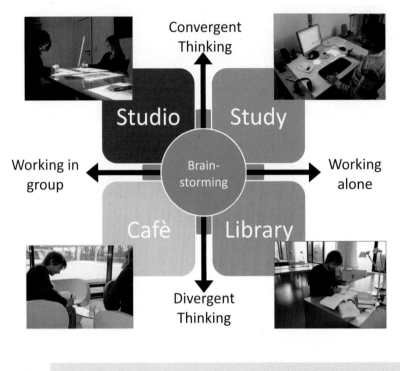

FIGURE 1   Brainstorming happens in many different environments. Thus, we need tools that are embedded in convenient, everyday furniture such as tables, walls, armrests etc.

sions. While this practice is not ideal in co-located environments (as someone often must later translate the results into digital format), using traditional media also restricts contributions from remote colleagues. Future collaboration environments will provide opportunities to access and manipulate data both locally and remotely, enabling substantive contributions from even geographically distributed team members (see Figure 1).

The increasing number of videos of multi-touch surfaces available on YouTube, show that users' expectations about using these devices in their daily lives have increased. The reaction to these natural interface implementations has been very positive. This is because people are still interested in a simpler way of navigating information and content where the computer interface is not a barrier, but enables them to accomplish tasks more quickly and easily. Multiple metaphors and interaction paradigms using pen, touch, and visual recognition are coming together with the other elements to create a new experience. In education, intuitive interfaces lower the barriers to using IT, allow for a better understanding of complex content and enhance opportunities for collaboration. In the near future it is likely that emerging display technologies such as electronic paper and OLED (Organic Light-Emitting Diode) screens will be delivered on flexible substrates. This will enable bendable/rollable displays that can be made larger than the dimension of the mobile device they are used with. E-paper could also enable inexpensive, very large digital displays to be incorporated into walls and other surfaces more widely. Speech recognition, gesture recognition, haptics, machine vision and even brain control are all improving rapidly to support more natural interactions with these new display technologies. This article concentrates on developments in different multi-touch surfaces and related applications. It also describes particular challenges and solutions for the design of tabletop and interactive wall environments and presents possible solutions for classrooms.

With the increasing development of interactive walls, interactive tables, and multi-touch devices, both companies and academics are evaluating their potential for wider use. We see that display technology is not just improving in quality, but also in the way that we interact with large surfaces. These newly emerging form factors require novel human-computer interaction techniques. Although movies such as Minority Report and The Island popularized the idea of futuristic, off-the-desktop gesture-based human-computer interaction and direct manipulation-based interfaces, in reality, making these interfaces is still a challenge. Conventional metaphors and underlying interface infrastructures for single-user desktop systems have been traditionally geared towards single mouse and keyboard-based WIMP (Windows, Icons, Menus and Pointing) interface design. However, a table/wall setting provides a large interactive visual surface for groups to interact together. It encourages collaboration and coordination, as well as simultaneous and parallel problem solving among multiple users and therefore needs new kinds of interface.

Interactive Surfaces 1

In late 1988, Xerox PARC developed the Live-Board, the first blackboard-sized touch-sensitive screen capable of displaying an image. Many in education will now be familiar with the interactive whiteboard. SMART Technologies Inc.[1] introduced its first interactive whiteboard SMARTBoard in 1991. The tracking is based on the DViT (Digital Vision Touch) technology and uses small cameras mounted in each of the four corners of the panel to track the user input. The system is mainly designed to be used with pens, but it can also track finger touches. A great number of digital whiteboards have also been sold to universities and educational institutions.

---

[1] http://www.smarttech.com

A similar technology is the touch frame provided by NextWindow[2]. Again, embedded cameras track up to two points at the same time. The MIMIO[3] and eBeam[4] ultrasonic tracking devices, where participants use special styli, are a good and cheap alternative tracking surface. However, they are limited in their range, and line-of-sight restrictions reduce the tracking performance.

More recently, touch interfaces have been able to respond to multiple touches and gestures, increasing the possibilities for interaction and for multiple users to collaborate. Interactive tables, for example, have begun to move from prototype to product and combine the benefits of a traditional table with all the functionalities of a digital computer. Although interactive tabletop environments are becoming increasingly common (see for example Diamond-Touch from Mitsubishi Electric Research Laboratories (MERL), Surface from Microsoft), there are few applications which fully show their potential. One area where they could be expected to be very useful is in supporting creative collaboration. In the creative process, people often sketch their ideas on large tables. A digital tabletop set-up could therefore provide an ideal interface for supporting computer-based collaboration. To better understand the design requirements for interactive displays in a business setting, we carried out an exploratory field study at Voestalpine, an Austrian steel company, which wants to use a tabletop surface for brainstorming sessions. We found the following design recommendations for an interactive, large vertical/horizontal display:

- multi-point interaction and identification,
- robust tracking under non-optimal conditions,
- hardware robustness,
- physical objects should not interfere,
- user can interact directly with the system,
- reasonable latency, and
- inexpensive to manufacture.

Related projects have demonstrated the possibilities of digital tabletops in different scenarios. These approaches vary in the enabling technologies as well as the applications that are implemented for these surfaces.

1.1 DiamondTouch

Up to four users can sit on special chairs around the DiamondTouch table interface developed at MERL [DL01]. The sensing technology behind DiamondTouch is an XY pair of antenna arrays embedded in the surface of the

---

[2] http://www.nextwindow.com

[3] http://www.mimio.com

[4] http://www.e-beam.com

table. Each user sits in a wired chair that broadcasts a unique radio signal. These signals are capacitively coupled through the user's body and into the antenna array whenever touches occur. Since each user sits in a different chair, the table is able to distinguish touches among the users.

The DiamondTouch Table. Based on an array of antennas embedded in   FIGURE 2
the touch surface, the DiamondTouch can detect up to four different
users simultaneously.

The DiamondTouch is not only able to track multiple touches, but also able to identify different users (we can therefore call the system a multi-person system). The digital content is always projected onto the table's surface. Another advantage of this table is the fact that additional objects placed on the surface do not interfere with the system. The interpolated resolution of the DiamondTouch is 2736×2048 points (with a physical screen size of 42 inches) and the table can read out tracking information with a refresh rate of 30Hz. A similar set-up is presented by Rekimoto with the SmartSkin project, where he uses a mesh-shaped sensor grid to determine the hand position.

FIGURE 3   The Microsoft Surface. All pictures are sent to the table's surface, once the Wi-Fi-based camera is put on the table. Alternatively, RFID tags on the devices can help for tracking devices on an interactive large surface.

1.2 Microsoft's Surface

More recently, Microsoft presented the Surface table[5]. The system enables interaction with digital content through natural gestures, touches and physical objects. The Surface can track up to 40 simultaneous touches. In contrast to the DiamondTouch, the Surface is based on an optical tracking set-up, where five embedded infra-red cameras track the entire table (the current prototypes have a screen size of 30 inches). A special rear-projection surface and an embedded projector allow an optimal image. With the special projector, the engineers developed a relative low-sized table with a maximum height of 56cm. The Microsoft team demonstrates the table's advantages with effective demonstrations developed for Sheraton Hotels, Harrah's Casinos, and T-Mobile. In the photo-sharing application, for instance, friends can put their WiFi digital camera on the table and share their photos in a very natural way.

An alternative is to recognize and pair a device with RFID (Radio-Frequency Identification) tags or NFC (Near Field Communication). In this case, the table includes RFID readers which in combination with RFID tagged objects can be used to save and load different content. NFC allows devices

---

[5] http://www.surface.com

to set up a link when brought together in close proximity. It is primarily designed to be used on mobile phones. The content, however, has still to be sent over Bluetooth or another suitable link), since the NFC technology is not designed to transfer large amounts of data. RFID/NFC is likely to be included in increasing numbers of mobile phones and other devices, so in the future it may be possible for a user to have content from a mobile device appear on a large screen just by bringing their device within close range of the display.

Other Interactive Tables 1.3

Similar to the Microsoft Surface, the LumiSight table captures the objects on the table using cameras and a projector mounted inside the table [MIO+04]. The InteracTable, a single-user system, allows interaction using a stylus. In contrast to related research, this system is based on a plasma display. The DViT cameras mounted in each of the four corners of the table track the users' input. The lens of each camera has an approximately 90° field of view. The current version allows two simultaneous touches. Similar to the Microsoft Surface, people cannot place any physical objects (a coffee mug, for example) on the surface without achieving un-wanted touches. Stanford's iRoom table, an interface mainly designed for brainstorming discussion in schools, is another example, which is also based on the DViT tracking with multiple DViT frames.

One of the first larger tabletop setups has been presented by Ullmer and Ishii [UI97]. In their installation, they implemented a set-up for engineers discussing urban planning. The system supports multi-layering of 2D sketches, drawings and maps in combination with 3D physical (tangible) objects, and is primarily designed for group sizes up to 10 people. The setup consists of two projectors hanging from the ceiling. Two cameras (also mounted above the setup) capture all the users' activities. Finally, Han [Han05] demonstrated an impressive scalable multi-touch interaction surface that takes advantage of frustrated total internal reflection (FTIR), a technique used in biometric applications such as fingerprint scanning. When light encounters the interface to a medium with a lower index of refraction, the light becomes refracted and beyond a certain angle, it undergoes total internal reflection. In contrast, another object (such as a finger) at the interface can frustrate this total internal reflection, causing a visible blob on the backface of the surface. This tracking system is highly scalable and very accurate—even under different lighting conditions.

As seen in this section, many companies and research laboratories are working on interactive tables, since they combine the advantages of a traditional table (face-to-face communication) with the advantages of a computer (easy archiving of data, and sharing of content for example).

1.4 Digital Pens

Pens have been used as tools for interacting with horizontal as well as vertical digital surfaces in various research projects. The affordances of a pen make it a suitable input device for tasks like writing or sketching. Users are well practiced with traditional pen use, and can easily translate their knowledge to the digital surface with minimal cognitive impact. Moreover, pens provide a precise tool for pointing and can further include extensions like buttons or pressure sensors.

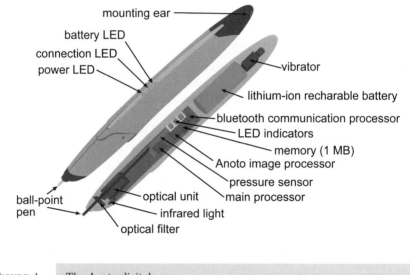

FIGURE 4   The Anoto digital pen.

The Swedish company Anoto[6] developed the *Digital Pen and Paper* technology. The main tool for interaction is a pen with a small infrared camera integrated in the tip that derives the pen's position on a unique high-resolution dot pattern. Figure 4 depicts the components of the Anoto digital pen. The Anoto pattern consists of tiny dots that are slightly displaced from a regular grid. By setting the dots with offsets in horizontal and vertical position from the grid, each dot encodes two bit of information. The combination of

---

[6] www.anoto.com

several dots makes a unique sequence that defines the position on the paper. To enable stable tracking, the digital pen has to see at least an collection of six by six dots. In practice, the camera in the pen's tip manages to see this minimum 36 points with a high frequency (70Hz). Once the dots are recognized, the pen not only sends its coordinates, but also additional information about the current page ID and a pressure level.

(a)   (b)

Anoto pens are available in two versions: a USB only version (a) and a   FIGURE 5
Bluetooth streaming version (b).

The Anoto digital pens are available in two different types: a USB and a Bluetooth streaming version. Figure 5 shows the two different versions of data transfer from the Anoto pen to the PC. The USB pen, which is commonly used for storing a digital copy of ones handwriting, can only be synchronized with the PC when placed in a docking station. Once the pen is connected to the PC via the docking station, all stored data from the pen is transmitted in a single step. Afterwards, the memory in the pen is emptied. The second version of Anoto pen not only stores handwriting in the pen, but also allow one to stream data in real-time over Bluetooth to the PC. With this streaming input, the user can get feedback from the PC in real-time. Moreover, this real-time streaming makes the Anoto technology suitable for direct interaction on large digital surfaces. Currently, three commercial pens with Bluetooth are available from Nokia (SU-1B), Logitech (io-2), and Anoto (PenIT).

Design Challenges 2

In order to gain a better understanding of the requirements and potentials for interactive workspaces that arise from real meeting and workshop situations, an explorative field study at a big Austrian steel company has been carried out in fall 2005. The field study has been focused on the collaborative interactions between the participants and how these are mediated by the documents and tools used as well as the physical setup of the meeting room itself. The field study included six meetings and workshops of the company's IT-service division with internal and external customers. The meetings took between 1 and 3 hours and covered topics such as business process modeling, requirements specification, evaluation of mock-ups, and project coordination. Both participants and locations varied across the meetings. Data collection included the notes taken manually during non-participant observation in the meetings as well as qualitative interviews with the chairs before and after the meetings. In order to structure the data collection and allow for comparison across the meetings a self-devised protocol was used. The protocol draws on cultural-historical activity theory (e.g. [Eng99, BCT95]) and provides a set of questions aimed to identify

1. core activities addressed in the meeting,
2. relevant stakeholders and communities as well as
3. actors involved,
4. rules and values guiding the interaction,
5. specific actions performed,
6. the artifacts and tools used,
7. physical properties of the meeting venue as well as
8. problems and breakdowns occurring in the meeting.

Based on the data collected a set of preliminary design challenges was formulated. Afterwards the outcomes were validated against the judgment of the meeting chairs as well as prior research on synchronous collaboration.

The following section provides a synopsis of the design challenges that emerged from our analysis. A brief description of the design challenge itself is given, and the resulting requirements for the design of interactive spaces and collaborative tabletop devices are outlined.

2.1 Interactive Spaces

Interactive rooms incorporate different digital surfaces such as tabletops, digital walls and portable devices in a single space to facilitate work processes [SGH+99, JFW02]. However, the design of such a room and the according applications can hardly accommodate the requirements posed by the huge variety of collaborative work activities. For instance, a workspace for presentations and customer meetings will pose different demands on the system than a creative brainstorming session. Considerations about the room design must involve various situation specific aspects such as work group size, group characteristics, required tools or used media during the meeting.

Multiplicity and Heterogeneity of Tasks

Even though workshops and meetings are usually focused on a limited set of topics, they regularly encompass a multiplicity of heterogeneous tasks. For example one and the same session might entail phases of presenting, brainstorming, decision-making, collaborative modeling, and planning. As each of these tasks requires different types of collaborative behavior, a meeting room has to be adaptable according to the changing needs. While during a presentation it might be useful that the presenter can guide the participants through a set of documents other tasks such as collaborative modeling might require active contribution to the development of a shared artifact by all participants. The change from one task to another often occurs spontaneously based on the situational demands emerging in the meeting. Consequently, interactive spaces and collaborative tabletop devices for meetings and workshops have to account for the diversity of tasks at hand. Input and output devices should be selectable on demand and there need to be seamless mechanisms for floor and access control. Furthermore, it has to be possible to switch between different tasks, and to save the current system status to come back to a task later on.

Integration of Individual and Shared Spaces

Most collaborative tasks also include subtasks to be carried out by the different participants in parallel [JK01]. Accordingly, all participants have to have access not only to a shared but also to an individual workspace where they can create and store their own documents. In order to integrate individual and collective activities a smooth transition between individual and shared spaces has to be ensured while the integrity of the personal workspace must be ensured. For example, the notes taken might not be intended for the eyes of the other participants. The use of multiple documents renders the coordination of activities more difficult. In order to prevent misunderstandings it is important to support natural pointing gestures and direct manipulation of objects [WCFB06].

Fostering the Creation of Shared Documents

Shared documents play a fundamental role in collaborative working environments as they foster the creation of a shared understanding, support the coordination of activities and provide a shared memory for the group [Sch01]. The creation of shared documents also fosters the objectification of thoughts and ideas, a process highly relevant for creative and constructional tasks [Hac02]. Therefore, an interactive workspace also has also to provide means to create and manipulate shared documents collectively. In order to foster the joint creation of documents concurrent document manipulation should be enabled and documents should be readable by all attendees simultaneously.

Multiple and Interrelated Documents

The set of documents used in professional workshops and meetings are often quite extensive and heterogeneous in nature. For example software mock-ups, requirements specifications and business process models might be used in parallel. In addition these documents are often highly interrelated and relevant information is often spread across the various resources. The use of multiple and interrelated documents requires interaction metaphors that allow for easy navigation across documents. Furthermore, the relation between documents should also be visible to ease orientation [WCFB06].

Integration into Overarching Activities

Meetings and workshops usually do not constitute an end in itself, but are part of more overarching activities such as project work, or other ongoing work processes. Hence, it is important that meeting attendees can easily access previous information and store the results of the meeting for further processing. The access to one's own information is especially relevant when different organizations are attending a meeting.

2.2 Interactive Tabletops

The horizontal layout of a table along with the possibility of multi-user interaction requires new concepts that have been researched under a variety of different perspectives. Assuming that the hardware supports interaction with the table's surface, the main attention has been focused on the application design for digital tabletops. The following summary shall provide an overview of the most important features and related published approaches.

Shared Input and Display Surface

As related work on interactive tabletops has shown, it is possible to use standard Windows applications on a horizontal surface [ER06]. But such an approach will never explore the full functionality of a tabletop, since the input is restricted to a single cursor and the output is tailored for viewing from only one distinct orientation. In an interactive tabletop setup, multiple users expect to interact simultaneously without restricting their workflow to turn taking. Studies about traditional tables and the interaction of groups around them have shown that table surfaces encourage people to use physical objects simultaneously [Tan91, Sco05, KCSG03]. This behavior must be supported by the design of a digital tabletop by providing mechanisms that allow for concurrent input. With a horizontal surface, people tend to develop new forms of collaboration and communication when working with applications that are tailored for this kind of surface [RHBL04]. The DiamondSpin tabletop groupware [SVFR04], for example, supports the development of such applications for tabletops. Among others, it provides a feature to replicate the system menu for each user at the table and place it at an appropriate position on the surface. Projects like the Personal Digital Historian [VLS02, SLM+01] and the UbiTable [SER03] show implementations based on the DiamondSpin toolkit with different duplicated personal menu layouts. The menus provide the tools for multiple users to interact with the table. This process also involves the digital artifacts that are manipulated by the group. Since multiple users work simultaneously, the concurrent access of objects must be handled. The DiamondSpin groupware allows for this collaborative interaction so that users can manipulate objects and enlarge them to gain shared access. A different approach has been explored for the InteracTable within the i-Land project [SGH+99]. Their table is based on the BEACH software [Tan04, SPMT+02], which allows for the making of copies of an object for each user and further manipulating the object through these references.

In contrast to the collaborative manipulation of objects on the shared surface, hand-over techniques have been investigated for tabletops. In such applications, only one user has the right to work with an object. To grant access for other users, the object must be passed on. Four different hand-over strategies have been explored with the release, relocate, resize, and reorient techniques [RRS+04]. All four techniques suffer from the strong dependency of the hand-over action on the user currently owning the object. Without the action initiated by the owner, any other user that hinders a fluid interaction in a group cannot access the object.

Use of Space and Accessibility

The use of space during collaborative sessions is shaped by several partially competing factors. The access to and manipulation of objects requires them to be in reach of the meeting attendees [TT06]. Accordingly, collaboration around a tabletop device requires the attendees to be relatively close to each other. At the same time, this vicinity is at least partially at odds with social norms in professional settings where distance can demonstrate respect for each other's privacy and interests. Furthermore, having direct access to a document or input device often provides an essential prerequisite for active participation but also for control over the situation. As a consequence, the meeting attendees should be able to regulate their distance but also the access to documents and input devices on demand. As Scott's studies on territoriality in collaborative tabletop workspaces suggest, the management of data on the table leads to the effect of partitioning in the user's personal space [Sco05]. This observation has influenced the implementation of separated workspaces for digital tabletops. DiamondSpin, for example, allows for the creation of *personal* and *public spaces* that are visually demarcated in the application. But Scott noticed that visible boundaries of the workspace might have a negative effect on the territorial behavior on a tabletop. Moreover, our field study revealed, that in traditional meeting-rooms a significant proportion of the tabletop is covered by objects irrelevant to the task at hand, such as additional documents, beverages, day-timers or mobile phones. In order to reduce the amount of unused documents on the tabletop attendees should be able to easily store, search, and retrieve the digital artifacts currently unused.

Orientation of User Interface Elements

With a table setup, people will naturally sit or stand around the table. Once people sit at different sides around the table, individual views onto the surface vary, creating the problem of orientation of visuals on the table's surface. This is the reason why traditional Windows interfaces cannot be simply ported onto the table, because they rely on a distinct orientation. A lot of research into the field of tabletops has been invested on this issue already [KCSG03, Sco05, WB05, FSWB06, SVFR04, FS05, HCV+06].

Privacy

With a single large display that is visible to all users in the room, a lack of privacy exists. There are possibilities to arrange the space of the surface in a way that each user has at least a visual boundary of his workplace

[Mor06, Sco05]. But there are only a few prototypes that allow for real privacy. The *LumiSight* table uses orientation dependent views on the surface, for example [MIO⁺04]. On the other hand there is a natural constraint to work in the proximity space of another user. This is supported by the work of Scott [Sco05] who noticed that users avoid reaching into the personal space of others.

Shadow and Occlusion Problems

Front-projected tabletop systems suffer from shadow and occlusion problems once a user reaches with his hand over the surface. But interestingly, the assumed problems are not affirmed in practical tests. Consistent with Ashdown's observations of the *Escritoire* setup [Ash04], we found out that shadow and occlusion problems turn out to have less effect than expected. This is due to the fact that people are used to cast shadows in illuminated rooms. They are not surprised if the same happens while interacting with a front-projected table. Moreover, if they occlude information on the surface with their hands, it is again a familiar effect that also appears with physical objects.

Table Size and Group Size

When building a table for collaborative work, the physical size is of course an important factor. The size of the table is related to the size of the group that is expected to use the table for their work. Ryall et al. [RFSM04] conducted an interesting experiment that gives valuable insights about the correlation of table and group sizes. They identified three main effects: first, the table size had no effect on the speed a task could be completed. Second, the group size effected collaboration; smaller groups collaborated more strongly than larger groups. Finally, they noticed that other users respected personal spaces so that they did not reach into their proximity. This is in tune with the findings reported from Scott [Sco05].

2.3 Digital Whiteboards

Due to the different physical orientation of horizontal and vertical surfaces, the user's perception of the workspace will vary. Hence the design parameters from digital tabletops cannot be directly applied to wall displays.

Vertical vs. Horizontal Display

Rogers and Lindley [RL04] report about the effect of physical affordances of an interactive workspace on the social interactions and collaborations. On the tabletop, they observed that users would switch more roles, explore more ideas and have a stronger perception of the other user's actions. In contrast, horizontal displays tend to disturb the collaboration aspect in groups as the physical distance between the person at the whiteboard and the rest of the group becomes larger. To compensate for this effect, we included a close connection between the digital whiteboard and the digital tabletop in our room design. For example, interaction with the digital whiteboard should be possible while being seated at the table without the need to physically walk to the whiteboard. To support this feature, the applications running on both displays must have a technical connection on a protocol layer as well as tools for the user to allow the transfer of data between them.

One Person as Presenter Role

Through the changes in collaboration between horizontal and vertical displays, the role of the users during a work session is altered. The fluid role changing that Rogers and Lindley [RL04] observed on tabletops changed to a "one person as presenter" situation when they used a digital whiteboard. The same behavior of one person taking the lead and the others stepping back was noticed by Russel et al. [RDS02].

Turn-Taking Behavior

Since most interactive whiteboard solutions are still designed for single person usage [SMA03], turn taking is required in these environments. But looking at the way people work with traditional whiteboards [Tan91] suggests that this turn-taking behavior would not change even if the technology would support multi-user interaction. This is again in tune with the findings of Rogers and Lindley [RL04] who observed that it is generally difficult to notice what other people are doing at the wall without stepping back. Moreover, people felt uncomfortable working too close together at the wall display.

Tasks on the Whiteboard

A vertical display is well suited for presentation tasks as all viewers have the same view on the displays. In contrast to a tabletop setup, there are no rotational problems with a vertical display. Although the exact task will depend on the context of the work group, there is a tendency towards using the digital whiteboard for displaying information that is relevant for everyone in the room. This is coherent with the role of a single person taking control over the display instead of multiple persons working simultaneously. This person is normally the presenter, which is also communicated through his standing position in contrast to the sitting position of the users at the table. If the whiteboard is used in a creative task together with an interactive table, Rogers and Lindley [RL04] noticed that the connection of the person at the whiteboard to the table group was disturbed. The whiteboard requires the user to turn his back at the others while his body occludes parts of the display, making it harder to follow his actions. To re-establish the connection to the group, a specific effort was necessary. In a presentation situation, this might be less of a problem, because everyone is paying attention to the presenter instead of working on a different task simultaneously.

Design of the Whiteboard

Guimbretière [Gui02] describes in his work about large interactive walls that they faced three major challenges when building a wall for brainstorming sessions: First they had to find a command mechanism that allows for working with the wall with a minimum distraction from the task. Moreover, they describe the need for a novel space management to support creative sessions without the limitations of a conventional analogue whiteboard. And finally, a digital whiteboard will only be accepted when the latency is minimized and the user can experience fluid interaction. We found similar expectations from our users in the partner company when we discussed the requirements for the digital whiteboard. Since traditional whiteboards and flipcharts are frequently used during meetings and discussions in this company, the standard of a digital whiteboard should at least meet the known quality. Therefore, ease-of-use and fast input processing were basic features for a successful implementation of the whiteboard.

UI design

In contrast to the digital table, UI elements on the digital whiteboard are closer to the traditional WIMP paradigm. With the vertical setup, there is one specific orientation for the elements, so users face the display like in a desktop computer situation. This is the reason why products like the SMARTBoard[7] offer WIMP style applications for their digital whiteboard. Although rotation is not an issue for a vertical display, the placement of UI elements is a key factor for the design. Unfortunately, the commercial software solutions for interactive whiteboards are following a too traditional WIMP implementation, which leads to obvious problems on large surfaces. The top located task bar, for example, is hard to reach on a SMARTBoard, and for smaller persons it may be even impossible to reach. The user interface design has to account for the large size of the digital whiteboard, especially in terms of reachability.

2.4 Input Devices

Digital Pens

To complement the design of the interactive room that includes a digital tabletop and a digital whiteboard, we explored the potential of several input devices. The aim was to incorporate a selection of input devices that enable convenient interaction directly with the table and whiteboard as well as the transfer of data between them. Our research focused on digital pens as the primary input device for the tabletop and the whiteboard. In addition to the pens we thought of direct touch as ancillary input for the interactive surfaces.

Tangible Palettes

Other types of input devices are tangible objects. Previous studies suggest that tangible objects can enhance collaboration among groups, as the perception of the others' actions is naturally supported [RLH06]. Although these studies have been based on tabletop setups, we thought of an extension to our interactive room concept. As demonstrated by Streitz et al. [SGH+99] in the i-Land project, tangible objects can also be used to transfer data between

---

[7] http://www2.smarttech.com/st/de-DE/Products/SMART+Boards/

surfaces. They used wood blocks that could be recognized by every surface and linked data to the blocks. Consequently, they could transfer data through the physical placement of these blocks. In our concept, we designed tangible palettes as control interfaces for the digital surfaces in the room. The functionalities assigned to the palettes are shortcuts for frequently used actions or tools that allow for a fluid interaction with the system. By defining the number of available palettes, different parameters of the collaboration can be influenced. First, if options are only available on a unique palette, a group has to share that object which again leads to stronger collaboration. Second, multiple palettes with the same function will require a distribution across the table or the whole room with respect to the screen estate and reachability. Compared to a digital menu, a hardware palette is a very natural control object. It can be easily accessed and also removed on demand. Moreover, the tangible aspect makes it easy to share and hand over.

Interactive Paper

A special kind of tangible device is paper. Despite the predictions of the paperless office, we still see paper as part of many activities in office environments. Sellen and Harper have explored the reason why paper has not been replaced by digital systems until today in their book *The Myth of the Paperless Office* [SH01]. They report about the concept of *affordances*, which describes the activities that an object allows or affords. Using this concept, they compare the affordances of paper to the digital world. Paper is tangible; it is easy to pick up and flip through the pages while getting a sense of the length of a document. While navigating in a paper document, the reader gets feedback about his location from the amount of pages already seen and the ones still to be read. Paper can be tailored; it is easy to annotate a paper document, which can be done simultaneously to reading it. It is a common practice to use a notebook for taking notes while reading in another paper document [SGP98]. Furthermore, paper is spatially flexible; it can be spread out and organized in a structure that suits our needs for a specific task. We are able to read across multiple pages at the same time and can further structure them to define a new order. Finally, paper has its own affordances in collaborating groups. Because paper is a tangible object, the actions performed with the paper are visible to the other group members. The exact content of a user's note on the paper may not be recognizable by the others, but the action of taking a note is clearly visible. This affordance especially makes paper a highly interesting tangible device in an interactive room context. Referring to the proximities and orientations that people used to establish personal and group spaces on tables [Tan91, KCSG03], paper provides an ideal device through its affordances. The transition from personal to group space, for example, can be easily accomplished by putting a paper document on the table's surface. The action with the paper document already informs the group about the intention and the social context.

Switching of Devices

Input devices like digital pens, tangible palettes and real paper serve as the connection between the single digital surfaces in the room. One key factor for the successful integration of the input devices is the fluidity of interaction and consequently the effect on the work flows. A common approach is to associate different input devices with different activities, like wireless keyboards for text input and pointing devices for selecting and manipulating digital objects [FJHW00, SLV+02, SGS+02]. However, switching between a variety of different devices distracts the natural work flow because the attention is focused on the handling of the devices instead of the process itself. Therefore, a consistent integration of devices with a minimum of necessary switches is desired. In our observations of work processes with our partner company, we noticed that digital pen interaction allows for a great variety of different actions. Handwriting and free sketching are tasks that are well suited for the affordances of digital pens. Moreover, a pen offers a highly accurate device for precise pointing and selection tasks. User interfaces for digital pens can be generally smaller than for direct touch, for example.

2.5 Discussion

The design challenges outlined before are not dissimilar from the guidelines for interactive spaces and collaborative tabletop devices that can be found in the literature. In fact, the design challenges can be mapped quite easily to the guidelines put forward by [SGM03]. According to this guidelines, tabletop displays for co-located collaborative work must support:

1. natural interpersonal interaction,
2. transitions between activities,
3. transitions between personal and group work,
4. transitions between tabletop collaboration and external work,
5. the use of physical objects,
6. accessing shared physical and digital objects,
7. flexible user arrangements, and
8. simultaneous user interactions.

The design challenges described here, nevertheless go beyond the existing guidelines in that they put emphasis on the requirements that arise in professional meeting and workshop situations. Towards that end the following points appear to be particular noteworthy:

- The development of interactive spaces and collaborative tabletop systems cannot be reduced to the question of the most appropriate interface technology or interaction design, but inevitably has to take into account the dynamics of the social activities to be supported. For example, moving between activities is not only a question of the appropriate input device, but also about the assignment of roles and the internal division of labor.
- Collaborative activities are not always consensus oriented nor can it be assumed that participants work towards the same objectives. Questions of territory, access, and control over documents or input-devices, therefore have direct bearing on the scope of actions of the various participants.
- Finally, when used in support of professional meetings and workshops multiple types of mediation have to be taken into account simultaneously (see [BR00]). This is to say that the creation and work with knowledge artifacts, the organization and coordination of the collaborative effort as well as the shaping of the social relations among participants cannot be treated in isolation. For example to allow for concurrent document manipulation does not only affect the content of the document created, but also the work processes as well as the relation among those involved in this exercise.

Design and Implementation of a Multi-Display Environment for Collaboration 3

To gain a better understanding of how present meetings are held and how our vision of an interactive room could improve collaboration, we observed several meetings in one of our partner's companies (see Section 2). Through this approach, we collected valuable insights about the current situation and further iteratively refine our designs and implications. Once we collected data from the observations, we designed a prototype that addressed potential aspects of the workflows which were then tested in the company again. The first setup of our interactive room is shown in Figure 6.

The interaction with the surfaces in this room is enabled through Anoto technology (see Section 1.4). Since the pen tracking is relying on the special dot pattern, a surface can be made interactive by overlaying it with a printout of this pattern. Our first demonstration, the Shared Design Space, was accurate, fast, and highly scalable [HLL+06].

Figure 7 (a) depicts the top-projection table in combination with the Anoto pen. The middle layer consists of the pattern, which is protected by a scratch resistant Plexiglas, placed on the top of the surface. For the Plexiglas, a maximum thickness of 3mm is recommended, since thicker layers on top of

454   Michael Haller et al.

FIGURE 6   The interactive room consisting of a digital tabletop, a digital whiteboard and a presentation display.

the pattern interfere with the tracking. To prevent ink traces from the pens on the Plexiglas, we exchanged the ballpoint pens with plastic stylus tips.

Alternatively, we also implemented a rear-projection solution for digital tables and walls, see Figure 7 (b). Since the Anoto pen tracking technology is designed to be used in combination with a special dot pattern that is printed on traditional paper, materials that allow for rear-projections are not initially supported. We faced this problem when we tried to print the dot pattern on different surfaces such as transparent foils. The optimal base-material should reflect the IR light that is emitted from the pen's integrated IR-LED. For the camera in the pen's tip, the area appears as a bright surface with a high contrast pattern on it. If the material is too transparent or too glossy, the contrast between background material and dot pattern is not high enough to ensure stable pen tracking. A transparent surface would not reflect enough infrared light and therefore appear as a dark background with nearly invisible black dots on it.

We found a solution that allows to apply Anoto pen tracking to large rear-projected surfaces. The tracking is realized by using a large Anoto pattern printed on a special rear-projection foil. This foil diffuses the illumination from the rear LCD projector resulting in an image with no visible hotspots at the front of the screen. Backlit foil is used in order to produce an image with sufficient contrast for the embedded Anoto pen camera to recognize the dot pattern. This provides translucency for projection while being opaque

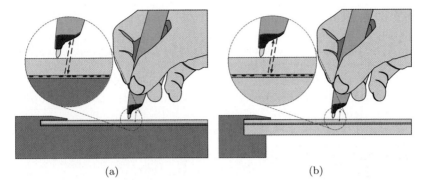

(a)   (b)

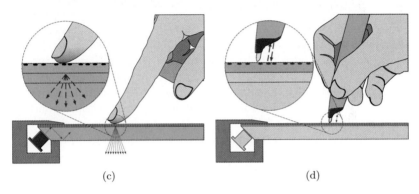

(c)   (d)

The front-projected layer composition (a). Anoto pattern for a rear-   FIGURE 7
projected interactive surface (b). The three layers needed to track the
finger touches (c). In the final layer composition only the top layer is
relevant for the Anoto tracking (d).

enough to enable the Anoto IR-tracking. Figure 7 (top right) depicts the
final layer composition that provides good results for the pen tracking. The
dot pattern on the backlit foil is placed between two acrylic panels. The panel
in the back has a width of 6mm and guarantees a stable and robust surface
while the panel in the front has a width of only 0.8mm to protect the pattern
from scratches.

To augment the Anoto input tracking with the advantages of direct, multi-
touch interaction, we further extended the rear-projection layer composition.
For the touch tracking, we used an approach based on FTIR. Unfortunately,
a user must press hard on the surface to trigger the FTIR effect. The fric-
tion caused by dragging a finger on the surface, such as to perform a motion
gesture, can also decrease the FTIR effect. Therefore, we used an additional
layer (compliant surface layer) on top of the polycarbonate material to improve the sensitivity of the surface. We use a thin layer of latex to provide
a soft, transparent compliant layer. Figures 7 (c, d) highlight the relevant

layers of our final composition. When pressure is applied on the surface, the coupling of the diffuse top layer and the bottom polycarbonate surface triggers the FTIR effect; this effect is intensified by the middle compliant surface layer (c). The latex must be combined with the projection layer with an air gap between the latex and the polycarbonate base plate. As shown in Figure 7 (d), the digital pen tracking is enabled through the dot pattern printed on the top projection layer.

3.1 Design of an Interactive Table

Our goal was to integrate a table into the room in a way that traditional work flows are supported with the possibility to use the additional features of a digital system. The table should provide space for four people and it must allow to place additional objects on the surface without interfering with the application. It should be possible to turn the digital tabletop off and use it like a normal table.

There are basically two different display-based hardware solutions that can be used to build an interactive table: a front projected or a rear-projected setup. LCD or plasma screen-based solutions as used by Streitz et al. for the InteracTable [SGH+99] were not relevant in our case, because they were too limiting in size and shape factors. Compared to a front-projected solution, rear-projected setups are normally more restrictive in terms of materials that can be used for the table's surface. This is due to the fact that the surface must be suitable for a projection with sufficient contrast and brightness qualities while minimizing the effect of a visible hotspot. Moreover, a rear-projected setup restricts the possible size of the table because the stability of the surface is only guaranteed through the surrounding edges of the table's frame. In a front-projected setup, the projection surface can be placed on top of the table, thus supporting the sturdiness over the whole surface area. The choice of possible materials for a front-projected setup is broader compared to rear-projected solutions; for example, a simple white surface already fulfills the requirements. These considerations led us to the design of a front-projected setup for our interactive table.

Through an additional requirements analysis with our company partner, we identified another important feature that the table design had to address. As the domain was focused on meetings, people would sit most of the time around the table, with occasionally exceptions when someone walks to the whiteboard or joins the side of another person. For a sitting position, however, appropriate space for the feet under the table is very important, as staying in an awkward position at the table for an extended period of time has a negative impact on the user's comfort. These ergonomic issues are supported by a front projected setup, but they are hard to satisfy with a rear-projected setup if users should be able to sit around the table.

The table is a modified product provided by the company Team 7[8], featuring a 170×90cm large surface with digital pen interaction as primary input technology. In order to allow users to interact with the table, we extended the surface with a large Anoto pattern printout. This modification provides a high accurate input solution for the tabletop with the additional advantage of robustness and independence of environmental conditions. Moreover, the digital pen solution offers an input device that is tailored for fast sketching input and annotations. The modification of the table still allows to use it like a traditional table, as there are no electronic parts integrated into the table. Finally, the top projected setup enables users to sit in a comfortable position with enough space for their feet under the table. To achieve a high resolution projection on the tabletop, three projectors are mounted above the table.

Personal workspaces on top of a common shared space.   FIGURE 8

In our interactive room context we implemented two different versions of tabletop GUIs, one based on separated personal workspaces and another one with a common shared space. For the first version the whole table served as public space that was overlaid with multiple personal workspaces (see Figure 8). Each user could manipulate the layout of his personal workspace. By clicking on an empty spot on the surface the workspace would appear at this

---

[8] http://www.team7.at

position. Each workspace was uniquely assigned to a digital pen, thus each user could configure his workspace independently. Options for manipulating the workspace included resizing, rotating and showing/hiding. The workspace was automatically rotated towards the nearest edge of the table seen from the activation position. To exchange data between workspaces, the object had to be placed in the public space where the other user could pick a copy of it.

FIGURE 9   Tabletop with one large common shared space.

Our second approach was based on a common shared space concept. Without the visible boundaries of personal workspaces, each user has the same rights to work on the surface, to create, manipulate and share data. Without the need to actively grant access to objects for other users, we expected the workflows to be more fluid compared to the separated workspace version. Figure 9 shows the tabletop with the shared public space across the whole surface. Since the tabletop is equally shared by all users, the interaction is influenced by the *social protocol* of the group. But previous studies showed that the *social protocol* among users is not always sufficient on multi-user tabletops [MRS+04]. Actions that effect the whole workspace, like changing the view or clearing it for example, are critical if controls are replicated and each user has the right to perform them. In this context we experimented with tangible palettes that can physically restrict controls to a single user, if there is only one palette available for a certain task. With this one copy it is assured that only one person takes over the control. Moreover it is visible for the group who is in charge of it and when it is used.

Tangible Palettes   3.2

The tangible palettes were also used to change the properties of the digital pens for interacting with the tabletop [HBL+07].

Tangible palettes are used for changing pen properties such as color and stroke width.   FIGURE 10

The palettes are based on the same Anoto technology that is integrated into the table's surface. The single color and stroke width areas of the palette include the Anoto pattern in the background of the printout. The overlaid graphics are the visible hint for the user to distinguish between different functions that are invoked by the area. There is no interference of the graphics with the tracking. Figure 10 shows the two palettes for picking different colors and stroke widths on the tabletop.

3.3   An Adaptable Rear-Projection Digital Whiteboard

The digital whiteboard is installed as a replacement for the traditional paper flip chart. The activities that are assigned to the digital whiteboard include presenting and brainstorming. As shown in Figure 11, our display features a novel combination of digital pen technology from Anoto with a rear-projected setup [BHH+07]. Using the Anoto pen tracking, not only multi-user functionality is possible, but also the identification of each user.

FIGURE 11   The digital whiteboard combines Anoto pen tracking with a rear-projected setup.

In our setup we used HP Colorlucent Backlit UV foil to generate the pattern. The Backlit foil is mainly designed for rear illuminated signs so it generates a diffuse light. Thus, no spotlights from the projectors are visible at the front of the screen. Moreover, the rendering and the brightness of the projected image is still of high quality. In our setup, we used one A0 sized pattern sheet (118.0cm×84.1cm). The pattern is clamped in-between two acrylic panels. The panel in the back has a width of 6mm and guarantees a stable and robust surface while the panel in the front has a width of only 0.8mm to protect the pattern from scratches. The front panel is made of a special scratch resistant acrylic. We noticed that the acrylic cover in the front does not diffract the Anoto pattern at all. However, using thicker front panels (e.g. 4mm) produced bad tracking results.

Application for Collaborative Tasks 3.4

The room application is designed to support typical activities during a meeting. The application features one large workspace that is organized in pages across a session. A page represents the current work area that is accessible for all users. Each page is treated as an infinite large work space which can be controlled through the two functions Move() and Zoom(). With these controls, the current view on the page can be either translated or scaled. As shown in Figure 12, these functionalities provide the flexibility to create new space if needed and to spatially organize data within the workspace. Since the control of the current view changes the whole workspace, it affects all users in a multi-user session. Therefore, the control over the view locks the current workspace and can only be used by a single person exclusively. The same exclusive control is used when when skipping pages or changing to the page overview.

Controlling the view on the session. Original view (left), and zoomed in view (right).   FIGURE 12

The main session control functions can be either used through the appropriate item in the user menu or by performing a simple gesture. The gesture area inside the user menu allows for these shortcut navigation. Possible gestures include stroke up (new page), stroke down (page overview), stroke left (previous page) and stroke right (next page). The page overview provides a collection of all pages of a current session. By clicking on a specific page the session manager appropriately sets the view on it.

During a session, multiple users can work on the current page simultaneously. Each user has a menu that can be used to set custom parameters for the interaction. Different colors and stroke widths are available to customize the input. In addition to the tangible palettes, selections can be made through the projected menu. The palettes provide shortcuts (as there is no navigation in a menu necessary), but the same parameters can also be set through the digital menu.

3.5   Occlusion-Aware Menu Design

Interaction with large direct digital surfaces is strongly influenced by physical restrictions. Reachability of items or occlusions through the user's body require novel design considerations for appropriate interfaces. As Apitz et al. noticed for example, traditional menus are not very well adapted to direct pen interaction. Menus that appear on the location where they are activated seem to be a better choice for large interactive surfaces, where the input is normally done with a pen or a direct finger touch. Circular context (or pie) menus are a convenient solution, as they fulfill most of the requirements of direct input on large displays. As described by Hopkins, pie menus pop up at the users' click location and due to their circular layout, the motion required to make a selection is minimized.

Direct input on digital tabletops is strongly affected by the handedness and the position of the user. Hancock et al. [HBS04] studied selection times for pop-up menus with pen input and noticed that adapting to the user's handedness is necessary. Otherwise, either a left or right-handed user will be discriminated, depending on the application settings. In their study, the authors noticed a slower performance for occluded areas. These are mirrored for left and right-handed users. This observation shows that occlusion is strongly related to handedness and hand posture. Moreover, the study showed that not occluded menus are better accepted by the users and can enhance performance.

Based on these results, we designed a menu for direct input surfaces with the key design criteria to avoid occlusions and to adapt the menu placement to the user's handedness and position on the tabletop. To address the occlusion problem, we observed several users and noticed that the visibility of the menu is mainly influenced by the occlusion caused by the user's hand. Figure 13 shows the results of our observation. The mirror effect of occlusions for left and right-handed participants is clearly visible.

Referring to a full 360° circle of possible item placements around an invocation point, we found that 92° of the circle are occluded on average. According to this result, we designed a menu with items placed only in areas that are not occluded by the hand. Our design is inspired by the layout of circular menus [Hop91]. The position of the menu is centered at the point of activation (see Figure 14).

We propose to use the occluded area as part of an interactive area for gesture input inside the menu. Our observations showed that occlusions are not a problem in this case if the area can be recognized and the user knows

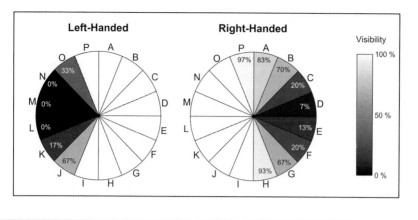

The visibility of each segment for left-handed and right-handed users shows a mirror effect.   FIGURE 13

where he can start a gesture and which gestures he can use. The outer region of the menu should be used for the items which can be accessed with a simple point-and-click.

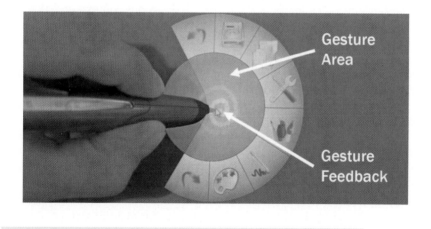

Users can perform gestures on the circular gesture area inside the menu.   FIGURE 14

3.6   Bridging the Gap Between Real Printouts and Digital Surfaces

Sketching ideas and taking notes is a basic task that is performed frequently in the phase of preparing or during a meeting or presentation. For this reason, tablet PCs have been used as a good alternative to notebooks, because they allow an easy-to-use interface for sketching ideas. However, they are currently too heavy and too big to be used in different environments (e.g. people still do not like to use a tablet PC during a flight for making a quick note - instead, they still prefer pencil and paper).

This is the reason why paper still has a lot of advantages: it is lightweight, easy to navigate, people get a fast overview, it is easy to annotate, it is socially well accepted, and it does not need any power. The usage of real paper and digital information combines the advantages of paper and additionally enhances them through the possibilities of the digital world.

The integration of real paper into our interactive room concept is supporting the rule to avoid frequent switching of input devices. Based on the Anoto tracking technology, we could use the same digital pens to interact with our digital surfaces as well as the paper interfaces. This allows for a very fluid work process even with the integration of such different input sources as paper and digital surfaces.

The benefits of paper for interaction in the room context are plentiful. Firstly, paper supports the storage of written information on a page automatically, with the additional advantage to easily archive pages. Secondly, paper is lightweight and can be moved around the room and spread out to access an overview of the content. It can be handled in different working positions like sitting or standing. Depending on the placement of paper in relation to the group, it can be used to define workspaces that support private, personal and public boundaries. Previous research on tabletop setups has shown that users are frequently transitioning between their private space and the group space [EKHH+90, MO94]. With paper, this continual transition between the spaces is a very natural process that happens by simply changing the arrangement of paper documents. To transfer a document from a public position on the table to a private view, the document can be simply picked up from the table, restricting the group further seeing its content. Another advantage of paper is the immediate feedback of written content without latency or resolution problems. Digital systems that capture handwriting are commonly facing the problem of input latency, which hampers the experience of fluid interaction.

Moreover, digital systems require switching between tools to support different activities such as writing, sketching or manipulating digital object, whereas studies that focused on traditional tabletop work sessions showed that people are frequently transitioning between writing and drawing without making a distinction of their activities [Bly88, Tan91]. Sketching and writing on paper is naturally supporting this work practice, as there is no difference in the type of input. A sketch or a note is treated equally on a sheet of paper. With paper as the input surface, interaction is not effected by additional technology imposed overhead.

Motivated by the opportunities and challenges that paper could offer together with a digital environment, we investigated the potential of this combination. We present a new paper-based interaction device which enables a seamless usage of a digital pen for manipulating real printouts and for controlling digital surfaces [BHOS08].

Pick-and-Drop

Similar to Rekimoto's Pick-and-Drop metaphor with mobile devices [Rek97], users can pick up data from a printed document and drop it on the interactive surface. Once in selection mode, each item of the printout becomes a selectable content and can be transferred without losing quality - since we transfer the raw data. In our scenario, users have to click with the pen on the corresponding data of the real printout. By using the digital pen, we can calculate the exact position and we can identify the according item. The data gets transferred when clicking again on the digital surface (see Figure 15).

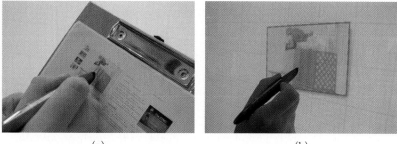

(a)   (b)

Users can pick up content from the real printout (a) and drop it on the   FIGURE 15
digital surface (b).

Remote Control

Influenced by the ideas of PaperPoint [SN07], the real printout can also be used as an alternative *input device*, where all sketched notes are sent to the digital whiteboard in real-time over Bluetooth.

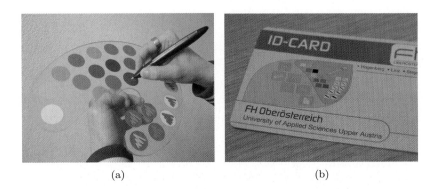

(a)   (b)

FIGURE 16   Different possibilities for the additional interaction. We either support a unique palette (a) or special ID cards where the additional functions are printed on the backside of each card (b).

In addition, special printed control elements on the paper allow further operation with the digital wall (e.g. adding a new page/changing the ink color of the digital flipchart etc.). In our demonstration, we implemented different possibilities for changing the ink properties (see Figure 16).

We tested our application by using a tangible tool palette, which was either embedded in an acrylic palette (a), or by adding the functions on the back of an ID card (b). In each scenario, we simply had to put the Anoto pattern on the corresponding surface (e.g. embed it into acrylic, or to put it on the backside of the ID card). Therefore, our solution is really cheap and does not require any additional electronic sensors.

Sketch-and-Send

The first method allows to send a group of strokes on demand. The strokes are transferred to the system in a single step and appear on the digital surface. In this mode, the user has the control over the moment when the sketches should be sent. The alternative way to send sketches to the system is via a real-time streaming paper. In this case, the strokes show up on the digital surface immediately. For example, this mode is useful for explanations that require to develop a sketch in front of the group step by step. The group can watch the digital representation of the sketches that the presenter draws on his paper.

Our system supports additional annotations on the real printout that can be performed with the real ink of the pen. The digital version of the ink can be either visualized in real-time on the digital surface or stored on the pen's integrated memory. In both variations, all data that is entered with the pen while in inking mode is processed in one or the other way.

Real-time streaming is useful for explanations that require to develop a sketch in front of the group step by step, for example. The group can watch the digital representation of the sketches that the presenter draws on his paper. The data transfer is accomplished through Bluetooth streaming from the Anoto pen to the server PC. Figure 17 shows an example where a user is annotating with real ink on the paper document.

Annotations on the real printout are immediately visible on the digital whiteboard.   FIGURE 17

Offering remote sketching in our system allows the participants of a meeting to keep seated around a table and share their ideas by sketching with real ink directly on a paper while the digital whiteboard acts as presentation area. This means that the users have two possibilities: they can either sit at the table and work on the digital whiteboard from their place; or they can stand up, go to the flipchart but still make their comments on the paper, which also automatically get transferred to the digital whiteboard. In both cases, all sketched information is sent to the whiteboard in real-time, regardless of the user's location. In our system, multiple people (we tested the scenario with 7 participants) can interact simultaneously - independently if they are sitting or standing.

Working in offline mode, the sketched notes can be stored in the pen's integrated memory in advance and moved seamlessly to the whiteboard during a presentation. People can sketch offline on the real paper, come to the meeting and send all sketched data to the digital whiteboard. In this case, the pen allows to store up to 70 full-written pages. This whole functionality can of course also be used during a meeting to prepare sketches on the paper without displaying them in real-time on the whiteboard; presenting it to the audience can be done at any time later during the meeting.

4 Conclusions

Multi-touch and interactive surfaces are becoming more interesting, because they allow a natural and intuitive interaction with the computer system. These more intuitive and natural interfaces could help users to be more actively involved in working together with content and could also help improve brainstorming activities. As these technologies develop, the barrier of having to learn and work with traditional computer interfaces may diminish. It is still unclear how fast these interfaces will become part of our daily life and how long it will take for them to be used in workplaces and classrooms. We also have sill only quite vague understanding of how these technologies will change the way we work and learn together and which practices will actually emerge. However, we strongly believe that the more intuitive the interface is, the faster it will be accepted and used. There is a huge potential in these devices, because they allow us to use digital technologies in a more human way. We are just at the beginning of a new decade, where books can be displayed on e-paper devices such as the Sony Reader.

On the other hand, we will still work with traditional interfaces including paper. The integration of real notes, for example, in a digital environment seems to be a very important motivation for people using these new technologies, since it combines the affordances of a traditional medium such as paper with the capabilities of digital content and displays.

Acknowledgements

The presented projects are sponsored by the Austrian Science Fund FFG (FHplus, contract no. 811407), voestalpine group-IT, Team 7, AMS Engineering, and Nortel. The authors would like to express their gratitude to the users who tested the implementation and all the team of the Media Interaction Lab.

References

[Ash04]   Mark S. D. Ashdown. Personal projected displays. Technical Report UCAM-CL-TR-585, University of Cambridge, Computer Laboratory, March 2004.

[BCT95]   S. Boedker, E. Christiansen, and M. Thüring. A conceptual toolbox for designing cscw applications. In *COOP '95, International Workshop on the Design of Cooperative Systems*, pages 266–284, Juan-les-Pins, January 1995.

[BHH+07]   Peter Brandl, Michael Haller, Michael Hurnaus, Verena Lugmayr, Juergen Oberngruber, Claudia Oster, Christian Schafleitner, and Mark Billinghurst. An adaptable rear-projection screen using digital pens and hand gestures. In *IEEE ICAT '07: Proceedings of the 17th International Conference on Artificial Reality and Telexistence*, page 49–54, Washington, DC, USA, 2007. IEEE Computer Society.

[BHOS08]   Peter Brandl, Michael Haller, Juergen Oberngruber, and Christian Schafleitner. Bridging the gap between real printouts and digital whiteboard. In *AVI '08: Proceedings of the working conference on Advanced Visual Interfaces*, page 31–38, New York, NY, USA, 2008. ACM.

[Bly88]   Sara A. Bly. A use of drawing surfaces in different collaborative settings. In *CSCW '88: Proceedings of the 1988 ACM conference on Computer-supported cooperative work*, pages 250–256, New York, NY, USA, 1988. ACM.

[BR00]   P. Beguin and P. Rabardel. Designing for instrument-mediated activity. *Scandinavian Journal of Information Systems*, 12:173–190, 2000.

[DL01]   Paul Dietz and Darren Leigh. Diamondtouch: a multi-user touch technology. In *UIST '01: Proceedings of the 14th annual ACM symposium on User interface software and technology*, pages 219–226, New York, NY, USA, 2001. ACM.

[EKHH+90] Mary Elwart-Keys, David Halonen, Marjorie Horton, Robert Kass, and Paul Scott. User interface requirements for face to face groupware. In *CHI '90: Proceedings of the SIGCHI conference on Human factors in computing systems*, pages 295–301, New York, NY, USA, 1990. ACM.

[Eng99]   Y. Engeström. Activity theory and individual and social transformation. In Y. Engeström and R. Miettinen, editors, *Perspectives on Activity Theory*, pages 19–38. Cambridge University Press, Cambridge, 1999.

[ER06]   Alan Esenther and Kathy Ryall. Fluid dtmouse: better mouse support for touch-based interactions. In *AVI '06: Proceedings of the working conference on Advanced visual interfaces*, pages 112–115, New York, NY, USA, 2006. ACM.

[FJHW00]   Armando Fox, Brad Johanson, Pat Hanrahan, and Terry Winograd. Integrating information appliances into an interactive workspace. *IEEE Comput. Graph. Appl.*, 20(3):54–65, 2000.

[FS05]   Clifton Forlines and Chia Shen. Dtlens: multi-user tabletop spatial data exploration. In *UIST '05: Proceedings of the 18th annual ACM symposium on User interface software and technology*, pages 119–122, New York, NY, USA, 2005. ACM.

[FSWB06]   Clifton Forlines, Chia Shen, Daniel Wigdor, and Ravin Balakrishnan. Exploring the effects of group size and display configuration on visual search. In

CSCW '06: Proceedings of the 2006 20th anniversary conference on Computer supported cooperative work, pages 11–20, New York, NY, USA, 2006. ACM.

[Gui02]   Francois Victor Guimbretière. *Fluid interaction for high resolution wall-size displays*. PhD thesis, Stanford, CA, USA, 2002. Adviser-Terry Winograd.

[Hac02]   W. Hacker. Konstruktives entwickeln: Psychologische grundlagen. In W. Hacker, editor, *Denken in der Produktentwicklung: Psychologische Unterstützung der frühen Phasen*, pages 11–26. VDF, Zürich, 2002.

[Han05]   Jefferson Y. Han. Low-cost multi-touch sensing through frustrated total internal reflection. In *UIST '05: Proceedings of the 18th annual ACM symposium on User interface software and technology*, pages 115–118, New York, NY, USA, 2005. ACM.

[HBL+07]   Michael Haller, Peter Brandl, Daniel Leithinger, Jakob Leitner, and Thomas Seifried. Large interactive surfaces based on digital pens. In *10th Interantional Conference on Humans and Computers, HC-2007*, pages 172–177, 2007. [INVITED PAPER].

[HBS04]   Mark S. Hancock, Booth, and Kellogg S. Improving menu placement strategies for pen input. In *GI '04: Proceedings of Graphics Interface 2004*, pages 221–230, School of Computer Science, University of Waterloo, Waterloo, Ontario, Canada, 2004. Canadian Human-Computer Communications Society.

[HCV+06]   Mark S. Hancock, Sheelagh Carpendale, Frederic D. Vernier, Daniel Wigdor, and Chia Shen. Rotation and translation mechanisms for tabletop interaction. In *TABLETOP '06: Proceedings of the First IEEE International Workshop on Horizontal Interactive Human-Computer Systems*, pages 79–88, Washington, DC, USA, 2006. IEEE Computer Society.

[HLL+06]   Michael Haller, Daniel Leithinger, Jakob Leitner, Thomas Seifried, Peter Brandl, Jürgen Zauner, and Mark Billinghurst. The shared design space. In *SIGGRAPH '06: ACM SIGGRAPH 2006 Emerging technologies*, page 29, New York, NY, USA, 2006. ACM.

[Hop91]   Don Hopkins. The design and implementation of pie menus. *Dr. Dobb's J.*, 16(12):16–26, 1991.

[JFW02]   Brad Johanson, Armando Fox, and Terry Winograd. The interactive workspaces project: Experiences with ubiquitous computing rooms. *IEEE Pervasive Computing*, 1(2):67–74, 2002.

[JK01]   A. Johannsen and H. Krcmar. Parallelität. In G. Schwabe, N. Streitz, and R. Unland, editors, *CSCW-Kompendium: Lehr- und Handbuch zum computerunterstützten kooperativen Arbeiten*, pages 438–446. Springer, Berlin, 2001.

[KCSG03]   Russell Kruger, Sheelagh Carpendale, Stacey D. Scott, and Saul Greenberg. How people use orientation on tables: comprehension, coordination and communication. In *GROUP '03: Proceedings of the 2003 international ACM SIGGROUP conference on Supporting group work*, pages 369–378, New York, NY, USA, 2003. ACM.

[MIO+04]   Mitsunori Matsushita, Makoto Iida, Takeshi Ohguro, Yoshinari Shirai, Yasuaki Kakehi, and Takeshi Naemura. Lumisight table: a face-to-face collaboration support system that optimizes direction of projected information to each stakeholder. In *CSCW '04: Proceedings of the 2004 ACM conference on Computer supported cooperative work*, pages 274–283, New York, NY, USA, 2004. ACM.

[MO94]   Munir Mandviwalla and Lorne Olfman. What do groups need? a proposed set of generic groupware requirements. *ACM Trans. Comput.-Hum. Interact.*, 1(3):245–268, 1994.

[Mor06]   Meredith June Morris. *Supporting effective interaction with tabletop groupware*. PhD thesis, Stanford, CA, USA, 2006. Adviser-Terry Winograd.

[MRS⁺04]   Meredith Ringel Morris, Kathy Ryall, Chia Shen, Clifton Forlines, and Fred-
           eric Vernier. Beyond "social protocols": multi-user coordination policies for
           co-located groupware. In *CSCW '04: Proceedings of the 2004 ACM confer-
           ence on Computer supported cooperative work*, pages 262–265, New York, NY,
           USA, 2004. ACM.

[RDS02]   Daniel M. Russell, Clemens Drews, and Alison Sue. Social aspects of us-
           ing large public interactive displays for collaboration. In *UbiComp '02: Pro-
           ceedings of the 4th international conference on Ubiquitous Computing*, pages
           229–236, London, UK, 2002. Springer-Verlag.

[Rek97]   Jun Rekimoto. Pick-and-drop: a direct manipulation technique for multiple
           computer environments. In *UIST '97: Proceedings of the 10th annual ACM
           symposium on User interface software and technology*, pages 31–39, New York,
           NY, USA, 1997. ACM Press.

[RFSM04]   Kathy Ryall, Clifton Forlines, Chia Shen, and Meredith Ringel Morris. Ex-
           ploring the effects of group size and table size on interactions with tabletop
           shared-display groupware. In *CSCW '04: Proceedings of the 2004 ACM con-
           ference on Computer supported cooperative work*, pages 284–293, New York,
           NY, USA, 2004. ACM.

[RHBL04]   Yvonne Rogers, William Hazlewood, Eli Blevis, and Youn-Kyung Lim. Finger
           talk: collaborative decision-making using talk and fingertip interaction around
           a tabletop display. In *CHI '04: CHI '04 extended abstracts on Human factors
           in computing systems*, pages 1271–1274, New York, NY, USA, 2004. ACM.

[RL04]   Yvonne Rogers and Siân E. Lindley. Collaborating around vertical and hori-
           zontal large interactive displays: which way is best? volume 16, pages 1133–
           1152, 2004.

[RLH06]   Yvonne Rogers, Youn-Kyung Lim, and William R. Hazlewood. Extending
           tabletops to support flexible collaborative interactions. In *TABLETOP '06:
           Proceedings of the First IEEE International Workshop on Horizontal Inter-
           active Human-Computer Systems*, pages 71–78, Washington, DC, USA, 2006.
           IEEE Computer Society.

[RRS⁺04]   Meredith Ringel, Kathy Ryall, Chia Shen, Clifton Forlines, and Frederic
           Vernier. Release, relocate, reorient, resize: fluid techniques for document shar-
           ing on multi-user interactive tables. In *CHI '04: CHI '04 extended abstracts
           on Human factors in computing systems*, pages 1441–1444, New York, NY,
           USA, 2004. ACM.

[Sch01]   G. Schwabe. Gemeinsames materia und gruppengedächtnis. In G. Schwabe,
           N. Streitz, and R. Unland, editors, *CSCW-Kompendium: Lehr- und Handbuch
           zum computerunterstützten kooperativen Arbeiten*, pages 447–454. Springer,
           Berlin, 2001.

[Sco05]   Stacey D. Scott. *Territoriality in collaborative tabletop workspaces*. PhD
           thesis, Calgary, Alta., Canada, Canada, 2005.

[SER03]   Chia Shen, Katherine Everitt, and Kathleen Ryall. Ubitable: Impromptu face-
           to-face collaboration on horizontal interactive surfaces. In *In Proc. UbiComp
           2003*, pages 281–288, 2003.

[SGH⁺99]   Norbert A. Streitz, Jörg Geißler, Torsten Holmer, Christian Müller-tomfelde,
           Wolfgang Reischl, Petra Rexroth, Peter Seitz, and Ralf Steinmetz. i-land:
           An interactive landscape for creativity and innovation. pages 120–127. ACM
           Press, 1999.

[SGM03]   S.D. Scott, K.D. Grant, and R.L. Mandryk. System guidelines for co-located,
           collaborative work on a tabletop display. In *Proceedings of ECSCW'03*, pages
           159–178, 2003.

[SGP98]   Bill N. Schilit, Gene Golovchinsky, and Morgan N. Price. Beyond paper:
           supporting active reading with free form digital ink annotations. In *CHI
           '98: Proceedings of the SIGCHI conference on Human factors in computing*

systems, pages 249–256, New York, NY, USA, 1998. ACM Press/Addison-Wesley Publishing Co.

[SGS+02]   Stacey D. Scott, Karen Grant, M. Sheelagh, T. Carpendale, Kori M. Inkpen, Regan L, and Terry Winograd. Co-located tabletop collaboration: Technologies and directions, November 16-20 2002.

[SH01]   Abigail J. Sellen and Richard H. R. Harper. *The Myth of the Paperless Office*. MIT Press, Cambridge, MA, USA, 2001.

[SLM+01]   Chia Shen, Neal Lesh, Baback Moghaddam, Paul Beardsley, and Ryan Scott Bardsley. Personal digital historian: user interface design. In *CHI '01: CHI '01 extended abstracts on Human factors in computing systems*, pages 29–30, New York, NY, USA, 2001. ACM.

[SLV+02]   Chia Shen, Neal B. Lesh, Frederic Vernier, Clifton Forlines, and Jeana Frost. Sharing and building digital group histories. In *CSCW '02: Proceedings of the 2002 ACM conference on Computer supported cooperative work*, pages 324–333, New York, NY, USA, 2002. ACM.

[SMA03]   SMARTTech. Digital vision touch technology. Technical report, http://www.smarttech.com/dvit/, 2003.

[SN07]   Beat Signer and Moira C. Norrie. Paperpoint: a paper-based presentation and interactive paper prototyping tool. In *TEI '07: Proceedings of the 1st international conference on Tangible and embedded interaction*, pages 57–64, New York, NY, USA, 2007. ACM.

[SPMT+02] Norbert Streitz, Thorsten Prante, Christian Müller-Tomfelde, Peter Tandler, and Carsten Magerkurth. Roomware: The second generation. In *CHI '02: CHI '02 extended abstracts on Human factors in computing systems*, pages 506–507, New York, NY, USA, 2002. ACM.

[SVFR04]   Chia Shen, Frédéric D. Vernier, Clifton Forlines, and Meredith Ringel. Diamondspin: an extensible toolkit for around-the-table interaction. In *CHI '04: Proceedings of the SIGCHI conference on Human factors in computing systems*, pages 167–174, New York, NY, USA, 2004. ACM.

[Tan91]   J. C. Tang. Findings from observational studies of collaborative work. pages 11–28, 1991.

[Tan04]   Peter Tandler. The beach application model and software framework for synchronous collaboration in ubiquitous computing environments. *J. Syst. Softw.*, 69(3):267–296, 2004.

[TT06]   A. Toney and B. Thomas. Considering reach in tangible and table top design. In *Tabletop 2006*, pages 57–58, 2006.

[UI97]   Brygg Ullmer and Hiroshi Ishii. The metadesk: Models and prototypes for tangible user interfaces. pages 223–232. ACM Press, 1997.

[VLS02]   Frederic Vernier, Neal Lesh, and Chia Shen. Visualization techniques for circular tabletop interfaces. pages 257–263, 2002.

[WB05]   Daniel Wigdor and Ravin Balakrishnan. Empirical investigation into the effect of orientation on text readability in tabletop displays. In *ECSCW'05: Proceedings of the ninth conference on European Conference on Computer Supported Cooperative Work*, pages 205–224, New York, NY, USA, 2005. Springer-Verlag New York, Inc.

[WCFB06]   D. Wigdor, C. Chen, C. Forlines, and R. Balakrishnan. Table-centric interactive spaces for real-time collaboration. In *Proceedings of the working conference on advanced visual interfaces, AVI 2006, May 23-26*, pages 103–107, Venezia, 2006.

Index

particle physics, 40
pathology fitting, 353
pattern, 441
  based programming, 88
PCS reasoner, 75, 80
performance, 335, 367
PHIDIAS, 12
pick-and-drop, 465
PILLWEIN, VERONIKA, 15
pipelining, 336, 368
piping system, 325
plan-do-check-act (*PDCA*) model, 168
planning, route ∼, 128
plasticity-stability dilemma, 249, 251
platform, 176
polynomial
  ideal theory, 17
  invariant, 89
population, 137
post-optimization, 259
predicate logic
  higher order, 68
predicate, fuzzy ∼, 255
prefabricates, 176
premature convergence, 121
process, 160
  assessment model, 167
  capability, 161, 175
  capability (continuous), 167
  control, 160, 210
  definition, 160
  dimension, 167
  evolution, 172
  execution, 163
  implementation model, 167
  improvement, 160
  improvement paradigm-cycle, 168
  instantiation, 163
  maturity (staged), 167
  measurement, 160
  modeling, 163
  quality, 164
  reference model, 167, 172
processor
  many-core, 368, 369
  multi-core, 368, 369
product
  algebra, 239
  characteristics prediction, 160
  development, 173
  family development, 161
  lifecycle management, 161, 173
  logic, 239
  quality, 164

profitability, 160
program
  definition, 91
  formal analysis, 96
  specification, 89, 91
  transformation, 83
ProgramExplorer, 96
programming
  by contract, 91
  functional, 88
  genetic, 136
  imperative, 89
  parallel functional, 338, 345
  pattern based, 88
proof
  failing ∼, 70
  situation, 95
ProofNavigator, 94
proper parametrization, 26
  inversion of, 26
Prove-Compute-Solve method, 75
proving, 5
  assistant, 93
  highschool ∼, 70
  quantifier free ∼, 70
  rewrite ∼, 70
push forward insertion heuristic, 133

q-class method, 53
quadratic assignment problem, 132
quality
  assurance, 187
  in use, 164
  inspection, 271
quantifier
  alternating ∼, 75
  elimination, 79
quarter plane, 33–39

rational
  curve, 25
  parametrization, 24, 25
  series, 35
reasoning, 63
  automated, 63, 65, 83, 366
recurrence
  relation, 47
  solving, 44
recursive fuzzy weighted least squares, 251
regression
  model, fuzzy, 245
  test, 326
regularization, 259
  parameter, 247

List of Editors and Authors

Michael Affenzeller
Heuristic and Evolutionary Algorithms Laboratory
Upper Austria University of Applied Sciences
michael.affenzeller@fh-hagenberg.at

Wolfgang Beer
Software Competence Center Hagenberg (SCCH)
wolfgang.beer@scch.at

Andreas Beham
Heuristic and Evolutionary Algorithms Laboratory
Upper Austria University of Applied Sciences
andreas.beham@fh-hagenberg.at

Peter Brandl
Media Interaction Lab
Upper Austria University of Applied Sciences
peter.brandl@fh-hagenberg.at

Bruno Buchberger
Research Institute for Symbolic Computation (RISC)
Johannes Kepler University Linz (JKU)
bruno.buchberger@risc.jku.at

Georg Buchgeher
Software Competence Center Hagenberg (SCCH)
georg.buchgeher@scch.at

Christina Buttinger
Institute for Application Oriented Knowledge Processing (FAW)
Johannes Kepler University Linz (JKU)
cbuttinger@faw.jku.at

Károly Bósa
Research Institute for Symbolic Computation (RISC)
Johannes Kepler University Linz (JKU)
Karoly.Bosa@risc.jku.at

Bernhard Dorninger
Software Competence Center Hagenberg (SCCH)
bernhard.dorninger@scch.at

Christina Feilmayr
Institute for Application Oriented Knowledge Processing (FAW)
Johannes Kepler University Linz (JKU)
cfeilmayr@faw.jku.at

Alois Ferscha
Department of Pervasive Computing
Johannes Kepler University Linz (JKU)
ferscha@soft.uni-linz.ac.at

Bernhard Freudenthaler
Institute for Application Oriented Knowledge Processing (FAW)
Johannes Kepler University Linz (JKU)
bfreudenthaler@faw.jku.at

Adam Gokcezade
Media Interaction Lab
Upper Austria University of Applied Sciences
adam.gokcezade@fh-hagenberg.at

Michael Guttenbrunner
Institute for Application Oriented Knowledge Processing (FAW)
Johannes Kepler University Linz (JKU)
mguttenbrunner@faw.jku.at

Michael Haller
Media Interaction Lab
Upper Austria University of Applied Sciences
haller@fh-hagenberg.at

Christian Hawel
Software Competence Center Hagenberg (SCCH)
christian.hawel@scch.at

Johannes Himmelbauer
Software Competence Center Hagenberg (SCCH)
johannes.himmelbauer@scch.at

Melanie Himsl
Institute for Application Oriented Knowledge Processing (FAW)
Johannes Kepler University Linz (JKU)
mhimsl@faw.at

Daniel Jabornig
Institute for Application Oriented Knowledge Processing (FAW)
Johannes Kepler University Linz (JKU)
djabornig@faw.at

Tudor Jebelean
Research Institute for Symbolic Computation (RISC)
Johannes Kepler University Linz (JKU)
Tudor.Jebelean@risc.jku.at

Lena Kartashova
Research Institute for Symbolic Computation (RISC)
Johannes Kepler University Linz (JKU)
Lena.Kartashova@risc.uni-linz.ac.at

Manuel Kauers
Research Institute for Symbolic Computation (RISC)
Johannes Kepler University Linz (JKU)
Manuel.Kauers@risc.uni-linz.ac.at

Erich Peter Klement
Dept. of Knowledge-Based Mathematical Systems, Fuzzy Logic Laboratorium Linz-Hagenberg (FLLL), Johannes Kepler University (JKU)
ep.klement@jku.at

Monika Kofler
Heuristic and Evolutionary Algorithms Laboratory
Upper Austria University of Applied Sciences
monika.kofler@fh-hagenberg.at

Gabriel Kronberger
Heuristic and Evolutionary Algorithms Laboratory
Upper Austria University of Applied Sciences
gabriel.kronberger@fh-hagenberg.at

Temur Kutsia
Research Institute for Symbolic Computation (RISC)
Johannes Kepler University Linz (JKU)
Temur.Kutsia@risc.jku.at

Josef Küng
Institute for Application Oriented Knowledge Processing (FAW)
Johannes Kepler University Linz (JKU)
jkueng@faw.jku.at

Andreas Langegger
Institute for Application Oriented Knowledge Processing (FAW)
Johannes Kepler University Linz (JKU)
Andreas.Langegger@jku.at

Daniel Leithinger
Media Lab
Massachusetts Institute of Technology (MIT), USA
daniell@mit.edu

Werner Leithner
Institute for Application Oriented Knowledge Processing (FAW)
Johannes Kepler University Linz (JKU)
wleithner@faw.at

Jakob Leitner
Media Interaction Lab
Upper Austria University of Applied Sciences
jakob.leitner@fh-hagenberg.at

Thomas Leitner
Institute for Application Oriented Knowledge Processing (FAW)
Johannes Kepler University Linz (JKU)
Thomas.Leitner@jku.at

Edwin Lughofer
Dept. of Knowledge-Based Mathematical Systems, Fuzzy Logic Laboratorium Linz-Hagenberg (FLLL), Johannes Kepler University (JKU)
edwin.lughofer@jku.at

Bernhard Moser
Software Competence Center Hagenberg (SCCH)
Bernhard.Moser@scch.at

Stefan Parzer
Institute for Application Oriented Knowledge Processing (FAW)
Johannes Kepler University Linz (JKU)
sparzer@faw.jku.at

Peter Paule
Research Institute for Symbolic Computation (RISC)
Johannes Kepler University Linz (JKU)
Peter.Paule@risc.uni-linz.ac.at

Josef Pichler
Software Competence Center Hagenberg (SCCH)
josef.pichler@scch.at

Gustav Pomberger
Institute of Business Informatics – Software Engineering
Johannes Kepler University Linz (JKU)
gustav.pomberger@jku.at

Nikolaj Popov
Research Institute for Symbolic Computation (RISC)
Johannes Kepler University Linz (JKU)
Nikolaj.Popov@risc.jku.at

Herbert Prähofer
Institute for System Software
Johannes Kepler University Linz (JKU)
herbert.praehofer@jku.at

Birgit Pröll
Institute for Application Oriented Knowledge Processing (FAW)
Johannes Kepler University Linz (JKU)
bproell@faw.jku.at

Szilárd Páll
Software Competence Center Hagenberg (SCCH)
Pall.Szilard@gmail.com

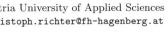

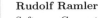

Rudolf Ramler
Software Competence Center Hagenberg (SCCH)
rudolf.ramler@scch.at

Christoph Richter
Research Group Knowledge Media
Upper Austria University of Applied Sciences
christoph.richter@fh-hagenberg.at

Carsten Schneider
Research Institute for Symbolic Computation (RISC)
Johannes Kepler University Linz (JKU)
Carsten.Schneider@risc.uni-linz.ac.at

Wolfgang Schreiner
Research Institute for Symbolic Computation (RISC)
Johannes Kepler University Linz (JKU)
Wolfgang.Schreiner@risc.jku.at

Thomas Seifried
Media Interaction Lab
Upper Austria University of Applied Sciences
thomas.seifried@fh-hagenberg.at

Fritz Stallinger
Software Competence Center Hagenberg (SCCH)
fritz.stallinger@scch.at

Robert Stubenrauch
Softwarepark Hagenberg
stubenrauch@softwarepark-hagenberg.com

Reinhard Stumptner
Institute for Application Oriented Knowledge Processing (FAW)
Johannes Kepler University Linz (JKU)
rstumptner@faw.jku.at

Roland Wagner
Institute for Application Oriented Knowledge Processing (FAW)
Johannes Kepler University Linz (JKU)
rwagner@faw.jku.at

Stefan A. Wagner
Heuristic and Evolutionary Algorithms Laboratory
Upper Austria University of Applied Sciences
stefan.wagner@fh-hagenberg.at

Stefan Wagner
Institute for Application Oriented Knowledge Processing (FAW)
Johannes Kepler University Linz (JKU)
swagner@faw.at

Rainer Weinreich
Institute of Business Informatics – Software Engineering
Johannes Kepler University Linz (JKU)
rainer.weinreich@jku.at

Gerhard Weiss
Software Competence Center Hagenberg (SCCH)
gerhard.weiss@scch.at

Volkmar Wieser
Software Competence Center Hagenberg (SCCH)
Volkmar.Wieser@scch.at

Wolfgang Windsteiger
Research Institute for Symbolic Computation (RISC)
Johannes Kepler University Linz (JKU)
Wolfgang.Windsteiger@risc.jku.at

Franz Winkler
Research Institute for Symbolic Computation (RISC)
Johannes Kepler University Linz (JKU)
Franz.Winkler@risc.uni-linz.ac.at

Stephan Winkler
Heuristic and Evolutionary Algorithms Laboratory
Upper Austria University of Applied Sciences
stephan.winkler@fh-hagenberg.at

Wolfram Wöß
Institute for Application Oriented Knowledge Processing (FAW)
Johannes Kepler University Linz (JKU)
Wolfram.Woess@jku.at

Printing: Krips bv, Meppel, The Netherlands
Binding: Stürtz, Würzburg, Germany